Douglas Shomburger

Feed My Sheep

A History of the Hispanic Missions in the Pacific Southwest District of The Lutheran Church—Missouri Synod

Feed My Sheep

A History of the Hispanic Missions of the Pacific Southwest District
The Lutheran Church – Missouri Synod

By Michael Doyle

Dragonflyer Press · Upland, California

Photography Research: Michael Doyle
Design: Sue Campbell
Layout: Scott Harmon

ISBN 10: 0-944933-17-3
ISBN 13: 978-0944933-176

DRAGONFLYER
press

592 North Euclid Avenue
Upland California 91786
909-981-9522

Printed in Hong Kong

In Nomine Jesu!

Dedicated To
Rev. Dr. David Stirdivant

The Father of Hispanic Ministry,
who worked tirelessly to spread God's Word
to the Hispanic population of the Pacific Southwest District.

To God alone be the Glory!

CONTENTS

This project, *Feed My Sheep: A History of the Hispanic Missions in the Pacific Southwest District of The Lutheran Church — Missouri Synod*, came about at the suggestion of Jean Beres, the former director of communications of the Pacific Southwest District, with the approval of the District Board of Directors. Her idea was to tell the story of the Hispanic ministry in the District over the past seventy-five years. In order to compile the book, information was gleaned from periodicals and pictures in the Pacific Southwest District Archives; the minutes of the Mission Board; the Board of Directors; Synod's Board of Home Missions housed in Concordia Historical Institute in St. Louis, Missouri; summary reports of the Mission Board in the District Convention Proceedings; and District periodicals: *The Southern California Lutheran, Southern California District Digest, The Lutheran Witness Supplement, This Month, In Focus,* and PSW e-News. Assistance was given to me by many wonderful people who supplied me with vast amounts of information and a variety of pictures. The story could be told only with the help of the many dedicated people who were involved in the creation of the history of Hispanic ministries in the District.

First of all, I wish to thank my beloved wife, Mina, who was my chief proofreader and advisor. Second, I wish to thank my son, Matthew, who assisted me with technological guidance on the computer when it failed me, and my sister-in-law, Mary Smith, for the hours she spent transcribing all the oral interviews. Third, I want to thank Jean Beres and Eldrid Hinton, who donated hours and hours not only devising a style manual for the book but also using their editorial expertise to proofread the text. Finally, I want to thank all the pastors and lay people who gave me assistance by supplying information and pictures of their ministries and churches, especially Rev. David Stirdivant, who assisted me with interviews, supplied various pictures of his ministries, and gave loyal support to the project. Without these dedicated people, the project wouldn't have materialized.

A very special thanks goes to the staff at the Pacific Southwest District office; Concordia Historical Institute, St. Louis, Missouri, staff who opened their files for research; the Upland Library for materials; Jeanne Rankin, librarian at the Cypress Branch of the Los Angeles Public Library; Carolyn Cole for use of the Los Angeles Public Library pictures; Cheryl Eberly for use of the Santa Ana Library pictures; Ann Jones, librarian at the Fallbrook Public Library; and Mary Stevens, secretary of Trinity Lutheran Church of Whittier, California, for use of the church's archives. Their assistance was invaluable and deeply appreciated.

I'm also indebted to the following people for information and pictures they gave for the book: Vera (Gandara) Saldaña, Belen (Gandara) Perez, Flora (Flores) Chavez, and Gilbert Flores on the Santa Ana Mission; Mrs. Grace Rennegarbe on old St. John's of Boyle Heights in Los Angeles; and Catalina Broyles on El Mirage Mission in El Mirage, Arizona.

I am especially thankful to my publisher, Carolyn Hayes Uber, for all her time and assistance and her staff: Sue Campbell, for her design of the book; Scott Harmon for the layout of the book; Chris Wheeler for designing the publicity; Jason Collins for scanning all 480 pictures; Phil Hayes, Natalie Willison, and Rachel Ruiz for all their assistance in handling the sales of the book. Through their efforts, the book is what it is.

In order for the book to be published, funds had to be secured. I am deeply indebted to Rev. Dr. Larry Stoterau, president of the Pacific Southwest District; the Pacific Southwest District Board of Directors, Rev. Dr. Jacob Preus III, president of Concordia University, Irvine; and all the donors listed in the Appendix for contributing the down payment. Without their support, the book would not have been published.

My prayer is that all who read this book may see God's hand of blessing on the District's Hispanic mission as His people did His work of proclaiming His love for mankind through His Son, Jesus Christ, not only to the large German and Anglo populations that arrived in California in the late 1800s but also to all the Hispanic people who live in the Pacific Southwest District consisting of Southern California, southern Nevada, and Arizona.

Soli Deo Gloria!

Upland, California
Second Sunday in Lent 2006
Michael J. Doyle

**"I remember the days of old,
I meditate on all Thou hast done."**

— PSLAM 143:5

The story of the Lutheran church's mission to the Hispanic population of the Pacific Southwest District must begin in the late eighteenth century, when the Spaniards decided to minimize the threat of possible Russian and English encroachment of their territory by establishing settlements in Alta California. They began by founding Mission San Diego in 1769 and then sent an overland expedition northward under the leadership of Gaspár de Portolá, the Californias' first governor, to look for a harbor (Monterey Bay) that had been described by Viscaino in 1602. On August 2, 1769, the first European visitors reached the Los Angeles area with Portola who named the Los Angeles River, Nuestra Senora de Los Angeles de Porciúncula. Father Juan Crespi commented on the excellence of the site for a settlement because of its rich and fertile valley, because of a copious river flowing through it, and friendly Indians living nearby. They in turn recommended this area for settlement. Twelve years later King Carlos III of Spain ordered Governor Felipe de Neve to establish a *pueblo* or small town on this site. As early as 1777, he had proclaimed Monterey as the capital of the New World north of Mexico. Later that year, a settlement was established at San Jose in northern California. The second civil settlement, near Rio Porciúncula, would eventually become Los Angeles. Settlers were recruited in what later became the Mexican states of Sonora and Sinaloa on the northwest coast of Mexico.

, The humble colonists, led by Spanish soldiers, came up from Mexico by boat, mule, horse, and on foot. They were poor and had nothing to lose, but hoped to gain a new life in Alta California. The Spanish government promised a salary of ten pesos a month plus rations to volunteers who were willing to make the long trek north. Governor Neve was looking for 24 families but only 14 applied. With their families and their livestock and in parties escorted by soldiers, they made the long journey on foot and by horseback to Mission San Gabriel. They arrived between the months of July and September of 1781. Two of those families quit before the journey began, and another dropped out along the way when a child was stricken with smallpox. The 11 remaining families traveled more than 8 months to reach their new home. Corporal Jose Vicente Feliz led the founding party from San Gabriel Mission to El Pueblo de Nuestra Senora la Reina de Los Angeles de Porciuncula (the Town of Our Lady the Queen of the Angels of Porciúncula). Of the founding fathers, two were Spaniards, four Indians, two blacks, two mulattoes, and one mestizo with the accompanying wives who were either mulattoes or Indians. A total of 44 settlers founded a multi-cultural and multi-ethnic tradition, which has continued in the city to the present day. It is doubtful that any other city in California or possibly the United States had such a multi-ethnic beginning.

In August of 1781, Felipe de Neve, a remarkable administrator who realized that the fledgling community would need water and protection from the wind, laid out the new pueblo. He designed a plaza, 200' wide by 300' long, with building lots for the settlers, a large space set aside for a church, and surrounding land for agriculture. He allowed house lots and two planting fields for each family and fields to be cultivated in common. Mules, mares, cows, calves, sheep, and goats were distributed to the colonists, beginning their new lives in Los Angeles.

The day which is recognized as the city's birthday is September 4, because it was on that day in 1781 that the settlers were given their house lots and their planting fields. Felipe de Neve gave the name of El

Pueblo de la Reina de Los Angeles sobre el Rio Porciúncula (the town of the Angels on the River Porciúncula) to the new little settlement. The word *porciúncula* means "little portion" and refers to the small portion of land near Assisi in Italy which St. Francis and his followers were given in the thirteenth century. This was later associated with a religious feast day, August 2, 1769, the date that Portola and his expedition had arrived in the Los Angeles area.

In 1782, Father Junípero Serra, no stranger to the area, visited the new settlement as well as San Gabriel Mission. He had left his post as professor of philosophy at Majorca to come to the New World. In 1769, Serra and Captain Gaspár de Portolá led a small group of friars from Mexico to the Californias. The priest helped found San Gabriel Mission in 1771, 10 years before the settlement of Los Angeles. During his visit in 1782, he expelled three families from El Pueblo de Nuestra Senora la Reina de Los Angeles for shirking their community duties.

Father Junípero Serra, the founder of the twenty-one mission system of California.

Since the church and state worked hand-in-hand in the Californias, Catholic missionaries wanted to save the souls of the "heathen" Indians to the north, and Spanish authorities wanted to secure bases in the Californias in order to promote trade and control territory that was open to Russian forays from the north. Franciscan padres and Spanish soldiers together led the early expeditions out of Mexico northward into the Californias, Alta and Baja (Upper and Lower).

El Pueblo de Nuestra Senora la Reina de Los Angeles was, at first, just a tiny commercial outpost for Spain and a struggling little community of support for army presidios and missionary padres. No one — not even the farsighted Neve — dreamed of Los Angeles as a potential paradise. Since rainfall was rare, life was forever dependent on the waters of the Porciúncula (Los Angeles River). Padres and *pobladores* (settlers) had come to a land where survival would demand struggle, sacrifice, and even heroics in establishing a farming community.

By 1784, this struggling little pueblo of Los Angeles was only three years old when soldiers stationed in the area began asking for land grants.

One of the first applicants was Jose Manuel Nieto, who requested a "grazing place situated at three leagues distance" from San Gabriel Mission. He promised "not to harm a living soul" and pledged respect for the friars nearby as well as for the settlers in town. Governor Pedro Fages, Neve's successor, granted the request providing that Nieto promise not to harm either the "pagan Indians" or the inhabitants of the Spanish enclaves. Nieto's holdings eventually increased to 167,000 acres — the beginnings of the ranches and a foretaste of what would become Los Angeles sprawl. In time, ranches surrounded the pueblo, becoming the social and trading center of the area. By 1790, the pueblo had grown to a population of 139 people.

Education was not a high priority in the pueblo, since the settlers who struggled north from Mexico were illiterate. School, in fact, was a threat to ranching, as the children were needed to work in the fields. Los Angeles did not open a school until Governor Pablo de Vicente de Sola ordered one to be built. The first teacher, Mazimo Piña, a former soldier with a disability, was hired in 1817 to begin teaching. The governor wanted reading and writing to be emphasized, but the community stressed religious training, with the children receiving instruction in religious matters only. After trying to teach for two years at a salary of about $140 per year, Piña left town, which meant the school closed and education remained a low priority in the minds of the citizens of the little pueblo.

In 1815 after 10 nights of rain, the Los Angeles River grew from a trickle to a raging torrent, washing away the original plaza in a brutal flood. Since a new church was needed, this called for a new and uncluttered public square, moving the plaza farther west of the Los Angeles River. The new church building was started in 1818 on community-owned land, with the citizens helping to fund the construction by donating cattle. Joseph Chapman, who became the first important American resident in Los Angeles, came to town using his expertise of felling trees to construct the new church roof. In the early 1820s, the finished church dominated the new plaza, as it still does today. On

The first school in Los Angeles is opened in 1817 with a former soldier, Mazino Piña, hired as the teacher.

the other three sides of the plaza rose the town houses of the *rancheros*. The Avila Adobe, the oldest residence in Los Angeles, was built on Olvera Street in 1818. By 1820, the pueblo's population had increased to 650 people.

During this time, news traveled very slowly. In 1821, Mexico declared her independence from Spain, with this startling news not reaching the Pueblo until six months later in the month of March 1822. The reaction of the sleepy little village was to change the flags; down came the lion of Spain and up went the serpent of Mexico, and a new oath of allegiance was sworn to Mexico. Other changes to take place were the addition of a treasurer and a secretary to the local government now called *ayuntamiento*, the municipal council in Los Angeles. The revolution hardly touched the life of the little town.

The next decade in 1830 saw the pueblo's population swell to 770, excluding Indians. During this period, more *gringos* came to town: Yankees, Germans, Frenchmen, Scotsmen, Jews, Irishmen, and Swedes, each joining the Roman Catholic Church, renouncing their allegiance to whatever country from which they came, swearing their allegiance to Mexico, and most often marrying the *senoritas* and receiving large dowries of land that went with these young maidens. Having become an official *ciudad* or city in 1835, the first official census in 1836 recorded a population of 2,228 in Los Angeles and its environs, including 603 men, 421 women, 651 children, and 553 Indians. Among the population were 50 foreigners — 29 Americans, 4 Englishmen, 5 Frenchmen, 3 Portuguese, 2 Africans, and one each Canadian, Irishman, Italian, Scot, Norwegian, Curacao native, and German.

The decade of the 1840s brought huge, drastic changes to the populace of Los Angeles, with more gringos arriving and gaining a firmer foothold in the city. One of these gringos was John J. Behn, a German sea captain who arrived in Los Angeles in the 1840s and married the daughter of General Castello of Enseñada, Lower California. Their daughter, Louisa, the first white child to be born on Catalina Island in 1857, wed in 1873, Heinrich (Henry) Stoll, a German immigrant, who came across the plains as a pioneer and arrived in Los Angeles in 1867. During the following year, he established a soda-water plant, which gradually became the largest on the West Coast. By 1889, H. W. Stoll & Co., proprietors of the Los Angeles Soda-water Works, produced "3,000 to 5,000 dozen per day of sarsaparilla, soda mineral water, syrups, cordials, and other temperance beverages." In May of 1870, he and other Germans established the Teutonia Concordia Turnverein, a gymnastic club. Their daughter, Wilhelmine H. Stoll, was born in October of 1875 in Los Angeles and was baptized by a Lutheran pastor, Rev. A. Geyer, on November 9, 1875. The family became charter members of Trinity Lutheran Church in Los Angeles when it was organized in 1882.

With the Treaty of Guadalupe Hidalgo signed on February 2, 1848, California was acquired for the United States as part of the Mexican Cession. By 1850, the county and city of Los Angeles were established by the state legislature making California the 31st state with the city's first mayor, Alpheus P. Hodges, elected. The first federal census recorded a city population of 1,610, and a county population of 3,530, including 2 Chinese, 334 Indians, 15 Negroes, and 699 foreign born. The

> Louisa Behn is the first white child to be born on Catalina Island in 1857. She becomes a charter member of Trinity Lutheran Church in 1882

Los Angeles in 1853, the first known sketch of the city taken from an official railroad survey report to the then Secretary of War Jefferson Davis. The Church of Our Lady of Angels faces the plaza surrounded by adobe buildings of the period.

lure of gold to northern California had drawn so many inhabitants from the pueblo that the town's growth practically stood still from 1850 to 1860. The figure in 1860 was 4,399, which meant that the gold fever was over, and many, who would otherwise be back East, were stranded here.

The Reverend Adam Bland, a Methodist minister, conducted the first Protestant services in 1853 where he had five discouraging years preaching in a small adobe building that was also used as a school. Then came Rev. James Woods, a Presbyterian minister, holding services in a carpenter shop near the plaza. Rev. Freeman organized the first Baptist church in town. In 1858, the Rev. Elias Birdsall ministered to the Episcopalians in a real church building, the first Protestant building, at the corner of New High and Temple streets. Los Angeles was such a sinkhole of iniquity that the four Protestant preachers, Methodist, Baptist, Presbyterian, and Episcopal, closed their churches in disgust in 1858 and abandoned Los Angeles to the Devil. A new Methodist preacher soon appeared on the scene and attempted to organize a general Protestant church. A brick building was started, but before it was well under way, six Mexicans were lynched, the preacher left town, and

the project faded, leaving the Catholics as sole survivors. The Presbyterian pastor, the Reverend James Woods, contributed this sad benediction to the press as he departed:

> To preach week after week to empty benches is certainly not encouraging, but when in addition to that a minister has to contend against a torrent of vice and immorality which obliterates all traces of the Christian Sabbath; when he is compelled to endure the blasphemous denunciations of his divine mission, to live where society is disorganized, religion scoffed at, where violence runs riot, and even life itself is unsafe — such condition of affairs may suit some men, but it is not calculated for the peaceful labors of one who follows unobtrusively the foot-steps of the meek and lowly Savior.

The town's angelic name was too ridiculous for such a "den of iniquity." Throughout the state, Los Angeles became known as *Los Diablos*, or The Devils, and letters thus addressed had no difficulty in reaching their proper destination. Colloquially,

Since Los Angeles is such a sinkhole of iniquity, the four preachers, Methodist, Baptist, Presbyterian, and Episcopal, close their churches in disgust in 1858 and abandon Los Angeles to the Devil.

The vicinity of Los Angeles as it looked in 1850, surrounded by agriculture. (SECURITY PACIFIC COLLECTION/Los Angeles Public Library)

the town was simply called Los, meaning "The" — perhaps implying "The What Is It?" — which seems to have been appropriate, for, during this period, there was hardly any other name to give Los Angeles except "the Hell-hole," and the "Pest-house," as it was frequently called.

Out of the terrible muck of Los Angeles, tough, strong, persevering individuals nevertheless sprang beautifully forth in establishing wonderful, new institutions. Like lilies in a dank, dark swamp that took root and came into full bloom, some of the city's most useful institutions came forth. In 1851, the first newspaper, the bilingual *Los Angeles Star*, was published. The public school system was re-established in 1852 with the first two schoolhouses opened in 1855, one at Second and Spring streets, costing $6,000, the other on Bath Street. In 1856 came the Catholic Orphans Asylum, to be followed in 1858 by the Sisters Hospital. Wells-Fargo opened two offices, one in 1857 and one in 1859. The first library association opened a reading room at Court and Spring streets in 1858. The French Benevolent Society was funded in 1860. In 1865, St. Vincent's College (now Loyola Marymount University) began on the plaza, to be moved two years later to Sixth and Broadway.

In 1860, more changes occurred in the pueblo: telegraph service linked Los Angeles via San Francisco to the rest of the nation, bringing Los Angeles out of its sleepy little village mentality; bull and bear fights were outlawed; and pro-slavery Los Angeles gave its vote to Breckinridge and Douglas 2–1 over Lincoln, demonstrating its sympathies for the South. The population was 4,399,

more than double the previous decade. When the Confederate forces fired on Fort Sumter in 1861, Rebel sympathizers raised Confederate flags over the plaza. In the end, Los Angeles, like all of California, remained loyal to the Union. The war itself had a minor impact locally. Southern Californians knew there was a war going on far away, pitting the North against the South, but they had more immediate problems of their own. The great flood of 1861–1862 was followed by two years of unparalleled drought, permanently destroying the cattle industry, breaking up the ranches, and beginning the agricultural era, which included commercial planting of orange groves. By 1867, the Los Angeles City Gas Company began placing gas streetlights at the city's principal intersections. In 1868, the first artesian well was dug and iron pipes were used to supply water to the public.

Demographic and cultural changes of the pueblo came slowly. For 2 decades, Mexican-Americans remained strongly represented in the population at 47 percent (2,069 out of 4,385) in 1860, and 38 percent (2,160 out of 5,728) in 1870. Bilingualism continued even among Yankees, and school children, if they were taught at all in the 1850s, were taught mostly in Spanish. Some local judges used English and Spanish interchangeably in their courtrooms, and at least one of them, District Judge Joaquin Carrillo, used Spanish exclusively for the 14 years he sat on the bench. Local journalist Horace Bell referred to Los Angeles in those days as a "semi-gringo" town. By 1870, Los Angeles had gained only 2,000 people and most of its 5,728 inhabitants were of Hispanic origin. Many of

> For two decades, 1860 and 1870, Mexican-Americans remain strongly represented in the population, 47 percent and 38 percent.

The Los Angeles Plaza where the city was born, as it looked in 1869 with the Church of Our Lady of Angels on the left.

these newcomers were Civil War veterans, here to start life once again. That they were largely Confederates was indicated by the vote for Seymour in 1868, which was 1,236 to Grant's 748. Yet, there was harmony between the races with a Yankee mayor occasionally elected, but never a Yankee city council. Between one-half and one-third of the population was Mexican, and residential segregation was not yet practiced. No one spoke of a "Mexican *barrio*," although north of the plaza was a distinctive neighborhood founded in the 1850s by Mexicans returning south from the gold country. Here, in what was called Sonora Town, the poorer Mexicans settled into adobe houses, and by 1880 it would form the nucleus of the first Mexican barrio in this or any other U.S. city.

> In Sonora Town, the poorer Mexicans settle into adobe houses, and by 1880 it forms the nucleus of the first Mexican barrio.

Of the two cultures, Mexican and American, represented architecturally in Los Angeles, the Mexican predominated into the mid-1870s, according to Ludwig Salva-

Pio Pico, the last Mexican governor of California.

dor, who wrote about his travels in and around Los Angeles in the 1870s in his book, *Los Angeles in the Sunny Seventies*. As new tracts developed, particularly in the southern parts of town, more homes were constructed of wood, until the number of frame buildings quickly surpassed adobes. The old ranches bearing Spanish names that once ringed the pueblo, gave way to farms and new communities. Even the hills north and west of the plaza were crowned, in the 1870s, the 1880s, and the 1890s, with Victorian and ornate homes of the well-to-do, offering a view of orange groves, gardens, orchards, and vineyards.

The old plaza retained its identity as the center of town until about 1870 when commerce began moving steadily south. Pio Pico, the last Mexican governor of California, and several associates invested a considerable fortune constructing the elegant hotel known as the Pico House on the south side of the plaza. This

An advertisement of the Pico House built in 1869 on the Plaza by Pio Pico, billed as "the only first-class hotel in California." (SECURITY PACIFIC COLLECTION/Los Angeles Public Library)

handsome masonry structure, completed in 1869, was the first three-story building in Los Angeles. It ranked, for a while, as one of the West's most fashionable and popular hotels. Its developers hoped it would anchor the town's business community to the plaza, but the Pico House's success faded as the city advanced and moved south.

The year 1876 saw a centennial celebration in the plaza making history with some 30,000 persons living in Los Angeles County, which, until 1889, included Orange County. Protestant churches had begun to function once again. The Presbyterian church was on Second and Broadway; the Episcopalians reopened their activities at their original church at Temple and New High; the Congregationalists located nearby on New High; and the Methodists occupied a building on Broadway between Third and Fourth. The Church of Our Lady of the Angels continued to be a gathering place for Catholics on the plaza, as St. Vibiana Cathedral at Second and South Main streets was under construction. In the 1875 Los Angeles City Directory, there is a listing for a Lutheran church holding services at 9:50 a.m. with Sunday school at 12:30 p.m. in the Good Templars' Hall on Main Street with Rev. Gustav Borchard as pastor. Neither he nor the church appears in later city directories.

When the Southern Pacific Railroad built a line from San Francisco to Los Angeles in 1876, giving Los Angeles its transcontinental rail connections, the last chapter in the pueblo's history ended and the modern chapter began. The railroad ended Los Angeles' era of isolation, paving the way for new immigration. A more direct connection with the East was established in 1881 when the Southern Pacific completed construction work between Los Angeles and El Paso, Texas. The city's continued growth in the late 1870s was also due to the people already living in Los Angeles writing glowing letters to the relatives and friends back home, a practice that is said to have continued to this day. In 1873, Charles Nordhoff, grandfather of the Nordhoff of *Mutiny on the Bounty* fame, published a volume, *California: for Health, Pleasure, and Residence.* This work was given credit for having sent more people to Southern California than any other book ever written.

Through the use of clever and sometimes deceiving advertising, promoters, colonizers, and professional boosters soon after 1880 discovered that more and more settlers and buyers of lots could be brought into Southern California. Soon books, pamphlets, newspaper and magazine articles, and more-or-less honest advertisements extolling the virtues of the semi-tropical climate and inexhaustible resources of California, flooded the United States and Europe. Ben F. Taylor's *Between the Gates* had reached his 11th edition by 1883. This rosy prose is a sample:

> The railroad ends Los Angeles' era of isolation, paving the way for new immigration.

The first Southern Pacific train to arrive in Los Angeles from San Francisco in 1876 was greeted by the town band.

Whoever asks where Los Angeles is, to him I shall say, Across a desert without wearying, beyond a mountain without climbing....

Where the flowers catch fire with beauty; where the pomegranates wear calyx crowns; where the bananas of Honolulu are blossoming; where the chestnuts of Italy are ripening; where the almond trees are shining…in the midst of a garden of 36 square miles, there is Los Angeles!

Due to the publicity given about the mild climate of Southern California, much attention was given to the beneficial effects on all manner of respiratory diseases, especially tuberculosis, or consumption as it was then called. William Henry Bishop, widely traveled in California during the boom years, held out great hope to every invalid: "Many advantages offer to the invalid. The climate permits him to be almost constantly outdoors. The sky is blue, the sun unclouded, nearly every day in the year, and he can go into his orchard…."

The railways retained their own advertising staff writers. Major Benjamin C. Truman was chief of the literary bureau of the Southern Pacific

and wrote in the *Southern Pacific Sketchbook*, which had a circulation of 10,000 copies. Already in 1874, he stated in his *Semitropical California*: "The purity of the air of Los Angeles is remarkable.... The air, when inhaled, gives to the individual a stimulus and vital force which only an atmosphere so pure can ever communicate."

The pastoral landscape charmed both residents and visitors, but Salvador's travel account, *Los Angeles in the Sunny Seventies*, painted an idyllic picture of flowering gardens, fragrant orchards, and handsome mountain vistas, all blessed by clean and healthful air. Among Salvador's most pleasant memories were horseback outings in the canyons, wagon rides to the Santa Monica seashore, bird hunting in the marshlands (what would later become Venice), and year-round agricultural enterprises. So it was that Angelinos awoke and discovered their climate; astute travel writers had pointed it out to them. Charles Nordhoff and Ben C. Truman and others likened Southern California to Greece, Italy, Palestine, and other Mediterranean lands. Here, in the "semi-tropical" part of the state, they wrote, was a glorious climate for growing nearly every known crop with a minimum outlay of land, labor, or capital. Here, throughout

Writers liken Southern California to Greece, Italy, Palestine, and other Mediterranean lands.

A view of Los Angeles in 1880 looking north on Main Street from Commercial Street. (SECURITY PACIFIC COLLECTION/Los Angeles Public Library)

the year was an outdoor environment where people could climb mountains, bask at the seashore, or explore the desert without ever encountering the dangerous sleet or paralyzing snowstorms that plagued the Midwest and East. Even insects (with the notable exception of fleas) seemed more benign than elsewhere. Here gentle nature served to cure every illness including tuberculosis, or consumption, so it was said.

With this new migration, the city continued to grow to a population of 11,183, according to the 1880 census. This decade brought significant demographic and cultural changes. The Mexican American population slipped to 19 percent, as the Midwestern Anglo culture sank deeper roots. Also that year, the city's first cement and asphalt pavement was laid on Main Street north of First, and the University of Southern California, the first Protestant school of higher education organized by Methodists, was chartered. Ozro Childs, a Protestant, donated 308 lots to raise construction money. The former governor, John Downey, a Roman Catholic, and Jewish businessman, Isaias Hellman, also helped this endeavor. Dr. Joseph P. Widney, brother of a major donor, left his medical practice to become the university's first president, personally guaranteeing payment of the school's debts within four years.

By 1880, Los Angeles had 172 industrial establishments employing over 700 workers, a marked increase from 1850 when the town had supported only one lonely factory, a bakery with two employees. The age of electricity was ushered into Los Angeles in 1882 when Mayor Toberman threw a switch that lighted lamps affixed to seven tall masts in the downtown area. Their glow was bright enough to provide a landmark for sailors miles offshore, despite objections from the gas company and those skeptics who feared that artificial light would cause blindness or damage eyes in other ways.

Within a few short years, the city's image had changed from a fallen angel to that of a Sunday school teacher living in a "new paradise" or in the "Promised Land." Overnight, the Los Angeles climate became a saleable item, along with the land. Hucksters grew fond of saying, "We sold them the climate and threw in the land free." Many newcomers lured to Los Angeles by descriptions of this "new paradise" were Danes, Swedes, Norwegians, French, Germans, and Swiss. Among them were numerous Lutherans, and those who would eventually be won to the Lutheran church. Among those health seekers coming to the area were pastors of The Lutheran Church — Missouri Synod, who the Lord had sent to plant the church in this "blooming garden." In Rev. John William Theiss' manuscript, *The History of the Lutheran Churches and Missions of Southern California 1881–19–*, is the following description:

> Southern California is naturally a desert and only when water is poured upon the sandy soil and flows in glistening diamonds from place to place moistening, permeating, and saturating the ground, vegetation springs up in its wake and the desert valleys are turned into blooming gardens which delight the eye of man and offer rich returns for his labors. In like manner, Southern California would today be a spiritual wilderness had not, by the grace of God, the living waters of the Gospel of Christ Jesus been poured out upon it and had not this water of life gradually flowed from city to city, from village to village by means of our mission until also this part of the United States, the Southwestern extreme of our beloved land, had been converted into a blooming garden of the Lord bearing sweet fruit unto life eternal.

The time was ripe and the harvest was waiting for establishing The Lutheran Church — Missouri Synod in Southern California in the new "Promised Land." Where the 1880s would bring the biggest "boom" to Southern California in its two hundred-year history, God's messengers would bring the Good News of His salvation.

Within a few short years, the city's image has changed from fallen angel to that of a Sunday school teacher living in a "new paradise" or in the "promised land."

As lab'rers in Thy vineyard,
Lord, send them out to be
Content to bear the burden
Of weary days for Thee.

The Seed Is Cast

od's inevitable plan was that one invalid pastor should be instrumental in establishing two Lutheran congregations in sunny Southern California. Unlike northern California, where for almost 20 years one single congregation had carried on the work of The Lutheran Church — Missouri Synod, the work in Southern California began simultaneously with two Lutheran groups, one in Los Angeles and the other in the city of Orange. These two congregations, which developed from missionary beginnings during the "Land Boom" of unprecedented proportions changing the course of history of Southern California in the 1880s, can be considered twin daughters, having had one spiritual father who was instrumental in proclaiming the Gospel ministry to both of them. One might add that they even had the same spiritual "grandfather."

The nature of Christ's kingdom manifested itself in the missions of Southern California with its small beginnings, "like unto a grain of mustard seed." In no case did God give great increase at once, but by slender, small beginnings and slow growth He proved that through faith and prayer the church would grow and mature. The Lord also showed His church that His strength is made perfect in weakness, for it pleased Him to have His pioneer work performed by pastors who came, as invalids, to California for their health.

In the fall of 1880, when Los Angeles numbered 11,000 people, Rev. Martin Luther Wyneken, formerly of Cincinnati, Ohio, arrived in Los Angeles in order to benefit from the mild climate; he was suffering from consumption and a throat problem. While in

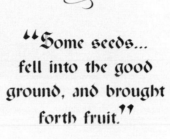

> "Some seeds... fell into the good ground, and brought forth fruit."
>
> — MATTHEW 13:8

Cincinnati in December of 1876, he began suffering with a severe cough causing a disabling throat condition, growing worse, necessitating his resignation as pastor of Trinity Lutheran Church in that city in 1878. His plan was to seek a warmer climate for the restoration of his health. With his wife and children, he traveled to Louisiana where his health continued to deteriorate. After finding no relief in that climate, he moved to San Francisco, California, where his brother-in-law, Rev. Jacob M. Buehler, the first Missouri Synod pastor on the Pacific Coast established the mother church, Saint Paulus Lutheran Church, where he was pastor. As Pastor Wyneken's health continued to decline, his brother-in-law suggested he try the milder climate of Los Angeles. There is little doubt, as subsequent events were to prove, that Brother Buehler sent Wyneken south on an exploratory trip not only as a means to improve his health but also to build the Kingdom of God.

Pastor Wyneken arrived in Los Angeles in either the late summer or fall of 1880. Despite his physical ailments, he was well aware of the important developments that were taking place in Southern California, especially in and around Los Angeles. Not only did he gather some Lutherans about him to hold reading services and family devotions, but he also interested himself in real estate developments in the Sierra Madre foothills where he wanted Lutherans to settle; since the Lutherans were slow to move and characteristically cautious, the plans did not materialize. At the same time, many other religious groups were establishing colonies in the area — the Quakers in Whittier and the Brethren in La Verne. For this purpose he, too, became one of the press agents for the great southland, writing various articles telling of the virtues, beauties, and possibilities of Southern California for the Milwaukee *Rundschau* and the St. Louis *Abendschule* papers that were read in Lutheran circles. In the fall of 1881 and 1882, a few Lutherans from St. Louis, Missouri, relocated in Los Angeles and the "mission efforts" of Rev. Wyneken prospered.

Pastor Wyneken, although in poor health, did much of the missionary work, which led to the founding of Trinity congregation, the first Missouri Synod Lutheran

Pictured in 1882, Rev. Martin Luther Wyneken, the missionary who did work leading to the founding of Trinity Lutheran Church in Los Angeles. (Pacific Southwest District Archives)

church in the Los Angeles area. He was described as having a "winning personality," "very conservative disposition of mind," and being "amiable." Day by day, Mr. Julius Schmidt, a German Lutheran, took him by horse and buggy to make many house calls on prospective German members. When Schmidt was not available, the 35-year-old "retired" pastor had the services of Los Angeles' first rail transit line, "The Spring & West Sixth Street Railroad," which was operating 11 miles of track within the city, from the plaza to Sixth Street and out to Lincoln Heights. This was a horse-drawn streetcar with open sides that must have required a great deal of fortitude on the part of the passengers to be trundled over the dusty streets of the time. He conducted reading services in German in his home for the pioneer Lutherans throughout 1881 and into the spring of 1882, as he couldn't preach due to his severe throat problems. His sister, Miss Emma Wyneken, a teacher at St. John's, Orange, in the early 1900s, reported in an interview many years ago that a Sunday school of between eighty and ninety pupils was conducted during those years in a rented hall. She also stated that his throat condition did improve somewhat.

Wyneken did get around, however, for he found Lutheran settlers on the subdivided lands of the Rancho Santiago de Santa Ana, particularly the present town of Orange, also part of Los An-

geles County at that time. Although his physical condition did not permit him to provide this group with regular services, he nevertheless visited them and encouraged them to seek an eventual congregational organization.

In November of 1881, another Lutheran minister, Rev. Jacob Kogler, came to Los Angeles from Belle Plaine, Minnesota, also for the climate that would restore his health and in hopes of restoring throat problems that forced him to resign his pastorate in Minnesota. Due to his health problems, he couldn't think of returning to active ministry immediately. After a short time, Pastor Wyneken drew Pastor Kogler's attention to the plight of the shepherdless flock in Orange, inducing him to visit them at once. Pastor Kogler preached his first German sermon to the Orange group on December 10, 1881, followed by several more Sundays in January when they organized *Ev. Luth. St. Johannes-Gemeinde U. A. C. zu Orange, California*, "St. John's Lutheran Congregation of the Unaltered Augsburg Confession at Orange, California," and then called him as their pastor on February 12, 1882. The Rev. J. M. Buehler installed him as pastor of the congregation in May of 1882. With renewed health, Pastor Kogler could attend to all the spiritual needs of this little flock.

God's strength is mighty in the weak, which was demonstrated in the spring of 1882 when a bronchial affliction compelled Rev. J. M. Buehler to rest and recuperate for some six weeks in the milder climate of Los Angeles. He did not find much rest, since he would recuperate by taking charge of the young mission in Los Angeles. The group rented Leck's Hall at 116 South Main Street between Second and Third streets for public worship on Sundays, where Buehler held the first public service of The Lutheran Church — Missouri Synod on Sunday, May 28, 1882. He reported his impression at length in the letter to the Northern Conference, which met in Oakland early in June:

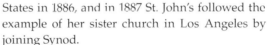

Last Sunday we had our first service here. Since Los Angeles does not enjoy a good reputation with regard to church life and religion, I did not expect too much of an attendance. But we had notices in all local newspapers and had notified all friends and acquaintances. Thus to our great joy a not inconsiderable congregation came together. There were 52 adults and some children. It appeared that the people were greatly pleased at the prospect of having services for several Sundays more. In the service itself, there were indeed fine evidences of true devotion. However, I shall not become too optimistic but shall rather wait to see how the attendance turns out on the Sundays to follow....

Neither Buehler nor Wyneken were disappointed, as the services continued to be well attended and appreciated. On the fifth Sunday, June 25, a short meeting was held after the service where it was decided to meet that same afternoon for purposes of organizing a congregation.

The minutes of this meeting have been preserved and state:

The divine services conducted by Pastor Buehler on the previous four Sundays have furnished ample testimony that there is a general desire to establish a congregation of our faith in this locality. Be it resolved, therefore, to call a meeting for this afternoon in this Leck's Hall in order to deliberate on the feasibility and preparation for the establishment of a congregation.

At the appointed time, the men met with Buehler, who served as chairman of the meeting, and under his guidance *die Deutsche Ev. Lutherische Dreieinigkeits Gemeinde U. A. C., zu Los Angeles* (The First German Evangelical Lutheran Trinity Congregation U.A.C. of Los Angeles, California) was organized. Fifteen members had appeared for the historic meeting, and elected F. Witte, president; J. A. Schumacher, vice president; Julius Schmidt, secretary; and H. W. Stoll became treasurer, an office he held for 22 years until the time of his death. Los Angeles now had its first Lutheran congregation under the auspices of the Missouri Synod, but it was a church without its own resident pastor, since Pastor Wyneken's health did not permit him to serve in a full pastoral capacity. Trinity request-

ed St. Paulus in San Francisco to allow Pastor Buehler to remain in Southern California until a permanent pastor would come. The request was regretfully denied.

Thus it happened, when the Lutheran work in Southern California began, that Martin L. Wyneken became the pioneer in the south and gave impetus to the simultaneous establishment of two Lutheran congregations, Trinity in Los Angeles and St. John's in Orange. Both mother congregations began to meet for prayer and praise in 1881, and both were organized in 1882. Trinity became a member of The Lutheran Synod of Missouri, Ohio, and Other States in 1886, and in 1887 St. John's followed the example of her sister church in Los Angeles by joining Synod.

Since Rev. M. L. Wyneken's health continued to decline and he could not serve as pastor of this flock, Rev. Hoelter of Chicago was, therefore, called. He declined the call. Trinity congregation called Rev. J. M. Buehler of San Francisco, but he also declined. Next Rev. George Paul Runkel of Aurora, Indiana, was sent a call. Four days before Christmas on December 21, 1882, he sent a telegram announcing that he had accepted the call. The first Christmas of this new little Los Angeles congregation was a very happy one, even though the Runkel family did not arrive until March 1883. When Rev. Runkel (1883–1905) arrived in Los Angeles, he was installed as pastor of Trinity by Rev. J. M. Buehler of San Francisco with Rev. J. Kogler of Orange assisting.

The next step for this young congregation, under

Rev. Jacob Matthias Buehler, California's pioneer Lutheran missionary who also served as the first President of the California and Nevada District, 1887–1901.

Rev. George Runkel, first pastor of Trinity Lutheran Church, Los Angeles, 1883–1905. (Pacific Southwest District Archives)

Trinity builds first church building in 1883.

Trinity's first church and school building located on Broadway (then Fort Street), between Sixth and Seventh streets where the property was on the southern edge of town. (Pacific Southwest District Archives)

the energetic leadership of its own pastor, was to look for property to erect a church building. On May 7, a building committee began to function. Within two weeks, the first $1,000 was pledged for this purpose, and within another two weeks a lot, 58' × 150', had been purchased for a sum of $1,700 at 540 South Fort Street (now Broadway), between Sixth and Seventh streets. The first church-school building, 34' × 60' with a 70-foot spire, a beautiful altar and pulpit built to match, constructed by the builder, Mr. P. Witte, and built on the property at a cost of $3,000, was dedicated to the service of the Triune God on November 25, 1883. A unique feature of this edifice was that instead of pews, the nave had benches with collapsible desks attached. Now this little flock could rejoice in the words of Psalm 83: "The sparrow hath found an house, and the swallow a nest, where she may lay her young, even Thine altars, O Lord of hosts, my King and my God!" The congregation would worship in this church building for only four years.

Immediately following the dedication, Pastor Runkel opened the first Christian day school of 27 pupils in the new structure. Besides performing his heavy pastoral duties with the constant influx of people into the area, he taught school in German for 5 years, with school attendance increasing to 45 children. Since the property was inadequate to accommodate a new school building, a city ordinance with zoning restrictions that prohibited the erection of a school building on Broadway helped spur the cause of finding a larger piece of property.

On October 19, 1884, in Los Angeles, California, the beloved Pastor Wyneken at age 39 breathed his last breath and was called by his Lord to the Church Triumphant leaving his wife Clara of 12 years and 4 children, Concordia, Clara, Martin II, and Arthur who later became pastor of First Lutheran of Long Beach. The obituary in *The Lutheran Witness*, November 7, 1884, stated, "But neither climate nor the care and assistance of his relatives and friends, nor his own resoluteness to fight against the inroads of the lingering malady, could snatch him from an early grave. His departure is a cause of bereavement not only to his family, but to all who knew him, especially to his classmates in college and seminary...." His death was a great loss to the church at that time. Even in severe sickness, he continued to do the Lord's work! One of the last things he did for Trinity was to prepare a constitution that was accepted by the congregation in April of 1884.

When the church property was purchased on Broadway at the south end of town in 1883, the city numbered 12,000 inhabitants. By 1887, just four years later, the Los Angeles City Directory listed 55,488 citizens, and by 1888 the estimated population was 80,000. A rumor was circulating that the Post Office was going to be moved to Broadway near Seventh, and business frontage in that section brought $875 a foot, enabling Trinity to sell the property for a handsome $15,000.

What was causing this phenomenal growth? A more direct connection with the East was established in 1881 when the Southern Pacific completed construction on a line between Los Angeles and El Paso, Texas. Henceforth, the story of Los Angeles is of newcomers constantly pouring into its expanding area, an influx that continued year by year, resulting in agricultural development, especially citrus, and the rise of tributary communities.

The exceptional growth of Los Angeles in the mid-1880s can also be attributed the Santa Fe Railroad linking Los Angeles to the East. Ten days after Santa Fe Railroad reached Los Angeles, driving the last (golden) spike at Cajón Pass on November 9, 1885, it reduced the straight fare from Mississippi Valley points to Los Angeles from $100 to $95, and the round-trip fare from $150 to $140. The Southern Pacific met this cut and went its new upstart competitor one better — and the greatest railroad "rate war" ever seen in America was on. Fares continued to be cut, first by one road and then by the other, a matter of 5 or 10 dollars at a time. As business started to pick up, people began packing their bags and trunks to come west. Newspapers kept the price war going using ads like "Land! Cheap land, in sunny California!" The one-way fare went down to $85. Personally conducted tours were organized, starting at Chicago and St. Louis, bringing people west. Freight rates went down proportionately; for example, the rate on salt from New York was 60 cents a ton; coal was transported from Chicago for one dollar a ton.

Starting in little dribbles, the movement to Southern California gained volume rapidly as fares went down, and, shortly thereafter, when transportation was offered practically free, it assumed the proportions of a mad rush of people, leaving the cold Midwest for "Sunny California." For several weeks, one could buy a ticket from any Mississippi Valley point to the City of the Angels for $15; for one week it was $5, and at the very peak of this "bitter, cut-throat competition," for one day, in the spring of 1886, the fare was $1. "Kansas City to Los Angeles for a dollar!" The crowds rushed to it, first scores, then hundreds, then thousands. The "California Boom" was in full progress! Among these passengers were many Lutherans drawn by the lure of cheap land and sunny, warm weather.

In 1887, Trinity congregation, numbering 240 souls with 34 voting members, moved farther west and purchased a 120' × 167' lot on the northwest corner of Eighth and Flower streets in order to erect a Christian day school. The lot on Fort Street (Broadway) was too small to accommodate both church and school, and the Broadway property had gone from a residential area to a commercial block. The cost of the new lot was $7,000 with an outlay of $2,900 to construct a chapel on Eighth Street with an addition to the structure used for the school. In 1888, a parsonage was erected by the builders of the school, Messrs. Witte and Ihlo, on Flower Street leaving the corner for the new church. The Fort Street property was then sold for $15,000, thus liquidating the congregation's debts. The ensuing years were years of financial depression for Southern California, as the great land boom had "burst." During the depression

of the 1890s, the congregation had difficulty making ends meet and was not able to erect a suitable church. However, in 1898, the congregation took a bold venture of faith and dedicated to the Lord, a church measuring 80' × 44' × 52' with a 100 foot spire costing $6,000, having the same contractor, Mr. P. Witte, who built the other buildings on the property. Memorial windows, chandeliers, two bells, and other items were donated. The church, with a two-manual pneumatic pipe organ built by Schuelke of Milwaukee, Wisconsin, was dedicated on the Sunday after Easter in 1898. The congregation rejoiced over the progress made with the help of the Lord in difficult times. There was only one sentiment among the parishioners that day: "This is the day, which the Lord has made; we will be glad and rejoice in it." Psalm 118:24. The congregation now numbered 437 souls with 55 voting members

By 1903, the congregation had 91 voting members and numbered 456 souls with Los Angeles no longer a semi-rural town of 12,000, but rather a city of over 100,000 inhabitants and a large German-speaking population. Every winter, Mid-

Trinity moves to Eighth and Flower streets in 1887.

Trinity's Christian day school building on Eighth Street with new church building on the corner of Eighth and Flower streets. Students with Teacher Albert Schendel and Pastor Runkel behind fence, circa 1900. (Pacific Southwest District Archives)

Trinity's second church building on the corner of Eighth and Flower streets, dedicated on the Sunday after Easter in 1898. (Pacific Southwest District Archives)

The interior of Trinity, circa 1900. (Pacific Southwest District Archives)

Rev. John W. Theiss becomes Trinity's assistant pastor in 1904.

western tourists came in greater numbers to Los Angeles to escape cold weather. As the area of the city encompassed more land in 1903, it became an impossibility for the aged Pastor Runkel to attend to much-needed missionary work. He was instrumental in establishing congregations at Palmdale in 1887, Pasadena in 1890, Oxnard, and also preaching in different areas in Los Angeles as far east as Pomona. Rev. John William Theiss of Santa Rosa, California, was called to be the Los Angeles missionary and assistant pastor; after accepting the call, he was installed in March of 1904. He immediately did mission work in the Vernon District of Los Angeles and in East Los Angeles. In 1905, Christ Evangelical Lutheran Church was organized in the Vernon District with six members of Trinity dismissed in peace to become charter members of Christ Church. Also in Long Beach, the mission work of preaching a few sermons by Rev. Runkel was continued by Pastor Theiss, where a congregation (Zion) was organized in 1905.

Trinity's assistant pastor, Rev. John Theiss, would be another man of great missionary zeal and vision in Southern California, helping to establish many new congregations. He was born on September 29, 1863, in the parsonage of his father, Rev. John George Theiss, in Zelienople, Pennsylvania, where his father was pastor. He was the 8th of 10 children. Two brothers become pastors and four become parochial school teachers. Following Confirmation, he entered Concordia College, Fort Wayne, Indiana, and graduated from Con-

cordia Seminary, St. Louis, in 1886. His first call was to Madisonville, Ohio, now a part of Cincinnati. Three years later, he received a call to Portland, Oregon, where he established Trinity congregation. After four years of service in Portland, a throat ailment forced him to resign. Within a year, he had recovered and received a call in 1893 to Trinity Lutheran Church, Santa Rosa, California. In 1890, he married Mattie Broadhurst of Cincinnati, Ohio. Their happy marriage resulted in the birth of four daughters. In 1911, his beloved spouse was called to her heavenly home. After 14 lonely years, he married Mrs. Theodora Stumpf of Springfield, Ohio.

John Theiss was known as a man of prayer, a true theologian, a model preacher and teacher. During his active 34 years in California, he was a prominent pastor, District president (1920–1924), poet with published works, pencil and watercolor artist whose pictures were exhibited in art museums, historian, writer, and pioneer in being the first to regularly preach in English. He established the first English-speaking congregation, Grace Lutheran, in Los Angeles during 1906. He would also accept the call to be the pastor of Christ Lutheran in Los Angeles where he remained 24 years. After a severe stroke forced him to resign in 1928, he and Theodora returned to her hometown of Springfield, Ohio, where they lived four years. On March 3, 1932, while taking a nap, he quietly departed this life after having a second stroke.

In May 1905 while calling on the sick, Pastor Runkel stepped from an electric tram, slipped, and fell, aggravating an old rupture and sustaining internal injuries. On his deathbed, he said, "Tell my congregation that I am dying in the faith in Christ Jesus. The same [faith] that I preached at Trinity's pulpit. I am tired and want to go to sleep. Tell them a poor sinner is going home to his Savior." His wife of 40 years was not at his bedside as she was in the East attending her mother's funeral. On May 30, it pleased the Lord to call Rev. George P. Runkel to his eternal reward after he had faithfully served Trinity congregation for 22 years. At his funeral, Rev. Kogler spoke in German and Rev. Theiss preached in English. During his ministry in and around Los Angeles, he had baptized 700 persons, confirmed 213, married 346 couples, and Trinity had numbered 675 souls with 523 communicant members. Through his missionary zeal, many new congregations were established in the Southern California area.

Rev. John William Theiss was called in 1903 to be the Los Angeles city missionary and Trinity's assistant pastor. (Pacific Southwest District Archives)

The Lord had blessed Trinity with only a short vacancy; a month later on July 9, 1905, a new pastor, the 43-year-old Rev. Arthur E. Michel of Lockport, New York, was unanimously called to serve Trinity as its pastor. He was a man of wide experience, having served Immanuel Church of Pensacola, Florida, from 1885 to 1891, and Lockport until 1905. While in the Buffalo area, he served as circuit visitor. For the rest of his life, he served

In 1905, the 43-year-old Rev. Arthur A. Michel of Lockport, New York, became Trinity's second pastor where he served until his retirement in 1941. (Pacific Southwest District Archives)

the mother church of Lutheranism in Los Angeles until his retirement in 1941. He was described as a quiet, firm, serious, almost stern man. All who knew him respected him. He had seen much grief in his life: losing his first wife, the former Sophie Borman of New York, after six years of marriage and having three infant children taken from him in early deaths. His second helpmate, Elise Brandt of Fort Wayne, was called to her eternal home in 1929, causing him to live his remaining 29 years as a widower.

On September 24, 1905, Pastor Michel was installed as Trinity's second pastor by Rev. August Hansen of Pasadena, assisted by Rev. J. W. Theiss and Rev. E. P. Block. Since this celebration was a joint effort of all the Southern California Lutherans coming from East Los Angeles, the Vernon District, Long Beach, Oxnard, Pasadena, and Azusa, every seat in the church was filled. Under his guidance, Trinity would experience internal and external growth with membership reaching 1,000. He would also be another missionary pastor helping to establish congregations in Whittier, Pomona, Glendale, and other cities.

As the Flower Street property was inadequate for the expansion of the Christian day school and playground for the children of the school, which had grown to 95 students in 2 classrooms, Trinity resolved to sell the property and move to larger quarters. In 1904, 5 lots were purchased for $20,000 with a total expanse of

238 feet on Eighteenth Street and 170 feet on Cherry Street, moving farther southwest from their original property as the city continued to expand north, south, east, and west. A two-story wood-frame structure, including a five-classroom school and a large parish hall, was erected in 1906 at a cost of $13,000. This venerable and loved building would serve the congregation and District for 46 years, hosting meetings, conventions, conferences, and banquets. The old Flower Street property was sold for $110,135 in 1907, giving the congregation a substantial profit. In 1910, a large two-story parsonage was built for $5,000 next door to the school on Eighteenth Street in Swiss chalet style matching the school building. Since God had visibly blessed Trinity congregation, the congregation in gratitude donated $1,400 during 1910–1911 to the Church Extension Fund of the California and Nevada District of the Missouri Synod.

After much anticipation, the cornerstone for Trinity's magnificent, grand, new church building on the corner of Eighteenth and Cherry streets was laid on May 12, 1912, with Pastor Edward J. Rudnick of San Bernardino, another pastor who came to California because of tuberculosis, delivering the sermon in classical German oratory and Rev. Arthur Wyneken of Long Beach delivering an English address. Pastor Michel performed the official act. The beautiful, dark-brick and sandstone-

trimmed church of modified French Gothic style was designed by a member, Elimar Meinardus, built at a cost of about $60,000. Mr. F. Witte was supervisor of construction. The building boasted twin spires rising to the heavens 138 feet and 107 feet respectively. The nave, together with the loft, seated 900 people with 1,000 people present that joyful dedication day on Palm Sunday, March 16, 1913, to praise and thank God. The nave measured 73 feet in length with a transept of 61 feet, having a large memorial window on the east side depicting the resurrection of Christ given in memory of Mr. J. Mohn. The west window portrayed St. Peter sinking in the water and was given in memory of Mr. Henry Stoll. In the chancel was a high, white altar with gold trim containing three statues with Christ in the center and the interior walls painted to look like graceful, elegant hanging draperies. In the center of the altar was a woodcarving of the Last Supper. The ornate pulpit also had carved statuettes on each side. At the foot of the chancel steps was a large, white, Italian marble-angel baptismal font. Exquisite Austrian crystal chandeliers hung from the ceiling of the nave illuminating the splendid sanctuary. In the front, east of the chancel, was the sizeable choir stall with an Austin pipe organ, which led the congregation and choirs in praise.

In the morning service on Easter Sunday, March 23, 1913, Pastor Michel preached in German on "Christ the Lord is Risen," and in the evening service, he preached in English on "Folly of Not Believing in the Word and Works of Christ, Since He is Risen from the Dead." On Monday evening, the new $7,600 pipe organ and chimes were dedicated with Professor G. H. F. Holter of San Francisco giving a concert on the new instrument assisted by Professor G. Retz and a choir of 30 voices, and with Rev. G. H. Smukal as violin soloist. Following the dedication of the new church, English services were introduced and continued in the Sunday evening services while German services were conducted in the morning.

By the time the 1920s arrived, many changes took place at Trinity: beginning in 1921, English services were conducted at 11:00 a.m. and German services at 9:30 a.m.; in 1923, an English constitution was adopted, and in 1926, the congregation reincorporated under the name of "Trinity Evangelical Lutheran Congregation U.A.C. of Los Angeles, California." The congregation had gone from a predominately German-speaking parish to a congregation that was conducting its worship and

> Trinity's new majestic church is dedicated on March 16, 1913.

Laying of the cornerstone of Trinity's third church building at 18th and Cherry on May 12, 1912. Pictured are Rev. Michel, (center), Mr. Schreiber, (right) chairman of the Building Committee, and Rev. Edward Rudnick, (left) holding derby. (Pacific Southwest District Archives)

Trinity's new modified French Gothic style church built at a cost of about $60,000 was dedicated on Palm Sunday, March 16, 1913. (Pacific Southwest District Archives)

The interior of Trinity's new church which would seat 900 people. Pictured are the Italian marble-angel baptismal font, altar, and new Austin Pipe Organ, circa 1917. (Pacific Southwest District Archives)

business in the dominant language of the country, English. Years later, she would become bilingual again meeting the needs of Koreans, Brazilians, and Hispanics in her neighborhood, known as the "Church of All Nations."

After serving Trinity for 35 years and 7 months, Pastor Michel retired from the active ministry, giving his farewell sermon on June 1, 1941. He departed this life on March 9, 1955, having walked this earthly pilgrimage 92 years, 8 months, and 25 days. On June 8, 1941, Trinity's third pastor, the Rev. Immanuel F. Hodde of South Bend, Indiana, was installed. His father, the Rev. William Hodde, and mother, Marie, provided his elementary education in parish schools where his father was pastor. He attended St. Paul's College in Concordia, Missouri, and Concordia Seminary in St. Louis. He graduated in 1926 and served parishes in Indiana. His ministry at Trinity would be some of the more troubling years because of World War II, the Korean War, the "cold war," the spike in membership, and finally the decline of membership with the beautiful historic building at Eighteenth and Cherry sold and dismantled to make way for a freeway interchange. During the Annual Every Member Visit on Sunday, December 7, 1941, the members learned that Japan had bombed Pearl Harbor. On December 8, 1941, Germany declared

Mr. E. G. Dankworth directing the Junior Choir, students in grades five to nine, in 1943. (Pacific Southwest District Archives)

war on the United States, and 10 days later, during a mournful congregational meeting, it was resolved to discontinue German services and offer the facilities to the government in the event of an emergency.

In 1958, Pastor Hodde accepted an appointment to the chaplaincy of hospitals in Santa Monica, Huntington Beach, and for Casa Descanso Retirement Home in Santa Monica. He died in 1974, leaving his wife, Rose, 5 children, and 12 grandchildren. Rev. William J. Seebeck of Dover, New Jersey, who would oversee the transition from the old location to the new site, was installed on November 16, 1958, succeeding Pastor Hodde as the

Rev. William J. Seebeck becomes pastor in 1958.

fourth pastor of Trinity. He was a graduate of Concordia Collegiate Institute, Bronxville, New York, and Concordia Seminary in St. Louis. He served congregations in High Ridge, Missouri, St. Louis, Springfield, Illinois, and Mendon, New York. He and his wife had two children, Dorothy and John.

Trinity reached its peak in membership with an all-time high of 1,076 in 1948 and decreased to 447 in 1957. After World War II, the neighborhood around the church experienced many changes as it deteriorated. In 1952, the church was compelled to sell for $44,000, the eastern section of the property (where the school, parish hall, and schoolyard were located) to the state of California for the construction of the Harbor Freeway. The old parsonage next to the church was demolished and a new school and parish hall were constructed in 1954 at a cost of $109,167. By 1959, with the mortar of the new building hardly set, the state "cast its eyes" on the remainder of the property for use as the interchange of the Santa Monica and Harbor freeways, paying $505,700 for the property with the magnificent, historical landmark destroyed. With the property sold, the congregation's dwindling membership of 232 members moved farther west to South Gramercy Place off Wilton Place to begin a new ministry.

Trinity certainly deserved her title as the "mother" of Missouri Synod Lutheranism in Los Angeles, as she spawned many congregations giving her members to establish new parishes. The Boyle Heights area, one of the older sections of Los Angeles east of the Los Angeles River, had streetcar connection with the heart of the city. It was only natural that this promising section of the city should receive consideration when Trinity congregation employed a city missionary, Pastor J. W. Theiss in 1905 to make

a canvass of the greater part of Boyle Heights. He began services in a hall at the northwest corner of Chicago and First streets. Though various members of Trinity Church lived in Boyle Heights, the attendance at times was very slim, consisting chiefly of members of the R. Eichhorn family. In 1906, the John Harlow family, the Jeske family, and Mrs. Freitag joined the little mission, which was then transferred to Corbell's Hall.

On May 13, 1906, Rev. H. M. Tietjen of Crockett, California, accepted the spiritual leadership of the new Boyle Heights congregation, while serving as pastor of Emanuel in Lincoln Heights. A Ladies Aid Society was organized in August 1906, and services were conducted in Bevione's Hall at First and Indiana streets that same year. Catholics, who had their separate section with a special altar, also used this hall. As the work of Rev. Tietjen in East Los Angeles grew, the services in Boyle Heights could be held only around noon or later with substitutes — a retired pastor, Rev. Sapper, and the teachers of Trinity Church — frequently serving. The little mission at the same time suffered much through the changes of service times and spiritual leaders. Because of this, they applied in 1908 to Synod for support of a local pastor. Since Synod's financial position was not strong, the request couldn't be granted, but in 1909, the petition was renewed. St. John's mission, with the aid of the Mission Board, was now able to call a pastor, the Rev. Gotthold H. Smukal of St. Mark's Lutheran Church, Ruskin, Nebraska, where he had served since 1908. He was installed on December 4, 1910, and spent the rest of his pastoral life at St. John's.

Rev. Smukal was born to Rev. Robert J. Smukal and his wife, Laura, on December 7, 1886, in a parsonage where his father was pastor in Iron Moun-

Trinity's third pastor, Rev. Immanuel Hodde, was installed on June 8, 1941, and served until 1958. (Pacific Southwest District Archives)

Rev. William Seebeck, Trinity's fourth pastor, was installed on November 16, 1958. (Pacific Southwest District Archives)

St. John's Lutheran Church, Los Angeles, is begun by Rev. Theiss in 1905.

tain, Missouri. After his father accepted a call to Bethany Lutheran Church in Detroit, Michigan, young Smukal received his early Christian education training in Bethany's day school. His father instructed him so well in the classical languages that when he applied to Concordia College in Fort Wayne, he was admitted to the third-year class. He graduated from Concordia Seminary, St. Louis, in 1908. He was also a proficient violinist of concert caliber, who, some said at the time, could have won international fame not only as a violinist but also as a baseball coach. He was a man of many talents. In the beginning of his early career in Los Angeles, he served missions in Upland, Hollywood, Hawthorne, Inglewood, and other suburban areas including the development of St. Matthew's in East Los Angeles. From 1917 to 1927, he was secretary of the Sub-Mission Board for Southern California, serving as its chairman from 1927 to 1930. From 1920 to 1927, he served as editor of *Lutherische Bote* and contributed articles to the *Concordia Theological Monthly,* the *Concordia Pulpit, Der Lutheraner,* and *The Lutheran Witness.* When the Southern California District was formed, he was elected president,

Rev. Gotthold H. Smukal, first pastor of St. John's in Boyle Heights, was installed on December 4, 1910, spending the rest of his pastoral life in the congregation until his retirement in 1957. (Pacific Southwest District Archives)

serving from 1930 to 1942.

One of Pastor Smukal's first undertakings was the organization of the congregation in 1911, so that it could purchase property at East Second and Dacotah streets with borrowed funds. That year also saw the formation of the Walther League and the organization of the first church choir. On September 26, 1911, he was united in marriage to Lena Ruether, who became his helpmeet for many years. Their union was blessed with one daughter, Lorna, who also served the church and married Pastor Robert Schaller, the veteran pastor of Arizona.

With $500 in subscriptions, the chapel was built and dedicated on February 18, 1912; in the dedication service, English was used for the first time. The pews, altar, and chancel furnishings were a gift from Trinity's old church building on Eighth and Flower streets. Through the assistance of the Walther League, a parish hall was constructed at a cost of $600 and dedicated on June 19, 1913. In the fall, the first school with seven pupils was opened in the parish hall, a small frame building, still in the rough, unplastered, unfurnished state. Rev. Robert P. Kaiser, pastor emeritus, served as the first teacher.

English is used for the first time in St. John's dedication service on February 18, 1912.

St. John's first church built at a cost of $500 and dedicated on February 18, 1912. (Pacific Southwest District Archives)

Interior of St. John's at Easter, showing the pews, altar, and chancel furnishings. (Pacific Southwest District Archives)

On May 29, 1917, the congregation resolved to dismiss the current teacher, Mr. Theodore Schroeder, and close the school, as it had shown no growth between 1914 and 1917. Since Pastor Smukal felt Christian education was vitally important, the school continued with him teaching in the one-room school through 1920. Seeing a need for a larger school building and parish hall in the late 1920s, a lot adjourning the church property was purchased for $4,200 and a new structure was built and dedicated on Sunday, April 12, 1931, with Rev. A. G. Webbeking and Dr. W. H. T. Dau delivering the sermons. To accommodate overflow attendance, a loudspeaker system was installed for the day. The service was carried to the audience seated outside. November 20, 1938, was a day of great rejoicing for St. John's, as Pastor Smukal placed the last note and mortgage upon the altar in grateful recognition that the school debt had been paid in full.

During Pastor Smukal's early years at St. John's, he and Pastor Theiss became good friends, walking the hills of Boyle Heights, viewing and admiring the beautiful, large residential homes with views of the city and attractive Hollenbeck Park in the center of the heights. One day during one of these strolls in the late teens or early twenties, they noticed the overwhelming influx of Jews, Mexicans, and Japanese into the immediate neighborhood of the present church, and the ensuing exit of Germans and Anglos from the area. Pastor Theiss remarked as early as 1906 that the church should be doing mission work among all the Mexican people who lived in the area. Pastor Theiss had an interest in bringing the Gospel to the Mexicans when, in 1911, he and Rev. August Hansen were elected by the Los Angeles Pastoral Conference to explore Old Mexico. They answered: "As soon as the bullets stop flying, we'll go. Right now not a cactus is

> Pastor Theiss remarks as early as 1906 that mission work should be done among the Mexican people in the area.

safe in Mexico." At that early date, Southern California was going to enter the foreign mission field, occupying itself with the spiritual plight of the southern neighbor. However, it seemed the bullets never stopped flying long enough, as a series of revolutions kept occurring in Mexico. Considering the continued turmoil, the District waited thirty years to send envoys to Mexico.

In the meantime, the East Los Angeles field was "ripe for the harvest" as more and more Mexicans moved into the area surrounding the church. Rev. David Stirdivant remembered how his grandfather, the Rev. John William Theiss, would remark, "How many of these people are Spanish-speaking people?" as he and Pastor Smukal visited in Boyle Heights. They would also say, "We ought to be doing some Spanish mission work here, but we don't have anybody." Since it was in this area that thousands of Mexican-Americans were living and seeing the opportunity for Lutheran work among these people, Pastor Smukal opened a branch Sunday school in 1929 with the aid of his daughter, Lorna, as a teacher; he rented or used a member's garage on Marietta Street off of Atlantic Street (a short street that was taken when the Santa Ana Freeway went through) for the Sunday school. This was quickly followed with a Wednesday evening Bible hour for Spanish-speaking adults, and later he held regular preaching services, according to the 1934 Mission Board report to the Southern California District Convention. He must have had some skill in Spanish, but he stated in a letter some time later, that it was limited.

In 1930 when Pastor Smukal was elected president of the newly formed Southern California District, he had a real dilemma since he was serving as pastor of St. John's, doing missionary work among Mexicans, and now was president of the new District. He asked people what he should do in this situation with some giving the advice of dropping the Mexican mission work and finding someone who could speak Spanish more fluently. He did not want the mission to die. He recalled how his friend, John Theiss, used to look over this neighborhood and say, "These people deserve to hear the clear Gospel, too. It shouldn't be just for us Anglo-Saxon people. It should be for the Mexican people." Rev. Stirdivant recalled the previous quote in an interview in 1991.

In 1930 entrusted with new duties, Rev. Smukal turned to Synod's Foreign-Tongue Missions Board for assistance. They had promised to place a missionary in the field as soon as a suitable man could

St. John's new brick school building dedicated on April 12, 1931. (Pacific Southwest District Archives)

be found, but they begged the District Mission Board to find a way to meet the other expenses. The District Mission Board suggested that the contributions of the District Sunday schools be directed to the new Mexican mission venture in East Los Angeles, which had a Sunday school enrollment of 16 children with 2 women teachers, and a Bible class with an enrollment of 6 Mexicans. Also the District Mission Board reported they "have found an open door also at Pico which at present is under the supervision of Rev. R. Jeske" of Trinity, Whittier. This is the only recorded mention in any District material of the little known Hispanic mission work in the town of Pico. It was also mentioned once in Trinity's (Whittier) Announcement Book in 1930.

This forward-thinking and very talented man, Rev. Smukal, was to be the "father" of mission work among the Hispanics in Southern California, as St. John's Church was not ready to open its doors to the neighborhood at that time. The Texas District of the Missouri Synod was in the lead, beginning work among Hispanics in San Antonio, Texas, in 1926. Dr. Robert Scudieri, Synod's director for North America Missions stated in 1994, that The Lutheran Church — Missouri Synod is the largest immigrant church in the United States. Between 1840 and 1940, ministry was directed only to German immigrants. The language of worship and parochial education was changed from German to English because of World War II. He emphasized this heritage should direct fellow Lutherans to an understanding and acceptance of these new mission fields.

With the church established in Los Angeles and other areas of Southern California in the 1930s, some attention was given to work among the Hispanic population in Southern California. Through these humble beginnings, the life of the church in sharing the Gospel with the Hispanic population of the District will now be chronicled.

Almighty God, Thy Word is cast
Like seed into the ground;
Now let the dew of heav'n descend
And righteous fruits abound.

CHAPTER TWO

Genesis

1931-1946

ith the seeds of the Word being established in the Mexican community by Pastor Smukal in East Los Angeles, the request for a Spanish-speaking pastor by the Southern California District to the Synod's Foreign-Tongue Missions Board was granted when the Rev. Bruno Martinelli left New Orleans on the Santa Fe Railroad, Tuesday, May 12, 1931. In a May 4, 1931, letter to Pastor Smukal, he described himself as having a stature of 5 feet, 6 inches, weighing 158 pounds and wearing glasses. He also stated that he was coming alone, as he left his two little girls in the charge of the Lutheran Orphan Home in New Orleans where they had been living the previous two and one-half years. This orphan home may have been his first contact with the Lutheran Church — Missouri Synod. Even though his daughters didn't come with him at that time, they later lived in California with him and his wife.

Rev. Martinelli's background had been in band and orchestral music. His early education was at the Christian Endeavor Academy, Endeavor, Wisconsin, and Evansville Junior College, Evansville, Wisconsin, where he was a student and taught orchestra and band instruments; he attended the University of Wisconsin at Madison, Wisconsin, as a special music student and leader of two bands. He was in U.S. Army Band School and 15th Infantry Band, Tientsin, China, receiving

Pastor Bruno Martinelli in 1929. (Pacific Southwest District Archives)

"In the beginning was the Word,..."

— JOHN 1:11

an honorable discharge, November 11, 1916. In 1919, he received a diploma from the Moody Bible Institute in Chicago and received a diploma from the University Extension Conservatory in Chicago graduating in 1921; in 1938, he received a Bachelor of Divinity degree from Concordia Seminary, St. Louis, Missouri.

In 1922, Rev. Martinelli went to Bryan, Texas, where he was a Methodist missionary to Italians, building an $8,000 church and $3,500 parsonage. While in Bryan, he also served as bandleader, junior orchestra director, and at the Bryan Military Academy, serving as a tutor to some of the faculty. In 1925, he went to St. Mark's Church in New Orleans, Louisiana, as a missionary to the Latin people and assistant pastor to the English congregation, as well as being the choir director. In 1927, he became the music director at one of the leading Protestant churches in Bernice, Louisiana, and taught music at Bernice Louisiana High School. In 1928, he started a piano repair and tuning business in New Orleans, Louisiana. While in New Orleans, he became acquainted with The Lutheran Church — Missouri Synod. Since he came from a Methodist background, he studied with three Lutheran pastors under the direction of the Southern District president, Rev. M. W. H. Holls, New Orleans, Louisiana, in 1928–1931.

After Pastor Martinelli arrived in Los Angeles, he was installed on May 17, at 7:45 p.m., in the largest church in Los Angeles, Trinity, with the Rev. Hugo Gihring, secretary of Southern California District Mission Board, delivering the sermon, and Rev. Smukal performing the Rite of Installation. In the July–August 1931, edition of the *Southern California Lutheran*, the following was stated: "With the installation of the Reverend Martinelli as missionary for our church to Italian- and Spanish-speaking people of this region, our District has made a distinct gain. May his coming to these people be like unto the coming of the sainted Pastor Buehler among the Germans of the San Francisco Bay region and may God bless his labors."

At Rev. Martinelli's suggestion, he was sent to Los Angeles as an Italian missionary who would give attention to the Spanish mission as a "sideline" until his Spanish skills were more proficient and he could take full charge of the Spanish work. He felt that the Mexicans would not expect too much of him if they knew that he was an Italian missionary who was helping out in Spanish and would be willing to overlook some of his mistakes in his Spanish grammar. If he came as a full-fledged Spanish missionary, they might demand more of him than he could give with his limited knowledge of Spanish.

When Martinelli arrived, he was eager to enter the work of the Spanish mission field, with no intention of deceiving the Mission Board as to his ability to speak Spanish. He was up front with the Board, frankly stating that he did not feel competent at that time to take full charge of a Spanish mission, although he had already begun to add to his knowledge of the Spanish language. Even with the assurance of his lack of Spanish abilities, the Mission Board thought he was more proficient in Spanish than Pastor Smukal was. Pastor Smukal even wrote to the Foreign Mission Board that Martinelli's Spanish was no better than his. With the misunderstanding of the language problem, Pastor Martinelli didn't have the confidence of some of the Mission Board members, which would create some problems in the future.

In a January 26, 1932, letter to Rev. L. Wambsganse, Secretary of the Board of Foreign-Tongue Missions, President Smukal wrote the following:

On the report you had from the Southern District relative to the ability of Brother Martinelli, you also reported to us that his Spanish needed but a general polish. But when the brother arrived here, we found that he knew hardly more Spanish than I did. This is the reason why he could not enter upon regular mission work until recently. He took instruction from several teachers, and applied himself very faithfully. At times, he was rather downcast and discouraged, and he feared that he had been misunderstood. I believe that he overworked during the month in the fall of last year. While he applied himself to the language and the study and practice of it, he also sought contact with such Mexicans whom he hoped to invite as soon as he would gather that courage necessary to address them on spiritual things in the Sunday school, Bible class, and divine worship. Such Mexicans and Spaniards whose mutual acquaintance he and I share have expressed great surprise at the progress he made in this short [time] in the acquisition of the language. He now speaks a much better Spanish than English. The work he did in a missionary way during his intense study was merely personal and individual.

With missionary zeal, Pastor Martinelli, acting on Pentecostal injunction to preach the Gospel in all tongues to all peoples, opened the Mexican and Italian mission in October of 1931 in a rented four-room house at 2661 Atlantic Street. The little mission was furnished with an altar, candlesticks, and a lectern from the portable chapel that was once used not only at First, Van Nuys, but also at Bethany, Hollywood, and Trinity, San Bernardino in 1908. St. John's Sunday School of Los Angeles presented a beautiful crucifix to the chapel and the institutional chaplain, Rev. E. G. A. Wachholz, gave an attractive pulpit. The first service had an attendance of eight people, mainly children. In 2 months, the attendance had grown to 34. Pastor Martinelli reported in the 1932 *Southern California Lutheran* that at the Christmas festival, they were 65 people present. Bethany Lutheran Church of Hollywood and its Walther League supplied a Christmas tree, candles, and oranges, and the Ladies Aid of St. John's in Los Angeles decorated the tree and gave cookies and candy for the Sunday school children. On Christmas morning, an 11-year-old girl was baptized. Her father was so impressed that he said to the pastor, "I was baptized in the Catholic Church, but I want to be baptized again." Ten people were preparing for Confirmation, and he organized a young people's society.

Mexican and Italian Mission in Los Angeles is started in October 1931.

In addition to Sunday services and Sunday school for children and adults, there was a Wednesday evening Bible class, and a Saturday morning religious instruction class with the missionary using three languages (Italian, English, and Spanish) in his work. According to Rev. David Stirdivant, each year Martinelli had a big parade in the neighborhood with a band to advertise the Lutheran mission.

In order for the mission to have some financial support, the District Board of Directors in their February 1932 meeting, resolved: "That we endorse the plan to use [the District] Sunday schools' [offering] for the support of our Mexican Mission work." The District Sunday school offerings paid $21.60 per month for the house, water, and lights. In the May 19, 1932, meeting, they gave Pastor Martinelli permission to solicit the Ladies Aid Societies of the District for financial support of the Mexican mission work, "provided the general Synod does not appropriate necessary funds."

San Pablo congregation in front of the rented four-room house at 2661 Atlantic Street that was used as a chapel. Pastor in back row. (Pacific Southwest District Archives)

During the first few months of the little mission's existence, President Smukal reported,

> Brother Martinelli was not preaching at the time, but was still studying the language. Within a few months, he will be ready to deliver sermons. At present, he gets his instruction at the seminary for Mexicans conducted by the Baptist Church, because the instruction is very thorough and because it is cheap. If I am not mistaken, he pays tuition out of his own pocket. Martinelli, having worked in a sectarian church until he became a Lutheran, has a tendency toward organizing and conducting a mission in the manner of the sectarians. He is with me often, and we talk over these things, and I try to give him the proper direction in the work toward organization. He feels that the prospects must be more or less socially entertained, and that such social activity gives more opportunity for new contacts. But he is gradually shifting to see our viewpoint, and he is beginning to stress the Word and the message immediately. He effected a temporary organization of young people and seems to have success with them. I visited the mission two weeks ago, and I must say that I was agreeably surprised to find so many in attendance on so cold an evening as we had that date. There were over 30 present, young and old, all interested in the lesson, and very well behaving, not as boisterous and loud as Mexicans sometimes are. I believe that Brother Martinelli has them well in hand, and I assure you that a prayer of thanksgiving rose in my heart when I saw their interest and lively discussion, now after all the time and work I had put into this endeavor. And I wish that your honorable Board may feel about this first success even as I do, and to thank the Lord for His past blessings and guidance in this matter, and to pray that His abundant mercy may continue with you and with us to the salvation of souls.

In the January 1932 *Southern California Lutheran,* the following article described work at the mission:

> Even on a cold night such as January 13, you will find as many as 31 adults and children at the Bible hour conducted by Rev.

Martinelli, at 2661 Atlantic Street, Los Angeles. Little Antonio and Senorita Maria, sturdy Alberto and studious Juan, and all others diligently learn the *"no por orbras, pero por la fe* (not by works, but by faith)." If you can do nothing else for this Mexican mission, at least pray for its success. The expense for the mission to the District does not exceed $25 per month at this time. The estimate of a population of 250,000 Mexicans in Southern California is quite correct. What a field for us! Rev. Martinelli is giving private instruction to several adults. Several Italians show interest in the work. His Sunday school is already contributing to mission work. Let us help him build a cathedral, a habitation of God through the Spirit.

Members of San Pablo gathered for Christmas with Pastor Martinelli in back row, second from the left. (Pacific Southwest District Archives)

On January 22, 1932, there was great joy in the little mission's rented rooms on Atlantic Street in Los Angeles, as the congregation of 37 witnessed the Confirmation of 3 new members who had been converted to the love and forgiveness of Christ. The activities of one month at the mission were attended by an aggregate of 340 attendees. Pastor Bruno Martinelli wrote in the March 1932 issue of the *Southern California Lutheran*: "I was surprised to learn how much good can be done through the weekend school which we conduct. A little girl of about seven years came the other day and recited an entire hymn, thus carrying the Gospel into the home on wings of songs. Another little girl came to me after religious instruction, saying, 'We prayed so beautifully this morning.' I hope we can arrange to conduct a summer school this year."

In the May 1932 edition of the *Southern California Lutheran*, it was acknowledged that Rev. Martinelli attended a recent meeting of the Mission Board to report on the progress of the Mexican and Italian work. It stated, "He radiated a dynamic enthusiasm for his work and its prospects." Among other items, he reported that a Confirmation service in the near future would bring his membership total to 15. The board resolved at its meeting to give the mission 24 additional folding chairs with the cost taken from the "Conference Treasury" and $15 was given to the mission for other purposes.

In December of 1932, a truckload of enthusiastic Lutherans from the little Mexican mission led by their loyal pastor, Rev. Martinelli, attended the Pastoral Communion Service. Some of the members, who live a distance from their place of worship, were too poor to afford bus fare. Since it was too far to walk, what were they to do? Pastor Martinelli found a man who was willing to furnish the truck, if Pastor Martinelli would pay for the gas. Having found his truck, the missionary found the "gas" in the special mission treasury for non-budgeted items. The little Mexican mission was among the first in the District that year to contribute to the synodical emergency collection.

At the 1933 Southern California District Convention, the Mission Board reported that the supervision of the Los Angeles Mexican mission had been placed back into their hands at that time. The salary and rent of $125 per month for the missionary, Rev. Martinelli, was being paid by the Synod with the District furnishing the rent of $16 per month for the chapel. During the summer of 1933, a Vacation Bible School was conducted with an average attendance of 27 Mexican, Syrian, Armenian, and Italian pupils. At the closing service, the pupils gave a program in Spanish and recited three poems from *The Lutheran Witness* in English. The year at the mission concluded with 52 souls, 20 communicants, 4 voting members, and a Sunday school enrollment of 56 pupils.

By 1934, the mission was known as San Pablo Iglesia Luterana Mexicana (St. Paul's Mexican Lutheran Church) and required a subsidy of $1,687 a year with the District providing $15 per month and Synod giving $125. The cost of operating the mission was $1,654 with $33 a year given for the synodical budget. The pastor received a salary of $100 per month plus a house was rented for him at $25 a month. Sometime before 1934, a small house at 1047 Marieta Street off of Atlantic Street in Los Angeles was rented for a chapel at $15 for

By 1934, the mission is known as San Pablo Iglesia Luterana Mexicana.

the mission to conduct services and use the facilities for other activities. The house was demolished during the early 1950s when the Santa Ana Freeway went through East Los Angeles. During two weeks in July, San Pablo conducted a Vacation Bible School with an enrollment of 31 pupils. Regular mid-week services were conducted in Spanish with an average attendance of 30. At Christmas, the Spanish-Italian chapel celebrated Christmas Eve with great joy in a three-hour double service beginning at 8:00 p.m. and ending at 11.00 p.m. with one service in Spanish and the other in English. Several Italians were present. The beautifully decorated little chapel was filled to capacity with some people standing outside. The next morning, Christmas Day, the service was also well attended. Since Pastor Martinelli was trained as a band director, special instrumental music was provided for the services.

By mid-1935, the mission had grown to 65 souls, 20 communicants, and 6 voters with a Sunday school enrollment of 62, having an average attendance of 40. A morning service was conducted each Sunday in Spanish, with an average attendance of 34. A Saturday school with catechetical instructions for children was held regularly for a period of nine months, and on each Thursday a short period of time was devoted to Bible reading and memorizing Bible passages. When the children finished reading a book of the Bible, the best-prepared pupils received a reward, thus encouraging them to continue memorizing passages of Scripture. Regular mid-week services were conducted in Spanish with an average attendance of 30.

In the October 1935 *Lutheran Witness*, the following article by Rev. Bruno Martinelli appeared describing Spanish mission work:

Spanish Mission Work
Native Background

The Mexican people in the United States comprise two general elements: the immigrant newcomer from Old Mexico and the long-time residents.

As a people, the Mexicans are what we naturally think of Latin Americans, a mixture of good and bad, of culture and ignorance, of the emancipated and superstitious, of prosperous and very poor, practically all reared under the influence of the Roman Catholic Church, which has never liberalized in the least degree.

The Mexican Belief

"The Mexicans are a Roman Catholic people without a religion," said a Catholic priest who had just come from Mexico.

They may be divided into five classes: the Roman Catholics, the positivists or freethinkers, the Evangelicals, the modern fanatics, and atheists. The Roman Catholics claim about 60 percent, made up for the most part of the women, the aged, and the ignorant peons. The Evangelicals, or Protestants, make up about 10 percent. They are handpicked, awakened people, most who are products of missions and mission school.

Mission Work Among the Mexicans

Two questions are constantly being asked: Are Mexicans ever really converted? and How do you start a mission among them?

Locating the mission plant is half the battle. Mexicans by nature are plaza people. Become familiar with their racial traits and their beautiful language. It is essential to know these well. They love music. Formulate a cheerful and natural cultural order of church service, with full prominence given to the Word and little stress put on symbolism.

Influence of Song

One element in the Protestant worship that has proved a special attraction to music loving Mexicans has been singing. Most people can sing. The hymns have sung their way into the hearts of the people. In our congregation, I was surprised to find how many could sing and recite an entire hymn. They have nothing of the sort before. The Catholic worship, aside from the chanting of a few litanies, has no popular singing.

The Gospel in Its Element

It was the common people who loved Jesus gladly. Publicans and harlots flocked to Him to learn from Him how they could be saved.

The Gospel gives most to those who need most. The Mexicans rejoice over it as over the pearl of great price. They are sometimes slow to accept its offers of free grace, having been accustomed to a religion of good works as a basis of salvation. But when faith has been kindled in their hearts by the Gospel, their happiness is great. The message of salvation through Christ Jesus brightens their faces, sets them singing, lights up their poor homes, and makes their poverty and disease more tolerable.

They become heroes and martyrs. More than 60 have laid down their lives for Christ's sake. It makes them apostles to their kinsman and neighbors. And they bear testimony with their last breath that Jesus Christ is to them Wisdom, and Righteousness, and Sanctification, and Redemption.

At the 1936 Southern California District Convention, the Mission Board reported the following about the work of Rev. Martinelli at San Pablo Mexican Mission: In 1933, the mission had numbered 52 souls, with 20 communicants, and 4 voting members, having a Sunday school of 56 pupils. The latest report of the mission in 1936 showed 56 souls, 21 communicants, and 5 voters with an average 26 at Sunday services. The Sunday school had an enrollment of 50 with an average attendance of 30.

The budget for the mission in 1935 was $1,770 with the congregation bringing offerings of $127.95, or an average of $6.39 per communicant member and giving $12 to the synodical budget. The subsidy was $1,682 or $140.17 per month with general Synod furnishing $125 per month and the balance being given by the District. The same amount was required for the following year.

They concluded by saying, "It is the opinion of your present board that the missionary should be encouraged to expand the work among the Spanish-speaking people of Southern California and to that end to seek out other Mexican settlements in Los Angeles or other cities and towns for the purpose of opening a preaching station in such places as present the most favorable opportunities and prospects. The District should appropriate certain funds and authorize its Mission Board to meet the expenditures, which such a venture would involve." After this report was filed, a period of suspicion and mistrust followed between Martinelli and the Mission Board.

At approximately the same time, the Foreign-Tongue Missions Board reported that there were 20 languages being used by missionaries in preaching the Gospel, "To every man in his own tongue," which was the aim of the church from its very beginning. Synod had always been interested in spiritual welfare of immigrants coming to the United States from Europe and other parts of the world, in keeping with the command of the Lord to "preach the Gospel to every creature."

Among "the foreign-tongued people" served by missionaries were Poles, Lithuanians, Estonians, Latvians, Finns, Norwegians, Slovaks, Italians, Spanish, Portuguese, French, Assyrians, and other nationalities. The largest group of foreign-tongued people served by the Synod was of German descent, which was dwindling quickly due to a change from German to the English in the work of the church. According to a report issued in 1936, Synod had 177 congregations that conducted their services exclusively in the German language, 277 congregations that made more use of the German than of the English language, 1,096 congregations that made equal use of both languages, 998 congregations that gave preferences to English, and 1,800 congregations whose services were conducted exclusively in the English language. They concluded by stating, "There are other foreign-tongue peoples who cling to their native tongue, having made little advance in the acquisition of English language."

In the September 29, 1936, Mission Board Meeting, President Smukal reported that Pastor Martinelli had expressed a willingness to assist the California and Nevada District in organizing a new Mexican mission. Pastor Michel of Trinity, Los Angeles, informed the group that he had received a communication from the mission director of the Northern District, Pastor Hansen, but it was decided that Pastor Martinelli be asked "to expand his Mexican mission in some place where he might use the buildings of an established congregation, and thus save the mission treasury the additional expense, save that of mileage."

San Pablo's Sunday school with Mrs. Martinelli standing in the back row. (Pacific Southwest District Archives)

In an October 9, 1936, letter to Pastor [George] Theiss of First Lutheran of Pasadena, a Mission Board member, Rev. Martinelli defended his work by explaining what he had done at the mission. In 1934, he had printed 1,000 fliers describing the mission. Shortly after the fliers were distributed, 16 people of different nationalities began to call. Four played the violin, others played the cornet, saxophone, drum, meloxiophone, and the piano. They used a book containing choral melodies of the Lutheran church for the purpose of having music in the church services. Some parents had ask him to give private lessons in their homes, but he had refused as the music was for church use only. From this group, one was baptized and confirmed. They also had four Syrians boys and one Syrian girl and an organist who was Armenian.

He then stated they now had Mexican parents attending services, because it was in Spanish. For the previous two years, 95 percent of those attending were Mexican, since all the services were in Spanish. He said, "You don't think [that] is progress; when I started we had nothing." He had 25 Confirmations, 6 Baptisms, and one marriage in 2 years. The mission also had a small orchestra. He further acknowledged that the preceding 14 months, the District had not paid the rent on the house, nor paid the organist, but only his salary. From the beginning, the mission made contributions, between one to five dollars each month, to Mission Board and reduced the chapel rent from $22.50 to $15 a month.

He also declared that he had distributed over 10,000 tracts, 2 Bibles, 20 New Testaments in Italian and Spanish, and 500 portions of the Bible. He had 5,000 other materials printed and distributed. In the first service, there were six children who had stayed with the mission, were confirmed, and were in the school choir; he even officiated at marriages for some of them. He concluded by saying:

I have conducted [an] evening school for adults, [and] summer school; last year at [the] end of summer, two were confirmed. On Christmas morning, two children were baptized. This year we had 24 pupils in summer school and almost all were new pupils. [I] Canvass every week, from [for] three years. I have not missed one Sunday. This is not personal sacrifice I made by myself, as [I made] many — 300 visits in one week.

Please call on me, and I will show the records and talk the things over.

Fraternally,
B. Martinelli

P.S. I visited in the hospitals and Olive View, etc. I have delivered lectures in the District as many [as] two a week. I have finished two courses from the Concordia Seminary–Grade 98 percent.
B. M.

In another letter to Rev. George Theiss dated November 5, 1936, Pastor Martinelli tells of the places he had visited at the urging of the Mission Board. That week in order to expand the Mexican mission work, he visited the following places with Pastor Reno Jeske of Trinity, Whittier: Whittier, North Pico, Jim Town, Rivera, La Habra, and Los Nietos. In Whittier, they found very few Mexicans; and in North Pico in the small Mexican community, there was a Roman Catholic chapel, but they found no place to rent. In Jim Town, the Friends church had a nice building for the Mexican people. There was also a Pentecostal and a Foursquare church there with no building to rent. In Rivera, there was a fine Methodist church serving that community.

He also visited La Habra where there was a Baptist and a Roman Catholic Church, each with a good church building, but he found no place to rent. Los Nietos had a Pentecostal and a Catholic Church. He visited Inglewood, but there was nothing there to rent. El Monte had two Mexican Presbyterian laymen working the area. In Bell, the Friends were doing active work but had no pastor.

He stated he would visit other communities the following week and would be out of the city for three days. He closed by saying, "Therefore, until further instruction from the Mission Board, I will not visit other communities outside of Los Angeles."

At the December 22, 1936, Mission Board meeting, Pastor Michel reported that he and Pastor George Theiss had made their regular visit to the Mexican mission. They agreed that the Rev. Martinelli was working diligently and faithfully. "However, in order to circumvent possible irregularities, the Visitation Committee deemed it advisable to confer periodically with the missionary." President Smukal reported the following: "The investigation of the Spanish mission has begun."

By the October 25, 1937, Mission Board meeting, the board expressed "doubt as to the qualifications of our Spanish missionary, Pastor Martinelli." The

Rev. Streufert of St. Louis recommended that there be a close supervision of that field. It was decided that "the investigation of the Spanish mission be continued under the supervision of the mission department. Emphasis was to be placed upon establishing whether the missionary was "apt to teach." The secretary of the Mission Board was instructed to confer with the Conference Program Committee and request to assign a paper to Pastor Martinelli on the subject, "Confirmation Instruction." Pastor Martinelli consistently refused to prepare this or any other paper for the conference, thus upsetting the board, which referred the problem to the president's office and the mission department for action.

At the February 22, 1938, board meeting, President Smukal reported the following: "In a communication from the Colloquy Board, the latter's stand of the missionary's aptness to teach was affirmed." The president had visited the mission and in the examination of members of the parish, yet incomplete, reported that he had found them correctly informed on many of the Lutheran doctrines. Basing his remarks on this evidence, Pastor Smukal also expressed his opinion that the missionary was qualified to teach. However, the opinion was expressed that "he would be of greater service to an Italian rather than a Mexican mission." It was decided to request that the Eastern Home Mission Board place Pastor Martinelli into an Italian field.

At Synod's Board of Home Mission meeting on March 24, 1938, a letter was read from the secretary of the Southern California District Mission Board that the board was of the opinion that Pastor Martinelli, the Mexican missionary at Los Angeles, upon investigation was doctrinally sound and "apt to teach," but that he was not doing successful work among the Mexicans because he was an Italian. Because of this racial difference, there was not that bond between pastor and people as there should be. The Mission Board suggested that consideration be given to transfer Rev. Martinelli to an Italian mission field. The synodical board informed the Southern California District Mission Board that at that time, there was no such opening available, but that they would keep the suggestion made in mind.

In the April 26, 1938, Mission Board meeting, Pastor Smukal submitted his final report on the investigation of the Mexican mission. In general, the report stated that the missionary was working under handicaps, but served his church as well as could be expected. That summer, Pastor Martinelli offered a special Spanish summer school (Vacation Bible School) program that met for four weeks and had an enrollment of 40 pupils.

Five months later on September 27, 1938, the mission department reported that the young people of St. John's Walther League of Orange were initiating a move to begin a Mexican mission in their neighborhood. The board commended them for their efforts and would stand ready to offer any advice needed. By October, Rev. Martinelli had been asked by the Walther League of Orange to conduct services for a group of Mexicans in Santa Ana under the supervision of St. John's congregation of Orange, thus beginning a second attempt in the District to do work among the Hispanic population.

In late 1938, a canvass in Puente was conducted by a mission-minded member of Trinity, Whittier, "revealing the presence of some 18 interested Mexicans." Pastor Martinelli began conducting a Spanish Bible class there on Tuesday evenings.

Once again at the Mission Board meeting on December 17, 1938, the matter of the Mexican mission was presented with some feeling that a change was necessary, because Pastor Martinelli was not producing the desired results — that was increasing membership in the mission. It was stated that he was conscientious in his work but not capable, nor qualified, nor apt to teach.

Because Pastor Martinelli had opportunities to work in other fields of a secular nature, as he himself stated in a letter to Pastor Theiss, the mission department recommended that he be encouraged to enter another field at the beginning of 1939, with the District supporting him for a period of six months, if necessary, after he entered upon another vocation. After a lengthy discussion of the recommendation, it became evident that opinions of the qualifications of the missionary were divided and the matter was tabled at that time. At the 1939 Southern California District Convention, the Mission Board reported that during 1938, the Mexican mission work at the mission in Los Angeles consisted of Sunday service, Sunday school, Bible class, mid-week service, Confirmation class, Saturday school, Vacation Bible School with 40 attending and that 3,000 pieces of literature were distributed in 3 languages. The missionary used three languages, but predominantly worked in Spanish. Work was also started in Santa Ana, Orange, Puente, and Belvedere by Pastor B. Martinelli. The subsidy for the mission was cut from

> At the Mission Board meeting on December 17, 1938, the matter of the Mexican mission is presented with some feeling that a change is necessary.

$1,680 to $1,500 for the next year with the pastor receiving a salary of $1,200 per year. The mission had contributed $80 for home purposes and $25 for outside purposes.

On August 13, 1939, the little chapel of Iglesia San Pablo was filled beyond capacity when they celebrated the mission festival. The Rev. O. E. Naumann of Three Rivers, Texas, a missionary to the Mexicans, was the guest speaker. Worshipers came from far and near to hear the Gospel proclaimed in faultless Spanish. The following month at the Mission Board meeting, the mission department requested information as to whether it should make an investigation of the Spanish mission. It was decided that a proper investigation should be made and the investigation be conducted by Rev. Hillmer, Rev. Webbeking, and Rev. Smukal. At the February 20, 1940 Mission Board meeting, the investigation committee on the Spanish mission rendered its report, recommending the closure of the mission for the time being with the provision to continue the missionary's salary for six months.

At the April 16–21, 1940, Southern California District Convention, the Mission Board reported:

Following a careful investigation covering a period of three years, at the direction of the Home Mission Board, the Spanish-Italian mission in Los Angeles was closed. The Board looks forward to a renewed consummation of Mexican missionary activity.

Mexican Mission

Your committee is in hearty agreement with the report concerning this mission as offered by the Mission Board and recommends that Mexican mission work be resumed immediately, and that the Board approach the General Foreign-Tongue Missions Board for the support of this mission.

As of April 1, 1940, San Pablo Iglesia Luterana Mexicana mission was closed, never again to open its doors to the populace of Los Angeles. Rev. Martinelli received $100 per month for 6 months with his services discontinued. Since he had expressed his willingness to cooperate with the District board, it was recommended by the board "to give his time to individual spiritual advice as far as his time and personal interests will permit." The furniture and miscellaneous equipment of the Spanish mission was moved to the mission in Garvey.

The following article appeared in the Southern California *District News* on May 15, 1940:

…Our readers will learn with deep regret that the Home Missions Board found it advisable to close our Mexican mission in Los Angeles, a city of more than 100,000 Spanish-speaking inhabitants. Rev. B. Martinelli has been retired from his work, yet he graciously offered his assistance and cooperation to the District. Lest our readers think, however, that there is no heart for missionary work among the Mexicans in our Southern California District, let them remember the fine work by St. John's Missionary Society of Orange.

On September 11, 1940, Pastor Martinelli wrote the following letter to President Smukal:

The time is approaching, that all connection will be sever[ed], with regret, (with Southern California Mission Board, Evan. Lutheran Synod). I have remained with my work in a fashion, because of the misunderstanding of the Mission Board of So. Calif. and also at times, I have not felt good at all.

However, I will remain with the work until the very day, September 30, 1940. Then I will search, if it is possible, for some kind of work, etc.

As a rule, they want recommendation and the reason when and why the applicant was discharge[d] from his work,[;] personally, I do not know the reason, some intimate, that I did not have enough education, I could enthusiastically dislike their dissonance, that I have studied Lutheranism for over 12 years with an average grade [of] B+. However, perhaps this [is] outside the point. What I would appreciate at this time [is] some kind recommendation, which would state why and when I was discharged if [it] was on account of personality, failure, character, or education, only the truth; I hope at your early convenience, that you can conscientiously send me such a recommendation of discharge. I hope that I am recommendable, I wish to state conscientiously I am very sorry, that, I fail[ed] and I did not come up to the expectation of the Mission Board, and if I had foreseen such ending, I would have take[n] other step[s] to prevent so.

My hope and desire is that I may remain Lutheran always, however, if destiny should design differ[ently], my hope is that you will

San Pablo Iglesia Luterana Mexicana closes on April 1, 1940.

not be disappointed you can realize readily how hard [it] will be for me, but be only a Lutheran Christian.

Very sincerely yours,
Bruno Martinelli

P.S. I have in my possession the transcripts of my work but only will send [an] outline for your scrutiny.

After Martinelli was dismissed, another tragic event befell him. Since the mission was so poor, he had been paying the chapel rent out of his salary and the mission hadn't paid any money into the pension fund for him. He stated in a letter to the Synodical Pension Fund that he had a physical examination on September 4, 1940, by three physicians, who advised that he needed a long rest, a vacation. In a letter to President Smukal, he said that his last pastoral visit was on September 30, 1940. He had given away one Bible, portions of the Scriptures, and 10,000 tracts. He also stated that "we felt a moral obligation to keep together what we had, etc.," up to September 30, 1940. From his words, it can be inferred that he kept the small group together in some type of worship.

President Smukal also sent the following letter to the Pension Board stating the District's position and gave some insights into Pastor Martinelli's problems:

October 9, 1940
Board of Support and Pension
Rev. F. G. Kuehnert, Chairman
Crystal Lake, Ill.

Dear Brother:
The Home Mission Board and our District Mission Board decided to close, for a time, the Mexican mission, because it did not yield the growth to be reasonably expected. This action was under advisement for more than two years. Our District resolved to re-open the Mission immediately. The District Mission Board is planning ways and means of carrying out this resolution, awaiting a conference with Secretary Streufert, who expects to visit here in November. Martinelli was informed at the beginning of the year of the contemplated action of the Mission Board in regard to the closing of the mission and of his ensuing release from service at

that Mission. The reason given him was as above, and he ought not write that he knows no reason. However, our Mission Board, in all fairness to Martinelli, after the closing of the mission, paid him his salary for six months to give him opportunity to adapt himself to new conditions. In the meantime, he rendered individual service to the members of the "orphan mission." But Martinelli is a sick man not far from a nervous collapse. The closing of the Mission and his loss of the regular salary, which ceased some two months ago, heightened his disappointment, timidly, and detection, and further broke his health making him quite unfit for any paying position. His lack of success is not due to any lack of effort and sincerity. During the past ten years, he was one of our busiest and most active men. The failure is due in part to the field itself, and in part to his own personality. I am sure that the Mission Board made arrangements for the pensioning of Martinelli. That the Mexican Mission did not respond to the pension system, according to Martinelli letter of September 11, is true and sad. I would advise that you send him an application and, if his request is granted, to limit it nevertheless to temporary relief only, say about six months.

My reply is late because I did not return home immediately after adjournment in St. Louis.

With kindest wishes,
Yours,
Smukal

Pastor David Stirdivant visited Martinelli in the mid-1950s when he started a mission in East Los Angeles. He said that Martinelli spoke fluent Italian and broken English; Martinelli claimed he could speak Spanish, but it sounded like "Hispanized" Italian. Every time Pastor Stirdivant took him to the doctor or his wife to the hospital or did something for them, Pastor Martinelli would give him books from his library. While Rev. Martinelli lived in East Los Angeles, he gave private music lessons in his home. Pastor Stirdivant recalled that Martinelli moved to Petaluma where he died.

In the November 19, 1940, Mission Board meeting, it was moved and carried to secure a worker for the Spanish mission field, and that, if possible,

The Southern California District sends Rev. Smukal and Rev. Du Brau to Mexico to explore mission opportunities in 1941.

Pastor and Mrs. Bruno Martinelli pictured with their two daughters during the 1930s. (Pacific Southwest District Archives)

a Mexican worker be obtained; if that was not possible, an American worker proficient in the Spanish language would be hired. This worker was to begin missionary activities in Santa Ana, Bell, and later in Los Angeles, and his salary was to come from the Expansion Fund of the General Board. The mission department in conjunction with the president's office was to study the situation in the Santa Ana field "with the prospect of rendering adequate service to the field." The Santa Ann field will be discussed at length in the next chapter.

The District's zeal for mission work in Mexico was still great at this time. In the May 15, 1940, edition of the *District News*, the following article appeared:

The *District News* also has knowledge of a number of true mission friends in our District who are supporting the excellent and impressive work of our Lutheran missionary, J. M. Vallejo, in Mexico City with their gifts and their prayers. Your Editor [Rev. R. T. Du Brau] is in possession of a number of communications from high governmental officials, including a telegram from the *Palacio National*, from President Cardenas, and several *Senadores* of the Mexican Republic in commendation of Sr. J. M. Vallejo's good work in Mexico. Vallejo, a former general was converted to our faith by the instrumentality of our pastor, Geo. Klein, then at Springfield, Illinois, a few years ago. Your Editor, who confesses to a great heart for the

Gospel in Spanish, bespeaks your prayers in behalf of our Spanish missionary work, both here, and *Viejo Mexico* (Old Mexico).

Finally in 1941, just before World War II restricted travel, the Southern California District sent two envoys, President G. H. Smukal, with his interpreter and editor of the District newspaper, Rev. R. T. Du Brau, to Mexico to investigate the mission opportunities. At about noon, Monday, May 12, they crossed into Nogales, Sonora, were they met Señor Manuel Bernal, the general agent of the Mutualista de Mexico, Compania Seguros sobre la Vida, "Mexican Mutual," in short, an agent for the state of Sonora. While the customs inspection was going on, Manuel Bernal and Francisco Reyes discussed the mechanics of a Lutheran tract mission in Sonora with the Los Angeles pastors. As Bernal's work gave him entrance into many homes, a Lutheran tract would also go with him.

After a journey along the west coast of Mexico, the American pastors arrived at the Buena Vista station in Mexico City on Thursday morning, May 15, 1941. They were met by a Lutheran lay missionary, the former general and governor of Campeche, José Maria Vallejo, and his co-worker, Alfonso Lopez Gonzales. Then followed many hours of theological conferences and visits to people and parishioners. The committee of 2, spending 10 days in Mexico, traveled 4,300 miles. The groundwork had been preceded by the parish societies of Christ Lutheran Church of Los Angeles, who had sent some 5,000 Lutheran tracts in Spanish to Missionary Vallejo. Little did they realize that those tracts would actually cover 28 states in Mexico. Señor Vallejo had redistributed them to his friends and co-workers who had been instructed in the Lutheran Catechism. Among these were the committee's friend Bernal, and Perfecto Villanuova in Queretaro, Agapito Pacheco in Aguascalientes, Conrado Ruiz in Torreon, and the venerable 72-year-old Señor Onquay in the state of Campeche, where J. M. Vallejo had been governor, which included 34 workers. It was an inspiration to the committee to learn from these workers that when they ran out of their supply of tracts, they would laboriously copy them by hand, and thus distribute them.

The Los Angeles colloquy committee had seen Señor Vallejo's registry of souls, an extremely neat record of people visited and instructed by him, and examined Vallejo's theological library; the Southern California pastors were satisfied that he had under his care 262 adults, who would be ready for Confirmation and Holy Communion along with numerous children of these families. The Los Angeles pastors met with 120 of them who lived close to Mexico City. The committee was unanimous in calling upon the Southern California District to serve them with Word and Sacrament.

As it was the conscientious conviction of the Southern California emissaries that the brethren in the faith in Mexico City should no longer be deprived of the Holy Communion, they were promised a celebration of the Sacrament for the following evening. On Monday, May 19, 1941, was the great historical moment for Spanish Lutheranism in Mexico City when the Holy Sacrament of the Altar was celebrated there in Spanish for the first time using the Lutheran form. Pastor Du Brau read the entire service in Spanish and distributed the elements. When in turn President Smukal communed him, he read the words of distribution in Spanish also: *"Toma y come; esto es el verdadero cuerpo de nuestro Senor Jesucristo...."* It proved to be a deeply moving occasion for all those present. After the solemn Aaronic benediction, the little congregation departed quietly with these words: "Now you know that you have not only friends in Mexico City but brethren in the faith who love you."

Since Señor Vallejo was recognized as pastor by three mission stations, the committee attended the divine services of all three of these groups. They discovered that people sought the church not for social diversion or relief, but by conviction for the pure Gospel of Jesus Christ. The aggregate membership of the 3 stations was about 260 souls. The committee saw no social distinctions demonstrated by any group, but hearty appreciation of all. Pastor Du Brau spoke words of encouragement and Christian greeting in Spanish and President Smukal addressed the mission in English, which was translated into Spanish, but he did quote Scriptures in Spanish. Each group extended to the Southern California District, through lay representatives, their appreciation of the visit and the earnest plea for further consideration to recognize a divine call to the District and Synod.

In 1942 at the ninth convention of the Southern California District at St. Paul's Church, Pasadena, the Mission Board briefly reported: "Mexico City, J. M. Vallejo. This is our foreign mission endeavor. The history of how we came to take over this work and of the trip of investigation of pastors Smukal and Du Brau has been reported in the *District*

District President Smukal on the right and Rev. R. T. Du Brau in the Floating Gardens of Xochimilco on May 19, 1941, during their trip to Mexico. (Pacific Southwest District Archives)

News. We have been supporting the work with a contribution of $65 a month. Rev. Vallejo passed his colloquy recently, and the work will be taken over shortly by Synod's Board of Missions."

The colloquy referred to above was the "official" synodical examination of Vallejo, which confirmed the preliminary colloquy held by Smukal and Du Brau. As subsequent events were to prove, it was perhaps premature for the Southern California District to release this work to Synod's Board of Missions. The District was acting upon a synodical resolution (37th convention, 1938, p. 191), which read:

> Resolved, That Synod authorizes the Home Mission Board either through the Texas District or the Southern California District or through both Districts, as the case may be, to begin missionary work in Mexico when the opportune moment has come.

From a synodical viewpoint, the Board for Missions feared a "collision, duplication of efforts, overlapping of work," in the Mexico City area with over two million inhabitants. Since the Texas District was closer to St. Louis than Los Angeles, it was authorized to carry on the work in Mexico at the exclusion of Southern California. The Texas District had its own man, and the executive secretary of missions of the Missouri Synod, in a report dated March 17, 1944, made no mention of the Southern California efforts and the excellent preliminary work of J. M. Vallejo. From that report, it was stated that "the first service was held in Mexico City on August 31, 1941; eighteen were in attendance. The first three adults were accepted into the Lutheran Church by Confirmation on December 2, 1941."

Du Brau wrote in his book, *The Romance of Lutheranism in California*, "After much heartbreaking correspondence dealing with jurisdictional priorities, the wonderful Southern California contacts in Mexico were lost to our Synod. Despite this misfortune, a number of Southern California Christians continued to support Vallejo and his growing work individually. History's task must be to record failures as well as successes. We loved the brethren, and we failed them."

In Rev. Roberto G. Huebner's "Historical Account of US/Mexican Border Ministry" 2002 research paper, Rev. Bernard Pankow of the Missouri Synod and Rev. David Trejo of the Mexican Synod, "told me that they had no knowledge or had any contact with the leaders or groups that Vallejo claims to have shepherded. The 34 ministerial assistants who supposedly worked in 28 states, nor any of the 262 persons Vallejo claimed to have served, asked to join with the other existing Lutheran groups, after Vallejo resigned from the ministry." Huebner noted that Vallejo's assistant, Rev. López Gonzales, served in the Nazarene Church in the state of Chiapas and was not a Lutheran. According to Pastor Hueber, during a search of the national archives Web site in Mexico City there was no trace of Vallejo serving in the Revolutionary Army as a general nor was he listed as a governor of the state of Campeche.

As soon as the Mexico report appeared in the Southern California *District News*, the District editor, Rev. Du Brau, wrote: "With the new and great enthusiasm that Mexico creates in us, we must not overlook our Spanish mission obligations close at home. We are still praying for the reopening of the great Los Angeles field."

As eyes were turned from the mission field in Mexico because it was released to the Texas District, once again the mission vision was refocused on the city of Los Angeles which was not only more than great but it was phenomenal. The major problem was finding a man who was fluent in Spanish to work the field. With the closing of San Pablo Mission in 1940 and the ensuing war years, the Los Angeles field lay dormant. At the December 14, 1944, Synod's Board of Home Mission meeting in St. Louis, the board approved the appointment of two vicars to start work among Mexicans in Los Angeles. At the December 19, 1944, District Mission Board meeting, it was resolved to call three workers for the Mexican mission, one vicar for San Diego, one vicar for the Imperial Valley, and a permanent man for the Los Angeles area. Alfredo Saez, who formerly served as a vicar in the Mexican mission in Santa Ana, was suggested for the permanent call. These three workers were to be called in accordance with the plan and promise of the Board of Home Missions. No vicars were sent, but Rev. Saez was called to the Los Angeles Hispanic mission field, arriving the first of March to begin work in the Spanish mission in Los Angeles where he received a salary of $100 per month with a housing allowance of $50 per month.

Rev. Alfredo Saez was born in Naranjito, Puerto Rico, on August 27, 1917, the youngest of four children by his mother's second husband. She had 6 other children by her first husband with the oldest child 17 years older than Alfredo. After his father, mother, and sister died, his oldest sister sent him to a Methodist orphanage where he learned of the love of Christ. While at the orphanage, he was an avid reader and was given a Bible, which he read all the time, leading him to the decision of becoming a minister.

When he was about 11 years old, he was sent to live in Texas with one of his sisters, who had become a Lutheran. After he disembarked from the ship from Puerto Rico in Galveston, Texas, and while riding on the train, mosquitoes bit him and infected him with malaria. Since he had graduated from eighth grade in Puerto Rico, he was sent to Concordia High School in Austin, Texas; while there he became very ill and was diagnosed with malaria, a disease he carried with him the rest of his life. While at Concordia, his roommate was John W. Behnken. He earned part of his tuition and room and board by doing dishes in the cafeteria. He continued his education at St. John's in Winfield, Kansas.

In 1939 while attending Concordia Seminary in St. Louis, he met Rev. Jargo, a missionary in St. Louis and Illinois, who taught first- and second-year Spanish classes with 14 students in each class. He invited Alfredo to attend the class. When Jargo took a call, Alfredo not only took over his Spanish classes but also became a missionary conducting Spanish services at an Illinois mission on Sunday mornings and in the evening preaching in an extremely poor section of St. Louis. He received a Walther League scholarship from the Texas District, assisting him with his tuition.

At about the same time, a letter arrived from Quinto, Ecuador, requesting the English "Lutheran Hour" be translated into Spanish. Since Dr. Maier had Alfredo in a Hebrew class, he gave Alfredo the job of translating his sermons into Spanish. He then became the "Spanish Lutheran Hour" speaker and taught four Milwaukee boys (Edwin Wiebel, Gerard Kohn, Paul Lessmann, and Robert Moehring) to sing hymns in Spanish for the radio broadcast. He also preached the Spanish sermon, a translation of Dr. Maiers's English sermon, for "The Lutheran Hour" every Saturday evening. A layman, Mr. Zarndt, would take him from the seminary to Concordia Publishing House where the broadcast was recorded.

In 1941, he completed his vicarage at Mission San Juan in Santa Ana and returned to the seminary in 1942. While riding the streetcar in St. Louis one day, he met his future wife, Theodiste, daughter of Rev. and Mrs. Theodore Herrmann of Brownstown, Indiana, who was living with an aunt in St. Louis. When she got on the streetcar he was riding, she fell and he assisted her, and a friendship developed. They were married on June 24, 1943, and had four children, two sons and two daughters, who years later, presented them with four grandchildren. Following his graduation from the seminary in 1943, he worked for "The Lutheran Hour" for $60 a month where he printed excerpts in Spanish and would chauffeur Dr. Walter A. Maier to the train or drive him to southern Illinois. He was the first Spanish-speaking student to graduate from a Lutheran Church—Missouri Synod preparatory school and seminary.

Following his work at "The Lutheran Hour," he was called to start a Spanish mission in East Los Angeles. The District Mission Board had requested that Pastor Smukal's congregation, St. John's in Boyle Heights, allow the new mission to worship in its facilities. The Mission Board paid $5 a month to St. John's to help defray the cost of utilities. Since St. John's had a very German membership, they at first were hesitant in allowing Pastor Saez to hold services in their church building. After giving permission for use of the church, they stated that neither the organ nor the restrooms could be used by the "other people." Finally, the details were

ironed out so that both congregations could use the organ and restrooms.

In the March 20, 1945, Mission Board meeting, it was reported that Pastor Saez and Pastor Moehle had been at work for several weeks in the Mexican mission field. Pastor Saez had purchased a home for $7,000, and Pastor Moehle was making his home with members of St. John's. At the following meeting in April, even though Pastor Moehle had been assisting Pastor Berner at Faith in Los Angeles, the Board resolved to retain his services for Spanish work. At the next meeting in May, again it was resolved to permit Pastor Moehle to divide his time between Faith Lutheran Church of Los Angeles and the Mexican mission. It was also stated that "Pastor Moehle was not inclined to make the Spanish or Mexican mission his principal work." These were the last words on Rev. Moehle's work among the Hispanics of East Los Angeles.

On March 24, 1945, the first service was to be conducted, but no one came. On April 8, Candidate Alfred R. Saez was ordained and installed as pastor of the Spanish mission in Los Angeles at St. John's Church. By Sunday, April 15, 21 people attended an English service; 9 were adults, which included 3 men. The new congregation, Concordia Evangelical Lutheran Church, set a goal of having 25 communicant members in a year. They started a program of one motion picture per month, which was well attended. Another goal was to be able to start paying either for a church building of their own or to purchase St. John's facility should St. John's move out of the area. When the American Lutheran Church's brick church building in East Los Angeles was placed on the market for $7,000, the Mission Board declined to purchase it even when Pastor Saez stated he would help by teaching school full-time.

By September 1945, the Mission Board was concerned that Pastor Saez had been called to do work in the Mexican field, but he felt that his work should include all nationalities in English. The Mission Board decided to inform Synod's Board of Home Mission regarding the problem. At Synod's Board of Home Mission meeting on October 26, 1945, Rev. L. H. Jagels' letter was read regarding the problem in Mexican missions. "The Rev. Saez, called to do mission work among Mexicans, is laying more stress on developing a mixed congregation of whites and Mexicans, than upon the Mexicans themselves. He seems to meet with considerable success in this. The matter becomes disturbing because he is using the church build-

Rev. Alfred R. Saez, the pastor of Concordia Lutheran Church, Los Angeles, from 1945–1946. (Pacific Southwest District Archives)

Rev. Saez conducts first service on March 24, 1945 to begin Concordia Lutheran Church in East Los Angeles as a Hispanic congregation.

ing of St. John's Congregation and is neglecting the Mexicans who live in the neighborhood." Dr. Streufert, the head of the Board of Home Missions, in his answer, "pointed out that the call to Mexicans dared not be overlooked. If opportunity presents itself to bring in others, this is no doubt very commendable in itself, but perhaps these people ought to be urged to join St. John's congregation rather than form a mixed congregation. If Pastor Saez neglects the work for which he has been called, then he should be told so by the board."

At the 12th District Convention of the Southern California District in 1946 in Resolution No. 2, the Convention adopted a resolution stating "that Pastor Saez should devote his efforts primarily to the Spanish people and that he conduct preaching services in the Spanish language." At the Mission Board meeting on April 16, 1945, a recommendation was made to present an overture to the District Convention in regard to establishing educational facilities for Mexican children.

Pastor Saez wrote, in a March 18, 1946, report to the Mission Board, that "there are enough people in East Los Angeles to have a Lutheran church every four blocks, most of them unchurched! Should St. John's move and the Mission Board purchase the property, we intend to start a Boy Scout troop in conjunction with our mission expansion. We also believe a school is necessary to make up our being behind the time.... [Since] We begin our service [at 11:00 a.m.] right after theirs ends, our people are reluctant to come in while the people stay in front of the church — sometimes you have to push your way through. Our people, themselves, have estimated that we are being kept from a hundred percent gain. I constantly admonish patience and Christian love."

In his one-year ministry at the mission, Pastor Saez said he had confirmed 49. He had given a former policeman, an Irishman who lived only a block from the St. John's Church, Confirmation instruction. He reported that from March 18, 1945, to January 13, 1946, Concordia had 7 communicant members, one Baptism, 4 Confirmations, 44 services with an attendance of 836 [an average of 19 per service], offerings of $203.86, and a Sunday school having an enrollment of 11 with a maximum of 23 in attendance. The Ladies Aid of Grace Church, Los Angeles, contributed money for Sunday school materials. The little congregation had gathered people of German, Irish, French, Spanish, Mexican, and Armenian descent, worshiping in English only. By March 18, 1946, the mission had 29 baptized souls of whom 16 were adults with a communicant membership of 9 adults. He had confirmed two more people and was instructing two more adults.

In the summer of 1946 when Valparaiso University issued a second call to Pastor Saez to teach in the Foreign Language Department, he decided to accept the position where he stayed for 18 years. While at Northwestern University working on his doctorate, he taught part-time to help defray the cost of tuition. His doctorate was on "The Scriptures and the Perez Galdos's Novels." After receiving his doctorate from Northwestern in 1964, he took a teaching position at California Lutheran University, where he taught in the Foreign Language Department as a full-time professor retiring in 1984. He continued at CLU for 10 more years as a part-time professor.

Pastor Saez left Los Angeles in August of 1946. On September 17, 1946, the Mission Board recommended "that we do not call a worker into the East Los Angeles area immediately. If the group [Concordia] wishes to continue with separate services, then some assurance from the group in regard to financial help and moral support should be received. In the event that separate services are desired, Pastor Elfman has consented to serve them." At the following meeting in October, the department recommended that no subsidy be allotted for the Mexican mission in East Los Angeles area for the year 1947 with no action taken. In subsequent meetings of the Mission Board, no mention is made of the Spanish mission, Concordia Evangelical Lutheran Church of Los Angeles. Another chapter in the life of the Los Angeles mission work to the Hispanic population closed, but it would soon be revived some six years later on a more solid base.

"Lord, Thou hast been our dwelling place in all generations.
Before the mountains were brought forth, Thou art God."
— PSALM 90:1

CHAPTER THREE

Feed My Lambs

1938–1956

The second attempt to do work among the Mexican population in Southern California had its beginning in a much different manner than the first. The Mexican missions in Los Angeles were all started by pastors who saw the need of proclaiming the Gospel to the huge Mexican population in East Los Angeles. The Santa Ana Mission was conceived not by pastors but by a group of young women interested in bringing the Gospel of Christ's redeeming love to the Orange County Mexican population, especially in the Santa Ana area.

The area where the present city of Santa Ana is located was explored on July 26, 1769, by Don Gaspár de Portolá, a Spanish expedition party leader who discovered a picturesque valley and river in Southern California. He christened the valley and river, Santa Ana, in honor of Saint Anne (Santa Ana). José Antonio Yorba, a youthful expedition soldier and his nephew, Juan Peralta, were given a Spanish land grant for the area developing Rancho Santiago de Santa Ana for cattle grazing and productive farmland. In 1869, William H. Spurgeon purchased 70-acres from the Yorba family and plotted a town site, giving the new town the name of Santa Ana. In 1886 during the great land

"He will feed his flock like a shepherd, he will gather the lambs in his arms, he will carry them in his bosom, and gently lead those that are with young."

— ISAIAH 40:11

boom of California, Santa Ana was incorporated as a city; when Orange County separated from Los Angeles in 1889, Santa Ana was designated the county seat and remained an agricultural area until the late 1940s, devoted to citrus groves requiring the help of Mexican laborers.

By the late 1930s, Santa Ana had a population of nearly 4,000 Mexicans living in 3 Mexican colonies or barrios. On the west side of town was the Artesia Colony, on the south side was the Delhi Road Colony, and on the east side was the Logan Colony, in the middle, between the three barrios, was the town of Santa Ana where all the Anglos lived.

The key person in instigating work among the Mexicans in their barrios was -. Her keen concern for the Mexican people began with her Christian education and with her high school Spanish class. She utilized her Spanish as she worked part-time during her high school years in a grocery store, serving Mexican customers. Late one evening, a Mexican man, tired from a long walk, returned to the store. As he gave Alice five dollars, he said, "My change should have been one dollar instead of five." This and similar experiences deepened her understanding and love for the Mexican people.

Miss Alice Fiene at her office desk where she translated Spanish letters, which led her to organize a group to begin mission work among the Mexicans in Santa Ana. (Pacific Southwest District Archives)

During Christmas of 1937, Alice received a Spanish Bible as a gift from her parents. As she read it, she meditated on the words of Scripture and thought of the more than 4,000 Mexicans living in Santa Ana who had no opportunity to hear the pure Word. Poverty, fights, murders, and prostitution among the Mexicans often made the headlines; countless poor Mexican children lived like orphans. She thought: "That was an inspiring mission sermon I heard at St. John's, Orange, last Sunday! But what is being done to take the Gospel to these Mexicans?"

Some time later, Alice was employed by a firm, which exported articles and goods to Spanish-speaking countries. She observed that the Spanish letters had to be sent to an outside firm for translation. One day Alice asked the manager if she could try to translate the letters. From that time forward, she became the chief translator of letters and the Spanish correspondent for the company.

In the spring of 1938, Alice had a party for a group of 29 young Lutheran women from Saint John's Lutheran Church of Orange. She explained to them her missionary zeal for beginning mission work among the Mexicans in the area. These women formed a mission society, which met weekly for several years. Their project was to do Mexican mission work in Santa Ana. Inspired by Alice's zeal and enthusiasm when she presented the plan to start a Sunday school for these children, the ladies decided to ask their pastor for his consent and blessing on their plan. Pastor Bode went to their next meeting and said, "I have no objection to you forming a mission society, but not for Mexicans. Let's take care of own people first." With Alice's continued persistence for a Mexican mission, Pastor Bode, finally, dared her to go knocking on doors.

On October 9, 1938, Doris Schannon and Alice went with tracts in hand to distribute in Santa Ana. At first, they didn't know where to begin; after noticing more Mexicans at an apartment building than they had seen on other blocks, they decided to enter it. That first Sunday they felt like they accomplished nothing as they passed out literature, but people couldn't read it, and Alice couldn't speak Spanish well enough to evangelize. Through Alice's encouragement, though, they did not give up their goal of establishing a mission.

The following Sunday the mission society ladies drove throughout Santa Ana asking the children in the streets if they would come to Sunday school if they had one. They recorded names and

addresses of children and promised the children a Sunday school in two weeks. They didn't know where it would meet, but they were determined to have a Sunday school, even if it was in the street.

They saw an abandoned and dilapidated store building, which looked suitable, at the corner of West Second Street and Daisy Street in Santa Ana. After questioning people about the owner, the four spinsters were told to go into a saloon on the east side of town; when they entered the saloon, all drinking stopped as the patrons where shocked to see the four Anglo ladies in this place of business. At last, they found the owner, Juan Ramirez, and hurriedly rented the building for $1 for each Sunday afternoon it was utilized. A Negro lady was preaching in the same building in the mornings. Afterwards they gathered discarded Sunday school lessons and chairs from St. John's, a piano from Mrs. Nolin, and they mimeographed some fliers to be distributed the following Sunday.

On Sunday, October 23, the ladies enlisted seven cars, going back into the neighborhood, leaving fliers at doors, and talking to people about the service and Sunday school to be held on October 30. On Reformation Sunday, October 30, Rev. Bruno Martinelli from Los Angeles came to conduct and preach at the 3:30 p.m. church service, bringing instrumental players with him to lead the singing. The first service had 43 children and 2 adults preceded by a Sunday school at 2:30 p.m. Since it was too hot to have Sunday school in the building in the afternoons, they moved it to mornings; Pastor Martinelli served the little mission from October 1938 to June of 1939. During all the interim periods where there was no pastor, Raymond Andersen, a layman from Immanuel of Orange, read sermons in Spanish, that had been prepared by pastors in the area, and conducted services in the evening.

The Sunday school had an average attendance of 38 children the first few months. Before Christmas, Alice Fiene with her limited knowledge of Spanish along with others members of the mission society, visited 20 homes of Mexican children on Saturday afternoons installing paper scenes of Bethlehem. On Christmas Day, 69 people were present to celebrate the birth of the Christ Child. At this time, the little church was named Mission San Juan Luterana with 15 consecrated ladies of St. John's, Orange, serving in the mission society.

In 1940, two key families, Flores and Gandara, were brought to the mission. Gilbert Flores recalled, when he was about seven years old, Alice Fiene picking up Gilbert's neighborhood friend for

---

The mission in Santa Ana is called San Juan Luterana in the beginning.

Sunday school. When she asked him if he wanted to come along, he said that he didn't. The following Sunday, after Alice asked him again, he consented and attended. While attending the Sunday school that Sunday, he discovered that it was interesting. The next Sunday when Alice arrived to pick him up, all of his sisters were there, too, and went to the mission Sunday school with him. Both he and his sister, Flora, had fun and enjoyed Sunday school. Each Sunday morning, the ladies would send Gilbert out on the street to ring a small hand-bell announcing that Sunday school was ready to begin. He said he was very embarrassed doing that job. As Flora was so touched by Alice's kindnesses to her family, she said that her mother, grandmother, and other members of the family requested to be and were buried just above Alice and her family in St. John's Cemetery in Santa Ana.

The Flores family brought the seven Gandara children, Ephren, Vera, Belen, Joe, Jesús, Tila, and Adam to the mission. Later on, their mother, Victoria, also became a member of the mission. Both Vera, age 11, and Belen, age 6, remember coming to the mission for Sunday school and Vacation Bible School, where they received candy, a real treat since they were very poor. Christmas had special memories for each of the children as their parents came to the Christmas program along with all the neighborhood to hear them recite Bible verses they had memorized; the ladies from St. John's would bring them stockings filled with candy, nuts, and fruit. They recalled it was a joy going to church, "especially when my mother joined" the mission.

Vera recalled that since the family was so poor, they had no clock; at about 8:30 a.m. on Sunday morning, the ladies from the mission society would come around the barrio in three cars honking their horns to get the children up for Sunday school. They would come into Vera's house to help them get ready, because their mother had eight

Mr. Raymond Andersen, a layman from Immanuel of Orange, who was one of the leaders in establishing the Mexican mission in Santa Ana. (Pacific Southwest District Archives)

children. She recalled the kindness of all these ladies and that the first organist at the mission was Annie Guerrello.

In the summer of 1940, the Sunday school teachers took 22 children from the mission Sunday school to Santiago Park for a picnic in the park, as reported by Miss Inez Kogler, secretary of the St. John's Mission Society. On November 3, 1940, San Juan Mission Sunday school celebrated its second anniversary with Rev. William Schmoock of Trinity, Santa Ana, preaching in English, while Raymond Andersen translated the address into Spanish. The 45 Sunday school children in attendance recited Scripture passages they had memorized, and also gave very good answers to points of doctrine when questioned.

For the first three years, the women of the mission society assumed the entire responsibility for the mission, financing the project and planning the services, which included some rather elaborate Christmas and Easter observances. Some of the women taught Sunday school continually for 10 years. Under Alice's leadership, the women studied Spanish and "soul winning," issued publicity, canvassed, and worked to overcome numerous obstacles. Stories were told of how some nuns came and took children from the Sunday school, and how rocks were thrown into the building during Sunday school hour. Miss Fiene used her excellent musical talent of playing the piano for the mission, which was a great asset. As time passed, other church organizations lent financial assistance, making it possible for the first resident missionary to be called.

Not to be disheartened or discouraged, this relatively small mission society showed countless kindnesses to the Mexicans. When agricultural workers followed the fruit harvest, they sent their addresses to the mission society where the women of the society then sent the workers Sunday school materials; these workers, in turn, taught the lessons in camps where they were living. This is just another example of the society's zeal for sharing the love of Christ with the little Mexican children.

In 1941, at the request of the women of the mission society, the Southern California District Mission Board took over the mission. In a January 9, 1941, letter from Pastor Webbeking, to Rev. F. C. Streufert, the head of Synod's Mission Board, the District mission director said:

> In the last regular meeting of our Mission Board, it was resolved to take up work again among the Mexican population of our District particularly in Santa Ana, Bell, a small town about half way between Santa Ana and Los Angeles, and, later on, in Los Angeles proper.
>
> Santa Ana has a Mexican population of nearly 4,000, at Bell there are nearly 1,000, and Los Angeles has some 15,000. It is estimated that Southern California, from Los Angeles to San Diego, has some 75,000 Mexicans.
>
> In Santa Ana, work has been carried on for over a year by a group of mission-minded people from Santa Ana and Orange. They have done some very fine work, particularly with the children. They have been holding Sunday school every Sunday morning, a sort of a Bible hour on every Sunday evening, and religious instructions on one evening during the week. As a result, they have gathered 32 children who are definitely enrolled in their group, about half of which have been attending regularly from the beginning. I attended one of the meetings recently and found that the children have a fine knowledge of Bible passages and are also quite well versed in Bible history. A number of the children are advanced sufficiently that they should be receiving instruction preparatory to Confirmation; a number of parents have also asked for Baptism of their children, and also want the ministration of the Word and Lord's Supper for themselves. Our board is convinced that Santa Ana should prove a very fertile field.

In April of 1941, the Rev. Harry H. Smith of Brownsville, Texas, was called to serve Santa Ana, Bell, and Los Angeles. In his first reply to the Mission Board, he asked if there were chapels in Santa Ana, Bell, and Los Angeles. The reply was "not really." In May, he stated that he couldn't leave the Brownsville area because of the great need for a Spanish-speaking pastor there and the work he was doing not only as a pastor but also as the writer and business manager of both *Noticiero Luterano* and *Sociedad Luterana De Tradados* with no one to replace him. He stayed in Brownsville his entire ministry, ministering to the Mexican people on both sides of the border.

In the June 15, 1941, issue of the *District News*, the following was reported:

> …Good news continues to come from Santa Ana, and here is the latest story:
>
> It all began when our faithful pupil, Vera Gandara, came with a question from the lady who lives next door, "How much does it cost to be baptized?" Upon learning that this blessing can be obtained without any money at all, her surprise was very great. So on the evening of May 18, Mrs. Ruiz brought her two children, Andrew, age two, and Consuelo, age six months to our church, Mission Evangelica Luterana San Juan in Santa Ana, and the Rev. William Schmoock of Trinity, Santa Ana, baptized them. Pastor Schmoock read the ceremony in English and Raymond Andersen read it in Spanish. It was a solemn moment when the baptismal formula, *"Yo te bautizo en el nombre del Padre, y del Hijo, v del Espiritu Santo"* was pronounced by Pastor Schmoock who had studied these words for the occasion.…
>
> It is our desire that all who read this may remember the grace of God is something which cannot be bought with gold or silver, but through God's mercy, it is a free gift to all who believe and trust in it. May God hold his guiding hand over Andrew and Consuelo in order that they may faithfully keep their baptismal vows.

The Mission Board placed a Spanish-speaking vicar, Alfredo Saez, that year, filling the request for a pastor by the Santa Ana mission. On August 24, 1941, he was commissioned as pastor of Mission San Juan by Rev. Du Brau of Christ Church, Los Angeles, with Pastor William Gesch of St. John's, Orange, assisting in the little chapel building, which had a front door between two large storefront windows that had been boarded up. The ceiling was old cardboard that covered the studs

Vicar Alfredo Saez is commissioned on August 24, 1941, as pastor of Mission San Juan.

Commissioning of Vicar Alfredo Saez (third from the left) on August 24, 1941, in Mission San Juan's storefront building with Rev. Du Brau (third from the right) of Christ Church, Los Angeles, and Pastor William Gesch (right) of St. John's, Orange. (Pacific Southwest District Archives)

Vicar Saez with the 1942 Confirmation Class that included Angelita Velardes, Teresa Martinez, Mrs. J. Gandara, Vera Gandara, Ofelia Flores in front of the San Juan Mission at Second and Daisy, Santa Ana. (Pacific Southwest District Archives)

of the building. A small library table served as an altar having a small cross with two candles on each side. Behind the altar was a velvet curtain.

Vera (Gandara) Saldaña recalled Vicar Saez as being very young and patient, speaking Spanish well, and instructing her in the Confirmation class. Both Flora (Flores) Chavez and Gilbert Flores remember the vicar conducting the young people's meeting and planning hikes to Santiago Park; the young people's group also planned the annual picnic at Santiago Park where they always had hot dogs, a treat for them. In 1941, the Junior Walther League was organized with 5 members, growing to 11 members in 1946 and 17 members in 1947.

Pastor Saez, in an interview, recalled that while in Santa Ana he met the Gandara family and their little son Jesús (Chui), who couldn't move his fingers and who couldn't walk or talk. Pastor Saez took him into the small room of the chapel that served as an office, and used a small ruler to help him move his fingers and massaged his legs. In a year, he had little Chui walking, talking, and manipulating his fingers. He also remembered that in order to raise funds for the mission, he and the members of the mission society recycled newspapers.

On that December 7, 1941, a quiet second Sunday in Advent, everything changed with the bombing of Pearl Harbor at 7:55 a.m. Hawaii time, 9:55 a.m. California time. No one knew, as they sat in chapel that morning, about the incident that would change everything in their lives and the mission's

life. That afternoon fear gripped the hearts of the people on the West Coast as they were fearful of a Japanese attack.

On Monday, December 8, radios were brought to schools and in homes and businesses people gathered at 9:30 a.m. to hear President Roosevelt give his famous "Day of Infamy" speech declaring war on the Axis powers. Beginning with a blackout on December 10, 1941, civil defense officials began enforcing air raid drills and blackout regulations with some 65,000 people volunteering to serve as block wardens in the Los Angeles area alone. Local police distributed incendiary-bomb extinguishers to residents fearful of Japanese air attacks. The year ended not only with much apprehension and concern about the future but also with trust in God for His protective care.

The New Year, 1942, began with many changes in the mission and the country. The country changed from a peacetime economy to a wartime production economy. In January 1942, the OPA (Office of Price Administration) instituted rationing limiting the amount of food, gas, and clothing that could be purchased with the use of little books and stamps. Gasoline rationing was especially unpopular. The average driver received an "A" card limiting him to a mere "patriotic" three gallons of gas a week. Almost everything that Americans liked to eat — meat, coffee, butter, cheese, sugar — were strictly rationed by a point system that drove housewives and grocers crazy.

The OPA issued ration books of stamps with point values and assigned specific point values to food, which turned into a heroic nightmare. Many grocers had to cope with some 14 billion points a month, actually handling 3.5 billion tiny stamps. Listed below are examples of the point system:

Wartime Shopping Guide

Item	Weight	Point Value
Porterhouse steak	1 lb.	12
Hamburger	1 lb.	7
Ham	1 lb	7
Butter	1 lb.	16
Peaches	16 oz. can	18
Carrots	16 oz. can	6
Tomato catsup	14 oz. bottle	15

Even though there were shortages of goods and food during the war, it was said the American people had never eaten as well.

On February 23, 1942, a Japanese submarine shelled the coast near Santa Barbara, and three nights later Los Angeles succumbed completely to war jitters as sirens blared, search lights flooded the skies, and anti-aircraft batteries fired 1,440 rounds of anti-aircraft shells into the sky at "Japanese bombers" in what turned out to be a false alarm, subsequently dubbing it the "Battle of Los Angeles," a very frightening experience for those living in the area. The next day residents woke up to the startling headline, "L. A. Battles Air Raids," in an extra edition of newspapers being sold on the street that morning. By February 1942, people locally were getting used to reading about the monumental events exploding all over the world, but this one brought home the fact that the Second World War had finally arrived in Orange County. A second headline that day said, "Heavy Fire Turns Back Two Flights of Enemy Planes." The story reported how anti-aircraft gunners had fired more than 1,400 shells at what were believed to be Japanese planes above the South Bay area.

A blackout throughout Santa Ana and all of Southern California had been ordered during the air raid, requiring every home and business to extinguish or cover any light, including all street lights and billboard lights. Those living closer to the coast that night were shaken out of their beds by anti-aircraft guns firing into a dark sky crisscrossed with searchlights. Shrapnel from exploded shells rained down, and at least two duds from guns made craters in south Los Angeles and Santa Monica when they landed without exploding.

After it was all over, no one was ever able to find "those enemy planes," and there was no trace of bombs. The night of widespread military action

World War II brings blackouts and an air raid to Santa Ana and all of Southern California.

and terror was just one very big and wild false alarm. Residents were still on edge as they read in the paper almost daily of Japanese gains throughout the Pacific. Many were certain they would soon have to beat off an enemy attack in their own city. The war had come to the backyard of Orange County, giving actual fear to everyone as they faced a new daily life during World War II.

During the War, Vicar Saez stayed in Santa Ana with a German woman, Aunt Rose, a German citizen. When World War II broke with the populace afraid that the Japanese were going to invade the West Coast, a law was passed in Congress that no German citizen could travel and had to register at a local Post Office. Aunt Rose was a cousin of Pastor Wachholz, the institutional pastor in Los Angeles. Vicar Saez took her to Los Angeles to register her at the Los Angeles Post Office so that she could visit her relatives. He recalled that, at night when he was out making calls, a blackout would occur forcing him to drive in blackness of the night through Santa Ana and Orange, isolated little country towns at that time.

The mission society was made up of 15 people mainly from St. John's of Orange. One of the leaders, Alice Fiene, would take her mother and the Vicar to dinner each Sunday at the best restaurant in town, Thrifty Drug Store. Belen (Gandara) Perez also recalled Alice's inspiration and how it touched her heart for the rest of her life.

The vicar's California mother, Mrs. Eva Magnusson, a Norwegian who loved fresh fish and the Mexican people, was the widow of Dr. Magnusson. They were both very mission-minded in sharing the Word with the Mexican populace. Mrs. Magnusson was also very active in the mission society, teaching sewing classes, making cookies and punch for the children, speaking to them in Spanish, keeping the youth group going, and sometimes having them to her modest home in Santa Ana to play volleyball in her big backyard. Flora Chavez also remembers cleaning Mrs. Magnusson's house in Santa Ana, which Flora thought was very large compared to her little house with very small rooms.

Some other members of the mission society were Dora Kogler, who was there at the very first meeting, and her sister, Inez, both Sunday school teachers for many years (daughters of St. John's first pastor); Mary Szegethy did crafts and taught Sunday school, bringing crayons for the children to use; Miss Margaret Fitschen taught Sunday school, had a beautiful voice, and sang in St. John's

Mrs. Eva Magnusson, an active member of the mission society, in front of her Santa Ana home. (Pacific Southwest District Archives)

The children of the mission with Vicar Saez (back); on his left are Mary Szegethy, Raymond Andersen, and Edna Bandick on the end with other members of the Mission Society. (Pacific Southwest District Archives)

Mr. and Mrs. Raymond Andersen with their twin daughters.(Pacific Southwest District Archives)

choir; Miss Mary Hillebrecht, taught Sunday school and Vacation Bible School and had a green Ford that she used to pick up the children for Sunday school; Edna Bandick and Doris Schannon both taught Sunday school; the others included Mrs. Lenora Stock, Mrs. Selma Kothe, and Miss Thelma Prellwitz.

Another key person who played an enormous role in the mission was Raymond Andersen, a young man from Immanuel, Orange, who was not in the original mission group when it first met. He read sermons in very broken Spanish and played the accordion and pump organ for services. Gilbert and Flora recalled that one Sunday while Raymond was playing the small pump organ, the three-legged stool collapsed and spilled him to the floor. He got up while the congregation continued to sing, and began to accompany them again on the organ. After a couple of years, he married and he and his wife had twin girls. The children of the mission grew up with them, as they were also members of the mission. Eventually, he and his family moved to the state of Washington.

In 1942, Vicar Saez wrote the following report to the District convention about the Santa Ana mission:

> Mission work among the Mexicans is slow because of their ignorance and their reluctance to give up pet sins and their fear of the Roman clergy. Our Spanish mission is small, began with group of Sunday school children gathered in by the mission society of St. John's, Orange. In spite of discouragement, the young women of the mission society and others, particularly Mr. Andersen and Mrs. Magnusson of Santa Ana, faithfully continued the work. August of 1941, Vicar Saez was put in charge of the work. The number has grown. Four have been confirmed and two more will be confirmed by the time this report is published. Two additional Confirmation classes are being held.

Young people's society organized, sewing classes for women and children and singing class being conducted. Sunday school is conducted in English, evening services in Spanish. Needs of this field are a decent place of worship, a permanent pastor, a day school. The missionary feels that 50 children could be enrolled in such a school. The missionary has also been seeking to reclaim the Los Angeles field. Subsidy: $72 per month.

During the War, Vicar Saez and helpers started formal worship services with about 10 women doing the work. Vicar Saez returned to the seminary in June of 1942. During the interim period between him and the next pastor, Raymond Andersen would conduct the services and read the sermon in Spanish.

In the March 1943 *Walther League Messenger*, an interesting article appeared in regard to the mission in the summer of 1942:

A very interesting sidelight on the convention of the Southern California District is brought to us by President Irene Schroeder.... She tells of two Mexican girls of the Spanish mission in Santa Ana who were brought to the convention by Margaret Fitschen and Mary Hillebrecht of St. John's Church, Orange.... As Irene tells the story, "these girls were confirmed together with three others this summer, the first confirmands of our little mission. The following week they had their regular young people's society meeting. Both girls wore their convention badges and asked Margaret where hers was. Fortunately, she had it in her purse. The girls got up and told the others about the convention, explained 'The Lutheran Hour,' Mr. McFadden's talk about 'The Power of God' and the chaplain picture, told about our Wheat Ridge Sanitarium, the Lutheran Youth Building which had just been dedicated at Chicago, besides mentioning the social features of the Sunday part of the convention.

Margaret also told me that their little society has five-cent dues in order to help defray luncheon expenses. In this way, they are trying to teach them to give and not always expect something. Just as soon as the members arrive, they pay their nickels, saying, 'Here's my nickel.' They are proud of their contributions. Last Wednesday, one girl forgot her money and asked to be taken home again to get it. When one of our other young women heard about this, she remarked, 'Why, I would have given her a nickel.' Margaret replied, 'I could have, too, but it is better for them to assume their own responsibilities.' They are now planning to have little banks in which to save money for missions."

Also during that summer, the Mission Board wrote letters to the St. Louis Seminary requesting a candidate to fill the vacancy in Santa Ana. Dean Richard Jesse had recommended Candidate Robert Gussick, who had served in the Spanish mission, San Pedro Church, at San Antonio, Texas, the previous year. He was described as "a capable individual and a terrifically hard worker" who was given charge of the school, and when Pastor Melendez left to go into government service, he was also given complete charge of everything else including the church. During that time, he married and was assisted by his very capable wife. While there, he had translated the Communion and Vespers liturgies into Spanish. With this recommendation, the Mission Board immediately called him for a period of one year.

In the call papers, the Santa Ana area was described as approximately twenty families under the influence of the existing mission; the mission had a communicant membership of 6 with an average Sunday school attendance ranging from 18 to 20 children and the Sunday evening service was attended by 25. Santa Ana had a total population of about 40,000 with over 8,000 Mexicans, and Los Angeles had a population of about one and

The Mission Society with the Sunday school children at a park. In the back row, Vicar Saez (right) and Pastor Bode (left) of St. John's, Orange (Pacific Southwest District Archives)

one-half million with some 150,000 Mexicans. The mission society had promised to raise at least $20 per month for general expenses. After deliberation, Candidate Gussick declined the call and later went to Guatemala where he served as a missionary for many years. He is presently affiliated with the Lutheran Border Concerns Ministry.

In December of 1942, Rev. Erhardt Henry Riedel, a missionary from China, was placed in charge of the mission where he stayed until December 1945. He was the son of Erhardt Helnrich Theodor and Caroline nee Goetcke Riedel born on June 12, 1889, in Lincoln, Illinois, where his parents were members of Zion Lutheran Church. At the age of 17, he went to Chicago to learn the printing trade. While working in St. Louis, Missouri, in 1908, he met The Rev. F. Herzberger, city missionary, who encouraged him to enter the seminary in Springfield, Illinois. He graduated from that institution in 1915.

Having received a call from the Evangelical Lutheran Missionary Society for China, an organization consisting of pastors, teachers, and members of the Synodical Conference in Minnesota and a number of other states, Graduate Riedel was commissioned as the second missionary of the society on September 19, 1915, in St. Paul's Lutheran Church at New Ulm, Minnesota. On October 28, 1915, Missionary-elect Riedel married Carmelia Becher at Westgate, Iowa. The Lord blessed this union with six sons and two daughters. One son, Erhardt Paul, also became a pastor. Following their marriage, the young couple set sail from San Francisco, California, for the mission field in China on board the *S. S. Awa Maru* on December 13, 1915, arriving in Shanghai on January 12, 1916; they proceeded to the mission field in Hankow, arriving on January 16, 1916, where he ministered in the China mission field. Due to tuberculosis, he left free China at the end of February 1941. From Dr. Riedel's book, *From the Land of Sinim — A Memoir*, he describes his ministry in the Santa Ana Mission:

After about 10 months rest, I received an appointment from the Southern California District Mission Board to work among the Mexicans, using a rented chapel at Santa Ana, California. All the preaching was done in Spanish. There was at that time a nucleus of a congregation consisting of four–six families, all of whom had severed relations with the Catholic Church into which they had been baptized. The reasons for leaving the Catholic Church usually involved marriage problems or adherence some time to national Mexican church groups such as spiritualists or the Assembly of God. The Sunday school was well attended.

It is not difficult for one to learn Spanish to be able to preach. At first, I engaged a Mexican gentleman as a tutor; he had recently been in a drinking bout, breaking a leg, and thus was free to give assistance at a reasonable salary. As a rule, I was welcomed and my Gospel message was well received, especially by the men, who often seemed resentful of the high charges of the Catholics for Baptism, Confirmation, marriage, and funeral services. In one case, a man who was a habitual drunkard had lived for years with his wife in a common-law marriage. They had six children, who, together with the mother, were members of the Lutheran church. Through efforts made in his behalf, he was granted a belated marriage license, and they were finally married by me. Later, while working in northern California's fruit and vegetable harvest, this man, who was signally blessed with his Protestant wife and children, was said to have ended his almost continuous spree of drinking by jumping into a river while drunk. No one but God knows whether or not he deplored his sins and turned to Christ in faith, receiving pardon; his precious soul, bought by the blood of Jesus, entering paradise.

…During my time, a class of four young Mexicans was confirmed. Also for a while, the Mexican children, who attended public school, were granted time in the afternoon to attend religious instruction. If I did at least some effective preaching (Gospel), and if a few souls were saved, I can be satisfied and happy with my work with a gentle and hospitable people.

Since Pastor Riedel wasn't proficient in Spanish when he began his work at the mission, he would take Gilbert Flores along with him to translate as he went canvassing the neighborhood. After canvassing, they went to Pastor Riedel's modest home in Orange for dinner where Mrs. Riedel served knackwurst and sauerkraut. Since Gilbert had never seen knackwurst before, he thought it was a large hot dog, and he didn't like the sauerkraut; Gilbert said his family was so poor that he used

Rev. Riedel, a missionary from China, takes over the mission in 1942, staying until 1945.

to eat tortillas and beans and beans and tortillas for every meal; Flora Chavez said she couldn't eat the sauerkraut either. Flora remembered the girls in the Confirmation class going through the lunch Mrs. Riedel had prepared for pastor and sampling some of the things like pumpernickel bread. They had never seen it or tasted it before. Pastor told them all they had to do was ask and he would give them some food. His wife then prepared food for the class, since the children were so poor and had little to eat.

Belen Perez remembered Pastor Riedel as a very patient man who instructed her in her Confirmation class where he told them, "When you grow up, go to China." He was also able to communicate with her mother in Spanish. After church, he'd take the children to his home for dinner where they feasted on roast and homemade pies his wife had prepared. At the time, Pastor had three children at home, John who was in the service, Marie, and Joe. All the children from the mission thought that Pastor was really rich and lived in a big house. In realty, he had very little and had difficulty making ends meet. Since the children came from very poor, small homes, his house seemed like a mansion to them, especially eating in a dining room.

Pastor Riedel reported to the District Convention in 1943, that the average Sunday evening attendance at the mission from March 1942 to May 1943 was 20 Mexicans with the smallest attendance at 14 and the largest at 35. Outstanding progress was made in the Sunday school from a noisy, disorderly one to a quiet and orderly one. "There was a marked attitude of the children, and a noticed growth in grace among the regular members. In general, the outlook for the future is good — the progress, naturally, will be slow." The subsidy was $189. In the spring, the synodical Board of Foreign Missions approved the temporary assignment of the Rev. Riedel to the Spanish mission in Santa Ana.

In a June 6, 1943, letter from Eva Magnusson to Pastor Webbeking, she stated:

It has become a burden on my heart to read of the hundreds of Mexicans coming in directly from Mexico to harvest our crops. According to the [*Santa Ana*] *Register* of last week, the number in our county is already over 1,700. Our quota is 2,000. Two camps are mentioned — at Irvine and at Orange, but Pastor Riedel has made inquiries and

says there are more camps housing groups.

...Pastor Riedel is doing valiantly learning Spanish. In May, he began preaching his sermons in Spanish. He writes them and has a Mexican check over his Spanish. And he does truly well. But he hasn't reached a place where he can converse in Spanish, except in simple things. I can't either. Also they usually know no English. But these laborers are men and know no English as a rule. To reach them would take a man who freely uses Spanish.

In the summer of 1943, an African Methodist Episcopal church building on 1820 West Second Street was rented for $8 per month and used until 1946. Pastor Stirdivant recalled the building was lovingly called the "Hen House," as its cardboard ceiling filtered the winter rains. It was truly a "holy" place on Sundays; as the African Methodists occupied and worshiped there in the mornings followed by the Lutherans in the late afternoon, and ending with the Mexican Pentecostals in the evening. On the third Sunday in August, Mission San Juan held its annual picnic at Santiago Park, where Rev. Riedel conducted the service with twenty-three children and three Mexican adults present. The mission observed its fifth anniversary on Reformation Sunday. At that time, the Sunday school had 30 pupils; four children had been baptized and five adults were confirmed. Mr. Fridling made and gave the baptismal font at Santa Ana Spanish Mission, which had formerly been used at Bethany, San Diego.

Rev. Erhardt Riedel, a missionary from China, with the San Juan Mission's Confirmation Class on Pentecost Day in 1944: (left to right) Flora Flores, Lupe Flores, Belen Gandara, and Jesús Gandara. (Pacific Southwest District Archives)

The rented church building on West Second is lovingly called the "Hen House," as its cardboard ceiling filters the winter rains.

Not only was Pastor Riedel working in the Santa Ana field, he was also going into the East Los Angeles field two to three days giving instructions in people's homes. At the Santa Ana mission in 1944, he reported that he had an average attendance of 18 and was giving Confirmation instruction to seven or eight adults, with five children being instructed privately. The Mission Board provided mileage to East Los Angeles along with his salary of $120 per month plus $10 a month car allowance and free rent. On Pentecost Sunday of 1944, he confirmed Flora Flores, Lupe Flores, Belen Gandara, and Jesús Gandara.

In late fall of 1944 and into the early spring of 1945, the main discussion of the Mission Board regarding the Santa Ana mission was the purchase of property for the congregation. The Inner Mission Department recommended that the Santa Ana Mission Society be encouraged to purchase the proposed site for $3,800 and that the society be permitted to solicit funds from the congregations within its circuit. These recommendations were adopted. The matter of the purchase of a lot and the building of a suitable mission chapel in Santa Ana was left to the discretion of Mr. Martens and the members of the Church Extension Department. By August of 1945, the Mission Board learned that the African Methodist Episcopal church building in Santa Ana where the mission was worshiping, could be purchased for $2,000. The department felt that it would not be wise to spend that amount of money in Santa Ana at that time. In the October 16, 1945, Mission Board meeting, a report was made stating that the property of Trinity Lutheran Church in Santa Ana could be purchased for the mission for $12,000, and that a Mexican school could be started in Santa Ana. The board wrote to Synod's Home Mission Board to see if they would be interested in the project. Unfortunately, no building or school was purchased or established at this time.

At the same time, the Lord laid a very heavy burden upon the shoulders of Missionary Riedel due to the illness of his dear wife, Carmelia, who had two operations for brain tumor and suffered excruciating seizures until the Lord in His grace and mercy released her from her suffering and granted her a blessed end on January 18, 1946. Her funeral services were conducted in St. John's Lutheran Church of Orange, California, where the Rev. William G. Gesch delivered the sermon and conducted the burial rites in the Orange County Cemetery with St. John's assuming the cost of the hospital bills and helping the family in many other ways.

Although Missionary Riedel had his hands full with his ailing wife and household chores, not to mention serving the Santa Ana Mission, he did not forget his dear China and its needs. He busied himself with preparing a rough draft of the *Thorough Declaration of the Formula of Concord* and also translated the first three lectures of Dr. Walther's *Law and Gospel*. After Carmelia's death, Missionary Riedel continued his translation work, kept house for his two boys who were still at home, and engaged in pulpit supply work in Orange and Santa Ana, California, and in Pocatello and Haley, Idaho. He served St. John's Lutheran Church near White City, Kansas; St. Peter's Lutheran Church of Davenport, Nebraska; and First Lutheran Church of Sommerfield, Kansas. In 1951, he married his second wife, Frieda Graf, of Orange, California. He welcomed the opportunity to return to his "first love," China, having been recalled by the Board of Foreign Missions to serve in Taiwan, arriving in November of 1956, where he was assigned the task of teaching in the seminary and was in charge of three preaching stations—Tainan, Bai Chuan Din chapel, and Bei Hsin Chie chapel. For his work in dogmatics, he translated Dr. John T. Mueller's *Christian Dogmatics*, at first mimeographed and some time later 1,500 copies were printed. A copy was presented to President Chiang Kai-shek, who expressed wonderment at the fact that a foreign missionary had done such a lengthy and worthwhile work in the Chinese language. In 1962, the Springfield seminary conferred on him an honorary Doctor of Divinity, citing him "for long years of service as missionary, teacher, and translator."

The marvelous fruit of his labor was the translation of the entire *Book of Concord* in Chinese, a project he was able to finish within one year — a gigantic accomplishment. Despite delays and that no funds had been appropriated for publishing it, and even some opposition to printing the complete *Book of Concord* in Chinese, it was printed in its entirety. Five hundred dollars came from his son's congregation in Wenatchee, Washington; one hundred dollars from his daughter Marie and her husband; and, through the good offices of the area counselor, another five hundred dollars was procured from the Mission Board.

Doctor Riedel's heart must have leaped with great joy and with deep satisfaction when, on April 17, 1971, 1,000 volumes of the Chinese edition of the *Book of Concord* were delivered to his home

Missonary Riedel translates Dr. Mueller's *Christian Dogmatics* and the *Book of Concord* into Chinese, in Chia Yi. Instead of promoting the book for sale, it was decided to send the *Book of Concord* gratis to all pastors and church workers who would respond to an ad in the leading Protestant paper of Taiwan. About 600 pastors, deacons, theological students, and youth workers responded, and were indeed grateful to receive the book. In addition to the *Book of Concord*, a free copy of the Chinese *Dogmatics* and the Chinese version of Dr. Edward Preus' *The Justification of a Sinner Before God* were included in the offer. Dean Victor Hafner of the Hong Kong Seminary ordered two hundred copies of the *Book of Concord* for the seminary.

Doctor Riedel returned to the States for the last time in May of 1971, where he made it a point to visit his children, grandchildren, and great-grandchildren as well as other relatives and friends. While in Los Angeles, he suffered a stroke on December 10, 1971. The Lord called His faithful servant to his heavenly home on the day after Christmas in Los Angeles, after spending his life serving the mission fields of China, Santa Ana, and Taiwan. His son, the Rev. E. Paul Riedel, officiated at his funeral in the Orange County Cemetery Chapel, where he was buried in the Orange County Cemetery. A granddaughter sang "Now Sing We, Now Rejoice" and the congregation sang "Jesus Lives, the Victory's Won."

In December of 1945, a new vicar arrived on the scene to serve at the Mission San Juan to replace Pastor Riedel. This vicar was not only the fulfillment of Rev. John W. Theiss's dream of sharing

The new vicar, David Stirdivant, who arrived at the mission in January 1946. (Pacific Southwest District Archives)

the Word with the Mexican people but was also his grandson, David Stirdivant. David was born on November 10, 1923, in Huntington Park, California, and came from a rich heritage of Lutheran pastors — his great-grandfather, Johann Georg Theiss; his grandfather, John Theiss; and the husband of his mother's cousin, Reno Jeske, of Trinity, Whittier. In his family, it was assumed he would follow in their footsteps, and became a pastor.

At the end of the eighth grade while in junior high school in Redlands, teenage David had to select a foreign language for high school. One evening, he asked his father if he should study Spanish or Latin. His father stated, "Well, maybe it would be a good idea for you to take Latin because if you ever become a minister you'll have to study Latin." After he was confirmed at 16, his Aunt Helen took him to visit Rev. Burkhardt in Lynwood. She told Pastor Burkhardt, "This is David and he would like to become a minister but his parents are too poor to send him to a school like Concordia." Pastor Burkhardt took him into his little office and said, "Now, if you're too poor and your parents are too poor to get the money, your aunt doesn't have any money, and I sure don't, but, we have a God in heaven who is very rich and if He wants you to study and become a pastor, He will help you, but we have to pray." So he told him to pray all the time, praying every day about it. David did pray, and little by little he began to see that God was guiding him in the direction of being a pastor.

David couldn't go to Concordia in Oakland, California, to study for the ministry, as he didn't have $150 for tuition. His dad advised him to work in the orchards of Yucaipa harvesting fruit and to work in his neighbor's berry patch. All the money he saved, he placed in an old coffee can. At the end of the summer, he counted the money, which amounted to only $75 — not enough to go to Concordia. He was very discouraged, and his father told him to work the following summer to augment his funds. The next summer when he was about 17 or 18, again after he had worked hard, he stood by the side of his bed and prayed, "Well, Lord, if I'm supposed to go to Concordia, show us how it can be done." The next day after his father went to the mailbox, he came walking up the driveway with a letter in his hand from a cousin, Carl Muller of Oakland, thinking it was strange to be receiving a letter from him in August as he never sent anything but a card at Christmas. His mother excitedly tore open the letter and read:

Dear Ben and Ruth,

I suppose you'll be surprised at me writing to you at this time of the year, but there is a rumor that you have a son who might be interested in coming to Concordia, Oakland. As you know, we live only three blocks from the school and if it would be of any help to you, let David come and live at our house; we have a bedroom that's unoccupied and there is only our one son, Ernie, who would be good company for David. David could walk to the school, attend there, and be a day student. That would save expenses and what's more we wouldn't expect any pay from you people. David could mow the lawn and take care of our garden for us here and help my wife with the cleaning and things like that. I'm sure that we could make it.

His mother put down the letter and exclaimed, "Can it be!" David was thinking, "Boy, I've just been praying these recent nights about this, wondering whether this would be the year I would get to go to Concordia." It was as though the Lord was really answering a prayer that he'd been saying regularly for several years. His father opened the coffee can to see how much money he had. Fortunately, there was enough to fund not only his first bus trip to northern California (where he was so surprised seeing all the moss on the old barns and so much moisture) but also for tuition for his last year of high school at Concordia, Oakland. The Lord does answer the prayers of the faithful in His own way and in His own time! In this case, He was setting aside teenage David for the ministry in proclaiming the Word to the poor people of Mexico and Latin America.

After graduating from Concordia High School and Concordia College at Oakland and two years at the Seminary, he was sent to the border town of Calexico, California, to start a Mexican mission with his 300-word Spanish vocabulary learned at the seminary. His field supervisor was Pastor Edgar Heckenberg of St. Paul's in Holtville, who was a missionary among the Swiss and didn't understand how to do mission work among Mexican Catholics but tried to help as much as he could. He was there from mid-summer of 1945 to the end of December. The plan was that he would rent a building, start a Sunday school, and conduct services, but when he got there, he discovered that none of the people could speak English. Each day he would go out to the park and try to converse with the Mexicans, working to expand his 300 words of Spanish. Toward the end of the year, the Mission Board called him to Los Angeles to give a report on his work in Calexico. At the Mission Board meeting, it was decided to send him to Santa Ana as a replacement for Pastor Riedel.

Since Vicar Stirdivant had never previously worked in Santa Ana, the mission society made arrangements to rent the front bedroom of a house in Orange from a lady by the name of Minnie Grote. Following his stay at Minnie Grote's, he lived with Mr. and Mrs. Henry Weir of Orange. The St. John's Mission Society was very delighted because they now had a worker who would do regular preaching on Sundays and lead the Sunday school. When he got to Santa Ana in January of 1946, the group consisted of thirteen people, Doña Victoria Gandara and her five children plus Doña Teresa Martinez and her five grandchildren in the Flores family and a few other individuals. These people were already acclimated to the Sunday school and the Lutheran Church because St. John's Mission Society had been working with them for several years. These two ladies, Doña Victoria and Doña Teresa, gave their approval of the vicar and let their children attend activities at the mission. Pastor Smukal had advised the vicar, "When you start to work with the Mexican families, you have to zero in as early as you can on the grandmothers. If you can win the grandmothers over to at least go along a little bit with letting their grandchildren go to your mission, you've made a lot of headway. But if she opposes you and says, 'No, we are Catholic and I do not want any of my children under any influence that is Protestant,' well, you're pretty well licked from the start."

One day in mid-1946, when the vicar arrived at the small rented chapel building, he met Pastor Buenrostro of the Pentecostal group who told him that African Methodist Episcopal was selling them the building, proposing that the Pentecostal and Lutheran groups combine as one church to pay for the building as they were both very small. If the Lutherans didn't join them, they would have to be out of the building in three weeks. The target date came, and out went the Lutheran mission, which would not join the Pentecostal group. The next problem was where to worship. In an October 3, 1946, letter, Margaret Fitschen, a member of the mission society wrote to Pastor Jagels of Grace, Escondido, who was a member of the District Mission Board, the following:

In 1946, the small rented chapel building is sold, leaving the mission with no place to worship.

In lieu of Raymond's [Andersen] absence, I will try to give you a brief outline of the past month's activities at the mission.

Sunday, September 1, we held our last service at Johnson chapel, recently purchased by the Pentecostals. We were evicted after a one-month notice according to state law. During the following week, we searched for another suitable location in which to hold services. After consulting Pastor Duerr, Vicar Stirdivant obtained permission to use the old Trinity Lutheran Church on Sunday evenings. Dr. Johnston, the present owner, asked for an "offering of gratitude" in the amount of $5 for 1½ hours use each Sunday afternoon. The following Sunday, September 8, we held our first service there and continued holding services there for three Sundays, the last being September 22. To our regret, we had to abandon regular Sunday school and Saturday Bible school, because we could only get the church on Sunday afternoons. This reduced our activities to regular weekly visiting and instruction of two adults in their home.

During the week, Mr. Martens came down and closed the escrow deal. We then filed eviction notice application with the OPA office in Santa Ana.

We started putting out weekly bulletins on Sunday, September 15, copies of which are enclosed. (I hope you can read them and any suggestions will be appreciated). Vicar Stirdivant enrolled in Santa Ana Junior College to study intermediate Spanish four hours per week.

We continued looking for a hall which we could use not only on Sunday evenings for church services but also during the week for young people's meeting and instruction classes and on Sunday morning for Sunday school. Vicar Stirdivant asked for permission to use the Negro Baptist church at the corner of Second and Baker Streets, just a block away from our new location. Two Baptist church councils had to be consulted. Both were highly in favor of helping us, BUT a certain clause in one of their constitutions restricts use of Baptist property solely for Baptists. (Pastor Thornhill is most amiable towards us, offers to help us in any way he can and says we couldn't have picked a better location in Santa Ana for doing future Spanish work).

We still have no time for Sunday school, so Vicar Stirdivant deemed it advisable to present some special educational feature for the children in connection with the regular evening service. On Sunday, September 29, he presented a one-half hour colored slide-lecture on "The Unjust Steward," immediately after the close of the church service. Vicar Hillmer attended our services and operated the projector. Future slides will be obtained from Pastors Duerr and Busdiecker of St. Peter Lutheran Church in Santa Ana, an American Lutheran Church.

Vicar Stirdivant and Mr. J. J. Troester (our pianist) have worked on a complete Spanish liturgy with music for the congregation. We tried it out Sunday evening and were amazed to hear how well the Mexicans sang it for the first time.

Last week we received another letter from the O.P.A. requesting the following information:

Since we plan to remodel said property, have we had our plans O.K.'d by the Planning Commission and are we able to get priority, etc.?

Vicar Stirdivant took the letter to the OPA and explained to them that we did not plan any big remodeling project at this time but just a few changes to fulfill our needs at present. We're now patiently awaiting a reply as to when the six months' eviction period will start.

The collections for the past month have been as follows:

Sunday school	Sept. 1	$1.81
Church	Sept. 1	$3.76
Church	Sept. 8	$3.70
Church	Sept. 15	$4.67
Church	Sept. 22	$5.01
Church	Sept. 29	$6.06
		$25.01

The attendance has been as follows:

Date	Mexicans		Visitors
	Adults	Children	
Sept. 1	14	13	4
Sept. 8	11	5	9
Sept. 15	10	6	6
Sept. 22	12	7	9
Sept. 29	14	6	7

The people from the mission after a service in Santiago Park in Santa Ana where they worshiped following their eviction from the Pentecostal church in 1946. Vicar Stirdivant (right) and Mr. Troester, (left) a teacher from St. John's who played the piano for the mission. (Pacific Southwest District Archives)

The interior of the small chapel at 1103 West Second Street and Shelton showing the altar with the relief of the Lord's Supper built by Mr. Andersen. (Pacific Southwest District Archives)

After using the Baptist church, the mission began holding Sunday school and church services in a park by Parton Street in Santa Ana and then moved to Jack Fischer Park in Orange, located between Orange and Santa Ana with a creek running through it. Since it was getting into fall and the weather was turning cold, services were conducted at St. Peter Lutheran Church (ALC) of Santa Ana until March 16, 1947. The vicar also worked in the Orange County Hospital where about one-half of the patients were Mexicans. The average attendance for November was about 18, which included adults and children. At the Christmas Program in 1946, 33 children participated by reciting Bible verses and singing Christmas carols.

In order to place the mission and its work on firmer foundation, the Mission Board finally decided to purchase an old, two-bedroom house located on a corner lot at 1103 West Second Street and Shelton for $3,750. It was built in the late 1800s with square nails. With the help of Raymond Andersen, a carpenter, the old house was remodeled at a cost of $500. Walls were removed to make room for a small chapel, which would seat about 40 with an adjourning room for another 40 people; two other rooms were used for Sunday school purposes. The building also included a small office and a kitchen. Raymond also built the altar, inserting a relief of the Lord's Supper in the center, the pulpit, and all the pews. On the altar was a silver crucifix with one silver candlestick on each side with a velvet curtain hanging behind it. When a sign was to be placed on the roof of the building, it was decided not to use the name San Juan Mission, but instead to rename the congregation Iglesia de Nuestro Salvador, Church of Our Savior Lutheran.

On March 16, 1947, the joyous day for the mission to dedicate its own facilities had finally arrived after nine years of laboring in rented quarters shared with other religious groups. Vicar Stirdivant gave the Spanish sermon, Rev. William G. Gesch of St. John's of Orange delivered the English sermon, and Missionary George Miller of Brazil presented a lecture in Portuguese. Other pastors from the area who also came and participated in the service were Kurt Brink, William Duerr, Victor L. Behnken, Helmut Wiechmann, Erhardt Riedel, and D. Schneider, along with the church choir from the mission. Since there was such a huge crowd that day from different parts of Southern California, people had to be seated on the front porch of the Mission as 250 people filled the small chapel. What a joy-filled day that was, thanking God for giving them their own building!

The following appeared in the March 16, 1947, dedication bulletin:

Iglesia de Nuestro Salvador was started in the fall of 1938 through the mission efforts of Mrs. Alice [Fiene] Krahnke, a member of St. John's Lutheran Church in Orange. She, with the help of other ladies from St. John's Lutheran Church, formed the mission society of St. John's, which is still sponsoring this iglesia together with the Mission Board of the Southern California District.

The following pastors and vicars have served the Iglesia:

Rev. Bruno Martinelli	1938–1939
Vicar Alfred R. Saez	1941–1942
Rev. E. W. Riedel	1942–1945
Vicar D. M. Stirdivant	1946–1947

The Mission Board purchases an old two-bedroom home on West Second Street for the mission in 1947.

Lack of suitable quarters has been the greatest handicap to progressive work. In spite of this and other difficulties, progress has been slow but substantial. Hundreds of souls have received the Bread of Life within our doors and eternity alone will reveal the fruits of our labors.

We, the members of Our Savior's Lutheran Church, wish to thank especially:

The congregation and pastor of St. Peter's Lutheran Church for the use of their parish hall during the past six months as our house of worship.

The congregation and pastor of Trinity Lutheran Church for use of their temporary church building in south Santa Ana these past months for our Sunday school.

The many, many friends who have given their money, time, and special talents in helping us acquire and repair our new church property.

May the Lord reward you for your kindnesses.

Following the dedication of the new building, this article appeared in the Wednesday, March 19, 1947, edition of the newspaper:

Dedicates Spanish Lutheran Church

With members and officials of both St. John's and Immanuel Lutheran Church of Orange participating, dedication services of "Iglesia de Nuestro Salvador," Spanish Lutheran church of Santa Ana, were conducted Sunday afternoon. Seventeen Lutheran pastors from all parts of Southern California attended the services.

Vicar David M. Stirdivant of Orange delivered the sermon in Spanish on the subject, "Christ, Our Sure Foundation."

Rev. W. G. Gesch, pastor of St. John's Lutheran Church, was guest speaker, and Rev. G. Miller, missionary from Brazil gave a lecture on his work in that country.

Vicar William Luecke of St. John's Lutheran Church, sang "Bless This House," accompanied on the organ by Theo. M. Hopmann, St. John's organist; E. T. Pingel, principal of Immanuel Lutheran School, served as guest organist.

Services will be held each Sunday at 10:00 a.m., with Saturday school at 9 a.m., in Spanish.

When the church is dedicated, the name is changed to Iglesia de Nuestro Salvador.

Dedication of the small chapel with the crowd of people seated not only in the chapel but also on the porch and lawn for the service. (Pacific Southwest District Archives)

The June 3, 1947, issue of *The Lutheran Witness Supplement*, stated, "The lack of suitable quarters was a great handicap to the mission. Progress has been slow, but since the dedication of the new chapel, church attendances have averaged 35 and Sunday school attendance is about 32. Most of the members and worshipers are under 20 years of age."

During Vicar Stirdivant's year and a half ministry at the mission, Vera Saldaña and her sister, Belen Perez, recalled that the kids couldn't understand the vicar's Spanish at first. He would go into the homes and eat with the families, and, as the year progressed, his Spanish improved enough for him to communicate with their mother who couldn't speak English. After the vicar purchased an old car, he cut off the top, making it a permanent convertible. Vera remembered going with him on his trip to San Francisco in the old car, where he dropped her off in San Jose to visit relatives.

Gilbert Flores remembered that the vicar taught him how to make a crystal radio, since the Flores family didn't have a radio, and how to make wallets and belt items from leather. On summer evenings, the vicar conducted hikes in the park, as he loved to hike. He took Gilbert, Tony Gutierrez, and Joe Arzate to his parents' ranch in Yucaipa on weekends and on vacations to help pick fruit from the apple and peach trees. Vera and Belen also recalled going to his folk's home. In the winter, he took the young people on snow trips to the mountains. On one trip, Gilbert Mercado broke his leg while sliding down the mountain 15 minutes after arriving. That ended the snow trip since everyone had to turn around and return home to Santa Ana.

One day while the vicar was canvassing the area around the church inviting people to come to the new church, he discovered the Vasquez family living across the street from the church. There were many young people in the family. The mother told him she was a Christian and that she was a member of the Mexican Methodist Church in Santa Ana. She also said she would be happy to let her children and young people attend the Young People's Society. Through this invitation, her family did come and he met his future wife, Belen. She went to the church, played volleyball, and eventually joined the church. Through this large family, seven children joined the mission and Pastor Stirdivant found a wife. Pastor Stirdivant commented, "I recommend to all unmarried vicars that they should go canvassing." While Pastor Stirdivant was at the seminary, Belen received Confirmation instruction from Pastor Hodde of Trinity in Los Angeles. After he was ordained, Rev. Hodde performed their wedding ceremony in the little mission chapel in Santa Ana. Their union was blessed with seven children.

The old car of Vicar Stirdivant, mentioned by Gilbert, Flora, Vera, and Belen, was a 1932 or 1933 Model A Ford Cabriolet. Pastor Stirdivant recollected that it had a canvas roof on it originally. One day while he was living in Orange, he saw smoke coming from an orange grove outside of the city. When he got to where the fire was, firemen were rolling up their hoses and leaving a poor disheartened young boy standing by this scorched car. Two tires on one side had burned, and all the wires on the engine were also burned. He asked the fellow what had happened. The young man said he was trying to look into the gas tank with a kerosene lantern and the car caught fire. After the vicar purchased this shell of a Model A Ford from him for $35, he started to rebuild it, bought a V8 engine from a wreck, and had a fellow from St. John's Church who owned a garage, put the V8

Vicar Stirdivant in the old Model A Ford, known as "The Bath Tub," taking the children to Sunday school. (Pacific Southwest District Archives)

engine in it. Now, it had so much power and speed that the brakes wouldn't hold it. This old vehicle became very popular with the youth of the mission and was used for all types of outings, especially picking up children for Sunday school.

In August of 1947, Vicar Stirdivant left the mission to return to the seminary at St. Louis leaving behind his old car for the new vicar, Martin Friedrich, who arrived in July. Vera and Belen recalled that Vicar Friedrich's Spanish wasn't very good at that time, but he always encouraged them to attend Sunday school and church; Belen said, "You always wanted to go to church." Flora Chavez remembered that Vicar Friedrich was a bit shy and hilarious. Since he was living at the church at Second and Shelton, Gilbert and Leo would sneak into the building and drink some of his milk. They tried to fool him by filling the jar with water. When the vicar drank the milk, he knew he had been deceived. He also loved to play volleyball with the young people.

Vicar Martin W. Friedrich was born on June 29, 1925, in Audubon, Iowa, and attended Concordia, St. Paul, Minnesota, graduating in 1945. When he came to the mission, he continued where Vicar Stirdivant left off, taking the youth to the beach in the old car during the summer and using the old car to pick up the children for Sunday school. Following his vicarage in August of 1948, he returned to Concordia Seminary in St. Louis and graduated in 1949. He received a call to serve as the Spanish missionary at Immanuel, Mercedes, Texas, where he was installed and ordained. The call included Our Redeemer, Harlingen, Texas, and he served both of these congregations until 1962. In 1949, he married Ruth Mary Kramer. They had five children. He accepted a call to San Pedro Lutheran Church in Houston, Texas, and served until 1977. He accepted a call to Salem Lutheran, Gretna, Louisiana in 1977, where he continues to serve.

February 17, 1948, Mission Board minutes record a communication was received from the mission in Santa Ana signed by 36 members requesting that Candidate Stirdivant be called to serve them as their pastor. The department recommended that this request be granted and the recommendation was adopted. By May 18, the Mission Board had received word from the seminary that Candidate Stirdivant had been assigned to serve the mission in Santa Ana. At the June 15 meeting, the Mission Board was informed that Vicar Stirdivant had accepted the call to serve in Santa Ana and his installation would be in the first part of August.

Vicar Martin Friedrich arrives in July of 1947 to take over the mission for one-year.

In a newspaper article the first of March 1948, appeared the following:

Sunday School to Present Program Tomorrow

Under the direction of their teachers, Sunday school children of the Church of Our Savior, Lutheran Spanish Mission in Santa Ana, will give a post-Easter program at Trinity Lutheran Church, 902 South Broadway, Santa Ana.

The program will consist of songs and recitations.

Martin Friedrich is pastor of the church. Teachers in the church school are Mary Szegethy, Dora Kogler, Thelma Prellwitz, and Raymond Andersen, all of Orange, and Alice Krahnke of Tustin.

Easter, 1948, at Trinity, Santa Ana. Front row: ____, ____, ____, ____, ____, Tila Gandara, ____, ____, Frankie Bennette, Ophelia Aceves, Marina Aceves, Aurora Aceves; Second row: Lupe Flores, Belen Gandara, Esther Arzate, Valentina Acuña, Flora Flores, Ophelia Flores, Vera Gandara, Bernie Aceves; Back row: Alice (Fiene) Krahnke, Vicar Martin Friedrich, Leo Callaros, Raymond Andersen, Gilbert Mercado, Mary Szigethy. (Pacific Southwest District Archives)

In July, Candidate Stirdivant was honored in his home congregation in Redlands where his parents were charter members. Mr. Henry Benit, chairman of the congregation, congratulated him upon his graduation from Concordia Theological Seminary, bade him Godspeed upon his entry into the Lutheran ministry, and also presented him with a purse from the members of the congregation. On behalf of the congregation, Mr. Benit congratulated Mr. Stirdivant and said prayers of the home congregation would go with him as he entered on his life work. He also made a plea for other young men and women of the church to follow Stirdivant's example and enter full-time service in the church. In return, the youthful minister addressed the congregation on "Mission Work Amongst Spanish-speaking People." Previously, he had demonstrated his leadership skills as the first president of Redlands' Junior High School.

In August of 1948, after ten years of struggling and waiting, the mission was to have a permanent pastor. The following newspaper article appeared in August announcing this long-awaited event:

New Pastor to Be Installed

Rev. David M. Stirdivant of Yucaipa will be installed as the new pastor of Our Savior Lutheran Church, 1103 W. Second St., August 8 at 3 p.m. in ceremonies at the church.

Rev. Stirdivant was graduated this June from Concordia Lutheran Seminary in St. Louis, Mo. He also studied at Concordia College in Oakland and served as student pastor of Our Savior Church from January 1946 to August 1947.

Ordination and Installation Service of Rev. David Stirdivant on August 8, 1948. Front: Pastors ____, Vicar Martin Friedrich, David Stirdivant, E. Riedel, William C. Gesch, D. Schnieder. Back: Kurt Brink, William Duerr, Victor Behnken, H. H. Wiechmann. (Pacific Southwest District Archives)

Choir at Pastor Stirdivant's Installation Service, August 8, 1948. Front: Bernie Aceves, Ophelia Flores, Leo Callaros, Flora Flores, Gilbert Flores, Joe Gandara, Belen Gandara. Back: Vera Gandara, Rosie Flores, Lupe Flores. (Pacific Southwest District Archives)

The installation ceremony will include a sermon in the English language by Rev. William Gesch of St. John's Lutheran Church of Orange and a sermon by Martin Friedrich, student pastor of Our Savior Church.

The choir will sing "The Lord's Prayer" and the Benediction in Spanish. Special music during the offertory and processional will be presented by Miss Thelma Prellwitz, organist; Mrs. Alice Krahnke, pianist; and Raymond Andersen, accordionist.

More than 200 members and friends filled the small chapel and porch to witness the impressive Spanish-English services on August 8, as Rev. David Stirdivant was ordained and installed as the first resident pastor of Iglesia de Nuestro Salvador in Santa Ana where he had previously served his one and a half year vicarage.

The church choir of 12 members led the procession into the chapel, singing "Santo, Santo, Santo." Vicar Martin Friedrich, who served the congregation for the past year, was liturgist. The entire service was conducted in both English and Spanish so that the large assembly could participate fully. Rev. W. C. Gesch, visitor from Circuit Six, gave the English address, and Vicar Friedrich gave his last sermon at the mission in Spanish. Rev. E. Riedel, who served the mission from 1942 through 1945, read the charge of ordination and installed Candidate Stirdivant as pastor of the congregation.

In a 1949 mission report, Pastor Stirdivant stated that the congregation numbered 71 souls with 21 communicants. Since there were only three men who could be voters, the parish was not yet organized. Because of the nature of the work, much emphasis was placed on winning children and young people. The Sunday school enrollment was 59 and Mr. Henry Steinbrink of Anaheim had loaned a Sunday school bus to the congregation. In 1946, a lot and house to serve as the church were purchased for $3,750 and had a debt of $415.14 on the property at that time with a parsonage rented for the pastor.

The organizations within the mission were a Young People's Society, a boy's club, a sewing class, and a prayer circle. Hindrances to the work of the mission were that not a single member had a Lutheran, or even a Protestant, background, and Catholic relatives were constantly using their influence against the mission. Most of the members lived in abject poverty and could scarcely read English or Spanish. "Much credit should be given to the few faithful members of St. John's Mission Society, and especially to Raymond Andersen of Immanuel, Orange, who stepped in and held the mission together during the interims between each worker." The subsidy during the first six months of that year was $225 per month. Subsidy was requested for the following six months at $250.

When Pastor Stirdivant returned from the seminary, the ladies of the mission society didn't think it was proper for the pastor to be driving an old car with no roof, so they bought him a used Dodge. Gilbert Flores recalled that after Pastor Stirdivant was installed, the attendance was so large that the little church couldn't hold all the worshipers. Flora Chavez said that pastor performed her wedding ceremony in the little mission chapel and baptized all her children. When Gilbert went into the Army in 1952, he was stationed in San Antonio and stayed there for 44 years, never to return to the little mission.

In the summer of 1949, Pastor Stirdivant was invited to attend the Latin-American Conference for missionaries held in Texas, with the District Mission Board paying the expense of $75 and any other additional bill. By December, it was reported to the Mission Board that Pastor Stirdivant favored the idea of dividing the work, combining the Santa Ana and the Los Angeles field. He would like to make a survey of the Los Angeles field to ascertain where the most suitable area would be to conduct services.

Iglesia de Nuestro Salvador's tenth anniversary, October 31, 1948. Front: ____, ____, ____, ____, ____, ____, Tila Gandara, Bernie Aceves; Middle: Teresa Martinez, ____, Joe Gandara, Leo Callaros, Gilbert Flores, Clara Mawson; Back: Ophelia Flores, Bertha Bennette, Vera Gandara, Joe Arzta, ____, Flora Flores, Lupe Flores, Rosie Flores, Mr. Lugo, Raymond Andersen. (Pacific Southwest District Archives)

In the late spring of 1950, Rev. Stirdivant launched a publicity campaign to let the Spanish-speaking population of Santa Ana know about the Lutheran mission. Every Friday morning, before dawn, Pastor Stirdivant and the boys of the congregation distributed a thousand tracts in Spanish and English weekly in the Spanish districts of the community. By the end of this campaign blitz, planned for three months, he hoped that every Spanish person in Santa Ana would have heard of the Lutheran mission. He also reported to the Mission Board that the building was adequate, but that it could be made more presentable in appearance. The dilapidated house, used for a church, was anything but a drawing card to the middle-class Mexicans the Mission Board wished to win.

Throughout the years, the favorite youth activities at the mission were beach trips to Corona Del Mar in the summer and Halloween parties and volleyball tournaments at the church. The Young People's Society, or YPS as the youth group was called, often went to Yucaipa and camped. Gilbert Flores recalled going on hikes with pastor where he would practice his sermon with Gilbert giving him Spanish words he didn't know.

One day Mrs. Magnusson, a mission-minded member of the mission society, was riding on a bus going to Garden Grove when a man boarded the bus and sat beside her. As she was riding along, she observed that he was a Mexican. She immediately thought of the mission in Santa Ana and asked him if he went to church, and he stated that he had neglected all of that. Next she asked if he had children; he replied he had four children. She questioned him again, asking if they went to Sunday school; again, he answered that they didn't go to any church. She then proceeded to say, "Well, you know you really ought to go to church, don't you think? Don't you owe that much to God?" By this time, it was time for her to disembark from the bus, ending her conversation with the man.

During the week after the brief bus encounter, Mrs. Magnusson told pastor the whole story even giving him the man's name, Amos Lopez, and told him that he should go out to visit him. One evening as he called on the Lopez family, Amos remembered the lady on the bus and the discussion of the mission. He gave permission for pastor to pick up his four children, two girls and two boys, for Sunday school. A couple of Sundays later, the Lopez children asked if they could invite the three Murrillo girls who lived across the street. The next Sunday pastor picked up three Murrillo daughters

along with the four Lopez children. He discovered that the Murrillos had two more sons. It turned out that pastor gave those people instruction and baptized the three youngest children who had never been baptized. Then they brought Phil Murillo's mother, whose name was Senovia Godoy, who had an alcoholic husband. Pastor talked him into having Bible class at his house. Senovia then told him she had another daughter with four children who lived nearby. She ended up taking them to Sunday school in her old 1936 Chevy. Through Mrs. Magnusson's chance encounter with Amos Lopez and because of her missionary zeal for Christ, over 30 people came to the Mission.

One day before Christmas, Amos Lopez came to church and told pastor that he wanted to be Santa Claus at the Christmas program so he could invite all his *compadres* and pass out the presents. He had a *compadre*, Jess Guerrero, living way out on the west side of Santa Ana with his wife, Micaela or Miki, and three children who also started coming to church and took instructions for joining the church in 1952, all through the results of Mrs. Magnusson's contact. About two or three months later, Jess Guerrero bought an old Plymouth from pastor. One night in 1953 while Jess was crossing the Rio Hondo River on the First Street Bridge, the car suddenly stopped due to a dead battery, leaving Jess stranded on a dark two-lane bridge. When he got out of the automobile to try to push it to the other side of the bridge, another car came speeding along in the darkness, hit the back of the car and crushed Jess to death. He had often told pastor that he wished that all his friends could hear this Lutheran Gospel. On the night of Jess's funeral in the Vega Funeral Home on Seventeenth Street, his dream came true through his death as 300 people crowded into the small funeral home chapel, which included all his family and friends who had heard of his sudden and tragic death. All his friends finally had the opportunity to hear the Lutheran Gospel proclaimed in Spanish with Pastor Stirdivant preaching the Lord's Word of hope and salvation to all in attendance. To add to this misfortune, the night that Jess was killed, Mrs. Miki Guerrero had buried her father that same day.

Another sad incident occurred some time later on a winter morning; Amos Lopez was home alone. His children had gone to school and his wife was at work. Being despondent over the loss of his job and his inability to find a new one, he went in the bedroom, lay on his bed, took a revolver, and shot

Through Mrs. Magnusson's chance encounter with Amos Lopez on the bus, 30 people are brought to the mission.

himself in the head. He committed suicide after making it possible for so many others to be introduced to God's healing love at the mission. In the short life of the mission, there were many joys and many tragedies, but the Word was always preached proclaiming the forgiving love of Christ and bringing hope to the faithful.

In the summer of 1950, the annual Vacation Bible School was conducted with 80 Mexican children receiving instruction in the Word of God. Assisting in the project were teachers from St. John's, Orange, and Trinity, Santa Ana: Miss Jean Leichtfuss, Miss Ruth Schnackenberg, Miss Billine Fitschen, Miss Bonnie Griffin, Miss Ruth Vasquez, Miss Anna Kahlert, and Mr. Wilbur Barnett. Pastor Stirdivant found that the Vacation Bible School program was the best means available for gaining entrance into Mexican homes to discuss the Word of Life. That fall Miss Bertha Bennett and Bernard Aceves were confirmed at the mission.

In his 1951 mission report to the District Convention, Pastor Stirdivant wrote that the congregation numbered 51 souls with 16 communicants and was not yet organized. Sunday school had an enrollment of 46 children. The old converted house served as a place of worship with the property valued at $3,750 and was debt free. A four-room parsonage was rented for the pastor and his family at $45 per month. Monthly subsidy was $290. "Progress in this work has been extremely slow in spite of the great amount of money and effort expended. In working with the Mexicans, we meet the nominal Catholic, who for centuries has left the work of the church up to the clergy and who considers himself to be churched but in most cases is not.... Severely felt is the lack of a Lutheran nucleus to stabilize the group. Most discouraging of all is the comparatively large number of backsliders even among those who have been well instructed. An intensive canvass and house-to-house solicitation is under way at present."

As the decade of the 1950s unfolded, no one would have dreamed of the demise of the little mission, Iglesia de Nuestro Salvador, especially since it was growing. This death was brought about when the mission director, Pastor Webbeking, requested Pastor Stirdivant to divide his time between Santa Ana and Los Angeles, a distance of some 30 or more miles before the Santa Ana Freeway was built. He was requested to do a very thorough survey of East Los Angeles showing maps of the population, colonies, districts, neighborhoods, and interests, and lifestyles of the people living

there. After the survey was completed, he was instructed by the mission board to move to East Los Angeles. Pastor Webbeking said, "The 5,000 or so Hispanic people living here in the Santa Ana area is only a drop in the bucket compared to what there is in Los Angeles. Why are we working here in Santa Ana when we've got hundreds of thousands of Mexicans in Los Angeles?" Pastor Stirdivant replied, "A bird in hand is worth two in the bush," alluding to the fact that there was a well-established mission in Santa Ana with absolutely no mission or any building for a mission to begin work in Los Angeles. There was only a huge mission field.

By March of 1952, Pastor Stirdivant was living in East Los Angeles and was conducting a thorough survey of the field as well as working in

Vacation Bible School held in the summer of 1950. (Pacific Southwest District Archives)

the Santa Ana field. He stated later in life, "That first year of living in Los Angeles was the saddest, hardest year of my life. All year long I walked around the Los Angeles streets hunting for people who would be interested in coming to a Lutheran church. And they would say to me, 'Well, where is your church?' I would say, 'I don't have one yet but I live over here on Rosalind Avenue and we're going to build one someday, probably, if you will start coming.' They said, 'Well, when you get a church built, you let us know. We'll come and see.'" During this time, he started English services at Iglesia de Nuestro Salvador in Santa Ana along with a Spanish service.

The following 1953 letter from Pastor Stirdivant best described his and his family's life serving the two missions of Santa Ana and East Los Angeles:

> 1119 Rosalind Avenue
> Los Angeles 23, Calif.
> December 7, 1953
>
> Mission Board
> Southern California District
> Lutheran Church — Missouri Synod
>
> Dear Brethren:
>
> We have a problem and I am writing this to you at the suggestion of Rev. Webbeking. As you know, I have been living in Los Angeles since last year. However, two or three days of each week (including Sundays) I spend in Santa Ana in order to serve the people there. I take my wife and family with me because Mrs. is a real help to me in the work. We wanted to save the expense of renting a house or apartment so we put a bunk bed and some sleeping bags in one of the back rooms of the church and thus managed to spend a night or two each week in Santa Ana.
>
> This worked out fairly well for a while. We used the kitchen facilities for breakfast and lunch; went to restaurants for other meals. But the whole arrangement became complicated when last July the back porch and kitchen burned. Church supplies and equipment were piled into the bedroom where we had been staying. Since then, we've been sleeping on the floor in another room.
>
> We have thought of various solutions to this problem. One would be to purchase a house trailer and park it behind the church, but we discovered on further investigation that Building Department of Santa Ana would not permit us to do this. Another solution would be to rent an apartment or a small house. Could money be made available for this? We have hesitated for a long time to ask for any additional financial help, since this work is costly enough, but on the other hand, we see that the present arrangement is too inconvenient for satisfactory work. Your advice on this would be appreciated.
>
> I have another question and Rev. Webbeking has recommended that I bring it to you. Could some adjustment be made with regard to my monthly car allowance? For the past seven months, I've been averaging 2,174 miles per month (this, naturally, does not include the 2,500 mile trip to Portland for the LWML convention in July). I believe that at least two-thirds of this mileage is in the service of the church, i.e., about 1,400 miles per month. The thirty-dollar allowance, which I receive, doesn't even pay for the gasoline consumed, so here again I would appreciate your consideration.
>
> Most sincerely,
> David Stirdivant

The Mission Board did grant pastor's request and rented a small apartment for him and his family to use while in Santa Ana. The fire he mentioned in the letter was caused when newspaper and old clothing stored in the back porch of the church ignited by spontaneous combustion. It was also in 1953, the ladies of the mission organized an LWML and received a charter.

In the April 13, 1954 edition of *The Lutheran Witness Supplement*, Pastor Stirdivant, made the following remark about the work of the mission society: "These women did not have a Lutheran nucleus among the Mexicans with which to begin. Had it not been for the constant God-given interest of the mission society, this work would have been terminated many a time." Later in that same year at the October 19 Mission Board meeting, it was recommended that the Church Extension Department make the necessary study to determine the proper solution to the problem of providing adequate facilities for the Santa Ana mission as the present house-chapel was not conducive to gaining prospective members. In order to help develop better facilities, the District LWML had pledged a grant of $5,000 to apply toward the new chapel project.

Growth was apparent at the mission, as it had grown at the end of 1950 to 16 communicants, 51 baptized members, an average church attendance of 32, and an average Sunday school attendance of 28. By 1954, the communicant membership was 23 with a baptized membership of 65. Church attendance was averaging 40, and Sunday school attendance was averaging 25 with an enrollment of 28. That year two juniors were confirmed, along with one adult, with another adult gained by profession of faith. Offerings for 1954 were $415 for Home Purposes and $389 for District and Synod. The mission received $202 in monthly subsidy. The District supported the Mission with a total of $33,430 in its sixteen years of existence.

By June of 1955, the Mission Board recommended that the Orange County zone of the LWML and the pastors of Orange County meet to discuss plans for building a modest chapel with available funds. With this interest, it was hoped that the little mission would go forward with a building program and continue to grow, reaching the Mexican community of Santa Ana.

In the fall of 1955, the District Mission Board position on the Santa Ana mission had shifted as is reflected in the November 9 letter of Rev. A. G. Webbeking, the District's mission and stewardship counselor, to Dr. H. A. Mayer, Synod secretary of missions. He wrote the following:

>...If you will check our records, you will find that we indicated a decrease in our subsidy request for this field [Santa Ana] for 1956 as compared to the current year. The increase for our Spanish work was requested for the Los Angeles field. In view of recent agitation in the Santa Ana area for improvement and possibly even a replacement of the present place of worship with a new building, our Mission Board has again devoted itself to conscientious study of the advisability of continuing and, as to say, throw "good money" after bad.
>
>In the course of the discussion of this problem, the Mission Board has recently resolved to make a restudy of our entire Mexican mission both in Santa Ana, in Los Angeles, and in other sections of our District. Preliminary work again seems to indicate very definitely not only the advisability but also the urgency of discontinuing the work in Santa Ana. The reasons for this are: (1) the small potential. In the Santa Ana field, there are only about 4,000 Mexicans in the city of Santa Ana — two large Catholic churches, one Methodist, one Baptist, and several others and only about 8,000 Mexicans in the entire county of Orange. (2) Our man, Rev. David Stirdivant, who during the past years has divided his time between Santa Ana and Los Angeles, will have to devote all his energies to the vast Los Angeles field where there are approximately 100,000 Mexicans in the immediate area where our new facilities are now being constructed through a grant from the National Lutheran Women's Missionary League (3) To continue in Santa Ana would mean a continuation of approximately $200 per month subsidy and possibly even $400, if a full-time worker is to be placed in charge plus the additional cost of renovating the present place of worship or replacing it with a new building at a cost of approximately $25,000. These are only a few of the important facts, which play into this situation.
>
>...I am very fearful, however, that your communication is going to make it more difficult for our Board to cope with this situation in view of considerable opposition that is being set up on the part of a very small group of the original workers in the Santa Ana field. A representation of our Board had a meeting with the entire LWML Orange Zone several weeks ago when this matter was completely aired. The majority of the women were very sympathetic with the thinking of our Mission Board, yet there are a few who are determined not to give up and they are resorting to many different means for the purpose of strengthening their cause.

By the end of the year on December 28, 1955, members of the LWML wrote the following letter to the Mission Board of the Southern California District expressing their concern about the future of the Santa Ana mission:

The Orange Zone LWML tries to save Iglesia de Nuestro Salvador from closing, but the Mission Board closes it in 1956.

The Zone LWML Executive Board met recently to plan the zone LWML activities. An important topic of discussion was the mission of Our Savior's in Santa Ana.

A prayerful discussion of this topic took place; in the light of the report given by the Mission Board at the Fall Rally (Trinity, Santa Ana), a resolution was passed at the rally to the effect that a committee from the LWML is to meet with the Mission Board to discuss the future of Our Savior's.

All of the women present are vitally interested in the future of Our Savior's. Discussion included the value of a soul, "what might have been" had Our Savior's had an attractive chapel and a full-time pastor for the last five years. We support foreign missions in many countries of the world, and yet the need for our Orange County FOREIGN MISSION in Santa Ana is not realized. We have a foreign mission in our backyard.

The Zone Executive Board then passed the following resolution: "that we request the Mission Board to give prayerful, careful, and thorough consideration to the future of Our Savior's, Santa Ana." The thought was expressed that if $5,000 is not sufficient amount to build the proper chapel, then making Our Savior's the district project for the next two years would give them $10,000 or more for their chapel.

There are various ways to help Our Savior's, rather than closing the doors. Greater amounts of money have been spent elsewhere with lesser results.

We plead with you to again consider the matter prayerfully so that the kingdom of God will be strengthened.

Yours in Christ,
Velma Schmidt,
Zone Secretary

Attached:

These members of the Zone Lutheran Women's Missionary League executive board are vitally interested in Our Savior's, Santa Ana. All of the undersigned have agreed upon the contents of the accompanying letter.

Mrs. William R. Bayer, Trinity, Santa Ana

Mrs. Leona Rodicak, Immanuel, Orange
Mrs. L. V. Tornow, Christ, Costa Mesa
Mrs. E. Mueller, St. John's, Orange
Mrs. David Stirdivant, Our Savior's, Santa Ana
Mrs. E. Oldenburg, Zion, Anaheim
Mrs. W. Kniggs, Zion, Anaheim
Mrs. Wm. Gehring, St. John's, Orange
Irene Schroeder, St. John's, Orange
Alma Trinken, St. Paul's, Orange
Olive I. Lemke, St. Paul's, Orange
Velma Schmidt, St. John's, Orange

In the January 17, 1956 Mission Board meeting the fate of the mission was sealed with the following resolution, "Since the work in this mission over the many years has not proven sufficiently fruitful that the mission be discontinued, that the present members apply to Trinity of Santa Ana for membership, and that Trinity be encouraged to concern itself with the spiritual welfare of this group." So on Easter Sunday, April 1, 1956, the final worship service was conducted at Iglesia de Nuestro Salvador. What a sad day for the mission even though it was on the great festival of the Resurrection! The painful decision to discontinue this mission and sell its property had been made by the District Mission Board. The little old, dilapidated house where the mission worshiped was sold by the end of the year. At the 1957 District Convention, the following was reported, "In the interest of good stewardship, your board saw fit to terminate the Mexican mission in Santa Ana (requesting established parishes to serve the souls of such who were connected with this mission) in order to use the service of the missionary in the larger field of Mexican missions in Los Angeles."

What was the reaction to the closing of this 16-year venture of taking the Gospel to the Mexican community in Santa Ana? Flora Chavez remembered that the members all felt terrible about the closing. Vera Saldaña recalled feeling devastated and that the Gandara, Lopez, Murrillo, Flores, and Guerrero families all went to Trinity, Santa Ana, even though there were no Spanish services. Mrs. Senovia Murrillo, who didn't speak any English, would go to Trinity each Sunday with her Spanish hymnbook, sit next to Vera who would find the hymns in the Spanish hymnbook, and sing the hymns in Spanish while the congregation sang in English. Vera's mother, Victoria Gandara, moved to East Los Angeles so that she could attend Pastor Stirdivant's church, La Santa Cruz, becoming an active member in that congregation. The other members were lost to the Lutheran church and attended Spanish services at the Baptist and Methodist churches with one young fellow becoming a Methodist minister.

What impact did the mission have on its members? Belen Perez realized later in life that "I needed Christ in my life to carry me through many trials. The seed was planted in my heart, since childhood. What a blessing! The memory verse that inspired me: He never leaves us or forsakes us. He gives us whatever we can handle. He is always with us. Thank God for the mission and all the people that blessed us." Vera Saldaña expressed it this way, "I am very grateful for all the servants in the mission work. If it had not been for the mission, I would not know Christ. I learned to tell others." Flora Chavez expressed her feelings saying, "The mission changed my life; I learned about Jesus and it made me feel better about my life."

In 1999, there was a Mission Reunion Dinner in Santa Ana at Trinity's parish hall with about 35–40 people in attendance. Pastor Stirdivant, their beloved pastor, showed slides and pictures

Iglesia de Nuestro Salvador's Reunion Dinner in 1999 at Trinity's Parish Hall, Santa Ana, with 35–40 people in attendance. Pictured are Pastor Dave Stirdivant (middle) and sisters, Phyllis (Murrillo) Morales (left) and Pat (Murrillo) Grey (right).

Iglesia de Nuestro Salvador is closed, with the members invited to become members of Trinity, Santa Ana, where there are no Spanish services.

of the Mission with all present reliving their precious and joy-filled years at Iglesia de Nuestro Salvador. Even at this writing, there is still sorrow in the hearts of the pastor and his flock at the closing of this little mission in Santa Ana.

I am Jesus' little lamb,
Ever glad at heart I am;
For my Shepherd gently guides me,
Knows my needs, and well provides me
Loves me ev'ry day the same,
Even calls me by my name.

Let Us Rise Up and Build

1950 – 2003

> And they said, "Let us rise up and build." So they strengthened their hands for this good work.
>
> — NEHEMIAH 3:18

After a period of four years while the Los Angeles mission field lay fallow, a third attempt was made to re-establish a Lutheran mission among the Mexican people of East Los Angeles. This mission had some of the same ingredients of the Santa Ana Mission — Pastor Stirdivant and the ladies of the Lutheran Women's Missionary League working hand-in-hand.

After doing a survey of the Los Angeles area, Pastor Stirdivant reported the results of that survey to the Mission Board at its February 21, 1950, meeting. With the aid of maps, he showed the board the concentration of the Mexican population in Los Angeles County. He stated that the greatest concentration was in the Boyle Heights area extending east of the Los Angeles River and going into East Los Angeles. If work was to be done, this seemed to be the logical area. It was estimated that over 200,000 Mexicans and other Hispanic people were living in this area. At that time, Pastor Stirdivant was encouraged to make contact in the Los Angeles area. By April, the Mission Board encouraged him to start services as soon as possible, as he was of the opinion that services should be begun at Los Angeles as soon as a suitable place of worship could be found. By surveying the churches in greater Los Angeles, Pastor tried to locate Lutherans in the area for the nucleus of a Lutheran church. He found only two families living in that vicinity who were members of Trinity, Los Angeles, and didn't want to leave Trinity, as they had been long-time members there.

In October 1950, the Mission Board asked Pastor Stirdivant to begin work in the Los Angeles area as soon as possible using the building for the Japanese mission work as a place of worship. At the November meeting, the board decided to lease the building where the Japanese mission was being attempted for another six months in order for the work among the Hispanic community to be commenced. By December, it was reported that a Spanish mission was being conducted next door to the building that was planned for Spanish work, changing the plan to extend the lease on the building. Apparently no building was rented for the new mission. As was stated in the previous chapter, by March 1, 1952, Pastor Stirdivant rented a house and moved to East Los Angeles and continued to work in the Santa Ana field. During May and June, he conducted a thorough survey and a spot canvass of the Little Mexico area and reported the findings to the mission and stewardship counselor. He discovered that there were 18 Roman Catholic churches in the area, but not a single Lutheran church. The strength of the Catholic Church was demonstrated in 13 Catholic parochial schools, averaging 10 classrooms per school. In this report was included the District's request for funds from the "Conquest for Christ," a Synodical campaign to raise funds for Synod's missions and educational institutions.

On Saturday afternoons, Pastor Stirdivant would do street preaching in East Los Angeles, standing on First and Rowen at the end of the streetcar line where the taxicabs loaded the people and took them away. People would look at him and say, "Man, look at this guy, another street preacher." He would go then to Brooklyn Avenue and First Street, preaching in front of a barbershop. The men inside the barbershop would listen to him preaching on the sidewalk while they were getting their haircuts. He recalled, "The first year of living in Los Angeles was the saddest, hardest year of my life. All year long I walked around the Los Angeles streets hunting for people who would be interested in coming to a Lutheran church. And they would say to me, 'Well, where is your church?' I would say, 'I don't have one yet, but I live over here on Rosalind Avenue and we're going to build one someday, probably, if you will start coming.' They said, 'Well, when you get a church built, you let us know. We'll come and see.'"

Finally after a year of canvassing and talking to people, Pastor Stirdivant got one person to take instruction. That person would go to Pastor Stirdivant's home and receive instructions in the Lutheran catechism at his kitchen table. He stated in an interview, "Boy, this isn't working out too well. Here we have 250,000 Latin American people living on the east side of Los Angeles and I live among them one year and I've gotten one person who comes for instruction. I am a total failure." Due to the lack of results from all his hard and frustrating work, he really felt terrible. As he was thinking and praying daily about the

situation, he received a phone call one day from a wonderful lady named Mrs. Arthur Holmberg, who was president of the Lutheran Women's Missionary League. She said "Pastor Stirdivant, we understand from the Mission Board that you are living in East Los Angeles and that you have been surveying that field and would like to start a mission there. Could we be of any help? We're the Lutheran Women's Missionary League."

With an expressed interest of the Southern California LWML in the work in East Los Angeles, Pastor Stirdivant made a report on the mission needs and opportunities of Little Mexico to the LWML Executive Board on February 9, 1953. They unanimously decided to propose the Mexican mission work of Los Angeles to the National LWML as a project worthy of their financial assistance, asking for a grant of $75,000. The next problem was getting publicity and information to all the zones of the LWML in the United States. To meet this need, the Southern California LWML wrote a descriptive brochure telling of the East Los Angeles mission possibilities with 10,000 copies printed, distributing them across the country. A flip chart was designed with ten sets made and circulated throughout the Southern California District; the pastor presented 29 illustrated lec-

> The Southern California District LWML helps start Mission Work in East Los Angeles in 1953 through canvasing the area.

The East Los Angeles neighborhood one block from where La Santa Cruz Church was built. (Pacific Southwest District Archives)

tures on Little Mexico in every zone of the District. An article was written for *The Lutheran Witness Supplement* with a thousand reprints of the article made and distributed at the National Convention. On Saturday, June 12, a tour of Little Mexico was conducted for all the ladies and other interested persons. Several announcements were made over the "Southern California Lutheran Hour."

Pastor recalled how much the women helped in the Santa Ana Mission. Maybe they could do something in Los Angeles. He asked them to do canvassing with him, which they organized, getting publicity ready in order to go from house to house. Did they get organized! Through their

organizational skills, the women went to 6,000 homes, canvassing the hills of East Los Angeles. That summer four two-week Vacation Bible Schools were held in four different neighborhoods of Little Mexico. The first school was held in a United Brethren Church of Boyle Heights. The next two were held at Emanuel Lutheran in Lincoln Heights. The last was conducted at St. Matthew's in East Los Angeles. To locate families in the hundreds of homes canvassed, 58 canvassers came from 15 different congregations and worked on Saturday mornings and Sunday afternoons. The teaching staff for the 4 schools consisted of 30 persons from 12 congregations who volunteered their time and services, thanks to the LWML and many pastors. In all, 205 children had attended, representing 100 families.

Pastor Stirdivant said he felt like a circuit rider as he raced from Santa Ana, after conducting an early Saturday morning Bible school to conduct another morning Bible school in Boyle Heights, and then finally going to St. Matthew's in East Los Angeles and having a Saturday afternoon school for children. The women would prepare the children for Christmas programs and for Easter programs where their parents would be invited to come, making the first contacts for the church. With the success of the Vacation Bible Schools and Saturday schools, Mrs. Holmberg, and other influential women in the LWML, including Mrs. Emma Theiss, the wife of Pastor George Theiss in Pasadena, saw that in order for the mission to grow, it

District LWML ladies receiving instructions and materials for canvassing of the Boyle Heights area. Back row third from the left is Mrs. George E. Thiess, the president of the District LWML, and Mrs. Belen Stirdivant on the right. Middle right is Miss Lois Wenschlag, a teacher from Zion Lutheran School in Maywood.

The children and teachers at Emanuel Lutheran in Lincoln Heights in one of the Vacation Bible Schools held in East Los Angeles in 1953. Back center is Pastor Stirdivant and back right is Mr. Estel Sitze.

needed to procure its own property and building. A Lutheran building was urgently needed instead of renting and borrowing buildings from a variety of other churches. Through the means of the ladies and their work, a congregation was started. Pastor Stirdivant once reflected, "So, don't let it ever be said that women can't start things. They really can do a lot when they put their minds to it. I saw it at Santa Ana in the St. John's Mission Society and I saw it here at La Santa Cruz with the Lutheran Women's Missionary League. "

At the Mission Board meeting on March 17, 1953, acting upon a request of the board at its December 1952 meeting to the District LWML that the group consider giving support to the Los Angeles Spanish work even to the extent of proposing this as a mission project to the National Convention in July 1953, the Executive Board of the District LWML had resolved to give the project their whole-hearted support. To this end, it prepared necessary publicity for circulation in other districts and completed a set of resolutions which was to present the project to the coming convention in July. The resolutions were submitted to the Mission Board and approved. Upon request of the LWML, the board resolved to make up to $300 available for the financing of necessary publicity.

It was also resolved to bear the expenses involved to send Pastor Stirdivant to the convention to appear before the ladies in Portland to make a personal appeal. It was further resolved that the Mission Board through a communication by the chairman, appeal to the synodical and to the general Home Mission Board to give favorable consideration to approve the undertaking of the District LWML as a national project.

In the June 23, 1953, issue of *The Lutheran Witness Supplement*, Missionary Stirdivant stated the following in his article about "Little Mexico:"

Last year I moved to Los Angeles. Everywhere I looked, I saw Mexican people. I wondered to myself, "How many Mexican persons live here?" I went to the Mexican consulate and asked them. They didn't know. I asked the city library, the city housing authority, the planning commission, and the welfare department. All had the same answer. They didn't know. Finally I went to the statistical department of the Chamber of Commerce. They didn't know either but they said they'd like to find out. Together we sat down with adding machine and 1950 census figures before us. We worked a long time, and what we discovered amazed us!

We found that at least 250,000 Mexican-Americans live in the city of Los Angeles. Another 200,000 live in the suburbs surrounding Los Angeles. We discovered that one single area, 011, the east side of the city is the home of 93,000 Mexican persons: a veritable "LITTLE MEXICO" in the heart of Los Angeles! Actually, Los Angeles has the second largest Mexican population of any city in the world. In all Mexico, only one city has more Mexican population than we have in the Los Angeles area — that's Mexico City, the capital of Mexico.

Our Synod and the Mexicans

Sad to say, very few of these people have ever been directly invited to join the Lutheran Church. Their names are seldom found on our church membership lists. Most of them do not even know our Church exists. What's more, in the densely populated area where the 93,000 Mexican-Americans live, there is not a single church of our Synod to which we might invite them.

Someone might conclude that our Church is not interested in the souls of these people. This is not true. Our Church is very much interested in the salvation of these Mexican-Americans, but it is always the same old problem: money.

As a Synod, we've been doing Mexican mission work for twenty-seven years. With God's blessing, we have been successful too, for today we have sixteen missions among the Mexicans. Hundreds of souls have found their Savior through our Church. But experience has taught us some lessons. We have learned, for instance, that this is one mission field where, if we hope to see substantial gains, we must make an outlay of money at the start. We have learned, too, that a parochial school is the most effective method for indoctrinating and holding the Mexican youth to our Church.

Southern California's Problem

Hence our problem in Southern California has been and still is: funds for mission work. What else might we expect in an area where the population is increasing 736 persons per day and where we've been privileged to open 54 new Lutheran churches in 13 years! How we would like to reach these

The International LWML in convention at Portland votes to give the Hispanic mission in Los Angeles funds to build a chapel.

thousands of persons in "Little Mexico" at Los Angeles, erect a church and a school for them! But our church extension funds are exhausted. Twice before, our District started Mexican mission work in Los Angeles, but each time the work came to a halt, mainly because there were not sufficient funds to purchase property.

Despite this, our Church has felt a deep Christian concern for these people God has placed this foreign mission field at our doorstep, and our District feels that this is a field too great to simply pass by and ignore. A thorough mission survey has been conducted, and our missionary in charge has been asked to divide his time between Our Savior Spanish Mission in Santa Ana and the Los Angeles field.

The LWML Takes Action

Backed with the full consent and encouragement of our District Mission Board, the Southern California Lutheran Women's Missionary League has decided to aid this work by holding four Vacation Bible Schools at different locations in "Little Mexico" this summer. The women with the help of Walther Leaguers from two nearby zones are doing the canvassing. Children have always been effective keys for opening the doors to Mexican homes. Our prayer is that many families will become acquainted with our Church by means of these Bible schools this summer.

A Project Proposed

Realizing the need for having a Lutheran church in "Little Mexico" as soon as possible, the LWML of Southern California has gone one step farther. They have submitted Mexican mission work at Los Angeles as a mission project to be voted upon at the International LWML convention being held in Portland, Oregon, this month. A grant of $75,000 is being asked for, so that we may build a parochial school and chapel in "Little Mexico." Thus our work among the world's largest concentration of Mexicans will by God's grace be done thoroughly and become permanent.

With excitement and enthusiasm, 75 women from the Southern California District Lutheran Women's Missionary League, attended the fifth biennial convention of the International LWML, held in Portland, Oregon, July 28 and 29, testifying to the fact that it was a memorable convention. This was the first convention at which the District had an elected delegate from each of the 10 zones. Mrs. George Reed of Whittier handled all reservations and arrangements for the 37 women who traveled by chartered bus to Portland. Regular devotions were held on the bus, and the women learned several hymns in Spanish while traveling. A display of "Little Mexico" was prepared for the convention and a brief demonstration and prayer was made before the convention guests assembled at Concordia College, Portland. Day-by-day calendar cards were printed and offered at the International Convention. At the first evening of the convention during the social hour, the group dressed in Mexican costumes, helping to promote the proposed project of "Little Mexico" by singing several hymns in Spanish. The music director was Mrs. Arthur Kreidt of El Monte. Another traveler was Mrs. Al Gallegos, a member of Emmaus in Alhambra, who made her home in the heart of "Little Mexico."

At the convention, 48 overtures were considered with 15 concerned with grants of money. Of these 15, the National Executive Board with 5 submitted to the assembly eliminated 10. Of the five, three would be selected. When the convention voted, the Mexican mission work at Los Angeles took the top vote with over 80 percent of the delegates voting for it. The Southern California project, "Little Mexico" of Los Angeles, as proposed to the International Convention, was chosen by the 276 delegates as one of the 3 projects to receive a $60,000 grant during 1953 — 1956. As the announcement was made, hearts leaped with joy, and eyes filled with tears, knowing that with God all things are possible. The dream of having a house of worship to take Christ to the Mexican neighbors had finally become a reality. Pastor Stirdivant and his family drove to Portland to attend the convention. They were the special guests of the Southern California District on the closing evening of the convention when the Southern California District held an open house in the Marine Room in the Muthnomah Hotel. At the close of the evening, Pastor Stirdivant offered a prayer of thanksgiving for the gracious support that the International Convention had given, that work might begin in "little Mexico" in a suitable chapel.

The International Convention Delegates of the LWML in Portland, Oregon, adopted the following resolution:

SUBJECT MATTER: MEXICAN MISSIONS in Los Angeles

WHEREAS, a heavy concentration of persons of Mexican descent is found in Los Angeles County, respectively in the City of Los Angeles, and

WHEREAS, our church has recognized the mission opportunity among these people, even though progress is often slow and discouraging, by placing a missionary in this area; and

WHEREAS, our work among these people is tragically handicapped by the fact no suitable place of worship or Christian education is available; therefore be it

RESOLVED, that we make available to the Southern California District of Synod a grant of $60,000 for the construction of a church with educational facilities for people of Mexican descent living in Los Angeles, California; and be it further

RESOLVED, that we call the attention of the Southern California District Mission Board to the necessity of emphasizing constantly to those who join our mission, their responsibility as personal witness and faithful stewards of the gifts and talents with which God has endowed them.

In this action, a direct and overwhelming answer was given to Pastor Stirdivant's three years of personal prayer for guidance and wisdom as to what should be done for a church building in Little Mexico. Not only were the prayers answered but also the prayers of hundreds of others throughout the District and nation were answered. It was the strongest indication that the Lord wanted a church to be at developed in Little Mexico. Seeing the mission challenge of this second largest city of Mexican people in the world on the District's doorstep, it was often lamented that there were no funds to buy equipment for this important work. The Lord, through the National LWML, had given $60,000.

The major problem confronting the mission was two-fold: a congregation had to be gathered and established and property had to be purchased for the erection of a church building with suitable

Children singing at a Saturday school conducted at St. Matthew's Lutheran Church in East Los Angeles.

educational facilities. Plans for the immediate future were to invite all Mexican children who attended the Vacation Bible Schools to enroll in Saturday schools, which opened on October 3. Two Saturday schools were operated with two separate staffs of volunteer teachers using the standard Concordia Sunday school lessons and preparing the children for two Christmas programs. The important task at hand was the follow-up visitation of children in their homes, making contact with their parents. To insure a steady flow of new contacts and prospects, on Tuesday, October 13, and every Tuesday thereafter, a canvass was made. Each Tuesday was set aside as "Canvass for Little Mexico Day." The LWML was asked to help with this and continued to canvass until all the 93,000 people living in Little Mexico had been reached.

By January of 1954, various properties had been investigated with the most desirable one selected at 6th and Euclid, at an asking price of $20,000. As various people were consulted, their opinion was that the asking price of $20,000 was excessive. An offer of $12,500 was made to the owner who promptly refused and continued to insist on the asking price of $20,000. The Mission Board Expansion Department and a committee from the LWML agreed upon a plot of ground, measuring 150' × 170' at 2747 Whittier Boulevard and Camulos Street, in Los Angeles, that was suited to the needs of the Mexican mission. The property was purchased for $20,000 and was in escrow by May. At the November 16, 1954, Mission Board meeting, it was recommended that Mr. Bruer be asked to draw up plans for a chapel to cost $40,000 with donated labor.

The day for which all had been praying finally arrived on March 27, 1955, when the ground was broken for the new church of La Santa Cruz. The following was taken from the bulletin for that day:

SANTA CRUZ LUTHERAN CHURCH
IGLESIA DE LA SANTA CRUZ

GROUDBREAKING SERVICE

SUNDAY, MARCH 27, 1955 — 4 P.M.

2759 E. WHITTIER BLVD.
LOS ANGELES, CALIFORNIA

THE HYMN — BY CONGEGATION:
We all believe in one true God,
  Father, Son, and Holy Ghost,
Ever-present Help in need,
  Praised by all the heavenly host,
By whose mighty power alone
  All is made and wrought and done.

We all believe in Jesus Christ,
  Son of God and Mary's Son,
Who descended from His throne
  And for us salvation won;
By whose cross and death are we,
  Rescued from all misery.

We all confess the Holy Ghost,
  Who from both for-e'er proceeds;
Who upholds and comforts us
  In all trials, fears, and needs.
Blest and Holy Trinity,
  Praise forever to be Thee! Amen.

THE READING OF HOLY SCRIPTURE

THE PRAYER

THE HYMN — BY CHILDREN OF THE CONGREGATION:
  "The Church's One Foundation"

THE SERMON ADDRESS:
  The Rev. William Duerr,
  Trinity Lutheran Church, Santa Ana

THE CHORUS — LUTHERAN WOMEN'S MISSIONARY LEAGUE
  "O Christ, Our True and Only Light"

THE CEREMONY OF GROUNDBREAKING:
  Rev. David Stirdivant,
  Pastor Santa Cruz Lutheran Church.

THE PRAYERS

THE LORD'S PRAYER

THE BENEDICTION

THE CLOSING HYMN — BY CONGREGATION:

Beautiful Savior,	Querido Salvador,
King of Creation,	Rey de la creacion,
Son of God and	Hijo de Dios, y del
Son of Man	hombre
Truly I'd love Thee,	Si, yo te amo,
Truly I'd serve Thee,	Si, yo te sirvo,
Light of my soul,	Luz de mi alma,
my Joy,	
My crown. Amen.	gozo y fe. Amen.

PLEASE REMAIN QUIET A MOMENT FOR —
THE SILENT PRAYER

* * * * *

Participating in the Ceremony of Groundbreaking:

The Rev. Harold Tietjen,
Chairman of the Mission Board
Southern California District
Lutheran Church — Missouri Synod

Mrs. George E. Theiss
President of Southern California
District, Lutheran Women's
Missionary League

Mr. Reuben Carabio,
Representing the congregation of
Santa Cruz Lutheran Church.

Director of Children's Chorus:
Mrs. Betty Northwick,
Bell Gardens

Director of LWML Chorus:
Mrs. G. H. Janes,
Maywood

Organist:
Mrs. Dorothy Perkins,
Bell Gardens,

ARCHITECT — O. J. BRUER, MONTE-
BELLO

BUILDER — SANDAHL-SCATLETT,
PUENTE

* * * * *

Construction of this beautiful church and parish center is realized through the prayerful and financial efforts of the Lutheran Women's Missionary League, an international organization dedicated to carry our Lord and Savior's command, "Go ye into all the world and preach the gospel to every creature."

My God speed the erection of this church to His glory!

For Information:

Phone: ANgeles 9-7364 or
ANgeles 9-7839

Pastor David Stirdivant
1119 Rosalind Ave.
Los Angeles 23, California.

By October of 1955, Pastor Stirdivant had secured a building that was formerly used by the YMCA as a place for worship and Sunday school. In order to conduct services, he requested funds of $194.52 for chairs, which the Mission Board granted. The first formal church service was conducted on the Sunday after Easter, April 8, 1956, in a lunch room of a YMCA building near the present church site with 13 persons in attendance. Services continued at those facilities until the new church was dedicated. Growth was slow but constant. In May of 1956, the LWML of the Minnesota District provided some funds to assist in completion of the National LWML project. At the May Mission Board meeting, Mr. Schlueter, chairman of the Church Extension Department, asked for more volunteer help to complete the mission chapel, stating that if 15 men would come for two Saturdays, the work could be finished. At the next meeting in August, he reported at length that the completion of the building was costing considerably more than had

been anticipated due to the fact that the city was demanding walls surrounding the property and also because volunteer labor to finish the building did not materialize. The Board of Directors was asked to approve a further loan of $15,000 to complete building and improve grounds. In order to complete the building, a number of individuals and organizations within the District, as well as several outside, made appreciable contributions in either cash or donated labor. The magnificent new facilities included a sanctuary, two schoolrooms, a kitchen, offices, and a patio, built at a cost of $75,000.

After two years of waiting, praying, and building, the day had finally arrived to dedicate this beautiful new building. It was the answer to the work and prayers of Lutherans, not only in Southern California but also throughout the United States, for many had taken a part in the building of this house of worship. Hundreds of Lutherans from churches throughout Southern California attended the formal dedication of La Santa Cruz Lutheran Church. A chorus of more than 150 women of the Lutheran Women's Missionary League of Southern California under the direction of Mrs. Walter Lemmermann of Rialto, sang "Come, Holy Spirit" and "Bless This Temple." A highlight of dedication day was the presentation of an additional $5,000 from the Minnesota District of the Lutheran Women's Missionary League to the pastor, Rev. David M. Stirdivant, by Mrs. Walter Rosenbrock, Ontario, the Southern California District LWML president. Following the afternoon

Sign on the new church property at 2747 Whittier Boulevard and Camulos Street in Los Angeles advertising new church.

Pastor Stirdivant receives a $5,000 check from the Minnesota District of the LWML by Mrs. Walter Rosenbrock, president of the Southern California District LWML. On the left is Mrs. George Theiss and Rev. Andres A. Melendez, D. D., and on the right is Mr. Leo Leon, chairman of the congregation.

La Santa Cruz church building is dedicated on May 19, 1957.

service, ladies of La Santa Cruz Church and members of the El Rancho Zone LWML served a buffet supper of Spanish and American food to guests in the church patio. The menu included tamales, enchiladas, Mexican beans, and Spanish rice furnished by the members of La Santa Cruz. The ladies' organizations of neighboring congregations provided potato salad, sandwiches, relishes, and cakes.

The following is taken from the May 19, 1957, Dedication Booklet:

"LA SANTA CRUZ" LUTHERAN CHURCH
2747 WHITTIER BLVD.
LOS ANGELES 23, CALIFORNIA

REV. DAVID M. STIRDIVANT Pastor

FESTIVAL OF DEDICATION
May 19, 1957

"La Santa Cruz" Lutheran Church is located in the heart of Little Mexico at Los Angeles. "Little Mexico" is a name we fondly

use to designate the heavily populated area where nearly 120 thousand persons of Mexican descent make their home. Geographically, the district begins around historic Olvera Street and Old Plaza and extends eastward to beyond Belvedere and East Los Angeles. Of course, thousands of persons of other national backgrounds live in this portion of the city, but the Latin-Americans predominate.

In erecting "La Santa Cruz" (Holy Cross) Lutheran Church, we pray that two objectives will be accomplished: first, that thousands of Latin-Americans will have the opportunity to know the Lutheran Church and the Gospel which she proclaims; secondly, that residents of this community, no matter what their nationality might be, will have the privilege of worshiping in a Lutheran church. To this end, we offer our services in both the Spanish and English languages.

Some History

Los Angeles has long been a strongly Mexican community. In fact, in 1781 when California's Governor Felipe de Neve decided to found our city, he imported seven families from Mexico to establish the colony. Since that day, the Spanish-speaking portion of our populace has grown to number one-half million in Los Angeles County. Regretfully we must admit that hardly any of these people have ever been directly approached and invited to meet the Lutheran Church.

In 1952, the Southern California District Mission Board conducted a thorough survey of this mission field. In spring 1953, mission work was begun by conducting Bible schools for children. This led to our contact with the first prospective adults for instruction. Then the LWML of So. California became interested and gave their assistance. It soon became evident that if this mission was to prosper and become permanent, a building we could call our own would have to be secured.

Today this hope and prayer has become a reality, thanks to God and his work through the National Lutheran Women's Missionary League. On July 30, 1953, the League assembled in convention at Portland, Oregon voted to make "Little Mexico at Los Angeles" one of their mission projects. A grant of $60,000 was given for the purchase of property and the construction of the church facilities being dedicated today.

Divine services were first conducted in what had formerly been a YMCA building. In summer 1956, our congregation elected its first congregational officers and drew up a constitution. Growth has been slow but constant so that today 118 baptized members are numbered within our fold. The gracious hand of God has been clearly seen in the past blessings to our young congregation, and it is with humble and grateful hearts that we dedicate this building today, proclaiming now and always

To God Alone Be The Glory !

The Dedication Service
Sunday, May 19, 1957 4:00 P. M.

All having assembled at the door of the new Church, the Pastor shall offer the following prayer:

O eternal God, who dwellest in the high and holy place and with him also that is of a contrite and humble spirit, we beseech Thee, graciously look upon us, and let us enter this Thy house with Thy blessing, through Jesus Christ, Thy Son, our Lord. Amen.

Then shall the keys be handed to the Pastor by the chairman of the Mission Board, and the Pastor shall say:

Our Help is in the name of the Lord, who made heaven and earth. Whereas, by the grace of God, we are permitted this day to dedicate this house of God, I herewith open the gates of this house for the preaching of the saving Word of God in accordance with the Confession of our Church, for the administration and use of the Holy Sacraments according to the institution of our Lord Jesus Christ, and for offering to God's majesty the sacrifice of prayer and thanksgiving, in the name of the Father and the Son and the Holy Ghost. Amen.

The Pastor shall then unlock the door, which shall then be opened by the Chairman of the congregation. The Pastor shall then read Psalm 100.

The Pastor and the Dedication Speaker, followed by the Church Officers and the Congregation shall, during the organ processional, enter the Church.

HYMN BY CONGREGATION
1. From all that dwell below the skies
    Let the Creator's praise arise;
    Alleluia! Alleluia!
    Let the Redeemer's name be sung
    Thro' ev'ry land, by every tongue
    Alleluia! Alleluia!
    Alleluia! Alleluia! Alleluia!

2. Eternal are Thy mercies, Lord;
    Eternal truth attends Thy Word:
    Alleluia! Alleluia!
    Thy praise shall sound from shore to
       shore
    Till suns shall rise and set no more.
    Alleluia! Alleluia!
    Alleluia! Alleluia! Alleluia!

(The Congregation shall remain standing)
THE RITE OF DEDICATION
Pastor: O God, our Father, Creator of heaven and earth, by Whose favor we have built this house,
Congregation: To Thee we dedicate this Church.
Pastor: O Jesus Christ, the Son of the Living God, our Lord and Saviour,
Congregation: To Thee we dedicate this Church.
Pastor: O Holy Ghost, Source of life and light, our Sanctifier and Converter,
Congregation: To Thee we dedicate this Church.
Pastor: To the preaching and teaching of Thy Holy Word, the proclamation of the Law and Gospel,
Congregation: We dedicate this Church.
Pastor: To the proper administration of the Holy Sacraments of Baptism and the Lord's Supper,
Congregation: We dedicate this Church.
Pastor: As a house of prayer for all who would call upon Thy name and worship Thee in spirit and in truth,
Congregation: We dedicate this Church.
Pastor: As a place where Thou mightest manifest Thy presence unto men,
Congregation: We dedicate this Church.
Pastor: As a place where sinners may receive comfort and assurance, where men

may be turned to repentance and to faith in Thee, the only true God, and Jesus Christ, Whom Thou hast sent, where saints may be strengthened and encouraged, where Thy praise may be chanted, Thy Kingdom extended, Thy glory revealed, and Thy power manifested,

Congregation: We dedicate this La Santa Cruz Lutheran Church.

Pastor: As a place where the lambs of the flock of Christ may be fed, where little ones may increase in wisdom and favor with God and man, where the young may be taught to remember their Creator in the days of their youth, where a generation may grow up fit for citizenship on earth and in heaven,

Congregation: We dedicate this "La Santa Cruz" Lutheran Church. And we beseech Thee, O eternal God, Creator, Redeemer, and Sanctifier, accept this house, with all its furnishings and appointments, now dedicated to Thy honor and glory as Thy dwelling place. Amen.

THE GLORY PATRI

Glory be to the Father and to the Son and to the Holy Ghost; as it was in the beginning, is now, and ever shall be world without end. Amen.

(The congregation shall be seated)

THE CHOIR ANTHEMS:

"Bless this Temple" Mrs. Eva C. Magnusson Music by May H. Brahe

"Come Holy Spirit" arranged by Morten J. Luvaas; Chorus of the Lutheran Women's Missionary League, So. Calif.

THE COLLECT

Congregation: Amen.

THE LECTION: 1 Chronicles 29:10–16

Pastor: But Thou, O Lord, have mercy upon us.

Congregation: Thanks be to Thee, O Lord.

HYMN BY THE CONGREGATION

1. Christ, Thou art the sure Foundation,
   Thou the Head and Cornerstone;
   Chosen of the Lord and precious,
   Binding all the Church in one;
   Thou Thy Zion's Help forever
   And her Confidence alone.

2. To this temple, where we call Thee,
   Come, O Lord of hosts, today;
   With Thy wanted loving kindness
   Hear Thy servants as they pray
   And Thy fullest benediction
   Shed within these walls always.

3. Here vouchsafe to all Thy servants
   What they ask of Thee to gain,
   What they gain from Thee forever
   With the blessed to retain,
   And hereafter in Thy glory
   Evermore with Thee to reign.

4. Praise and honor to the Father,
   Praise and honor to the Son,
   Praise and honor to the Spirit,
   Ever Three and ever One,
   One in might and one in glory,
   While unending ages run. Amen.

THE DEDICATORY SERMON
The Reverend Andres A. Melendez, D. D.
"Striving together for the Faith of the Gospel" — Philippians 1:27b

THE DEDICATION OFFERING
THE DEDICATION PRAYER AND LORD'S PRAYER
THE CHOIR ANTHEM:
"Go and tell them, I am Jesus" Mrs. Eileen Klimes; Chorus of the So. California Lutheran Women's Missionary League

HYMN BY THE CONGREGATION (the congregation shall stand)

1. Holy God, we praise Thy name
   Lord of all, we bow before Thee.
   All on earth Thy scepter claim,
   All in heav'n above adore Thee.
   Infinite Thy vast domain,
   Everlasting is Thy reign.

2. Lo, th' apostles' holy train
   Join Thy sacred name to hallow;
   Prophets swell the glad refrain,
   And the white-robed martyrs follow,
   And from morn to set of sun
   Thro' the Church the song goes on.
   Amen.

THE BENEDICTION
Congregation: Amen.

SILENT PRAYER
THE ANNOUNCEMENTS
THE ORGAN POSTLUDE

The Dedication Speaker:
The Rev. Andres A. Melendez

Our guest speaker, Rev. Melendez, is internationally known for his work since 1941 as the official speaker on the Spanish Lutheran Hour radio broadcasts. In addition to his regular weekly program "Bringing Christ to the Nations", he serves our Church as Editor of Spanish Literature. He is native of Puerto Rico where he attended schools, including the university. In 1925, he entered Concordia Seminary, Springfield, Illinois. After his graduation in 1930, he served as missionary to the Mexicans in the Texas District until 1941. He is the author of numerous religious books, pamphlets and tracts and is an authority on the economic, social and spiritual conditions in Latin America. In 1953, he was awarded the degree of Doctor of Divinity from Concordia Seminary, Springfield. We certainly are honored in having Rev. Melendez, his lovely wife and family present with us today, and we shall always be grateful to him for his service to us on this occasion.

The organist:
Mr. Ray Linson of Eagle Rock
The LWML Chorus director:
Mrs. Walter Lemmermann of Rialto

We cordially invite all attending our afternoon Dedication Service to inspect the church and grounds and to partake of refreshments to be served in the Parish Hall across the patio immediately after the service.

TO OUR VISITORS

We extend a most cordial welcome to all visitors worshiping with us today. We invite you to join us often for worship. If you have not registered as our guest in some previous service, we would appreciate having you do so today. For this purpose, you will find a guest register in the narthex and guest cards at the pews. The guest cards may be filled in and handed to the Pastor or one of the ushers.

Worship service in English is held each Sunday at 9 o'clock A. M. Worship service in Spanish is held each Sunday at 11 o'clock A. M. Sunday school and Bible Classes in both languages meet each Sunday at 10:20 A. M.

Servicio de Dedicación y Acción de Gracia
el domingo, 19 de mayo, 1957, a las 8 P. M.

HIMNO POR LA CONGREGACION
1. ¡Santo! ¡Santo! ¡Santo! Señor Omnipotente,
Siempre el labio mio loores Te dará;
¡Santo! ¡Santo! ¡Santo Te adoro reverente,
Dios en tres personas, bendita Trinidad.

2. !Santo! ¡Santo! ¡Santo! en numeroso coro
Santos escogidos te adoran con fervor,
De alegría llenos, y sus coronas de oro
Rinden ante el trono glorioso el Señor.

3. ¡Santo! ¡Santo! ¡Santo la gloria de Tu nombre
Vemos en tus obras, en cielo, tierra, y mar.
¡Santo! ¡Santo! ¡Santo! Te adorará todo hombre
Dios en tres personas, bendita Trinidad.

EL ACTO DE DEDICACION
Pastor: A la gloria de Dios, nuestro Padre, por el favor de quien hemos edificado esta casa; para la honra de Jesús, el Cristo, el Hijo de Dios Viviente, nuestro Señor y Salvador; para la alabanza del Espíritu Santo fuente de luz y vida:
Congregación: Dedicamos esta casa.
Pastor: Para el consuelo de aquellos que lloran,
Para fortaleza de los que son tentados
Para el socorro de los necesitados,
Congregación: Dedicamos esta casa.
Pastor: Para la salvación de los seres humanos.
Para guiar a la niñez y la juventud,
Para rectamente dividir y proclamar la ley y el evangelio,
Congregación: Dedicamos esta casa.
Pastor: Como una ofrenda de amor y gratitud, una acción de gracias y loor de aquellos que han probado tu salvación y experimentado las riquezas de tu gracia; nosotros, los miembros de esta Iglesia y Congregación,

volviendo ahora a consagrarnos de nuevo a nuestro Dios, dedicamos todo este edificio en el nombre del Padre, del Hijo y del Espíritu Santo. Amen.

GLORIA PATRI

Gloria sea al Padre, y al Hijo, y al Espiritu Santo. Como era al principio, es ahora, y será siempre, por los siglos de los siglos. Amen.

HIMNO POR LA CONGREGACION

1. Tu reino amo, ¡Oh! Dios,
   Con todo e' corazón,
   Y el pueblo que en Jesús halló
   Completa redención.

2. Tu Iglesia, mi Senor;
   Tu templo espiritual;
   La Iglesia que guiando vas
   Con mano paternal.

3. Por ella mi oración,
   Mis lágrimas de amor,
   Y mis cuidados y mi afán
   Por ella son, Señor.

4. Un gozo sin igual
   Me causa en ella estar;
   Por siempre allí tu comunión
   Anhelo disfrutar.

5. Yo sé que durará,
   Mi Dios, cual Tu verdad;
   Y victoriosa llegará
   Hasta la eternidad.

LA LECCION: I Crónica 29:10–16
EL CORO DE LA LIGA DE LAICOS LUTER-
ANOS — Profesor Herman Meyerhoff, director
"De Boca y Corazón, Load al Dios" — Cruger-Bach
"Bless the Lord, O My Soul" — Ippolitov-Ivanoff
"Lord, When at Thy Command" — Geo. W. Martin

EL SERMON por el Rdo. Andrés A. Meléndez, renombrado orador sagrado y director de "La Hora Luterana"
"Un Mensaje del Señor" —Apocalipsis 3:7–12

LA OFRENDA DEDICATORIA reservada

para los gastos de la construcción.

HIMNO POR LA CONGREGACION

1. Querido Salvador
   Rey de la creación,
   Hijo de Dios y del hombre;
   Si, yo Te amo,
   Si, yo Te sirvo,
   Luz de mi alma, gozo y fe.

2. Bellos los prados,
   Grandes los bosques,
   Adornados con primor,
   Jesús mas puro,
   Jesús mas grande,
   Hace mi espíritu cantar.

3. Querido Salvador,
   Señor del mundo,
   Hijo de Dios y del hombre
   Gloria y honra,
   Loor y preces,
   A Ti ahora y siempro. Amén.

LA ORACION DEDICATORIA
LA BENDICION
Congregación:"Amén, Amén, Amén"
EL CORO DE LA LIGA DE LAICOS LUTER-
ANOS: "The Lord's Prayer"
LOS ANUNCIOS

The Building

Our church structure was designed by the Lutheran architect, Mr. O. J. Bruer of Montebello. Designed along the lines of our early California Spanish missions, the building is built around an open patio. The substantial red tile roof, the long covered corridors with porticoes, the ornamental wrought iron porch railings and gates, the patio camellia garden and the adobe tan of all exterior walls combine to give this modern building a truly "old Spanish" flavor. On the one side of the patio is the church sanctuary proper with its chancel furniture and pews of Philippine mahogany. To the rear of the chapel and above the worshipers is a large statue of the resurrected Christ with his hands extended in blessing. Across the patio are two standard size classrooms for our future parochial school. Filling in the remaining space surrounding the patio are the church offices, the lavatories, the children's nursery and a spacious modern kitchen. Complete in every respect, the building has forced air heating and asphalt tile floors throughout. Building and furnishings cost some 75,000 dollars.

In Appreciation
THE CONGREGATION OF "LA SANTA CRUZ" IS DEEPLY GRATEFUL:

TO GOD, for His unbounded and undeserved mercy in Christ Jesus, our Savior, for the privilege of erecting this new house of worship to His Glory; for providing for us in abundance all that has been necessary to complete this project.

TO THE NATIONAL LUTHERAN WOMEN'S MISSIONARY LEAGUE, which at their 1953 Portland, Oregon Convention voted to grant $60,000 of mite offerings for the purchase of land and the erection of this mission church and school.

TO THE LUTHERAN WOMEN'S MISSIONARY LEAGUE OF THE MINNESOTA DISTRICT, for the gift of an additional $5,000 for the purchase of furnishings and equipment.

TO THE LUTHERAN WOMEN'S MISSIONARY LEAGUE OF THE SOUTHERN CALIFORNIA DISTRICT, which under the most capable leadership of Mrs. George Theiss and Mrs. Arthur Holmberg served the Lord with gladness by canvassing thousands of homes, teaching and transporting hundreds of children to Bible schools, publicizing the project and helping in every way possible to extend the cause of Christ in Little Mexico at Los Angeles.

TO THE MEMBERS AND FRIENDS OF THE CONGREGATION, who came from far and near to support this project with their prayers and hundreds of hours of volunteer labor.

TO THE ARCHITECT, MR. O. J. BRUER, for the attractive early Spanish mission style design and most serviceable plans.

TO MR. HAROLD HANSEN, for faithfully and untiringly executing the plans for this building and supervising the construction thereof.

TO THE MISSION BOARD OF THE SOUTHERN CALIFORNIA DISTRICT, and in particular, THE CHURCH EXTENSION DEPARTMENT, under the chairmanship of Mr. Carl Schlueter, for their continual direction and advice.

In every project of the church there are many who deserve words of appreciation. It would be utterly impossible to single out each and everyone who has in some way helped with this project. May we simply give an all-embracing "Thanks" to everyone who participated, and may the abundant blessings of our gracious God rest upon your labors for Him. After all is spoken and done, we can only bow our heads before the Master and say, "We are unprofitable servants; we have done that which it is our duty to do." Luke 17:10.

GIFTS TO THE GLORY OF GOD AND THE EXTENSION OF HIS KINGDOM
ALTAR — In memory of Mr. Ernest Jennings Moe from his wife Bertha
PULPIT and LECTERN — LWML of First Lutheran Church, Pasadena
BAPTISMAL FONT — Sunday school of First Lutheran Church, Pasadena
HOLY COMMUNION VESSELS — Mr. and Mrs. John J. Bredenkamp, Evansville, Ind.
PULPIT BIBLE — Junior Bible Class of First Lutheran Church, Pasadena
OFFERING PLATES — Mr. and Mrs. Robert H. Schatz
ALTAR VASES — In memory of Mr. Fred Kringle by Mr. and Mrs. F. A., Torkelson, Inglewood
ALTAR PARAMENTS — Altar Guild of LWML of First Lutheran Church, Pasadena; LWML of First Lutheran Church, Fontana; Mary and Martha Society, St. John's, Montebello; Mr. and Mrs. E. Lloyd
CANDELABRA — Mr. and Mrs. Clarence J. Stirdivant, Downey
STATUE OF CHRIST — Trinity Lutheran Church, San Bernardino
ORNAMENTAL IRON WORK — In memory of Mrs. J. N. Stirdivant from sons, Clarence J. Stirdivant, Downey and Ben F. Stirdivant, Yucaipa, and families.
SPANISH BIBLES — Mrs. Maria López and daughter, Jean
HYMNALS — Miss Thelma Prellwitz, Culver City; Iglesia de Nuestro Salvador, Santa Ana

FOLDING TABLES — Mr. Herman A. Meyer
SLIDE PROJECTOR, SCREEN, and CHAIRS — Sunday School of First Lutheran Church,; Pasadena
TYPEWRITER — Concordia Circuit LWML, Oakland
OFFICE EQUIPMENT — Dr. and Mrs. Earl C. Muck, Portland, Oregon; Mrs. R. A. Mills, Whittier
SPECIAL LIGHTING — Mr. and Mrs. Atillo Ratarro, Oakland; Mr. and Mrs. Ralph Romero
KITCHEN RANGE — Mr. and Mrs. Robert Schatz
PATIO SHRUBS — Mrs. Mary Michael, Baltimore, Md.; Mr. Herman A. Meyer
GARDEN EQUIPMENT — Mr. and Mrs. Ruben Carabio
VOLLEY AND TETHER BALL EQUIPMENT — Mr. and Mrs. Leo Leon
CHANCEL CARPETING — Mount Calvary Lutheran Church, Beverly Hills; Bethany Lutheran Ladies Aid, Hollywood; Zion Lutheran Ladies Aid, Maywood
NURSERY PLAY PEN — LWML of St. Paul's Lutheran Church, Council Bluffs, Iowa
TREES AND PLANTS — Mrs. Antonia Gallegos; Mr. and Mrs. William Nye, Riverside; Mr. and Mrs. Morehouse, Whittier; Mr. and Mrs. Robert E. Roan, Alhambra; Mr. and Mrs. Leo Wood, Garden Grove

THE ORGAN — Since 1954, numerous love offerings from individuals and organizations have been sent to "La Santa Cruz" Lutheran Church to be used for any need the mission might have. These contributions were placed into an organ fund, because we knew of no other way we could ever hope to obtain such an expensive item for our church. One day in January of this year, we received the almost incredible news that a Hammond organ (their largest model) had been given to us by a sister congregation — St. John's of Montebello. The organ had formerly been the property of St. Matthew's in East Los Angeles.

Receiving such a costly gift made possible the release of our organ fund monies for the purchase of pews for our chapel. We shall ever remain deeply grateful to the members of St. Matthew's and St. John's for this wonderful gift.

THE PEWS — In memory of Mrs. Wm. Eifert from Gertrude E. Lavitt, and family friends.; Mr. and Mrs. Fred Euhus, Yuma, Arizona; Rev. L. J. Rausch, Wapakoneta, Ohio; Mr. Wm. Bornhoeft, Dundee, Illinois; Mrs. Anora M. Denmiger, Los Angeles; Mrs. Margrete Gross, St. Louis, Mo.; Mrs. Gertrude Brauer, Norman, Oklahoma; Mr. and Mrs. Ruben Carabio, Los Angeles; Mrs. Busch, San Diego; Mrs. B. J. Richardson, Oxnard; Mrs. Jeanette Alexander, Los Angeles; Lina H. Hommel, Alhambra; May E. Nobs, Santa Barbara; Annette B. Carillo, Santa Barbara Lutheran Business and Professional Women, Los Angeles; Women's Guild, First Lutheran, Ventura; Calvary Lutheran Church, Yuma, Arizona; First Lutheran Sunday School, Long Beach; Emmaus First Lutheran Sunday School, Alhambra; St. Paul's Lutheran Sunday School, Garden Grove; Mary and Martha Society, First Lutheran Church, El Monte St. Paul's Evangelical Lutheran Sunday School, Ashland, Kentucky Faith Lutheran Church, East Whittier; Trinity Lutheran Walther League, Whittier; Lynwood Lutheran Sunday School, Lynwood; Dorcas Society Christ Lutheran Church, Los Angeles; LWML Society, Fort Smith, Arkansas; Redeemer Lutheran Sunday School, Waukegan, Illinois Concordia Lutheran Church, Los Angeles; Mite Box Circle, Grace Lutheran Church, Atlanta, Georgia; St. Matthew's Lutheran LWML, Wilmington; St. Paul's First Lutheran Sunday School, North Hollywood; Trinity Lutheran Sunday School, Reseda; First Lutheran Parochial School, Culver City; Grace Lutheran Ladies Aid, Santa Maria Bethany Lutheran Sunday School, Hollywood; Sunday School and Bible Class, St. John's, Orange

Our Speaker
(Nuestro Orador)
Rev. Andres A. Melendez, D.D.

SPEAKER OF
"BRINGING CHRIST TO THE NATIONS"
Editor of Spanish Literature for the
Lutheran Church — Missouri Synod.

ORADOR DE
"CRISTO PARA TODAS LAS NACIONES"
Redactor de Literatura en Español de la
Iglesia Luterana — Sinodo de Misuri.

Rev. Andres A. Melendez, D. D., of St. Louis, was speaker on "La Hora Luterana," the Spanish Lutheran Hour, for 17 years at the time of the dedication. He was also a native of Puerto Rico, serving the church as editor of Spanish literature and was an authority on economic, social, and spiritual conditions in Latin America. In his sermon based on the text Phil. 1:27b, "Striving together for the faith of the Gospel," he pointed out that the word *Gospel* runs like a golden thread through all of Paul's letters and that the world's greatest need, especially south of the border in all Latin America, is the Gospel. An Indian in South America was asked by one of our missionaries, "Who is your Savior?" He pointed to the Virgin Mary statue and replied, "That is my savior." Dr. Melendez stated, "There they know Christ as the lord of death and an object of pity, and Mary as the lord of life, holding out her hands and smilingly saying, 'Come unto me, all ye that are weary and heavy laden.' Many Latin Americans look to the Virgin Mary as their Savior, and this is the prevailing belief in South America; ignorance, idolatry, superstition, and modernism are common in Latin America, but the same evils, although not as bad, are also present in Los Angeles."

Dr. Melendez pleaded for gifts or loans to the Church Extension Fund to build more chapels and churches and concluded that by faithful attendance at worship services and by testifying to others "we strive together for the faith of the Gospel."

After the service, numerous letters and telegrams of congratulation were read — letters from Dr. J. W. Behnken, President of The Lutheran Church — Missouri Synod, from Mrs. Arthur Preisinger, president of the International Lutheran Women's Missionary League, from congregations and individuals near and far, and from almost every district of the International LWML.

An unprecedented crowd of 900 worshipers came that afternoon for the dedication service. Since the church grounds were so overcrowded, many went home to return for the evening service where there were 260 people present. Everyone rejoiced that here was finally a place where the Word of God could be proclaimed for the guidance of immortal souls and the sacraments administered as instituted. The evening service, conducted in Spanish, was very impressive. Dr. Melendez addressed the congregation on the text

Worshipers entering the new La Santa Cruz Church on Dedication Day, May 19, 1957.

On August 6, 1961, the Spanish Lutheran Hour is first broadcast in the Los Angeles area.

Revelations 3:7–12, exhorting members to be faithful and active in the service to the Lord. Preceding the sermon, two children were baptized, bringing the membership to 120 souls. Seven adults were received as communicants, giving this young mission a total of 37 communicant members.

Pastor Stirdivant described the area surrounding the church as a very mobile population with many poor and low-income renters. It was like ministering to a procession or a parade going by. Nobody wanted to settle in East Los Angeles or buy a house. Another obstacle to the ministry was a conservative estimate that the populace was 75 percent Roman Catholic. Even with these challenges, La Santa Cruz touched the lives of many people. Pastor recalled Moses Garcia and his wife who came in to solve their differences of opinions. They decided to become Lutherans because she was Catholic and he was Methodist. They said, "We'll get a church that's half Methodist and half Catholic and you've got a Lutheran." He became active in the church before moving to the Yakama Valley in Washington. One lady who attended services at Pastor Johnny Lopez's church, Christo Rey in Orange, told him, "Because of Pastor Stirdivant, I was enrolled in Lutheran High School and received a good education. Due to a good education and Pastor Stirdivant, I was given a chance to break out of the ghetto of Central Los Angeles. We now live in Anaheim in a nice home, and we have a nice family. It was that education, that contact which did a world of good."

In 1957, the congregation was organized with 10 voting members and continued with slow and steady growth; two services were held each Sunday, one in English and one in Spanish. At that time, approximately 85 percent of members were of Mexican descent. During the year, a suitable 80' × 120' lot was purchased at a cost of $7,000 for the building of a four-bedroom parsonage that was constructed at a cost of $23,000 in 1960. The need for the new parsonage was urgent as Pastor and Mrs. Stirdivant (who recently had twin boys, Donald and Ronald) were residing in a two-bedroom home with four children. Their family would eventually grow to seven children: Lorraine, David Mark, Timothy, Donald, Ronald, Kevin, and Lisa. These children gave them fifteen grandchildren and 12 great-grandchildren. Also in 1957, the church had grown to 93 communicant members, 162 baptized souls, with 50 in the Sunday school. The church budget was $16,440 with the members giving $4,440 and the District providing a subsidy

of $12,000. In 1961, there were 70 communicant members, 151 baptized souls, 15 voters, and a Sunday school of 45.

On Sunday morning, August 6, 1961, with much joy and grateful fervor, Pastor Stirdivant led a joint service in the crowded church of La Santa Cruz. He preached both in English and in Spanish about our Lord's serious command, "Occupy till I come." This began an all-day festival of missions to welcome the first broadcast of the Spanish Lutheran Hour, *Cristo Para Todas Las Nacions* (Bringing Christ to the Nations), in the Los Angeles area. The first broadcast was heard on radio station KWKW at 8:45 a.m. that morning with Rev. Andres Melendez, speaker of the 15-minute broadcast, preaching on peace of heart and mind, which everyone seemed to be searching for but few could find, because they did not turn to Christ and His Word.

Holy Communion was celebrated that morning with both Spanish- and English-speaking members kneeling at the altar rail side by side. Prayers for the future success of the radio mission were offered. Following the service, the crowd streamed into the parish hall to view the handicraft of some 90 children who had attended daily Vacation Bible School which concluded with the festival. A delicious chicken dinner was prepared by the ladies of the Dorcas Society, under the supervision of Mrs. Jo Price, president. After the dinner, chairs were whisked around in the parish hall and patio, and all settled down to enjoy the program prepared by the children, young people, and friends of La Santa Cruz. The children sang action songs led by Rev. Toshio Okamoto, pastor of St. Thomas, Los Angeles, who had helped Pastor Stirdivant with the VBS, even as Pastor Stirdivant had helped at the St. Thomas VBS.

A variety program was presented which included a demonstration by the church's Boy Scout troop under the leadership of Scoutmaster Henry Ledesma, piano solos by talented Larry Rodriguez, a vocal solo by Mrs. Olga Lakin, and a number of Mexican folk dances and songs. The program concluded with music by an up-and-coming musical group from the neighborhood, the Benny Montez Band, with some instrumental numbers by Frankie Vasquez and Boby Lujan.

Also present at this historical event was Rev. Daniel Wooten, pastor of Our Savior in Bellflower, a former immigration officer and now a Lutheran missionary. He told of his conversion to the Lutheran church in 1953; his graduation from Concordia, Springfield, in 1961; and his subsequent call to

Bellflower. He shared how he had learned Spanish in high school but had to relearn it later on for his work as an immigration officer. The interview of Pastor Wooten was conducted in Spanish with the Spanish-speaking members remarking on his good accent and clear speech in Spanish.

A short time later, Julio Soria, KHOF announcer for the Gospel radio program "In the Shadow of the Cross," interviewed Pastor Stirdivant. After an introduction and questions about La Santa Cruz Lutheran Church and its activities, pastor was given time to make a personal testimony about his life and ministry and concluded with a five-minute devotion for the day. On Sunday, November 26, he and Rev. Toshio Okamoto of St. Thomas Japanese Mission, Los Angeles, presented a mission education program for the mission festival of Good Shepherd Lutheran Church, Yucaipa, at the Woman's Clubhouse, where members and many guests were in attendance. Following a delightful potluck dinner served in the Patio Tea Room in late afternoon, the two missionaries used colored slides to illustrate their informal talks. His inspiring message, "You Can Be a Missionary," was accompanied with colorful pictures of work within his mission since its beginning. In his inimitable manner, Rev. Stirdivant vividly told of how his Santa Ana parish grew almost spontaneously, "all because a little old lady going to Garden Grove on a bus talked about her church to a young man who then brought his family and friends to that church, and they likewise, until there was an ever-widening circle." At his side assisting him was his wife Belen. Their family consisted of six little missionaries. It was noted at the event "this young, enthusiastic minister of the Gospel attended the Yucaipa Elementary School and Redlands High School where he received oratorical honors. He continued his higher education at California Concordia College, Oakland, and later graduated from Concordia Seminary, St. Louis, Missouri."

In the spring of 1962, the Mission Board paid expenses of $300 for Pastor Stirdivant to attend a two-week Latin American Conference in Guatemala City. On May 20, 1962, La Santa Cruz was privileged to celebrate the fifth anniversary of the dedication of the building. Amid rejoicing and prayerful thanks to God for His blessings the previous five years, a beautiful scroll, especially drawn by the talented young artist, Albert Bates, and signed by all the members of La Santa Cruz, was presented to Pastor Stirdivant on behalf of the congregation by the president, Nick Shmakoff. It stated:

IN GRATITUDE TO GOD, the Lord of the Church, even our Lord Jesus Christ, the Chief Shepherd,

WE ACKNOWLEDGE the faithfulness of our devout Pastor, David M. Stirdivant, His servant, who has instructed us in His ways, counseled and comforted us with His Gospel, and sought the lost, and

WE BESEECH GOD to illumine the heart of His faithful ambassador to lead and guide him with the strength of His right hand that he may continue to perform the ministry committed unto him to the glory of God's name and to the edification of all believers in the church; and

WE PLEDGE with the help of God to show towards our Pastor such love, honor, and fit obedience in the Lord as are due to a minister of Christ.

The dream of Rev. John W. Theiss in 1906 as he walked about a neighborhood, known as "Little Mexico," on the east side of Los Angeles and prayed that some day a Lutheran church would be built there had been fulfilled. This church would be dedicated as a mission to the glory of God and the winning of many souls for Christ among the large group of Latin-American people living there. God, who hears and mercifully answers the prayers of His true and faithful servants, made Pastor Theiss's dream a reality on May 19, 1957, when the doors of La Santa Cruz Lutheran Church were joyfully opened, and Rev. David M. Stirdivant walked up the aisle followed by his rejoicing congregation and visitors when that first Sunday morning worship service was conducted. Pastor Stirdivant's becoming the first pastor of La Santa Cruz was, in itself, a special blessing God granted Pastor Theiss. Pastor Stirdivant was Rev. Theiss's grandson.

During the late fifties, a Lutheran family, the Hernandez, who had five or six children at the time, arrived in East Los Angeles from Texas. Since they had no lodging, three of the children lived with Pastor Stirdivant and his family in the parsonage for a few weeks while the rest of the family lived with other people. After they found a house, Pastor Stirdivant would take Carlos, the oldest child, and his brothers and sisters along with his children to the Christian day school at St. John's in Montebello each day. One of the Hernandez children, Carlos, became a Lutheran pastor after attending Lutheran High School in Los An-

Rev. John W. Theiss's dream is fullfilled when La Santa Cruz opens its doors on May 19, 1957 with the pastor, Rev. David Stirdivant, his grandson.

Carlos Hernandez, a student at Concordia Senior College in Fort Wayne, in 1964, who later became a pastor serving many churches in the Missouri Synod. (Pacific Southwest District Archives)

Rev. Toshio Okamoto is honored in a "farewell" supper given by the congregation on February 23, 1962.

geles, Concordia College, Portland, Oregon, and Concordia Seminary, St. Louis. In the summer of 1962 just before his second year at Concordia, Portland, Carlos was honored for his Americanism before the City Council of Los Angeles. He was singled out for this exceptional award in honor of his efforts in oratory (He also won the national speech award at Kiwanis International in Philadelphia in 1961). The contribution he has made to his community was highlighted for this singular commendation. He was presented the award, a handsome hand-lettered scroll reserved for outstanding people whose civic-mindedness had proved an inspiration to others, by Councilman Royball of East Los Angeles. In August of the following summer, Carlos competed in the national finals in another oratorical contest in Ohio.

This wasn't the last family to live with Pastor and Mrs. Stirdivant in the parsonage, as they took in many people who were in need of support. One Friday afternoon, Pastor received an urgent call from Lutheran Social Services in Los Angeles, stating they had a young fellow from Tijuana needing a place to stay for a few nights. Pastor went downtown to get him and took him home for the "few nights" that lasted for a few months. During his stay with the Stirdivant family, it was discovered that this young man wasn't a very nice fellow. Finally, after a few months, he was given other lodging where he did some things that caused him to be deported to Mexico. Even though this wasn't a very positive experience, the Stirdivant parsonage continued to be open to those who needed aid.

On Sunday evening, February 23, 1962, Rev. Toshio Okamoto was honored in a "farewell" supper given by the congregation. Rev. Okamoto, former pastor of St. Thomas Lutheran Church and missionary to the Japanese, had accepted a call to Our Master Lutheran Church, Inkster, Michigan. At the supper, Mr. George Schwartz, spokesman for La Santa Cruz, presented Rev. Okamoto with a gift — a briefcase — and said, "For the past ten years, La Santa Cruz has benefited from the interest and help of Rev. Okamoto. Year after year our Pastor Stirdivant and Pastor Okamoto have cooperated in helping each other with Vacation Bible Schools, sometimes conducting as many as three or four schools in one summer. Whenever the services of two pastors were needed for presenting special worship services, as on Good Friday, Christmas, or Mission Festival, Rev. Okamoto gave us his help. When we needed counsel and advice, we knew we could turn to Rev. Okamo-

to with complete confidence. He has been a true Christian friend to our pastor and to us, and we share with our Japanese brethren the loss of this missionary from our midst."

A cake that was baked and decorated by one of the men of La Santa Cruz, Mr. Ahlberg, was presented to Pastor Okamoto. It was decorated with yellow roses and forget-me-nots and read, "God be with you. Farewell, Pastor Okamoto." Mr. Louis Holguin was master of ceremonies for the informal program following the supper. The Sunday school children sang some favorite songs, which Rev. Okamoto had taught them. Rev. Stirdivant, using colored slides from the congregation's history, reviewed God's blessings over the years and showed how Pastor Okamoto had helped the parish in countless ways. In the audience were persons from Mexico, Puerto Rico, Honduras, Persia, Sweden, and Denmark. Mr. Nick Shmakoff closed the memorable evening with a prayer of thanksgiving to the Savior and for continued blessings upon Pastor Okamoto and his family.

In the 1964 Mission Report to District Convention, Pastor Stirdivant revealed that La Santa Cruz had a baptized membership of 170 with 95 communicant members and a Sunday school enrollment of 60. It took $16,440 to operate the parish with the congregation giving $4,221 and the District providing a subsidy of $12,219. He stated that for the previous three years the congregation had shown very little growth, gains scarcely keeping pace with losses. In an effort to halt that trend, they were initiating more home visitation programs and adding an evening service to the Sunday schedule of two morning services, one in English and one in Spanish. During the past year, they were brought into contact with a new segment of the Latin American populace now having 12 members of Puerto Rican extraction. He concluded by writing, "The history of the Lutheran Church's work among the Mexican people has proven to be costly, slow, and uphill all the way. In Mexico, where work was begun in 1940 and we currently have 8 missionaries at work, we still have less than 500 communicants. Despite the slow numerical growth in Los Angeles, our church is spiritually helping hundreds of Latin Americans and we look for continued — though not spectacular — but solid growth in this field."

During the summer, La Santa Cruz had its annual fiesta and Vacation Bible School closing program where people from various parts of Southern California met with representatives from Puerto

Rev. Toshio Okamoto pastor of St. Thomas Lutheran Church and missionary to the Japanese with Pastor Stirdivant in 1962.

Rico, Colombia, Mexico, and other South American countries. The day began with Holy Communion, where the first portion of the Communion liturgy was spoken in Spanish and the latter part in English. Both the English "Take eat" and the Spanish *"Tome comer"* were used in the distribution of the Sacrament. The choir sang anthems in both English and in Spanish. Rev. Robert Fiore delivered the address urging his listeners to realize that Christ is always a matter of life and death and emphasized the need to be truly "followers of the Way," as the early Christians were called. After the service, the visitors enjoyed a Mexican-style dinner served in the patio where VBS handcraft was on display with some woven pieces by the children available as souvenirs. The children not only presented a play and sang a number of songs but also had a piñata.

Even though La Santa Cruz, located in the heart of Little Mexico at Los Angeles, was thought of as serving only Spanish-speaking persons, she was also an inner-city congregation and as such was called upon to minister to persons of many other racial backgrounds. In the spring of 1965, Pastor Stirdivant instructed and baptized an 84-year-old gentleman, Mr. Archie Hudgens, whose granddaughter, Mrs. Patricia Bede, was a member of Peace Lutheran Church in Pico Rivera. That summer some 250 delegates to the International Lutheran Women's Missionary League convention in San Diego took time out to go to La Santa Cruz to inspect one of their projects that was begun 12 years earlier. The women of the congregation welcomed them to La Santa Cruz Church with Spanish-American hospitality, Mexican food, and Mariachi-style music. Following the dinner, a service of thanksgiving and praise was conducted with the church choir singing a Spanish hymn and Pastor Stirdivant presenting slides and reviewing the history of the congregation.

In the January 17, 1967, Mission Board meeting, the board approved a lease agreement on the La Santa Cruz property with the Standard Oil Company for $30 per year until drilling operations produced oil; thereafter royalties of 16⅔ percent were to be paid. The following spring, young people from Lutheran churches throughout the Los Angeles area and Orange County responded to the challenge in the East Los Angeles community. Since Pastor Stirdivant had seen many Protestant churches in the area cease to exist as functioning parts of the community, he was determined to make a contribution where the need was so obvious. Nineteen young folks helped set up play days with teams of youth starting a parade in the morning by banging on metal pans to get the attention of the neighborhood children. After gathering the children, they assembled at the church for films, Bible stories, lunch, and play activity. The original 40 children increased to 106 before the special one-week effort came to its climax.

Steve Watkins of Los Angeles related an incident of a 15-year-old boy named Tony. Much of his time was spent in the streets, because he had been expelled from school. He knew the police, and they knew him very well. On the first night, shouting from the roof of the church, he said he would bring his gang and wreck the place. The next day he came back, but without his gang. The following day it was thrilling to hear Tony singing "Rise and Shine and Give God the Glory." When he brought his gang, instead of causing trouble, he witnessed to them. When they disrupted the Bible class, it was Tony who quieted them. He also participated in a church play. The young people who had come to East Los Angeles said: "We never saw anything like it before." As the staff was leaving, Tony offered them a place to stay — his home. The staff helpers were Paul Watkins, Los Angeles; Ken Neal, Stanton; Debbi Miller, Torrance; Greg Raley, Gardena; Rhonda Evans, Palm Springs; Sandy McFadden, Downey; Jeanie Stohlman, Montebello; Ralph Cruz, Los Angeles; Mr. and Mrs. Sam Prentiss, Orange; Rick Trombley, Woodland Hills; Chris Tweil, Norwalk; Wayne Pitzler, Fullerton; Tom Johnson, Whittier; Sandi Edwards, Long Beach; Carol Thornberg, Pico Rivera; Sharon Maxwell, Long Beach; Armando Hamilton, Los Angeles; and Patty Knaack, Whittier.

With the fluctuation of membership at La Santa Cruz (160 baptized members, 90 communicant

A gang member is converted to Christ and changes his life.

members with a Sunday school enrollment of 59 in 1966 and 135 baptized, 87 communicant members, with a Sunday school enrollment of seven in 1968) the Mission Board wanted to re-evaluate the program in the Mexican mission field, as it had failed to achieve the predicted results in terms of numerical growth. One of the primary factors in the growth of La Santa Cruz was the extreme mobility of economically depressed Mexican-Americans living in the area, making an effective mission outreach almost impossible.

In the April 1, 1973, edition of the *District Digest*, it was reported that more and more lay activity with personal evangelism was taking place. In La Santa Cruz Lutheran Church, earlier that year, the Rev. Harold Deye, former missionary to Venezuela, conducted a bi-lingual evangelism clinic in the parish with a number of the members of the mission better equipped to witness to their Savior, Jesus Christ, than ever before. In the September 4, 1977, *Lutheran Witness Supplement*, another evangelism effort was reported. On eight successive Friday and Saturday evenings a dozen or more people came to La Santa Cruz, driving 60 miles round trip on two successive nights for courses offered to lay members of Lutheran parishes in the greater Los Angeles area who were especially interested in reaching Hispanic families in their neighborhoods with the Gospel. All but two of those enrolled had a Hispanic background.

Rev. Robert F. Gussick; Rev. Daniel Saavedra, Mexican pastor under the supervision of the Lutheran Baja California Mission; and the host pastor, Rev. David Stirdivant, presented the courses. They dealt with the objectives of evangelism and the communication of the Gospel, as applied to the Hispanic cultural situation, and a study of the Gospel according to St. Luke. The latter material prepared the group for beginning Bible study in their homes with Hispanic friends and neighbors. Such informal Bible study groups were encouraged and guided by Rev. Saavedra and Rev. Stirdivant in the following months with some already functioning at the time. This new strategy was being tried under the auspices of the Mission Board of the Southern California District, under the guidance of Rev. Vernon Trahms who was on the Commission on Urban Ministries. The experiment was called the Center of Cultural Lay Evangelism Ministry with refresher courses for the first students and new classes for new recruits in that fall.

At the May 20, 1975, Board for Missions meeting, it was decided to honor the request of the

Bell Gardens Lutheran Church with the part-time services of Rev. David Stirdivant in order to initiate a Hispanic mission outreach in that parish. By June, Pastor Stirdivant was endeavoring to reach the Spanish-speaking people, utilizing the membership in follow-up contacts. Since the very successful means of reaching Spanish children was through a Vacation Bible School, he conducted a VBS in August of that year. It reached many children, most of whom were Anglos.

About this time, a young man, Hilario Deniz, arrived at Pastor Stirdivant's door. He was from the state of Colima, Mexico, where he was raised as a Catholic. When he came to the United States, some Protestant evangelicals, who encouraged him to go to the seminary, influenced him. While studying for the ministry, one of the Protestant pastors told him that Lutherans had a book of sermons for all occasions from which they read sermons. When Hilario went to visit Pastor Stirdivant, he explained to Hilario that the book was only for ideas and not read for services. As Pastor worked with Hilario, he became more and more interested in Lutheran doctrine and wanted to become a Lutheran minister. Through Pastor's teaching and coaching, he started helping at the church, gaining more members for the congregation through his

Rev. David Stirdivant at his desk in the church office, circa 1960.

Rev. Deye conducts evangelism clinics at La Santa Cruz in 1973.

very personal ways. When a need was expressed by the Arizona congregations to start a Hispanic mission in El Mirage west of Phoenix, Hilario was sent under Pastor Stirdivant's guidance to begin the mission in that area. The mission will be discussed later in the book.

In the *District Digest* of May — June 1977, the following article gave a prelude of the shift in the District's strategies regarding Hispanic ministry:

The Center of Cultural Lay Evangelism Ministry (CCLEM) is in its fourth week of operation. The lay people enrolled are responding nobly and home Bible classes will be starting very shortly. An evaluation will be made on June 4 and plans for Phase I will then be laid.

The Pastoral Conference this fall will emphasize cross-cultural ministry with heavy emphasis on Hispanic work.

The Southwest contains about 70 percent of the 14 million Spanish surname people who live within the borders of the United States. Of all 50 states, California has the largest number of Spanish surname residents (3.2 million), with more than 1.2 million in the Los Angeles area alone.

The object of Hispanic mission work is not to pull people out of the society in which they find themselves, but rather to reconcile them to God and their neighbors so that the will of God might be done in that society.

The board is determined to provide a program of mission outreach relevant to the needs of the Spanish surnames that live among us. We seek to develop communities among them, to preserve and enhance their culture, and to share with them the blessing and command of Christ that we love one another.

Since the Hispanic population was increasing not only in California but also throughout the United States, the Hispanic Advisory Council meeting in St. Louis, Missouri, passed the following Resolution 4-24-01 on April 24, 1978, in order to meet the needs of the church in its ministry to the Hispanics:

WHEREAS, The Hispanic Council endorsed the resolution adopted by the Board for Missions at its meeting on April 21 as follows:

WHEREAS, Concordia Theological Seminary, Fort Wayne, has offered to carry on a program of Theological Education by Extension for Hispanic candidates for the pastoral ministry; and

WHEREAS, such a program would amount to another dimension of the Hispanic-American Seminary Extension Program which is scheduled to begin in September in the Chicago area, specifically on the campus of Concordia Teachers College, River Forest; and

WHEREAS, this new facet of the program will add a flexibility to the Seminary Extension Program, which will enable Hispanics to begin their preparation for pastoral ministry without leaving their homes and local congregations; and

WHEREAS, this latest development will furnish the Synod with a well-rounded program for training Hispanics for ministry, since an institute for the Training of Lay Workers has been established on the campus of Concordia College, Austin, Texas; therefore be it

RESOLVED, that the Board for Missions commend Concordia Seminary, Fort Wayne, for the progressive steps of establishing Theological Education by Extension for Hispanics in many locations in the fall of 1978 and be it further

RESOLVED, that the Board for Missions plead with Concordia Seminary, Fort Wayne, not to fail to implement the basic Hispanic-American Seminary Extension Program at River Forest in September, 1978; and be it finally

RESOLVED, that the Board for Missions, in the interest of effective Hispanic-American ministry, and in solidarity with the Hispanic-American Regional Advisory Council, pledge its most vigorous support for the total training program for Hispanic-American Ministry; therefore be it

RESOLVED, that we ask the President of the Synod to use the powers of his office to make provision for the establishment, coordination, and implementation of a total program for the training of Hispanic workers in consultation with the Hispanic Advisory Council; and be it further

RESOLVED, that we ask the Division of Higher Education, the Colloquy Committee, the Fort Wayne Board of Control, as well as all other institutions of higher learning of the Synod, the Councils of Presidents, and the Board of Directors to implement the resolution given us by the Mission Board; and be it further

RESOLVED, that the President of Concordia Seminary, Fort Wayne, be thanked for his assurance that the program of Theological Education by Extension can be implemented with Synodical schools at Christ College, Irvine; Concordia, Austin; Concordia, River Forest; Concordia, Milwaukee; and Concordia, Bronxville; or with selected individuals with Hispanic expertise; and be it further

RESOLVED, that the Colloquy Committee use the flexibility authorized in the Synodical Handbook, 4.61 — f.2, to expedite Hispanics (ethnic minorities) entering the colloquy program; and be it further

RESOLVED, that the entire program, once in operation, be reviewed every two years according to synodical procedures by the Board for Higher Education.

RESOLVED, that we ask the Board for Higher Education to prioritize the allocation of funds so that the total training program for Hispanic-American ministry be implemented; and be it finally

RESOLVED, that the entire project be in operation no later than September 1, 1978.

The Second National Hispanic Conference of The Lutheran Church — Missouri Synod met in Los Angeles at the Hyatt House in the City of Commerce on September 13 — 15, 1979, using as its theme "Forward In Community and Growth" with nearly 100 pastors, laymen, and mission personnel. Coming from the five Hispanic regions of the United States and representing the multifaceted Hispanic background in America of Cubans, Puerto Ricans, Mexican-Americans, and Central and South Americans, the delegates conducted business solely in Spanish. Although, representing different regions and backgrounds, the unity of faith in Jesus Christ and Lutheran teaching was apparent, as the delegates heard papers and passed resolutions, which dealt with the urgency of the Lutheran church in reaching the 19 million Hispanics with the Gospel of Jesus Christ.

Gene Hernandez, campus chaplain at East Los Angeles Community College and member of St.

John's, Montebello, and the Rev. Carlos Hernandez, Watsonville, California, made arrangements for the conference. Bus trips were conducted by the delegates to various parts of Los Angeles and to Redeemer Lutheran Church and School in South Gate to acquaint those from other regions with the immense challenge in ministry to the Hispanic, which was before the congregations of the Southern California District.

Following the National Hispanic Conference and because the dramatic need for Hispanic ministry was so great in the Los Angeles area, pastors and laymen met on October 9, 1979, to form the Hispanic Support Conference at La Santa Cruz Lutheran Church, East Los Angeles, which met monthly at various locations for the purpose of mutual support, encouragement, and idea sharing in Hispanic ministry. In attendance at this formation meeting were Rev. Cris Artigas, Rev. Charles Brady, Rev. Philip Molnar, Rev. Mike Drews, Rev. Larry Stoterau, Rev. Harold Deye, Rev. Woody Mather, Rev. Wil Glade, Rev. Lothar Tornow, and teacher Geraldine Fellwock.

"The conference is to include those who are directly involved in Spanish language ministry, those who have the desire to begin work, as well as those who have a heart for the many Hispanic people in Southern California," stated Rev. Phil Molnar. There was no specific membership, and therefore pastors and lay people could attend to discuss problems, opportunities, and successes in Hispanic out reach.

"Sensitizing an Anglo Congregation to Hispanic Culture" was the title of the paper presented at the conference by Rev. David Stirdivant where he stated:

… As pastors of such churches [Anglo], we do well to prepare ourselves for leading our people through these four stages. It may be a delicate process — sensitizing an Anglo congregation for entering Hispanic work.

First, we must expect the realization of the reality to hit. "We're surrounded." "There's thousands of them moving in! Our people are moving out. It just isn't like it used to be. Hardly any children come to Sunday school. Nobody wants to be an officer. Finances are an increasing worry." All of this has to sink in, to shock us out of our dreaming and into reality — the reality of seeing the situation like it really is.

Then will come the thoughts of rejection. "What's going to happen to us if we start letting those people in?" "Well, we've still got some transfers coming in." "Wonder why the District Mission Board doesn't do something about the Spanish people?" "Oh, they're all Catholics anyway."

Then come the ideas of withdrawal. "Let's sell out, pack up, and move." Last Palm Sunday, I sat with Brother Carl Lampitt and a committee from his church, First Lutheran of Pasadena. "What should we do? Ten years ago our neighborhood turned black. We finally had to close down our school. Now we're renting the facilities to the Presbyterians. But now another change is happening. The Hispanics are moving in and the blacks are moving out. Pastor Lampitt said, "Personally I think it's high time we get going in Hispanic work. But most of our members feel we should sell out and go east…maybe even join with one of the other Lutheran churches."

Yes, we've heard this tape before. In Lincoln Heights, at the corner of Griffen and Alturas, stands a building, which used to be Emanuel Lutheran Church. Today it belongs to some Latin American evangelical group. On Euclid Avenue, a few blocks from La Santa Cruz, there is a Japanese Seventh-day Adventist church. It formerly was a Lutheran church, (A.L.C), but they sold out and moved to the suburbs. At Second and Dacotah is a Mexican-American Free Methodist church with a Light and Life Christian School. This was the original property of St John's Lutheran Church, which sold and relocated in Montebello. For a couple of years, we conducted a Saturday morning Bible School for Hispanic children in a nice building known as St. Matthew's Lutheran Church of East Los Angeles. That building now houses Len's Body and Fender Shop.

As we Lutherans continue to withdraw and sell our real estate, others will show us how we could have stayed on and continued to work in Latin-American communities.

Finally, Marge Wold tells us, there will be pastors and congregations who will say, "Shucks no! We won't go! We're not pulling up stakes and running. Let's roll up our sleeves and get to work!"

When we arrive then at this stage, what's the next step? Where to must we lead our people now?

The November meeting was held at Angelica Lutheran Church in Los Angeles. Rev. Mike Cooper demonstrated through slides and commentary the early efforts of an established Lutheran congregation to reach out to its Hispanic neighborhood. For over thirty years, Pastor Stirdivant was the sole person in the District doing ministry among the Hispanic population. Through this new organization, more pastors and congregations would become involved in ministering to the Hispanic population in their neighborhoods.

As was stated in chapter one, Pastor Smukal was the father of Hispanic work in the District, because he established the first Sunday school for Mexican children. One could also say that the Rev. David Stirdivant is the true father of Hispanic ministry in the Pacific Southwest District as he has been involved in the establishment of most of the Hispanic congregations through his actual presence or through his advice and support. This dedicated man of God has given his whole life to share the Gospel with the Hispanic culture.

Through the end of the 1970s and into the early 1980s, Pastor Stirdivant divided his time working in the Hispanic fields in East Los Angeles and Bell Gardens. He would preach at the Spanish service at La Santa Cruz and then go to Bell Gardens to preach in the Spanish service there. He was assisted by the Rev. Phil Molnar who would preach in the English services in each of these congregations. By 1982, La Santa Cruz had only 75 baptized members and 40 communicant members serving immigrants arriving steadily from Mexico, Puerto Rico, and other Spanish-speaking countries, bearing a strong witness to this portion of the community. In 1980, the sad day arrived when Pastor Stirdivant left La Santa Cruz to become Pastor at Bell Gardens Lutheran Church. As the only pastor of that parish, he had baptized, confirmed, married, and buried members of this parish for almost 30 years. For 30 years, this congregation had been the heart and center of the District's Hispanic outreach.

The second pastor to serve La Santa Cruz, the only church in the District with an official Hispanic name, was Rev. Cristiano Artigas who was born and raised in Nicaragua where his father, Rev. Napoleon Artigas, was a pastor. He had received his college and seminary training in the United States and spent his vicarage year at Redeemer Lutheran Church in South Gate, California. Following his graduation from the seminary in 1980, he was called as missionary-at-large with

Rev. Artigas becomes second pastor of La Santa Cruz in 1983.

assignment to begin a Hispanic congregation at Zion Lutheran Church in Maywood. The day school was re-opened in 1981. He served as principal and also conducted a Saturday doctrine school for children. In 1983, he accepted the call to be the pastor at La Santa Cruz. He and Pastor Stirdivant continued to work together in some aspects of ministry between the Bell Gardens and La Santa Cruz churches.

Pastor Artigas's Latin American background gave him something in common with the people of the community he served. In his evangelism efforts, he worked primarily with those who had recently arrived in this country, who were establishing ties and deciding where they belonged. Since almost all of the people of the congregation were converts, he found that Bible instruction had to be very basic. His Sunday school classes for both children and adults provided simple insights into the Bible. Since many were not well educated, even in Spanish, it was difficult for them to read words and learn new music, which was another reason for using traditional melodies. The worship service was traditional in form, but the liturgy was simplified, using modern wording. The greatest success had been with young people who met jointly at Bell Gardens every other week with about 40 youth serving, studying, and sharing activities. At that time, La Santa Cruz had 30 — 40 people at Sunday services with 40 young people at the Monday Youth Program and 12 or more at the Thursday adult Bible class.

In the March 1984 edition of *THIS MONTH*, the following story was written about Hispanic ministry:

Pastor Stirdivant welcoming Pastor Artigas to La Santa Cruz as pastor of the parish.

"Hispanic Ministry is probably the most important outreach for the Lutheran Church of this District in the 1980s. We must meet that challenge now or count ourselves out with these people," the Rev. Kenneth Behnken, Administrative Assistant to the President-Missions, believes.

"It is a challenge because we are dealing with a different culture and a different language, and we must train lay people to minister to their own," the District executive elaborates.

Although Hispanic ministry is not new in the District, a glance at the statistics quickly reflects the reason for its burgeoning growth.

In 1950, Anglos comprised 86.13 percent of the Los Angeles population; by 1980 they represented less than 49 percent. In 1950, less than 7 percent of the population of the city of Los Angeles was Hispanic. Today 3 out of 10 are Hispanic. Of the Spanish speaking Americans living in the U.S.A., 15 percent are active Roman Catholics, 5 percent are practicing Protestants, and 80 percent are unchurched.

The Rev. Behnken believes that the church cannot limit the methods and models used. Pastors must be given the freedom to use the gifts and talents they have to allow the Lord's direction in their ministries.

People come from many countries, from Central and South America, and Cuba, not only Mexico. All speak the Spanish language.

In the November 1984 edition of *THIS MONTH*, the article states:

Opportunity — Like Never Before

The decade of the 1980s, to a national magazine, was described like this:

"What lies ahead is a 10 year period unlike any in this century. It's challenges for constructive change are great, and immense progress is almost certain.... Of all the factors that will affect people's lives in the '80s, few will have a bigger impact than the shifts ahead in American population."

In a few words, that's the opportunity for our "Unlimited Partnership" in the Southern California District. Consider:

+ from 1970 — 1980, the Anglo population in Los Angeles County declined from 89 percent to 76 percent;

+ the Hispanic population of California increased by 92 percent to 4.5 million....

In his 1983 report, Frank Brundige, a field worker at La Santa Cruz and Bell Gardens, recorded that his experience as a lay worker in Hispanic ministry began on June 20 and concluded on August 21. One of his responsibilities was to read the lessons and prayers at the English service. In time, he also read the lessons at the Spanish service and attended Spanish Catechism, Youth Night, and Adult Bible Study, setting up audio-visual equipment and helping wherever possible. In Pastor Artigas's absence, he taught Catechism class. An unsuccessful attempt was made to start a Bible study group for English-speaking Hispanic youth. In the summers of 1985 and 1986, as a young seminarian, he was contracted for $700 to again help Rev. Artigas at La Santa Cruz and Rev. Stirdivant at Bell Gardens. Since he had a degree in child development, he worked in the preschool at Bell Gardens.

During 1987, Pastor Artigas reported that La Santa Cruz had 76 baptized souls and 30 communicant members. By May of that year, the Department of Mission Services decided to call Candidate Frank Brundige as missionary-at-large to the Southern California District for Hispanic ministry. Frank came to the Lutheran Church as a young adult after being raised in the Roman Catholic Church. After Frank's birth on December 12, 1959, in Glendale, California, he lived in El Monte and was baptized at Nativity Catholic Church. At the age of four, his parents moved to Alhambra where he attended San Gabriel Mission Catholic School for eight years. He attended high school and junior college at Don Bosco Tech in Rosemead, California. One of the pivotal things that changed his life was attending a Boy Scout summer camp on Catalina Island when he was 16. He continued participating in the camp for seven summers, eventually becoming the camp director. While at the camp

Rev. Frank Brundige at the time of his graduation from the seminary at Fort Wayne in 1987.

one summer, he met a young Baptist seminarian, the acting chaplain. This fellow brought up some questions that made him really see free grace in Jesus Christ. A New Testament the seminarian gave him helped Frank see the truth of the Gospel.

While Frank was at California State University Los Angeles, a friend informed him that Pastor Larry Stoterau of Emmaus Lutheran Church in Alhambra needed a person to work in the day-care center. After he obtained the job, he met Eleanor Hoffman, a fellow staff member, who would talk about the Christian faith. One day she opened the Bible to Ephesians 2:8 — 10 and explained the relationship of grace versus works. All of a sudden, he started finding excuses to attend church at Emmaus in Alhambra as well as Mass at the Catholic Church; he soon became a member of Emmaus. After he graduated from California State University Los Angeles in 1982 with a Bachelor of Arts degree in Child Development, he attended Christ College, Irvine, receiving another Bachelor of Arts in Liberal Arts. He continued his education at Concordia Seminary in Fort Wayne, Indiana, serving his vicarage at St. Matthew's in little Havana, Miami, Florida. Following his graduation from Fort Wayne, he was ordained and installed in a 3:00 p.m. service on June 28, 1987, at La Santa Cruz, Los Angeles. Preaching at the service was the Rev. Cristiano Artigas of La Santa Cruz Church with Rev. David Stirdivant, pastor of San Pedro y San Pablo Lutheran Church, Bell Gardens, installing him. The area pastors participating in the service were Rev. Felipe Luna of Trinity, Los Angeles; the Rev. William Brunold of Alhambra; and the Rev. John Jaster of Grace, Los Angeles.

In an interview some years ago, Pastor Brundige talked about his ministry. Since he lived close to the church, he said, "I feel safe, but I go where I know people. I can walk to church. I make pastoral calls at the laundromat. I see people in the community as neighbors and they see me that way, too. I live, breathe, and mix life and ministry. You begin to really understand their perspective and they really talk to you; it's acceptance and some of it comes from just living here. I listen, and in the process I get to share. My goal is that they know Christ. I don't drive hard; I don't extract promises. But they hear that the door is open ...and Christ cares."

When Pastor Brundige first arrived at La Santa Cruz, he stated, "I walked the streets and talked to the neighborhood kids who were writing on the church." The church parking lot was dirty, littered with broken glass, dirt, and writing on the walls. After he started working with those teenagers and talking to them, they began going to church helping him paint and loading the trunk of his Ford Fairmont with chunks of cement and old tires from the parking lot. They built a little retaining wall and planted some fruit trees in a small play area. They soon stopped writing on the church building and started going to a Friday Bible study, where they read a small portion of the Gospel of Mark, had it explained, and then spent time singing and praying. This Bible study not only attracted the youth but also their parents and neighbors of the church. After three years, there were about 60 people in church all because 17 or 20 youth, who were gang members, came in from the street. Pastor also spent time visiting young people in jail, going to court as an advocate, and talking to teenagers on the street; he walked the neighborhood, sharing the Gospel with people and strengthening them as Christians. He related, "I think the Word and Sacrament strengthens; you're a part of whatever process God is doing out there. Your church is bigger than your walls and that's really what you are doing in East Los Angeles."

A third of Pastor Brundige's church membership was gang members who were Spanish-speaking youth; most lived with their parents but a few were living on the street. That group of youth brought other people into the church because they thought if these kids were welcomed, they would also be welcomed. That was how he met Rey and became his legal guardian. Around Christmas when Pastor was at the church, he noticed that the old, abandoned car in the church parking lot had a young teenager sleeping in it. Since he had been talking to Rey and developing a friendship, he was able to get the boy back into school, going to church, and out of the gang. He became his foster father, bringing him into his home, raising him, and supporting him.

During Pastor Brundige's ministry, the Hispanic community was very transient with many of the people from La Santa Cruz, the mother congregation of Hispanic work, transferring to other Lutheran congregations throughout the District

as they moved from the East Los Angeles community, which had become an entrance point for many of the Hispanics coming from Mexico. He also observed the tension between gang loyalty and loyalty to the home and family in the Hispanic community. The idea of conducting a Saturday school came from the members of the parish, since Saturday was a traditional time for instruction of children and youth in the Hispanic culture. They pointed out to pastor that they wanted to be home with their families after church on Sunday, because there was strong loyalty to the home and family and to each other.

Even though La Santa Cruz was a mission congregation, it returned 10 percent of its budget to the District and made regular mission offerings supporting several smaller ministries, as it was able. They believed in putting into practice what they asked others to do. Pastor Brundige advocated having a Christian day school as a primary key to acceptance, involvement, and growth of La Santa Cruz in the neighborhood. In order to have a school, financial assistance was necessary to make it become a reality. The day school teachers were the most effective when they had an on-going relationship with the congregation and community, as the teacher was a highly respected member of the community. The parish was saving $125 a month as seed money for a school. He felt that a school was one of the best witnesses to bring the community close to the church, as the school demonstrated the church cares about children. Since the community was so poor, a District subsidy was needed in order to make this a possibility, but the school never became a reality.

At the beginning of 1988, Pastor Brundige was assisting both congregations at Bell Gardens and La Santa Cruz while Pastor Artigas was attending chaplaincy training school and Pastor Stirdivant was hospitalized. By October, Pastor Artigas had accepted a call to serve as chaplain in the U.S. Army and was commissioned on November 6, 1988, at La Santa Cruz, to serve as a chaplain in the U.S. Army for three years. Pastor Brundige also served as volunteer chaplain at the Central Juvenile Hall in Los Angeles. He conducted the chapel service at Zion in Maywood for the Christian day school during the interim period between Pastor Mather and Pastor Kay.

In the summer of 1990, Pastor Brundige received a call to become pastor of San Pedro y San Pablo in Bell Gardens. He met with leaders in order to consider the call. Through this productive

Rev. Frank Brundige becomes Pastor of La Santa Cruz in 1987.

and helpful meeting, he made the decision to accept the call. During the months of July and August, he began to work in Bell Gardens, as well as doing an interim ministry at La Santa Cruz and conducting Bible classes and services in Baldwin Park, a preaching mission which was growing and had great potential as a church.

After Victor Artavia had declined the call to serve as a contracted lay-pastor at La Santa Cruz, the Mission Department contacted Pastor Ron Kusel of First Lutheran of Long Beach about Jesús Martinez, lay minister at First, working at La Santa Cruz. Since it was agreeable with First, Long Beach, and with Jesús, he was contracted as lay minister, meeting with Pastor Brundige in the latter part of the summer to convey information relating to La Santa Cruz so that he could begin his ministry. He was dedicated as pastor and began working alone on August 19. He and Pastor Brundige met about once a week as their situations had enough in common to work together on worship materials and other needs.

Pastor Martinez was born in San Pedro, Coahuila, Mexico, on January 2, 1938. In 1944, his family moved to El Paso, Texas, where they lived for one year before moving to Los Angeles; in Los Angeles, he received his education, graduating from Fremont High School in south Los Angeles. As a boy, he was raised a Roman Catholic. After graduating from high school, he attended East Los Angeles Community College graduating in 1959. While attending college, he worked as an x-ray technician. He served in the Army as a chaplain assistant to a Presbyterian chaplain, typing bulletins and also counseling soldiers. While serving in that capacity, he met a Lutheran chaplain who assisted him in his time of difficulty and made a deep impression on him, causing him to become a Lutheran later in life. On November 30, 1963, he was united in marriage to Katherine Flores with their union producing three children, Paul, Eric, and Reuben.

In a September 25, 1990, letter to Rev. Ken Behnken, assistant to the president — missions, Pastor Brundige again stressed the need to keep La Santa Cruz open. He stated, "We are in a prime Hispanic (Mexican) crossroads in an established and traditional neighborhood. Numbers may not climb at the church, but many people pass through and return when there is a need to re-establish bearing. Needs are great, so are the opportunities, so is the Gospel's relevence and power. Finally, thank you for the privilege, blessing, and

opportunity of serving in East Los Angeles at La Santa Cruz. There is a piece of me that I have left there and a piece of it that I carry." Also in the letter, he stated that the average Sunday attendance in the Spanish service was 50 with 6 in the English service. In the Bible study classes, he had around 4 in English and in Spanish there were usually 14. The Ash Wednesday Service was attended by 100 people while the Good Friday Service had 60. The Catechism classes had between 7 to 15 students and 2 teachers with 3 youth confirmed. In July, a Vacation Bible School was conducted with 12 students and 2 teachers and a church picnic was held with 2 families attending. In July and August, instead of having separate Spanish and English services each Sunday, there was one bilingual service conducted averaging 41 per Sunday. In the middle of August, membership was recorded at 28 confirmed members with 9 baptized members for a total of 37 souls. He accounted for the transfers and losses of active families as follows: 10 households were referred to LCMS churches, 6 households went to Roman Catholic churches, 6 households went to other Christian churches, one man became a Jehovah's Witness, one household went to the Mormon church, and 2 households stopped going to church.

Since Pastor Martinez owned his own home in Santa Fe Springs, the District Board of Directors in its September 26, 1990, meeting decided to sell the La Santa Cruz parsonage and distribute the proceeds in the following manner, as requested by the congregation: 10 percent ($13,000) to be given to the Pacific Southwest District for use in general mission and ministry activity; 35 percent ($50,000) to be used as a partial reimbursement to the Pacific Southwest District for subsidy support of La Santa Cruz through the years; and 55 percent ($55,000) to be used to create the "La Santa Cruz Professional Workers' Support Fund." These funds were to be invested jointly by the District and La Santa Cruz in Lutheran Church Extension Fund at the best possible rate of interest. Earnings were to flow to the congregation and District as a means to offset the costs of providing a professional worker to serve the La Santa Cruz congregation. As long as the salary for the worker was paid directly by the District, the earnings would go to the District; when the congregation was able to assume the cost to support the professional worker, the earnings would go to the congregation.

In Pastor Martinez's first report to the District, he wrote that since he was installed as pastor on

Jesús Martinez is dedicated as Pastor of La Santa Cruz in 1990.

August 19 and through October 31, 1990, he had three weddings and four Baptisms; there were two worship services on Sunday, 9:30 a.m. in English and 12:00 noon in Spanish with Pastor Stirdivant playing the music for the Spanish services. Every other week, he led a Bible study in Baldwin Park with Rev. Brundige and on Fridays at La Santa Cruz; they had a family night Bible study, viewing a filmstrip on the life of Christ, singing, and praying. He also taught Bible studies at the homes of several families. The monthly receipts were $1,000 for the rental of the parish hall from a preschool program at La Santa Cruz and $400 from Odon's Meat Company for weekly use of the church parking lot. The total income for September was $1,957 and for October $2,591. He was enrolled in the Theological Education by Extension (TEE) Program of the District, studying sermon preparation and a music course. By the end of December 1990, he would be eligible to become a certified lay worker of the church. He was in the process of getting to know the people on the prospect list with a goal of gathering "a core of loyal, stable, Mexican and Latino Lutheran Christians at La Santa Cruz so that we can carry out an effective ministry to the community."

In his January 22, 1992, report, Pastor Martinez stated that the Lord was blessing the Mexican-American ministry where the attendance had grown from 3 in September 1990 to between 15 and 25 in December 1991. There were four young families attending the English service who were second generation Mexicans, preferring English services, as they did not speak Spanish. Most of the young families lived in Santa Fe Springs or in the Whittier area and were friends of Pastor Martinez's sons. Through his son Paul and wife Cynthia, the Lord used them to bless other young couples, and the growth in the English service was through their efforts. A Sunday school was developed for small children with Pastor Martinez's wife, Katy, teaching and teenage girls serving as helpers. An adult Bible study was to be started in February 1992. The Spanish ministry was in a transition period as several families moved from the area and were unable to attend because they lacked transportation. The attendance went from 50 in September 1990 to between 15 and 25 in December 1991. Pastor Stirdivant was still supplying music for the service, but since he lived in Yucaipa, he was often unable to be in Los Angeles. There was a need for a musician in the Spanish service.

Pastor Martinez continued to lead a worship service and Bible study in homes in Baldwin Park every Wednesday, and he conducted Sunday worship in Spanish. He led the adult Bible study, while one of the young people taught the children's Bible study in English. He concluded by saying, "I thank the Lord for blessing us. We are growing spiritually, and several leaders are emerging. It was their idea to take up an offering and they have used much wisdom in administering the monies. One of my dreams is to develop cell group leaders to lead small group worship and caring groups."

Pastor Martinez stated in his October 23, 1993, report that, for the most part, the congregation was serving a very transient community with about four congregations having come and gone. They served many hurting people. He gave a case in point with Mr. Silva:

When we first met him [Mr. Silva], he was homeless, sleeping in a van. He was paranoid, thinking people were conspiring to do him harm. He avoided people, and preferred being alone. Later he told me that he had been divorced and had been an alcoholic. The day I met him, he was hungry so I fed him, gave him a couple of hours work, and had a short devotion with him. Slowly, he began coming to worship with us. He would drop by during the week, and we would have a short devotion and pray for his needs and the needs of the congregation. After a couple of months, one of the families offered him part-time work and a room in which to sleep. Mr. Silva would help clean the church grounds. He responded to the love of the congregation. We discovered that he was an educated man. He participated in the worship services reading the scriptures. He reads like a professional actor. We also discovered that he had years of artistic training and experience. He hadn't drawn or painted for years. The love of Christ and the love of the congregation inspired him to draw again and he left us a couple of artistic treasures. Mr. Silva received word that his mother was very ill. He has returned to Ecuador to see his mother and to heal the broken relationship with his brother. We miss Mr. Silva. Although he was only with us for about eight months, he has left a lasting impression on our lives.

He further stated, "We serve a hurting and passing community. Some, we only see for a day and others for a few months. Still others, who are around for a couple of years, are baptized, confirmed, and as they become financially able, move out to the suburbs." The challenge was to evangelize, nurture, and equip Christian leaders who had roots in "our neighborhood to serve the many people who are in spiritual darkness all around us." He said that he was becoming part of the community. In September 1993, a mother from the neighborhood asked him to do a memorial service for her son who had been shot while sitting in a car in front of his house. The young man, a member of the White Fence gang in the barrio, would have celebrated his 24th birthday. About 30 young people attended the graveside service with about 40 people attending the memorial service at La Santa Cruz. Pastor's prayer was "that the Lord of the harvest would bring all who heard God's Word to believe that Jesus Christ is their Lord and Savior too!"

On September 26, 1993, nine children received their First Communion after being instructed in the Apostle's Creed, the outline for the course of study, and Bible stories to tell of Jesus, with *Luther's Small Catechism* explaining the basic doctrines of the church. Six of the nine children who made their First Communion were from Baldwin Park with about five families from Baldwin Park who continued to worship at La Santa Cruz. Much of his ministry was done in the community, sharing God's Word, and showing love in the homes, in hospitals, parking lots, porches, alleys, restaurants, or just "hanging around" where the people were congregated. He said that sometimes he felt overwhelmed by the problems of alcoholism and drug abuse in the neighborhood. He had started an hour of prayer on Friday evenings.

In 1996, the congregation developed the following three-year plan:

THREE-YEAR VISION STATEMENT

By 1999, La Santa Cruz Lutheran Church will have constructed a solid foundation of program services that attracts the unchurched and develop faithful disciples of Jesus Christ. These programs will range from Christian Worship, Christian Growth, social and culture, health and safety, job skills and employment, social services, and leadership development. This will be augmented by an effective outreach program designed to locate, identify, reach, and influence our target population. A comprehensive fundraising plan will be implemented to support programs and outreach efforts.

MISSION STATEMENT

We, the members of La Santa Cruz Lutheran Church redeemed by Christ, thank God for choosing us to be His own. We humbly submit to Christ and His Word. We are committed to building a united loving congregation by actively seeking the unchurched, so that they too may know Christ and have the abundant life, which He gives. We will offer, and participate in programs that promote individual spiritual growth and strengthen family relationships. We will be a loving community of people that shares our Christian life and faith with one another, our neighbors, and the world at large.

In order to implement the goal of reaching the unchurched, La Santa Cruz established the program entitled "I AM HE", with a goal to identify, locate, reach and influence a target population around the church to become disciples of Jesus Christ and members of the church. There was great spiritual darkness in the community surrounding La Santa Cruz due to the fusion of superficial Catholicism and ancient superstitions and rites were brought by Mexican immigrants. Since most of the target population did not have a true knowledge of God and His Word and were unchurched, demonstrating idolatry, evil, and sinful acts such as abortion, rape, incest, domestic violence, unwed-birth, drug and alcohol abuse, robbery, and murder, the need for a Gospel outreach and a Lutheran presence in the community was great.

Starting in 1997, the main emphasis would be to reach the critical target group of 50,000 people located in postal zone 90023. The people there were primarily of Mexican ancestry, poverty stricken, Spanish-speaking, under-employed with dysfunctional lifestyles. The major focus would be on Mexican families with children but would also include couples, singles, youths, and seniors. The objective was to reach many of the 50,000 residents of Boyle Heights within the next three years and have 180 new families join the church by the end of that period.

In Pastor Martinez's March 12, 1997, quarterly ministry report, he stated that for the previous

In 1999, La Santa Cruz has a Three Year Vision Plan for work in the parish.

three years a bilingual worship service was conducted on Sundays at 11:00 a.m. with the congregation singing two hymns in English and two hymns in Spanish, reading the Sunday texts in Spanish and reading the Gospel in English. The sermon was preached in Spanish and summarized in English. Since this approach did not seem to fit the needs of the community, the congregation felt that what was needed was a worship service in Spanish that communicated the Gospel to the hearts of the Mexican people and another worship service in English that satisfied the needs of the English-speaking Mexicans who lived in the neighborhood. The average attendance at worship services varied from between 15 to 35. The last Sunday in February, an English service was held at 1:00 p.m. with seven people attending. The week prior to the service 200 invitations to worship were distributed.

Pastor concluded his report by telling of his pastoral activities: In the past three months, he had marriage counseling with eight couples, working in depth with two couples. Once a week, he taught a four-month ESL class with seven adults; three students attended worship regularly at La Santa Cruz. On March 9, five of the students worshiped the Lord at the regular worship service. On Saturdays, he taught Catechism classes to 10 children where he presented a simple Bible story, prayed, played, sang, and did a craft. The children were growing spiritually and enjoyed going.

He concluded his report with the following story:

> When I first met Jaime five years ago, he was an alcoholic. He drank hard liquor every day. He worked every day and was able to carry on a conversation. Jaime lives near the church. I sought him out and became his friend. We went out for lunch a couple of times. One day when we were at his house, he asked me if I would hear his confession. I said I would. He confessed sins that had been burdening him for many years. I gave him absolution of his sins and assured him that God forgave him all his sins. Jaime is presently studying for his Confirmation. He worships regularly at La Santa Cruz. He no longer drinks any liquor.

At La Santa Cruz, Pastor worked in a very transient community. One day as he was walking up the wooden stairs from the parking lot to the alley

At Las Santa Cruz, Pastor Martinez worked in a very transient community.

with a 19-year-old fellow, he noticed that the wall that had just been painted had graffiti sprayed all over it. In disgust, he made a comment to the young fellow about it. The young man bowed his head confessing he was the one who had done it. Pastor told him that he needed to put such childish things away. The man later married, had three children, and owns a video store in the area.

One evening while Pastor was at church, a young man came into the church and asked him to drive out demons he claimed he had. After Pastor asked him why he thought he had demons, the fellow told of all the vile and terrible things he had done in his life. After hearing all these appalling things, Pastor was convinced that he was indeed possessed by the demons. He told him of the story of Jesus casting out the demons and asked if the man believed that Jesus could cast the demons from him. Since the man believed that could happen, Pastor commanded the demons leave "right now." As Pastor could see that nothing visibly had happened, he asked the man if the demons had left and he responded that three had left. From that moment on, he was a changed man even coming to church each Sunday. Since he had such a vile reputation, the congregation didn't want to associate with him and didn't treat him well. He began attending the Pentecostal church not far from La Santa Cruz and he became a missionary to Mexico.

While at La Santa Cruz, Pastor Martinez also ministered to the people in Baldwin Park. During this time period, Pastor Brundige was helpful to him in teaching him how to do ministry in a Spanish community sharing with him aspects of the Mexican culture. In 1997, he was contracted to do ministry at Holy Cross in La Puente, which was situated in a middle class Hispanic neighborhood.

In 1997, La Santa Cruz celebrated its fortieth anniversary, continuing to be a viable ministry for the Hispanic community, which was led by Pastor Raul Saldaña. When he left Maywood to go to La Santa Cruz in East Los Angeles in 1997, the Maywood parish died. Three families from Maywood went with him, as there was no one left at La Santa Cruz after Pastor Martinez left. He had to begin to build a new congregation from scratch placing fliers on doors, walking the streets, meeting people, knocking on doors, and doing follow-up calls on relatives of members. He placed only biblical pictures representing the Stations of the Cross in the church. He gathered people in Bible study to help them understand the true nature of the church and what the Bible said about the Virgin Mary, when people asked why there wasn't a statue of her in the church.

Pastor Saldaña was born on a farm in Tepechitlán, Zacatecas, Mexico, on November 11, 1950, where he was raised with six brothers and four sisters. When he attended a Catholic school in Mexico, one nun read the whole Bible to the class in the course of a year introducing the Bible stories to him as a young child. His brother, who became a priest, sent a large illustrated Bible to the family home where Raul could learn more of the Bible. His brother studied at a seminary in San Luis Potosi, Mexico, where Raul also went to study for the priesthood for one month. He would assist his brother with the Mass even becoming a deacon in the church. In the 1970s, he worked building homes with a group in Mexico that assisted the poor. He married Maria del Carmen on March 23, 1975, with their union blessed with three children two of whom died in infancy. Their son, Raul V. Saldaña who was born in 1982, now works in a bank in Los Angeles. In 1977, a cousin invited Pastor to come to the United States to work. After a few months time, Carmen also came to be with him in America. He eventually became a gardener, establishing his own business.

When Pastor Saldaña went to the Bell Gardens church to inquire about showing a video on the problems in El Salvador, Pastor Stirdivant allowed it to be shown one afternoon and introduced him and Carmen to the Lutheran church. They soon became involved in the church, as they were very unhappy in the Catholic Church. In 1984, he was installed as a deacon in the church. In 1990, he became interested in the TEE program through Pastor Artigas.

To help promote good stewardship at La Santa Cruz each Sunday, Pastor Saldaña placed information in the bulletin about tithing and giving to the Lord. The resolution for January of 2003 was that everyone should attend Bible study to grow in the faith. In order to keep the church on a sound financial footing, two of the church's classrooms were rented to the International Institute of Los Angeles to run a preschool on the church property. During 1999, he conducted four services on Sundays, two at La Santa Cruz, one at Wayside Chapel, and one at Trinity, Los Angeles. In 1998 through 1999, he started a mission at Wayside Chapel, an old Methodist church on Ford Boulevard and Caesar Chavez owned by an elderly lady who let him use the building rent-free. He gathered 20 people for worship services that lasted only one year. He was also the vacancy pastor at Trinity in Los Angeles from October 1998 to April 1999 when Pastor Alfonso Conrado was called to Panorama City. After Pastor Conrado's departure, leaving only two families, Pastor Saldaña was able to build attendance up to 20 people a Sunday before Deacon Edgar Arroyo arrived to take over the Trinity parish. One of the problems in Hispanic ministry is that when a pastor leaves, the people in the congregation either follow him or leave the church altogether.

In a 1975 report, Pastor Stirdivant declared, "Ministering at La Santa Cruz is like preaching to a passing parade." In the twenty years, East Los Angeles hadn't changed, as it was the port of

> In 1997, La Santa Cruz celebrates its fortieth anniversary and is led by Pastor Raul Saldaña.

Mrs. Saldaña, Pastor Stirdivant, and Pastor Raul Saldaña in front of the church in 2003.

The congregation at a Maundy Thursday service in April of 1998.

La Santa Cruz in 2003 with Pastor Stirdivant, Mrs. Saldaña, and Pastor Saldaña.

The chancel of La Santa Cruz with large statue of Christ given by Trinity, San Bernardino, at the time of the church's dedication in 1957. The statue was in Trinity's first church built in 1914.

"Ministering at La Santa Cruz is like preaching to a passing parade," declared Pastor Stirdivant in a 1975 report.

entry for thousands of Latin Americans who arrived there each year, not only from Mexico, but from all of the Spanish-speaking countries as well. Surprisingly, East Los Angeles has become even more densely populated and more Spanish speaking than it was 40 years ago when La Santa Cruz began its work. Membership listed persons from Cuba, Puerto Rico, and almost every Central and South American country, except Brazil. La Santa Cruz has always been there to welcome arriving immigrants as well as to serve those who have chosen to settle in the neighborhood. La Santa Cruz has been a feeder congregation for many Hispanic ministries throughout the District.

One large change that had taken place since the birth of La Santa Cruz was that by 1997, the District had 19 Hispanic ministries with 17 workers. This was a dramatic increase from one congregation with one lone worker, Rev. David Stirdivant, who was recognized in 1995 by Concordia Seminary in St. Louis with an Honorary Doctor of Letters for his groundbreaking Hispanic work on the West Coast. At the time, the programs in the District to train Hispanics for ministry were the TEE program (Theological Education by Extension) through Concordia University at River Forest, Illinois, which included five students from the Pacific Southwest District, and the Institute Biblico Concordia de las dos Californias. That institute trains students for ministry and was directed by Dr. Esaúl Salomón of Chula Vista. Students had the option to continue their studies certification program at Concordia University in Irvine or through one of the two synodical theological seminaries at either Fort Wayne or St. Louis. According to government statistics at the time, the Hispanic population of California would grow to 31 million by 2040, representing half of California's total population. The need was great for Hispanic ministers to take the Gospel to the growing Hispanic population in the Pacific Southwest District.

I love Thy kingdom Lord,
The house of Thine abode,
The Church our blest Redeemer saved
With His own precious blood

A New Beginning

Bell Gardens Lutheran Church
Iglesia Luterana San Pedro Y San Pablo
Bell Gardens, California

"Though thy beginning was small, yet thy latter end should greatly increase."

— JOB 8:7

The name, Bell Gardens, evokes visions of bright, plump, red strawberries, delicious oranges, and rows of bountiful, green vegetables. Despite this pastoral connotation of Bell Gardens, the city is a residential community surrounded by a sea of light industry. Although the city's mostly blue-collar, Hispanic residents had an average income that made Bell Gardens, once known as Billy Goat Acres, the third-poorest suburb in the nation in 1996, the civic finances of the community were very solid due to the revenue from legalized draw poker.

There could be no history of Bell Gardens without including the story of the Lugo Spanish Land Grant that encompassed what is now the city of Bell Gardens and is a vital and colorful part of the area's history. An important figure among the early Spanish settlers of the region and a cavalry corporal for the King of Spain was Francisco Lugo, whose son, Don Antonio Maria Lugo (1783–1860), was granted 11 square leagues of land in 1810 by the King of Spain in appreciation for his father's service to the crown. This vast estate was known as the Rancho San Antonio Land Grant and extended from the low range of hills, which separated it from the San Gabriel Valley, to the old Dominguez Ranch at its south, and from the eastern boundary of the pueblo of Los Angeles to the San Gabriel River. The Lugo Family began construction in 1795 on their casa that became known as Casa de Rancho San Antonio or later, the Henry Gage Mansion. The house, located at 7000 East Gage Avenue in Bell Gardens, was built to qualify the younger Lugo, a former Spanish colonial soldier, for a land grant

from the Spanish crown. In 1810, Antonio Maria Lugo completed the house and received the grant, naming his new grant Rancho San Antonio. The ranch eventually grew to encompass 29,513 acres, including what are now the cities of Bell Gardens, Commerce, and parts of Bell, Cudahy, Lynwood, Montebello, South Gate, Vernon, and East Los Angeles. When California became part of the United States in 1850, Lugo, as did all recipients of Spanish/Mexican land grants, began losing portions of his land to the growing population of Yankee newcomers. The ranch adobe, however, continued to be owned and used by the Lugo family.

Don Antonio María Lugo died at the age of 85 in 1860. By 1865, most of the Lugo ranch, divided among five sons and three daughters, had been sold for as little as one dollar per acre. The original adobe ranch home, however, remained in the family. In 1880, attorney Henry T. Gage, a transplant from Michigan, married one of Lugo's great-granddaughters, Francis "Fanny" Rains. The original adobe ranch home was given to Gage as a wedding dowry, and became known as the Gage Mansion. In 1898, Gage was elected governor of California serving in that office from 1899 to 1903. In 1910, he was appointed by President William Howard Taft to serve as U.S. minister to Portugal. He resigned after only one year due to his wife's health problems. Gage lived in the adobe ranch house until his death in 1924. In the twentieth century, the Gage Mansion was all that remained of the once grand Rancho San Antonio. In 1983, the Casa Mobile Home Park, a cooperative of mobile home owners renting lots on the property, purchased the land and the house from their ailing landlord. Although they were aware of the historical significance of the old house, they had no means of maintaining it. In 1987, then Bell Gardens City Councilwoman Letha Wiles began working to get the house listed on the state historical registry, making it eligible for maintenance grants. The Gage mansion is now California Historical Site Number 984.

As the land grant was handed down from generation to generation, it was divided among offspring and eventually parceled and sold to people outside the Lugo family. Don Antonio's son, Vincente, (1820–1889) built his adobe dwelling in the 1850s on five and one half acres, known as the Lugo Ranch, situated on the modern day intersection of Gage and Garfield avenues in the city of Bell Gardens. Before the end of the 1870s, 40-acre tracts had replaced much of the original land grant. By 1880, cattle raising had been replaced by agriculture as the most important local industry.

When parts of the area were a vast orange grove in 1924, developer John Joseph Woodworth built himself a spectacular mansion with the intention of constructing other large homes, envisioning a community that would rival Beverly Hills. He was forced to scrap his ambitious plans because of the Great Depression. Instead of the wealthy, Woodworth's community was settled by Midwesterners and Dust Bowl refugees who sought a better life and ended up living in piano crates, tents, and tar paper shacks on vacant lots. In 1930, vegetable gardens that had been developed by Japanese entrepreneurs were subdivided and named after nearby Bell, which was founded by James G. Bell and his son, Alphonzo Edward Bell. The Bells also founded Santa Fe Springs and Bel Air.

During the 1940s and 1950s, the area was under the Los Angeles County government's control, which granted blanket zoning allowing everything from factories to homes to be built in proximity. When the city was incorporated in 1961, it inherited a planning mess but set about to rectify it. Residents wanted their city to contain neat geographical areas designated for business, homes, and light manufacturing. A decade later, in an attempt to clean up the hodgepodge, the city changed commercial zoning in predominantly residential areas to residential zoning. Officials gave commercial property owners and operators in the rezoned areas a two-year grace

> Developer, John Joseph Woodworth, envisions Bell Gardens would rival Beverly Hills.

The Lugo family in front of their adobe home in Bell Gardens built in 1849 by Vincente Lugo, son of Don Antonio Lugo, circa 1890. (SHADES OF L.A. ARCHIVES/Los Angeles Public Library)

period before the new regulations were enforced. In the 1980s, the city launched an ambitious redevelopment program, tearing down more than 300 homes and leveling entire neighborhoods for park space and commercial development.

As tensions ran high, a grassroots coalition of mostly Latino residents confronted an all-white City Council in 1991, accusing the members of trying to reduce Bell Gardens' Latino population by legislating lower legal densities in neighborhoods. Within months, the "No Rezoning Committee" ousted four of the five council members, bringing to power the first Latino council majority in Bell Gardens' history. Regardless of the city's political turmoil, the municipality remained stable with tax revenue from the large and popular Bicycle Club Casino, although its proceeds have declined over the past few years. According to the 2000 census, Bell Gardens had 44,054 inhabitants, 93.37 percent Hispanic and 4.37 percent Anglo.

By 1940, a number of Lutherans had established residence in the area and were worshiping at Zion Lutheran Church in Maywood. Seeing a need for a Lutheran presence in Bell Gardens, Pastor Roland Finke of Maywood decided to start a Sunday school in Bell Gardens. He persuaded a number of Maywood people and those from Bell Gardens to canvass the area in April and May of 1940. Following the canvass, the American Legion Hall was rented for $8 a month where the first service was conducted on May 19 and averaged about 20 in the Sunday school and between 10 and 20 at the church services for the few months it existed. Since the American Legion Hall facilities were entirely inadequate, no other hall was available, and the Maywood congregation was also a young, struggling mission, all work in Bell Gardens ceased.

Another attempt was made in 1944 to establish a Lutheran church in Bell Gardens, when the area was partially canvassed by vicars Paul Lemke and Carl Last. At that time, there were about 18,000 people living in the area with 17 churches: a Latter Day Saints, a Catholic, a Christian Reformed, a Presbyterian, a Nazarene, two Church of Christ, five Baptists, and six Pentecostal. An Episcopal

The first pastor of Bell Gardens Lutheran Church, Rev. Wayne Thomsen (1945–1954). (Pacific Southwest District Archives)

pastor began services in 1947 but was not successful in establishing a church. The first Lutheran service conducted by Vicar Last in Bell Gardens on October 1, 1944, had an attendance of 11 and a Sunday school of 54. The average attendance for 1944 was 17 in church services and 29 in Sunday school.

Wayne Thomsen entered the field on February 16, 1945, and in March was ordained and installed as District missionary of the Bell Gardens Lutheran Church. He was born in Nebraska and graduated from high school in that state. He attended St. Paul's College at Concordia, Missouri, and Concordia Seminary at St. Louis. Before going to Bell Gardens, he spent 10 months as assistant pastor at Trinity Lutheran Church in Los Angeles. He returned to the East to wed Evelyn Firnhaber, who had graduated from the College of Dental Hygiene at the University of Minnesota. While in Bell Gardens, their union was blessed with five children, Lynne, Steven, Gayle, Craig and Jill. Rev. Thomsen had planned to enter the foreign mission field, but a combination of circumstances guided him away from foreign countries and led him to Bell Gardens.

By June of 1945, a duplex was purchased on Colmar Avenue with one side remodeled for a chapel, seating 70 people, and the other side became a three-room apartment for Rev. Thomsen and his bride (the three rooms served as home, church office, and Bible class meeting room). On June 10, 1945, the first service was held in the chapel; a double garage that provided four Sunday school rooms and was also used as a meeting hall, augmented the facilities. By 1949, the average attendance had increase to 100 necessitating the need for two services with the Sunday school averaging 55.

When the congregation was organized in January 1947, it had 59 communicants. By 1950, the parish had grown to 180 communicants, of which 75 percent were confirmands or Lutherans regained for membership, with a Sunday school enrollment of around 150. Though the original plan was to use the duplex as living quarters for a day school teacher and the pastor and to erect a combination

Wayne Thomsen becomes the first pastor of Bell Gardens Lutheran Church.

The attractive church facilities of Bell Gardens that were built with volunteer labor and dedicated on October 15, 1950. (Pacific Southwest District Archives)

The first Easter Sunrise service is held in 1949 at the Gage Drive-in Theater.

church and school building in 1945, it was not until October 15, 1950, that a permanent church building was completed. This building was built almost entirely by voluntary labor at a cost of about $22,000 and was valued at over $40,000. The building, though beautiful and churchly, accommodated 320 people for church services; the combination church and parish hall, with an office, and Sunday school rooms were inadequate. The building lacked about $1,000 worth of equipment at the time. It was hoped by the congregation that the duplex unit, on the same lot as the church, could be used for Sunday school, meeting rooms, parish hall and, perhaps, as a day school. This seemed especially advisable because the church property measured only 195' × 70' and would not

accommodate another building. Since funds were unavailable in the treasuries of both the congregation and the Church Extension Department to acquire a parsonage, the three small rooms served as home for Pastor Thomsen's family of five (with another child expected) and was inadequate. The Church Extension Department, therefore, made $1,000 available to the congregation to convert the duplex into a three-bedroom home with the congregation augmenting the loan with $400 contributions from members. In order to accommodate the huge Vacation Bible School in 1948, a massive canvas tent was placed on the church property for the summer event. The first outdoor Easter Sunrise service was held in 1949 at the Gage Drive-in Theater, just before the theater's formal opening. This new venue was filled with cars and people who had gone to worship the risen Savior on that Easter morning.

In Pastor Thomsen's 1951 report to the Mission Board, he stated, "Bell Gardens is a community of 20,000 in an industrial area. Alcoholic, marital, criminal, and juvenile delinquency problems are among the highest in number on record." By January 1952, the church became self-supporting and was no longer a mission congregation. In March of 1953, a beautiful oil painting, "The Calling of the Apostles," was done by the artist B. Brownell McGrew of Palm Springs and placed in the church. Church members were pleased to have an original painting by McGrew, an outstanding master painter of mountains and lakes. The scene, por-

The children of the huge Vacation Bible School in the summer of 1948 gathered in front of the massive canvass tent placed on the church property to accommodate the group. (Pacific Southwest District Archives)

traying Jesus as the central figure with the apostles coming down the mountainside to join Him, gives a third dimension feeling. It still hangs in the narthex. Pastor Thomsen left Bell Gardens in 1954.

The second pastor to serve Bell Gardens was Rev. Reinhold H. Kalthoff who was born in Alma, Missouri, on March 18, 1909. He received his elementary education in the Christian day school of Trinity Lutheran Church in that community. In the fall of 1924, he enrolled at St. Paul's College, Concordia, Missouri, and graduated from Concordia Seminary, Saint Louis, Missouri, in 1934. That fall he accepted a temporary assignment to the northern New Mexico mission field, with preaching stations at Raton, Springer, and Dawson, New Mexico. On November 12, 1935, he was ordained and installed at Raton, New Mexico. Also that year he married Marie Louise Bockelman of Dallas, Texas. They were the parents of two children, Robert and Ruth Jean (Mrs. Donald Detviler).

In 1940, he accepted a call to Grace Church of El Dorado, Kansas, where he remained until 1943, when he was commissioned as chaplain in the United States Army. His military tour of duty took him over most of the United States and into the Pacific, serving with the 27th Infantry Combat Division. In 1946 following his separation from the military, he accepted a call as institutional chaplain in the Leavenworth-Topeka, Kansas, area, with the major portion of his work confined to the prisons located in that vicinity. In 1950, he accepted a call to serve as institutional chaplain for the Colorado District in the Denver area and also as chaplain of the Lutheran TB Sanatorium at Wheat Ridge, Colorado. In 1954, he was called as pastor of Bell Gardens Lutheran Church. While there, he also served as speaker for the "Southern California Lutheran Hour" and was a delegate to the House of Delegates for the Southern California Hospital Association. In 1958, he accepted the call to First Lutheran Church in Culver City. Before leaving Bell Gardens, plans had been made for an expansion of the Sunday school facilities, as the present one was totally inadequate.

By the end of 1958, the third pastor, Rev. La Mar Miller, formerly of Victorville, was installed as pastor of the Bell Gardens Church. He began his ministerial career by serving the dual parishes at Barstow and Victorville for two years and then he served only Victorville for an additional three years. He and his wife, Eunice, had two children, Robbyn and La Mar Jr. His ministry at Bell Gar-

dens was very fruitful with the congregational membership peaking at 250 communicants.

After a year of negotiations with the owner and fervent prayers by the congregation, the property east of the church building was purchased. The realization for larger facilities, Faith Annex, finally became a reality with the ground breaking on January 21, 1962, at the close of the regular morning service. Because of the heavy rain that morning, the congregation remained inside the church while the pastor and building committee broke ground during the singing of a special ground-breaking hymn. The men then returned to the church, presenting the shovel before the altar, witnessing that the ground had been broken. Pastor Miller declared all had been begun in the name of the Triune God and the various men of the building committee represented various phases or groups: James Cook, chairman of the committee, broke ground as chairman of the volunteer workers who would build the annex; Omar Garvin broke ground in the name of the entire congregation; Arvid Gorder represented the stewardship program of the congregation; Sy Reddemann, the founders of the congregation; Guy Sagert, the Sunday school; Louis Summers, Sr., represented the architect and all those who drew and completed the plans; and George Whitehouse, the neighboring congregations of Circuit Nine and of the Southern California District of The Lutheran Church — Missouri Synod.

The congregation named the annex Faith Annex because it was only by faith that the program could begin. The 5,600-square foot Faith Annex was incorporated into the plant by a lobby attached to the original building. The new building had two classrooms, which were to be used for a parochial school in the future when the congregation was financially able, a smaller meeting room, a parish hall, a kitchen, restroom facilities, and office space.

Rev. Reinhold H. Kalthoff, the second pastor of Bell Gardens Lutheran Church. (1954–1958) (Pacific Southwest District Archives)

Rev. La Mar Miller, the third pastor at Bell Gardens. (1958–1970) (Pacific Southwest District Archives)

The new annex formed a U-shape with the center patio used for outdoor activities. Most of the work was done by volunteer labor with the cost less than $50,000 to construct the building that was valued at well over $75,000 without furnishings. With a parking variance granted for a lighted and paved parking lot located at the back of the property, by faith, the congregation was prepared to build, using largely volunteer labor and salvaged lumber for the rough construction of the building. Members of the congregation drew the plans for the building with the consultation of Dennis Wehmueller, architect.

On June 9, 1963, Pastor La Mar Miller conducted the Service of Dedication for the congregation's new educational facilities. The children of the Sunday school sang the festival hymn, "Come, Children, and Join in Our Festival Song." Rev. Reinhold H. Kalthoff, former pastor from 1954 to 1958 and then pastor of First Lutheran, Culver City, spoke at the afternoon service as guest speaker. Assisting in the dedicatory service were James Cook, building chairman; Raymond Biemeret, chairman of the congregation and the building committee; Guy B. Sagert, Sy Reddemann; and George Whitehouse. Following the service an informal reception was held in the new parish hall with the Walther Leaguers and Boy Scouts serving as tour guides.

The next plan of the congregation was a renovation of the parish hall-chapel interior, built in 1951, and the addition of padded pews. The final service in the chapel was held on October 3, 1966, with Kirco beginning the renovations on October 4, and Dennis Wehmueller serving as architect for the project. In order to extend the chancel the entire width of the building, two interior walls had to be removed with the addition of a large beam in the ceiling to support the roof. Besides the new chancel furnishings, the renovation also included new floor tile, carpeting, pews, and a two-manual Allen organ. The newly renovated house of worship was dedicated on a rainy Sunday, December 12, 1966. Even with the rain, the spirit of joy and thanksgiving of the congregation could not be dampened. Mr. James Cook, chair-

The 1966 renovation of nave and the enlarging of the chancel with new appointments at a cost of $22,000.

man of the building committee, received the key for the front door of the church from Raymond Biemeret, chairman of the congregation. The other members of the building committee included J. Robert Dilley, James L. Powers, Jr., and Frank Luebcke. Pastor Miller preached at the dedication service, and Rev. Oswald A. Waech, the Southern California District Executive Secretary of Stewardship, preached during the afternoon service of praise and thanksgiving. Guest organist for both services was Alan Kennedy, teacher of St. John's School, Covina, and a son of the congregation. His mother served as one of the two regular organists. This $22,000 renovation program was made possible by a partial loan from Lutheran Mutual. In 1970, Pastor Miller accepted a call to Salem Lutheran Church and School in Blue Island, Illinois, where he served for 22 years, leaving Bell Gardens after twelve years of service. While at Salem, he received his doctorate degree. In 1992, Dr. Miller, semi-retired, received a call to serve The Lutheran Church of Our Redeemer in Ojai, California.

In 1970, Rev. Oswald W. Mieger was installed as pastor of Bell Gardens Lutheran Church. He was born in Olive, California, in 1910 where his father was pastor of St. Paul's from 1908 to 1915. He received preparatory education for the ministry at California Concordia College in Oakland, California, completing his studies at Concordia Seminary in St. Louis, Missouri, graduating in June 1934. The following two years he served Pilgrim Church, at Oakland, California, and then moved to Oroville, California, in October 1936, where he was installed as pastor of the newly organized Calvary Church in 1937. During the same year, he was united in holy wedlock with Miss Edna Doerrer of Chicago, Illinois, and their union was blessed with three children. In March 1941, he accepted a call to Santa Maria and there organized Grace Church in October of the same year. Under his direction a $25,000 parish hall was dedicated in August 1945. In the same month, he accepted the call to Grace Church of Visalia. On Sunday, September 3, 1950, he was installed as pastor of Calvary Lutheran Church in Yuma, Arizona.

In 1970, Rev. Mieger was installed as pastor of Bell Gardens Lutheran Church as the fourth pastor. By June 1972, with the controversy over Seminex and the problems that ensued in Synod, the congregation was split by the secession of more than half of its membership to FAL (Federation of Authentic Lutheranism), establishing a church a few blocks from the recognized parish. In order to assist the Bell Gardens congregation, Rev. Dr. Arnold Kuntz, President of the Southern California District wrote the following June 19, 1972, letter to the Board for Missions:

The current concern revolves around our congregation in Bell Gardens. Approximately 50 communicants remain loyal. Most of these are ladies. The entire group of officers, with possibly some minor exceptions, has determined to go with FAL. Our Board of Directors has retained counsel for our people at Bell Gardens and has advanced funds to reimburse the pastor who remains with us but whose salary was stopped on a three-day notice because he is remaining with Missouri. The Board of Directors has voted unanimously to ask the Board for Missions to take the group of loyal Missourians from Bell Gardens under wing and provide them with as much support by way of subsidy as may be necessary to enable them to do what is required at least until they have gotten themselves on their feet again.

Consequently, this letter is to be regarded as an official request from our Board of Directors for the kind of assistance for these people in Bell Gardens as might be required. We thank you for the consideration, which you will give to this request.

With the approval of this request, the congregation received subsidy from the District. In October, the congregation was reorganized with 8 voting members and the LWML was also reorganized with 12 women; the Sunday school averaged 14 to 24 children and Sunday worship attendance of 26 to 37. The communicant membership had dropped to 64 with 88 baptized souls. With the resignation of Pastor Mieger from his pastorate at Bell Gardens in 1973, the direction of the ministry at the parish was carried on under the supervision of Redeemer Lutheran Church of South Gate until the congregation and Board for Missions established goals for the mission. During that same year, the District had provided a part-time ministry with Rev. Richard M. Brandt. The congregation felt its progress was being hampered by a half-time ministry and requested support of the Board for Missions to call a full-time pastor. Since the community was changing to a larger Hispanic population, the Board for Missions and the congregation were searching for an effective mission

The congregation receives a District subsidy in 1972.

outreach among the Spanish-speaking people in the community.

Two meetings were held with the Board for Missions and with 23 members of the congregation. At the meetings, it was reported that within five to ten years, Bell Gardens would be in a totally Spanish-speaking community. It was decided that a committee of four congregational members and four Board for Missions members, plus a moderator be formed in order to arrive at a pilot plan for the direction and ministry of the congregation. The chairman of the Board for Missions appointed the following Committee to meet with Bell Gardens: Rev. Arthur Kollmeyer (Faith, Whittier), Rev. Lothar Tornow (Christ, Costa Mesa), Rev. Harvey Lehman (St. Paul's, Los Angeles), Rev. Paulus Voelzke (First, Culver City), and moderator, William Duerr (Trinity, Santa Ana). Later in October, the board seriously considered dissolving the Bell Gardens congregation by transferring its members to neighboring congregations. By November, the board recommended that a call be extended to a missionary-at-large in the service of the District at Bell Gardens, who was conversant in Spanish, for a three-year pilot program.

In the January 1975 *District Digest*, it was stated that the Bell Gardens congregation was regarded as the "springboard" to a more intensive Spanish

Rev. Stirdivant begins Hispanic work in Bell Gardens in 1975.

Pastor Stirdivant and Señor Ricardo Sarria, who was commissioned at Bell Gardens on April 10, 1978, to be a non-salaried neighborhood worker.

ministry among the increasing numbers of Mexican-Americans residing in the area. A call was extended to Rev. Frederick G. Boden Jr. of Corpus Christi, Texas, to assume direction of this work. Since he declined the call, a call was issued to Rev. Robert Gussick who also declined.

Since the Board for Missions decided to defer calling of a missionary-at-large to serve Bell Gardens, the congregation filed a request for the part-time services of the Rev. David Stirdivant to initiate a Hispanic mission outreach in the parish. By June of 1975, Pastor Stirdivant was endeavoring to reach Spanish-speaking people in Bell Gardens by utilizing the membership in following up contacts and conducting a VBS in August. With the board supplying $50 to help defray the costs of the Bible School, he was invited to conduct the Vacation Bible School with the interim pastors. He recalled there were a lot of little blond haired children that first year, and the next year there were fewer blond children. The third year they were all dark, black haired children with no blondes among them. He stated, "This was an overnight change that took place here." Pastor Stirdivant was also given $30 for his mileage expenses, and 100 copies of the Spanish version of *Little Visits with God* for distribution in Bell Gardens. During this time period, Pastor Richard Brandt served the congregation part-time. In the fall of 1977, a cross-cultural ministry team was to be emphasized, initiated by Pastors Stirdivant and Daniel Saavedra, a CCLEM student (Center of Cultural Lay Evangelism Ministry, a program designed by the Board for Missions, with assistance of the Lutheran Baja California Mission, to train Hispanic lay people to be effective witnesses and how to conduct home Bible classes for the entire family). On April 10, 1978, Señor Ricardo Sarria, a product of CCLEM, was commissioned at Bell Gardens to be a non-salaried neighborhood worker.

In 1978, Pastor Phil Molnar (Bethlehem, Santa Clarita) wrote a letter to Dr. Arnold Kuntz, District President, and stated that if the District didn't start work in Hispanic ministries, they would end up closing more churches than opening. Dr. Kuntz's response was to designate Pastor Molnar as the chairman of a committee that eventually gave birth to the Hispanic Ministries Task Force. He listed high Hispanic population areas and invited those pastors to the District office for a meeting. This group continued to meet as an ad hoc committee with no District direction. They brainstormed approaches for Hispanic ministry and made recommendations to the Mission Board. Carlos Puig, Director of Hispanic Ministries LCMS, St. Louis, came from St. Louis for a meeting with the committee and Ken Behnken, District Mission Executive (who served as an encourager), where they brainstormed goals for a Hispanic ministry with Ken Behnken providing the underlying philosophy — there was no one way to do Hispanic ministry.

The meetings were always conducted at the District office. The main agenda item at those meetings was brainstorming different approaches used in Hispanic ministry. They saw that there were differences between pastors Stirdivant (La Santa Cruz, Los Angeles), Woody Mather (Maywood), Chuck Brady (South Gate) and Cris Artigas (Maywood) in their styles of ministry, bringing them to the conclusion that there was no way to set up a standardized approach. So the District started experimenting by moving people around: Pastor Stirdivant was moved from La Santa Cruz to Bell Gardens; Pastor Artigas was moved from Maywood to La Santa Cruz.

On October 5, 1980, Rev. Phil Molnar was commissioned as missionary-at-large in Bell Gardens where he served the English-speaking congregations of Bell Gardens and La Santa Cruz. He was born in East Los Angeles in 1935 where he attended St. John's Lutheran Church and School and was confirmed by Pastor Smukal. He graduated from St. John's College in Winfield, Kansas, in 1955 and Concordia Seminary, St. Louis, Missouri, in 1960, with the Bachelor of Arts and Master of Divinity degrees. While serving a dual parish in Spearfish, South Dakota, and Sundance, Wyoming, from 1960 to 1967, he also served as chairman of the South Dakota Board of Parish Education and was a member of the Board of Directors. From 1967 to 1978, he served Emanuel Lutheran Church, Santa Barbara, California. During his first three years, the congregation completed a $350,000 relocation and building program.

While in Santa Barbara, Pastor Molnar instituted a Black Studies Seminar among the churches and was active on the Ad-Hoc Committee for Low Cost Housing. He served, by appointment of the Santa Barbara County Supervisors, on the County Senior Citizens Advisory Commission, the County General Hospital Study Committee, and was instrumental in the inception and qualification for federal funding of the Tri-County Area Agency of Aging. He also served as a board member of the Santa Barbara Y.M.C.A. and as consultant to the

Honors Student Program of Westmont College. In 1978, he served Bethlehem Lutheran congregation, a suburban Los Angeles County congregation, which experienced continuing growth in the Newhall/Saugus area. At the time of his commissioning, he served in the Southern California District of the Lutheran Church — Missouri Synod, (later to become the Pacific Southwest District) as convener of the Hispanic Ministries Task Force, and was a member of the Urban Ministries Department of the Southern California Mission Board.

Pastor Molnar's wife, Sally, a native of Wichita, Kansas, was a graduate of St. John's College in Winfield, Kansas, where they met, and she taught in Lutheran elementary schools in St. Louis, Missouri. The Molnar family included three children: Suzanne, Sharon, and Thomas. The worship officiants for the commissioning service were:

Installing Officer: The Rev. Gulfrey Laurent, Circuit Counselor

Preacher: The Rev. Lothar Tornow, Chairman of the Mission Board, Southern California District

Rev. Phil Molnar with his wife, Sally, was commissioned as missionary-at-large on October 5, 1980, in Bell Gardens to serve the English-speaking congregations of Bell Gardens and La Santa Cruz.

Liturgist: The Rev. Elwood Mather III, Zion Lutheran Church, Maywood

Lector: The Rev. David Stirdivant, La Santa Cruz Lutheran Church, East Los Angeles

Organist: Mr. Alan Kennedy

Pastor Molnar's call was:

1. To serve as pastor of the Bell Gardens congregation, serving the people who make up the present congregation and to develop this ministry to its full potential.

2. To initiate, with the help of Rev. David Stirdivant, a Hispanic ministry to the Bell Gardens community with the hope of developing models that could be shared with other congregations in the District.

3. To serve as a resource person and facilitator for Hispanic ministry in the Southern California District as he worked with the Hispanic Standing Committee and the Administrative Assistant to the President.

4. To work with Rev. David Stirdivant to carry out an effective team ministry between La Santa Cruz and Bell Gardens so that an English ministry could be continued in both congregations.

In November of 1980, Pastor Stirdivant was asked to work in Bell Gardens among the Hispanic community. With some helpers, they canvassed the area, inviting people to church. In the middle of January, Hilario Deniz returned from Mexico and began assisting Pastor Stirdivant with the Hispanic work, using his musical abilities in worship services. They began an intense canvassing of the community, inviting boys and girls to a Saturday morning Catechism class preparing for First Communion — something Pastor had never done before. On the first Saturday, there were about a dozen pupils and the following Saturday 18. Since so many children began coming, they had to divide the group. Hilario took the older children and Pastor took the younger ones; in four weeks they had 24 to 30 children attending. They started a Young People's Society on Wednesday nights with ball games in back of the church. This developed into starting a little church service with 8, 10, and a dozen going. When Lent arrived, what a surprise awaited them! Among Latin Americans, suddenly everyone becomes spiritual on Ash Wednesday, as that is when Lent begins. When the Ash Wednesday service was announced, the

people asked, "Do you give ashes on the forehead, and the mark of ashes on the forehead?" Pastor thought, "Well, I guess we could do that. What's wrong with that? It's something that the people are used to, but it isn't too Lutheran." To their amazement, the evening of Ash Wednesday in 1981, the church was packed; 140-some people who had come to church were lined up all the way out the door of the building.

To take advantage of this large attendance needing spiritual nourishment, a Lenten program was announced with three Bible classes during the week: one on Monday night and Wednesday night and Friday night with a doctrine class on Saturday mornings and then church on Sunday. Hilario also suggested that the crucifix hanging on the sidewall of the church be moved to the front and hung over the altar, which the Anglo congregation resisted. For the six weeks of Lent in 1981, they talked with people and encouraged them to come to Bible study. Through this, they had a nucleus of people who were going to church regularly. This was followed with Confirmation services and First Communion services, which continues to be used at the present time.

Through this experience, Pastor Stirdivant learned some valuable lessons in dealing with the Hispanic community. He said:

For the first 30 years of my ministry, I tried to do things exactly the way I had been taught and the only thing I'd been taught was the way my teachers had always known to do them. I followed my Lutheran Agenda, my Lutheran hymnbook, my Lutheran Catechism, and anything else that was Lutheran; I followed it as closely as I could. And I didn't know anything about the Catholic background except what I had learned in contacts with Latin-American people that usually was on my turf, Lutheran. I didn't know their customs too well, I didn't know what their religious customs were, and I had grown up as a child to have a great horror of Roman Catholicism. So, I grew up with this belief that Catholics are just like off limits and you don't think about that stuff. Here at Bell Gardens, I began to revise my thinking about it and I said, "These people have customs; they've got traditions. Maybe I should learn a little bit more about it." And instead of insisting that everything be done the way I've always done it, maybe I could do well by listening a little bit to them and asking them. So I started listening instead of talking so much. I became a much better listener.

Through listening to Hispanics, Pastor Stirdivant learned the Latinos' customs of Lent, Good Friday, and Christmas with its *Posadas*. He remembered how Martin Luther developed the Deutsch Massa, or German Mass deleting the unscriptural parts and keeping the basics ingredients of the Mass. He thought, "Why not try it here?" If people know some songs that they appreciate from their childhood, we'll sing them if they're not too unscriptural, maybe even changing some words or revising them. At Christmas, he instituted Posadas where, nine nights before Christmas, songs were sung, while people were walking the streets going from door to door at different homes each night. He thought about the thirty years of silence on these customs during his ministry and revised some of them.

Pastor Stirdivant recalled the words of Bob Gussick, "We missionaries are bridge builders. And if we're going to build bridges, any bridge engineer knows that when you build a bridge, you have to study the soil on both sides of the river. So you take a study on one side, you see how Lutheran it is. And you study the soil over on the other side and you see how Catholic it is. Now you're going to build the bridge. And across this bridge you're going to go with the Gospel, but first the bridge has to be a strong bridge of love and trust. If they don't trust you, you can have all the stuff in the world to offer them and they're not going to be listening to you."

The first bridge to be built was that of trust and friendship with changing the name of the church from Bell Gardens Lutheran Church, as it wasn't the right name in the Spanish world. At first, the name San Martín, Saint Martin, was used, but people would come in asking for pictures of Saint Martin. When they received pictures of Martin Luther, they walked away disgusted; it was decided to change the name, again, to San Pedro y San Pablo and, when requested, gave pictures of two great men of the Bible, Peter and Paul. When people came to the church, they weren't told of saints or purgatory, but instead they heard the Word of God and were taught God's Word in Bible studies with the Holy Spirit working in them through the use of the Bible. Pastor was most successful in sharing the message of the Gospel by letting people feel at ease and at home. Since most of them

came from a Roman Catholic culture, he concentrated first in areas of agreement: the Apostles Creed, the Ten Commandments, and the Lord's Prayer, all of which were carefully explained. He emphasized in his teaching the open Bible, the constant use and study of God's Word with all of this making a big difference. In all of these little things that were learned in dealing with Mexican families, the children were very, very important. No Baptism was done without classes for the parents and *padrinos*, Godparents, who were a special glue in the Hispanic family.

Some of the customs had changed, but the church service still retained its liturgical form. The services consisted of an 8:30 a.m. English service, a 9:30 a.m. Spanish service, and an 11:00 a.m. English service on Sunday mornings, and a 5:30 p.m. Spanish service with between 90 to 120 people in attendance. Some years later, an early morning service was also conducted at 7:00 a.m. with fifty people attending. In the June–July 1982 *District Digest*, the following was stated:

> BELL GARDENS LUTHERAN (HISPANIC) — The Word and Sacrament services led at this congregation are presently being attended by 125–180 Hispanic people each Sunday morning. A Saturday School of over 100 Hispanic children is meeting every Saturday and numerous Bible classes and teaching classes are held throughout the week. This is presently one of the most ex-

1981 Children's Christmas Service with Hilario Deniz (right) playing the accordion and Pastor Stirdivant (left).

citing Hispanic ministries happening in the entire Synod.

On April 25, 1982, the Rev. Philip Molnar was installed as the pastor of Our Savior Lutheran Church in Bellflower where he served Bellflower and Bell Gardens as a dual parish not only preaching the English service at Bell Gardens but also preaching the English services at La Santa Cruz in Los Angeles. He did all of the administrative work at Our Savior, San Pedro y San Pablo, and La Santa Cruz so that pastors Artigas and Stirdivant could spend their time preaching, teaching, and reaching the Hispanic communities. At this time, Pastor Stirdivant received an official call to become missionary-at-large with assignment to full pastoral responsibilities at the Bell Gardens' church.

A 1982 grant from Lutheran World Relief of $4,000 seed money, enabled the congregation to begin a preschool. The preschool opened in May of 1982 with Penny Williams, director, who was a volunteer taking no pay. Initially, a monthly fee of $120 per child was established, about $30 less per month than any other preschool in Bell Gardens. Since the fee was too high for Hispanic families, not one person enrolled a child in May or June. On the advice of Pastor Stirdivant, the fees were cut in half to $60 per month, and immediately ten Hispanic children were enrolled. This was accomplished when Pastor Stirdivant and Director Penny Williams walked through the barrio talking to people in Spanish about the preschool. By October, the enrollment had increased to 15 children with the addition of some Anglo children from low-income families. Since they were drawing heavily on the school's Revolving Fund, by January 1983, the fee was raised $10 per month and again in September bringing it to a total $100 per month. Even though this was still very low, the enrollment dropped from 36 to 26 children.

About two-thirds of the preschool were Hispanic with usually four to six children who couldn't speak any English. All schoolwork was done in English, as that was what the parents requested. The preschool was still not financially sound because of fluctuations in enrollment primarily due to the employment of the parents. The school had received permission from the Los Angeles County Department of Social Services, Child Care Division, to increase the enrollment to 58 children.

The preschool had touched approximately 60 families through the children who were enrolled, creating an avenue for the Gospel to be proclaimed. Once a week immigration counseling was done by Kathy Howe (through a partial World Relief Grant) and the Word and Sacrament ministry of Pastor Stirdivant made the preschool one of the brightest mission places in the Southern California District at that time. Pastor Stirdivant, who loved children, conducted weekly morning chapel services in the church for the preschool children and the children had daily Bible story time. Two related projects of the preschool were to purchase two adjoining lots for increased playground and parking space and to start a kindergarten through sixth-grade elementary school, as a request of some preschool parents. These elaborate plans never materialized.

During the summer of 1982, Mark McKenzie, a first-year seminary student, did an internship at Bell Gardens for eight weeks where he lived in the parsonage of Pastor Stirdivant in East Los Angeles as Pastor continued residing there through his ministry in Bell Gardens and until his retirement. Mark recalled going camping with the young people of the congregation along with some of the parents and their children. He assisted in the worship services and with Bible study classes.

In the summer of 1983, Pastor Albrecht instead of Pastor Molnar began preaching at the English services at La Santa Cruz and Bell Gardens. By having this arrangement, Our Savior would be able to have an earlier worship time and an adult Bible class, which they desperately needed. Pastor Albrecht did not ask for any payment or a gasoline allowance for his services, since he considered it a privilege to preach God's Word. However, it was decided it would be fair to have the congregation where he preached give him a token gas allowance of $25 each time as he drove over 100 miles in order to perform this service for them. Pastor Molnar still continued to administer the business affairs of Bell Gardens under Pastor Stirdivant, and Pastor Molnar aided Pastor Artigas at La Cruz at his request. Everything that Pastor Albrecht did was under the authority of Pastor Stirdivant who was the head pastor at Bell Gardens, and Pastor Artigas who was the head pastor at La Santa Cruz.

Also, during that summer, Frank Brundige, a summer intern from Christ College, was a lay worker in the Hispanic ministry at Bell Gardens, beginning on June 20 and ending on August 21. One of his responsibilities was to read the lessons and prayers at the English service, and, in time, he also read the lessons at the Spanish service. He at-

During the summer of 1982, Mark McKenzie did an internship at Bell Gardens.

tended Spanish Catechism, youth night, and adult Bible study setting up audio-visual equipment and helping wherever possible in the preschool. In Pastor Artigas's absence, he taught the Catechism class. He made some evangelism calls to English-speaking people, and with Pastor Stirdivant, they called on Spanish-speaking parents of preschool children. They were welcomed by the families and found that the people were honored by the "visit of a priest" and interested in what a teacher had to say about their children. The results of the visits were that two families started attending the Spanish worship service. He also assisted with grounds' maintenance and gained a basic understanding of the culture while working in Hispanic ministry at Bell Gardens.

In a November 1983 report to the Department of Mission Services, Pastor Stirdivant reported the following statistics about Bell Gardens:

8:30 a.m. Anglo Sunday Service
    8 adults
9:30 a.m. Spanish-language
    averaged 75
11:00 a.m. Youth Service
    5 Anglos & 25 Hispanics
5:30 p.m. Spanish-language
    35–75
Tuesday Adult Bible Study
    averaged 20
Saturday Children's Catechism
    averaged 150–160 children

In the summer of 1984, the First Hispanic Convocation was held at the Bell Gardens church, attracting 130 who gathered to meet the need for fellowship among Spanish-speaking members of Southern California congregations and featured some aspects of a Fiesta but boasted far more significant values. Rev. Ricardo Sarria led a Bible study on "Family Life and Faith." The youth had their own Bible lessons, music, and handcrafts, directed by teachers Lola Dino of South Gate, and Luisa Hernandez of San Diego. Johnny Lopez, youth director of Trinity, Santa Ana, led singing, playing both guitar and piano. Pastor Stirdivant participated along with the ladies of the congregation who served the meal. Also in 1984, Raul Saldaña was installed as deacon at Bell Gardens where he served as a worker-deacon continuing to do his paid work in his gardening business and assisting Pastor Stirdivant at the church until 1990.

During May of 1985, Pastor Stirdivant had surgery, recuperating enough to attend the June

1 commencement ceremonies at Christ College, Irvine, along with more than 1,100 persons hearing Dr. Oswald Hoffmann, *Lutheran Hour* speaker, challenge students to be the "salt of the earth and the light of the world." The Christus Mundo award was given to him for his 40 years of service in developing Spanish missions in Southern California. He was described as a pastor of pastors who loved people, cared for them, and ministered to them most effectively. That summer Frank Brundige returned to serve as a summer intern for Rev. Artigas and Rev. Stirdivant at La Santa Cruz and Bell Gardens being paid $700, continuing in the work he had done the previous summer.

On Saturday, April 26, 1986, Bell Gardens was the host to the "Vision for Churches in Changing Neighborhoods" conference with the event designed to help both churches in communities which were already ethnically different, and those in neighborhoods which were just beginning to change by helping them understand demographic factors that affected growth and to identify the root problems they encountered. It also outlined practical ways to minister to "old" members and "new" ethnic groups at the same time and described several methods by which a church could grow in a changing neighborhood. The keynote speaker at the conference was the Rev. James Duren, who was pastor of a church with both Anglo and Hispanic congregations. He had also helped plant many churches as the area mission executive for the Conservative Baptist denomination. Other speakers included Church Growth Task Force members John Krueger, John Juedes, Mark Behring, Ron Kusel, and Larry Alb, almost all of whom had been pastors of churches in changing neighborhoods.

By September of 1989, Bell Gardens continued to be one of the most active Hispanic ministries in the District, serving 250 to 325 people in worship services a week. Pastor Stirdivant's Saturday school had about 200 pupils on Saturday mornings and a trained staff of 8 to 10 teachers who helped him with the school. Since his coming to Bell Gardens, the Saturday school was a tremendous success. He used that time to instruct the children for their First Communion and for Confirmation. Since he had First Communion and Confirmation services with classes of 30 or more children, the church was so packed that people were even standing outside looking through the windows.

When Pastor Stirdivant announced that he would be retiring from active ministry in January

Pastor Stirdivant receives Christus Mundo Award.

First Communion and Confirmation class of almost 50 children and young people, circa 1985.

Pastor Stirdivant
retires in 1990.

Rev. Brundige becomes
Pastor to San Pedro y
San Pablo in 1989.

of 1990 after serving in three Hispanic churches for over forty years, the Hispanic pastors gave him a special appreciation lunch on December 7, where he received many letters of congratulations and approximately $800. Until 1980, when Rev. Cris Artigas was called to assist in the ministry to Hispanics, Pastor Stirdivant was the sole Spanish-language voice in the District. During the previous 20 years, 18 additional pastors had joined in that ministry. In spring of 1996 at the 157th academic exercises at Concordia Seminary, the following words were expressed about his ministry: "Pastor Stirdivant is held in deep respect as a pastor, a mentor to young pastors and a loving and caring shepherd, who, at great personal sacrifice, was a pioneer in Lutheran work among Hispanic people living in the United States." With these words, he was the recipient of an honorary Doctor of Theology degree.

Dr. Stirdivant used various evangelistic techniques, such as meeting people on the streets becoming friend and "pastor" to them, taking youth camping and fishing, and leading countless Bible classes and leadership training courses in the Spanish language. Today many congregations in the area have second-generation members who had their Christian roots in his work at La Santa Cruz. He modeled a ministry that today has multiplied all over the United States and continues to grow with the expansion of Hispanic communities. In Pastor's retirement, he started Spanish

services at Messiah, Highland, moving the group to Trinity, San Bernardino, where he continued to assist Pastor McKenzie in the Hispanic ministry there. In 1998, Concordia University at Irvine also recognized his pioneering work with an honorary doctorate.

In order to fill the vacancy at Iglesia de San Pedro y San Pablo in Bell Gardens, in the October 1989 meeting, the Department of Mission Services voted unanimously to call the Rev. Garry McClure of Tucson, Arizona, to serve. Because Rev. McClure declined the call, Rev. Frank Brundige of La Santa Cruz in Los Angeles received and accepted the call. Bell Gardens was not a new experience for him as he had worked there two summers and had assisted Pastor Stirdivant at various times. During his first year at Bell Gardens, Pastor Stirdivant forgot to mention to him that on Ash Wednesday everybody went to church. He had planned a regular Communion worship service like the ones that were done on Sunday mornings. There were only a very small handful of regular Sunday worshipers there that night in the church, as he discovered, most of the people who attended regularly knew not to come that night, because there would just be such a big crowd. Since it was a balmy evening, the doors and windows of the church were all open. When it was time for the offering, only three plates were brought forward to the altar. Then comes this fellow, looking very forlorn, bringing an offering plate up to the altar. He had been out on the street passing the plate among the line of people who were waiting outside of church for ashes. Due to the large crowd, Pastor said he was almost mobbed at the altar. He was not prepared for it, and didn't know what to expect, but was glad so many people came to church.

In order to deal with the "mobs" of Ash Wednesday, making it a more meaningful and lasting experience, Pastor Brundige stated, "In later years, we held three to four short services that were comprised of confession and an evangelical sermon inviting the people to walk with us through Lent, Easter, and beyond. Our people at San Pedro y San Pablo provided coffee and cake and welcomed our neighbors to church. Attendance is often between 400 to 500 people. Over the years, Ash Wednesday visitors have become members or friends of our church."

Pastor Brundige discovered the way to win children and people to Christ was to open the church playground, letting them play, getting to know them, and sharing the love of Christ. He said, "I think people are needy of relationships so that's where the cults make their big impact. They give meaning and relationship to people while they chew them up, basically, and then close them down to everybody else. The secular crowd is sometimes resistant, but what happens is they become hungry, and all of a sudden 'Jesus loves me this I know for the Bible tells me so' isn't a little child's song, but it's a deep confession of faith. Waiting for that moment to happen, you then win them for Christ. So we stand on this little corner here in Bell Gardens and we hold the Gospel up for everybody to see — those who want to and those who don't. Even when people finally tell you why they don't come to church, you're still a friend to them and tell them that they are welcome. You still love them; you still say hello to them and ask them about their children. There is the Great Commission, 'Go and make disciples of all nations, baptizing them in the name of the Father, Son, and Holy Spirit,' but there is also the command to love one another and by this be known as Christ's disciple." In order to be a welcoming church in the community, he opens the church door every morning allowing people to come in and pray and he is outside the church greeting parents as they take their children to school. His ministry is one of having a presence in the community, letting people know him, and that he is there to help them.

At the end of 1991, Bell Gardens received a LCEF (Lutheran Church Extension Fund) loan of $25,000 to repair the roof and repave the church parking lot and playground. In a 1993 report, Pastor Brundige wrote that Word and Sacrament services were conducted each Sunday in an English service attended by 30 and a Spanish service attended by 140 with the Hispanic ministry being the focus of the congregation in both languages.

During 1996, the windows in the church were replaced, and Pastor led the chapel services at Southeast Lutheran High, and Redeemer, South Gate. Twenty youth organized and participated in a Good Friday drama, which had been previously organized by their mothers. He wrote to Ken Behnken, "No matter how hard we work, teach, and preach there is always a turnover and a lack of faithfulness.... We often work alone, with volunteers with a primary education, no secretary or janitor,... while the roof leaks, typewriters are stolen, the building is vandalized, and people simply reject or loose interest in the Gospel; our best bet is on our own prayerfully in the Word seeking God's will and ministry for us."

When the 1997 Lenten season began with Ash Wednesday, there were four services attended by 500 people. Following the service cake, coffee, and punch were served and members shared and mixed among visitors. Beginning with Lent, the Sunday attendance increased by 40. After Easter, it decreased by 30, giving a net gain of 10 people. Holy Week attendance was also up, with Maundy Thursday having 57 and Good Friday, 78. Pastor reported that the turnover at the church was tremendous and stated:

> We are often given a short amount of time to touch people's lives with the Gospel. We receive people with family and personal crises, very little education (sometimes third-grade-educated adults), and a minimal, often confused, concept of church. Sometimes it can take a relationship of five years of visiting for someone to begin to read the Bible and see that even in the midst of drugs, gang banging, fornication, and stealing, God still loves, provides, and wants to forgive. Many times someone who was taught as a youth, returned with joy to the church seeking to be married or to baptize a child. The Gospel planted produced fruit. Even with the high turnover, we have sent members who were prepared with the Gospel and left here in the infancy or adolescence of their faith, yet blossomed to ma-

Pastor Brundige discovers the way to win children and people to Christ is to open the church playground.

turity at their new congregations. There are many things here that sadden, discourage, and make things difficult. You have to live in and around these things to truly grasp their ugliness and pain. We are called to live in the Lord who lives in us in this time and place that He has privileged us to show Him to people He wants and loves and who very much need Him. *¡Alzad la Cruz!* Lift High the Cross!

In late spring, Pastor Brundige received a call to Mt. Olive in Miami, expressing that it was an interesting opportunity; the more he heard the more interesting it became. Since he was going to get married that summer, he decided it was not a good time to move, as he felt the call was to stay in Bell Gardens. That summer on August 4, 1996, a beautiful day around four in the afternoon as the sun came through the church windows and turned it kind of gold, Pastor was united in marriage to Reyna Orozco, who he met on a call when her sister was renting the parsonage next to the church. Also coming into this union were his foster son, Reynaldo DeHijar, and Reyna's two sons, Jose Ibarra and Luis Neri, and finally the birth of their son, Patrick Brundige. They lived in a small house west of the church, finally moving into the parsonage in 2001. Reyna is a helpmate, supporting church work and providing a warm and caring home for the family. In the fall, in order to model a self-supporting congregation, Pastor committed himself to live as his people do and become a worker/priest.

In November, the church received a $6,000 LCEF net-operating-results check, which they divided, giving Southeast Lutheran High School $3,000 and using the other $3,000 to make a principal payment on the church loan. Since a number of families from San Pedro y San Pablo were living in Maywood, Pastor Brundige asked Zion in Maywood for permission to use its church building on Sunday afternoons for worship services in Spanish; Zion denied the request. After Zion closed its doors in June of 1997, Pastor Brundige began conducting services in Zion's old building in the fall, beginning a new Hispanic ministry in the Maywood area, having 17 in the Spanish service, 3 in the English Bible study, and 8 in the Wednesday school.

During 1997, one of the needs of the congregation was to have simple, reasonably priced Spanish-written resources to supplement classes offered on Saturdays for grades 1–12. That fall, Ruben Vasquez, a TEE student, proved a blessing in helping in the work of the parish. Attendance at worship continued to increase — 53 at the Thanksgiving service, 65 in the Posada, and 55 Christmas Eve.

The new year of 1998 began with an increase in average attendance: 96 in the Spanish service, 8 in the English service, Bible study class, 18, and Saturday school, 30. A 5:30 p.m. Sunday worship service in Spanish was begun and reached 40 people by the end of Lent. Ruben Vasquez had increased the Saturday adult Bible study and was visiting in the community. He proved to be a good Bible teacher as well as a good caller, making him an asset to the ministry. By fall, the District had granted him permission to consecrate the elements and administer Sacraments at the church. The major goal for the year was to be an independent, self-supporting congregation and entirely free of District subsidy.

As the new year of 1998 developed, the congregation continued to grow in worship attendance averaging 112 per Sunday, and the Ash Wednesday services continued to have an attendance of 500 with some of the frequent faces at Ash Wednesday service eventually becoming part of the church. In June, Dia de San Pedro y San Pablo was an outreach open house, where donated used articles and food were for sale, drawing in the community with a rented "jumper" and free arts and crafts for the children. People came, stayed, and visited. All proceeds were given to two projects: the building of a Sunday school room at el Divino Emanuel in Guasave, Sinaloa, Mexico, and the installation of toys and a basketball hoop in the church yard for the neighborhood children. A free raffle of a Bible was held, and people from the church visited those who submitted raffle cards. As a result of the event, new people were in Sunday worship and Saturday school. Since there was no one to play the organ, compact disks were used to accompany the congregational singing.

A monthly women's Bible study was well received with 11 in attendance. The Fall Festival was designed as an outreach where many new contacts were made. The Planning Council was able to devise a mission plan in one meeting, versus four meetings the previous year, where they also discussed in detail finances, stewardship, and pastor's salary, which was all new territory for them. Eighty-four people attended the annual Christmas Posada. Generally, new people were

Pastor Brundige marries Reyna Orozco in 1996.

seen as a result of the mission plan, with some staying and becoming very dedicated members. The turnover of people living in the area was high, with 80 percent living in multiple units and 95 percent of the community renting as they couldn't afford to purchase homes; some stayed in the area with the Gospel and blossomed, while other were scattered as seed.

In the first quarter of 2000, average church attendance had increased to 104 with 11:30 a.m. English service growing. The fellowship hour following the service had become a weekly event and was supported by the congregation. The Ash Wednesday service was attended by 463 worshipers, and a Communion and Confirmation service was conducted on Maundy Thursday with increased attendance at this service. The Quinceñeras and weddings were used as another outreach along with the community use of the playground. A Friday Bible devotion was held with the playground basketball players; also, the evening was broadened to offer arts and crafts, computers, and crochet. Through this outreach, new contacts were made with people going to church services. The proceeds from the open house on Dia de San Pedro y San Pablo were sent to missions in Mexico. Ruben Vasquez, a trained lay person, continued serving with Pastor Brundige in Bell Gardens. During the year, the congregation was instrumental in helping to plant new ministries in Mexico, Maywood, and Norwalk. At the end of the year, God had blessed the five Posadas that were used as outreach tools with two of them supporting other missions.

The year 2001 began with some changes in community; it became more secularized and materialistic as people were Americanized, better educated, and financially more prosperous. Attendance at worship services continued to grow, with an average attendance of 116 on Sundays, 363 on Ash Wednesday, 44 Maundy Thursday, and 61 on Good Friday. An English Sunday school was established in addition to bilingual Saturday school. The Friday after-school program continued with games and Bible stories and reached 14 children and 3 adults. In the fall, Pastor Brundige taught the seventh and eighth grades three days a week at Redeemer Lutheran School in South Gate instead of five half-days. He also went to Grace in Los Angeles to help canvass the area with the goal of establishing a Hispanic church there. The December Posadas held in a Bell Gardens home cultivated new friends and evangelism prospects. Another

The 10:00 a.m. Saturday Doctrine and Bible class in 1998 with Pastor Brundige at top right.

Pastor Brundige conducting a Father's Day Service in 2000.

Posada was held at a home in Baldwin Park, and this group wanted to continue Bible study in the coming year. The Posada at the church brought in neighborhood children and parents from the Friday after-school group as well as evangelism prospects from other visits.

The year 2002 began with successful church council/planning meetings where members shared ideas and leaders were identified and trained. Since the Lord had blessed the parish with funds from the previous year and the member giving had increased, necessary building repairs were being made without securing new loans. Ash Wednesday service was large at 343; Maundy Thursday, 44; and Good Friday, 70. In the fall, the Bell Gardens facilities were used by the Hispanic Institute of Theology to conduct four-hour classes on Saturday afternoons that aided Hispanics for ministry. The Lord has truly blessed the Bell Gardens mission in its work to the Spanish-speaking people in the area!

Redeemer Lutheran Church
Iglesia Luterana El Redentor
South Gate, California

The city of South Gate was also part of the large Lugo Spanish Land Grant that encompassed the entire area extending from the low range of hills that separated it from the San Gabriel Valley to the old Dominguez Ranch at its south end and from the eastern boundary of the pueblo of Los Angeles to the San Gabriel River. A little more than 100 years after the establishment of the Lugo Spanish Land Grant, the area at the south gate of the ranch became the city of South Gate. As Don Lugo's family grew, he obtained San Bernardino Rancho and other grants in his children's names.

The future South Gate site with its adjacent mesas presented a colorful spectacle when countless heads of cattle and horses were herded from all directions to a common point for the annual great spring rodeo. Lugo would direct the proceedings and settle disputes regarding ownership of contested animals as well as adjudicate agricultural disputes. The land grant, handed down from generation to generation, had been divided among his offspring and eventually parceled and sold to people outside of the Lugo family.

Before the end of the 1870s, 40-acre tracts had replaced much of the original land grant. By 1880, cattle raising had been replaced by agriculture as the most important local industry. During the years between 1910 and 1940, homes and factories replaced most of the agricultural land. Today,

> The area at the south gate of the Lugo Rancho became the city of South Gate.

with the land divided by numerous freeways, it is difficult to imagine it as it was in those early years, a vast plain stretching from the mountains to the sea.

The Tweedy family, headed by R. D. Tweedy, had played an important part in South Gate's history. Mr. Tweedy was born in 1812 in Illinois and came to California by ox-drawn cart in 1852, while Mrs. Tweedy rode across the prairies perched on her rocking chair in the ox cart. Since several generations of the large family lived in the city, family members bought some 2,000 acres of the land on which much of South Gate was built. The "downtown business district," Tweedy Mile, in South Gate was named after the family.

In the late 1800s and early 1900s as far as the eye could see, Rancho San Antonio was covered with thousands of head of grazing cattle, sheep, and horses; large fertile fruit orchards; fields of cauliflower, beets, barley, and beans as well as dairy farms producing rich butter and cheese. But change was in the air. At noon on September 23, 1917, an important event took place — the selling of land as "Southgate Gardens — Gateway to the Sea," that would eventually be the foundation for the beautiful city of South Gate. When this sale was highly advertised from Santa Monica to Santa Ana, Realtor Charles B. Hooper had arranged for 12 buses to pick up people along routes through various towns. Excursionists traveled

An early view of South Gate before it was subdivided in 1917. (SECURITY PACIFIC COLLECTION/Los Angeles Public Library)

in everything from the latest Model "T" Fords to high-powered Packards. The buses traveled in a procession east from Long Beach Boulevard down a dirt road about a half-mile to the Cudahy Ranch House located on present-day Santa Ana Street surrounded on three sides by cauliflower fields. Realtor Hooper sold 268 parcels, mostly in one-half acre lots, in a subdivision with no streets, no sewers, and no water system. Parallel furrows had been plowed 50 feet apart, to indicate streets of the future; amazingly, the signs that were stuck in imaginary intersections bore the same names that many of the city's streets carry today. Some $25,000 worth of land was sold on opening day.

By the end of 1918, 125 houses had been constructed with shade trees and flowers planted along the parkways, and the city population was estimated at 500. The community of Southgate Gardens now extended east from Long Beach Boulevard to Otis and south from Santa Ana to Independence and was still growing. The first school, now known as State Street School, was established with 52 pupils and opened September 8, 1919. America's famous aviatrix, Amelia Earhart, learned to fly at Kinner Field, a dirt field located on Century Boulevard at Long Beach Boulevard. She became the first woman to fly solo across the Atlantic Ocean in 1932, and she vanished without a trace in 1937 during an attempt to fly around the world.

In the autumn of 1922, a petition for incorporating the town of South Gate was circulated by I. W. Lampman. The petition was signed by more than 50 qualified voters and presented to the Los Angeles County Board of Supervisors. An election was held on January 2, 1923, to determine the will of the people. On January 20, 1923, the Board of Supervisors formally declared the incorporation of the "City of South Gate," population of 2,500. The years following incorporation in 1923 were boom years with families finding contentment in this fertile little suburb. As early as 1922, several small industrial plants had moved to South Gate. Since families moved there needing employment close to home, businesses, factories, and industry soon followed. One of the largest local industries was Firestone Tire and Rubber Company

Rev. Hugo Gihring, Redeemer's first pastor, who led the congregation from 1922 until 1935.

built on a 40-acre former bean field; the first tire rolled off the assembly line on June 15, 1928. Since the company was so famous, the street running along the factory property was renamed Firestone Boulevard. In 1936, the General Motors plant went into production in South Gate with 1,000 employees, soon increasing to 4,000, building three lines of cars, Pontiac, Oldsmobile, and Buick.

Schools and churches were being established with many Lutherans moving into this new suburb. Following the War, a great boom of migration bought more people from the Midwest to South Gate. In the late 1970s, the population of the area shifted from a middle-class Anglo community to a Hispanic area. By 2000, the city had a population of 96,375, 92 percent of the city Hispanic and 6 percent Anglo. There was also a change in owner occupied dwellings with only 47 percent owning their own homes and 53 percent renting.

Redeemer Lutheran Church was born in the great population explosion of the 1920s in March 1922, when Mrs. Long and Mrs. Gilmore, Sunday school teachers at Grace Lutheran Church, Los Angeles, received the consent of the Rev. R. Jeske, visitor of the circuit, to organize a Sunday school. They made a house-to-house canvass resulting in a Sunday school of four large classes. Services were also conducted in the homes of members where, on June 29, 1922, a group of men met in the home of Mr. and Mrs. Gilmore in Walnut Park for the purpose of forming a Lutheran congregation of the Missouri Synod, voting to call the new congregation Redeemer English Lutheran Church, making it the mother church of Lutheranism in the area. On August 16, the congregation was officially established and organized at the home of Mr. and Mrs. P. M. Long of Walnut Park. Two weeks later at a Voter's Meeting, the members adopted the following resolution:…"that we, the members of Redeemer English Lutheran Church, heartily endorse the action of the Mission Board in extending a call to the Reverend H. Gihring as pastor of our church and cordially welcome and receive him as our pastor, so help us God."

Pastor Hugo Gihring was born on April 15, 1894, at Freedom, Missouri, where his father, Immanuel, was pastor, and his

> Redeemer Lutheran Church is born in March 1922, during the great population explosion of the 1920s.

mother was Pauline (Wiedmann) Gihring. He did his vicarage at Ayrshire, Iowa, for two years, 1915–1917. Following his graduation from Concordia Seminary, Springfield, Illinois, in 1918, he received a call as a missionary to China where he served at Hankow and Shinanfu from 1918 to December 1921. He married Adella C. Matthias on August 14, 1918, before leaving for the Chinese mission field. Their marriage was blessed with three children, Leonard born October 5, 1919; Verona Marie born January 12, 1924; and Dr. Melvin Charles D.D.S. born July 13, 1927, who preceded Pastor in death on January 3, 1952. His ministry in China caused much pain as his little eleven-and-a-half month-old son died of dysentery and was buried in Hankow International Cemetery. Pastor and his wife also contracted dysentery. Mrs. Gihring was later diagnosed with breast cancer, and they were forced to return to the United States for treatment. He accepted the call to be pastor of Redeemer, South Gate, in August of 1922, and served there until 1935. While serving at Redeemer, he was elected secretary of the Southern California District Mission Board from 1930 to 1933.

Since the congregation had outgrown homes for worship, services were held in the K. P. Hall in Huntington Park, and the Lyric Theater on Long Beach Boulevard near Florence Avenue was leased in April 1923 for the Sunday services at a fee of $20 per month. In July of 1924, a special congregational meeting was called for raising funds to purchase a lot. In 1926, a lot at 2720 Santa Ana Street was purchased to build a church. This property was on the southern border of Walnut Park, a wealthy section

of Huntington Park. From then on, developments followed in quick succession. A groundbreaking ceremony was held in March 1927. The next month a contract was signed for a new church building at a cost of $13,400. In August 1927, with much praise and joy, the Spanish mission-style church and parish hall were dedicated. In November of 1930, a pipe organ was purchased and placed in the sanctuary, and in 1931, an addition to the parish hall was completed to meet the needs of the growing Sunday school. In 1938, the congregation accepted the gift of a beautiful marble altar from Edmund B. Lohr.

In November of 1935, Pastor Gihring resigned his pastorate and was called to First Lutheran, Long Beach, as associate pastor from April 1936 to October 1939. After leaving the full-time ministry, he became an insurance agent in Gihring and Associates, a profession he pursued from 1946 until his death on June 29, 1966; this insurance agency established the District's first medical plan. He also served as an assistant pastor at St John's in Montebello beginning in 1941. His successor at Redeemer was Rev. A. M. Loth of Aurora, Illinois, who was installed in May of 1936. Pastor Loth was born September 14, 1875, in Germany, and gradu-

Redeemer's first church built in 1927 and located at 2720 Santa Ana Street in Huntington Park. The church was moved to the Long Beach Boulevard. property in South Gate in 1948. (Pacific Southwest District Archives)

The interior of the church with its beautiful marble altar. The building was sold to the Unitarian Church in 1956 and moved to State Street where it now stands. (Pacific Southwest District Archives)

ated from Concordia Seminary, St. Louis, Missouri, in 1898. He had served the Aurora congregation from 1898 to 1936. He was pastor of Redeemer from 1936 to 1941 where his stormy ministry was filled with strife, internal pain, and dissension ended with a court case to settle who had the rights to the congregation's property. Through these and other problems, a split in the congregation occurred, and a small group established Gloria Dei Lutheran Church in Huntington Park some time later. Pastor Loth died on October 22, 1946.

At the close of Pastor Loth's ministry in 1941, the Rev. Tobias H. Joeckel was called and arrived in June of that year. He was born on May 17, 1900, in Chicago, Illinois, where his father was a pastor; he attended elementary school in Garlin, Texas; he was a graduate of St. Paul's College, Concordia, Missouri, and the St. Louis Concordia Seminary in 1923. Before going to South Gate, he held pastorates at Presho and Huron, South Dakota, and at Saint Paul's Church, Williamsburg, Iowa. He and his wife, Esther, were married on June 7, 1924 and were blessed with four children: Raymond, Ralph, Barbara, and David, who also became a pastor. Under his positive and dynamic leadership, the congregation grew and prospered.

Rev. A. M. Loth, the second pastor of Redeemer from 1936 to 1941. (Pacific Southwest District Archives)

Rev. Tobias H. Joeckel, the third pastor of Redeemer from 1941 to 1965. (Pacific Southwest District Archives)

With the bombing of Pearl Harbor and the growing influx of people into Southern California, a scarcity of rental homes resulted, making it imperative that a parsonage be purchased for the pastor and his family. In 1942, the house at 3010 Broadway, Walnut Park, was purchased for $6,300. During the War years, the congregation continued to grow in unprecedented proportions, demanding more space and more room. In September of 1945, a parcel of land facing Liberty Boulevard and bordered by Long Beach Boulevard and Seville Avenue was purchased for $35,000; in January of 1946, the congregation resolved to erect an entirely new church plant, a reinforced concrete building of Gothic architecture that would accommodate 700 worshipers at a cost of approximately $175,000, which didn't occur at that time. In 1948, the congregation moved its first Spanish mission-style building onto the new property and sold the Santa Ana Street property. On June 5, 1949, the large parish hall was dedicated. It included a two-room parochial school to accommodate 80 pupils; a 80' × 49' gymnasium auditorium for social, educational, and athletic purposes; a spacious lounge with a fireplace room; a stage for performances; two offices for the church staff; storage facilities; and a large, modern kitchen.

The large parish hall/gymnasium with two rooms for a parochial school, a spacious lounge with a fireplace room, a stage, two offices, and a large, modern kitchen, was dedicated on June 5, 1949. (Pacific Southwest District Archives)

By 1947, the parish had grown to over 700 baptized members and 525 communicant members with 50 voting members. At the silver anniversary celebration during the week of September 7 to 12, the Rev. Hugo Gihring, first pastor of Redeemer, delivered the sermon in the morning service, on Sunday, September 7, and the Rev. Reno Jeske, circuit visitor, of Whittier, was the preacher at the evening service. A family buffet supper was served free of charge to all in attendance and the new LLL sound film, "Messenger of Peace," was shown to a large audience assembled on the church lawn. Other events of the week included duplicate banquets on Tuesday and Thursday evenings, with the mayors of South Gate and Huntington Park, respectively, in attendance and programs presented by the congregation's two Walther League groups; an evensong service on Wednesday night, featuring the church choir and soloists under the direction of Robert A. Lange, director of music; a family night on Friday, including program numbers presented by various auxiliaries and a con-

gratulatory address by District President Walter F. Troeger. The anniversary offering reached the $7,000 mark, making the congregation debt free. In two years, the church had liquidated its entire indebtedness on the new property, purchased in September 1945, for a sum of $35,000.

In the summer of 1949, the congregation celebrated the 25th wedding anniversary of Pastor and Mrs. Joeckel, presenting them with a silver coffee service set with other silver pieces at an open house. In the spring of 1950 on May 21 and 22, the Third Biennial Convention of the LWML, having a theme of "Thy Kingdom Come," was held in the new parish hall of Redeemer with an attendance of over 700, which included 124 delegates and 375 visitors. The convention voted to assist Zion Church of Victorville with $5,000 to build a new chapel. By 1950, three services had to be conducted at Redeemer in order to accommodate all the worshipers in the small church with Rev. Herman Atroops assisting.

Plans, designed by Ainswoth & Westberg, Pasadena architects, were formulated in 1954 for a new 9,000 square foot, imposing, moderate Gothic church building, which was designed for a cathedral effect. The construction of this large edifice began in late December 1956. The framework consisted of nine concrete arches 45 feet high, weighing 17 tons each. Forty-five foot-high concrete panels formed the church's end walls, each panel weighing more than 35 tons. The roof, capping the building, was formed with concrete panels between the arches, covered with wood shakes. The secondary concrete structure also formed with concrete panels, provided aisles running the length of the nave. The structure was mounted on 71 pilings, some of which were 32 feet deep. The first section of the 75-foot slender tower was erected using a Swedish-patented slip-form

Redeemer's large, modern Gothic church seating over 550, was dedicated on December 8, 1957. (Pacific Southwest District Archives)

The interior of the new church with the white marble altar in the spacious chancel. (Pacific Southwest District Archives)

process eliminating laps and joints. The upper 25 feet was a steel framework covered with glass mosaic. The tower of the new church was visible for several blocks in all directions from the strategic location of the church at Liberty and Long Beach Boulevard. In excess of 2,400 tons of concrete was used in the building.

A beautiful marble altar, carved with Agnus Dei relief, provided the focal point as worshipers entered the magnificent building. Twelve hand-carved wood symbols on the altar screen were taken from the pages of *Luther's Small Catechism*. The church had a seating capacity for over 550 persons, plus a large narthex and a spacious chancel of generous proportions. The pipe organ, located in the chancel area, was a rebuilt Robert Morton instrument of 14 ranks. Pastor Joeckel, who was assisted by his father, Rev. T. Joeckel Sr., of Lincoln, Nebraska, performed the Rite of Dedication for this inspiring house of worship on Sunday, December 8, 1957. Rev. Victor L. Behnken, President of the Southern California District, preached in the afternoon service, and an organ recital presented in the evening by Mr. LeRoy Urseth featuring the soloist, Robert Baker. Approximately 2,100 members and guests attended the three festival services. An afternoon buffet dinner was prepared and served by the Dorcas Circle, the Business Women, and other members of the congregation.

Since many members of Redeemer were moving into the growing community of Downey, Redeemer congregation decided to establish a branch church in Downey. While members had retained their membership and attendance at South Gate, many of them asked that their congregation begin work in their area both as a conservation measure and as a missionary endeavor. As a result of this request, a study of the possibilities in this fast-growing city, was made, with Redeemer resolving to begin work there starting worship services and Sunday school in September 1959 in the Women's Club building at 9813 South Paramount. The congregation obtained the services of Rev. Harold Kupke, a Los Angeles Lutheran High School teacher, who assisted with additional preaching requirements. Beginning in July 1960, Rev. Edward C. Beyer, formerly of Alcester, South Dakota, assisted the congregation. Worship services were conducted at 10:15 a.m. with attendance reaching 60, and Sunday school was at 9 a.m. averaged 39 pupils. This branch later merged with Messiah in Downey.

In order to accommodate the large number of children in the day school and to expand the school to eight grades, the voters decided that if all cooperated, the new room, 25' × 35', could be built for less than $5,000. Under the direction of Edmund B. Lohr, member of the Board of Education, and with the help of a large number of volunteers, the building was completed in time for the 1960–1961 school year. "Do it yourself" was the motto for building additional room for an expanding school program. The congregation responded so generously to the call for funds that it was also possible to purchase new robes for the church choirs. At the time, Leroy F. Hotz was principal of the school.

On June 6, 1965, Pastor Joeckel retired from active ministry after serving Redeemer Church for 24 years; in his retirement, he continued to serve the District in numerous vacancy positions, Mt. Calvary, Lake Arrowhead, and concluding his ministry at St. Matthew's in Irvine. He was called to the Church Triumphant in 1982. Mrs. Joeckel had also served in many capacities in the congregations of which her husband was pastor. In addition, she was elected the first president of the District's Lutheran Women's Missionary League and was also instrumental in establishing the Greater Los Angeles Business and Professional Women's organization.

Rev. John Schumacher served Redeemer for two months of the vacancy. On November 28, 1965, the Rev. John Charles Rumsey from Trinity, Woodward, Oklahoma, was installed as the fourth pastor of Redeemer. He was born August 15, 1928, in San Diego, California. After graduating from high school, Pastor Rumsey attended San Diego State College, where he received his B. S. degree, majoring in psychology and sociology. He did one year of post-graduate work toward a master's in clinical psychology and later attended Concordia, Oakland, for a special semester. After that he graduated from Concordia, Springfield, in 1957. His ministry began in a mission congregation in Fort Lauderdale, Florida, until 1959, when he accepted a call to Trinity Church in Woodward, Oklahoma. On June 1, 1956, he was united in marriage to Dorothy Mae Meyers of Oklahoma City. They were blessed with five children: John III, Rebecca, Judith, Grace Ann, and David. He served Redeemer until 1974 when he took a call to St. James, Imperial Beach.

Redeemer school expands in 1960.

Redeemer decides to build a branch church in Downey in 1959.

Rev. John Rumsey (right) installed as the fourth pastor of Redeemer on November 28, 1965, by Rev. L. Miller, circuit counselor (left). (Pacific Southwest District Archives)

Vicar Brady is commissioned to initiate a Hispanic ministry in South Gate in 1977.

After a two-year vacancy, Rev. Paul Adams accepted the position as Redeemer's pastor and was installed on January 2, 1977. Rev. Martin E. Lundi of Tempe, Arizona, delivered the sermon and Circuit Counselor Rev. Gulfrey Laurent conducted the Rite of Installation. The church choir under the direction of Kenneth Heitshusen sang "O Sing to the Lord." Also participating in the installation service were Rev. Robert Wolter; Rev. John Cassidy; Rev. Alvin Young; Rev. Robert Wobrock; Rev. Tobias H. Joeckel, former pastor of Redeemer; Rev. Elmer Boxdorfer; and Rev. Daniel Wooten. Following the service, a reception for Pastor, his wife, Janet, and their eight-year-old daughter, Cherish, was held in the parish hall. Pastor Adams came to South Gate from Trinity, Prescott Valley, Arizona, where he had served as missionary-at-large for the Southern California District after graduating from Concordia Seminary, Springfield, Illinois. His short ministry at Redeemer ended in May of 1978, as he accepted a call to Nevada.

By the 1970s, the South Gate area was beginning to witness an ethnic change with Anglos retiring and moving from the area and Hispanics replacing them. Seeing the change in the community surrounding Redeemer, in 1977, the parish requested that the Board for Missions send a Hispanic worker to work in their area. This request was granted in December when Vicar Charles Brady, a student from Concordia Seminary, Fort Wayne, Indiana, was commissioned to initiate a Hispanic ministry in South Gate where the community was nearly 70 percent Hispanic. A reception including a food shower was held for the vicar, his wife Sandra, and son Aaron. This Hispanic vicarage was aimed at determining effective means of outreach in a community that had changed rapidly in the previous 10 years. Also that fall, the 20-year mortgage on the church facilities was burned during a special service attended by members and former members of the congregation. Two previous pastors of Redeemer, Tobias Joeckel and John C. Rumsey, as well as the pastor at that time, the Rev. Paul M. Adams, officiated at the ceremony.

During the summer of 1978, the Hispanic Concerns Network of Los Angeles, a pan-Lutheran organization, held a Hispanic youth camp, "Campamento Hispano." Its sole purpose was to provide inner-city young people with in-depth exposure to Christian life including Bible studies, devotional and worship experiences, and a diverse recreational program. The idea was to provide Hispanic children with real alternatives to gang activities and other aspects of life on the streets in the "concrete jungle." The camp was for Hispanic youth ages 10 to 16. Recruitment was especially focused on children from low-income families and youth under the influence of gangs in the local barrios.

The first Campamento Hispano was held in the summer of 1977 where 56 young people and 14 counselors spent 3 days at Camp Yolijwa in the San Bernardino Mountains. The one-week camp adventure cost $55 for one child. Vicar Brady was in charge of raising funds for the camp. Following his graduation from Concordia Seminary, Fort Wayne, Indiana, in 1978, he was ordained at his home congregation, Our Savior Lutheran Church, San Jose, California, and installed as the pastor of Redeemer, South Gate, in November 1978.

Pastor Charles Brady was born in Glendale, California, on April 23, 1941, and attended Fremont High School in Sunnyvale, California, where he graduated in 1959. On June 28, 1968, he married Sandra Ojeda, and their marriage was blessed with four children. While serving as pastor of Redeemer, he also served as police chaplain, Commission for South City of South Gate, president of Ministerial Alliance, president of Churches in Action, and he participated in the Optimist Club.

Participating in the installation of Pastor Adams were Rev. Laurent, Rev. Robert Wolter, Rev. Lundi, Rev. John Cassidy, Rev. Alvin Young, Rev. Adams (center), Rev. Robert Wobrock, Rev. Tobias Joeckel, Rev. Elmer Boxdorfer, and Rev. Daniel Wooten. (Pacific Southwest District Archives)

In the early part of 1979, Rick Sarria was employed as a full-time lay assistant to the pastor at Redeemer. He was born on November 16, 1934, in Havana, Cuba, where he studied at University of Havana and graduated in 1952. He was drafted into the United States Army in 1961 and met his German wife, Anna Warner, from Frankfurt, Germany. They were married on April 2, 1961. Their union was blessed with one daughter, Jennifer. In the summer of 1979, Pastor Sarria was enrolled in a program at Concordia, River Forest, starting a Hispanic mission, San Pablo, at St. Paul's in Melrose Park, Illinois, which he served until 1981. Needing only 90 units to qualify for a colloquy, he continued his theological studies at Concordia Seminary, Fort Wayne, Indiana.

In the fall of 1979, Christian Education Month was celebrated at Redeemer including the installation of Cristiano Artigas as vicar with special emphasis on his ministry to the Spanish-speaking community. Rev. Kenneth Behnken, Mission Executive of the District, preached on the theme "Be Prophets with the Spirit." Vicar Artigas, a native of Ecuador, and his wife, Sherrie, were honored at a reception. The school's new eighth- and ninth-grade classroom was dedicated, and the new fifth- and sixth-grades teacher, Fred Brauer, was installed. Heading the construction of the classroom, which was located in the church basement, was a member of the congregation, Herb Grober. Assisting in the work were Jack Fergason and George Kaspar Sr., along with many other church and school families who donated time and talents. The classroom, built to accommodate 25 students, contained a science lab organized by Richard Whiteside, who taught in the room. All of the teachers were re-commissioned, including Virginia France, Wyaneta Timm, Lorraine Bergeman, and Timothy Peters, principal. The teachers were honored at a reception, together with the School Board and those who worked on the classroom. The school had grown from 72 students to 133 in the previous four years with the ninth-grade opening that fall with six students. Notes were sold to congregation members to finance the construction.

The pastor, Rev. Brady, praising God for the many blessings He had bestowed on Redeemer in its Christian education program, conducted a special worship service. The first and second graders sang "We Are the Church" under the direction of Wyaneta Timm. A number of students from the sixth through eighth grades participated in the service with readings and ushering.

In the middle of September 1979, the Hispanic Convention was held at the Hyatt House, City of Commerce. Included in the three-day convention was a tour of Redeemer Church and School in South Gate. Pastor Brady addressed the group, telling of the church's history and what the congregation was doing in its work among Hispanics. Also speaking on the work of the Hispanic congregation was Vicar Cristiano Artigas. Vicar Artigas was installed at Redeemer Church to work with Hispanic people in the area. Much communication between the church and the Hispanic people was accomplished through an outreach program that began with the Christian day school. Principal Tim Peters told the group that approximately one-third of the enrollment consisted of Hispanic children. By 1990, the day school had the highest Hispanic population of any school in the District, having 132 pupils or 77 percent of the student body Hispanic. In 1974, the day schools in the District had only 239 Hispanic students out of a student population of 8,417.

After completing his studies, the Rev. Ricardo Sarria was called by Redeemer as associate pastor in 1982 to direct the Spanish ministry. Pastor Sarria, a former Roman Catholic raised in Cuba, wanted only to bring the strength of the Gospel to the hearts of the people. He said, "Through this, their eyes are opened so they are no longer in bondage." He found such strength and beauty in the Lutheran liturgy and hymns in which "we are speaking directly to the Lord," that he conducted a traditional service using a Spanish translation of the liturgy. He believed that familiarity with the traditional also helped his people feel at home in any Lutheran church. Most of his evangelism was done through Redeemer's day school. "The key is the children, to reach the families and bring them the Word," he

Rev. Charles Brady was installed as the pastor of Redeemer in November of 1978, where he presently serves the English and Hispanic congregation. (Pacific Southwest District Archives)

Vicar Cristiano Artigas (left) being installed by Pastor Stirdivant at Redeemer Church to work with the Hispanic people in the area.

Rev. Ricardo Sarria was called as Redeemer's associate pastor to direct the Spanish ministry in 1982 and remained to 1989.

On September 3, 1993, a radio program known as "Spanish Radio Ministry: Ayer, Hoy, y Siempre" (Yesterday, Today and Always), is inaugurated.

stated many years ago. Confirmation classes and Bible studies for children and adults, and a youth group of 25 to 30 were part of his busy ministry. Miss Lola Denow, bi-lingual teacher in the day school, worked in the youth program with Pastor Sarria, as did three young men who were training for lay ministry. Additional contacts were made by visits to businesses in the community where Pastor left signs that invited people to worship services at Redeemer or Iglesia Luterana El Redentor.

By 1983, the 11:30 a.m. Spanish language Sunday service was averaging between 60 and 65 worshipers with the 10:15 a.m. Spanish language Bible class averaging between 12 to 15 adults. The Tuesday lay ministry training had 6 students enrolled and the Wednesday evening New Member Class had 12. The Friday Spanish adult Bible class was averaging 25 to 35 adults with the youth Bible study averaging 20 to 25 young people. Saturday afternoon Catechism class had 11 children enrolled. When Pastor Sarria left in 1989, he and the Spanish congregation moved to Pico Rivera. Work began anew under Pastor Charles Brady where the congregation had a solid and growing core of active and committed people working to share the Gospel of Jesus with the community and beyond. The worship services at Redeemer were lively and featured a worship band and church choir. "La Infanteria de Cristo" made calls on people in the community. The congregation also had active men's and women's groups.

Pastor Brady's ministry at Redeemer touched another man, Marcelo Gómez. He immigrated to the Los Angeles area in 1988, when he was 35 years old, having had a career as an accountant and bank auditor in Mexico. He recalled his first contact with the Lutheran church, "God had been good to me, and I wanted to offer my service as a volunteer to the church. But nobody would accept my offer; they turned me away. Then Pastor Charles Brady of Redeemer Lutheran Church in South Gate listened to my story, and before long I joined his church." Mr. Gomez became interested in a deeper study of theology and in 1994 began attending classes of the Hispanic Institute of Theology, taught in the Los Angeles area by Rev. Bob Alsleben, formerly a pastor in the NID. "I was in it because I loved the study of the Bible, not because I planned to become a pastor," he recalled. "But after four years of study, Pastor Alsleben told me that I had completed the pre-seminary work and was now ready for the seminary level. Maybe I

shouldn't have been surprised, but I was. That's when I had to decide whether or not to become a Lutheran pastor. Well, after, four more years of study, here I am. And my wife Andrea and I are very happy with that decision." The couple has a son who lived in Pasadena. At Pastor Gomez's ordination in 2002 at St. Paul's Lutheran Church in Harvard, Illinois, Pastor Alsleben, who lived in Milwaukee, was the preacher.

On September 3, 1993, a radio program known as "Spanish Radio Ministry: Ayer, Hoy y Siempre" (Yesterday, Today and Always), was inaugurated, broadcasting from Ventura to La Jolla at 5:00 to 5:30 p.m. each Friday, sharing the Gospel message with more than 6,000,000 Spanish-speaking people in metropolitan Los Angeles alone. The broadcasts were the result of work accomplished by the Hispanic Worker's Support Group. Contributing significantly to the establishment of Lutheran Spanish radio for the Pacific Southwest District were the Rev. Charles Brady of South Gate, the Rev. Douglas Jones of Montebello, and the Rev. Johnny Lopez of Orange. The ministry was sponsored primarily through the International Lutheran Laymen's League, which sponsored similar Spanish-language ministries throughout the United States, Central and South America, and the Caribbean. The Lutheran Women's Missionary League saw it as a significant way to join hands with the LLL in fulfilling the Great Commission.

The Good News of Jesus Christ was simultaneously broadcast to Spanish-speaking people of the Pacific Southwest District on stations KAXX 107.1 FM, Ventura; KMAX 107.1, Arcadia; and KBAX 107.1 FM, Fallbrook at a cost of $40,500 for six months. Pastor Douglas Jones, secretary of the Hispanic Worker's Support Group, explained the program this way, "We call the program a radio ministry because we will not only be proclaiming the Gospel over the radio, but we will be inviting people to call an 800 number to request helpful literature produced in the Spanish language by the Lutheran Laymen's League. The callers would then be referred to one of our churches in their area for continued Gospel ministry." The format of the program began with a dramatic presentation on a number of issues important in contemporary living, followed by a live discussion with Pastor Brady, who served as host of the program, and pastors Jones and Lopez. Among program highlights were the appearance of the Sweet Salvation Sanctuary Band with Johnny Lopez, the St. John's Worship Band of Orange, Singer Claudia Aguirre

Morrison, and Master Storyteller Tom Rogers, pastor of Abiding Savior, Lake Forest. Guest appearances were made by President Loren Kramer of the Pacific Southwest District and Dr. Norbert Oesch of the host congregation, St. John's, Orange.

By 1997, the Spanish radio program, "Ayer, Hoy y Siempre" (Yesterday, Today and Always), was aired weekly on KLXT (formerly KGER) 1390 AM every Friday evening at 10:30 p.m. Listeners were invited to call, talk over problems, and receive materials. Pastor Brady, the show's director, quoted a listener's words, "Pastor Brady, I don't have a phone, but when I heard the show, I went out to a pay phone. Your program really touched a nerve. I think I'm ready to give my marriage a new try." He later commented, "These words from a listener to 'Ayer, Hoy y Siempre,' the District's Spanish program, shows the power of radio to reach people." The show's format featured a theme song recorded by Pastor Johnny Lopez, then an introduction, followed by a drama enacted by professional actors, illustrating contemporary problems — family, marital, abortion, substance abuse — with Gospel solutions.

At Christmas time of 1995, AAL grants of $500 and $1,000, respectively, were presented to Redeemer Lutheran School and Southeast Lutheran High School immediately following a combined Hispanic and English worship service with carols sung in both languages. The grants were to enhance spring semester instruction at both educational institutions. John Thompson, district representative for Aid Association for Lutherans, made the presentation to both educational institutions. The $500 grant was used for general improvement at Redeemer to enhance its educational program.

Redeemer joined with close to 1,000 people from the District who gathered to celebrate diversity in the District and proclaim unity in Christ on May 9, 1996, for the "One in the Spirit" event organized by the Department of Mission Services at South Gate Municipal Auditorium. The joy filled day included sharing food, crafts, and entertainment, which helped all in attendance to experience the richness of each cultural group. With standing room only, the evening's entertainment brought culture, music, dance, song, and people together in a way that had never before been experienced in any other district in the United States. People from all cultures left that event saying, "This is our church, and we are glad to be a part of it. When are we going to do this again?" Another event was planned for 1999.

By 1996, Ben Parrales was hired as a part-time lay minister. Attendance at the Spanish service was up to 44 in 1997 with the Sunday school reaching 20 children. Pastors trained a core of leaders in the Spanish Bethel Bible series. One of the joys was receiving the Vargas family, Alejandro and Irma and their five children, as members of the congregation. When they first in lived in South Gate, they were members of the Apostolic Order Pentecostal — Jesus Only. When they moved to Davenport, Iowa, they met a Lutheran pastor who took them under his wing and instructed the father in the Lutheran Catechism. Since the father fell in love with Lutheran doctrine, they became members of Redeemer, when they moved back to South Gate.

In a devastating earthquake, Redeemer's sanctuary and gym were severely damaged. On Sunday, December 10, 1995, the people of Redeemer gathered to rededicate the gym wall that had been damaged in the quake. Pastor Charles Brady stated, "It was a great occasion. We have now come fully back from the disaster of the earthquake. With God's help we have rebuilt first the damaged sanctuary and now the damaged wall to our gym. The new wall is a testimony to God's grace to the spirit of our church and our people." The parish received love gifts from congregations all over Synod to repair the sanctuary and the gym wall. Especially helpful in the reconstruction were the gifts from Lutheran Brotherhood. "Lutheran Brotherhood was right there with a generous helping hand," declared Brady. The church also received tremendous help from investors in the Lutheran Church Extension Fund, with many investors dedicating the interest on their investment towards the rebuilding of churches. "It is a wonderful feeling to be able to rebuild. Everyone here at Redeemer, South Gate, is grateful to God who enabled us to come back from the earthquake," said Pastor Brady.

In order for the Spanish congregation to grow, three evangelism teams with six people each, "Infanteria de Cristo" (The Lord's Infantry), were formed to make weekly evangelism calls in 1998. They did a program, "Operation Celebration," in which 350 Bibles were distributed in the community. On Wednesday evenings during Lent, a program, "Free Family Dinners," was begun. The Lord blessed the efforts with attendance at worship services increasing to 59 and Sunday school going to 25. Luis Carrillo, a member of the congregation, decided the church needed a choir, so he began to

In a devastating earthquake, Redeemer's sanctuary and gym are severely damaged.

organize and develop one. He started with a brief rehearsal before Sunday service and then continued with a mid-week rehearsal on Wednesday evenings; the choir involved 6 to 10 people. Rafael Larios, who supplied Honduran food for "One in the Spirit," heard of an offer by the city of Filmore to donate seven bridges to Honduras in the aftermath of Hurricane Mitch. Through his efforts, this was undertaken as a congregational project and was adopted as "Bridges of Hope" with the goal of disassembling and reassembling the bridges in Honduras that year.

The "Redeemer Street Fair," a major community evangelistic event, was held on Saturday, August 7, 1999, with the street in front of the church closed for this big block party. During the Sunday service on October 7, a woman with a brain tumor, who had been battling cancer, got up in the church service and gave a testimony of the power of faith, moving everyone by her joy and sense of ultimate trust in Christ, her Lord. Through her conviction and great joy, she strengthened the faith of those present. Attendance in services continued to remain at 55 with the Sunday school reaching 25 students.

Attendance at the Spanish church services reached 62 during 2000 with a communicant membership of 238 in the English and Spanish churches combined. Through the school, two children were baptized along with one of the children's mother and her brother. In the spring, 6 were baptized and 12 children were confirmed. The stewardship goal for that year was to bring offerings of $250 per Sunday with the goal exceeded by $33 per Sunday. The church library grew with increased donations and new books. Prayer concerns were for a family whose father was working in Las Vegas, a boy struggling with drugs, and a family's car that was fire bombed. Gracieus Muñoz, dying of inoperable brain tumor, made a beautiful new robe (Alb) with embroidery and fine workmanship for the pastor. He said, "She barely had the strength to wish it, but finished it she did. What do you think of a gift like that?" By the end of the year, she seemed to be miraculously healed. At Redeemer, a good family atmosphere was exhibited among its members with people in the congregation caring for each other.

The first quarter of 2001 found attendance down somewhat due to several key and active families relocating. An extended family left the church, which decreased attendance even though new people were coming. The matriarch of the

clan didn't want to drive from Buena Park to South Gate any longer, as it was a long trip. As is the case with Hispanic families, when one leaves, the rest will follow. This sort of thing was not uncommon in Hispanic ministry. When the church janitor became ill and was unable to work, the congregation decided to do his work until he recovered. The congregation, including the Anglo church, planned a fabulous surprise birthday party for Pastor's 60th birthday with a Mariachi band, folkloric dancers, and piñatas. He was quoted as saying, "I never had a better time in my life." Once a month was "Friendship Sunday" where each member was encouraged to invite a friend, which worked very well and was a success. A new Saturday morning women's Bible class was begun. The choir and the other musicians made a music compact disk for the church. A new youth leader, Iszel Orozco, stepped forward to assist the youth minister and did a fine job. The youth did the Christmas play that year, which was very well attended and enthusiastically received. By the end of the year, attendance at the Spanish service increased to 65.

In 2002, the youth group had a successful "Kermés" (a kind of festival) in the church parking lot for outreach to the community. The Hispanic mission was growing in stewardship every quarter from the previous few years, bringing an increase in giving. The Spanish offerings and stewardship was up almost $1,000 from that quarter in the previous year. Victor Rico, who was Pastor's assistant, began his vicarage at Redeemer the first of the year. The overall church attendance was up 15 percent to 20 percent over the previous year with some of the Hispanic people going to the English service instead of the Spanish service. A stewardship/outreach campaign called "Apelación de Victoria" was conducted and included a talent show to reach the school children. The calling teams, "Infanteria de Cristo" went door-to-door canvassing the community on July 27. On a very sad note, one of the fathers in the Hispanic church, committed suicide as he couldn't deal with the loss of his job plus his rapidly deteriorating health, devastating the family.

During 2003, the mission continued to reach out to the community holding a special Epiphany service, "Dia de Reyes," where gifts were given to the children. During the Lenten season, starting with Ash Wednesday, the community was invited to a weekly service on Wednesday that was preceded by a light dinner. A potluck was held on February 16, "Domingo de Amistad." Fliers were sent

The "Redeemer Street Fair," a major community evangelistic event, is held on Saturday, August 7, 1999.

to the immediate area close to the church location, inviting them to the activities. At the beginning of the year, church attendance also increased to an average of 55. The church choir, "Coro del Espirito" sang two times a month to senior centers and a convalescent hospital with Vicar Rico also making calls every Saturday at a convalescent home. Ten ladies of the mission attended a District wide Hispanic Women's Retreat at Camp Arrowhead where they returned energized for the ministry of the church. A new women's Bible study met on Tuesday evenings, which was very well attended and continued to grow. The hope of the mission was to call Vicar Rico as pastor when he completed his vicarage. The Word continued to touch the lives of the people at Iglesia Luterana El Redentor in many different ways.

Zion Lutheran Church
Igelsia Luterana Sión
Iglesia Luterana San Pedro Y San Pablo
Iglesia Luterana Palabra De Dios
Maywood, California

Maywood, a 1.1-square-mile residential community surrounded by the more heavily industrialized cities of Vernon, Bell, Commerce, and Huntington Park in southeast Los Angeles County, is in a sea of industry. Some people describe it as being a lot like television's Mayberry, a small, warm, little town. Once a "lily white" community, it is now 2.63 percent Anglo and 96 percent Latino, consisting mostly of Mexican-Americans. A population of 28,083, makes it the most densely populated city in California. Maywood experienced a serious bout of white flight in the 1960s and 1970s when Anglo property owners moved to other areas and rented their homes.

Before there were any Lutherans in Maywood or a thought of Zion Lutheran Church or a city of Maywood, the land was passed from Indians to favorites of the Spanish Crown in 1781. Don Antonio Maria Lugo was one of those favorites who received the huge Spanish land grant, Rancho San Antonio, which encompassed the southeast area of Los Angeles County. Many years later, the Laguna Land & Water Company, owners and sub-dividers of Maywood, incorporated, under the laws of the State of California on December 3, 1912, with the intent of subdividing the land into half-acre farms and into city lots for residential use known as "Half-acre Garden Home Sites." It wasn't until May 1919 that the voters in the city named it Maywood, supposedly after a popular secretary, May Wood, who worked for the Laguna Land & Water Company.

By 1921, over 600 homes were built with a population of 1,100 having enjoyed life in Maywood garden homes. An average of 50 new homes per month were built in the area. The Pacific Electric Railroad also had a stop in Maywood and the main thoroughfare, Slauson Avenue, extended to Pacific Boulevard in the business district of Huntington Park. By 1924, the half-acre farms were being divided into city lots where the city enjoyed a business area on Slauson and Atlantic avenues, boasting the Maywood Egyptian Theatre. On September 2, 1924, the citizens of Maywood voted to incorporate, since there was a population of 1,000.

By 1933, the city had many large factories on the western border and many churches: United Methodist, 1920; St. Rose of Lima Catholic Church, 1922; First Baptist Church, 1922; and Bell's Grace Lutheran Church of the Augustana Synod, 1922. By this time, many Missouri Synod Lutherans had moved into the area. Since there wasn't a Missouri Synod church in Maywood, they attended St. John's Lutheran in Los Angeles, Redeemer Lutheran in South Gate, and Christ Lutheran in Los Angeles. One of the churches, Christ Lutheran, was planning to relocate since its neighborhood was in transition. On January 8, 1933, 24 members canvassed the vicinity of 54th Street and Western Avenue. On February 5, the Maywood area was canvassed by an equal number of members from Christ. On the following Sunday, Pastor Kuehnert conducted the first Lutheran service in Maywood at 58th Street and Carmelita Avenue. However, on May 28, the congregation resolved to choose

The first Lutheran service in Maywood is conducted by Pastor Kuehnert in 1933.

southwest Los Angeles as its future site, purchasing five lots on Chesterfield Square, at West 54th and Ruthelen streets, leaving the Lutherans in Maywood without a church. This situation would not last long, as God had a special plan for those Maywood Lutherans.

Maywood would see many changes in 1936 through 1938: a hospital, a $25,000 city hall built in 1938, a new post office building constructed in 1937, two fine, paved business streets 100 feet wide — Atlantic Avenue extending north and south from Pasadena to Long Beach and Slauson Avenue running east and west between Telegraph Road and the west beaches. The population of the city had grown to 9,000 people in 1936. From the Maywood Chamber of Commerce came these words: "Maywood is an ideal city in which to live and the fact that homes are greatly in demand is a testimony of its desirability as a place to make your future." So it was that God would plant His Word in Maywood through the establishment of a Lutheran church where the Word and Sacraments would nourish His faithful people.

In the depths of the Great Depression in 1936, a young candidate, Roland G. Finke, from Mayville, Wisconsin, who had graduated from Concordia Seminary, Springfield, Illinois in 1934, arrived to canvass the Maywood area. Not only did he canvass the area for six weeks but he also placed an ad in the *Maywood Journal*, the local newspaper, about establishing a Lutheran church in Maywood, announcing the first service of the new Lutheran mission was to take place on August 30 at the Townsend Club, 4344 East Slauson west of Pine

Rev. Roland G. Finke, Zion's first pastor, who arrived in 1936 and remained until 1949. (Pacific Southwest District Archives)

Avenue. On that first Sunday, 54 joyful souls attended the Mission with 35 children attending the Sunday school. This was the only church to be opened in the Southern California District in 1936 due to the Depression and lack of District funds. The first organizational meeting was held on October 11, 1936 at the Harold J. Billing's residence in Maywood where the name of the congregation, Zion Evangelical Lutheran Church, was unanimously selected. In November, Pastor Finke went back East to wed Miss Lorraine Ludeke, and their union was blessed with two children: Norman, who became a pastor, and Lois, who was a day school teacher. In the February 28, 1937, congregational meeting, the congregation voted to purchase the 122' × 145' property located at the corner of 61st Street and Pine Avenue at a cost of $2,100. On September 12, 1937, the chapel that would seat about ninety people and a one-room school was dedicated. The new teacher, Candidate Armin Hesse, opened the new one-room school the following day with 18 pupils. The cost of this chapel/school building was $3,604.58. The following year, the first called teacher, Mr. Earl Knaak, arrived to assume teaching responsibilities of the one-room school. By 1939, because the school and church had both grown, it was decided to add another classroom on the north side of the chapel, housing grades one through four.

Rev. Finke arrives in Maywood in 1936 to start Zion Lutheran Church.

Zion's first building, a combination chapel and day school, was dedicated in 1937. Picture taken in 1946. (Pacific Southwest District Archives)

Interior of the first church taken about 1939. When the building was dedicated, there was a statue of Christ on the altar. (Pacific Southwest District Archives)

Since the congregation continued to grow and all the classrooms and chapel were used for church services, the Planning Committee in March 1941 presented a proposal to build a new 400–seat sanctuary designed by the architect, Mr. J. H. Fleming of Glendale, on the recently purchased property on the corner of 61st Street and Clarkson Avenue, but December 7 put all plans of building aside until after the War. Following the War, in 1948, with the school enrollment at 120 students, the chapel was used for a third classroom to accommodate the enrollment. The architect, Mr. O. J. Bruer of Montebello, drew new plans to erect an Early English Gothic style church and parish hall. The day finally arrived for the groundbreaking service on Sunday, August 31, 1947, witnessed by 250 worshipers. At the time the ground was broken, $10,000 had been raised for the building that would eventually cost $60,000. Since the church didn't want to go into deep debt, part of the cost was financed with "the pay-as-you-go plan" adopted, having thirty members loan the congregation $19,700 at 3 percent interest.

Churches have been constructed in various manners, but Zion's is the most unique. Not that the method had never been used before, but that it functioned as it did. It was a cooperative endeavor,

with almost all work being done by the members of the congregation and other interested people in the community. Seldom was it necessary to employ professional help, and then only when such assistance was absolutely necessary by the nature of the job, or time deadlines to be met to permit other work to be done. The construction was not a simple task, and required many thousands of hours of labor and many prayers to the Lord for guidance, especially when, at times, it appeared that the project might never be completed. The project was under the direction of a building committee, composed of members of the congregation. Mr. J. Earl Daly, a Maywood building contractor, supervised construction and planned work for the crews. The crews were various members assigned to the different members of the Building Committee. Work was done after working hours in the evenings and on Saturdays with occasional groups working on Sunday afternoons. Every Saturday, the ladies of the congregation served lunches for the workmen. Finally, after two years of labor, the beautiful building was dedicated in the afternoon on Sunday, August 28, 1949, at 3:00 p.m.

When entering the imposing nave, the worshiper's eyes were drawn to the beautiful, fine-looking

Zion builds new church using all volunteer labor.

Men are laying the foundations for the church and side porch. In the foreground, Pastor Finke, wearing a white tee shirt, is bending over. (Pacific Southwest District Archives)

walnut altar with brass cross and candelabras and shiny walnut paneling in the chancel. Above the altar was a large, brightly colored stained glass window depicting Christ as the Good Shepherd flanked by two windows representing the two Sacraments, Baptism and the Lord's Supper. The rich looking 400-seat nave had 8,000 square feet of floor space in the church and parish hall. This style of architecture, originally used in England, gave full scope to the heavy scissors-type trusses. The interior trusses rising over 20 feet above the floor were made of steel by a member, Jake Schmidt, and covered with dark wood. Because of the low walls and high-pitched roof, drop-arch door openings of the Tudor period were used. The doorway in the tower, crowned with a tall octagonal, copper spire, rising 56 feet, made it the tallest building in Maywood at that time, giving dignity to the entrance. The modern developments, such as lighting and acoustics, were blended with the rustic early English design in such a manner that gave a truly churchly and devotional atmosphere

The tall octagonal, copper spire, rising 56 feet, makes it the tallest building in Maywood at the time.

for those who worshiped in the building. Pastor Finke had suggested the stained glass windows on the north side of the church depict the story of Christ from the promise to the Easter resurrection with those in the chancel representing the Word and Sacraments and the south side representing the Trinity, the Bible, Christian service and ending with the heavenly Zion, depicting the entire life of a Christian. The choir loft located off the chancel area would accommodate 30 choir members; an organ chamber was built into the south side of the chancel wall. The church office was off of the chancel and was also paneled in walnut stained wood.

When January of 1950 arrived, the congregation would receive the disheartening news that their beloved Pastor Finke had accepted a call to Trinity Lutheran Church, a large parish in Peoria, Illinois. The congregation gave the Finkes a farewell party on Lincoln's birthday presenting them with a cash farewell gift. He would serve a number of congregations in Wisconsin and Texas before retiring in

The new church on Dedication Day, August 24, 1949; the front steps needed brick trim and handrails, which were added some years later. (Pacific Southwest District Archives)

Arkansas where he died in 2002. With the departure of Pastor Finke, who would be the new pastor to follow in his tenure of almost 14 years at Zion? The pastor who followed him would double his tenure as pastor of Zion, staying 28 years. The new pastor was the Rev. Elmer C. J. Boxdorfer of Calvary Lutheran Church of Yuma, Arizona. He was born on February 11, 1909, in Perryville, Missouri, where he attended Immanuel Church and School. He attended high school and college at Concordia College in Fort Wayne, Indiana, where he met his future wife, Leona, and graduated in 1929. Following his graduation from Concordia Seminary, St. Louis, in 1932, he began his ministry in the hill country of his native state, Missouri, where he served Zion Lutheran Church of Gravelton, a congregation founded in 1857. In the fall of 1933, he was commissioned as a missionary in two sister congregations in two western Missouri counties, Henry and Johnson, where he served Trinity Lutheran Church in Clinton and Bethlehem in Warrensburg. In Warrensburg, he served as Lutheran

chaplain at Missouri State College and built a beautiful church in the town. Late in 1943, he accepted the call to Calvary Lutheran Church, Yuma, Arizona, and served as a Lutheran service pastor to thousands of Army and Air Force servicemen stationed at various bases on the southwest desert. In 1944, he assumed the Protestant chaplaincy among German and Italian prisoners incarcerated in a prisoner of war camp near Yuma. Under his guidance and ministry in Yuma, the congregation grew.

On the first of June, Pastor Boxdorfer left Yuma to travel to Maywood in his new 1950 Nash the Yuma congregation gave him as a farewell gift. He was installed as pastor of Zion on June 11, at a 3:00 p.m. service with Rev. T. H. Joeckel, circuit visitor and pastor of Redeemer, South Gate, in charge of the installation and Rev. E. C. Manns, Zion's vacancy pastor, delivering the address. A grocery shower reception was held following the service on the cement floor in the partially completed parish hall with an open ceiling viewing the clear,

> Rev. Boxdorfer arrives in Maywood in 1950 to begin his 28-year ministry there.

The beautiful interior of the church on Dedication Day, having no walnut panels, Communion rails, and choir loft screens in the chancel, as they had not yet been completed. The hymn boards were placed high to cover the furnace openings, because the furnace wasn't installed until 1950. (Pacific Southwest District Archives)

Pastor Elmer Boxdorfer honored at his twenty-fifth anniversary in the ministry in 1957. (Pacific Southwest District Archives)

In the 1950 Christmas Eve service, some 550 people fill the church pews and folding chairs for the day school service.

blue sky. At his first Christmas Eve service, some 550 people would fill the church pews and folding chairs in the aisles and back of the church to participate in the day school children's service, the largest attended Christmas Eve service in the history of the congregation. The following year, Easter festival service at 10:30 a.m. was attended by 428 worshipers, with 237 children in Sunday school; that evening at 7:30 p.m. the Easter program by the Sunday school, the "Joy of Easter" a story of Easter in 50 colored slides with a processional of 150 children carrying white crosses, and 3 groups of children singing, was attended by 243 people. The Vacation Bible School (July 9–20, 1951) had 203 registered with an average daily attendance of 194, with 50 prospects gained for the Sunday school and day school. Three hundred forty-two people attended the VBS closing service in the church on a hot summer evening and viewed the children's work following the service. The year ended with a congregation of 580 baptized members and 379 communicant members; this year would be the highest communicant membership even though attendance in Sunday morning services and Sunday school would increase until 1967. By 1956, the baptized membership had grown to 630 with a Sunday school enrollment of 345. During 1957, 41 baptisms were recorded; five Bible classes were maintained with 40 percent of communicants either attending a Bible-study class on Sunday morning or teaching one of the Sunday school classes.

In April 1952, the Christian Youth League, with the help of the congregation, filled 45 boxes, weighing over 800 pounds, with toys, clothes, and other personal items for the Korean War orphans, which were distributed by Lutheran chaplains serving in Korea. During this same period, the big priority was to not only complete the parish hall in 1951 but also finish the interior of the church. In 1956, a new beautiful two-story parsonage of 2,000 square feet was built next to the church to accommodate Pastor and Mrs. Boxdorfer and their two children, Janet and Tom. The house had a large living room, dining room, den, study, large kitchen, and half bath downstairs with three spacious bedrooms and full bath upstairs. The following year, a set of Maas Cathedral Chimes was purchased for the old Wurlitzer organ. In 1961, the beautiful, 16-rank Casavant pipe organ was purchased at a cost of $18,000 to replace the electronic organ that had given the church problems for many years. At the time, the church choir numbered 30 and was un-

der the direction of Michael Doyle, organist and choir director for 12 years.

By 1969, the Maywood area was changing from a community with young families to a community of older people as so many families were moving to newer areas of Downey, Pico Rivera, Lakewood, and Whittier where there were larger and more affordable homes. With the changing community came a decrease in enrollment in both the public schools and at Zion, with the congregation making the painful decision to close the thirty-two-year-old day school. In 1966, the congregation had voted to drop the seventh and eighth grades making it a two-room school. By 1969, the two teachers had a student body of only 28 students. The school was forced to close. The declining neighborhood brought many changes to the congregation of 410 baptized members and the 265 communicant members. The 1970s would bring even more changes to Zion with a new change in the neighborhood. The Anglo population was moving away and a new group — Hispanics — would begin moving into Maywood.

In the fall of 1977, Pastor announced that he would retire at the end of January of 1978. With regret, the congregation accepted his resignation and began plans for his retirement farewell service on January 8. After 28 years of service as Pastor of Zion, it was difficult for the parish to accept the fact that he would be leaving them. The year ended with 204 Souls and 158 members. Even with all the changes in the neighborhood, loss of members,

The parsonage north of the church was built by volunteer labor and completed in 1956. (Pacific Southwest District Archives)

and a decrease in funds, Zion still remained firm in her trust in God and her mission to proclaim His Word. More than 250 members and friends honored Pastor and Mrs. Boxdorfer on his retirement in a service of praise and thanksgiving plus a farewell dinner in the parish hall on January 8, 1978. Pastor and Mrs. Boxdorfer moved to a new home in Riverside, purchased by their daughter and son-in-law, Janet and Gil Dyrr. Pastor started a mission church in nearby Sunnymead. It grew and became a large parish, Shepherd of the Valley, in the city of Moreno Valley. After the congregation called a permanent pastor, Pastor and Mrs. Boxdorfer became active members at Immanuel Lutheran in Riverside where they maintained their membership. In November of 2002, Pastor was called to the Church Triumphant at the age of 93.

During the vacancy period of eighteen months, the longest in the congregation's history, the Reverend W. Doering, a retired pastor from Our Sav-

Pastor Boxdorfer at Zion's altar on the occasion of his retirement in 1978, wearing the robes given to him by the congregation in 1957. (Pacific Southwest District Archives)

ior Lutheran Church in Arcadia, was hired as the interim pastor and began his service on February 1, 1978. It ended in August 1979, after he and his wife won the hearts of the people with their kind and loving ways. By summer, the congregation's prayers were answered when word was received that they had been given a candidate, the Rev. Elwood Mather III, a graduate of Concordia Seminary, St. Louis, who was a young man and would bring new vitality to the congregation. He arrived in August with his installation held on August 5. Pastor Mather was born July 11, 1952, in Kew Gardens, New York, the son of Rev. and Mrs. Elwood Mather Jr. After graduating from Concordia College in Bronxville, New York in 1969, he attended Central College in Pella, Iowa, receiving a B.A. in communications in January 1974. While there, he had an opportunity to participate in Central's overseas programs in Merida, Yucatan, Mexico, and in London, England. In June 1976, he graduated from Cambridge University in England with an Honours Degree in Theology and Religious Studies, concentrating in church history. In May 1979, he graduated from Concordia Seminary in St. Louis, Missouri, with a Master of Divinity degree. He later received a doctorate in history at the University of Southern California. On August 21, 1981, he married Sharon Hahn. Their marriage was blessed with two daughters, Christina and Michelle.

Seeing a need to do missionary work in the Hispanic neighborhood, the congregation requested the assistance of the Mission Board in making arrangements for a bilingual ministry in 1978. In September of 1979, word was received that the District was placing a Spanish speaking missionary-at-large at Zion. On Sunday, November 9, in a special service, the Reverend Cristiano Artigas was commissioned as missionary-at-large with the assignment to develop a Hispanic congregation using the facilities at Zion. Pastor Artigas was born on March 2, 1953, in Somoto, Nicaragua, Central America, to Rev. and Mrs. Napoleon Artigas, who were missionaries in El Salvador. He was baptized and confirmed in the Lutheran faith, attended schools in Managua, Nicaragua, and Panama City, Panama, and graduated in 1970 from Liceo Ruben Dario in San Salvador, El Salvador, with a Bachelor of Science and Literature degree. He received an Associate of Arts degree from Bethany Lutheran Junior College Mankato, Minnesota, attended Mankato State University in Mankato, and received a Bachelor of Science in Secondary Edu-

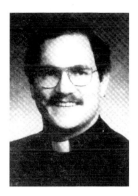

Rev. Elwood Mather III, Zion's third Pastor, 1979–1988.

Rev. Artigas is commissioned to develop a Hispanic congregation at Zion in 1979.

cation in Spanish and Speech in 1975. He next attended Bethany Lutheran Theological Seminary in Mankato, Minnesota, finishing his studies in 1978. His vicarage was at Northwood-Lake Mills Lutheran Parish in Iowa and at Redeemer Lutheran School in South Gate, California. In 1974, he married Sherrie M. Dannhoff of South Branch, St. James, Minnesota. She had a Bachelor of Science in Secondary Education from Mankato State University, Mankato, Minnesota. She held teaching credentials from three different states, teaching at the high school level for four years in Minnesota. They were blessed with a son, Cristiano Benjamin, on August 2, 1980.

The year ended with 127 souls and 110 communicants, an average Sunday attendance of 90 and a Sunday school enrollment of 33. The new year of 1981 began with Pastor Artigas forming a committee to investigate the reopening of the day school in order to minister to the Hispanic community surrounding the church. A temporary loan was made to the school fund to do some "temporary work at the school" with the election of School Board members held after the service on May 17. On September 8, the day school, closed for 12 years, was reopened with Miss Wyaneta Timm, principal and teacher of grades one through 3, teaching 15 students, 12 with Spanish surnames, 2 Anglos, and one American Indian. Pastor Artigas served as administrative assistant to Miss Timm and took over in the middle of the year as principal to give Miss Timm more time in the classroom. The money to support the school during the school year 1981–1982 came from the following sources: Flea Market, $4,500; AAL, $1,500; District, $5,000; Tuition, $11,250. Rev. Artigas also conducted a Saturday doctrine school for the children with astounding success.

The communicant membership had grown by 11 people that year with 8 children baptized and an average of 70 people attending services. In September 1982, the day school began with an enrollment of 48 with Ms. Anderson teaching kindergarten, Miss Timm teaching grades one thru three, and the new teacher, Donna Kay Winter, teaching grades four thru six. Pastor Artigas left in the fall to help Pastor Stirdivant in his ministry at La Santa Cruz in Los Angeles and in Bell Gardens; Pastor Rick Sarria came in 1985 to assist with the Spanish ministries at Zion and remained until 1987. Thirty people attended the first Family Life Night that was supplemented with films borrowed from AAL and Lutheran Brotherhood film

bank. Spanish worship services were being conducted each Sunday at 5:00 p.m. with an average of 15 to 20 in attendance. On Saturdays there was a visitation program in the neighborhood with Hispanic families. The Family Life Night and Spanish language class were held on Tuesdays, reaching 40 children and parents in the neighborhood. Some children attended Sunday school and parents expressed an interested in the church. In the fall of 1984, the school enrollment reached 69 pupils. In May, the youth painted the tower room and on June 23, the dedication of the Tower Youth Room was conducted giving the youth their special place for meetings with a new couch and chairs. Since attendance at Spanish services was so poor, the services were suspended the last Sunday in May.

On May 4, 1986, a tremendous, joyful celebration took place, the Fiftieth Anniversary Service and Dinner with Pastor and Mrs. Finke and their children, Norman and Lois from Texas. Pastor Finke preached on "Built on the Rock" from Matthew 16:13-18; Pastor Boxdorfer and Pastor Doering served as lectors and Pastor Mather was the liturgist. Michael Doyle was the organist and choir director directing the church choir in the anthem, "Built on the Rock." The beautiful, "Built on the Rock," stained glass anniversary and memorial window in the transom over the main entrance doors, designed and executed by Stan Hansen and

> On September 8, 1981, the day school, closed for 12 years, is reopened.

The church's 45th anniversary celebration with pastors: Front: E. Mather (1979–1988), R. Finke (founding pastor, 1936–1950), E. Boxdorfer (1950–1978), C. Artigas (missionary-at-large, 1980–1982); Back: A. Hesse (first teacher, 1937–1938), W. Doering (interim pastor, 1978–1979).

Associates of San Gabriel, was dedicated in that extraordinary 50th anniversary service. Following the service, a dinner was attended by such a large crowd, that people had to eat outside on the picnic tables and on the east porch of the parish hall. The decorations on the tables, the work of Ella Johnson, were gold placemats and golden churches as well as beautiful flowers decorating the parish hall. Ana Perez decorated large cakes, with images of Zion's church building on them. During the fellowship hour, the master of ceremonies, Bill Hamilton, Maywood mayor and councilman, introduced all of the speakers including the pastors. All the pastors' wives, Mrs. Finke, Mrs. Boxdorfer, Mrs. Doering, and Mrs. Mather, spoke of life in the parsonage. The former members, Miss Rolf, principal and teacher from 1953 to 1966; Don Buccowich; and Michael Doyle, reminisced on events of the past. Mr. Bob Nieweg, the original Building Committee chairman, shared how much the different materials cost at the time the building was built.

Hollywood came to Zion a second time on October 20, 1986, filming an episode of the "Lou Grant Show" with Ed Asner, star of the series, and Bob Prosky walking through a scene at Zion, simulating the setting of Grant's supposed hometown in Michigan. Two months later on Thursday, December 4, at 5:50 a.m., a greater-alarm fire caused by a faulty gas furnace did about $45,000 in damage to the school; eight fire companies brought the blaze under control in 20 minutes. Children in that classroom had class sessions in the parish hall while repairs were completed. On March 22, 227 people attended the school rededication with police and fire agencies invited to participate.

On June 6, 1988, the Congregational Farewell was held at Maywood Park after the church service for the Mr. and Mrs. Todd Jerabek, who had served as principal and teachers in the school for three years. Todd was going to study for the ministry at Concordia Seminary, St. Louis. The congregation would have to accept another departure that summer with the resignation of their beloved Pastor Mather; after nine years of service at Zion, he had decided to go into the university teaching profession full-time. Pastor Mather was granted a peaceful release, with the congregation gathering for a farewell potluck for him and his family on September 25. He taught part-time at universities in the area until he received a full-time position at the University of Montana at Billings where he stayed a number of years before accepting a call

to serve as pastor of St. Peters in Pine Island, New York.

Rev. Robert Foelber of Long Beach accepted the appointment of interim pastor as of October 2, 1988, with a special welcome for him held on October 10. Ben Parrales, "assisting pastor," was conducting Spanish services with 15 in attendance and also called on Hispanic families in the community; he was part of The Hispanic Institute of Theology program sponsored by the Missouri Synod to train men for Hispanic ministry. In 1989, he was under contract for $100 per week to help with Sunday services, build Spanish services, and canvass the neighborhood to invite prospective members. On Palm Sunday, three Hispanic youth were among the five members of the high school class accepted as communicant members during the service, which was conducted by the interim pastor, the Rev. Robert Foelber, and the assisting Spanish pastor, Ben Parrales. In the fall, school began with 67 pupils. Mrs. Bonnie Hoffschneider taught pre-kindergarten and kindergarten; Ms. Marilyn Coughran taught first through third grades; and Mr. Joel Hoffschneider taught grades four through six. The school children were also singing in the services, increasing church attendance. In December, Pastor Kay began serving as interim pastor at $900 per month. The year 1990 began with the congregation issuing Pastor Kay a call because of his sincere and kind manners, feeling he would be a good pastor for them; he accepted the position in February. He and his wife and children moved into the parsonage on March 10, and he was installed at an installation service at 3:00 p.m. on March 18 with Pastor Frank Brundige preaching the sermon. In March of 1991, Pastor Kay received a call to Trinity Lutheran Church in Wolf Point, Montana, which he accepted, leaving Zion on April 13, having stayed only thirteen months.

When Deacon Raul Saldaña arrived in Maywood from Bell Gardens to restart a Hispanic ministry at Zion in 1990, he visited people in the neighborhoods and invited them to come to church. In the nine months he was there, he developed a congregation conducting two services: one at 7:00 a.m. with about 35 people and another at 5:00 p.m. with 25 people. He instructed Saturday Catechism classes with 30 children and had a home Bible study for 25 adults. Due to economical and other problems at Zion, the Hispanic church was forced to leave Zion's premises, and many members of the newly formed Hispanic church

Raul Saldaña restarts a Hispanic ministry at Zion in 1990.

Deacon Raul Saldaña conducting services in the rented VFW Hall on Slauson Avenue in Maywood in 1996.

Spanish services are conducted in VFW Hall in 1992.

left the flock. The remnant worshiped in people's homes and in January of 1992 the small group moved to St. Phillip's in Compton where services were conducted for one month. They moved back to Maywood having services at a home on 53rd Street with Saturday Catechism classes. The deacon was also conducting Spanish Bible study classes in Norwalk and Bell Gardens.

In 1993, Deacon Saldaña rented the VFW Hall on Slauson Avenue in Maywood where he served 35 to 80 people by creating a small chapel in the hall and using the old altar from the Bell Gardens church. He also conducted Confirmation classes there. In 1997 when he left to go to La Santa Cruz in East Los Angeles, the Maywood Hispanic parish, which had worshiped in the VFW Hall, died.

With Pastor Kay's departure in 1991, Zion had a number of pastors filling the pulpit for Sunday services. Upon the suggestion of the principal and teacher of the day school, Joel Hoffschneider, the congregation called his father, Rev. Dale Hoffschneider from All Saints Lutheran Church, Slippery Rock, Pennsylvania, to be the Pastor of Zion with the vacancy period lasting a little over four months. Pastor Hoffschneider was installed on September 8, 1991. In the fall, the school year began with Mrs. Bonnie Hoffschneider teaching 15 kindergartners and first graders and a new teacher, Mr. Paul Barnes, teaching 10 children in grades 2–4, and Mr. Joel Hoffschneider teaching 17 students in grades 5–7. The year ended with a congregation of 104 souls, with 93 communicant members with a Sunday school of 5 students.

In the summer of 1992, Joel and Bonnie Hoffschneider accepted a call to St. John's, Oxnard. During

that summer, the parish hall was prepared for the arrival of Head Start in the fall with the Head Start leasing space in the parish hall for two classes in the morning and another in the afternoon. There were twenty in each class with the school paying $1,000 per month with a five-year lease. In the fall, the day school opened with Mr. Barnes as principal and teacher of grades four through seven and Mrs. Gert Hoffschneider as the teacher of grades one through three. On December 6, a planning session was held to discuss the future of Zion as the membership continued to decrease and the financial resources were also dwindling.

The year ended with 105 souls and 87 members and an average Sunday attendance of 35 per service. The year, 1993, began with the congregation showing their love by helping four homeless people. Due to a lack of men in the congregation, the constitution was amended to allow women to hold the office of chairman. Since the school had only 25 students and caused a financial drain on the congregation, it was decided to close it in June of that year. At the June 10 Closing Service of School, Joel Hoffschneider, former principal and teacher, was the guest speaker. Certificates of appreciation were sent to all 14 teachers who taught at the school since 1982. In January 1994, Head Start agreed to move to the school building where they used the east and west classrooms and the office. In February, Ana Sapien, a member whose family was gained through the school when Pastor Mather was there, agreed to teach the adult Bible class using Spanish/English side-by-side materials; in April, she began the English/Spanish Bible class on Friday evenings at the parsonage. In the spring, the parish began investigating the possibility of a joint ministry with another congregation. Since Zion's goal that summer was "To serve the community and make it a good place to live," they planned a free English class taught by Mrs. Hoffschneider advertising it in the *Industrial Post,* a local newspaper. The big event arrived on Saturday, July 30, with a Mariachi Band of Maywood musicians engaged from 2:00–4:00 p.m. along with Zion's members dispensing free ice cream to the 100 neighbors who came to register for the free ESL classes. The classes began on August 6 with 40 attending the Saturday morning class, and over 30 in the afternoon class despite the heat that day. Some returned on Sunday to repeat the class along with 19 new students, making almost 100 in attendance at the three beginning classes with 50 people at the second weekend classes. For a num-

Mariachi Band, in foreground, played for July 30, 1994, ESL Class Registration; Back: Vera Menge, Hulda Biel, Frances Clark, Pastor Hoffschneider, Gert Hoffschneider, Ronnie Potts, Gert Pritchard, Sonia Velasquez, Bill Hamilton, and Mildred Hamilton, seated. (Pacific Southwest District Archives)

ber of years, the name Zion Lutheran Church was also known as "Iglesia Luterana Sion" in order to appeal to the Hispanic community.

In August of 1994, St. John's of Montebello held a meeting for interested churches on merging all the Lutheran churches in the area forming one large church in a new location. This idea of merging all the Lutheran congregations never "got off the ground." The congregation did spend $140.89 per month to send letters in English and Spanish to new residents in the Maywood area to do evangelism work and develop a congregational self-study. On September 14, First Communion classes for Ashley and Felix Velasquez Jr. were started with their First Communion held on November 6; following the service, a potluck was held with the Sapien family providing the main dish. New English classes were started the first of October with fliers posted and given to members to distribute. In November, door hangers with the Gospel of John were printed in Spanish and distributed in Maywood and parts of Huntington Park advertising the church and its mission. By the end of that year, the congregation numbered 43 souls and 40 members with a Sunday school of 7 students with one teacher.

The New Year, 1995, began with Pastor sending letters to new Maywood residents from the automated neighborhood mailing list the church purchased. Invitational/information bags were prepared for neighborhood distribution. New "You Are Welcome" folders were given to visitors with

Sam Peña assisting visitors in Spanish. In February, the letters of welcome in Spanish and English were developed for Family Night. Because attendance was very poor at Family Night in April, mailings were sent in May to 447 people to tell about the Family Nights and the English classes. In July, the Family Nights were canceled due to a lack of interest and poor attendance on Friday nights. In June, 150 people registered for English classes with attendance running as high as 40. By July, 55 people were attending the English classes generating an interest in a Spanish service. One hundred one new people had moved into the area, and welcome letters sent to them from the church. In September, Head Start had its orientation in the parish hall and began using the third classroom in the school building. On September 19, the citizenship classes began on Tuesday and Thursday evenings from 6:00 to 9:00 p.m. English classes continued on Sundays from 7:00 to 9:00 p.m. with help from Ana, Alberto, and Sydney Sapien. In the late fall, the last session of the English class was held on November 12, with a new session beginning on January 17. The citizen classes had 36 registered with an attendance of 20 to 22; Pastor and Mrs. Hoffschneider, who taught the classes, invited people to services. Preparations were begun for the 60th anniversary celebration using the same theme and logo as the 50th, "Built on the Rock;" the committee was planning many special events in 1996. The year 1995 ended with 34 souls and 34 communicant members with the efforts to

The name Zion Lutheran Church is also known as "Iglesia Luterana Sion" in order to appeal to the Hispanic community.

reach the community through the Family Nights, English classes, and citizenship classes all intended to plant the seed of God's Word.

The New Year, 1996, began with much hope for Zion's survival. Since Peace Lutheran in South Gate, a congregation, which left the Evangelical Lutheran Church of America to affiliate with The Lutheran Church — Missouri Synod two years before, had lost its pastor, it was contacted to establish a joint parish arrangement with Zion. As Peace was interested in a joint parish, a general meeting was held at Peace on February 13, and on Ash Wednesday, February 21, a general meeting was conducted at Zion after the service to work out details. Following a meeting of Zion's council with the corresponding body of Peace, Pastor Hoffschneider was appointed interim pastor of Peace. In January before the arrangement with Peace, Zion decided to have the church property appraised for its sale value. They, also at that time, designated Ana Sapien as Zion's local mission liaison where she assisted in the adult instruction class with her Spanish skills. In order to accommodate the churches, Peace held its regular Sunday morning service at 8:30 a.m., and Zion changed its 10:30 a.m. service to 11:00 a.m. Mrs. Gert Hoffschneider became organist and choir director at Peace. In March, Ana Sapien provided assertive service — simultaneous Spanish translation — each Sunday at Zion. This was done when Pastor spoke the liturgy, the Scripture readings, and the sermon in English; Ana utilized a transmitter to translate his words into Spanish to listeners who were equipped with headsets. On May 26, the congregation began using Divine Service II, First Setting in *Lutheran Worship* as it matched the service in the Spanish Hymnal, *El Contad*. Also, at this time, Peace was ready to yoke with Zion officially sharing the same Pastor making Zion and Peace dual parishes.

The fall began with the citizenship classes relocated to other facilities due to a conflict in Zion's schedule. During the year, many of the long-time members had died. Congregation members lost hope and saw no way to survive. All the plans to yoke with Peace in South Gate were dropped. In November, the Board of Directors met with Gerald Bushore, a church real estate agent, to sell the church, suggesting a selling price of $895,000 with a 100 percent cash payment made by the purchaser and a real estate commission of 6 percent. The purchase price would include the church with pews, the pipe organ, and any other items

the congregation wished to designate, the school building, and the parsonage. A special Christmas Eve Carol Service was celebrated with Carol Morris-Lowe leading 45 people in a service of lessons and carols as Pastor and Mrs. Hoffschneider were out of town for Christmas. Pastor encouraged all the members to remain at Zion until the church was sold. The year closed with 31 members and a Sunday school of five pupils. All the plans to yoke with Peace and the big sixtieth anniversary celebration didn't materialize that year.

The last year of Zion's existence, 1997, began with the congregation's remaining remnant filled with deep regret and sorrow that the beautiful church they had worked so hard to build and support for sixty years was to be sold. The Designation of Church Property Sale Funds was to give the bulk of the proceeds to Concordia University, Irvine, for scholarships for church workers and "set aside a salary amount for Pastor Hoffschneider for a period of one year or until he found other permanent employment (whichever was less)." In March, the Tongan Seventh-day Adventist Church expressed an interested in the church property and was given until June 1 to secure funds to purchase the building, which they were not able to accomplish. By spring, all thoughts in the congregation were on two items: selling the property, or deeding it to the District if it wasn't sold, and developing plans for the big celebration of the 60th anniversary of the congregation on June 1. Letters were sent to former pastors inviting them to attend the anniversary and to participate in the "Book of Remembrance." In order to meet all financial obligations, funds were transferred from what money was left in the Church Extension Fund to the General Fund. On March 30, the members of Peace Lutheran of South Gate were invited to the Easter breakfast at 8:00 to 10:00 a.m.

The last anniversary celebration to be held at Zion occurred when 200 members, former members, and friends assembled on June 1 at 10:30 a.m. to thank God for 60 years of blessings at Zion. A choir of 11 former members, under the direction of Michael Doyle, organist and choir director, sang, "Let All the People Praise Thee" by Natalie Sleeth. Pastor Hoffschneider preached on "Seeds Sown Here!" Luke 8:15, and two infant children were baptized in the service. The chancel was filled with colorful bouquets of flowers and a large red banner made by the Jennings family, which all added to make it a festive service. What joy filled the hearts of the worshipers that day as they praised God for

Peace, South Gate, contacts Zion in 1996 to establish a joint parish.

all His blessings at Zion in its 60 years of existence. This happiness was overshadowed with sadness and remorse, as all present knew that the church would close its doors at the end of June and there would never be another Zion Lutheran Church in Maywood. Following the service, the congregation adjourned to the parish hall for a delicious luncheon served to 175 people. After the luncheon, they moved back to the church where Bill Hamilton, serving as master of ceremonies, introduced former members, Carolyn Sims, a former teacher; Arnold Porsch, a former member; Eugene Holtz, a son of the congregation who became a minister; and Hulda Biel, a member. They all told of their special memories of Zion. Joel Hoffschneider led the hymn sing with Karen (Menge) Robertson accompanying the group on the piano. Joel read a letter from the District President, Loren Kramer, who congratulated the congregation for its sixty years of blessing to the District. The afternoon ended on a very emotional note as Berneice Derscheid Peters accompanied the congregation as they sang "God Be with You 'til We Meet Again," the song that was sung for over thirty years to close Sunday school every Sunday morning. The fear that gripped the group was that they probably would never see each other or Zion Lutheran Church again. Some of those people sitting there

had been at the first service in the Townsend Hall some 61 years before. What a sad farewell!

At the last Voters' Meeting of the church on June 8, 1997, the treasurer reported that the receipts were $3,145, with disbursements of $4,672.34, leaving a balance of $199.19. The "Resolution of Dissolution" was accepted with a vote of 10 for the measure and 2 opposing it. When the corporation was dissolved on June 30, the District took possession of the property, worth almost $1 million, where they would develop a study for use of the property and make future plans for its use; the District rented the parsonage and continued to rent the school building to Head Start to cover expenses. This congregation had given over $1,700,000 to support the church at home and over $320,000 to the District and Synod for a total of around $2 million in its sixty-one year history to advance the Kingdom of God in the support of missions, charities, and educational facilities of Synod.

The last three services held in Zion were filled with melancholy, remorse, and sadness as each person present realized that the demise of this vibrant, caring, and giving congregation was near. On Sunday, June 8, about 20 faithful people came to worship. The following Sunday, June 15, about 30 people were present with Mary Stevens playing the organ for the last time. She served as

> Zion closes in 1997, giving the property to the District.

The final service at Zion conducted on June 22, 1997, with Pastor Hoffschneider in front pew and the 40 people who were in attendance.

temporary organist for over 25 years. On the last Sunday, June 22, over 40 members and former members came to worship at Zion for the final time, which was like going to the funeral of a beloved parent, experiencing the pain of a great loss. After the emotionally charged service, a potluck dinner was held where everyone said his or her sad farewells.

This final chapter in the life of Zion Lutheran Church as a congregation came to an end, a church that was blessed by God with dedicated pastors, teachers, and members who gave generously of their time, talents, and treasures to proclaim His love in Zion. Even though the congregation was disbanded and the church building sat vacant, God had plans to use the building again for a place to proclaim His Word in Spanish in the Bell-Maywood area. On July 3, 1997, a request was made by Pastor Frank Brundige of the Bell Gardens church to Rev. Ken Behnken, Administrative Assistant to the President, Missions, to use Zion for a mission station; he had 6 families (16 adults and 20 children and youth) who resided in the Maywood area and wanted to have Lutheran services conducted in their city. He had made the same request to Zion in 1996, but for some reason, it was denied. The District granted Pastor Brundige permission to establish a Hispanic mission in Zion's old buildings with a core of three families from San Pedro y San Pablo Lutheran Church in Bell Gardens who lived in Maywood; they began worship services on August 24, 1997, at 11:30 a.m. with 24 people. During this time period, many prayers were ascending to the throne of God not only by former members but also by a young boy in Maywood, Juan Arauz (age 14), who had prayed "for God to reveal Himself" to him, and who saw the answer in Bible study and worship on that Sunday in August of 1997.

Outreach began building on friendships built by the past ministries of pastors Mather, Kay, and Hoffschneider and "the establishing of a new Spanish-speaking Lutheran presence and identity in the community." Bible study and the instruction of children and youth began on Wednesday afternoons and evenings with Pastor Brundige serving from the Bell Gardens church; English classes were conducted on Friday evenings at 7:00 p.m. and worship services held on Sundays at 11:30 a.m.

Since the name Zion didn't have the same meaning for Hispanics as it did for the Anglos, the name Misión San Pedro y San Pablo was used tem-

porarily as the church consisted of members from the Bell Gardens congregation. To better reach the community, the mission decided to use the name Iglesia Luterana Palabra de Dios or Word of God Lutheran Church. The goal was to call a Spanish-speaking pastor to lead the group in outreach and discipleship. To accomplish this, the mission relied on the offerings of the members of Palabra de Dios, District stewardship of rents from the parsonage and the school building, and the prayers and donations of former Zion members who wanted to see the continuance of the Gospel preached in the community. In the fall of 1997, the mission's first officers were: President Elvira Mendez, Secretary Gloria Hernandez, Treasurer Zoila Leal; a budget of $6,430 was established with a tithe of $660 going to the District. (The Leal, Mendez, and Hernandez families were the three Lutheran families who chartered Palabra de Dios.) The year closed with an average attendance of 17 at services. In December, a Posada was held with 40 people caroling in the neighborhood and returning to the church for a service and potluck.

The New Year, 1998, began with the core of four families continuing to grow in God's Word through Bible classes conducted in English on Sunday after church and in Spanish in two homes on Wednesday nights. On February 14, the first Baptism took place with Michaelangelo Hernandez being baptized. On Ash Wednesday and throughout Lent, Wednesday afternoon Catechism and evening Bible classes were conducted. In the spring, the Zion Lutheran Mission Society was organized with the stated purpose of the "ongoing support for the continued preaching of the Gospel in the Maywood area." The Mission Society members were Pastor Brundige, Ana Sapien, and Michael Doyle. Through the newsletter, which helped keep former members and friends of Zion informed of the events and activities at the mission, over $2,600 had been contributed.

In the fall, Seminarian Antonio Lopez, a student from the Concordia University Irvine Ethnic Pastor Certification Program (EPCP), joined the mission staff. He had a B.A. and M.A. in history from Cal State Los Angeles. Antonio also was a teacher who was studying to be a pastor specializing in bilingual and bicultural ministry. While doing his vicarage and learning pastoral skills, he began English classes on Saturday mornings at the mission. Five hundred fliers were distributed in the neighborhood, generating 20 and 30 people at the first 2 classes. Antonio's wife, Rebecca,

Spanish work begins again in Old Zion in 1997 with new name, Misión San Pedro y San Pablo.

shared a Bible story and craft with the children while their parents learned practical English skills that would help them advance in employment and participate in the larger society. From a list of previous English/citizenship classes that were taught by Pastor and Mrs. Hoffschneider, calls and visits were made in the community. Pastor Brundige stated, "As was discovered time and time again, the seeds of the Gospel and friendship planted in the past opened doors to the ministry today." During the year, Compassion Southwest, a three-year-old group of LCMS churches made up of eight suburban congregations, which dedicated resources, time, and talent for the purpose of helping to begin new inner-city outreach ministries, came to begin work at the Zion site. Their first project was to begin a preschool outreach to the Hispanic neighborhood around Palabra de Dios in Maywood. Their goal was to bring resources into the area and start a self-supporting indigenous ministry. They refurbished the old school building and began a preschool program and daycare center under the leadership of Irazema Ojeda, who also became a member of the congregation.

On November 8, the first Confirmation held in the congregation was conducted with Nelsan Leal being confirmed in the faith. What a joyous occasion that was for the congregation! Throughout the year, a faithful neighborhood family, the Campos, watched the playground and opened it every afternoon so the neighborhood children could come and play. Young people frequented the playground to play basketball; children and parents often spent afternoons playing on the swings and riding bikes in the yard. A Cuban dance group used the parish hall to teach dancing to the youth where they prepared them for competitions and performances. Through this group, people were being exposed to the church. The year closed with the mission seeing many blessings of God and had an average attendance of 15 per Sunday with an average Bible class attendance of 3. They were reaching into the community with English classes and with a joyful Posada in December, with 50 people caroling in the neighborhood and returning to the church for a service of Word and song in Spanish and English followed by a delicious potluck in the parish hall.

The year 1999 began with much activity at the church: 30 people from the congregation, the basketball group, the Cuban dance group, and Compassion Southwest spent a Saturday painting the parish hall with the interior and exterior of the

Pastor Frank Brundige with Rebecca Lopez and Seminarian Antonio Lopez, who later became the vicar of Palabra de Dios.

church painted through offerings and donations of Palabra de Dios, Zion Lutheran Mission Society, and Sandy Strasbaugh of Compassion Southwest. Compassion Southwest painted the exterior and interior of the school building, and helped pay for the paint in the church building. They also slurry-topped the playground, installed an arbor over the lunch tables, and purchased all new equipment for the preschool to prepare for the opening of a Lutheran preschool, El Jardin de Niños, in May. The year continued with exciting plans for evangelism and outreach, canvassing the area with new fliers inviting people to attend Palabra de Dios, and visiting old and new members. Antonio Lopez conducted Ash Wednesday service with 20 people in attendance. In the spring, the congregation and the mission society had a tremendous festival celebration of the fiftieth anniversary of the dedication of the church building with a service of praise and thanksgiving on May 16 attended by 100 with Pastor Woody Mather, a former pastor, preaching, Pastor Brundige serving as liturgist, and a special choir of former members directed by the organist, Michael Doyle; after the service, a dinner followed in the parish hall where the book, *Sent Forth by God's Blessings*, *A History of Zion Lutheran Church, Maywood, California*, written by Michael Doyle, was presented to all those who had purchased it. All former members and friends of Zion were invited to attend this special event through the Zion Lutheran Mission Society newsletter.

Members of Palabra de Dios on March 21, 1999; Front: Selene Garcia, Lizette Garcia, Michael Hernandez, Elsie Pac, Carlos "Junior" Alvidrez, Xochitl Ojeda; Middle: Francisca Benavides, Francisca Garcia, Concepcion Lopez, Rebecca Lopez, Sylvia Guerra, Cynthia Alvidrez, Elvira Mendez, Irezema Ojeda, Graciela Ojeda, George Ojeda; Back: Jose Luis Gonzales, Antonio Lopez, Guillermo "Meno" Mora, Juan Garcia, Alvaro Henandez, Gloria Hernandez, Juan Arauz, Pastor Frank Brundige, Ruth Mendez.

Worship services on Sundays were attended by an average of 18 with compact disks used to expand the music in the service using the hymnals for liturgy and hymns with supplement pages for new songs. Antonio was leading the Service of Word by himself every other week, and leading Bible class of 11 every other week, as well. The coffee hour had proven to be fruitful as a gathering, planning, and fellowship time. English classes went well, with class members starting to attend church services. Through Irazema Ojeda's (preschool director) new mission plan, more students were attending the preschool. On Wednesday afternoons, a chapel service was conducted for the children in the preschool day care with the Word proclaimed to them. In December, the Posada, attended by 30 people, was making new contacts with follow-ups done. By the end of the year, the mission society had raised $5,282 for the church and baptized membership had increased to 40. The year ended with two Baptisms, one First Communion, and two Confirmations, all in the month of December.

January of 2000 began with Vicar Antonio Lopez serving full-time, as he had just finished his pastoral certification classes at Concordia University, Irvine, with Pastor Brundige serving as his mentor. During February and March, God blessed the ministry of Palabra de Dios with two Confirmations, one First Communion, and one Baptism. Since English language Sunday services were started in February aimed at the English speaking young people in the Maywood area, the Spanish language Sunday services were moved to 9:00 a.m. with Sunday school conducted from 10:00 a.m. to 10:30 a.m. English classes (ESL) were conducted on Saturday mornings with literacy classes, using Bible based materials, conducted on Tuesday evenings, and the Bible/Catechism classes met on Tuesday evenings. In addition to the activities, the vicar's wife, Rebecca, provided Bible lessons and activities for children and managed to put together a computer room using donated computer parts. Many of the area's young people became regular visitors and became quite proficient in operating computers. Irazema Ojeda, the director of El Jardin de Niños Preschool, reported that the school had an enrollment of 21 children. Teachers were instructing the children with Christian materials and the children attended weekly chapel services. There were also in-services conducted monthly where the teachers were instructed in the Lutheran doctrine and the Christian faith.

In the spring on May 21, 2000, at 3:00 p.m., the Second Annual Zion Lutheran Mission Society Reunion, attended by forty, was held with a special hymn festival where former members selected the hymns. Vicar Lopez served as liturgist, Pastor Brundige was the preacher, and Michael Doyle was the organist and choir director directing a choir of seven. By the fall, the Lord had blessed Antonio and his wife, Rebecca, with the birth of a baby daughter bringing much joy to the congregation. God had continued to bless the congregation with growth, as attendance had increased since spring. Two young ladies, 13 and 20, were baptized and were preparing for Confirmation/First Communion.

In the fall, the ladies of the parish had a yard sale, which also was an opportunity to share the church ministries with the community, making several new contacts. A portion of the funds that were raised was given to missions. El Jardin de Niños Preschool enrollment was at an all time high with twenty-three children and was supported by Compassion Southwest, Inc. of the Lutheran

Ministry. On September 23, the school had an open house for the members and community. The congregation had a joint service to hear a special speaker, Ted Martin from Apple of His Eye Ministry, who spoke in Spanish, giving a wonderful message to the people about his work in Jewish evangelism. The parish hall was used for general elections with hundreds of people coming to the church. At Halloween, candy bags with Christian materials and information about Palabra de Dios for the children in the area were distributed. The fourth annual Posada was celebrated during the Christmas season. The year ended with an average attendance of twenty-two in worship services, an increase of one over the previous year. The Bible study classes averaged eight with the Sunday school having five children and eight adults.

The year 2001 began with two Quinceñeras, 15th birthday celebrations, a tradition in many Latin American countries consisting of parents "presenting" their daughters at the 15th birthday to the church in a service done for the family with prayers said for the young girl focusing the service on the remembrance of one's Baptism. This service presented a wonderful opportunity to share the Gospel to extended family members who were often unchurched because each celebration, having between 75 to 100 family and friends, gathered at Palabra de Dios for the special occasion. That quarter, the average attendance at worship services increased to 33. During the municipal elections on March 16, the parish hall was used as a polling place with evangelistic materials available for people to take. Vicar Lopez stated, "One of the struggles in the ministry is getting people motivated to use their gifts. It seems that most people expect the pastor or his family to do everything. It's quite draining. Another problem is that people move very frequently. Our totals may be increasing then suddenly two or three families will move out of the area and we're back to our attendance totals of the previous year. So the appearance is that we haven't grown." The playground continued to be open with about 15 young people periodically using the basketball court.

Since the preschool wasn't supporting itself financially as the community couldn't afford the cost of tuition, Compassion Southwest was forced to withdraw its support and closed the school at the end of June. The next step for the congregation was to explore the possibility of having Head Start return to use the school building in order to generate funds to support the mission. The mission

continued to maintain a good average attendance in Spanish services; due to poor attendance at the English service, that service was suspended. The ESL classes continued with some people attending church services on Sundays as well. Over the summer, a group of 23 young people participated in a basketball tournament at Bethany Lutheran Church in Hollywood with 17 other youth; under the direction of Pastor Vern Wendt (Los Angeles Nehemiah Project), the event that took place had much success. The event proved to be a good outreach for the parish. At the end of the year, two Posadas (Christmas carol singing), one at church and one at a parishioner's home, were held making contact with several new families. An English Wednesday evening Vespers service was started with an average of 21 in both Spanish and English services.

The new year of 2002 began with attendance at worship dropping to an average of 16 with Bible classes staying at around 7. One sign of encouragement was that several of the young people had taken the initiative in helping with Communion and with the cleaning and up-keep of the parish hall. On Saturday, June 1, from 11:00 a.m. to 2:00 p.m., the mission society was invited to an open house to view the work being done in Maywood. Pastor Brundige and Vicar Lopez reported that over the four years of the mission society's existence, $19,525 had been donated for the work in Maywood and that the mission was beginning a time of transition since Antonio Lopez had completed his pastoral studies and vicarage and was awaiting a call but would continue to serve the ministry at Palabra de Dios for the short term. Pastor Brundige wrote, "We want to thank Antonio for his service and wish him God's blessings on his new call."

A lease was signed with a community service agency that would provide a preschool program in the school building. The playground area had been refurbished to attract neighborhood families, children, and youth to the site. With the swings up and the schoolyard opened, the children, youth, and parents came back! Some of the young men who were teens when the mission started in 1997 came by and helped get the yard and school ready. Some 11-year-old boys came to play and remembered attending preschool at the site when the Hoffschnieders were there. The people in the neighborhood were excited about the reopening of the preschool and the playground. The preschool repairs included paint, new toilets, repaired win-

Community service agency opens preschool in 2002.

dows, and electrical upgrade, all courtesy of the Institute for Leadership and Education who ran the preschool. When the complicated licensing was completed, the school opened in December with about 50 children enrolled.

Since Vicar Lopez had moved to Palmdale in the summer, Pastor Brundige and Ruben Vasquez, the Bell Gardens deacon, provided pastoral support from Bell Gardens beginning that October. An open house on Sunday, October 13, from 2:00 p.m. to 4:00 p.m. was held for mission society members to come, visit, and tour the refurbished school and playground. Region Two held a Spanish Reformation service at Palabra de Dios the following Sunday with Pastor Doug Johnstone preaching. The year ended with 23 people attending worship services and 15 people in Bible and Catechism instruction. At the end of the year, Vicar Lopez received a call from Good Shepherd Lutheran Church of Brooklyn, New York, which he accepted. Before leaving, Pastor Durkovic spoke with him about future plans he would have enacted at Maywood. His quick response was, "Begin to teach English again, as a second language, and help the people become bilingual."

In December, Pastor John Durkovic became the new pastor of Palabra de Dios. He was born on November 29, 1936, in Cheyenne, Wyoming, and on December 25, 1958, he married Janet Bahls; their union was blessed with five children. He attended Valparaiso University graduating in 1959 with an engineering degree. He later went to Concordia Seminary, Springfield, Illinois, graduating in 1969. Following his graduation, he and his wife Jan, and their three children, began their ministry as missionaries to Guatemala. While in Guatemala two more children were born, and his wife became ill in the early part of 1985, where it was discovered she had a brain tumor. The Lord called her to her heavenly rest in August 1985. After the family returned to the States in 1989, he began work in New York City, where he met Nancy Nowak in late 1992, and they were married in April 1993. They came to California in September 1994, where he served as pastor of Hispanic ministry at Trinity, Santa Ana. In 1997, he became pastor of both the English and Spanish ministries at Trinity. Since he was fluent in Spanish, he worked as a tutor with the Hispanic Institute of Theology (Concordia Seminary, St. Louis). He had also worked in New York City with Lutheran Social Services. His wife is a kindergarten/first grade teacher at St. Mark's Lutheran School in Anaheim. Pastor Brundige de-

John Durkovic becomes the new pastor of Palabra de Dios.

The new pastor of Palabra de Dios, Rev. John Durkovic, pictured with his wife Nancy.

scribed him as a pastor, who gave attention to details, cared for people, had the ability to be a mentor to leaders, and had a humble servant attitude.

By June 2003, the state funded preschool had three full classrooms in the old school building with a student body of 114 pupils. The preschool staff held monthly parent meetings in the parish hall. The rental from the school was collected and administered by the District, giving the mission one of its financial resources. The old parsonage next to the church was rented to a family of six, covering three generations: a mother, with three children and two grandchildren. She was one of 185 family units, which had been living in a nearby city block that was re-zoned for a new school. Each of these families had to relocate with the Los Angeles Unified School District helping them secure new housing. The mission also received a one-year District grant of $14,400 for 2003, helping to support the ministry.

This place, Zion Lutheran Church and Iglesia Luterana Palabra de Dios, has been a blessing to so many people and will continue to be a blessing with the help of God. "My Word… shall not return to Me void, but it shall accomplish that which I please, and it shall prosper in the thing whereto I sent it," Isaiah 55:11.

Bethany Lutheran Church
St. John's Lutheran Church
Montebello, California

he colorful and romantic history of Montebello dates back to the days of Franciscan missionaries, Fathers Angel Somera and Pedro Cambon, who, on September 9, 1771, established the original San Gabriel Mission near where San Gabriel Boulevard now crosses the Rio Hondo River. The mission, third in a chain of 21 to be established under the direction of Father Junípero Serra, managed to flourish under hardships, but heavy rains and flooding eventually drove the founding fathers to its present location in San Gabriel in 1776.

The city of Montebello originally consisted of sections of Rancho San Antonio, Rancho La Merced, and Rancho Paso de Bartolo. On the banks of the Rio Hondo, the last armed conflict, the Battle of the Rio San Gabriel, was staged with Mexico for possession of California on January 8, 1847. The old Juan Matias Sanchez Adobe, recently restored to its original splendor, stands just north of the intersection of La Merced and Lincoln Avenue, the heart of the old La Merced Rancho.

Following the Civil War, an Italian, Alessandro Repetto, built his ranch house on the hill overlooking his land, about a half-mile north of where Garfield Avenue crosses the Pomona Freeway. Since Repetto never married, when he died in 1885, his brother Antonio sold his inheritance to Harris Newmark, Kaspar Cohn, John A. Bicknell, Stephen M. White, and I. W. Hellman, a group of businessmen well-known in Los Angeles financial circles, for $60,000, about $12 per acre. Out of Newmark and Cohn shares, consisting of 1,200 acres, Montebello had its beginning in May 1899. The original town site of forty acres was bounded by First Street on the east, Fifth Street on the west, Cleveland on the north, and Los Angeles Avenue on the south. It was originally called Newmark, after the Newmark family. The remainder of the tract was divided into five-acre plots and named Montebello, meaning beautiful hills in Italian, at the suggestion of a gentleman, William Mulholland who also developed the water system, incorporated as the Montebello Land and Water Company in 1900.

Originally Montebello was known as an agricultural community; it boasted of having ideal climate, productive soil, and an abundance of water. From the turn of the century and through the 1920s, the area was renowned for its production of flowers, vegetables, berries, and fruits. In 1912, the Montebello Women's Club sponsored Montebello's first flower show in the high school auditorium. The discovery of oil by Standard Oil Company on the Anita Baldwin property in 1917 brought about a revolutionary change to Montebello. Soon the agricultural hills became a major contributor to the production of oil, with oil fields generating one-eighth of the state's crude oil by 1920. Since this new business brought a population explosion, Montebello was incorporated as the 35th of the present cities in Los Angeles County on October 19, 1920.

San Gabriel Mission, circa 1880, with wagon and carriage in foreground.

View of an orange grove and oil fields in Montebello on July 27, 1926. (HERALD EXAMINER COLLECTION/Los Angeles Public Library)

Rev. Norbert C. Mueller, who established a mission, Bethany, in Montebello in 1943.

Bethany Lutheran Mission is established in 1943.

By 1943 with many defense housing projects being erected in Montebello, Rev. Norbert C. Mueller, a 1938 graduate of Concordia Seminary of St. Louis, was called to conduct a field survey and establish a preaching station in this fast growing area. After making 459 canvass calls and leaving material and information at 216 dwellings of people not at home, he later sent cards informing them of the beginning of Lutheran services in the area with seventy-one Lutherans contacted who were prospects for the nucleus of the mission. He found 251 unchurched prospects with 61 prospects for a Sunday school. After a total of 305 follow-up calls were made, the first service was conducted in the Women's Clubhouse in Montebello on February 14 with ten people in attendance. The Lenten services were attended by an average of 13 persons with April attendance averaging 37; Easter Sunday had the highest attendance of 63. The mission, known as Bethany, continued to grow, but by December changes would take place. Since St. John's in Los Angeles wanted to relocate to Montebello, the District Mission Board suggested that Bethany Mission and St. John's amalgamate; the mission voted on Friday, December 10, to accept the Mission Board recommendation. Pastor Mueller conducted his last service at the mission on January 9, 1944, preaching his farewell sermon, "The Promise of God to You" based on Philippians 1: 6. The following Sunday, January 16, Pastor Smukal preached his first service in Montebello with Bethany now an integral component of St. John's.

Pastor Mueller was born on September 28, 1914, in Hubbell, Michigan, where his father, Rev. John T. Mueller, was pastor. When his father accepted a call to become a professor at Concordia Seminary, St. Louis, Missouri, in 1921, Norbert Mueller continued his education in Lutheran schools in the St. Louis area. After his second year at the seminary, he taught grade four at Trinity Lutheran School in Los Angeles. Upon graduation from the seminary in 1938, he was assigned to start a new mission in the suburbs of Omaha, Nebraska. Following the January 9 service in 1944, Pastor Mueller was assigned by the Mission Board to canvass the Lakewood area of Long Beach where he established Bethany Lutheran Church which would become a very large parish under his guidance and include a big Christian day school. In 1959, he took a call to Christ, San Pedro, where the church and school also grew. At both parishes, large, beautiful, new sanctuaries were built under his pastorates. He ended his ministerial career at Immanuel, Twenty-nine Palms, California where he retired.

Why did St. John's want to move from its location in the Boyle Heights section of East Los Angeles where it had been established in 1906? As was mentioned in Chapter One, the neighborhood in which St. John's was located was drastically changing with numerous ethic groups presenting difficulties in carrying on effective work. Since St. John's continued conducting German services, which were discontinued in December of 1941, along with English services, the congregation remained very German and not too mission minded even though Pastor Smukal had started a Sunday school among the Mexican population in 1929 some blocks away from the church. With this in mind, St. John's, on November 1, 1943, unanimously adopted three resolutions, namely, to relocate eastward, to buy a site in Montebello on Taylor Avenue, a plot of ground 135' × 600', and to pay as much as $12,500 if necessary. It was purchased for $12,300. Pastor Smukal reported, "Since it is true that the Lord wants us not merely to exist, but also to expand and to abound in His work, to advance and not to perish, it is our duty always to seek the most favorable opportunities. This must be done by every congregation with proper respect and regard for the rights, privileges, and welfare also of the surrounding sister congregations. In this spirit, St. John's held most amiable meetings with representatives of the sister congregations concerned in the growth of God's kingdom in the territory occupied by them. In these meetings, the District Mission Board also was represented. St. John's appreciates deeply the fraternal attitude of St. Matthew's [East Los Angeles], of the Montebello mission, and of Trinity, Whittier, and their pastors."

The St. John's Los Angeles church property was debt free and was not put on the market for sale. The congregation had need of it for some time, since the plan of relocation included two services on Sunday mornings, one in the Los Angeles church at 9:30 a.m., the other in the Montebello Women's Club at 11:00 a.m. Pastor Gihring was called as assistant pastor, conducting services in Montebello. At this time, the common cup and the individual cup were used alternately for Holy Communion. Sunday school was conducted at both places of worship in Los Angeles and Montebello. In 1945, a new school bus was purchased to transport pupils in the school and Sunday school to and from the different locations.

Also in 1945, Teacher J. R. Stenske tendered his resignation for health reasons after 17 years of faithful service as principal and teacher of St. John's Lutheran School. During this time, he also served the congregation as organist, secretary, and as a member of various boards and committees. The congregation regretfully accepted his resignation and called Teacher Henry W. Steinweg to serve as the new principal. He had served 10 years as teacher at St. John's. Vicar Robert Moehle was engaged for one year to teach in the second classroom. The third teacher was Mrs. W. J. Glatz of St. Matthew's, who served at St. John's School under the auspices of St. Matthew's congregation, Los Angeles. The school had an enrollment of 99 pupils.

In late 1945, St. John's submitted a request to the city of Montebello for rezoning of the Taylor Street property for school use. Since this was denied in January of 1946, the congregation subsequently withdrew its request in favor of a different approach. In March, they purchased a five-acre fig ranch on Beverly Boulevard and had to develop North Eighteenth Street from Beverly Boulevard to Harding Street. To open 18th Street from Harding to Washington streets, six members bought undeveloped property on the west side of the street and with the other owners developed that block. The congregation then set about to build its own facilities but was faced with high construction costs.

In June, preparations were made for the celebration of the congregation's 40th anniversary, which was observed in Montebello Park in a divine service on September 8, since neither the church in Los Angeles nor the chapel in Montebello offered sufficient seating capacity to accommodate St. John's on this occasion. The celebration extended over the month of September. On September 8, the congregation held an outdoor service of thanksgiving in Montebello Park. Visitor Reno H. Jeske, a son of the congregation, preached an excellent and animated sermon of thanksgiving on 1 Corinthians 1:21–24 with Pastor Hugo Gihring serving as liturgist. The choir sang two anthems under the direction of Principal H. W. Steinweg. Teacher Louis C. Eberhard was installed, and Pastor Smukal introduced him and Miss Frances Pieczynske, as teachers in St. John's Lutheran School. Teacher Eberhard was called by St. John's, and St. Matthew's engaged Miss Pieczynske. The folder entitled "The Answer of the Lutheran School to Five Great Questions," written by Arthur L. Amt,

was distributed at this service to all worshipers. After the service, members and friends enjoyed a luncheon and social gathering.

On September 15, the celebration continued in church and chapel with the congregation commemorating and giving thanks to God for His past and present blessings on the endeavor of Christian indoctrination by receiving five adults into membership by the Rite of Confirmation after they had completed 33 study periods. Since February of that year, 14 adults and 7 children were confirmed, and 3 adults and 19 children were baptized. The Sunday School Rally was also conducted in that service giving the children a prominent part by reciting the chief parts of the Christian doctrine, including the meaning and exposition, their favorite Scripture passages, and singing three songs. Pastor G. H. Smukal preached the sermon, using the text: "Your faith should not stand in the wisdom of men, but in the power of God" (I Corinthians 2:5). Through the sermon and prayer, the congregation was also reminded that St. John's Lutheran School entered its 34th year of educating the young. Since the school had such an excellent reputation, many applicants had to be denied for lack of room and teaching staff. The Sunday school in Montebello had doubled its enrollment over the first year, again over the second year, and doubled it again over the third year.

In the service on September 22, the Rev. R. Knaus, a son of the congregation, served as festival speaker where the congregation acknowledged God's many blessings granted by way of auxiliaries, the Ladies' Aid, the Walther League, the Mission Aid, and the Men's Club. These auxiliaries were cherished and fostered by the parish. An anniversary banquet was served under the auspices of the Men's Club on September 25, attended by about two hundred guests. On September 29, the anniversary celebration continued with particular reference to the mission work in which the congregation was engaged with a laudable interest in the spiritual welfare of others. The scope of the congregation's influence in missions continued to be widened through mission and synodical projects. The Rev. N. Mueller, first missionary in Montebello after that field was ceded to the Mission Board, preached the sermon, encouraging the congregation to render thanks to God by renewed, consecrated efforts in the fruitful work of His kingdom.

St. John's had intended to celebrate this grand anniversary in a new church, new school, and

In 1946, St. John's purchases a five-acre fig ranch on Beverly Boulevard.

new parish hall, but the two and one-half acres purchased in Montebello for purposes of relocation met with opposition and objections to the school on the part of several neighbors. The congregation withdrew its petition for rezoning, sold the property, and purchased five acres on Beverly Boulevard at 18th Street. As soon as the necessary material for buildings were available to the congregation, building operations were to be begun under the supervision of Architect O. J. Bruer.

On the occasion of the 40th anniversary of St. John's congregation, which Pastor Smukal had faithfully served for 36 years of those years, he stated:

> The history of St. John's bears the superscription: The Acts of Jesus for, in, and by St. John's. Else what a tragic and brief account it would be! But the history of St. John's does not consist in the members' own efforts, no matter how long or short a period of time they may have been affiliated with the congregation. Their faithfulness and brave work belongs in the record of their life in Christ. Jesus says: "Without Me ye can do nothing;" and St. Paul says: "Not I, but the grace of God which was with me." The works done by St. John's were not chosen by the congregation, but were before ordained that we should walk in them. (Ephesians 2:10) St. John's is learning more and more to depend for wisdom, knowledge, power, grace, success, and guidance to eternal salvation entirely on Jesus and to glory only in the Lord. The congregation also acknowledges with sincere thanks whatever favors it has received, especially in its formative period, from the sister congregations.

By 1947, the ladies had organized Mary-Martha Society, contributions in cash and pledges were in excess of $46,500 for the building fund, all street work on the Montebello property was completed in June, and an excellent pipe organ was purchased for $10,000, stored, and sold in 1950. St. Matthew's Church released Miss Pieczynske and St. John's engaged her as a teacher. Because the cost of erecting the three buildings became prohibitive, the congregation resolved to build the school and the chapel/parish hall. On May 23, 1948, an open-air Vespers service was conducted by Pastor Smukal, with Principal H. W. Steinweg breaking ground for the new day school of four classrooms.

On September 19, the school was dedicated to the service and glory of God with Pastor Smukal and Assistant Pastor Gihring officiating. Contractor Dwight Jones handed the master key to Architect O. J. Bruer, who passed it to the principal. Principal Steinweg opened all doors, the teachers entered their new classrooms, the Board of Education followed, bearing the flags and books, and the congregation and visitors crowded the building. The new school was entirely modern in its equipment at that time. The playground, about 135' × 275', was well surfaced and enclosed by an eight-foot fence. In September, the 36th consecutive school year was opened in the new school building with an enrollment of 113 children and the addition of the ninth grade. The relocation program was completed, except for the erection of a new church.

In another open-air Vespers service on August 15, 1948, ground was broken for the new chapel/parish hall. The soil was turned by Wilhelm Reisig, veteran Sunday school superintendent; Mrs. H. Kramer, vice-president of the Ladies' Aid, the oldest auxiliary; L. Rennegarbe, president of the Walther League; P. Jumey, president of the Men's Club; and Mrs. W. Schwalm, vice-president of the Mary Martha Society, with Pastor Smukal speaking an appropriate Bible passage as each person turned the soil. The building was to be used for Sunday school purposes and activities of the auxiliary groups. Until the church could be built, the chapel/parish hall was also to serve as the place of worship for the congregation. The prediction that school-minded St. John's would build the school first and the church last had come true. The cost of the school and playground was over $42,000 with the chapel-parish hall costing approximately $41,000. The prohibitive cost of labor, building material, and equipment deprived the parish of the joy of realizing the new church building at that time. The old property in Los Angeles was sold to the Mexican Free Methodist Church and the final act of relocation was to dedicate and occupy the new church hall. On January 30, 1949, the relocation was completed with the last service conducted in the old chapel on East Second and Dacotah streets. The chapel/parish hall was dedicated on February 6, completing the relocation program with both the school and chapel/parish hall buildings, designed by Architect O. J. Bruer, featuring a modified Gothic style. Another dedicatory service was held that afternoon, the message being delivered by Rev. H. Gihring, assistant pastor. A Vespers musicale concluded the day's festivities with

St. John's builds school and chapel/parish hall in 1948.

the dedication of the Wurlitzer organ, Series 20, a gift of Mr. and Mrs. E. J. Jensen.

The chapel/parish hall would seat 300 worshipers, with room available for an overflow of 100 people. A number of Sunday school rooms, a meeting room, and a large kitchen to accommodate social gatherings flanked the nave. A costly curtain, provided by the Walther League, was drawn in front of the chancel when the building was used as an auditorium for social events. When the curtain opened, the chancel with the white altar and pulpit, gifts of old Trinity of Los Angeles in 1912, and the white baptismal font, salvaged from a junk dealer back in 1907, was revealed. The lectern served as a pulpit in the temporary place of worship in Montebello the previous four years. The beautiful art-glass window, depicting the crucified Savior, was moved from the old chancel in Los Angeles and installed in the center of the altar of the new chancel.

The 3,000-pound bell, voiced to the deep C sharp, was a gift of the Sunday school children who saved their pennies by the penny-a-meal plan and the proceeds of Christmas card sales placed in the Bell Fund, earning the purchase price of $750, which on the open market would command a cost of $4,200. The bell, which was hung in a temporary belfry, was purchased from Bethany Lutheran Church in Detroit, Michigan, where it served from 1907 to 1941 before Bethany relocated. Since there was no belfry in the congregation's new church, the bell was stored in the church garden, standing silent, until the parish was persuaded to sell it. On St. John's dedication day, a trio of children, the choir, and the children's chorus sang "The Bell Song" written by Pastor Smukal, accompanied by nine rhythmical tones of the bell, tolling at the words Swing, Ring, Sing. The song was written as follows:

Hark! Hear our bell proclaim
Glory to God's great name,
Who in Christ Jesus came
To give us life and glory.
CHORUS
Swing, bell! Ring, bell! Sing, bell:
Glory to God in heaven.

Hark! Hear our bell's sweet call
Inviting great and small:
Come! Worship God! Come, all!
Come, and believe His Gospel.
CHORUS

Hark! Hear the solemn tone!
All hearts unite as one
In prayer before God's throne
To Father, Son, and Spirit.
CHORUS

In September of 1949, the fourth schoolroom was opened with Mrs. L. Eberhard engaged as teacher. In 1951, many changes would occur in the teaching staff: Mr. and Mrs. L. Eberhard moved to Wisconsin joining Peace Church in Antigo, Principal H. W. Steinweg accepted a position at First Lutheran Church of Venice, Candidate Donald Simpson was installed as teacher of grades five and six

The chapel/parish hall building, designed by Architect O. J. Bruer, was dedicated on September 19, 1948, and was used as the school building.

The altar from the old church with its beautiful art-glass window, depicting the crucified Savior. (Pacific Southwest District Archives)

staying many years and also serving as church organist, Teacher W. W. Wegener was installed as principal, and Mrs. Verna Buss was engaged as teacher of grades three and four. The following year, 1952, many members were released to start the new mission in Pico Rivera.

At the age of 68 and after serving St. John's since 1910, Pastor Smukal submitted the following undated letter to the congregation:

Dear Members:

At the request of the Voters' Assembly, I give reason once more for submitting my letter of retirement, or resignation — undated — on March ? 1955, as being the continuous undue references for the past five years by some officers and some members (1) to my age, which I cannot change; (2) to the long term of office, which is a divine act; (3) to my administration and leadership, which suffered interference; (4) the undue criticism of my sermons: all such references tending to repress and discourage people and pastor.

I submitted the document undated, because my own judgment in the matter of my retirement would be considered too subjective and personal, since my person and my office is involved, and I trusted the judgment of the congregation, in particular the judgment of the officers who gave oath at the Lord's altar to assist and not to oppose the Pastor. I do not believe that anyone could have chosen a wiser course than I in giving his congregation the opportunity of choice.

I shall always remain deeply grateful to all members and officers who have been truly helpful to me and to my office to the edification of the congregation, and to my joy and encouragement.

Your humble servant in the Lord Jesus Christ,

Pastor G. H. Smukal

The following was the response to Pastor Smukal's letter to the congregation:

June 25, 1956

STATEMENT OF REASONS FOR
ACCEPTANCE OF RESIGNATION

The following remarks in favor of the Pastor's resignation have been edited by the Board of Elders, but are not necessarily their own opinions:

We must all agree that no one person has all the talents required to please everyone; therefore, periodic changes in personnel will bring in persons with talents lacking in their predecessors.

It is generally agreed that changes in leadership will create new interest in any organization.

It is possible that one of our problems is the congregation itself, however, the consensus of opinion (verified by the recent voters' assembly action) is that a change is needed.

Final action on the Pastor's resignation will be taken at the regular voters' assembly meeting July 9, 1956.

All voters are reminded that it is their responsibility to attend all voters' assembly meetings.

The Voters' Assembly unanimously accepted the statement of retirement of Rev. G. H. Smukal, effective September 1, 1956, gratefully bestowing upon him the title of pastor emeritus ending his career as pastor of the church for almost 40 years. He continued to serve until May 5, 1957, when the Rev. William H. Ilten was installed as pastor, who served to 1976, giving the congregation the unique and happy distinction of having had only two called pastors in its seventy years of existence. On September 16, the congregation celebrated its golden anniversary with a service of thanksgiving in the Chapel that morning, and in the afternoon a special service was conducted in the Bowl of Montebello Park. The three pastors, R. F. Knaus, Reno Jeske, and Ken Molnar, who officiated at the services, were sons of the congregation. The fourth young man from St. John's to go into the ministry was Phil Molnar who was a student at the time of the anniversary. Also that fall, Principal W. W. Wegener accepted the call of First Lutheran Church of El Monte with Teacher Donald Simpson accepting the office of principal and minister of music of St. John's with Miss Gladys Voehl engaged as teacher of grades five and six.

The new pastor, Reverend William H. Ilten was born in Cedar Rapids, Iowa, on April 24, 1916, the son of Mr. and Mrs. Arnold G. Ilten. Following his study for the holy ministry at Concordia College in Milwaukee, Wisconsin, he entered Concordia

Pastor Smukal retires after serving St. John's for almost 40 years.

Theological Seminary, St. Louis, graduating in 1940. While a student at the seminary, he was active in musical circles, singing with the Lutheran Hour Chorus, the Concordia Seminary Chorus, the St. Louis Bach Festival Chorus, and the St. Louis A Capella Choir where he met his wife, Jean. During his vicarage year in 1939, he organized Zion Lutheran Church, Shellsburg, Iowa. He served as assistant at Trinity Lutheran Church, Detroit, Michigan, and was ordained on February 2, 1941, at Trinity Lutheran Church, Clinton, Iowa, where he served as pastor until 1957, before accepting the call as the second pastor of St. John's. He accepted a call to Mt. Calvary Lutheran Church, Diamond Bar, and was installed there on December 19, 1976, retiring from the active ministry at this congregation. His family included his wife Jean, the former Jean Wehmeyer of St. Louis, whom he married in October of 1941. They have two sons, Bill and Ted, and three grandsons.

Not only did Pastor Ilten serve as a faithful pastor, he also served the old Southern California District in various capacities, including chairman of the Child Life Department of the Board of Parish Education, director of the Public Relations Committee, advisor to the Sunday School Convention, pastoral counselor of the Lutheran Hour Float Committee, District Convention and "Forward in Remembrance" committees, executive director of the District's newspaper, *This Month*, chairman of the radio and television committee, a member of the Board of Religion in Media Association of Los Angeles, and he served as the president of the Montebello Kiwanis.

With the amalgamation of St. Matthew's congregation of East Los Angeles (a parish begun through the efforts of Pastor Smukal and St. John's in 1921 and 1924) with St. John's in December of 1956, an added impetus was realized for the construction of a new church building. The vision of many years was finally fulfilled by the members of the congregation, after a 10-year wait to construct a new church on the corner of Beverly Boulevard and North 18th Street. During the end of December of 1957, the congregation was involved in a fund-raising program to supply the necessary funds to construct the church, which was to cost

Rev. William H. Ilten, St. John's second pastor, who served from 1957–1976. (Pacific Southwest District Archives)

approximately $175,000, make necessary improvements on the school, and acquire a new school bus. The new church, designed by Mr. O. J. Bruer, also housed the pastor and secretary's offices, and a memorial chapel. Ground was broken on February 23, 1958, for the new church building with Pastor Ilten turning the first spade of earth assisted by Pastor Smukal and Mr. L. Reaber and Mr. F. O'Brien, members of the building committee.

On the afternoon of July 13, 1958, St. John's conducted the festival cornerstone laying service for the new $175,000 church edifice. The copper box, placed in the niche of the cornerstone, contained the Holy Bible, Catechism, *The Lutheran Hymnal*, Augsburg Confession, messages from the Honorable Goodwin Knight, Governor of California, and the Honorable Mayor A. S. Tutwiler of Montebello. Lists of communicant members, auxiliary members, officers, and school and church staff, 1958 coins, history of the congregation, the current issues of Montebello and Los Angeles newspapers, and editions of the Sunday bulletin were also placed in this historical container. Rev. R. Knaus of Fontana, a son of Saint John's, was speaker for the occasion with Pastor Smukal, emeritus pastor, serving as liturgist, and Pastor Ilten acting as the officiant. The junior and senior choirs under the direction of Donald Simpson, principal and minister of music, presented the music. Church officers and presidents of the various auxiliaries also participated in the formal ceremonies, which came to a climax when a representative of the builder secured the cornerstone in the building and the pastor struck the stone three times as the church bell tolled, signifying that the rites were being conducted in the name of the Holy Trinity.

On November 30, 1958, the culmination of the fondest dreams and prayers of the members of St. John's became a reality, when the new church of contemporary Gothic design, constructed of stucco with stone trim, was dedicated. The laminated wood structural arches supported the building and roof of asbestos shingles. The outstanding feature of the exterior of the building was the 50-foot tower with its 25-foot spire housing a 3,000-pound Memorial Bell, one of the largest bells of

St. John's builds a new $175,000 church edifice in 1958.

its type in Los Angeles County. As the worshiper enters the nave, he is impressed with the simple dignity of the building, which the architect expressed extremely well in the straight lines of the walls and ceiling. One's eye is drawn immediately to the beautiful marble altar surmounted by a huge 14-foot brass cross. Louvered walnut paneling accentuates the vertical line and height of the chancel wall with stone planters on each side of the altar enhancing the beauty of the chancel. The seating capacity of the building was 475 including the balcony that seated the choir and housed the $16,000 Kilgen Pipe Organ. Wide side aisles and a spacious narthex provided ample room for overflow seating.

Joining the main sanctuary were the new offices for the pastor and secretary, a boardroom, nursery, and prayer chapel with complete appointments. All windows in the sanctuary and prayer chapel were of leaded stained glass. The furnishings in the sanctuary were of ash with the exception of the altar and baptismal font, which were of marble. The aisles and chancel floor were carpeted. The church was designed by Mr. O. J. Bruer, architect, of Montebello, and was built by the Don R. Hill Construction Company of Inglewood, California.

After serving St. John's for nine years as a teacher, principal, organist and director of the children and adult choirs, and youth director, Don Simpson, accepted a call in 1960 to Hope Lutheran

School in Glendora where he helped open the new school, serving as principal, teacher, and organist and choir director. He helped build the two-room school with sixty children to a ten-classroom school servicing 260 students in preschool through eighth grade before he retired in 1996 after forty-five years of teaching in two Lutheran schools. His replacement as teacher and principal at St. John's in 1960, was Wesley C. Visser who came from St. John's Lutheran School in Oxnard where he taught the fifth and sixth grades after graduating from Concordia Teachers College, Seward, Nebraska, in 1954. He was born on November 5, 1932, in a rural community in north central Washington, a member of a family of 11 children. His family at the time included his wife, Roberta, daughter of Rev. Arthur W. Schelp of Corvallis, Oregon, and four children, two boys and two girls; the oldest son, Dennis, was a first grader at St. John's that fall.

In 1962, the congregation once again achieved peak membership of 515. Two years later, the theme, "Golden Praise," was selected by St. John's for the observance on January 26, 1964, of the 50th

The chancel of St. John's with a beautiful marble altar and huge 14-foot brass cross mounted above the altar. (Pacific Southwest District Archives)

St. John's church with its 50-foot tower and 25-foot spire housing a 3,000-pound Memorial Bell, was dedicated on November 30, 1958. (Pacific Southwest District Archives)

anniversary of the Christian day school with Pastor Ilten delivering the sermon at the 10:30 a.m. service, and District President Victor L. Behnken speaking at the 4:00 p.m. service. An evening reunion banquet of all the school graduates followed at the gymnasium of Emmaus Church, Alhambra, with the dinner program theme, "Those Wonderful Years." A highlight of the anniversary year was the addition of a kindergarten to the school with Mrs. Robert Kramer serving as the teacher. The staff also included Wesley C. Visser, principal; Frederic W. Kamprath; Arlene Haefker; and Mary Schnorr. The February 2 morning service was televised on "Great Churches of the Golden West" and was shown to the television audience on February 9. In 1964, another of St. John's Sunday services was telecast on "Great Churches of the Golden West."

Two years later, a festival service of praise and thanksgiving was conducted on February 6, 1966, when the congregation noted the silver jubilee of their pastor, Rev. William H. Ilten. Rev. F. Waldo Boettcher, pastor of Grace Lutheran Church, Escondido, and a former classmate of Pastor Ilten's at Concordia College in Milwaukee and Concordia Seminary, St. Louis, delivered the anniversary sermon on the theme "In His Service," taking his text from 1 Timothy 1:12, the apostle Paul's thanksgiving for his call to the ministry. Rev. Harold B. Tietjen, executive secretary of the Board of Missions, served as liturgist and choral numbers were provided by the junior and senior choirs under the direction of Ronald A. Fode, minister of music. After the service, the chairman of the Board of Elders, Mr. Mathew Stohlman, presented Pastor Ilten with a monetary gift from congregational members and a binder of the many greetings received. On February 2, the Mary Martha Society of St. John's sponsored a broadcast of the Southern California Lutheran Hour in Pastor Ilten's honor.

The 60th anniversary of the founding of St. John's was observed on August 14, 1966, a unique and unusual circumstance when the only two resident pastors participated in the service. Pastor Smukal, pastor emeritus, addressed the congregation and Pastor Ilten occupied the pulpit using as his theme, "God's Word to St. John's" using as his text I Corinthians 3:21-23.

Early Tuesday morning, May 28, 1968, St. John's beloved pastor emeritus, Rev. Gotthold H. F. Smukal, passed away at his home, 3017 East Fifth Street in Montebello at the age of 82. Funeral services were conducted the following Monday after-

noon at St. John's, with the Rev. Victor L. Behnken, president of the Southern California District, delivering the sermon, Rev. William H. Ilten assisting as liturgist, and Rev. Reno H. Jeske of Santa Barbara, a long time friend, giving the eulogy. A number of pastors from the District sang a selected hymn. He was survived by his wife of sixty years, Lena M. Ruether, and a daughter, Lorna, the wife of the Rev. Robert W. Schaller, pastor of Bethlehem Lutheran Church in Phoenix, Arizona. During Pastor Smukal's early ministry in Los Angeles, he founded and served a number of mission stations in Upland, Hollywood, Hawthorne, Inglewood, and Belvedere Gardens.

In 1971, the 65th anniversary of the church was celebrated with one of the prominent features of the celebration being the burning of the mortgage, which had been previously liquidated. Also in that year, the women of the congregation were given equal voting privileges in the Voters' Assembly. In 1976, Pastor Ilten accepted the call of Mt. Calvary Lutheran Church of Diamond Bar where he served until December of 1976 when he retired from the active ministry. He was called to his heavenly home in 1991 with funeral services conducted in the evening of December 2 at Good Shepherd Lutheran Church, Sun City, where he had lived in his retirement and a Service of Praise and Life and Joy conducted at St. John's in Montebello on December 3. Dr. Loren Kramer, president of the Pacific Southwest District, delivered the sermon with pastors James Blumhorst, August Hauptman, and Douglas Jones, pastor of St. John's, assisting. The children of grades four thru eight sang "I Love to Tell the Story" and the congregation sang a number of Pastor Ilten's favorite hymns.

With Pastor Ilten accepting the call to Diamond Bar, Rev. George Thomas Fisher accepted the position of vacancy pastor at St. John's in 1976, and was subsequently retained as assistant pastor until 1979. He was born on August 10, 1907, near Salt Lake City, Utah, on the farm of his parents, a German Lutheran mother and a father who had been a Mormon where George was baptized and raised in St. John's Lutheran Church of Salt Lake City. In September of 1920, at the age of 13, George boarded the train for Concordia College, Oakland, for his pre-ministerial training. He continued his education at the Concordia Theological Seminary, St. Louis, where, in addition to his studies, he also developed his singing talents as a member of several singing groups including the Municipal Opera of St. Louis. His first congregation was a

Pastor Ilten accepts the call to Mt. Calvary in Diamond Bar in 1976.

small church in Augusta, Wisconsin. Rev. A. Wahl ordained him in Eauclair, Wisconsin; soon afterward, he married Esther, Rev. A. Wahl's daughter. He moved to Bloomer and Eagleton, Wisconsin, where his children George, David, Gloria, and Nancy were born. Pastor Fisher was then located in Detroit, Michigan; Banning, California; and finally in 1951, he was called to First Lutheran Church, El Monte, California.

In 1977, the Rev. Paulus Voelzke was installed as the third pastor of St. John's. He was born in Arthur, North Dakota, on October 30, 1931, the son of Reverend Martin W. and Elsie (Glasnapp) Voelzke. Following his graduation from Fairmont High School in Minnesota in 1948, he attended Macalester College in St. Paul for one year. The next two years, he attended Concordia College in St. Paul, receiving an A. A. degree in 1951. He attended Concordia Seminary in St. Louis, graduating in 1956. During his vicarage year, 1954 to 1955, he served at Trinity Lutheran Church in Layton, Utah. He was ordained at his home church, Christ Lutheran of Minneapolis, on June 3, 1956.

Rev. Paulus Voelzke, St. John's third pastor, was installed in 1977 and remained until 1990. (Pacific Southwest District Archives)

He married Edna Pedersen on June 10, 1956, at Redeemer Lutheran Church, Salt Lake City, Utah; their union was blessed with four children, Susan, Rebecca, Joel, and Rachel. He became missionary-at-large for the Southern California District in the Tustin area in July 1956 where he organized Peace Lutheran Church in Tustin and was its pastor until October 1972, when he became pastor of First Lutheran Church, Culver City.

The year 1980 saw a new constitution adopted by the congregation, which redefined the church's governing authorities. Two new school classrooms were dedicated, and school enrollment reached a high of 181 pupils. The following year, St. John's marked the 75th anniversary of the congregation with four special services held in October of 1981. They not only celebrated the 75th year of the congregation's organization but also its 23rd year of the dedication of its house of worship. The theme was "In Him We Trust — Yesterday + Today + Tomorrow." Most of the speakers, liturgists, and organists for the services were sons of the congregation. The speaker on October 4 was Rev. Rheinold

F. Knaus with Rev. William H. Ilten speaking on October 11. Christian service was the topic of Dr. Richard L. Jeske's sermon, and first vice president of the District, Rev. Loren Kramer, used the theme "Our Challenge and Our Future." The climax of the month long celebration was a banquet at the Montebello Country Club on October 25 with the speaker, Dr. Arnold Kuntz, president of the District. Larry Batterman served as the master of ceremonies.

By 1981, the neighborhood surrounding St. John's was in transition with many Hispanics moving into the area. In April of 1981, Yolanda Rubio became a member of the congregation through adult Confirmation. Since she was so impressed with the Lutheran doctrine learned in 16 sessions that prepared her for her Confirmation, it convinced her of the need for Hispanic people to know and understand the teachings of Scripture that she had learned. Every Thursday evening, Pastor Voelzke conducted a Spanish Bible class even though he did not speak Spanish. The formation of the class and its continued success was the result of the talent and effort of Yolanda. Only three weeks after her Confirmation, Yolanda gathered 15 people in her apartment who were interested in learning the Bible but needed to learn it in Spanish. She prodded Pastor Voelzke into getting Spanish Bibles from the American Bible Society. Instruction manuals in Spanish, *La Iglesia Ensenna*, were ordered from Rev. Robert Gussick of Lutheran Baja California Mission. When the materials and students were all assembled, Yolanda instructed the pastor, "Now you teach what you taught me, and I will translate it into Spanish." That's the way the class had begun; from the first meeting, the class had been held weekly with attendance ranging between 12 and 17 people.

Through Yolanda, Pastor Voelzke was brought into contact with Lucia Armijo who had fled El Salvador bringing only her daughter Jenny to America leaving her son Alex behind. It was a very emotional moment when Alex Armijo, knowing no English, was brought from El Salvador to be reunited with his mother, Lucia, after more than six years of separation. Because of Yolanda, Alex

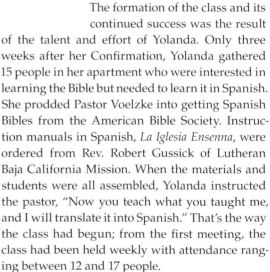

was learning the teachings of Christ. Members of the class were all anxious to learn English, but Spanish was their native tongue. Even though Yolanda came from Ciudad Hidalgo, Mexico, only ten years before, she was able to interpret what Pastor Voelzke said in English into Spanish with clear explanations. Plans were made to help the class members and other Hispanic people to understand the Sunday morning worship service by holding a 15– to 30–minute class after the service where people could explain and discuss in Spanish what happened in the service, what the pastor preached, and how they would benefit from it.

Pastor Voelzke stated: "Yolanda is proving to be a faithful teacher of the Gospel. She explains to the class that the biggest mistake that a church can make is to teach that you get to heaven by living a good enough life. Yolanda emphasizes heavily that word 'only' when she explains that we are saved only by believing and trusting in Christ."

Elba Knutson, a member, said that the reason Yolanda was such a good teacher was that she kept bringing simple, everyday illustrations into her interpretations and explanations of what Pastor Voelzke said in English. Elba, who was instrumental in helping the pastor minister to Yolanda, accompanied him on his calls the previous year when Yolanda was looking for God. Elba would explain the Gospel to Yolanda in Spanish as only one native Mexican can speak to another native Mexican. Because of pastor's need and inadequacy in Spanish, Elba and Yolanda became the nucleus of a small group of Hispanic people in St. John's who became real evangelists and missionaries. "Only by faith" got special emphasis at every class taught.

Since the congregational membership continued to steadily decline and the need became more apparent each year for a Spanish-speaking pastor at St. John's, Pastor Voelzke decided the thing he and the congregation had to do was change with the community, so he took a Spanish class in a community college. He noticed that people would begin to light up when he started saying words in Spanish, even though he didn't know very much Spanish at the time. When Rev. Kenneth Behnken, assistant to the District president for missions, asked Pastor Voelzke whether the congregation might like a Spanish vicar, he replied that they most certainly would but couldn't afford it. In 1983, the congregation requested the Board of Directors of the Pacific Southwest Directors at its May meeting to place a Spanish-speaking vicar

at St. John's. That spark set off a $10,000 grant from the Lutheran Women's Missionary League with Synod providing another $2,500, and the District, $6,000. Thus Mark McKenzie came as vicar for a year without a cost to the congregation.

Vicar McKenzie patterned his work after that of the Rev. David Stirdivant, the District's senior pastor in Hispanic ministry. Through the three families that were members or participating in the congregation, each Sunday at 10:30 a.m. he taught a Spanish-language Bible study attended by four to eight people and on October 31, 1983, a noontime Sunday Spanish language service was conducted along with a Tuesday evening Spanish language Bible study. While Vicar McKenzie was there, about 15–20 people attended Spanish worship services. He and the subsequent vicar were also given authority to consecrate the elements of Holy Communion in the Spanish worship service when the pastor of the church was unable to be present. Attendance continued to grow through the school and through friends and family of those people who were involved. After Christmas, Professor Albert Garcia of Concordia Seminary, Fort Wayne, Indiana, came to visit and commented, "You've got something good going here. You ought to keep going and not let it stop." Following his last year in the seminary, Vicar McKenzie returned to the District to work in the Hispanic mission field. After Vicar McKenzie returned to the seminary the following year, Vicar David Coles came to carry on the Hispanic ministry. More finances were arranged with St. John's contributing $6,000. David Coles, who came as the second vicar, had been raised in Venezuela until he was 15 years old; he spoke Spanish well. He had also earned a doctorate in history at an Ivy League university and, in the process, had studied in Spain. Voelzke said of him, "He was accepted. He was liked." While Vicar Coles was there, St. John's newsletter also included a Spanish section, typed with proper diacritical marks and signed by "El Padre David." Hispanic membership rose to the 20s and 30s. After graduating from the seminary, David Coles became a missionary in Venezuela, as that was where he had been raised as a child. Later, he became a professor at the seminary in Brazil.

Since there was no Spanish-speaking theology student in synodical schools, that third year of vicarage help at St. John's was eliminated, showing Pastor Voelzke that the crucial time had come for him to learn Spanish. He had been told, "'If you really want to learn Spanish, go to Mexico."

St. John's receives a Spanish speaking vicar, Mark McKenzie, in 1983.

As this was arranged with the congregation raising money through Mexican brunches and other events, in April of 1985, he began a nine-week course of studies in Morelia, the recognized center for linguistic work in Mexico. He could learn much, then come back, and keep practicing with help from Vicar Coles. The only problem was that nine weeks wasn't enough time for him to learn to conduct the worship service. He returned to Morelia again in August where this time he studied under the personal tutelage of Juan Manuel Perez. To meet the requirement that he lecture in Spanish, Voelzke chose the unit on the Holy Spirit from his adult instruction course where he had planned a 20-minute presentation. After he got through in half an hour with Perez's help and correction, Perez and the others present also became interested in Lutheran theology. To be able to preach in Spanish, Voelzke followed a pattern he observed in the practice of a pastor in Mexico City. After Pastor Voelzke worked out a draft of his coming Sunday's sermon by midweek, he and his secretary worked together on translating it into Spanish by Wednesday afternoon. He also taught a Bible class in Spanish with the members of the class helping him in expressing himself correctly in Spanish. One of his great satisfactions was to hear them say, *"Es increible como ha aprendido espanol"* — "It is unbelievable how you have learned Spanish!"

St. John's church secretary, Soraya Metamoros born in Ecuador, stated this about Pastor Voelzke, "The first time he came back from Mexico, it hardly seemed worthwhile. The second time he came back, there's no stopping him." She spoke both English and Spanish, but at church she and Pastor Voelzke conversed in Spanish making it a practical way for him to keep practicing the language while receiving correction from one who grew up speaking the language. At the time, he was the only pastor in the District who served both a Hispanic and an English congregation. The two groups worked closely together with a real desire to go out of their way to support each other, because they loved each other.

The Hispanic student population at St. John's Lutheran School continued to increase. At the graduation ceremonies and closing service held in the church on Thursday evening, June 7, 1984, 14 eighth grade students received diplomas and 24 kindergarteners received certificates. The Rev. Cristiano Artigas of La Santa Cruz Lutheran Church, Los Angeles, was the guest speaker pre-

senting a message based on the theme, "Continue in What You Have Learned," from II Timothy 3:14. At the service, the Eleanor Harabedian Lutheran High School Scholarship, left in memory of the late Eleanor Harabedian, was awarded for the first time to Cynthia Ramirez, who was to attend Lutheran High, La Verne. Also speaking at the ceremonies were the valedictorian, Gregory Placencia, and the salutatorian, Luz Rosas. In order to meet the challenges of the changing neighborhood, the congregation in 1989, opened a preschool in the parish hall. During the 1990–1991 school year, St. John's School had the third highest number of Hispanic students in the District with 119 or 70 percent of the 170 students having Spanish surnames. Of the 170 students, only 14 were from members of St. John's congregation. One hundred twenty-one students were from non-Lutheran homes, making a fertile field for mission work for a Spanish-speaking pastor or staff. In the fall of 1988, the congregation voted in favor of opening a preschool/day care for children ages two to kindergarten age. State requirements were met after much work with the preschool/day care opened in August 1989.

By 1989, it became apparent to the pastor and congregation that changes had to be made in the congregation's mission endeavor. Since the parish had struggled with a large decline in Anglo population surrounding the church, they realized that their only survival was an outreach to the Hispanic community. Pastor Voelzke, who was struggling with the Spanish language, intended to resign as soon as the new pastor came. There was no animosity on his part, he just felt inadequate for the task. The challenge of the ministry at St. John's was to continue to minister to Anglos but place a major emphasis on reaching the Hispanic community; the Anglo church attendance ranged from 40 to 90, and the Hispanic ranged from 18 to 20. To help the transition from Anglo to Hispanic take place gracefully, Pastor Voelzke would stay only a short time to help the new pastor get acclimated. He stayed until the fall of 1990 when he went to Panorama City to help at El Redentor. In January 1989, Jose Perez began Spanish services on Sunday afternoon, but this was discontinued after a short time. The parish decided they needed a pastor with the following special pastoral qualities: 1. Fluent in Spanish language; 2. Able to preach in English and Spanish; 3. Good pastoral heart; 4. Able to work with school and school staff. The person who met these qualifications was the

During the 1990–1991 school year, St. John's School has the third highest number of Hispanic students in the District.

Rev. Douglas Jones, who was assigned to St. John's as a missionary-at-large in 1989.

On July 16, 1989, Pastor Jones was ordained and installed as missionary-at-large at St. John's. He was born in Compton, California, in 1957, the oldest of four children; he has two brothers and one sister. Due to his father's work, he lived most of his life in Fullerton, and had been a member of Christ Lutheran Church in Brea. He received his B. A. in biblical studies from Biola University in La Mirada in 1983. He went on to graduate with a B.A. in philosophy from California State University, Fullerton, in 1984, along with studying at Talbot Theological Seminary. In 1988, he graduated with a Master of Divinity degree from Concordia Theological Seminary in Fort Wayne and remained there to do further studies towards his S.T.M. in missions.

During a seminary mission conference, Pastor Jones became aware of the needs in Hispanic ministries. Because of this interest, he was called to a Hispanic vicarage in Miami, Florida. However, the interest in the pastoral ministry, to which he dedicated his studies, began years before as a young child. To help pay for his education, Pastor Jones worked in various occupations including carpentry and general construction, factory work, warehouseman, Lutheran youth director, and as a psychiatric nursing technician at Lutheran Hospital's psychiatric unit in Fort Wayne, meeting his future wife, Sandra R. Halsey, at the nurses' annual harvest celebration at the Lutheran Hospital College of Health Professions where she was studying to be a registered nurse.

On July 28, 1985, Pastor Jones married Sandra at his home congregation, Christ, Brea. His wife was born in Montgomery, Alabama, in 1962 at the Maxwell Air Force Base Hospital, the oldest of

Rev. Douglas Jones, who was assigned to St. John's as a missionary-at-large in 1989, accepted the call to serve as St. John's full-time pastor in 1990 where he continues to emphasize work among the Hispanic population. (Pacific Southwest District Archives)

four children. She was raised outside of Memphis, Tennessee, for most of her life. When they arrived at St. John's, she was a full-time wife and mother, who cared for their 17-month-old daughter, Sarah Elizabeth, born February 24, 1988, and at the end of November of that year another child was born.

By 1990, Pastor Jones accepted the call to serve as St. John's full-time pastor where he continued to emphasize work among the Hispanic population. On May 15, 1993, the LWML Spring Rally at St. John's focused on "Hispanic Mission for the Year 2000"with the guest speakers, Dr. and Mrs. Esaúl Salomón of Iglesia Concordia, Chula Vista. In the spring of 1997, St. John's Lutheran School was among one of the Pacific Southwest District schools slated in national research commissioned by the national headquarters of The Lutheran Church — Missouri Synod. The purpose of the study was to determine the effectiveness of urban Lutheran schools as they pursued their mission course of developing and supporting the faith of children. While the study was about schools, the research embraced the entire congregation. Included in the research project was an examination of the faith development of Lutheran school children and how that impacts their homes. Other congregations and schools in the District that were included in the research were Good Shepherd, Inglewood; Redeemer, South Gate; and Trinity, Santa Ana. Many changes had taken place in the city of Montebello by the year 2000 as the population of 62,150 people had changed to a 74.57 percent Hispanic and an 11 percent Anglo populace. By the fall of 2002, big changes had taken place at St. John's with Pastor Jones serving both the church and school as pastor, preaching in two languages, English and Spanish, and teacher of grades four thru six, and principal.

By the fall of 2002, Pastor Jones serves as pastor, teacher of grades four through six, and principal of the school.

Peace Lutheran Church
Pico Rivera, California

Pico Rivera continues to be a fast-growing city of about 63,428 people having an 88.29 percent Hispanic and a 7.75 percent Anglo population in a more than eight-square-mile area located on the eastern border of the Los Angeles basin and in the southern border of the San Gabriel Valley. Native Americans who believed that the world began in this area where the city is now situated called it Sejat, meaning place where the bees burrowed in the ground. Pico Rivera today has changed from its original forested and bucolic state into an urban region easily accessible by car via the Pomona, Santa Ana, and San Gabriel freeways, by plane via Los Angeles International Airport, and by train via the Union Pacific Railroad, Southern Pacific Line, and the Atchison, Topeka and Santa Fe Railway Company.

The original San Gabriel Mission was first located on the northwest border of the city. Pico Rivera was also part of Jose Nieto's vast land grant, with Nieto allowing Juan Crispin Perez to graze his cattle on the land in 1805 or 1806. After the Mexican Independence in 1825, persons who held grazing rights to land were able to petition to receive the title of the land as their own. In 1835, Perez received title to the grazing land naming it Rancho Paso de Bartolo having present borders that are south of Whittier Narrows, with the Rio Hondo River bordering the west side, and extending as far east as Citrus Avenue in Whittier; the southern border was between Slauson Avenue and Washington Boulevard.

After Perez's death in 1846, Pio Pico, the last Mexican governor of California, began dealing with his heirs for the divided parcels in 1850,

A 4′ x 6′ oil painting by Herbert Hahn depicting early rancho life in the 1880s at Pio Pico's El Ranchito that is now part of Pico Rivera. (Whittier Historical Society)

eventually, purchasing all the property for $4,642. In 1852, he built an adobe casa on the property, a portion of it remaining today as the Pio Pico Mansion, giving it an affectionate and enduring name of El Ranchito. As time passed, Americans began settling the area purchasing the land for farming, with Pico selling parcels to early Pico Rivera residents. What land remained of the ranchito was lost in 1892 through a shameful court settlement taking all of Pio Pico's remaining property.

Pio Pico, an important figure in California's transition from Mexican to American rule, was born in a brush shelter at the San Gabriel Mission on May 5, 1801, the second son of ten children, whose father served as a mission guard. His father and grandfather had come to Alta California with Juan Bautista de Anza in 1776. When he was 18, his father died leaving Pio to support the large family who moved back to San Diego where he opened a general store. In 1826, he was appointed to the *diputacion*, an advisory committee to the governor. In 1834, he married Maria Ignacio Alvarado with their marriage producing no children. After she died and was buried on February 2, 1854, he never remarried. When he became governor on April 12, 1845, he moved the state capital to Los Angeles and stepped up the secularization of the mission lands. His term of office was cut short when Americans invaded in 1845. After going to Mexico, he returned in 1848, catching the American spirit as a staunch supporter of law and order using his wealth and influence for the development of education, banking, and town sites, serving as a Los Angeles councilman, building the Pico House, planning Picoville, and investing in California's first oil adventure. He died on September 11, 1894, and was buried next to his wife at the old Calvary Cemetery on North Broadway in Los Angeles. Their remains were later moved to the Walter P. Temple Mausoleum in the City of Industry.

The southern section of the city was part of Rancho Santa Gertrudes, which was sold to Lemuel Carpenter, a resident of Los Nietos, for 22 cents an acre, prior to the Mexican War. Before there was a Rivera, there was the Barton Ranch. This tract of land was bounded on the north by the Santa Fe tracks, on the south by Shade Lane, on the west by Rosemead Boulevard, and on the east by the San Gabriel River. This included most, but not all, of the present Rivera town site.

The Barton Ranch came into existence on December 28, 1852, when 170 acres was sold to James R. Barton by Lemuel Carpenter and his wife, Maria de Los Angeles Carpenter. The sale price was $2,315, a substantial increase in property value — jumping from 22 cents to over $13 an acre. Barton, an absentee owner and sheriff of Los Angeles County, was killed leading a posse in pursuit of the bandit Juan Flores. Eventually when the Barton's legal heirs were established, Joseph Hartley Burke bought the undeveloped land for $8,500 in 1878. The area, known today as Rivera, was first a farming community appropriately called Maiseland, due to the high yield of the corn crop. As the valley continued to be filled with newcomers, Joseph Hartley Burke and J. F. Isbell got the idea of developing 50 acres of the Barton Ranch into town lots. Accordingly, on October 29, 1887, an agreement was reached between these two gentlemen, establishing the township of Rivera. Isbell, a trustee for the Los Nietos Townsite Company, obtained the right to subdivide, "in such manner as he, Isbell, may deem best and most expedient for the sale of the same town lots."

The Southern California Railroad Company, later acquired by the Santa Fe Railroad, was laying track out of Los Angeles that would extend to San Bernardino by way of Anaheim, Orange, and Riverside. Burke was largely instrumental in having the railroad routed through the new town while it was being developed with the coming of a railroad providing the incentive for the town and depot to handle the shipments of grain and livestock. Rivera received its name from a Texan named Van Way, who suggested it be so named since Rivera means "between two rivers." The towns of Pico and Rivera, from which the city originated, officially began in the 1880s when the Union Pacific and Atchison, Topeka and Santa Fe railroads built rail lines through the region.

The arrival of Americans coincided with the demise of the cattle industry. Blessed with fertile soil, both communities became known for their walnuts, avocados, citrus, and other crops, retaining their agricultural character through the mid-1940s. When a growing influx of new residents came to Pico and Rivera after the end of World War II, development began supplanting farming as the landscape became dotted with housing subdivisions, schools, stores, and churches. The first churches in the area were the Baptist church in Rivera, building a church structure in 1888, still serving the congregation, and the Methodists who built their church in 1870 in the northern end of town called Pico after Pio Pico. Predating these two churches was Pio Pico's chapel in his Ranchito

Joseph Hartley Burke buys undeveloped land in Rivera for $8,500 in 1878.

for Catholic worshipers who lived in the area. As the population grew, the residents desired to blend the two separate towns, Pico and Rivera. On January 7, 1958, the majority of voters in Pico and Rivera voted to incorporate as one municipality with the decision becoming official on January 29, making Pico Rivera Los Angeles County's 61st city.

With the transition of Pico Rivera from an agrarian to an urban community, many Lutherans were purchasing new homes and moving into the area. The Southern California District canvassed the Rivera area on Sunday, April 20, 1952, for the purpose of beginning a new mission. In the summer of 1952, the Southern California District Mission Board assigned the Rev. Henry W. Schmitt to the field to begin the work and was assisted by Charles Manske, a vicar from St. Louis who would later serve as pastor at the University of Southern California campus church and the founding president of Christ College, Irvine. For 46 years, Rev. Schmitt served in the active ministry. He was born September 14, 1887, in Two Rivers, Wisconsin. Upon graduating from the Wisconsin Synod Seminary at Wauwatosa, Wisconsin, in 1912, Rev. Schmitt was ordained at his home church and installed as pastor of Christ Church, Eagle River, Wisconsin. In 1926, he accepted the call to First, Burbank, where he served until he was called to St. Paul's, North Hollywood where he retired in 1948. However, the rapid growth of the Southern California population moved the District Mission Board to request that he assist them as missionary-at-large, which he did for another 10 years, opening various missions in the Southern California area.

On August 10, 1952, the first service was conducted in the home of Mr. and Mrs. John Hoffman with 11 persons in attendance. Two Sundays later the congregation moved into the unattractive Legion Hall at 7702 Serapis, where services were held up to the time of the dedication of the new chapel in 1954. On September 14, 1952, a Sunday school was started with 14 children in attendance. The

Rev. Henry W. Schmitt was assigned to Pico Rivera, conducting the first service in the home of Mr. and Mrs. John Hoffman on August 10, 1952. (Pacific Southwest District Archives)

Rev. Schmitt conducts the first service in Rivera on August 10, 1952, in the home of Mr. and Mrs. John Hoffman with eleven people in attendance.

attendance in the church services and the Sunday school showed such steady growth that by the close of the year, the record showed an average attendance of 51 in church services and 44 in Sunday school with the congregation having 49 communicant members and 115 baptized members.

The first voter's meeting was held on Thursday evening, October 30, 1952, at 7:45, at the home of Mr. Alan Foster with seven members in attendance, at which time temporary officers were elected. At a meeting on December 2 with 17 present, the congregation voted to officially adopt its name, "Peace Lutheran Church of Rivera" with the parish formally organized at a meeting a week later on December 9, 1952, receiving 76 communicants and 68 children as charter members. On February 13, 1953, the congregation voted to purchase the property, comprising an area of 216.47' × 237.03', on Passons Boulevard and Shade Lane Avenue in Rivera. During the following months, Mr. O. J. Bruer was engaged as architect; after the approval of a loan from the District Extension Fund, groundbreaking ceremonies were held on Sunday morning November 22, 1953, following the regular service in the Legion Hall. Work on the chapel was begun on December 13, 1953, with hundreds of hours of volunteer labor given by members and friends of the congregation under the able supervision of Samuel Sinner, the builder and foreman, who was also a member of the congregation. At the time, 20 adults and 7 children had been received by Confirmation. Another adult class of six and a children's class of seven was started. Peace had more than 130 communicants and 30 voting members, with a Sunday school of 124 boys and girls. At the time, the congregation was calling a permanent pastor.

Pastor Schmitt preached his farewell sermon on January 10, 1954, with 168 persons present as he was beginning mission work in West Covina. He finally retired again in 1958 moving to Pasadena. In 1964, he and his wife entered the Lutheran Home at Anaheim, where he died on July 5, 1968. Pastor

William Klaustermeyer of Fullerton Junior College consented to preach on Sundays until a permanent pastor could be obtained. By late spring, Rev. Paul Lemke was called as the first resident pastor of Peace. He was born in 1920 in Holstein, Iowa, one of three sons of Mr. and Mrs. Fred Lemke. He attended Concordia College, Milwaukee, Wisconsin, and Concordia Seminary, Springfield, Illinois, graduating in January of 1945. He served his first year of vicarage in Geneseo, Illinois, the second in Long Beach, California with the trailer mission, from which the efforts resulted in the West Long Beach church being organized. He served congregations in Jefferson, Iowa, from April 1945 to October 1947 and St. Paul's Lutheran Church, Sac City, Iowa, until he accepted the call to Peace. He married Eleanor Kunz of San Diego, California, on February 18, 1945 with the Lord blessing their union with two children, Barbara and Steven Paul, who were eight years old and six years old at the time of his installation.

Rev. Paul Lemke became the first resident pastor of Peace in 1954. (Pacific Southwest District Archives)

The Rev. Paul Lemke was installed on June 6, 1954, at the same time the new sanctuary was dedicated, making it a grand day of joy and thanksgiving to God. On that day, the congregation assembled in front of the main entrance of the chapel at 10:00 a.m., where Pastor H. W. Schmitt conducted the opening service. Mr. S. Sinner, the builder, handed the key to the pastor, whereupon Mr. J. Wright, the president of the congregation, opened the door and the large congregation of over 300, led by the pastors and the choir, sang "Open Now Thy Gates of Beauty." The Rev. William Klaustermeyer officiated at the altar, and Pastor Schmitt preached the dedicatory sermon on the subject, "The Permanency of the Church Built on the Rock Jesus Christ." The choir, under the direction of Ken Fratzke, sang "Now Thank We All Our God" by Bach.

The chapel with a seating capacity of 250, was equipped with a Hammond electric organ donated by members and friends, had a pastor's study,

Peace Lutheran's first house of worship built by volunteers at a cost of $30,000 and dedicated on June 6, 1954. (Pacific Southwest District Archives)

five Sunday school rooms, and a kitchen, which were all located on the west side of the chapel entrance. A $30,000 loan made it possible to purchase the property and build the first building. With the new building completed, the church continued to grow. By June of 1954, a total of 99 adults had been confirmed with the communicant membership increasing to 330, and the baptized souls numbering 585. Nearly 110 baptized souls were added to the church of which 73 Baptisms had been performed the first 6 months of that year — 36 adults and 37 children. Truly "the fields are white unto the harvest," and the members and the pastor of Peace Church gave all glory to God alone in ceaseless praise for the blessings He had bestowed upon this 2-½-year-old mission. Pastor Lemke once said, "I came here from the Middle West in June 1954. To me it is almost unbelievable that there is so much mission work to be done in our Southern California District."

On May 20, 1956, a large, new parsonage of 1,780 square feet of living space with a 21' × 21' attached garage and covered patio was dedicated. It contained three bedrooms, a den with fireplace, a large living room/dining room combination, a large kitchen, service porch, and one and a half baths, built at a cost of approximately $9,200. Most of the work was done by volunteer labor with Mr. Sam Sinner, a member of the congregation, assuming the leadership, assisted by Mr. Charles Schultz, also a member of the congregation.

By 1957, the Sunday school and all other facilities were taxed beyond capacity with a Sunday school enrollment of some 450 pupils. At the time of purchase of the property in 1953, the seller had another plot adjacent to the one which was purchased, comprising an area of 99' × 216'. This plot had a large, two-story residence in good condition, which was about thirty years old. At the time of the first purchase, efforts were made to purchase this parcel, but the owner, an elderly lady, refused to sell her home when offered $18,000. After she passed away, the property was purchased for $22,500.

As the congregation continued to grow, there was a pressing need for a large sanctuary to house the congregation for worship services. Ground was broken for the new house of worship on May 15, 1960, with actual work begun on the construction of the building on June 8, 1960. The cornerstone for the new $215,000 sanctuary was laid on October 30, 1960, with 300 people attending the service. Rev. Paul Lemke laid the cornerstone with

members of the building and finance committees and Peace congregation assisting. Rev. William Graumann of Riverside spoke at the occasion. This new church was the fourth building project in the congregation's eight-year history — first, the unit which served as the chapel, then a Sunday school wing, next the parsonage, and, finally, the new church of a two-tone masonry construction providing seating for 450 people in the nave and 48 people in the balcony. Having paid off the $102,000 in debts in five years and with only $15,000 in the building fund, the members thought at first that the new church would be out of their reach financially, and yet, firmly believing that God would continue to bless them as He had in the past, they felt that the new church at its best would still be a very insignificant return to the Lord for the blessings which He had showered upon them.

On Sunday, March 12, 1961, another milestone in the short history of Peace Church was achieved when 2,300 people joined together in praising and thanking God at the dedication of the new church edifice. The services were inspiring with the Peace Lutheran Choir, the District LLL Chorus, and the Lutheran High School A Cappella Choir, blending their voices to fill the day with joy and gladness. At this joyous dedication day, the congregation had grown to 700 communicants in a short nine years. By June of that year, the Lord had blessed the congregation with 725 communicants with a class of over 50 children confirmed on Palm Sunday of 1961 and over 1,200 baptized souls with 600 children enrolled in the Sunday school.

The new church was constructed of white and oatmeal Norman brick throughout in a semi-contemporary design by architect Robert Inslee, with the nave measuring 126' × 40'. The altar, pulpit, lectern, and baptismal font were constructed of a very warm and soft walnut travertine marble. The 18' × 24' reredos was crafted with antique travertine marble with all the marble in the building imported from Italy. The marble work was beautified by cast-bronze symbols, and a 15-foot bronze cross, attached to the reredos, immediately calling attention to the focal point of the church — the altar. Although carpeting covered the aisles, the floors in the narthex, under the pews in the nave, and in the chancel area were of terrazzo. The oak pews of a new flex-o-steel construction were upholstered with beautiful golden fabric on the seats.

In addition to the main sanctuary, there was a sacristy workroom behind the reredos. Sinks,

On Sunday, March 12, 1961, 2,300 people join together to thank and praise God at the dedication of the large, new church edifice.

The nave of the church with the altar, pulpit, lectern, and baptismal font constructed of warm, soft walnut travertine marble, was dedicated on March 12, 1961. (Pacific Southwest District Archives)

closets, and cabinets had been provided for the storage of Communion ware, paraments, etc. To the right of the sacristy workroom were the private secretary's office, restroom facilities, and the pastor's study. The study, carpeted throughout, contained beautiful oak bookshelves plus a large sliding glass door, which led into an enclosed tropical garden. To the right of the study was an attractive private chapel with carpeted floors and oak furnishings. The chapel would seat approximately 25 people and was used for small weddings, private Baptisms, and private devotions.

A two-story structure attached to the narthex end of the church contained a ladies lounge or bride's room, together with restroom facilities, on the first floor. On the second floor, there was a mother's room, with sink and cabinets, restroom facilities, a closet for the choir robes, and a choir robing room. Three separate dimmer switches controlled all the lighting in the chancel area and the nave light fixtures. An intercom system was also provided at three separate stations in the structure. The building was designed for air-conditioning, but at the time of dedication, funds were not available for that project. The attractive three-legged tower housed something new in the church bell industry — four titanium bells, all tuned to four notes. A tape-player machine was added so that the bells could play a melody at set hours during the day. The bells were also controlled from the new Holtzinger pipe organ in the balcony, enabling the organist to ring them for services.

Members of the building and finance committees for the new church were Harry Guthormsen, chairman; Charles Schultz, Milton Krause, Edward Gottschalk, Walter Leichtfuss, James Wright, Ernest Nagel, and Alan Foster. The contractors were the Samuelson Brothers and the builder was Mr. Chet Umbarger.

During Pastor Lemke's 10-year ministry at Peace, the congregation had grown to 800 communicants. Pastor Lemke had Baptized 204 adults and 604 children and had confirmed 520 adults and 230 children. The parish decided to show their appreciation by providing Pastor and Mrs. Lemke with a Hawaiian holiday. On June 6, 1961, the members presented the Lemkes with a 32-foot scroll of signatures of all whose gifts were given to make the Hawaiian trip possible. To take care of any necessary pre-holiday shopping, Pastor and Mrs. Lemke were given 167 books of trading

During Pastor Lemke's 10-year ministry at Peace, the congregation grows to 800 communicant members.

In September of 1966,
Peace begins a weekday
school with 150 children
coming every Wednesday.

stamps. The presentation took place in a service conducted by Rev. Armand Mueller, who had installed Pastor Lemke 10 years before.

After Pastor Lemke took a call to Peace Lutheran Church in Rock Rapids, Iowa, in 1964, the Rev. Charles Birner accepted a call to Peace in Pico Rivera. He was born on December 1, 1922, in the parsonage of Zion Lutheran in Bunker Hill, Illinois, where his father was pastor. He attended Concordia College in Fort Wayne, Indiana, graduating in 1943. After his graduation from Concordia Theological Seminary, St. Louis, Missouri, in June 1947, he was ordained into the ministry by his father on August 31, 1947, in his home congregation in Mattoon, Illinois. He had served his vicarage year, August 1945 to September 1946, at Pilgrim Lutheran Church, Santa Monica, California.

On September 3, 1947, he began his ministry as missionary-at-large for the Oklahoma District where he and a classmate, Rev. Waldo Bentrup, moved their living quarters, a house trailer, from city to city, assisting local pastors in evangelizing existing congregations or establishing new ones. In January 1948, the District stationed Pastor Birner in Elk City, Oklahoma, to continue organizing a congregation that was started through the trailer mission. In October of 1948, he accepted a call to St. John's Lutheran Church, Hinton, Oklahoma, located 75 miles from Elk City, where he contined to serve both congregations for 3 years.

On April 24, 1949, Pastor Birner and Frieda Quade were married in Zion Lutheran Church, Oklahoma City. The Lord blessed this union with six children — David who became a pastor, Debbie, Kristen, Mary, Andrea, and Becky. Our Savior Congregation of Tulsa, Oklahoma, extended a call to Pastor Birner in January 1952. He served this congregation for 13 years until January 1965, when he accepted the call extended him by Peace of Pico Rivera, California. In Oklahoma, Pastor Birner served as pastoral advisor to the LLL, LWML, the Walther League, and 12 years as dean of camps and LSV (Lutheran Service Volunteer) schools. He served as circuit visitor and as secretary of stew-

Rev. Charles R. Birner became the second pastor of Peace in 1965 where he remained until 1976. (Pacific Southwest District Archives)

ardship for the Oklahoma District.

In the February 27, 1966 edition of *The Lutheran Witness Reporter*, Peace Lutheran Church was featured describing their weekday school that was started in September of 1966 to give children not attending a parochial school the best Christian education possible, as the congregation of nearly 1,200 baptized members did not have a parochial school. Space limitations, the erection of a new church, and the close proximity of Lutheran schools had deterred Peace from establishing its own school. Every Wednesday about 150 children in grades three to eight came for the newly established weekday religious school. Weekday classes, however, had drawn enough response to require 10 teachers including Pastor Birner and Raymond J. Mueller, superintendent of the weekday school and director of education in the congregation. Seven women and another man completed the staff.

The new weekday school materials from Concordia Publishing House formed the basis for instruction with each child bringing his own Bible and *Luther's Small Catechism* as a resource. The 4:00 to 7:30 p.m. period also included junior choir rehearsal, recreation, lunch, worship, and closing devotion. Pastor Birner stated in the article, "The weekday school is considered by all involved a very important agency to supplement the work of the Sunday school in providing effective Christian training for the children of the congregation." Parents and students who completed questionnaires on the school following the first semester endorsed his appraisal. The parents also were invited to inspect the program and materials as the first semester closed and the second began.

Jesús Martinez often walked and drove by Peace Lutheran Church and wondered about it but never went into the church. He wanted to go on Sundays, but he had never received an invitation. One Sunday morning in 1968, curiosity finally overcame his timidity as he decided to enter the church and attend worship where he was glad and felt at home. After taking his family to worship that Sunday, it started a new life for him, his wife, and two sons. He and his wife enrolled in the pastor's adult class to learn more about the Lutheran church. Their interest increased as they developed a strong faith and a desire to serve. As Confirmation Sunday approached, Jesús eagerly anticipated his reception into membership at Peace, but his wife, Katie, hesitated. To move from her Roman Catholic background to the Lutheran confession required a big "leap of faith." Many months later, Jesús asked the important question, "Could I become a pastor?" That proved to be a desire that would grow, but could not be satisfied for some years. When the Pacific Southwest District established the Ethnic Pastors Certification Program at Concordia University in Irvine, Jesús found his niche in 1976 as he began the lay ministry training program at St. John's in Covina, spending many months studying and preparing for the ministry. In 1987, he was contracted to work part-time as a lay minister at First Lutheran in Long Beach. From there he moved to Holy Cross Hispanic Church in La Puente where he continued to serve.

In the fall of 1968, Peace followed a Lutheran custom of bringing gifts of food to their Thanksgiving service. Pastor Birner in turn, gave the food to Dr. and Mrs. Erwin Kurth of Christ Church, Los Angeles, for distribution to needy families. Dr. Kurth stated, "It was our great pleasure to deliver boxes of gifts to 18 homes." By the late 1960s, Pico Rivera and the area surrounding the church experienced a shift in demographics from a dominant Anglo population of 70 percent in 1965 to a Hispanic population of 70 percent in 1974. In order to minister to the Hispanics in the area in 1971, Pastor David Stirdivant supplied assistance to Peace in reaching out to a greater number of Mexican-Americans who had taken up residence in the area. Also in that year, Mr. Carl Witt, was installed as director of Christian education and youth, during a special service on August 15 at 7:00 p.m. A reception followed immediately after the service to give the members an opportunity to get acquainted with Mr. Witt and his family. Attendance at services continued to remain good with the previous Sunday, August 6, having a total of 440 with 246 at the 8:00 a.m. service and 194 at the 10:30 a.m. service.

While at Peace, Pastor Birner contributed a great deal not only to the parish but also to the Southern California District and the community. He accomplished the following in his first seven years at Peace: midweek school from 5:15–7:15 on Wednesdays, ladies Bible class every second Tuesday at 9 a.m., Sunday night youth service, a Sunday night service with Communion the last Sunday of every quarter, Peacemakers Youth Choral Group, Dial-a-Prayer, Bethel Bible Study series, Speaker of the Southern California Lutheran Hour each Thursday at 9:00 a.m., and chairman of Stewardship Committee of Southern California District. The congregation thanked Pastor Birner for his participation in the projects as well as all the other committee tasks of guiding and leading Peace Lutheran Church in some troublesome times with a special 25th anniversary in the ministry service on November 5, 1972. The following participated in the service: The Rev. David Stirdivant, Pastor of La Santa Cruz Lutheran Church in Los Angeles, was liturgist; Mr. David Birner, Pastor Birner's son, a ministerial student at Concordia Senior College, Fort Wayne, Indiana, lector; The Rev. Oswald A. Waech, executive secretary of stewardship and youth ministries in the Southern California District, preacher; Richard Hoover, Organist; and Edna Foster directed the youth choir, Peacemakers. In the afternoon from 2:00 to 4:00 p.m. in the parish hall, a reception honoring Pastor Birner for 25 years of faithful service to the Lord was held with a special program presented at 3:00 p.m.

In 1974, Peace requested the Mission Board to use $6,000 of the Synod's 125th Anniversary Fund for the project of translating the Bethel Bible Series into Spanish in furthering an effective outreach to Mexican-Americans who had become the major populace in the area. In January of 1976, pastors and lay representatives of Bell Gardens Lutheran, La Santa Cruz in Los Angeles, Peace in Pico Rivera, and St. John's in Montebello, met at St. John's to discuss methods of more intensive mission outreach to the growing Hispanic population especially in the suburban areas adjoining East Los Angeles. As a result, the Mission Board made a request for the loan of services of the Rev. Robert Gussick, director of the Lutheran Baja California Mission, to make a survey of major centers of Mexican population and make recommendations for more effective outreach with an estimated completion date of six-weeks. On June 6, Rev. Daniel Saavedra of Tijuana, Mexico, was engaged to make a survey of mission potential in the Los Angeles's Mexican-American communities, beginning the assignment in Montebello and Pico Rivera. He recommended that the District begin, as soon as possible, to train lay people for a one-on-one ministry with the Urban Ministries Department recommending the establishment of a center for cultural lay ministry

By the late 1960s, Pico Rivera and the area surrounding the church experiences a shift in demographics from a dominant Anglo population to a Hispanic population

training within the District.

In 1976 after serving Peace for eleven years, Pastor Birner accepted the call to Abiding Savior in Lake Forest where he remained until his retirement in 1989. On September 30, 1977, Rev. Wilfred W. Glade was installed as the third pastor of Peace Lutheran Church. During the service, The Rev. Graeme M. Rosenau served as the liturgist, Rev. Paul N. Guebert was the lector, Rev. Arthur T. Kollmeyer was the preacher, Rev. James P. Poerschke was the officiant, Mr. Richard L. Hoover played the organ, and Mr. Leroy Blank directed the choir. Following the installation, a reception was held in the church parish hall for Rev. and Mrs. Glade.

Rev. Glade was the third eldest child of Mr. and Mrs. Alfred J. Glade born in Elmhurst, Illinois, on January 22, 1944. He attended primary grades at St. Matthew's Lutheran School in Lake Zurich, Illinois. In 1954, his family moved to Sharon, Wisconsin where Pastor Glade attended high school. His college years were spent at Concordia, Milwaukee, and Concordia Senior College, Fort Wayne, Indiana, receiving a B. A. degree in 1967.

Rev. Wilfred W. Glade was installed as the third pastor of Peace Lutheran Church on September 30, 1977. (Pacific Southwest District Archives)

He entered the seminary at Concordia, St. Louis, in 1967, where he also received a Master of Divinity degree in 1971. During the second semester of his second year at the St. Louis seminary, he went to Denver's Fort Logan Mental Health Center for Clinical Pastoral Education. While there, he met a student nurse, Sally Gonzales, from St. Joseph's Hospital who was doing her psychiatric affiliation there. As they were assigned to the same unit, they became friends and began dating. When he received a letter in 1969 telling him his vicarage would be at Trinity Lutheran Church in Pueblo, Colorado, he discovered that was her hometown. In the summer of 1970, he and Sally became engaged and were married January 5, 1971. They later became parents of two children. After graduating from the seminary, they moved to Decatur, Illinois, where he did a year of clinical pastoral education at the Decatur Mental Health Center.

After a year of post-graduate clinical pastoral education in Decatur, Illinois, he accepted a call to serve as pastor of St. Paul's Lutheran Church in Holtville, California, serving until 1976. Before being installed at St. Paul's, he was ordained in 1972

at Triune Lutheran Church in Sharon, Wisconsin. While at St. Paul's, he studied Spanish with Pastor Juan Rosas of Mexicali, Mexico, and took Berlitz courses at Concordia, River Forest, Illinois, and at San Diego. He taught an adult Confirmation class in Spanish in Holtville and traveled in Mexico.

During the Vacation Bible School held in the summer of 1977, Mr. David Ramirez, a college art professor and a member of Peace, guided the children in developing mosaic panels of various biblical themes as a result of the VBS experience. The original concept for the design of the theme, the Triune God, was conceived from research in various Lutheran publications dealing with symbolic references in the Bible. Each panel was completed by 8 children ranging from ages 8–12 years of age, under direction from Dee Gruver, Libby Mackiewicz, and Martha Rojas. The mosaic panels were permanently attached to the walls of the Sunday school classrooms and parish hall where they provided an inspirational background for worship and church activities.

In 1983, "The King's Klowns," a pantomime group, under the direction of Deaconess Cindy Martin, developed a new ministry at Peace. In the true tradition of clowns, each of the "King's Klowns" had chosen his or her own makeup and name, which then became that clown's permanent property. The clown, traditionally, brings a little laughter and lightheartedness so that others may momentarily forget their problems. "The King's Klowns" not only hoped to bring joy and laughter, but to point people to the Creator and loving Father who can give the only lasting joy and real solutions to problems. The group was available for outside clubs or organizations for a free-will offering or honorarium with the provision that they be able to share the Word of God.

Another outreach for evangelism at Peace in the summer of 1983 was the use of baseball-style caps. From Synod's Board for Evangelism, Peace's outreach committee took the idea of an iron-on rainbow T-shirt and changed it to a "God Promised" cap. The cap had a rainbow that was screened-printed with the words "God Promised," giving the wearers new opportunities to share "what God has promised." At the annual Sunday school picnic, one on-looker commented on the caps, visited with several members, and decided to join Pastor Glade's adult information class as result of the "God Promised" cap.

In September of 1988, Peace opened Peace Christian Preschool in a service of celebration attended by Congressman Esteban Torres and the Mayor of Pico Rivera. The preschool, under the direction of Mrs. Claudia Wright, a member of Faith Lutheran, Whittier, grew from an enrollment of only six students in the first year of operation to forty-eight pupils within five years. From its inception, the school's purpose was to offer a needed service to young Hispanic families in Pico Rivera, inviting those without an active relationship with Christ or in a local church to such a relationship. To aid Spanish-speaking parents and grandparents to be able to communicate with the teachers, every class had either a teacher or a teacher's assistant who was fluent in both Spanish and English. When the families of preschoolers were invited to hear their children sing simple Christian songs in Spanish such as "Amigos de Cristo" ("Friends of Jesus") or "Cristo Me Ama" ("Jesus Loves Me") as a part of each year's opening worship service about 20 families would attend.

In 1989, many new changes occurred at Peace. At the last service of each month, the new Yamaha Electric Piano Keyboard accompanied the congregation in fast-paced medleys of new praise songs and favorite Gospel songs. At the same time Peace was praying for a way to begin Hispanic ministry, Pastor Sarria was also searching for just such a place to move his ministry with many of the people in the Hispanic congregation at Redeemer, South Gate. Beginning in 1989, services were held in both English and Spanish, with the fifth Sunday of the month reserved for a joint bi-lingual service, creating an opportunity for shared worship and fellowship with bi-lingual Vacation Bible Schools held during the summers. One of the Spanish congregation's members, Lola Denow, was selected to teach a 10-week class in Russia in 1993. In November of 1994, the congregation was saddened when Anna Sarria, wife of Pastor Rick Sarria, was called to her Heavenly Home. During this same time period, Pastor Glade was on the Southeast Lutheran High Board in South Gate that served the area's large Hispanic populace.

Pastor Rick Sarria began a Hispanic ministry at Peace in 1989 and remained until 2001.

By 1997, the Hispanic congregation continued to grow with an average Sunday attendance of 50 people in worship services. In order to evangelize in the community, fliers were made, along with phone calls, and visiting in the community. Four members of the congregation went out two-by-two inviting the families of the community to the church with these visitors setting appointments with the families for the pastor to visit them. One of the members was studying in the District's TEE program and also working at Misión San Pedro y San Pablo in Maywood.

On the last Sunday in March of 1998, a woman from El Salvador passed by the church and saw the church sign in Spanish. Since she was looking for a parish, she chose to visit Peace. She was deeply moved by the service and experienced great peace. After the service, she shared with the pastor that she wished to continue attending and soon became part of the congregation.

On Easter Sunday, the congregation shared the double joy of Jesus' resurrection and the marriage of Pastor and Eugenia Nunes Sarria who was from Spain, with both Pastor Brady of South Gate and Pastor Glade officiating at the service. In the second half of the year, the director of the program, "Cristo Para Todas Las Naciones," selected members of the Spanish congregation to be in charge of a phone bank for the program. Through the calls received, it demonstrated that the need was great in the Hispanic community to know Christ and to do evangelism work. In the fall of 1998, Pastor Sarria was asked to begin a Hispanic ministry at Faith in Whittier. By the end of the year, the Hispanic congregation at Peace had grown to 65 people at worship services. Also, Claudia Wright became director of the preschool at Peace.

On Easter Sunday in 1999, the Hispanic church received six families as part of the family of God, making a commitment to the Lord Jesus Christ. By late spring five more people were attending worship services and Bible classes through the evangelism calls that were made. Attendance at worship services continued to be in the 50s. In 2001 when Pastor Sarria was called to Faith, Whittier, he and his congregation of 30 people left Peace in Pico Rivera and Spanish worship services ceased. With Pastor Sarria gone, Deacon Ben Parrales was

In September 1988, Peace Christian Preschool opens under the direction of Mrs. Claudia Wright.

enlisted to help with the outreach program to the large Hispanic population surrounding the church building. He had worked with Pastor Chuck Brady in South Gate for several years and studied in the TEE Hispanic program of Concordia Seminary, St. Louis. He worked with Pastor Glade but stayed only a short time as he was working at a regular job and had to relinquish his work at Peace. Rather than begin Spanish-language worship services immediately, the congregation concentrated on small group Bible studies, visits in the neighborhood, and offering various community services.

In February of 2002 when Vicar Zabdi Lopez came to Peace, he made many calls on people inviting them to the church, but nobody came. The vicar distributed 1,500 pictorial brochures in Spanish and English about the preschool, First Communion/Confirmation classes, and the church's ministries and classes. As a result of the fliers, he received six to eight phone calls inquiring about the First Communion classes, with two families attending the first class, then dropping out when they realized they were not in a Catholic Church.

In August, a lady by the name of Socorro Amigon (*socorro* means help or aid in Spanish) visited the English Sunday morning worship service, because the Baptist Spanish church she had attended split. Her fiancé, an ELCA Lutheran and a medical doctor in New York, suggested she find a Lutheran Church in Pico Rivera. Before she moved to New York to be married on April 13, she took Vicar Zabdi to the homes of relatives and former members of her church with the result of over 30 people attending one of the five home Bible classes the vicar led in Pico Rivera, East Los Angeles, El Monte, Whittier, and La Mirada. Also one of the couples that had established the Spanish Baptist congregation, enrolled in Pastor Frank Brundige's TEE classes as the husband wanted to become a pastor. The vicar paid half of that couple's enrollment fee and tuition. The vicar also conducted a Sunday morning bilingual Bible class with 40 people attending. By April, 544 people had attended the 68 Bible class sessions that were held; classes averaged eight per session.

Every Christmas the preschool children joined the children of the congregation in a children's Christmas worship service, doubling attendance that day, followed by the breaking of a piñata. When Vicar Zabdi Lopez joined the staff of Peace Lutheran, he taught everyone the song that is traditionally sung when the piñata game is played with the words:

> Hit it! Hit it! Hit it!
> Don't lose your aim,
> Because if you lose it
> You will lose the road.

Since Pastor Glade was curious about what was meant by "lose the road," he did some research, discovering the Spanish missionaries had brought to Mexico the piñata tradition that had come from China by way of Italy and then to Spain in the fourteenth century. Because the Aztecs and the Mayans had a tradition of breaking a clay pot in honor of their god of war, the missionaries introduced the piñata song with the words about "not losing the road." They taught the people that the piñata represented Satan with its seven horns representing the seven deadly sins. The piñata stick

Vicar Zabdi Lopez on the right with one of the Bible classes.

Vicar Lopez presenting Socorro Amigon a bouquet of roses from the Bible classes she helped to start.

was called the "virtue" or goodness stick with the child that was blindfolded named the "Faith." The "Faith" child had to listen carefully as many children would yell false directions with one child, the "True Word," calling the right directions. When the child obeyed the "True Word" and broke the piñata, the candy and fruit that poured forth were called "divine blessings."

Although the religious significance of the piñata has been lost in Mexico, the piñata game, called the "Dance of the Piñatas," was originally played on the first Sunday of Lent. Pastor Glade and Vicar Lopez brought back that tradition, teaching it to the congregation and preschool, and to the students at Trinity Lutheran School in Whittier. Pastor Glade stated, "What a wonderful symbol of the Lenten discipline of listening more closely to the Word, and fighting against the temptations of the devil, the world, and our sinful human nature!"

Since Claudia Wright and Pastor Glade had only a couple of children in the Sunday school in 1988, they started a family Bible class that replaced Sunday school. The family Bible class concept included children and parents from the preschool learning Bible stories together. As a result, the English congregation's membership directory has young families with surnames like Acosta, Grijalva, Moreno, and Perez. Because several community families liked the Lutheran Christian education of Peace's preschool so much, they continued it by enrolling their children in the elementary school of Trinity Lutheran Church in Whittier!

Vicar Lopez was active not only in the church but also in the community. He transported a wife and children of a prisoner to visit him in prison and pray with him. He did a home dedication/exorcism for the same family, gaining their respect. The lights of their home stopped going off and on as they had done previously. He also transported the same family to pray with a respected matriarch who lived in Ontario. He took the youth of the church to District Youth Gathering, as two of the youth were prospective members. One of them attended the adult Catechism class and all worship services. He explained to the Spanish-speaking parents the requirements for First Communion/Confirmation classes.

On Saturday, May 3, 2003, Vicar Lopez conducted a tour of Peace's facilities and began the first worship service where he had 120 people attending, of whom 80 were from Hispanic churches in Region Two. Once a month, the mission had a picnic in the park located next to the church. As a result of the Spanish worship services, he had two people in training in the deacon program. He was also in the District's Ethnic Pastor Certification Program at Concordia, Irvine, graduating in the spring of 2004. Since Pastor Glade's Spanish was very basic, he had to talk to people very slowly. He really appreciated having Vicar Lopez, who was from Mexico, take the lead in the Spanish outreach. One of the things Pastor did to improve his Spanish was to speak to people where he shopped and at the preschool and the church.

Again in the spring, nine members of Peace helped Vicar Lopez assemble enough Spanish and English preschool brochures, Peace ministry brochures, and Spanish First Communion class invitations to be distributed to 1,500 homes. This time the vicar didn't have to do it himself as he paid friends to help him hand them out in the neighborhood. Again the church received several phone call inquiring about the time and cost and again most of them asked if this was a Catholic church; when told it was a Lutheran church, they were no longer interested.

In order for Peace to receive support for the Hispanic ministry, Pastor Glade spoke at Lutheran school chapel services about the ministry. One day in the spring of 2003 after he told the students who had gathered for chapel service at Trinity Lutheran School in Whittier how the Holy Spirit brought Peace Lutheran Church a vicar from Mexico to start a Spanish speaking outreach, Adrianna Varos, a first-grade student at Trinity, went home and told her mother, "I want to give my money to help the vicar in Pico Rivera tell Spanish speaking people about Jesus!" When Adrianna and her mother brought Adrianna's life savings, more than $40, to school for the pastor to take to Pico Rivera, Pastor Bob Schroeder said, "I was blinking tears out of my eyes," as Adrianna knows how to say only "Yes, I can," in Spanish. When her parents, who were born in the United States and do not speak Spanish fluently, visited Mexico the previous summer, Adrianna became aware of the language barrier when she wanted to play with her cousins. Pastor Glade commented, "God's message to me from this event is to keep on telling people how your vicar has gathered more than 40 people into Bible study and worship this past year. Keep on asking them to help Peace Lutheran support a Spanish bilingual pastor!"

Trinity Lutheran Church
Faith Lutheran Church
Iglesia Luterana Fe
Whittier, California

he city of Whittier has grown from its beginnings as a small Society of Friends or Quaker Colony in 1887 to a fine residential city of 83,680 with shaded streets and well-planned residential developments — "a well-balanced city of spiritual, cultural, educational, and business interests." Originally conceived as a Quaker settlement to draw Quakers from the Midwest, especially Indiana, it has experienced a shifting demographics, going from a predominately Anglo city in the last century to a city with a Hispanic majority of 56 percent and an Anglo population of 38 percent.

In the second half of the eighteenth century, the area later to become Whittier, along with all land in California, became vested in the King of Spain. Don Gaspár de Portolá, Governor of Lower California, and Padre Junípero Serra were selected to head an expedition to protect the northern frontier of New Spain from ambitious Russians and English and to establish pueblos, presidios and missions. In 1771, the San Gabriel Mission was established and all of the Whittier section came under the jurisdiction of the mission. Here, where the rolling Puente Hills met the San Gabriel River, the Shoshonean Indians lived, fished, trapped, and trekked to the springs of Turnbull Canyon to catch a glimpse of the ocean in the distance. Here in this valley, known as the "place of the wild bees," whose hives were located in holes in the banks of the river, priests, farmers, settlers, and advancing soldiers on horseback traveled over El Camino Real, the main highway from San Diego to San Francisco that is now the present Whittier Boulevard.

Whittier was not on the immediate path of these first travelers, but it became a part of the series of land grants that began the area's pastoral ranch living. The territory passed from the hands of Jose Manuel Nieto with his lush vineyards, established in 1784, to Juan Perez and his cattle interests in 1835. Don Pio Pico bought out the heirs of Perez and built his hacienda El Ranchito. Here he lived until a few years before his death in 1894 where he watched from his ranch, with love and

interest, the rise of Whittier at the base of the Puente Hills.

Through purchase and foreclosure and homesteading, the land of Whittier came into the hands of John M. Thomas, a farmer from Indiana, where his ranch became a landmark. During this time in Chicago, Aquilla H. Pickering was making plans to embark on a trip to California to select the ideal community site for Quaker colonists from Indiana. Mr. Pickering and his wife Hannah traveled from Sacramento in the north to Enseñada in the south in search of their ideal land, a three-month quest. One afternoon, on a drive over the East Los Angeles area and up into the rolling hills, they first saw the Thomas Ranch with its graceful valley sloping toward the ocean miles away. They knew at once that this was the site for their colony. Since the ranch was for sale in 1887, it was purchased by the newly organized Pickering Land & Water Company with Jonathan Bailey as president, John Painter as vice-president, and Harvey Lindley as secretary.

The name of Whittier was selected for the new community in honor of the New England Quaker poet, John Greenleaf Whittier. On May 11, 1887, Jonathan Bailey and his wife, Rebecca, established their home on the 1,275 acres of ranch land at the base of the Turnbull Arroyo. The ranch house, surrounded by pepper trees, was Whittier's first building, a simple frame colonial structure surrounded by acres of mustard later to become known as the "Mustard Ranch." On Sunday, just four days after the Baileys moved into the old Ranch House, a Quaker church meeting was held on the front porch for all to attend along with the business of establishing the new colony. By the end of May, the sale of lots had started, with the town lots going for $100 to $200, and five-acre lots outside the town site selling at $1,000 each. Whittier was also caught up in the run-away land boom of Southern California in the 1880s.

Quakers were arriving from all over the United States; railroads enjoyed a brisk "fare war" with one-way tickets priced ridiculously low at $1. On July 18, 1887, the first tourist carload of Quakers

The name of Whittier is selected for the new community in honor of the New England Quaker poet, John Greenleaf Whittier.

reached the Norwalk train station. Jonathan Bailey, president of the land company, who welcomed newcomers with a gift box of apricots, personally greeted them. The Quakers were loaded into a horse drawn spring-wagon and driven six dusty miles up to Whittier. Halfway, the wagon party stopped at Fulton Wells, now Santa Fe Springs, for a refreshing taste of mineral spring waters. When they reached their town-to-be, they saw only tent houses, a small business structure and the Friends Church nearing completion. It was indeed a pioneer town, but it was a beginning. It was Whittier! Since the Quakers were great believers in higher education, they established Whittier College in the early years of the colony. It has grown to a large institution known throughout the country, having produced two occupants of the White House: the first was Lou Henry Hoover, President Herbert Hoover's wife, and the second was Richard Milhous Nixon, the 37th President of the United States from 1969–1974. Other notables from Whittier included renowned American authors, Jassamyn West, author of *Friendly Persuasion*, a story of Midwestern Quakers during the Civil War, who also wrote about Quaker life in Whittier; and MFK Fisher who became internationally known for her colorful culinary tales.

At the turn of the last century, German Lutherans began moving into this predominate Quaker community asking Rev. A. E. Michel, pastor of Trinity Lutheran Church in Los Angeles, to serve them with Lutheran services. On the first of January in 1908, a baptismal service was conducted in German by Pastor Michel in the home of Mr. and Mrs. Henry Kruse, laying the foundation of Trinity Lutheran Church of Whittier. It was at this gathering immediately following the service that a fervent desire for regular Lutheran services was expressed with Pastor Michel petitioned to conduct them. He readily consented, agreeing to come again in two weeks, conducting the second service on January 11 in the home of Mr. and Mrs. H. H. Nomann in East Whittier. Since interest and attendance grew in such a short time, it became apparent that a meeting place in Whittier had become a necessity. At first, the Moose Hall served as a gathering place, and later, the Free Methodist Church. Growing attendance and the ever-increasing interest filled the hearts of those who attended with a strong desire to have their own house of worship. The first step was to organize a congregation and choose the name that it bears today, Trinity Evangelical Lutheran Church of Whittier. The formal organization was affected with 5 voting members and 14 communicant members on January 24, 1909. These members then bought the property located at the southwest corner of Bailey Street and Newlin Avenue where the German-speaking congregation worshiped for about five years.

As early as 1908, the missionary prospects in this vicinity seemed to justify the petition for the placing of a vicar in Whittier, with the petition granted by the Mission Board of the Califor-

> Trinity Lutheran Church is established in Whittier with the first service in 1908.

A view of Greenleaf Avenue in 1902, a few years before the first Lutheran service was conducted in Whittier.
(SECURITY PACIFIC COLLECTION/Los Angeles Public Library)

nia-Nevada District. Mr. Theophil Haeuser, a student at Concordia Theological Seminary, St. Louis, Missouri, assumed the duties of a vicar in June of 1908. He continued his labors there until August 1910, when he returned to St. Louis to complete his preparations for the office of the ministry. While Mr. Haeuser was in St. Louis, Rev. C. F. Sapper, a retired pastor, acted as supply pastor. Exactly a year later, following his graduation from the seminary, Mr. Haeuser accepted a formal call and returned to Whittier to become Trinity Church's first resident pastor where he continued to serve until 1919. He took a call to Bethlehem Church in the Creston area near Paso Robles and then moved to Trinity Church in Paso Robles as pastor, staying 30 years. He also served parishes in Hayward and Richmond in northern California. He died in 1975 at the age of 90, having served the Lord in the ministry most of his life. In December of 1919, Reno H. Jeske, formerly pastor at Norman, Oklahoma, was installed as pastor of Trinity Lutheran Church, where he served as the congregation's spiritual leader until his retirement in 1957. Pastor Jeske was born on January 15, 1892, in Seymour, Wisconsin, the son of Herman Jeske and his wife, Bertha nee Hagen. With his parents and sister, he moved to Los Angeles at the age of 11 and attended Trinity Lutheran School on Flower Street. After being confirmed by Pastor Runkel, he attended California Concordia College in Oakland, graduating in June of 1910. He continued his studies at Concordia College in Milwaukee receiving his diploma in 1912. During his college years, he met his future wife, Emily Theiss the

Candidate Theophil Haeuser, a seminary student who served the Trinity mission from 1908 to 1910; following his graduation, he was called as Trinity's first pastor, remaining until 1919. (Pacific Southwest District Archives)

Rev. Reno H. Jeske in his 1915 Concordia Seminary graduation picture. He served Trinity from 1919 to 1957.

Trinity's first church building which served them until 1933. (Pacific Southwest District Archives)

daughter of J. A. Theiss, principal of Bethlehem School. They were married in 1916 and had two children, Elizabeth and Norman. His theological training was at Concordia Seminary at St. Louis where he graduated in 1915. After 66 years in the ministry — 36 at Trinity — he was called to his eternal home in 1981.

Since 1915, the congregation had worshiped at the corner of Penn Street and Pickering Avenue until 1960 when it was sold to St. Mary's Catholic Church. As the congregation continued to grow, a large new sanctuary, designed by the architect, John H. Fleming of Glendale, was built in 1933 at a cost of $11,000 plus another $5,000 for pews, organ, and chimes. In 1943, a Christian day school was established with 16 students in grades one through eight. Since the school and congregation continued to expand and outgrow the Penn Street property, land was purchased on Floral Drive for a new school in 1949 where the school and church eventually moved to the new site with a large parish hall built in 1958 and the present large sanctuary built in 1964.

After World War II, Whittier continued to grow and expand with the influx of new people coming to Southern California. As the orange groves and farmlands in East Whittier were rapidly being replaced with tracts of new homes in the 1950s with more Lutherans moving into the area, and since Trinity was located in the old downtown area of Whittier some distance from East Whittier, the Southern California District saw a need for a new parish in the area and called a young graduate, Candidate Marvin Suhr, from

Trinity builds a large new sanctuary in 1933.

Concordia Seminary in St. Louis in 1952. He was born December 1, 1926, at Staplehurst, Nebraska, the son of Mr. and Mrs. Herbert Suhr. Living in several sections of Seward County, Nebraska, he attended public schools until 1944 when he was enrolled at St. John's College, Winfield, Kansas, to begin his studies for the ministry in The Lutheran Church — Missouri Synod. He taught in a one-room Christian day school in Nebraska for one semester in 1947 prior to entering Concordia Seminary, St. Louis. In 1950, he was joined in marriage to Dawn Quam of San Bernardino, California, the culmination of a romance that had begun during a summer fieldwork assignment in 1948. The Suhrs had three children: Mark, born in 1953, and Gary, born in 1955, and Susan, born in 1959. Another summer was spent in fieldwork in Blythe and Needles, California, in 1949. His vicarage assignment was completed in 1950–1951 at St. Martini Lutheran Church, Chicago, Illinois.

Rev. Marvin Suhr, Faith's first pastor who served from 1953 to 1963. (Pacific Southwest District Archives)

Following graduation from Concordia Seminary in 1952 with a Master of Divinity degree, Pastor Suhr accepted his first assignment to begin a new mission in East Whittier, California, which became Faith Lutheran Church. He remained at Faith from 1952 to 1963 when he accepted a call to Epiphany Lutheran Church of Bothell, Washington, a suburb of Seattle. In 1964, he accepted a call to Our Savior's First Lutheran Church of Granada Hills, where he served until 1974 when he accepted a call to Faith Lutheran Church in Capistrano Beach. He later served a parish in Iowa before retiring and returning to California. He also served the church at large on the Family Life Department of the District Board of Education, chairman of the Program Committee for several district-wide Sunday school conventions, and circuit counselor of Circuit Two. He was director and announcer for the Southern California Lutheran Program, heard daily on radio station KGER, 1390 kc at 9:00 a.m.

When Candidate Suhr arrived in East Whittier on July 15, 1952, he began canvassing the area, holding the first service on August 31 in the American Legion Hall located at Beaty Avenue and Meyer Road, southeast of Whittier. It was rented for $35 a month. He borrowed 10 hymnals from the District office, hoping that another 10 that he ordered would supply the congregation's needs. Twenty hymnals weren't enough on that first Sunday as there were 42 children and adults attending Sunday school at 9:30 a.m. with 74 persons present for the initial church service at 10:45 a.m. In a special service held on Sunday afternoon, November 23, at 3:00 p.m., in the American Legion Hall, Candidate Marvin Suhr was ordained and commissioned as missionary-at-large of the Southern California District, temporarily assigned to serve in the southeast Whittier area with the Rev. T. H. Joeckel of South Gate performing the Rite of Ordination and Commissioning, and Pastor Luther Schwartzkopf of San Bernardino, preaching the sermon on "The Responsibilities of a Good Minister," basing his message on I Timothy 4:4–11., with others assisting including pastors Elmer Gunther, Luther Steiner, and Vicar Underwager. The members and friends of Faith Church joined in fellowship and refreshments following the service, during which time Pastor Joeckel spoke a few words of encouragement to the new mission. The average attendance at the morning services during the month of November was 75 with an average Sunday school attendance of 71. An adult membership class of six was started, and two children were attending a junior Confirmation class.

Palm Sunday, March 29, 1953, marked an important day for the new congregation as 81 charter members were accepted into communicant membership with four of these making their Confirmation vows on that Sunday. The congregation had also purchased a three-acre parcel of land for $5,000 an acre at the corner of Mills and Hawes in East Whittier just south of the new California High School and directly north of a shopping center that was under construction at the time. Rezoning of the property for the church's proposed development was completed with plans for the erection of the first unit of the proposed structure to include a chapel-parish hall with a kitchen, Sunday school rooms, and a church office. Members of the congregation, along with members of Zone 4 of the Lutheran Women's Missionary League, assisted in canvassing the large new area surrounding the church property. In an important congregational meeting held March 20, the congregation adopted

Candidate Suhr holds first service on August 31, 1952, in the American Legion Hall in East Whittier.

its permanent constitution and also extended a call for a permanent pastor. Pastors A. G. Webbeking, representing the Mission Board, and T. H. Joeckel, visitor of the circuit, were present to give their counsel and assistance. The call was extended to Rev. Marvin Suhr, who had served the congregation as missionary-at-large for the District. On Sunday, June 14, at 3:30 p.m., Pastor Suhr was installed in the American Legion Hall as the first resident pastor of Faith with the pastors T. H. Joeckel and A. G. Webbeking officiating.

On August 16, 1953, groundbreaking services were held in East Whittier for the new chapel-parish hall designed by Architect O. J. Bruer with about 150 people joining in the ceremony following the regular morning worship service in the American Legion Hall. The District Church Extension Fund made $30,000 available for the building with construction done primarily by means of donated labor from members of the congregation. The Building Committee consisted of Eugene Ireland, Walter Brelje, John White, David Herbold, Robert Tait, and Theodore Rurup, chairman of the committee, who was also a contractor in the East Whittier area. Mr. Rurup was on the job site every day.

Morning and afternoon services were held on March 7, 1954, to dedicate Faith's new chapel-parish hall. The congregation gathered in front of the main entrance at 10:45 a.m., where a brief door-opening ceremony was held prior to the morning dedicatory service. District President Rev. Armand Mueller, served as guest speaker for the afternoon service and delivered his message to more than 550 people with 1,030 people attending both the services. At the time of the dedication, the congregation numbered 169 communicants with 284 baptized souls; 30 children had been baptized, 16 adults had been confirmed, a Walther League, Women's Guild, Men's Club,

> Pastor Suhr is installed as the first resident pastor of Faith on Sunday, June 14, 1953.

and a choir had been organized, and there was a junior and an adult Bible class on Sunday mornings. The Sunday school, which had an average attendance of fewer than 150, including adults, saw a record-breaking attendance of 305 the first Sunday at the new location. At the American Legion Hall, church attendance averaged 170, and in the new chapel, attendance averaged 350 per service causing the congregation to take immediate steps to have two services every Sunday, at 8:00 and at 10:45 a.m. Under these circumstances, the congregation immediately made plans to raise money for a Sunday school annex and meeting room, which was completed and paid for by March of 1955. By 1956, the parish had grown to over 550 communicant members and was endeavoring to face the challenge of inadequate facilities. Members of the congregation pledged $122,000 for a new church and engaged Culver Heaton of Pasadena as architect for planning a new large sanctuary. In order to house the 883 Sunday school enrollees in 1957, 6 classrooms had to be rented from California High School, adjacent to the church, to accommodate the Sunday school. Three services were held each Sunday to accommodate the large attendance at the church services.

Five years after the first groundbreaking took place for the chapel-parish hall, groundbreaking ceremonies for the new church were held at 2:00 p.m., on Sunday, January 19, 1959, where the congregation gathered in the chapel for a brief worship service. After worship, members of the congregation assembled on the new building site to join forces in pulling a plow across the open field in a symbolic ceremony, pulling together as one body in Christ. Three long ropes attached to the plow represented the Trinity. Two furrows in the fashion of a cross, the cross of Christ, were formed to symbolize the foundation of faith and the church.

The new church of brick contemporary style, designed by Culver Heaton of Pasadena and constructed by Samuelson Brothers of Glendale, was built to seat 450 worshipers, 400 on the main floor and 50 in the balcony. Before entering the church, attention is focused on the large cross above the main doors, constructed of glass mosaic tile with 22-carat gold surfacing. On both sides of the entrance, Luther's seal is depicted on 12 sculptured white stones. Luther, as his own coat of arms, adopted this seal consisting of a cross on a heart, resting on the center of the Messianic Rose and surrounded by a circle to symbolize eternity.

Faith's new chapel/parish hall dedicated on March 7, 1954, where 1,030 people attended the two services. (Pacific Southwest District Archives)

Upon entering the nave of the church, one's attention is brought to the focal point of all of the Christian's worship, the altar in the center of the chancel area, flooded with light from the full length windows at either side of the chancel, and to the large wall cross hanging above the altar. To enhance the setting, native manzanita shrubs were placed on each side of the altar. The exterior side of the chancel wall, seen for approximately a half mile down the street, was decorated with a figure of Christ, constructed of wrought iron and gold tile, with the message for all who passed by to read, "I am the way." Other highlights of the church interior were the "floating" pulpit suspended from the wall, the bride's room in the narthex of the church, and a convenient working sacristy to the right of the chancel. The entire project including the new church, furnishings, Conn organ, parking lot, remodeling of parish hall, and concrete wall, was completed at a cost of $119,745.

Many Lutherans from the District helped swell the offerings of praise and thanksgiving on the occasion of the dedication of Faith's new church September 14, 1958, with nearly 2,000 persons attending the 4 services that day, making it a day of rejoicing in God's goodness. Two dedicatory services were held in the morning with Pastor Suhr speaking and Vicar Ronald Kudick serving as liturgist. Rev. William Graumann, pastor of Immanuel Church of Riverside, spoke at the afternoon festival service. The organ was dedicated in an evening service with Janice Mollenhauer presenting a program of music on the new Conn organ and the singing of the combined choirs of Faith Church under the direction of Kenneth Fratzke.

In January of 1958, feeling the need for helping mentally handicapped children who didn't have the privilege of being in the environment of the Good Shepherd Home of the West at Terra Bella, Faith began a Sunday school class for the mentally handicapped. A mother, connected with the Exceptional Children's Foundation, and a member of the church, had pointed out that there wasn't a Protestant church in the entire Whittier area serving these children. By observing the classes at several handicapped children's schools, Miss Marion Perry undertook the task of starting a Sunday school class for the 10 to 11 enrollees.

By 1960, seeing the need for a Christian day school at Faith, Mr. Gerald Uecker was called to start such a school. His installation as the new teacher-principal of the day school was held on Sunday, July 10, at 3:00 p.m. The dedication of a new Christian day-school building took place on September 11, when members and friends gathered in the church to hear Rev. William Ilten, pastor of St. John's, Montebello, and chairman of the Child Life Department of the District Board of Parish Education, preach on the text, "Bring them up in the nurture and admonition of the Lord." After the service, the congregation gathered at the school site, where official door-opening ceremonies were conducted. Participating were Fred Sauer, building committee chairman, and George Santy, chairman of the congregation. The four-classroom building, containing a principal's office

Faith's new church building is completed at a cost of $119,745 with 2,000 people attending the dedication services on September 14, 1958.

Artist's conception of Faith's new church dedicated on September 14, 1958, in four services with nearly 2,000 in attendance. (Pacific Southwest District Archives)

The chancel of Faith's new church with native manzanita branches flanking the altar. (Pacific Southwest District Archives)

On September 11, 1960, Faith dedicates its new Christian day school building.

and first-aid room, in addition to the other necessary facilities, was constructed by Robert Loewe, a member of the congregation, at a cost of $54,600. Classrooms were completely furnished including an intercommunications system. The new school opened the following day with 55 children enrolled in the four lower grades. Principal and teacher of grades three and four was Gerald P. Uecker, formerly of Redeemer, Ontario. Teaching grades one and two was Miss Gloria Lee, a recent graduate of Concordia Teachers College, River Forest, Illinois.

Another ministry to aid sick and shut-ins was begun in 1961. Members took recordings of the worship service to the homes of those members who, because of illness, could not attend church. Through playing the tapes in their homes, these members, who followed the order of service and the hymns in their hymnals, not only received spiritual strength, comfort, and instruction but also received the inspiration of group worship. The recording was taken to about six homes, which meant a great deal to those members. Many of them suffered from illnesses lasting months and years and were often overlooked by friends after the first few weeks of illness. Aside from the spiritual benefit, it provided a natural occasion for a short visit on a regular basis by different members of the congregation. In addition to the regular Sunday services, all special services and choir concerts were recorded, along with some weddings. The lightweight tape recorder was purchased with most of the funds donated by the shut-ins.

Faith School received national attention on Thursday, May 11, 1961, when four children, Craig Haas, Cynthia Sauer, Mary Jane Morris, and Mark Maloney from the first and second grades of the school appeared on "Art Linkletter's House Party" show on CBS TV, Channel 2. Their principal, Gerald P. Uecker, reported that their spirit and enthusiasm ran high for their first television appearance. Since the church and school continued to grow, Pastor Richard Goebel was called from the seminary as assistant pastor, and Robert Dueker was called as a teacher, organist/choir director, and youth director of the congregation. The following month on Pentecost Sunday, June 10, 51 young people, the largest class confirmed at Faith at the time, took their vows. On the last Sunday in June, ground was broken for the construction of additional classrooms for the Christian day school and an administration facility that included a general

office, workroom, library-conference room, pastors' offices, and a prayer chapel. This was the sixth building project the congregation had undertaken in nine years of existence. Although growth and blessing are so often measured mainly in terms of numbers and building projects, there was even more cause for rejoicing in the fact that giving by members of the congregation showed a 13 percent increase over the previous year.

During 1963, large events took place celebrating the 10th anniversary of Faith Lutheran Church with a Confirmation class reunion banquet on Saturday, March 16, at 6:00 p.m. in the parish hall, plus the 10th anniversary services and dedication of the new classroom, office, library and prayer chapel facilities on Sunday, March 17, at 8:30, 9:45 and 11:00 a.m. Pastor Suhr was the speaker for the anniversary and dedication services, delivering his farewell sermon prior to assuming his duties as pastor of Epiphany Lutheran Church of Kenmore, Bothell, Washington. As a farewell gift in appreciation of his 10 years of faithful service to the congregation, the parish assisted Pastor Suhr in the purchase of a new car. That evening a 10th anniversary banquet was served in the parish hall of Trinity Lutheran Church, Whittier.

On September 8, 1963, Rev. Eugene Schramm was installed as head pastor at Faith with Assistant Pastor Goebel preaching, Rev. Paul Lemke conducted the installation, area pastors participated, and the Senior Choir, under the direction of Robert Dueker, presented the anthem, "Come, Holy Ghost, Creator Blest." A reception was held in the parish hall for Rev. Schramm, his family,

The church and school staff in 1965: Standing: M. Reinertson, Pastor Brinkman, Pastor Schramm, G. Uecker, R. Cattau; Seated: Luanne Liefer, Janice Brinkman, Corinne Pingel, Beverly Leonhart. (Pacific Southwest District Archives)

and the day school teachers. Rev. Schramm came to Whittier from Bremerton, Washington, where he had served as pastor of Memorial Church for 19 years. He was born on January 30, 1908, in Cumberland, Wisconsin, attended Concordia College in St. Paul, Minnesota, and graduated from Concordia Seminary, St. Louis, in 1932. He served Zion, Roseland, Chicago, Illinois, from 1932 to 1934, and Grace, Eugene, Oregon, from 1933 to 1934. He married Ester M., nee Wollenburg, on September 12, 1934, with their union blessed with four children: David, Gordon, Natalie, and Steven. He was ordained on March 13, 1934, in Klickitat, Washington where he served Grace Church from 1934 to 1944. He remained at Faith, Whittier, from 1963 to 1966, before taking a call to Redeemer, Huntington Beach, where he served from 1969–1973. He became chaplain at the Walnut Manor Lutheran Home in Anaheim in 1974. He died on August 5, 1977.

Rev. Arthur T. Kollmeyer was installed as pastor at Faith in 1966. (Pacific Southwest District Archives)

The children's Christmas service in 1964 was very distinctive and creative as it was a filmed production which the members of the Sunday school staff prepared several months before Advent using information from *This Day* magazine with plenty of film, producing a Christ-centered Christmas service with emphasis on God's gift of His Son. Scenes were filmed at various locations in the area, making use of the hilly terrain as well as the historic Pio Pico Mansion. A burro for Mary as well as horses for the soldiers provided a touch of realism for the pictures with vividly colored costumes made by the women of the church, enhancing the richness of the scenes for the 279 children photographed on location. Also included in the script were classroom scenes as well as pictures emphasizing the missionary and sharing aspect of the theme of the presentation, "God's Gift of Love."

Following Pastor Schram's departure, Rev. Arthur T. Kollmeyer was installed as third pastor of Faith on September 11, 1966, where more than 550 persons attended the installation service and fellowship hour. Rev. Victor L. Behnken, District president, delivered the sermon, and the Rev. Roy Gesch, circuit counselor and pastor of Hope Church, Whittier, and Rev. Robert Wolter, Trinity

Church, Whittier, assisted in the service. Others participating were Pastors Frank Smith, Christ, Brea; William Ilten, St. John's, Montebello; William Fackler, St. Paul's, Long Beach; C. Rodger Meyer, Immanuel, Downey; and Armin Hesse, Faith, Pasadena. Under the direction of Rollin C. Cattau, minister of music, 60 members of the youth and senior choirs sang "My Shepherd Shall Supply My Need." Besides previously serving congregations in Texas and Oceanside, Rev. Kollmeyer had served on the District Public Relations Committee, the Rural Church Life Committee, Building and Loan Department of the Mission Board of the Southern California District, and as circuit counselor in the Texas District.

Rev. Arthur T. Kollmeyer was born on July 8, 1923, in Kingsburg, Texas. He attended high school at Concordia, Austin, Texas, graduating in 1941 and St. John's, Winfield, Kansas. After graduating from Concordia Seminary, St. Louis, in 1947, he was assigned to organize Peace, Texas City, Texas, where he was ordained and installed in August of 1947, serving there until October 1953. On July 20, 1947, he married Erna Kieschnick with their marriage blessed with two sons, Dennis and Ronald. He accepted the call to dual parishes, Trinity, Rosenberg, and St. Paul, Wallis, Texas, in November 1953 where he stayed until November 1961. In December of 1961, he was installed at Immanuel, Oceanside, where he ministered until 1966.

In order to celebrate both the 25th wedding anniversary of Pastor and Mrs. Kollmeyer and his 25 years in the ministry in 1972, the congregation transformed the patio of the church, with ferns, hibiscus flowers, seashells, soft lights, and fishnets, into an island dream for a surprise luau. The ladies of the congregation prepared a meal featuring Polynesian chicken, rice, fresh melons, and vegetables. The entertainment, also following the Hawaiian theme, was highlighted by the presentation of a monetary gift from the congregation and friends in Texas and Oceanside where they also served, for a vacation of their choice. Also that year, William Bade of Saginaw, Michigan, accepted the call to serve as principal of Faith School and organist and choir director of the church.

Rev. John Freitag was installed as the assistant pastor on September 16, 1979, with Rev. James Poerschke, pastor of Hope Lutheran Church of Whittier and counselor of Circuit 8, delivering the sermon; Rev. John S. Cassidy, pastor of First Lutheran Church of Culver City, serving as the lector; and Rev. Kollmeyer as the officiant. Pastor Freitag was born April 3, 1944 in Wyandotte, Michigan, and attended Lutheran day schools in Michigan and Inglewood, California. After graduating from California Concordia College, Oakland, with an A.A. degree in 1964, he attended Concordia Senior College, Fort Wayne, Indiana, receiving a B.A. in 1966. He attended Concordia Seminary, St. Louis, serving his vicarage at St. John Lutheran Church in Fraser, Michigan, graduating from the seminary in 1970 with a Master of Divinity degree. His father, Rev. Dr. Alfred Freitag, at Zion Lutheran Church, Glendale, California, ordained him into the holy ministry on July 5, 1970. Before coming to Faith, he served St. John Lutheran Church, Chester, Nebraska, in July 1970. In 1975, he accepted the call to Immanuel Lutheran Church, West Covina, California, and in August 1979, he accepted the call to Faith Lutheran Church, Whittier. In 1967, Pastor Freitag married Betty, nee Weber, who had taught grades three, four, and kindergarten. Since she was trained as a parish worker, she worked at the Southern California District Office. Pastor and Mrs. Freitag had three children, Chris, Anneliese, and Kiaran.

After serving Faith for 16½-years, Pastor Kollmeyer accepted a call to Bethany Lutheran Church in Leesburg, Florida. On April 10, 1983, he preached his farewell sermons. Later that day at the Candlewood Country Club in Whittier, Faith congregation feted Pastor Kollmeyer and his wife, Erna, with a banquet and a celebration. Festivities began with a welcome by Christian S. Ilten, chairman of the congregation, followed by some thoughts on the occasion by Rev. John Freitag, assistant pastor at Faith and Jim Reid, principal at Faith Lutheran School. Dr. Oswald Waech, pastor emeritus, gave a few humorous comments and Dr. Arnold Kuntz, president of the Southern California District, expressed thanks on the part of the District for the many contributions that Pastor Kollmeyer had

made, serving on the Mission Board, on the Convention Materials Committee, and on the District Board of Directors. Members of the congregation expressed their appreciation of the Kollmeyers in a series of vignettes highlighting Pastor Kollmeyer's ministry, which included a series of "appropriate" gifts, a description of the future of Faith in a humorous vein, and speculation about the Kollmeyers' new life in Florida. The congregation presented them with a picnic basket filled with green folding money. After serving Bethany, he spent his retirement years in Florida and was called to the Church Triumphant in 2003. Following Pastor Kollmeyer's departure, Pastor Freitag became the head pastor of Faith.

In 1988 Faith, was 35 years old and witnessed many changes in the neighborhood, facing a decline in membership. A special luncheon was held to commemorate this anniversary on Sunday, November 13. During this time period, twenty-five women gathered each Wednesday morning to prepare Braille materials for the blind to "Bring Christ to those in Darkness." They made Braille books, prepared packages to send to Braille service centers, and also prepared cards, note pads, place mats, and other blind-related items. In 1992, Rev. Daniel C. Parsons, assistant pastor, completed the requirements for the Doctor of Ministry degree and was awarded the doctorate in ceremonies at Christ College, Irvine. The title of his dissertation was "An Educational Program to Foster an Appreciation for the Style and Substance of Lutheran Worship." In his project, Parsons sought to demonstrate that education in the biblical and historical basis for Lutheran worship tradition would positively affect the attitudes of people toward traditional Lutheran liturgical style.

By 1992, Faith had turned 40, celebrating this anniversary on November 14, at a special 10:45 a.m. service with the theme "Mission to Mission" which included a joint worship with Faith Arabic Lutheran Mission. Pastor Kenneth W. Behnken of the Pacific Southwest District delivered the sermon. Following the service, a fellowship luncheon was held in the parish hall. In 1997, Pastor Freitag left Faith and Rev. Lee Settgast served as interim

Rev. John Freitag was installed as the assistant pastor on September 16, 1979, becoming head pastor in 1983. (Pacific Southwest District Archives)

In 1988, Faith is 35 years old and witnesses many changes in the neighborhood, facing a decline in membership.

pastor for two years. At the urging of Pastor Sett-gast, another mission was begun in 1998 to reach the Hispanic community when he asked Pastor Rick Sarria to begin a part-time Hispanic ministry at Faith along with serving the Hispanic Mission in Pico Rivera.

In 1999 after a two-year vacancy, Rev. Thomas St. Jean was called as the fifth pastor of Faith. He was born on August 11, 1947 in Providence, Rhode Island, and married Dorothy Nahlik on November 30, 1968. Their marriage was blessed with three daughters. He graduated from Faith Seminary in Tacoma, Washington, in 1980. After his ordination at First Lutheran Church in Tacoma, he was installed at Our Savior Lutheran Church in Temple, Texas, where he served until 1981. Following a year of study at Concordia Seminary in Fort Wayne, Indiana, in the colloquy program, he was called to Immanuel in Atkinson, Nebraska, in 1982 where he remained until 1986. He took a call to Redeemer in Chico, California, where he not only expanded the preschool but also established a K–6 Christian day school under the direction of his wife, Dorothy. A television ministry was begun that aired in over 30 cities in northern California, and Washington state. After a productive 13-year ministry in Chico, he accepted the call to Faith, Whittier, in 1999.

During the spring of 2000, Faith requested that the Mission Council of Region 2 of the Pacific Southwest District allow Pastor Rick Sarria to transfer the location of his District-funded Spanish-language ministry from Peace Lutheran Church in Pico Rivera to Faith Lutheran Church in East Whittier, because the community surrounding Faith had been transformed to a neighborhood that was essentially Hispanic in nature. As original owners in the neighborhood had retired, many Hispanic families had bought the homes as their first home. Faith noticed the change in the community, when many members of the congregation had Spanish surnames, and over 50 percent of the students enrolled in the day school were from the community rather than members of the congregation, as was the case in previous years. In addition to the numerous tracts of single-family homes, there were approximately 10 blocks of apartments. In canvassing these apartments, it was discovered that multiple families and/or extended families occupied a number of the units.

Surrounding Faith was the East Whittier City School District, which, according to October 1999 statistics, was 63.6 percent Hispanic. Of those students, approximately one in three was classified as an "English learner" indicating that their primary language was Spanish. Of the four surrounding elementary schools, the Hispanic proportion of enrollment varied from 57.8 percent to 82.4 percent. This ratio continued at a slightly lower rate in the middle schools and local high school. The trends indicated that the neighborhood had become primarily Hispanic and the early elementary school demographics suggested that the Hispanic community was continuing to grow. Review of demographics from the next two closest school districts, Whittier City and South Whittier, indicated that the areas closest to Faith were even more heavily Hispanic. Some schools reached as high as 94.7 percent Hispanic.

In recognizing this challenge in a changing community over the previous two years, Faith had gone door-to-door, hanging door hangers inviting the community to the church. During that time over 10,000 door hangers had been hung and in February of 2000, another 500 were distributed. In about 1997, Faith initiated ministries aimed at the local Hispanic community offering English as a Second Language (ESL) classes, which at one time had an enrollment of 30 students, distributing invitations in both English and Spanish to various activities at the church. Pastor St. Jean and the Bruses started a day-worker program to feed 110 workers Friday mornings where they distributed tracts and Bibles. Pastor Sarria was instrumental in the on-going development of the ministry as the language barrier limited the relationships that could be developed by the English-speaking congregation.

In August of 1999, Faith's Board of Directors approved the establishment of a Spanish language congregation. After having difficulty finding a qualified individual to assist in the development of a Hispanic ministry, Pastor Sarria offered to help establish a new Hispanic congregation. He served Faith without pay, although all facilities and resources necessary for the congregation were provided by Faith. For approximately 14 months, he worked at Peace Lutheran Church in Pico Rivera and led worship services at Faith on Sunday afternoons at 5:00 p.m. During this time, members of Faith repeatedly canvassed the neighborhood to find potential Spanish-speaking members. Slow growth was noticed, but repeatedly it was discovered that Pastor Sarria was over burdened by serving two congregations, and the worship times at Faith were very inconvenient for the community.

In 1999, Faith's Board of Directors approves the establishment of a Spanish language congregation.

In the fall of 1999, Pastor Sarria indicated that it was becoming too difficult for him to serve two ministries at the same time and that he was interested in leaving Peace congregation under the leadership of one of his students so he would devote more time to Faith. He also indicated that he would prefer to have Spanish worship earlier than 5:00 p.m. The congregation concurred with this proposal and worked for it to become a reality. The request was to allow Pastor Sarria to move his ministry to Faith and have the Spanish language congregation worship at 12:15 p.m. with all facilities and resources of Faith provided without charge to the Hispanic congregation.

The Board of Directors and congregation unanimously supported the establishment of a Spanish-language ministry at Faith and to continue to support the Arabic-speaking ministry at the church. The philosophy of ministry at Faith was that only one church should exist, although three language services and ministries were present and that all people attending any services at Faith would be equal members of Faith. The school policy was that all individuals attending the school, who were members of the English, Spanish or Arabic language ministries, were considered members for tuition purposes. The Board of Directors worked to include members of all ministries on the boards of the congregation. The pastor, Rev. Thomas St. Jean, continued as senior pastor for leadership purposes with each of the other pastors serving as associates of Faith.

In 1998, Faith also targeted the youth of the community through a weekly tract ministry to the local high school. These adolescents also participated in the newly formed Venturing Program, a single youth program to encourage relationship development between each ethnic group. Faith also reinstituted an English as a Second Language (ESL) program along with a Spanish language class that was developed for the English-speaking congregation.

With the granting of the request to move Pastor Ricardo Sarria from Peace, Pico Rivera, to Faith, Whittier, Pastor Sarria was installed at the new mission at Faith on Sunday April 30, 2000. On May 7, 2000, the first service in Spanish of the new mission, Iglesia Ev. Luterana Fe, was conducted with 22 people in attendance. After working full-time at Faith/Fe for about two months, Pastor Sarria reported, "It has been a great joy to see the help that the English congregation has given us along with their cooperation." He continued to form

In 1998, Pastor Rick Sarria began a part-time Hispanic ministry at Faith. He is pictured with small boy he baptized.

more Bible groups in homes, distribute tracts, and canvass the area. By the end of the first year, the Spanish services averaged 25 per Sunday with a Sunday school average of 7 children.

The Lord blessed the work of Fe with attendance averaging 33 in 2001. The new goal for the year was to meet with each member asking them to bring a new soul to the flock. Pastor Sarria could have retired that year. Looking back with satisfaction on Hispanic work begun in several locations during his years of ministry, he instead agreed to work with Faith in the new Hispanic ministry in the growing Hispanic community in the East Whittier area. Both he and Pastor Tom St. Jean worked closely together in this growing ministry. By the end of the year, the Spanish-speaking church attendance grew to 35 per Sunday and Sunday school grew to 10 children per Sunday with the Spanish congregation's giving increasing during the year. Ben Parrales also helped at Fe, doing the children's sermon, reading the lections, and sometimes doing the sermon.

According to Pastor St. Jean, Pastor Sarria was indispensable in dealing with the Hispanic community around Faith Lutheran Church. He filled the need for Hispanic outreach by communicating with people in Spanish and bringing children to be baptized. In February of 2002, he and his members set up a display in the Whitwood Mall distributing information about the various ministries offered by Faith to the Hispanic community. In March, a woman from Mexico saw the church sign and chose to attend a service. Since she was

On May 7, 2000, the first service in Spanish of the new mission, Iglesia Ev. Luterana Fe, is conducted.

deeply moved by the service and experienced inner peace, she informed Pastor Sarria she would continue to attend and became a member of Faith/Fe. The congregation's Hispanic members helped the LWML provide quilts to those in need and provided staples for the food bank. By the end of the year, attendance at Fe's services had increased to 38 and Sunday school was up to 8. Pastor Sarria developed tract teams to distribute Gospel information at the local Hispanic markets as well as grocery stores at the shopping centers. He and the participating Hispanic members touched many with the message of Jesus. Since he was working with people who did not move away from their Catholic roots very easily, his heart ached at times for those who could not turn from their errors to embrace the true Gospel. But he always liked to say, "If God is for him, who can be against him."

Faith kicked-off its 50th anniversary celebration, "50 Years in the Hands of Jesus" on December 29, 2002, with Rev. Roger Sonnenberg of Our Savior Lutheran Church of Arcadia, preaching at the service. They continued their yearlong 50th anniversary celebration with Rev. Dr. Larry Stoterau, president of the Pacific Southwest District, as guest preacher on Sunday, March 30, at the 10:00 a.m. service. The English church had 470 baptized members with an average attendance of 380 on Sundays and the Hispanic congregation had 60 baptized members. The Arabic church, established in 1992, had 40 baptized members. The school enrollment was 110 students with a preschool (established about 20 years ago) having 22. Through 50 years of grace, God had blessed the ministry in the East Whittier area with a growing church to the Anglos and now new ministries to the Spanish-speaking and Arabic communities. With the changing neighborhood, the parish had also changed its direction in evangelism, trying to meet the needs of a new community.

Messiah Lutheran Church
Iglesia Luterana El Mesias
Downey, California

The city of Downey is the home of the Apollo Space Program, a journey to the stars, the world's oldest McDonald's restaurant, and the first Taco Bell eatery, plus the pop recording artists, 'The Carpenters," who made many hit records. This unique city ten miles from Los Angeles and 10 miles from the beach in the heart of Southern California with a population of 107,323 people (57 percent Hispanic and 28 percent Anglo) combines the best of both a large and small city, and promotes a small town atmosphere. Before there was a thought of Downey in the late 1700s, ten Spanish missions and four pueblos had been established along the California coast by 1784 with these frontier outposts, a day's journey apart, forming the links to the development of the ranchos when Mexico gained independence from Spain in 1821. The city of Downey was part of the Los Nietos Grant of 300,000 acres of prime Southern California ranch land. In 1834, after the division among the Nieto heirs, a portion of this grant, between the banks of the San Gabriel and Rio Hondo rivers, became the Rancho Santa Gertrudes. In 1873, a 96-acre parcel of Rancho Santa Gertrudes became the central district of what became known as the community called "Downey City."

The town derived its name from John Gately Downey, an Irish immigrant who had come to California during the Gold Rush and succeeded in becoming governor of California, helping to keep the state in the Union during the Civil War. He helped build the economic foundation of Southern California, effecting a transition from open cattle range to an agricultural district of small farms, with Downey among the first to subdivide the vast ranchos into farms. John Downey and his associates called the property "Tract of the Downey Land Association." The agent for John G. Downey and attorney for the Downey Land & Improvement Association was Matson Duke Crawford, who would become a prominent member of the Christian Church, which built the first building in the new town. Crawford arranged for the church to acquire the lot on the corner of Fourth and New streets marking the beginning of the present downtown area. Although development of the new town proceeded slowly, the 1873

The city of Downey derives its name from John Gately Downey, an Irish immigrant.

tract map established 16 blocks, reserving 10 acres for a railroad station. The dense vegetation had been cleared and some 300 homes in the district had been established with the town continuing to grow having a courthouse, post office, schools, churches, businesses, and more houses located in the downtown. The typical Downey home in the 1870s was built entirely of unsurfaced knotty wood with pieces of tin nailed over the knotholes, and battens covered the gaps between the boards making the houses more livable. These California "box houses" had an average of two main rooms and a lean-to open-air kitchen with the windows closed with wooden shutters to keep out wind and rain.

The population, mostly of Southern origin, had come west in search of new opportunity, fleeing the ravages of the Civil War. By the 1870s, the farmers in the Los Nietos Valley had formed small communities with each of them building a school, a church, and a store at a central location. Two of these communities — Gallatin and College Settlement — later became a part of Downey. Gallatin was the first of the two communities (Paramount Boulevard and Florence Avenue area) to take the lead in commercial enterprise. Its date of origin is very sketchy, since it developed out of frontier conditions rather than as a real estate promotion. The Silver School District of Los Angeles County, formed in 1867, noted that Gallatin had a school "for some time." College Settlement began in the 1860s when John Ardis purchased a parcel of land in the southwest corner of Rancho Santa Gertrudes near today's Alameda Street and Paramount Boulevard, which was initially named College Avenue as Ardis opened a private school. In 1869 the Methodist Church established the Los Nietos Collegiate Institute there. This school-church centered community attracted settlers who had traveled west hoping to settle and raise families. John Ardis gave up his private school to devote his time to the college and to develop the new community. The sale of lots was not speculative, as they were purchased to build homes and commercial buildings. In less than a decade, College Settlement had the economic cornerstone of a thriving community of small farmers, educators, and merchants.

By the turn-of-the-century, Downey was the undisputed center of business and social life in the area. Downtown contained a Sunkist packing plant, a department store, banks, restaurants, and mercantile shops. It was also the site of Downey

Candidate Lawrence P. Rudolph conducts the first Lutheran service in Downey in October of 1942.

Union High School and Downey Grammar School. In the 1920s, wooden "Victorian" and "Craftsman" buildings were gradually replaced with Downey's first masonry structures. Downey was known for having the best agricultural soil in Los Angeles because the area was favored with a good climate, fertile soil, and an abundant water supply for irrigation. Cultivated fields of small grain, corn, castor beans, mustard, and deciduous fruit trees were producing excellent yields. At the beginning of the twentieth century, many Downey pioneers had achieved success in business and politics in Los Angeles County. The years 1900 through 1917 were perhaps the "Golden Age" of Downey. In this era, a citrus cooperative was formed, the Downey Board of Trade (later renamed the Downey Chamber of Commerce) was organized, and streets were lighted with electricity.

World War I brought a different sort of progress with local interest beginning to mount in the aviation branches of the military. By 1929, the "dare devil" period in aviation had ended as the industry began to consolidate in Southern California. Inventor E. M. Smith, whose family had reaped a fortune from a drill bit patent for oil exploration, pioneered aviation in Downey, purchasing the 73-acre Hughan Ranch located about one mile south of the Downey depot where he converted the ranch into an airstrip and formed his company, Emsco Aircraft, eventually leading to a huge aircraft industry employing over 30,000. The people of Downey suffered during the Depression years along with the rest of the nation, but its position as an agricultural center insured that food was available to sustain the local populace. Orange groves remained visible in the downtown area with dairies located along the banks of the two rivers.

In 1940, the population of sleepy, rural Downey had grown to 12,000 with many Lutherans counted in that number. By 1942 at the beginning of World War II, the Lutherans had requested the Mission Board to begin services in Downey with missionary work begun by Candidate Lawrence P. Rudolph conducting the first church service in October of 1942 with 36 people in attendance in a rented storefront building at 111 East Third Street. A Sunday school was organized, and, in spite of the city's scattered subdivisions among orange groves and limited transportation facilities, two of the Sunday school teachers solved the transportation difficulties by using their automobiles, helping to gather an enrollment of 25 pupils on the organization day. Messiah Evangelical Lutheran

Church was incorporated and organized as a legal corporation in January of 1943.

On March 21, 1943, at a 3:00 p.m. service, Candidate Rudolph was ordained at Trinity Lutheran Church in Whittier by Rev. Reno Jeske. He was later called by the congregation and installed as pastor on September 5, 1943, with his father, the Rev. Karl Rudolph of Watertown, Minnesota, performing the Rite of Installation. Pastor Rudolph was a graduate of Concordia College, St. Paul, Minnesota, and of Concordia Seminary in St. Louis, Missouri. After graduation, he served as one of the field men for Synod's Department of Publicity and Missionary Education, touring the West Coast during 1941–1942, showing the motion picture "The Power of God." On January 31, 1944, Messiah observed the first anniversary of its organization having a membership of 70 baptized souls, 40 communicant members, and 11 voting members. Thirty pupils were enrolled in Sunday school and eight attended the Saturday school. The average attendance in the Sunday service was 42. The congregation had a Ladies' Aid of 14 members, emphasizing Christian service. On the second Wednesday of every month, members assisted their pastor at near-by Rancho Los Amigos, where they took as many as 15 wheelchair patients to and from chapel services at a distance of 5 blocks; they made liberal contributions to home and deaf missions, and held biweekly meetings for sewing in one member's spacious garage.

On Easter Sunday of 1945, Pastor Rudolph announced his engagement to Miss Ethel Lundi of Ashtabula, Ohio, who was a resident of Pasadena. Her home church in Ashtabula was a member of the Finnish Lutheran National Church, affiliated with the Synodical Conference. Not only were the hearts of the congregation gladdened on June 24, 1945, when Pastor and Ethel were united in mar-

Rev. Lawrence P. Rudolph conducted the first church service in Downey in October of 1942. (Pacific Southwest District Archives)

Rev. John H. Hohengarten, Messiah's second pastor, was installed on September 28, 1947. (Pacific Southwest District Archives)

riage at First Lutheran in Pasadena but also when the parish had arranged for the purchase of a new site with a frontage of 187' for $3,500 in an excellent location on a wide, prominent thoroughfare of Paramount Boulevard and Sixth Street on the western edge of town. Due to a shortage of building materials after the war began, no building could be built. By 1946, the population of the area had increased to 22,000 with the congregation numbering 50 communicants, 150 souls, and 52 families having an average attendance of 51 with a Sunday school enrollment of 55 and an average attendance of 20. By this time, the congregation had liquidated its indebtedness on the Paramount Boulevard property. On August 19, 1946, Pastor Rudolph left the congregation that he had founded in 1942. During the vacancy of 1946 through September of 1947, Chaplain F. K. Finke conducted services at Messiah.

The year 1947 proved to be a banner year at Messiah, as the dream of having a new church building on the Paramount Boulevard property became a reality with ground broken for the new chapel/parish hall on January 26, and actual construction begun in June. The laying of the cornerstone took place on September 7, and the new pastor, Rev. J. H. Hohengarten, who would serve for almost 20 years, was installed as the second resident pastor on Sunday, September 28, by the Rev. R. Jeske, visitor, assisted by the Rev. G. H. Smukal, who delivered the sermon, the Rev. Wayne Thomsen of Bell Gardens, and the Rev. Roland G. Finke, executive secretary of the District Board of Missions. The service was held at the Montebello Women's Clubhouse, where the ladies of Messiah congregation also served a luncheon at the reception for their new pastor.

Before coming to Downey, Pastor Hohengarten served St. Paul's Church at Susanville, California, and stations in Lassen and Plumas counties

Messiah breaks ground for a new chapel/parish hall on January 26, 1947.

for over four and one-half years. Previously, he served in the Western District at Van Buren and Fort Smith, Arkansas, and at the Arkansas State Sanatorium in Boonville for ten years. He was a graduate of Concordia College, Fort Wayne, Indiana, and Concordia Seminary, St. Louis, in the class of 1931. He also did postgraduate work at Washington University, St. Louis, 1931–1932. He was ordained at First Lutheran Church, Fort Smith, Arkansas, on September 25, 1933, by Rev. Carl Kretzschmar. In 1939, he was united in marriage with Lorena Long of Fort Smith, Arkansas, with their marriage blessed with two sons, John and Karl. During his ministry at Messiah, an educational building was added to the church plant in 1955 and the church interior was redecorated.

On Sunday, November 2, 1947, the new chapel/parish hall of Messiah was dedicated to the glory of the Triune God in a special afternoon service, at which the Rev. F. K. Finke, vacancy pastor and Veterans' Administration chaplain, delivered the dedicatory sermon. Special music for the occasion was furnished by a quartet, singing the hymns "The Church's One Foundation" and "The Lord Is My Shepherd." The Rev. M. J. Bruer, chairman of the District Mission Board and pastor of First Lutheran, Long Beach, brought greetings of the District. The dedicatory service of the new chapel, seating 240, was attended by a capacity number of worshipers, including members and pastors of neighboring congregations.

The new church building, measuring 76' by 34', was prominently located on Paramount Boulevard at Sixth Street between Firestone Boulevard and Florence Avenue. In addition to the sanctuary, the new structure included five separate Sunday school rooms on the south side of the building, a nursery, restrooms, and a kitchen. The plan was that it was to serve as a parish hall when the congregation built its proposed larger church adjoining the present building. The newly dedicated unit was built at an approximate cost of $20,000 with many hours of volunteer labor donated by members of the congregation, and with many of the furnishings donated by members: carpeting for chancel and aisle, dossal curtains, altar, pulpit, and lectern hangings, a large art-glass window on the east end of the building. The congregation had also purchased a new, six-room parsonage at 11935 South Gurley for $10,500. At the time of dedication, Messiah had 78 souls, 49 communicants, 14 voters, and a Sunday school of 42 with an average attendance of 28.

By the mid-1950s, the city of Downey's population continued to increase with more orange groves and farmland being developed for tracts of new home. With the city growing, a second Missouri Synod congregation, Good Shepherd, was established in the very southeastern section of the city with Messiah also continuing to experience growth having outgrown their little chapel/parish hall. On March 13, 1955, in the morning service, at 10:30 a.m., the church was rededicated, with Rev. E. J. Brott preaching the sermon on the theme, "The True Glory of Your Beautified House of Worship" based on the text, Genesis 28:17. The entire interior of the church was redecorated in sea foam green paint, with 24 new pews made of Philippine mahogany, new asphalt tile flooring of simulated cork, and partitioned doors installed. The sanctuary was now used exclusively for worship purposes, as all social functions of the congregation were held in the new Sunday school building (65' × 26'), which was dedicated in September 1954. The new Sunday school building could be used as one large assembly room or 10 smaller classrooms. A public address system was installed in the Sunday school building and in the small nursery in the church in order to allow parents to bring their smaller children with them and hear the entire service. In addition to the $9,000 cost of the Sunday school building, the congregation had raised $5,000 for church beautification.

Duplicate services on Sunday mornings were scheduled at 8:00 and 10:30 a.m. with the Sunday school meeting at 9:15 a.m. The first Sunday of this new schedule on March 20, 1955, the attendances were 72 at 8:00 a.m. service, 200 in the

Messiah's new chapel/parish hall was dedicated on November 2, 1947. (Pacific Southwest District Archives)

Sunday school at 9:15 a.m., and 114 at 10:30 a.m. service. Six years later in 1961, Messiah remodeled the chancel area with a new custom-built pulpit, baptismal font, lectern, altar, with an indirectly lighted nine-foot cross, and a Communion kneeling rail, all of Philippine mahogany matching the 24 pews which the congregation had installed in 1955, with new carpeting extending the length of center aisle and a screen enclosing the organ. Ingolf Voge, a member of the congregation, was engaged by the congregation to do this work according to the plans of the architect. At the same time, the Connsonatta Concert Model organ, an electric organ with two manuals and a full pedalboard with a six-speaker system, was purchased and installed for $3,476.25.

By 1960, Downey's population had surpassed 86,000 with all the orange groves being replaced by light industry and tract homes. Even with this huge growth, Messiah wasn't growing. With so many members from Redeemer, South Gate, moving into Downey and the lack of churches in the fast growing city, Redeemer decided to begin a Downey branch as an extension of the South Gate church operating as one corporate unit. The branch church in Downey began on Sunday, September 27, 1959, in the Downey Woman's Clubhouse, 9813 South Paramount Boulevard, with Rev. Tobias H. Joeckel, Pastor of Redeemer, conducting worship services each Sunday at 11:00 a.m., with Sunday school sessions beginning on the first Sunday in October at 9:30 a.m. Since the initial services there, the group did very well both as to worship services and Sunday school with Confirmation classes being held there also. For a year, Pastor Edward Beyer, formally of South Dakota, assisted on a temporary basis. By August of 1961, 48 communicant members of Redeemer were released to form a new congregation organized under the name of Immanuel Lutheran Church of Downey, causing some friction between Messiah and them, since they worshiped only one mile north of Messiah. Immanuel had 48 communicant members, 16 voting members, and 65 enrolled in the Sunday school.

Rev. C. Rodger Meyer was called as the first resident pastor of Immanuel Church, Downey, worshiping in the Downey Women's Club. A special service of installation was held Sunday afternoon, December 2, 1962. Rev. E. C. J. Boxdorfer, pastor of Zion Church, Maywood, and counselor of Circuit Nine, performed the Rite of Installation; Rev. Edward C. Beyer, vacancy pastor, was liturgist, and Rev. Tobias H. Joeckel, pastor of Redeemer Church, South Gate, delivered the sermon. The choir of Redeemer Church, under the direction of Martin Bohlsen, sang the anthems: "Oh, that I Had a Thousand Voices" and "A Faithful Shepherd Is

> Redeemer, South Gate, begins branch, Immanual, Downey, on September 27, 1959.

The refurbished church with twenty-four new Philippine mahogany pews was rededicated on March 13, 1955. (Pacific Southwest District Archives)

My Lord." A reception hosted by Immanuel's Lutheran Women's Missionary League followed the service.

Pastor Meyer was born in Fort Wayne, Indiana, on July 19, 1934, and attended Concordia College, Portland, Oregon, completing his seminary training at Concordia Seminary, St. Louis, in 1959 with a Bachelor of Divinity degree. During his years of seminary training, he served congregations on the West Coast and in St. Louis. While in St. Louis, he met his wife, Elizabeth Howe, where they were married in December 1957; at the time of his installation at Immanuel, they had two children, Gretchen and Elise. Following his graduation from the seminary, he taught high school and college religion at St. Paul's College, Concordia, Missouri, and a year later was called as pastor at Immanuel Church, Boonville, Missouri. In November of 1961, he accepted a position as chaplain at the Missouri Training School for Boys, Boonville. The following year, he accepted the call to the Downey church.

Rev. C. Rodger Meyer, the third pastor of Messiah. (Pacific Southwest District Archives)

The congregation, under the leadership of its new pastor, embarked upon a complete stewardship program, making a study of the congregation's resources in preparation for securing a permanent location and for developing a program of outreach into the community. An intensive evangelism program was launched the first of February in 1963 and continued through Lent and the Easter season.

Beginning in April of 1964, negotiations were transacted with Messiah to effect a merger of the two congregations. When the matter came to a vote by the respective voter assemblies, Immanuel voted to approve a merger with Messiah. Messiah had 185 communicant members but rejected the proposal. The voters of Immanuel, with 140 communicants, felt that there was great potential for Immanuel in Downey, and took steps to develop a permanent program. Since the voters in their meeting on November 5, 1964, voted unanimously to ask to become a fully subsidized congregation of the District, they expressed the desire to be able to purchase property and begin construction of facilities as soon as possible. Redeemer subsidized

Immanuel until January of 1965, when the District assumed the responsibility in anticipation of land purchase, which never materialized. By 1966 as Immanuel continued to grow to 278 baptized members and 165 communicant membership, Messiah continued to decrease to 212 baptized members and 145 communicants, with giving decreasing to $14,000 a year.

In November of 1966, Pastor Hohengarten received a call from the Mission Board to become the Protestant Chaplain at Rancho Los Amigos Hospital in Downey, which he accepted staying at Messiah until the end of December as supply pastor. On December 21, 1966, in regular Voters' Assembly, Immanuel Lutheran Church of Downey, transferred all of her members to Messiah Lutheran Church of Downey and conveyed to Messiah all of her financial and physical assets, effective January 4, 1967. In a subsequent resolution, it was declared that effective that date, that Immanuel Lutheran Church of Downey be declared defacto dissolved. Messiah and Immanuel Churches of Downey officially united into a single congregation on January 6, 1967, when Rev. C. Rodger Meyer was installed as the new pastor of Messiah, taking the 280-member Immanuel congregation with him. Officiating at the installation were Rev. La Mar Miller of Bell Gardens, circuit counselor; Rev. Victor L. Behnken, president of the Southern California District, speaker; Rev. John Hohengarten, former pastor of Messiah; and Rev. George F. Duerr, Good Shepherd, Downey. Pastor Meyer tendered his letter of resignation to the congregation at the special voters' meeting on March 14, 1968, as he wanted to continue his education and work on his doctorate to prepare himself for the teaching ministry of the church; the voters accepted it with "deep and sincere regrets." He preached his farewell sermon on June 9, 1968.

With the merger of the two congregations, Messiah swelled to 461 baptized souls and 326 communicant members with a Sunday school of 187, necessitating additional space in the nave of the church for seating and more Sunday school rooms and office space. In order to enlarge the sanctuary,

Messiah and Immanuel merge on January 6, 1967.

the walls of the Sunday school rooms on the south side of the church were removed to provide more seating for worship services, and the office building south of the church was rented for additional Sunday school rooms and office space. Eighteen movable wall dividers were installed in the parish hall to make individual classrooms for the Sunday school. Replacing the previously used curtains made it a much more quiet learning environment for the children. With movable walls, the parish hall could be opened for large gatherings.

On June 30, 1968, Rev. Alvin Paul Young was ordained and installed as the fourth pastor of Messiah. Participating in the service were Rev. Ronald G. Timmons of Faith, Carpinteria, as liturgist; Dr. Merlin Newkirk of Messiah as lector; Rev. Oswald A. Waech, evangelism/ stewardship counselor of the Southern California District, as the preacher; and Rev. Thomas Faszholz, assistant professor at Concordia Teachers College, River Forest, Illinois, as the ordinator. Messiah was Pastor Young's first parish ministry after having done graduate work and teaching for three years at Valparaiso University in Indiana. He was

Rev. Alvin Paul Young was ordained and installed as the fourth pastor of Messiah on June 30, 1968. (Pacific Southwest District Archives)

baptized by his father, Rev. Alvin Young, attended California Concordia College in Oakland, California, Concordia Senior College in Fort Wayne, Indiana, and graduated from Concordia Seminary, St. Louis. Pastor Young resided in Downey with his wife, the former Nancy Jeske, and three children, Steve, Jeff, and Carrie. Mrs. Young was a graduate of Concordia Teachers College, River Forest, Illinois, serving as a Lutheran schoolteacher. In the fall, Messiah celebrated the 25th anniversary of its organization with a special service on Thanksgiving Day, November 28, 1968. Rev. Lawrence Rudolph of La Mesa, Messiah's first pastor, delivered the sermon called "This I Remember."

With the merger of the two congregations, Messiah continued to grow to 530 members, making it necessary to expand the building or find a larger piece of property. Dennis Wehmueller was selected as architect suggesting several ideas to solve the problem. The first was to build an entirely new building, but zoning restrictions made that impos-

sible, as there was inadequate property to provide necessary parking to meet Downey's new building code. Remodeling then became the means to meet the objective of a larger facility. In April of 1970, the city of Downey approved the plans of remodeling the church; the contract was signed in September with the contractor Stromberg & Sons at a cost of $115,000 for the entire project.

The church was enlarged by moving the north wall seven feet out; the east wall was moved about 10 feet closer to Paramount Boulevard, and the restrooms were removed from the back of the nave to the new office wing. The overflow area on the south side of the church was incorporated into the nave. The chancel area was opened, moved into the nave, and completely redecorated. A large narthex was built connecting a new office wing. Through the fall of 1972, into the Christmas season and spring, the members met in the parish hall for worship. On Easter Sunday, 1973, the first service was conducted in the newly remolded and enlarged church, which was not complete at the time. On Dedication Sunday, October 28, 1973, Pastor C. Rodger Meyer, pastor of Trinity, Santa Ana, preached at the 8:00 a.m. service and Pastor Hohengarten preached at the 10:30 a.m. service, and Robert Dueker served as organist at both the morning services. In the 3:00 p.m. dedication service, Rev. O. A. Waech was the preacher assisted by Rev. Tobias H. Joeckel, former pastor of Redeemer Church in South Gate, Rev. Alvin P. Young, and Rev. Lawrence Rudolph along with the Lutheran Chorale under the direction of Gregory Waite and the organist, Ron Doiron.

When entering the nave, the focal point of the building is the chancel with its white, free-standing, pedestal altar made of Italian Cremo marble in Italy, a gift from a friend of the congregation and designed by a member of Messiah. Carved in the front edge of the altar in gold letters is the alpha and omega symbol proclaiming Jesus Christ as the beginning and end of faith and hope. On the back wall of the chancel is the Celtic cross, drawing the attention of the worshiper toward the eternal Son of God, who died on a cross but conquered

In 1973, Messiah remodels the church, enlarging it to serve increased membership.

The old stained glass window is retained and placed in the prayer chapel.

death for all, the empty cross. On each side of the cross on the back wall of the chancel are the office lights (three candles), representing the six days of creation as recorded in Genesis 1. The dark walnut wood carvings on the back wall of the chancel and on the eyebrow above the chancel bear the symbol of a Greek cross over a circle, symbolizing Jesus Christ, the Lord and Savior of the entire world.

During the course of construction planning, the Building Committee resolved to preserve sev-

eral items for incorporation into the remodeled facility. When the original sanctuary was built in 1947, a special gift of a large, stained glass window was placed in the east wall of the nave facing Paramount Boulevard. After careful planning, the dismantled window was reduced to a rectangular shape and placed in the prayer chapel in the overflow section of the nave. Jesus Christ and His kingship is portrayed in the cross and crown symbol central to the main field of the window. Also,

The newly remodeled and enlarged church dedicated on Sunday, October 28, 1973. (Pacific Southwest District Archives)

The interior of the remodeled church with new marble altar and wood pews. (Pacific Southwest District Archives)

the old sanctuary lamp in the chancel was incorporated into a larger lamp fixture that hangs in the chancel area. Various pieces of furniture including the dark walnut pulpit, lectern, and padded pews, were custom built by the Overholtzer Church Furniture Company of Modesto, California. St. Luke's Lutheran Church of Westminster, California, took the old mahogany pews. A new custom built pipe organ was projected in the future through a generous gift of a former member who no longer lived in the area, and several memorials.

On Easter Sunday of 1975, Mrs. Eunice McKinney was installed as deaconess of Messiah Church by the pastor, Rev. Alvin P. Young. She was a graduate of the deaconess program at Valparaiso University with a degree in theology and additional training in nursing. She had lived five years in Brazil, where her father was a missionary. Her experience included coordination of volunteers and activities at the Lutheran Home for the Aging in Anaheim. She also served as deaconess at Bethlehem Church in Saugus for two years where she was active in the District's youth ministry and had been on the staff of the San Fernando Valley Area Confirmands' Retreat for five years. Her husband, Bob McKinney, was head of the religion department at Lutheran High School in Los Angeles. In the fall of that year, Messiah celebrated its 33rd anniversary with Dr. Carl Berner as guest speaker and the Lutheran High School Choir of La Verne, under the direction of Jim Klawiter, singing at the festival service. During this time, Nancy Young and Karen Loeber began a preschool for the children of Messiah that was conducted once a week.

The year 1978 brought Messiah many sorrows and joys with their pastor, Rev. Young, accepting a call to Trinity Lutheran in Simi Valley and Pastor Hohengarten passing away in December. The big joy of the year was the delivery of the new $38,694 custom-built pipe organ by the Schlicker Organ Company of Buffalo, New York, using specifications and designs by church consultant and organist Michael Doyle. After 12 years of saving, a dream came true for the congregation as the new 2-manual organ with 8-ranks of pipes and 29 stops arrived in July. Before its arrival, the carpets were removed, and members of the congregation installed new oak flooring throughout the nave of the church. The organ console and pipes were in the east end of the building with the choir area and included 494 pipes, ranging from ¾ of an inch to 8-feet high with a 6 small bell zimbelstern. The dedication of the organ took place on Sunday, September 10, 1978, in the 8:00 and 10:30 a.m. services where the church choir sang with the organist, Michael Doyle, playing the music of

> A Schlicker pipe organ is installed in Messiah in 1978.

The new two-manual, eight-rank Schlicker Pipe Organ with 29 stops was dedicated on Sunday, September 10, 1978. (Pacific Southwest District Archives)

J. S. Bach, Walther, and Buxtehude and the former pastor, Rev. Alvin P. Young of Trinity Lutheran Church, Simi Valley, preaching in both services. Rev. Charles Brehmer, interim pastor of Messiah also participated in the service.

During the 7:00 p.m. service, a special Dedicatory Choral Vesper was conducted with a well-known Southern California organist, Robert Prichard, at the console of the new pipe organ. Following the Lutheran tradition, he played the prelude on the hymn and the congregation sang while he used varied accompaniments to support the singing. Mr. Prichard, who consulted during the purchase of the organ, was a music teacher at Long Beach Community and Occidental colleges and had also played concerts in Germany and France and across the United States.

The year concluded with a brass choir consisting of high school boys, Bryant Buescher, Rick Burger, and Martin Freeman, playing at the Christmas candlelight service along with Harold Leistikow playing the violin. Also at that time, word was received that Rev. Thomas Windsor, pastor of St. Paul's, Laguna Beach, had accepted the call to become Messiah's fifth pastor. He was installed on January 21, 1979, in a joyful service with music provided by the church choir, trumpets, stringed bass, and flute and organ under the direction of Michael Doyle, director of music. Dr. Arnold Kuntz, president of the Southern California District was guest preacher and Rev. James Poerschke, pastor of Hope, Whittier, was liturgist for the service. A reception for the new pastor and his family followed the service and was sponsored by the Lutheran Women's Missionary League. Pastor Windsor was a native of Buffalo, New York, who attended Concordia College, Bronxville, New York, Concordia Senior College, Fort Wayne, Indiana, and Concordia Seminary, St. Louis, Missouri, where he graduated in 1968. He had served congregations in central Connecticut and Southern California and was a member of the Southern California District Committee on Worship and editor of the District's worship newsletter. When Mr. Doyle left in 1979, Pastor Windsor's wife, Sandy, became the director of music, assuming leadership of leading a large music program

Rev. Thomas Windsor was installed as fifth pastor of Messiah on January 21, 1979.

Messiah celebrates its 40th anniversary with the dedication of a carillon on November 28, 1982.

for the church with a children's choir, adult choir, and handbell choir. The Windsors had three children, Tim, Allison, and Andrea. Under Pastor Windsor's guidance, the congregation grew in worship with his creative and liturgical services, in the study of the Word, and in numerical growth. He later took a call to Gloria Dei in Escondido followed by a call to Redeemer in Honolulu, Hawaii, and most recently to historic Trinity in Gardnerville, Nevada.

In 1983, Messiah celebrated its 40th anniversary with the dedication of the 40th Anniversary Memorial Carillon on Thanksgiving Day, November 28, 1982; Rally Sunday at 9:30 a.m. with the famous "people movers" at 6:30 p.m.; presentation of "The Rainbow Express," a musical with over 100 singers, actors, and musicians, at 7:00 p.m., on September 23 and 24; and a 40th Anniversary Buffet Banquet at Bullock's, Lakewood, where Dr. Oswald Hoffmann, International Lutheran Hour speaker, was guest speaker on September 11. Other special events were special services on October 2 and 23, where former Pastors Lawrence Rudolph and Alvin Young were guest preachers. In 1985, Rev. Norman Stoppenhagen was installed as Messiah's sixth pastor with the Rev. Nathan Loesch, of Bethany, Long Beach, serving as officiant.

Pastor Stoppenhagen was born on September 15, 1940, in Wharton, Texas. After graduating from Concordia Senior College of Fort Wayne, Indiana, in 1963, he entered Concordia Seminary at St. Louis, receiving his ministerial degree in 1967. He was ordained into the ministry at St. John's Church in Wharton, Texas, in 1968 and was installed at Trinity, Taylor, Texas, the same year. In 1982, he took a call to St. Paul's in Agoura Hills, California, serving until 1982. He went to Messiah in 1985 where he continues to minister. In 1992, Pastor Stoppenhagen was a contributor of daily devotions to "Portal of Prayers" for October 1–10 and 14–31.

One of Messiah's long-time members, Dorothy Thompson, age 67, received the honor of being crowned Homecoming Queen at Cerritos College on October 24, 1987. Her husband, John, escorted her to her coronation while five of her six children and all of her eleven grandchildren watched from the crowded stands. A few years later, Messiah observed its 50th anniversary where many anniversary activities were held throughout 1993. During this time period from the 1980s and into the 1990s, the community of Downey was experiencing a demographic shift in population with more Anglos leaving and a large Hispanic population taking their place. As Messiah membership continued to decline, the congregation's leadership was looking for ways to minister to the new people in the neighborhood.

In the spring of 1996, Rev. Frank Brundige of Bell Gardens did a pulpit exchange with Messiah in preparation for the beginning of Deacon Ruben Vasquez's Hispanic ministry work there. The deacon was a TEE student in the Hispanic program, serving a group of Hispanics worshiping at Messiah when Messiah opened its doors for this ministry. He and his wife, Josefina, worked in the Hispanic community to bring people to Christ. In 1997, attendance at Spanish worship services averaged 17 to 19. In order to support the Spanish ministry, Messiah received a $10,000 grant from the Lutheran Brotherhood Foundation, which funded staff and materials for small-group Bible studies, worship, and outreach. Messiah participated in the Downey Street Faire with a booth for the distribution of information about salvation in Christ and about the Hispanic ministry of Messiah producing a prospect list of eight families, which the deacon and laity visited as a follow-up. On July 19, the church Parking Lot Sale was a success in creating a favorable impact on Spanish-speaking people who came to the sale where the Spanish congregation handled the food concession and distributed evangelism tracts.

The Rally Day Church Picnic on September 7 had a large number of Spanish-speaking members present, and the occasion built a sense of unity among the people of Messiah. The Spanish parish had a difficult time securing a musician to enhance the Spanish-speaking worship service, but some of the English-speaking musicians learned the Spanish hymns to provide music during the interim. When Pastor Stoppenhagen took a Spanish-speaking member of his English-speaking congregation to visit a couple who spoke only

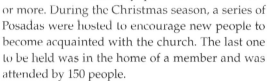

Rev. Norman Stoppenhagen was installed as Messiah's sixth pastor in 1985. (Pacific Southwest District Archives)

Spanish, she immediately asserted herself as the evangelist on the call and presented the Gospel and ministry of Messiah. After persuasion, the couple visited the church and their English-speaking son attended youth group activities.

In the fall, Pastor Stoppenhagen and Deacon Ruben Vasquez led a joint worship service; the deacon read the Gospel, led the confession of faith, prayed some of the prayers in Spanish, and helped with the distribution of Communion. Since the spirit and the unity of the worship made such a favorable impression on all the people present, they requested that such a worship service be conducted on the fifth Sunday of each month in 1998. In an attempt to reach more Hispanic people for Christ, an agreement was made with Marcelo Gómez to build on the work started by Ruben Vasquez who moved to Bell Gardens taking a few members with him. This increased the number of hours for ministry per week to nineteen or more. During the Christmas season, a series of Posadas were hosted to encourage new people to become acquainted with the church. The last one to be held was in the home of a member and was attended by 150 people.

The Mission Statement for 1998 stated: "El Mesias is the part of Messiah Lutheran Church that reaches out with the Gospel of Jesus Christ to the Spanish-speaking people of the community that they might believe and become involved in the church." In order to reach out, more evangelism calls, counseling, and Bible studies were conducted by the Spanish congregation. Music lessons on the keyboard and guitar were provided free of charge to attract people to the church. As Marcelo Gómez continued to draw more people to worship, he once stated, "My heart is filled with joy because two brothers in Christ have decided to become members of our congregation. In addition, they are attending classes in the Hispanic Institute of Theology, which gives me joy. I also baptized my first baby. He was the fruit of my visits to hospitals. The baby now is part of the great family of our Heavenly Father. I'm very happy. I know that working for our Lord is hard work, but he always provides and gives us opportunity and strength

Messiah begins a Hispanic ministry in 1996.

Vicar Ramon Contreras began his vicarage to the Hispanics at Messiah in the spring of 2002.

A Messiah mission society is launched among former members in 2003.

to accomplish to the best of our abilities His Great Commission." Worship at Spanish services had increased to 36 people per service. In the fall, the congregation continued visiting families of the community offering Bible study classes and ESL classes. During the Christmas season, 90 people attended the Posadas.

The New Year began with 14 new members being received into membership at El Mesias after they were instructed in Bible classes and membership classes. Through Deacon Gómez's continued visiting of families in two to three apartment buildings and through counseling of people, the parish was growing. In February and March, two-yard sales were conducted and Bible classes were offered every Friday along with Confirmation classes. From January to September of 1999, 24 Latinos declared their faith through Confirmation with the Latino congregation consisting of 40 members with a monthly average church attendance of 35. On October 23, 1999, and November 27, 1999, two parking lot sales were held. Resources were also used to reach teenagers in the community. During the Christmas season, Posada services were held at Messiah to encourage new people to visit the church. On Christmas Day, the first service for the Latino group was conducted in Spanish. For teenagers, there was a circuit party featuring four speakers and Christian music group where 30 young people were fed at no cost to the congregation, since all the Spanish congregations of the circuit co-operated. Worship services continued to maintain an average of 25 people.

The first quarter of the year 2000 saw church attendance increase to 35 per Sunday with yard sales conducted in February and March. On March 26, the first Quinceñera service was held and attended by 110 people. In the spring, the congregation joyfully celebrated its first marriage with everyone helping to make it a special event. Small-group home Bible studies were begun, equipping people so they could assist in church on Sundays. A women's group was formed as part of a program to serve the church in different areas. A congregational picnic was planned with the fo-

cus to be on unity within the two congregations. The small mission congregation grew by 13 members by the end of December, a 50 percent increase. The members were praying for musicians to assist with worship services. During the year, the congregation had helped 15 families who needed food and clothing.

In 2001, Marcelo Gómez was made a vicar studying in the Hispanic TEE program of Concordia Seminary, St. Louis, based in Chicago, Illinois, working under the supervision of Pastor Stoppenhagen at Messiah. Due to people moving, church attendance had decreased to 25 per Sunday even though 3 new families were attending worship services. On April 28, 2002, Candidate Marcelo Gómez, Messiah's former vicar, was ordained into the office of missionary-at-large to the Hispanic community of Northern Illinois, at St. Paul Lutheran Church in Harvard, Illinois. He was followed by Ramon Contreras, who began his vicarage in the spring of 2002 at Messiah. Since the average attendance had decreased to 13 per Sunday, Vicar Contreras did door-to-door visits in the neighborhoods of the members of the church, distributing fliers describing the church. Spanish services were conducted each Sunday at 9:00 a.m., with English services held at 8:00 and 11:00 a.m. There was also a Spanish youth group that met on Saturdays. By the year 2003, the average attendance at worship services had increased to 30 people per Sunday with Bible study classes being a good source to contact new people for the church. A Messiah mission society was launched among former members of Messiah to support the mission and ministry of the congregation.

In 1997 when Messiah began to reach out to the Hispanic community, it made the following statement in its Lutheran Brotherhood grant application: "While the growth in numbers is slow, the nature of ministry to Spanish-speaking people is to win their trust, which requires time, and then through friendship to win them to Christ. Then the door is open to reach the entire family." The initial statement continues to hold true today as they minister to their changing neighborhood.

St. Paul's Lutheran Church
Norwalk, California

Originally, the land that became known as "Norwalk" was home to the Shoshonean Indian tribes who survived primarily on honey, an array of berries, acorns, sage, squirrels, rabbits, and birds with their huts being part of the Sejat Indian village. In the late 1760s, Spanish settlers, padres, and missions flourished. In 1833 when the Mexican government passed the Secularization Bill, which returned the land to the Indian tribes, the Indian tribes had suffered the loss of much of their culture and were unable to successfully cope with the return of their land.

When the Rancho and mining days in California ended around the 1860s, the land was subdivided once again and made available for sale, with word of this land development reaching the Sproul Brothers in Oregon. They recalled the fertile land and huge sycamore trees they saw during an earlier visit to the Southern California area. In 1869, Atwood Sproul, on behalf of his brother, Gilbert, purchased 463 acres of land at $11 an acre in an area known as Corazon de los Valles, or "Heart of the Valleys." By 1873 when news of a railroad service was coming through the area, the Sprouls deeded 23 acres to the railroad with a clause in the deed stipulating a "passenger stop." Three days after the Anaheim Branch Railroad crossed the "North-walk" for the first time, Gilbert Sproul surveyed a town site, and the name Norwalk was officially recorded in 1874. While a majority of the Norwalk countryside remained undeveloped during the 1880s, the Norwalk Station allowed potential residents the opportunity to visit the "country" from across the nation. This pre-1900 era also brought the "first families" to Norwalk, including the Sprouls, the Dewitts, the Settles, the Orrs, and many others grouping together to shape the future of this little community. In 1880, D. D. Johnston was the pioneer of the first school system in Norwalk and was also responsible for the first real industry in town, a cheese factory, by furnishing money to Tom Lumbard to start it in 1882.

Norwalk celebrated the famous "Gay '90s" with the construction of a number of fine homes that were located in the middle of orchards, farms, and dairies. The D. D. Johnston family built one of these residential landmarks, a Victorian Eastlake,

in 1891. At the turn of the last century, Norwalk had become established as the dairy in the "Heart of the Valleys." Of the 50 local families reported in the 1900 census, most were associated with farming or with the dairy industry. Norwalk was also the home of some of the largest sugar beet farms in all of Southern California during this era. As the years passed, the community continued to grow; permanent educational facilities were constructed; electricity and telephones services were installed; and railroads and highways linked Norwalk to statewide markets. After World War II, the area changed from a rural, agricultural environment to land that was being subdivided into city lots with large tracts of new homes. After a special incorporation election was conducted, Norwalk was certified by the Secretary of State as California's 15th largest city and became Los Angeles County's 66th city on August 26, 1957. Today, Norwalk has 103,298 people within its borders in a city with a 62.89 percent Hispanic population and with 18.95 percent Anglo populace, according to the 2000 census.

As Norwalk was the most rapidly growing community in Southern California in the late 1940s, so was the Lutheran population. On Thursday, October 13, 1949, Rev. A. G. Webbeking, the District mission director, and Rev. H. W. Schmitt drove to Norwalk to survey the vast field that was "ripe for the harvest." The next day Pastor Schmitt called on four families who said they wanted to attend Lutheran services, if possible. On the following Sunday, October 16, the first service was conducted in the Veterans of Foreign War's Hall at 13952 South Pioneer, with an attendance of 18. The following Sunday, a Sunday school was begun with 15 in attendance and 22 in the worship service. On Sunday, November 20, the first church bulletin was issued to worshipers. In December, Pastor Schmitt and his wife moved from their home in Pasadena into an apartment at the corner of Rosecrans and Brink. On a very rainy Sunday evening, December 18, the first Sunday school Christmas program was given in the Norwalk Mortuary Chapel with some 76 in attendance. The first Holy Communion was celebrated on New Year's Day 1950, which fell on a Sunday.

Norwalk becomes the 15th largest city in Los Angeles County in 1957.

Since the District Mission Board and Church Extension Board both realized the great potential in Norwalk, they immediately purchased a fine piece of property at the corner of Rosecrans and Clarkdale with a 330' frontage on Rosecrans, a main intersection in Norwalk only several blocks from five-point. The first Voters' Meeting was held on Sunday evening, January 8, 1950, at the parsonage to consider organizing a congregation. On January 22, the election of officers took place, and the first articles of a constitution were adopted, marking the beginning of St. Paul's Lutheran Church of Norwalk, California. New officers were installed on Sunday, March 12, 1950.

Under the able leadership of Pastor Schmitt, there was a steady increase in attendance, both in Sunday school and in the services, which soon required larger quarters. Beginning with the first Sunday in May of 1950, the Sunday school and divine services were conducted in the Norwalk Women's Clubhouse. In order to reserve the rights to the hall on Sundays before the clubhouse was completed, the congregation signed a lease for one year. Also, in that month of May, the first children's and adult classes were confirmed. Right after this, Rev. Schmitt had to give up the parish, as the work was getting too strenuous for him. He later moved to Pasadena where he lived for six years before he and his wife moved to the Lutheran Home in Anaheim where he lived until his death in 1964, having served the church for 46 years in the active ministry.

During the vacancy, pastors F. K. Finke, H. Atrops, and W. H. Klaustermeyer served the parish. The congregation had grown to 62 communicants with an average Sunday attendance of 70, and Sunday school with 50 children enrolled. Pastor Robert Elmer Gunther was called from Trinity in San Bernardino and installed on November 19, 1950, in Norwalk. Pastor Gunther was born on May 30, 1901, in Des Moines, Iowa and was baptized on October 31, 1901, in St. Paul's Lutheran Church, Fort Dodge, Iowa. He was adopted into a Christian family that already had four older children, two boys and two girls. It was the father's fondest dream that one of his sons would become a minister. Because of the father's asthmatic condition, the family moved from Fort Dodge, Iowa, to Orange, California, in 1904, when the pastor-to-be was three years old.

Pastor Gunther attended St. John's Christian Day School in Orange and in the fall of 1915 entered California Concordia College, Oakland. In

1923, he entered Concordia Seminary, St. Louis, graduating in 1926. The following year, he did post-graduate work at the seminary. He was ordained September 18, 1927, in Ordway, Colorado, and installed as the pastor of Trinity Church. On June 7, 1928, he married Miss Agnes Welge of Chester, Illinois; they were blessed with three children, Robert, Sylvia, and Kenneth. In February 1934, he was called to Hope, Westcliff, Colorado, where he stayed until January 1940. In February 1940, Pastor Gunther was installed as pastor of Trinity Church in San Bernardino where he remained until April 1950. He became the first resident pastor of St. Paul's Church of Norwalk, on November 19, 1950, conducting his first service on Thanksgiving Day in the Women's Clubhouse, which stood where Sears and the Bank of America were located in Norwalk Square. At that time, the congregation was quite small, only 72 communicants.

On the church's Rosecrans property was a small house that was converted into a study and church office. It served as a meeting place for various board and voters' meetings, Sunday school teachers' meetings, and catechetical classes. By April of 1951, there were 210 souls and 110 communicants with an average Sunday attendance of 100. There were 216 at the Easter service where a 17-voice church choir sang 2 selections. Sunday school enrollment was around 175, with an average attendance of 101. Even in the spacious Women's Clubhouse, room was scarce at the rate the Sunday school was growing; the senior class had to meet outside.

The Women's Missionary Society was organized on January 10, 1950, the Junior Walther League on January 14, 1951, and the Men's Club on February 7, 1951. The clubhouse was reserved for a Vacation Bible School that was conducted the last two weeks of June. The District also purchased a parsonage, and the Building Committee was appointed along with the Finance Committee, where they discussed ways and means for a building program while the total indebtedness of the parish was $12,769 with a District subsidy of $300 per month.

On Sunday afternoon, February 24, 1952, at 2:30 p.m., ground was broken for the new 6,440 square foot church plant at the northeast corner of Rosecrans and Clarkdale with the ceremony conducted by the pastor, members of the building committee, and the chairmen of the various organizations also participating in the ceremony. In September, the Women's Clubhouse property was sold to Pa-

St. Paul's of Norwalk adopts a constitution on January 22, 1950, making it an organized congregation.

cific Mutual Insurance Company for business development and the clubhouse had to be moved off the property to another location some time in September. Two and half years before, the Women's Club purchased the two-acre site for $5,500, sold that same site to the Pacific Mutual for $76,000, and kept its building. Due to this situation, the members of St. Paul's were working day and night rushing to get their new structure to a stage where it could be occupied under temporary circumstances. With this moving pressure, they appealed for some outside voluntary help from members of sister parishes. The chapel was occupied for the first time on Christmas Eve in 1952.

Just one year and one month after groundbreaking, St. Paul's dedicated its chapel and educational unit on Sunday, March 22, 1953. Participating in the preliminary ceremony were Mr. Clayton Meglemre, construction superintendent, Mr. Robert Soule, president of the congregation, and Pastor Gunther. Mr. Paul Schreiber, organist, played the introductory strains of the processional hymn on the new Hammond organ, a gift to the congregation from Mrs. Schreiber's employer. Whereupon the pastor, the elders, who carried the Bible and Communion ware, the Building Committee, and the Finance Committee led the procession into the chapel singing "Open Now Thy Gates of Beauty." Immediately following them were the Chancel Choir, all other church officers, and the entire congregation. Arriving in the chancel, the pastor placed the Bible on the lectern and the Communion vessels on the altar, after which the pastor and congregation spoke the dedication responses, followed by the dedication of the chancel furniture and the organ. Pastor Gunther

delivered the sermon on the topic "Our Joy in the House of the Lord."

At 4:00 p.m., another dedicatory worship service was held with the local pastor as liturgist and Rev. Armand E. Mueller of Van Nuys, president of the Southern California District, as the guest speaker. Special organ selections by Mr. Paul Schreiber, organist, provided a festive and worshipful note for the occasion, while the Chancel Choir under the direction of Mr. L. Blank, with Mrs. R. Hoover as accompanist, rendered "We Gather Together," arranged by Davis, and then "The Lord Bless Thee and Keep Thee" by Lutkin. A baritone solo "How Lovely Are Thy Dwellings" by Little was sung by Rev. Gunther. Following the service, an open house was held with the ladies of the Priscilla Guild serving refreshments. Attendance in the morning was 240 and in the afternoon 375.

The new building was erected by volunteer labor at a cost of approximately $39,000. The nave of the chapel measured 59' × 32' and seated 260. The entire woodwork in the chapel was done in a walnut finish. There was a mothers' room and a spacious narthex, both of which housed Sunday school classes. The vestry and secretary's office also afforded room for Sunday school classes. The pastor's study was located directly behind the chancel, adjacent to the secretary's office. The choir loft was also utilized for a Sunday school class. In the educational unit, there were two sets of double rooms divided by folding doors, making space for four classes; a kitchen, which was also used as Sunday school space; a large meeting room 23' × 35', which housed four classes and provided a fine place for the various meetings of the Priscilla Guild, Walther League, and men's group;

St. Paul's builds a chapel for $39,000 with volunteer help.

St. Paul's chapel and educational unit at the time of dedication on Sunday, March 22, 1953. (Pacific Southwest District Archives)

The beautiful chancel with all the woodwork done in a rich walnut finish. (Pacific Southwest District Archives)

and well-equipped restrooms. St. Paul's could now proudly say that it had one of the most practical church plants in the Norwalk area.

Since church and Sunday school attendance continued to increase, an 8:00 a.m. service was inaugurated on May 23, 1953, and on June 13, 1953, a second session of the Sunday school for three-years-old to five-years-old, was begun during the main service. As the lot north of the church property with a small house was needed for future expansion, it was purchased in the fall of 1953 for $4,500 with special contributions and personal loans from individual members. On Sunday, January 23, 1955, an important milestone in the history of St. Paul's was marked by the fifth anniversary celebration of the congregation's existence. The occasion was observed with a special service in the morning with Pastor Gunther delivering the sermon. That evening the members of the congregation had a social with a potluck supper where Mr. L. Blank, newly elected chairman of the congregation, served as the master of ceremonies. The celebration closed with candlelight Vespers consisting of a litany of commemoration, the hymn "Blest Be the Tie That Binds," and the Benediction. The congregation had grown to 475 souls, 253 communicant members, and 44 voting members with a Sunday school enrollment of 361.

On Wednesday evening, September 18, 1957, Pastor Gunther walked to the front entrance of the church for what he thought was an ushers' meeting and choir rehearsal, to hear soft organ music coming from the chapel with the head usher greeting him at the door. As he entered the chapel, approximately 175 members and friends in this surprise gathering greeted him with the words "Happy Anniversary." Mr. Roy Phares, president of the congregation, extended congratulations to Pastor Gunther and expressed gratitude to God for the blessings during his 30 years of service. An address was given by Rev. Herbert Maas of San Pedro, pastor's long-time friend, who had left Orange with Pastor to attend Concordia, Oakland, and spent three years at the seminary with him. Rev. Alvin Wagner of North Hollywood, another close friend, was on hand to express his congratulations. In appreciation for Pastor Gunther's faithfulness, the congregation presented him a gift and plaque and his lovely wife thirty red roses, representing thirty beautiful years of faith, and cooperation, which she had so graciously given during his ministry. Rev. Karl Rudolph of Downey offered the invocation; anniversary cake and coffee were served.

On May 17, 1959, the two-classroom school was dedicated. In 1957, Rev. Gunther became ill with multiple Myeloma cancer, but served the congregation until July 1962, after tendering his resignation in January of 1962. Since his doctor had wanted him to retire two years before and since he was turning 60, he relented to his family's wishes that he retire from the active ministry effective as soon as another pastor could be installed. While he was ill, Pastor Luther Steiner had helped along with the assistant pastor, Rev. T. G. Gohike, who had celebrated his 50th anniversary of ordination that year. The Gunthers had purchased a home in Anaheim, where they retired and moved into it on May 17, 1962, along with him being commissioned as chaplain of the Walnut Manor in Anaheim. In the fall, approximately 400 members and friends of

Rev. and Mrs. R. Elmer Gunther in 1957 at the 30th anniversary celebration of his ordination in the ministry. (Pacific Southwest District Archives)

St. Paul's attended a farewell potluck supper program in honor of their Pastor and Mrs. Gunther with the highlight of the program being an interesting portrayal of "This Is Your Life, Pastor Gunther." Wallace Bean, president of the congregation, presented to Pastor and Mrs. Gunther gifts from the congregation: a mobile Zenith remote-control television and a check. Mrs. Julia Langevin, vice president of the Priscilla Guild, presented Mrs. Gunther a gift from the guild, a lovely and unique charm bracelet. When Pastor Gunther retired, the congregation numbered over 500 communicant members and had 850 baptized members with more than 300 children in the Sunday school.

A few months later on November 18, Pastor Gunther passed away after a lengthy illness at his home in Anaheim. Funeral services were conducted on November 21 at St. Paul's with the newly installed pastor of St. Paul's, Rev. Armand E. Mueller, officiating, and Rev. Tobias Joeckel, pastor of Redeemer Church, South Gate, delivering the funeral message. Pastors of the area sang the hymn, "Jerusalem the Golden," and Mrs. Dorothy Hafliger served as soloist, singing "I'm But a Stranger Here." Mr. Paul Schreiber served as organist. Members of the congregation acted as pallbearers and honorary pallbearers with those chosen having worked very closely with Pastor Gunther during his 12 years of pastorate in Norwalk. Rev. Victor Behnken, District president, delivered a message of consolation on behalf of the pastors and congregations of the District. Following the service at the church, the committal service was conducted at St. John's Cemetery in Orange.

The new pastor who replaced Pastor Gunther was Rev. Armand E. Mueller, who was installed in the 4:00 p.m. service on November 11, 1962. His brother, the Rev. Norbert C. Mueller of San Pedro, California, preached the sermon on "A Pastor's Pastor" (Ephesians 4: 11–13) with the Rev. Paul F. Lemke of Pico Rivera, counselor of Circuit 8, conducting the Rite of Installation. The church choir under the direction of Mr. Edward Lieb, sang "Praise to the Lord, the Almighty" by Neander. A reception followed the service for Pastor Mueller and his family.

Rev. Mueller was born November 30, 1908, the son of Professor and Mrs. John Theodore Mueller. (Armand's father was a noted professor at Concordia Seminary, St. Louis.) Pastor Armand Mueller graduated from the St. Louis Seminary and was ordained in 1931. His first assignment was that of an assistant pastor at St. John's Lutheran Church in Orange until 1932; from there he was called to First, Van Nuys. In 1933, he married Margaret, nee Miller, with their marriage blessed with four children: Thomas, Stephen, Marilyn, and Edwin. Edwin died at the age of 18. While serving as pastor of First, Van Nuys, for 23 years, he also served from 1948 until 1955 as the president of the Southern California District of The Lutheran Church — Missouri Synod, when he resigned due to ill health. In 1955, he accepted a call to Immanuel, Twin Falls, Idaho, and served two years. From 1957–1962, he served St. Luke's, Reno, Nevada, and in 1962 he began his ministry at St. Paul's, Norwalk. He was one of the founding speakers of the "Southern California Lutheran Program" serving as the Thursday morning radio speaker. He also served as a counselor to Lutheran Braille Workers, Inc.

Pastor Mueller's ministry at St. Paul's ended after a short illness, and he entered his eternal rest on September 29, 1968. He was greatly loved by people and they responded to him. This response was also evidenced at the funeral services conducted at the church in Van Nuys where he had served as pastor. He had worked well with his fellow pastors during his long ministry and during his years as District president. They too responded; more than 70 pastors attending the final rites

Pastor Mueller is president of the Southern California District from 1958 to 1955.

Rev. Armand E. Mueller, who served St. Paul's from November of 1962 until his death in 1968. (Pacific Southwest District Archives)

for "Tom," as he was affectionately known. His long-time friend and classmate, Rev. Elmer Ude, delivered the funeral sermon. The liturgists were Rev. Graeme Rosenau and Rev. Roy Gesch with Rev. Arnold Kuntz, first vice president, representing the District, and Pastor Elmer Klenk was in charge of the committal.

Following the untimely death of Pastor Mueller, Reverend Lambert E. Loock was called and installed as the third pastor of St. Paul's on September 29, 1965, with Rev. Graeme Rosenau, pastor of Mt. Olive, La Mirada, delivering the sermon based on Ephesians 4:11–12, "That Crippling Comma"; Rev. John Schumacher, vacancy pastor, serving as liturgist; and Rev. Robert Wolter, pastor of Trinity, Whittier, serving as installer. Pastor Loock, born July 31, 1934, in Rockford, Illinois, completed his elementary schooling at Trinity Lutheran Church, Peoria, Illinois, and entered Concordia College, Milwaukee, Wisconsin, to begin his studies for the holy ministry, graduating in 1954, completing his studies at Concordia Seminary, St. Louis, Missouri in 1959. From 1957 through 1958, Pastor Loock was vicar at Good Shepherd Lutheran Church in Inglewood, California. After graduating from the seminary, he accepted a call as missionary to Nigeria, West Africa, beginning his foreign missionary service in August of 1959. While in Nigeria, he taught for one year in the Lutheran High School at Obot Idim, and carried on evangelism work in Ogoja Province for two years. He returned to the United States in July of 1962, serving Grace Lutheran Church, Versailles, Missouri, and Hope Lutheran Church, Fort Worth, Texas, before accepting the call to St. Paul's. Pastor Loock married the former Marilyn Voigt of Peoria, Illinois, on June 9, 1957. Their marriage was blessed with four children, Kathryn, Timothy, Joel, and Paul at the time of his installation.

After Pastor Loock left St. Paul's in 1974 to accept the call of First Lutheran in Burbank, Rev. Paul N. Guebert was installed as pastor of St. Paul's in

In June of 1975, St. Paul's celebrates its 25th anniversary with day-long festivities.

Rev. Lambert E. Loock was installed as the third pastor of St. Paul's on September 29, 1965, and remained until 1974. (Pacific Southwest District Archives)

Rev. Paul N. Guebert served St. Paul's from 1975 until his retirement. (Pacific Southwest District Archives)

1975. He was born to a pastor in 1923, and moved to Canada when he was three years old. He and his wife, Marie, were blessed with four children, Linda, Julie, Elaine, and Timothy. After serving parishes in Canada, Nebraska, and Kansas, the Gueberts moved to California to serve St. Paul's where he retired from the ministry on April 24, 1988, having served St. Paul's for 13 years. More than 200 persons attended a dinner program on April 24, marking his retirement from the full-time pastoral ministry.

In June of 1975, St. Paul's celebrated its 25th anniversary with day-long festivities including the regular worship service, Sunday school, and a dinner served by the Lutheran Women's Missionary League Priscilla Guild, followed by a special anniversary service. Guest speakers for the afternoon service were Rev. James Poerschke of Hope Church, Whittier; Rev. Daniel Wooten, Our Savior Church, Bellflower; and Rev. Charles Birner of Peace Church, Pico Rivera. Movies along with narration were shown describing the church's history. Iola Turner led the Sunday school children, youth group, and senior choir in special music with Robert Petty serving as master of ceremonies. Also attending the celebration were Peter Fogarty, mayor of Norwalk and Mrs. Elmer Gunther, widow of the congregation's first pastor. In early 1977, members of the Gunther family, in memory of Rev. R. Elmer Gunther, gave beautiful new doors for the front entrance of the sanctuary. In dedicating the doors, Pastor Guebert stated: "The doors are to serve as a lasting tribute to the memory of Rev. Gunther, who served so well and with such dedication during the 12 years St. Paul's was privileged to have him."

In 1984, St. Paul's had a clown ministry called "Clowns for Christ," which led the Tenebrae Services on Good Friday, April 20. The liturgical clown troupe was composed of youth and adults who had been active in the area for a year, leading worship services and taking the Word of God to picnics, parades, hospitals, and convalescent homes. "Just being a member of such a group has opened many doors for sharing our faith, which we couldn't do before," the clowns said. "We look forward to more opportunities in 1984 for bringing smiles to people's faces as they see and hear about Jesus."

Following Pastor Guebert's retirement, Rev. Carl E. Nelson was called as pastor of St. Paul's and was installed on May 28, 1989. Participating in the service were the Rev. John Freitag; Dr. Eldred Dierker, who preached the sermon at the installation of his former member at Good Shepherd, Inglewood; Rev. Gulfrey Laurent; Rev. Norman Stoppenhagen; Rev. Paulus Voelzke; and Dr. Loren Kramer, District president; Rev. Daniel Parsons; Rev. Ethan Gebauer; and Rev. Charles Brady. Pastor Nelson had previously served a parish in Painesville, Ohio. During his ministry at St. Paul's, videos of the services were made in 1990 and circulated to those members who were unable to attend church. In 1997, St. Paul's with a communicant membership of 138 was among the top 10 percent in per capita giving in the entire Pacific Southwest District.

Rev. Carl E. Nelson on the day of his installation, May 28, 1989. (Pacific Southwest District Archives)

As the community surrounding St. Paul's continued to change, in 1996 Hispanic work was begun using a lay leader out of the TEE program.

In 2001 during a pastoral vacancy served by Rev. Edward Enu, St. Paul's moved forward to expand its mission outreach into the neighborhood by sponsoring a new Hispanic ministry with Vicar Abel Neyra, who worked full-time at another job. He served a two-year vicarage, ending on September 1, 2002, under the supervision of Pastor Frank Brundige. The Hispanic Mission Society assisted the congregation with initial funding. The congregation considered the Hispanic ministry to form an important part of their call for a new pastor. In February of 2001, the first Spanish service was conducted. The congregation had declined to 137 baptized members and 118 confirmed members. Sunday school enrollment of 21 averaged an attendance of 15. The membership was composed of laborers with a racial/ethnic composition of 66 percent Anglo; 19 percent Hispanic; 9 percent Asian Pacific; 1 percent black. Age profile by percentage: 8% 0–13; 7% 14–18; 6% 19–25; 10% 26–45; 23% 46–65; 46% 66 +.

During the year 2002, Spanish worship services averaged 20 people. At a baptismal service on February 17, 50 people attended with publicity handed to guests and letters mailed to all who signed the guest book. In March, Vicar Neyra conducted the first Spanish Good Friday ser-

During Pastor Nelson's ministry at St. Paul's, videos of the services are made in 1990 and circulated to those members who are unable to attend.

Vicar Abel Neyra, pictured with his wife Irma, began the Hispanic ministry at St. Paul's in 2001.

Rev. Carlos Hernandez, pastor of St. Paul's who took over the Hispanic ministry in January of 2003.

vice which had good attendance, and he held a children's Easter outreach showing the Lutheran Hour video, "The Puzzle Club's Easter Adventure," sang songs, made crafts, and later visited homes giving the children the book which accompanied the video. Through distribution of fliers at area elementary schools and personal contacts, 20 children attended the event. Using the Lutheran hymnal, *Cantad al Senor*, and the music CD helped to enhance and enrich the worship experience of parishioners. Bible classes were held at the church on Saturdays, at a home on Wednesdays, and Saturday Catechism instruction classes were given to two children with Bibles and catechisms offered at a reasonable price so that all could have their own copy.

The Lutheran Hour Ministries (LHM) Spanish booklets, "Project Connect," were purchased, and labels were pasted in them giving information about the Spanish service. They were distributed in various ways, at various times, and were also available in the church narthex. Business cards with information about the mission were printed and distributed. Tract size copies of *Luther's Small Catechism* in Spanish were purchased. A yard sale was held in May where English/Spanish brochures about the church and preschool were disseminated along with the Spanish copies of Lutheran Hour Ministry booklets. The Kids' Play Day Program held every Friday on the church grounds was launched in June in hopes of reaching area children, giving the opportunity to share Bible stories, using "The Invisible Sunday school" materials, which had 52 reproducible lessons in both English and Spanish. At that time, most of the children were being transported to church with the hope it would encourage neighborhood children to join in the activities.

The Lord blessed the Friday Kids' Play Day Program from two children that attended the Spanish service, branching out as the children invited neighborhood children with these children inviting others, averaging 18 children each week, but not always the same children. The ethnic background of most of the children was Hispanic and English speaking. In August, the second Vacation Bible School was held with many fliers distributed in the neighborhood. During VBS, a "Kid's Print" program was conducted where parents were invited to bring their children to have their fingerprints taken for their parents' records, providing a great opportunity to let them know St. Paul's was there.

In September of 2002, the prayers of St. Paul's were answered for a pastor who could serve both the English and Spanish congregations with Rev. Carlos Hernandez accepting the call and being installed on Sunday, September 8. Rev. Dr. Larry Stoterau, president, Pacific Southwest District, was the preacher and installer with Rev. Frank Brundige, Iglesia Luterana San Pedro y San Pablo, Bell Gardens, serving as the liturgist, and the lectors were Rev. Carl Nelson, emeritus; Dr. Abel Neyra, Hispanic ministry vicar, Iglesia Luterana San Pablo; Rev. Douglas Johnstone, mission and ministry facilitator Region Two; Rev. Robert Schroeder, Circuit Eight counselor, Trinity Lutheran Church, Whittier.

Pastor Carlos Hernandez was born on September 26, 1941, in Brownsville, Texas, the oldest son of 13 children of Charles and Juanita Hernandez. He was baptized and confirmed at San Pedro Lutheran Church in Houston, Texas, where he attended the day school from the first through the sixth grades and attended Immanuel Lutheran School in Houston for seventh grade. When the family relocated to Los Angeles, he continued his Lutheran education at St. John's in Montebello. Following his graduation in 1961 from Los Angeles Lutheran High School, he attended Concordia, Portland, Oregon; Concordia Senior College, Fort Wayne, Indiana; and Concordia Seminary, St. Louis, Missouri, graduating in 1969. In order to pay his tuition, his uncle, a baker, was able to obtain a baker's union card for him, enabling him to work in bakeries. He earned a Master of Sacred Theology from New York Theological Seminary in New York City and did four quarters of certified clinical pastoral education from Lutheran Medical Center in Brooklyn, New York. He also was granted an ecclesiastical endorsement from the LCMS Specialized Pastoral Care Ministries.

During his vicarage year at St. Paul Evangelical Lutheran Church of Tremont in the Bronx, New York, he met Maureen Remien and married her on December 21, 1968, at St. Paul, her home church. They were blessed with four sons, Matthew, Thomas, Andrew, and Michael, and one daughter, Jennifer. His first assignment after graduating from the seminary was Trinity and Zion, Wheatland and Douglas, Wyoming, where he served until 1973, establishing a Hispanic ministry at Wheatland. After a year of graduate school and service as interim pastor at St. Peter in Brooklyn, he accepted a call to Trinity, Watsonville, serving from 1974–1995 and also serving the California

Nevada Hawaii District as circuit counselor and second vice president. He and his wife started preschools in both Watsonville and Glen Cove and an elementary school in Watsonville. Maureen held a California State License as a children's center director and consults with centers on state regulations compliance. Pastor Hernandez accepted the call to Trinity, Glen Cove (Long Island), and Emanuel, Corona (Queens), where he also served as a part-time assistant to the District president, David Benke, in areas of strategic planning and conflict resolution. In 1998, he accepted a position as director of districts and congregations with LCMS World Relief and Human Care Ministries. In August of 2002, he completed his responsibilities at Bethlehem in Monterey as interim pastor before going to St. Paul's.

Pastor Hernandez took over the Hispanic ministry in January of 2003, with the group growing from 30 to 40 people on Sunday, celebrating Communion each Sunday, with the Anglo church having an attendance of 50 to 65. There are ESL classes conducted with Lutheran Social Services also conducting classes, Confirmation class on Saturdays, and a day-care center where religion is taught. An older lady goes on calls with pastor and a parish worker also makes calls on people in the area to help add members to the growing congregation. In August, a daily Vacation Bible School was conducted with many neighborhood children attending.

Southeast Lutheran High School
South Gate, California

The concept of Southeast Lutheran High School was conceived in 1982 both as an outreach to the communities surrounding Redeemer Lutheran School, South Gate, where a ninth grade had been established previously, and also as a response to the need of families living in municipalities that had such overcrowding in the public schools that pupils had to be on year-round session in buildings that were planned to accommodate less than half their student population. Since Huntington Park was over 90 percent Hispanic and South Gate over 60 percent, the Lutheran Church had a unique opportunity to reach out with its understanding and experience of Christian education on a secondary level. At Redeemer, there was a full-time pastor and a part-time lay assistant, Pastor Ricardo Sarria, who were directing their ministries to the Hispanic community. Because the surrounding Lutheran churches were not financially strong, the finances of the new school were based almost entirely on projected student tuition, $160 per month, which would meet the operating costs. Yet, start-up costs and renovation of the proposed building raised additional financial burdens to Redeemer and its partner churches.

At a Hispanic Task Force meeting in 1982, it was decided that the new, proposed Southeast Lutheran High School was to be located at the Huntington Park Methodist Church. Since the cost of renovating the old buildings at the Methodist Church were extremely high, buildings were rented at South Gate Baptist Church located at 8691 California Avenue which included a large number of classrooms, a nice-looking gymnasium, a chapel that would accommodate 150 people, and an attractive plant opposite South Gate Civic Center. A new constitution was adopted stating the purpose of SELHS as follows:

> SELHS shall be a means of outreach to the Southeast Los Angeles community, bringing the Gospel message to high school students and their families while providing them with a high quality, academically oriented secondary education.

The Planning Committee of the new Southeast Lutheran High School called Rev. Edward Rauff of New York in 1982 to be the founding principal with his installation held on Sunday, August 22, 1982, at 4 p.m. in Redeemer Lutheran Church, South Gate. He was born in New York City, graduating from Concordia College in Bronxville, New York. He later attended Concordia Seminary in St. Louis, graduating in 1956 with Bachelor of Arts and Bachelor of Divinity degrees. During an internship in New York, he taught science and religion at a Bronxville preparatory school. In 1958, he was awarded a master's degree in education from

In 1982, Southeast Lutheran High School is established on the campus of the South Gate Baptist Church.

Rev. Edward Rauff, the founding principal of Southeast Lutheran High School in 1982. (Pacific Southwest District Archives)

Columbia University. Following his ordination in 1956, he served congregations in Columbus, Ohio; Detroit, Michigan; and Patchogue, New York. In 1970, he joined the Lutheran Council in the USA, an agency that served the three major Lutheran church bodies where his duties included research and information gathering and was involved in national travel to help interpret census and religious statistics to church leaders. In 1980, Pilgrim Press published his book, *Why People Join the Church*. He and his wife, Naomi, who held graduate degrees in special education and was as an educational therapist in the education department of College Hospital in Cerritos, had six children.

Under Pastor Rauff's direction and guidance, Southeast Lutheran High School was opened on September 15, 1982, three months after his arrival, housed in the 12-room educational building of First Baptist Church of South Gate with 85 students in grades 7 through 10 and 5 full-time and 2 part-time teachers: Mr. Russell Belisle, Rev.

Jerry Lossner, Miss Tenlee Shortstall, Rev. Jack Risen, Mr. Larry Ayers, Mrs. Sherrie Artigas, and Rev. Cristiano Artigas, who was granted permission by the Mission Board to teach two courses at Lutheran High School that year. The school had a mainly Hispanic student body, which grew to 110 members within a year. In the fall of 1983, Southeast Lutheran High School opened its doors for a second academic year on September 14. As a token of regard by the trustees of First Baptist, the congregation used rental money from the high school to paint the exterior of its buildings and to change lighting to modern fluorescent fixtures. The educational building and gymnasium were built for a planned school for the Baptist church, which never materialized. Twenty years after the facility was built, the new Southeast Lutheran High School had made the site its home.

The high school had 6 full-time teachers; the administrator, Pastor Rauff; and a bilingual secretary who could relate to Hispanic parents who

The 12-room educational building at the First Baptist Church of South Gate was used for Southeast Lutheran High School. (Pacific Southwest District Archives)

were not comfortable speaking English, serving a student body of 100 students in grades 7 to 11, of which 60 percent were of Hispanic background. The newest member of the faculty was Tim McNiel, a graduate of Christ College, Irvine, who had done his student teaching at Los Angeles Lutheran High in Burbank and was the seventh-grade English and eighth-grade science teacher at SELHS.

Pastor Rauff served the high school for two years. By the third year, the high school had grown to a student body of 135. Rev. Rauff left SLHS to become the pastor of Mt. Olive in Pasadena, and the high school hired Mr. Michael Fischer as the executive director. Many of the policies and programs that were developed by him and the twelve teachers that year continued to be in force until the closing of the school. That year the school completed its constitution and was incorporated as a non-profit association of churches. At the end of that year, Mr. Fischer and five teachers left the high school. At the beginning of the 1985–1986 school year, enough teachers had been hired to serve the student body of 89 students in grades 7 through 12. Since a principal couldn't be secured, Sherrie Artigas, one of the original teachers who had served as dean of students the previous year, and Dr. Robert Meyer, chairman of the Board of Directors, served as administrators of the school.

Southeast Lutheran High School always had a very diverse student body, which fluctuated between 60 to 80 percent Hispanic over the years. It had less than 20 percent Lutherans with the majority being Catholics. By 1986, Peace, Pico Rivera; Messiah, Downey; Our Savior, Bellflower; Redeemer, South Gate; and La Santa Cruz, Los Angeles had ratified the constitution and bylaws allowing them to send delegates to the meeting of the SELHS Association of Los Angeles Incorporated.

Mr. Terry Carter, a 1968 graduate of the University of Oregon where he also obtained an M. A. degree, became director of the school. He had helped open Christ College, Irvine, in 1975, serving as head of the History Department and the only history teacher. In 1984, he left Christ College to work in the Newport Beach Library. When interviewed, Mr. Carter recalled that the school at that time had two types of students, above average and below average, with Dr. Robert Myers, the math teacher, creating tutorials for higher academic students. Dr. Myers favored having small ethnic Lutheran high schools across the Los Angeles area rather than a large one. There were two 7th-grade classes, two 8th-grade classes, one 9th-grade class, one

10th-grade class, one 11th-grade class, and one 12th-grade class with all the students required to wear uniforms.

In 1987, Jean Pierre Dumas, Ana Reyes, and Ana Espienera, all 11th graders at Southeast Lutheran High School, and Bobbi Lynn Anderson, a 12th grader were listed in *Who's Who Among American High School Students*. The high school enrollment had grown to 125 in grades 7–12. In the spring, 60 volunteers from the SELHS Thrift Shop were honored at a recognition dinner with Board Chairman Don Buccowich and Director Terry J. Carter thanking these dedicated Christians from area congregations for their many hours of service that benefited the school. During the early years of the high school's existence, the District also supported the institution financially.

Under Mr. Carter's leadership, the school added computers as a major part of the curriculum and administration; football and boy's volleyball were added to the already strong sports program; and the school applied for accreditation with the Western Association of Schools and Colleges. The high school offered 43 courses, fielded teams in football, basketball, baseball, softball, and volleyball with extra-curricular activities including chapel, counseling, student government, prom, weight training, and a functioning library. In addition to the usual sequence of courses that were offered by the average college-prep schools, Southeast offered several classes that were unusual for a small Lutheran high school: Marine Science, Film Appreciation, Spanish I, II, and III, Advanced Biology, Astronomy, and Western Civilization. When Mr. Carter left at the end of the 1988–1989 school year to continue to work in libraries as a librarian, Mr. Brent Baden, a teacher at the school since 1984 and guidance counselor, who became principal in 1989, followed him as principal.

By 1990, the school ranked second highest — 78 percent of the 160 student body — in the District in the number of Hispanic students attending a Lutheran school. That year the school was awarded full accreditation by the Western Association of Schools and Colleges and had its first balanced budget allowing a $20,000 surplus. Eight association congregations supported the school and the Thrift Shop netted $60,000 for the year. Southeast had the lowest tuition of any Lutheran high school in the United States, a maximum of $2,000. The lease was renewed with the Baptist church for an additional 10 months at $2,600 each month, with mobile classrooms being considered. Plans for re-

During the 1985–1986 school year, Mrs. Sherrie Artigas served as one of the school administrators. (Pacific Southwest District Archives)

Mr. Terry J. Carter served as director of Southeast Lutheran High School from 1987 to 1989. (Pacific Southwest District Archives)

Mr. Brent Baden, a teacher at the school since 1984 and guidance counselor, became principal in 1989. (Pacific Southwest District Archives)

Rev. Jerry Lossner conducting a weekly Wednesday chapel service. (Pacific Southwest District Archives)

Mr. Michael Grasz became principal in 1996. (Pacific Southwest District Archives)

modeling the building and for removal of asbestos were being discussed.

On May 16, 1992, at 3:00 p.m., Southeast Lutheran High School celebrated 10 years of educational ministry on the school campus. Among the events planned for the occasion were an art and science show, an open house, and messages by past and present administrators of the school. Light refreshments were served at 4:30 p.m. with the Rev. Charles Brady, one of the founders of the high school and pastor at Redeemer Lutheran Church in South Gate, officiating at the service. Principal Brent Baden stated, "With the nation's highest percentage of Hispanic students among LCMS high schools, we are in a unique position to serve a growing population in Southern California and the nation. We thank and praise God, not only for the opportunity to minister in a unique setting, but also for enabling us to persevere through the unexpected problems that accompany the starting of such a mission."

Southeast Lutheran was one of 9 schools selected to receive an AAL grant of $15,000 out of 69 schools that submitted applications. The grant was to develop a Hispanic Lutheran Schools Alliance of area Lutheran schools that served predominantly Hispanic communities. At that time there existed no formal network for predominantly Hispanic Lutheran schools to communicate, share resources, or foster a greater understanding of Hispanic culture within the parameters of the Lutheran educational system. The alliance would seek to increase awareness of Hispanic culture within area Lutheran educational institutions, provide training and skills relevant to Hispanic culture to educators, enhance chances for recruiting Hispanic youth to enter full-time church work, and create an organized unity for Hispanic ministry within the Lutheran educational system. Barb Kuxhaus, AAL grant program manager, stated, "We were very impressed by the quality and number of proposals submitted. Lutheran high schools provide an excellent education for their students. This grant program was an opportunity to take it a step further — to examine entire educational approaches to provide the best possible education for students." In 1996, SELHS received another AAL grant of $1,000, which was used to enhance the spring semester instruction through a special computer technology program created to help Lutheran high schools enhance their quality of education by obtaining additional computer hardware or software for administrative purposes. San Pedro y San Paulo in Bell Gardens also gave the high school $3,000 that year in order to help keep it operating.

By 1996, the high school had six teachers: Mr. Michael Grasz, principal, Mathematics Department and athletic director; Mrs. Tanya Grasz, guidance counselor, Foreign Language and Science departments; Mr. Joel Rahn, guidance counselor, Mathematics, Physical Education, and Computer departments; Mr. David Elliott, English, Art/Film, and Journalism departments; Dr. Robert Meyers, Mathematics Department; and Ms. Dian Flinn, History, Humanities and Science departments, Mrs. Lydia Lamarche served as school secretary. Even with all the grants and special money received, Southeast Lutheran High School couldn't survive. It had a $40,000 deficit, and the Baptist facilities that were built many years ago, were filled with asbestos, which would be very costly to remove. At the end of the 1996 school year, the high school, which had served the large Hispanic population of southeast Los Angeles, closed its doors after 14 years of proclaiming Christ to the teenage students of the area.

I love Thy kingdom Lord,
The house of Thine abode,
The Church our blest Redeemer saved
With His own precious blood.

New Challenges

Trinity Lutheran Church
Iglesia Luterana La Santisima Trinidad
San Bernardino, California

"*Lord, Thou hast been our dwelling place in all generations.*"

— PSALM 90:1

The city of San Bernardino, the only community to have an unlimited supply of sweet water thanks to a massive 1,000 foot deep underground lake fed by the San Bernardino Mountains, is located at the foot of the majestic San Bernardino Mountains near the Cajón Pass, having a population of 185,401 with 48 percent Hispanic according to the 2000 census. The city is noted for several things: First, it is the county seat of the largest county in the contiguous 48 states, having 20,000 square miles in area; second, The Arrowhead, one of the most famous attractions in the Inland Valley, a natural landmark easily seen near the base of the San Bernardino Mountains, is 1,115 feet in length and 396 feet in width, an outline so perfect it may appear to be man-made or artificial, the phenomenon is, in fact, natural; third, Route 66, a major highway completed in 1926 connecting Chicago and Santa Monica covering 2,448 miles passing through 8 states

and through San Bernardino on its way to Santa Monica where it ends, was THE major route for vehicle travel from the populated areas of the Midwest to Southern California making San Bernardino or "Gate City" the gateway for all of Southern California; and, fourth, the home of the world's first McDonald's restaurant was established by the McDonald brothers in 1940 on Fourteenth and E streets. The San Bernardino Valley has been a destination for pioneer families for over 150 years.

San Bernardino's colorful history began with the Serranos and the Cahuillas Indian tribes who lived in houses made of thatch and were the original occupants of the San Bernardino Valley. In the early years of the nineteenth century, Spanish missionaries were the first settlers to come to the region, choosing the fertile valley at the foot of a stately mountain range as an outpost for other missionaries who traveled throughout the California territory preaching to various Indian tribes. The first Spanish mission in the valley was established by Father Dumetz, a semi-retired Franciscan missionary of 40 years, on May 20, 1810, the feast day of Saint Bernardino of Siena, an Italian priest who was born in 1444. Father Dumetz was sent from the San Gabriel Mission to locate a possible site for a new mission; when he arrived at an Indian village west of Redlands, looking toward the towering mountains and the beautiful valley, he named the place San Bernardino in honor of the saint, where he erected a *capilla*, a small chapel, and celebrated mass. In his diary, Padre Dumetz mentioned the arrowhead on the mountain, describing the San Bernardino Valley and the Arrowhead Landmark as follows:

The Arrowhead, a landmark seen near the base of the San Bernardino Mountains, is a natural phenomenon.

The valley seems fertile and there is an abundance of water, both from the springs in the lowlands and from streams flowing from the mountains to the north and east. The valley will be found a one-day march east of here and is easily located by a mark on the mountain forming the north rim of the valley. This mark is in the shape of a large arrow, after the fashion used by the Indians of the region. It appears to be of natural origin and at the base of the mark is found a hot spring and some mud sinks, the hottest water that I have ever seen issuing from the earth.

The main concern of missionaries was the spiritual welfare of Indians, but they also took a part in their material well being for as the mission flourished, so did the Indians. By 1819, a mission rancho, and later an Asistencia, sub-mission of San Gabriel, were located near the Indian village where Father Dumetz first stopped. A ditch, or *zan-ja*, was dug to bring water to the rancho from Mill Creek 10 miles to the east, where all the Indians of the valley were invited to come to learn how to plant and irrigate crops. Since the Franciscan fathers dedicated themselves to the material and spiritual welfare of the Indians, the Indians were happy, and the Asistencia prospered. In 1830, a new asistencia mission building was erected close to the old buildings and almost on the location of the present reconstructed Asistencia on Barton Road; however, in 1834, all missions in California were ordered closed by decree of Governor Figueroa, and the mission period ceased. In San Bernardino, as elsewhere, the Indians were left to their own way of life, becoming demoralized and lawless.

By 1819, a mission rancho, and later an Asistencia, sub-mission of San Gabriel, are located near the Indain village where Father Dumetz first stopped.

An 1853 sketch of San Bernardino drawn by the Pacific Railroad artist, H. Orr.

After the secularization of the missions came the period of the great Spanish ranchos, giving birth to the grand Spanish rancheros. In 1843, Rancho San Bernardino, encompassing most of the area in the center of the valley, was granted to Antonio Maria Lugo, a well-known landowner and raiser of stock, and his three sons. An adobe ranch house was built on the site of the present courthouse where one or another of the Lugos lived for a number of years. One of the brothers repaired the old Asistencia Mission using it as his home. Life on the rancheros revolved around raising cattle, but there seemed to be plenty of time for celebrations and amusement since Indians from the villages were available to do the work. Accounts of life on the Spanish ranches stress the hospitality of the people, fiestas, rodeos, celebrations of religious holidays, bull and bear fights, and horse races. The abandoned missions didn't stay vacant for long as they soon became important posts on the trading route known as the Spanish Trail. Pioneer trailblazers like Kit Carson and Jedediah Strong Smith, among others, spent a good deal of time in the valley during those early years.

Among the biggest threat to the happy life on the ranches were horse-stealing raids of the desert Indians who usually came at the full of the moon and made life hazardous for Rancho San Bernardino. On some nights, the rancho would lose whole herds of horses. In order to try to prevent these raids, the Muscupiabe Rancho, a name from a Serrano Indian village nearby, Amuscupiabit, meaning "place of little pines" in Serrano dialect, was granted in 1843 to Michael White with the understanding that he would build a fortress-like house in the mouth of Cajón Pass and head-off the Mohave Indian horse thieves. Michael White did build his house overlooking Cajon Pass and the Mojave Trail, but he was not successful in stopping the raiders. Before long, the Indians had stolen all his stock, and Michael White had to abandon Muscupiabe after a short nine months. A more successful attempt to thwart the desert raiders came when a group of New Mexican colonists was invited to settle in the valley with the provision that they would give protection against horse-stealing raiders. These colonists did help fight off the raiders, but desert Indians continued to be a problem until the time of the Mormons.

In 1851, a company of nearly 500 Mormons arrived in San Bernardino Valley under the command of Amasa Lyman and Charles C. Rich, who had come across the desert in covered wagons.

The beautiful San Bernardino Valley seemed a welcome blessing to them. The group of Mormons who made camp at the mouth of Lytle Creek Canyon was so overjoyed by the abundance of water and the beauty of the spot that they named the stream for their leader, Captain Andrew Lytle. At that time, Lytle Creek flowed briskly through the valley to the Santa Ana River with dense growths of willows, cottonwoods, and sycamores along its banks. The hills and the valley were covered with wild oats, mustard, and rich grass. No wonder the settlers were pleased when the Lugos consented to sell 40,000-acre Rancho San Bernardino to them in 1852 for $77,500, with a down payment of $7,000. They were dedicated to expanding Brigham Young's religious empire.

Having heard about Indian raids and attacks, the Mormons built a stockade to house 100 families, calling it Fort San Bernardino. Located on the ground that is now the site of the present courthouse, the stockade consisted of log houses and stout pickets surrounding an enclosure in which there were other houses. The families lived inside the stockade for the first few years, growing wheat and other crops outside and building a grain mill inside. Since the Mormons weren't raising cattle or horses, the desert Indians were no longer a threat and soon families were able to move out of the stockade to build their own homes. At that time, there were two imposing buildings in the town: one was the Mormon Council House and the other the Amasa Lyman home, the old Lugo adobe which had been enlarged to take care of the large Lyman family, as Amasa was a polygamist who had brought five of his wives and their children with him to California.

In the fall of 1852, Colonel Henry Washington, a United States deputy surveyor, erected a monument on top of Mount San Bernardino and through it ran the base line from which surveys in the southern part of the state were, and still are, made. At first, Base Line Street was just a dirt track along that line; it took many years for the town to grow north to it. In 1854, San Bernardino was first officially incorporated as a city with Mormons comprising 75 percent of San Bernardino's population, 900 of 1,200, who very definitely ran the town, causing some friction with those of other faiths. San Bernardino was strictly a temperance town, no drinking or gambling allowed. The first trial in the new city was for drunkenness costing the offender $50. In 1857, Brigham Young recalled approximately 60 percent of the Mormons

to Salt Lake City, leaving San Bernardino with a diminished population. Some went, taking great financial losses, while others opted to remain and struggled to continue on their own. In the six short years that the Mormons followed their mission at San Bernardino Rancho, they made numerous achievements, establishing schools, stores, a network of roads and a strong government.

Gold was discovered in Holcomb Valley in 1862 with men pouring into the mountains through San Bernardino trying their luck at panning for this precious metal. For a time Belleville, in Holcomb Valley, was the largest city in Southern California with 10,000 residents, and it almost became the county seat, losing to San Bernardino by only one vote. Times were rough and hard, just like the men who came in search of instant wealth with numerous internal problems plaguing the God-fearing settlers. The community did survive with both a library and temperance associations created at the time.

As the last years of the nineteenth century waned, the giant railway companies eventually found their way to San Bernardino, changing it from a sleepy little town into an enterprising city. The Santa Fe, the Union Pacific, and the Southern Pacific railroads all converged on the city, making it the hub of their Southern California operations. Competition between the railroads set off a rate war, which brought thousands of newcomers to California in the great land boom of the 1880s. When the Santa Fe Railway established a transcontinental link in 1886, the already prosperous valley exploded with even more settlers flocking from the East with population figures doubled, from 6,150 in 1900 to 12,779 in 1910. In this mass population explosion were many German Lutherans who were in need of spiritual nourishment.

Gold is discovered in Holcomb Valley in 1862 with men pouring into the mountains through San Bernardino

A wagon train in downtown San Bernardino, circa 1870.

In the summer of 1906, Mr. R. C. Fischer and wife both of Bay City, Michigan, settled in San Bernardino, and to their great disappointment, found no Lutheran Church--Missouri Synod. They immediately communicated with the Rev. August Hansen of Pasadena, the nearest Lutheran pastor, who, after canvassing the field, conducted the first Lutheran service in San Bernardino at the First Baptist Church at Fourth and G streets on November 18, 1906. Since the field was ripe for the harvest, the Los Angeles Pastoral Conference-- which included the following pastors: J. W. Theiss, Olaf Eger, August Hansen, Arthur E. Michel, W. H. Tietjen--wrote a letter to the Mission Board of the California and Nevada District in January of 1907 stating the following:

We were happy to hear that you realize the potential and importance of the mission field in San Bernardino and its surrounding areas. It is not only the city of San Bernardino that is important but also Upland and Pomona....

In services in San Bernardino, we have had 13, 26, 28, and 14 depending on the weather, which was recently terrible. The city has between 14 to 15,000 people of which there is a large group of Germans; we have found seven families from the Missouri Synod. Since the city is so spread out, it is not easily accessible by streetcar. The "Evangelicals," who have been working there for four years, must be considered as an opposition. By far, the city has not been canvassed; but as of now, we have 10 families. Neither in Upland nor Pomona has anything been done. In any case, there is a lot of mission work to be done in these areas. At this time, there is no mission in either of these places. We are only telling you about these three cities, but there are many other towns in the area.

...As far as the church is concerned, San Bernardino is in the south far from the sea and blessed with hot weather throughout the year. A few years ago in March, we had extremely hot weather there. One hears that at time it can be as hot as 115–118 as it is the hottest field in California.

Later in 1907, Theophil Ferdinand Haeuser, a 22-year-old St. Louis Seminary student, was sent to San Bernardino and Upland as a supply preacher to the mission field. He conducted services in German on alternating Sundays in San Bernardino at 2:00 p.m. in the Baptist Church for a rental fee of $1.50 per month and in Upland in the Commercial National Bank building at 10:30 a.m. During the last months of 1907, he made the following calls: 72 in San Bernardino, 38 in Upland, 2 in Redlands, 2 in Riverside, 3 in Colton, and one in Claremont. In order to make the calls, he either took the train or streetcar, walked, or rode a bicycle. Transportation by automobile was difficult, since there were only dirt roads built for horses and buggies. Besides that, only the rich could afford a car, as the big expensive cars ran $3,000 and cost another $3,000 a year to operate. A Model T Ford cost $850 in 1908 with a worker at the Ford Plant making about $2.50 a day. By 1916, a Model T Ford cost $360 due to Henry Ford's installation of an assembly line with the autoworkers being paid $5 a day.

In Vicar Haeuser's December 12, 1907, mission report to the Mission Board in San Francisco, he stated he hadn't received his full pay, a problem which would also plague his successors. Since he wanted to go back to the seminary to complete his studies, he requested that he be released from the Upland and San Bernardino missions. Apparently between April and June, Student Haeuser changed his mind about going back to school, as the Mission Board employed him as the first resident pastor in Whittier from June 28, 1908, until August 1910, when he would finally be able to return to the seminary to complete his studies. Following his graduation from the seminary in 1911, he was called to Trinity Lutheran Church in Whittier where he stayed until 1920. He then took a call to Bethlehem Church in the Creston area near Paso Robles. He moved to Trinity Church in Paso Robles as pastor, staying 30 years. He also served parishes in Hayward and Richmond in Northern California. He died in 1975 at the age of 90, having served the Lord in the ministry most of his life.

Trinity's first called pastor, Rev. Edward J. Rudnick, was installed on March 29, 1908, by Rev. Arthur Michel, Pastor of Trinity Lutheran Church, Los Angeles, in the Baptist church in San Bernardino. Pastor August Hansen of St. Paul's Lutheran Church in Pasadena, who had started both missions in San Bernardino and Upland, also participated in the service bringing the choir from his church. The congregation of 100 people was the largest group of Lutherans ever to be assembled in the San Bernardino mission at that time.

Pastor Rudnick's first congregation, after he gaduated from Concordia Seminary in St. Louis in 1906, was St. Marcus Lutheran Church in St. Louis. However, he contracted a disease that was later diagnosed as tuberculosis and was advised by his doctor to relocate to a milder, drier climate. He wrote to his childhood pastor, Rev. Arthur Michel, who at the time was pastor of Trinity Lutheran Church, Los Angeles, and head of the Mission Board; Pastor Michel arranged for him to be called as the missionary to the San Bernardino and Upland missions. His parents were from Danzig, West Prussia (Poland), which at that time was part of Germany. They came to America in 1880, one year before Pastor was born. His father, John, a day laborer, had no education or money, and Pastor Rudnick went only through third grade in school. At 16, while working in a shoe store in Lockport, New York, he was confirmed by Pastor Arthur Michel, who suggested that he became a minister, as the boy was quite brilliant. Edward asked his father for permission, giving his father the promise that if he could go to school he and his mother could come and live with him after he graduated from the seminary and had a parish.

Rev. Edward J. Rudnick, who came to San Bernardino for his health in 1908, is pictured at his graduation from the seminary in 1906. (Pacific Southwest District Archives)

He entered the prep school at Fort Wayne with only a third-grade education, where he spent many extra hours of study so that he could matriculate to Concordia Seminary in St. Louis. While at Concordia Seminary, he was called to St. Markus Lutheran Church in St. Louis. When he attended a pastors' conference in 1907 in Perryville, Missouri, he stayed in the home of his future wife's parents, Peter and Margareta Sandler. Peter was Perryville's blacksmith, located a few blocks from the church. After the stay, he wrote to the pastor in Perryville and asked if Mr. Sandler's daughter, Natalie, would make a good pastor's wife. The pastor wrote back and replied she would, but that she also had an older sister, Barbara, who would be better. After he corresponded with Natalie, she and her older sister came to St. Louis to work as domestic help for a short time, where he would get to see her. He and Natalie were engaged before he was afflicted with an illness that wasn't properly diagnosed at the time.

In Pastor Rudnick's quarterly report for April, May, and June of 1908, he gave the following description of life in the mission field:

San Bernardino

To this area also belong the little towns of Redlands, Riverside, Colton, and Rialto. In San Bernardino, services are held every two weeks. In the past three months, they were held seven times. Twenty families and a number of singles bring a total of 65 adults of which 40 people regularly attend services. The train connection to the other cities is very good.

In the previously mentioned families, there are about 26 children. Of these, about 12 more or less regularly attend the Sunday school, which is held every Sunday. A well-trained lady gives me exceptional help. When I'm not here, she, with the aid of a young girl, conducts Sunday school. The greatest difficulty in teaching the Sunday school lessons is the language. Most of the children understand some German, but only a very few can read it. I'm trying to remedy this situation by teaching German and English. Right now, I have started a Saturday morning school to give German lessons. Since we don't have our own building, I have to teach the children at my house, which, of course, is very uncomfortable as we have very little room. If we had a suitable building, I would like to hold school during the summer to teach the children the Catechism and the German language.

…It becomes more obvious that we will very soon need our own building in which

Pastor Rudnick's 1908 quarterly report describes his work and problems. "Most of the children understand German, but only a very few can read it."

to worship. A reason has already been mentioned: the teaching of the children. But there are even more important reasons for a building, because we still use the Baptist church for the small rent of $1.50 per month in the afternoon, which is at a very unpleasant time due to the summer heat. At times here, it is 110 to 115 in the shade. It is then almost unbearable in the church. This is the reason that keeps many from coming. They would probably come in the cool of the morning. And those that do come, don't get much out of the sermon, because they constantly fight sleep and the heat.

Another reason for poor attendance is that there are families here that understand little or no German. If we do not have English services, it's the rule that we not only lose the English but part of the Germans to other sects or to the English opposition congregation of the General Synod here in the city. For both of these reasons I mentioned, I could give many sad examples. But I believe we have a good opportunity, with the help of the other dear sister congregations of Southern California, to have a small chapel.

By early July of 1908, a small portable chapel was purchased at a cost of $1,025 through the offerings of mission festivals that were conducted by Los Angeles area congregations. Since Trinity was not incorporated, the lot for the chapel at Sixth and Catick streets (Catick was later renamed Crescent), was purchased by G. Bublitz and William Maas, who promised to sell it back to the congregation at the purchase price. This little chapel, also known as the collapsible one, measured 25' by 32' including the narthex and the back room, having a tower that was 50' high. It served the San Bernardino congregation until 1914 when they built their first building and was later moved to Bethany, Hollywood, where it served for many years. Its final des-

> By early July of 1908, a small portable chapel is purchased at a cost of $1,025 through offerings of mission festivals conducted by Los Angeles area congregations.

tination was First Lutheran in Van Nuys, serving many years until it was retired and sold for secular use. In order to furnish the chapel, Mr. Fischer and Mr. Leonhardt each advanced a loan of $50 and Mr. Bublitz loaned $40. With this money, chairs and an organ were purchased.

The chapel arrived in San Bernardino on Tuesday, the fourth of August, and by Saturday evening, was erected, painted, furnished, and was beautifully decorated for the dedication with the pulpit, altar, and baptismal font given by a member, Mr. Richart. The joy-filled dedication day was on Sunday, the ninth of August, where Pastor Rudnick preached in the morning service with 75 people present, and in the evening, Pastor Lussky from Zion in Anaheim preached in English to 40 to 50 people. Also present were Pastor Bachus of Banning and student Blankenbuehler of Portland. Pastor Rudnick reported, "We would have had a better attendance, if the weather hadn't been so humid and rainy." The offerings were over $25, which was used to pay for some of the expenses of the chapel furnishings.

Pastor Rudnick also reported that the people had given generously of all they had in order to take care of the needs of the small chapel, as the furnishing cost more than expected. It was not only the cost of the furnishings, the small addition behind the chancel and the restroom that in-

Trinity's small portable chapel purchased through the offerings of Los Angeles area congregations' mission festivals in 1908 and later used in Van Nuys and Hollywood. (Pacific Southwest District Archives)

flated the expense but also the electric line from the chapel to the street, the sidewalks, the colored paper for the windows, screens, etc., that cost $300, which was a lot for people in the parish who were laborers and had hardly worked half of the time during that summer. Through this chapel, the German Lutheran presence was now known in the community with the help of a sign installed on the church as well as on the main street. Pastor Rudnick was now preaching monthly services in San Bernardino with two evening services in English and two German services in the morning while also conducting services in Upland every other Sunday. The chapel also proved to be a blessing for the children, because during the summer, he had been instructing the children, in the mornings in religion, singing, and German. The Sunday school, which was attended by 10 to 15 children, was conducted every Sunday with Confirmation class conducted in the chapel, whereas before all Confirmation classes were conducted in his home around the dining room table.

In 1909, he had started a mission in Chino along with preaching in Upland and San Bernardino, covering the field by train travel, horse and buggy, and transportation by members as he didn't know how to drive a car. While in San Bernardino, he made calls on his bicycle or used the streetcar. By the end of 1909, he was relieved of the Upland mission so that he could concentrate on establishing a mission in Riverside where he rented an Adventist church to begin services, thus establishing Immanuel Lutheran Church in Riverside. In June 1910, Trinity was formally organized and in October 1910 was incorporated as the "Evangelical Lutheran Trinity Church of the Unaltered Augsburg Confession at San Bernardino, California."

In Pastor Rudnick's 1914 mission report, he gave this description of his family, "My family has expanded; on August 16, a little son was born to us. We are now, altogether, eight souls like Noah and his family in the ark." When he arrived in San Bernardino, he had only himself and his parents and when he left in the later part of 1914 to accept a call to Trinity Lutheran Church in Santa Ana, he had a wife and four children plus his parents. After the move, a fifth child was born and the sixth was born in 1916. In May of 1918, tragedy struck the Rudnick household with two of the youngest boys dying of dysentery. By 1919, his tuberculosis recurred with the doctors prescribing a drier climate for him.

The place chosen by the Rudnick family to live was Banning, a small isolated desert town east of San Bernardino. Pastor's health improved enough for him to start a small preaching station there. Since they were so poor, they were given a mule and an old surrey with a horse from the churches in Los Angeles. Their son Martin recalls the family receiving barrels of clothing from the churches in Los Angeles, which helped to support them. They also raised chickens and goats, selling eggs and goat milk. Martin remembers an Indian who lived down the street coming to the house, asking Pastor to come and help deliver a baby. He took scissors and clean towels and delivered that baby.

Pastors are called to do many things in their ministry, but few are called upon to help deliver babies, which tells something about this man.

In 1922 with his health restored, Pastor Rudnick took a call to Emmanuel Lutheran Church in Fresno where he would minister for 24 years, until his retirement in 1946, shepherding the flock and increasing its size. From *The Romance of Lutheranism in California*, Rev. Richard T. Du Brau gives a beautiful description of Pastor Rudnick:

…He was a man of culture and learning, and yet he was a humble friend to his people, any people, and to his brethren in the ministry, especially the young men who still had much to learn. He was a lifelong student of the biblical languages. His expositions, whether popularly given from the pulpit or dispensed in a scholarly fashion at conferences, were listened to with interest, respect, and unforced attention.

…With all his seriousness in the work of the Lord, he had been blessed with a fine sense of humor. Some time after his heart attack, he died suddenly on February 18, 1947. His last sermon was on the text, "Be still and know that I am God."

This great man of God, who had taken his limited childhood education and become a scholarly minister, had been a true servant of the Word. He never gave in to poverty, illness, or sorrow, but remained true to the faith he proclaimed throughout his ministry trusting in the Lord, Jesus Christ, to the end. What a great gift he was to the church not only in Southern California where he served the Upland and San Bernardino missions and established missions in Chino, Riverside, Redlands, and Banning but also to California and Nevada District where he served Emmanuel Lutheran Church in Fresno for 24 years.

During Rev. Rudnick's pastorate at Trinity in San Bernardino, a beautiful church edifice was erected, with the cornerstone laid in October of 1913, and the new building was dedicated on February 22, 1914. A farewell service was held in the old chapel, which had been moved north of the new building, where Pastor Rudnick delivered a short address. This was followed by an impressive service conducted in German in the new church with Rev. John William Theiss of Los Angeles as the principal speaker; Pastor Rudnick conducted the evening service in English. The new church

Trinity's beautiful church is dedicated on February 22, 1914.

had a beautiful altar with a statue of Christ in the center, which is now at La Santa Cruz in Los Angeles and a baptismal font made of metal that also served the Mexican mission in Santa Ana and the Maywood Hispanic Mission which worshiped in the VFW (Veterans of Foreign War) Hall. The baptismal font is now on display in the Pacific Southwest District Archives.

In September 1914, Pastor Rudnick left San Bernardino to accept a call to Trinity, Santa Ana. The local congregation then issued a call to the Rev. William Joachim Lankow, who had resigned his charge at Santa Ana, due to throat problems. After accepting the call, he was installed as pastor of Trinity on September 20, 1914, by the Rev. L. Achenbach of Riverside. He was born at Fond du Lac, Wisconsin, on March 8, 1874, graduating earlier than the rest of the class from Concordia Seminary in Springfield, Illinois, on December 27, 1898, and was installed a few days later as pastor of Zion Church in Tacoma, Washington. During his ministry there, a parsonage and Christian day school were erected, where he also served Snohomish and Seattle. In 1905, he was called to Salt Lake City, Utah, where in the midst of Mormonism, he dedicated the first Lutheran church, school, and parsonage of St. John's

Pastor Rudnick is succeeded by Pastor Lankow in 1914.

Rev. William J. Lankow was installed as the second pastor of Trinity on September 20, 1914, and remained until his retirement in January 1940. (Pacific Southwest District Archives)

Lutheran congregation. Pastor Lankow served the congregation in Salt Lake City until 1913, when, due to his wife's ill health, he accepted a call to Trinity Church in Santa Ana. During his ministry there, the first parsonage was built and dedicated. In September 1914, he was called to Trinity Church, San Bernardino, where he also dedicated a school and parsonage. For many years, he served the county and state institutions around San Bernardino and also served the Redlands and Fontana fields. He was a charter member of the Oregon and Washington, the California and Nevada, and the Southern California districts, serving as the Southern California District's vice president, chairman of the Board of Support, and visitor of the Foothill Circuit until his retirement on January 1, 1940.

Pastor Lankow was united in marriage with Martha Fritze of Strong City, Kansas, in 1898 with their union blessed with three children, Arnold, Ella (Mrs. A. E. Warner), and Martin. During his retirement, Pastor Lankow made his home with his younger son, Martin Lankow, pastor of Bethany Lutheran Church in San Diego. Here he had an opportunity to continue in the work he loved: "laboring in the Lord's Vineyard." He taught Bible class and preached when the occasion arose.

Trinity's new church dedicated on February 22, 1914, with farewell service held in the old chapel, as shown north of the new building. (Pacific Southwest District Archives)

The chancel with the statue of Christ above the altar that is now housed in La Santa Cruz Church in East Los Angeles. (Pacific Southwest District Archives)

In the spring of 1916, the Trinity congregation erected a five-room bungalow, as the parsonage for their pastor. Having doubled membership in 1920 through 1922, the congregation voted to become self-supporting, and requested the Mission Board to relieve their pastor from serving the Riverside church, which was granted. As the congregation continued to grow, it was necessary to build a Sunday school annex in 1925 that was dedicated on June 15 as part of the 15th anniversary celebration of the parish. It was the intention of the congregation to use this room also for a Christian day school for which many prayers had been said.

The Lord heard the prayers of His flock, as the school was opened on September 12, 1927. With the assistance of the mission treasury of Synod, it was made possible to call a regular teacher,

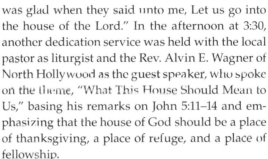

Rev. and Mrs. R. Elmer Gunther in 1943. (Pacific Southwest District Archives)

Mr. F. F. Herbst, who was installed on September 4, 1927. He was born on January 30, 1906, in Farmington, Missouri. After attending the Christian day school and the local high school in Farmington, he entered Concordia Teacher's College at River Forest, Illinois, where he graduated in June 1927. He served Trinity school as "the first teacher, with exceptional ability. His work was accompanied by a godly life, and is a fine example for young and old, worthy of imitation. He was a humble Christian of sterling character, always ready to serve His Lord." His service extended not only to the church, but also to the Synod, which he served as a member of the Board of Education. However, inscrutable are the ways of the Lord for on March 22, 1932, Mr. Herbst met with an accident on the highway near San Bernardino, and died two hours later. Funeral services were held for him on Good Friday, March 25, at 3:00 p.m., with the pastor addressing the sorrowing congregation on the basis of James 4:14, "What Is Your Life?" Ten colleagues sang three stanzas of the hymn, "Jesus Christ, My Sure Defense" and with the choir, which he had directed, sang "Jesus, Lover of My Soul," with a duet of two ladies rendering "Jerusalem, the Golden." His mortal remains were then shipped to Farmington, Missouri, his former home. After a call was sent to Concordia at River Forest for a teacher, Mr. H. E. Schock was assigned and installed on April 22, 1932. In 1935, the day school had 28 pupils, the Sunday school attendance had 68, and the congregation numbered 235 souls, with 163 communicants, and 40 voting members.

In January of 1940, following the retirement of Pastor Lankow, Rev. R. Elmer Gunther became the pastor. The church continued to grow and prosper during World War II from 1939 to 1945. As the city continued to expand northward and with the church outgrowing the Sixth Street facilities, the congregation voted to relocate to Twenty-ninth and Arrowhead Avenue. In less than four months after groundbreaking, a parish-hall chapel and educational unit was dedicated on June 5, 1949, at a cost of $52,000. In the morning service with 300 people in attendance, Pastor Gunther delivered his sermon on Psalm 26:8 and 122:1: "Lord, I have loved the habitation of Thy house, and the place where Thine honor dwelleth. I was glad when they said unto me, Let us go into the house of the Lord." In the afternoon at 3:30, another dedication service was held with the local pastor as liturgist and the Rev. Alvin E. Wagner of North Hollywood as the guest speaker, who spoke on the theme, "What This House Should Mean to Us," basing his remarks on John 5:11–14 and emphasizing that the house of God should be a place of thanksgiving, a place of refuge, and a place of fellowship.

The new building, designed by Architect O. J. Bruer, measured 70' × 31' and would seat 280. Mr. Alwardt, the contractor, donated the chancel furnishings, constructed of Philippine mahogany in a natural finish. Behind the altar was a beautiful crimson dossal curtain. In front of the altar rail hung a large draw curtain of the same material, which was closed to conceal the altar when the hall was not used for chapel purposes. A large meeting room measuring 32' × 23' in the front of the building had a fireplace and was furnished with draperies, comfortable chairs, and a spinet piano. A well-equipped kitchen was ready for any culinary needs of the parish. Off the hall were two rooms, one of which served as a classroom for the senior Sunday school class and Confirmation class, while the other, separated from the chapel by three arches, served as the choir loft and was used by one of the Bible classes. To the rear of the hall were the educational unit and well-furnished restrooms. There were nine Sunday school rooms,

Mr. F. F. Herbst is installed as Trinity's first teacher on September 4, 1927.

three of which could be opened into one unit, and four others could be used as two double units with appropriate religious pictures placed in each room.

In 1950, Pastor Gunther accepted the call to become the pastor of St. Paul's Lutheran Church in Norwalk. Following Pastor Gunther's departure, Rev. Luther Schwartzkopf of Oceanside was installed as Trinity's new pastor on September 10, 1950, with the Rev. Reno H. Jeske of Trinity Church in Whittier speaking for the occasion, basing his words of encouragement and inspiration on Malachi 2:7: "The priest's lips should keep knowledge." Pastor Schwartzkopf was born of missionary parents in Ichang, China, with most of his youth spent in the Chicago area. After graduating from Concordia College in Milwaukee, Wisconsin, he attended Concordia Seminary, St. Louis, Missouri. After graduating from the seminary, he took an assignment as missionary-at-large for the Southern California District, serving the Trona and Owens Valley areas in an experimental tent-trailer mission, leading to the establishment of congregations at Ridgecrest and Bishop. In 1948, he became pastor of Immanuel Church in Oceanside, with Fallbrook as a preaching station. Pastor and Mrs. Schwartzkopf were the parents of four children.

Rev. Luther Schwartzkopf was installed as Trinity's new pastor on September 10, 1950, and remained until 1972. (Pacific Southwest District Archives)

During his tenure, the congregation grew from 200 members to over 500 in 1959. Since no adjacent land could be purchased for a new sanctuary and room for the full development of the Christian education program at the Arrowhead property and for more parking, the congregation voted to acquire 12 individual parcels (all separately owned), a total of 3½ acres, at Twenty-ninth and E streets northwest of the Arrowhead property. Groundbreaking ceremonies for the magnificent sanctuary were conducted on Sunday, June 26, 1960, at 12:30 p.m.

Construction of the sanctuary and parish hall began on August 1, 1960, the first phase in a complete building and relocation program for Trinity with Culver Heaton of Pasadena serving as architect. The sanctuary, constructed of masonry with contemporary design, had a steep pitched roof rising to a peak at about 50-feet from the ground and topped by a delicate 50-foot fleche (spire) capped with a 12-foot gold cross. At the entrance was a large roof overhang providing shelter from the elements, particularly the hot sun in a semi-arid climate with a striking 10-foot mosaic sculpture of the victorious Christ greeting the worshiper, mounted against the large window area over the entrances. The interior of the sanctuary came into

The parish hall/chapel and educational unit at 29th and Arrowhead Avenue were dedicated on June 5, 1949, at a cost of $52,000. The expansive corner was reserved for a large sanctuary. (Pacific Southwest District Archives)

The interior of the new building with chancel furnishings, constructed of Philippine mahogany in a natural finish and folding chairs. (Pacific Southwest District Archives)

view as the worshiper approached the entrance where the cathedral glass wall became clear glass at eye level, permitting the eye to travel directly to the chancel. The architect had captured the eye of the worshiper by his use of receding planes and controlled light in the chancel, which drew the worshiper's gaze directly to the Cerrera marble altar from Italy and the large 14-foot freestanding cross, inlaid with gold glass tile, standing at the right of the marble altar. At the foot of the cross was the dedication stone of the church. A reredos was made of Dazz tile, 12 inch tiles whose surfaces were polished Italian stone, reaching 50 feet with its pointed top like a giant arrow pointing heavenward, providing a fitting backdrop for both the altar and the sculpture presenting symbolically the story of salvation in symbols of the Holy Trinity—the hand of the Father, upraised in blessing; the Holy Spirit as a descending dove; the Son as the Lamb of God, resting on the Book of the Seven Seals, all fabricated by the artist, Clifford Nelson of Pasadena. The altar candlesticks were three-sided with alternate faces of the candlesticks shown in white, green, or violet, according to the seasons of the church year. The baptismal font was connected by a copper pipe to a specially prepared area beneath the chancel to receive water after Baptism. The speakers for the public address system were incorporated into the graceful lighting fixtures. The building was designed to seat 342 on the ground floor with an additional 55 in the balcony.

A spacious chancel area provided for two dozen or more people to kneel at the Communion rail at one time for Communion. The entire north wall of the nave was of a special glare-proof glass, which opened the view to a symbolic garden of worship and the San Bernardino Mountains. The enclosed garden of worship brought the beauty of God's created world into the worship experience. A prayer chapel seating 25, off the narthex, featured a wall of chipped glass created by the Judson Studios, the same as was used in the Air Force Academy chapel at Colorado Springs, Colorado. The choir balcony at the rear of the nave was cantilevered, giving the impression of a "floating island." The sanctuary building also included a bride's room, a working sacristy, and the pastor's study.

The fellowship hall to the north had a completely furnished kitchen, stage, and fireside room. The fellowship hall could seat around 400 and handle about 325 when used as a dining room with special partitions enabling the auditorium to be divided for Sunday school use. It served as the Sunday school and educational facility of the church until classrooms were constructed some time later. The new facilities, including furnishings and ground improvements, were built at a cost of around $325,000. Dr. A. R. Kretzmann of Chicago served as liturgical consultant. The buildings were constructed by Hoefer Construction Company of Fontana with the local planning executed under the direction of the Building Committee: Ralph Maurer, chairman; William Yergens;

> The new church also has a prayer chapel off the narthex, featuring a wall of chipped glass created by Judson Studios.

The entrance to the church with a large roof overhang, sheltering a striking ten-foot mosaic sculpture of the victorious Christ. (Pacific Southwest District Archives)

The interior of the church with its spacious chancel and large cross. (Pacific Southwest District Archives)

Rev. William P. Rosenwald was installed on August 5, 1973, as the fifth pastor of Trinity and remained until 1978. (Pacific Southwest District Archives)

Rev. Martin R. Greunke was installed as pastor of Trinity on September 9, 1979, remaining until 1987. (Pacific Southwest District Archives)

Bernard Rabe; Sam Turner; O. A. Wall; Irving Quam; George Richter; William Hirsch; and Pastor Schwartzkopf, ex officio.

Over 2,500 people attended the various services held during the week of June 3, 1961, for the dedication of the new sanctuary and fellowship hall. The first 24 hours of the church use included almost all the official church acts — Holy Communion, adult and youth Confirmations, adult and infant Baptisms, reception by transfer, and a wedding. The dedicatory ceremonies took place in a special Holy Communion service on Saturday, June 3. On the next day, three special services were held with Holy Baptism administered to Mrs. James Carroll in the early morning worship and the guest speaker, Rev. Marvin Suhr, pastor of Faith Church, Whittier, who served Trinity Congregation during his "intern" year and later as a summer worker, preached the sermon. At the 11:00 a.m. service, 29 juniors and 5 adults were confirmed, the sermon was delivered by Rev. Daryl Wildermuth, pastor of St. Paul's Lutheran Church, Highland, a former assistant at Trinity, and infant Heather Miller was also baptized in this service. In the 4:00 p.m. festival service, the guest speaker was Rev. Armin Hesse, District vice president and former circuit counselor for Trinity congregation along with Rev. David Stirdivant, pastor of Santa Cruz congregation in Los Angeles and former member of Trinity, also taking part in the service. In the evening of June 4, the spacious, beautiful chancel was the setting for the wedding of Jerome Ringhofer and Janet Alonso, where the church was again almost completely filled.

A special candlelight Communion service was held on Wednesday evening with Rev. Graeme Rosenau as the speaker. On Friday evening, the youth-emphasized service featured an address by Rev. John G. Huber on the "Hope Chest for Youth." Joel Schumacher, director of religious education, installed newly elected officers of the Junior Walther League. The week of celebration came to a climax with a service recognizing the 50th anniversary of the founding of Trinity Congregation. At the morning worship, Rev. Martin Lankow of Reedsport, Oregon, son of Rev. William Lankow, who served as pastor of Trinity for 25 years, was the speaker. That evening a baked-ham dinner started the time of fellowship with Pastor Schwartzkopf serving as master of ceremonies and Rev. G. H. Hillmer of Hemet speaking, reminiscing about people and events familiar to him in the life of Trinity. On Sunday, June 18, Circuit Counselor

George Kettner brought the congregation a message stressing the mission challenges, opportunities, and responsibilities facing the church at that time, completing a full month of celebration and thanksgiving to the Lord for His many blessings.

Pastor Schwartzkopf served Trinity for 22 years; during that time, the congregation continued to prosper with the communicant membership reaching 644 in 1963. He resigned in 1972 to become full-time Lutheran camp director at the Arrowhead Lutheran Camp where he was on the original Lutheran Laymen's League Camp Committee when the campsite was purchased and participated in the groundbreaking and dedication ceremonies.

Rev. Curtis C. Stephan who had been appointed co-pastor in 1971, remained and served as interim pastor and as co-pastor until 1977. On August 5, 1973, Rev. William P. Rosenwald was installed as the fifth called pastor of Trinity in its 67 years in San Bernardino. Participating in the service were Rev. Curtis Stephan, interim pastor of the congregation who delivered the sermon on the theme "When Timothy Comes," and the circuit counselor, Rev. Richard Faerber, was the officiant. Rev. Rosenwald was born in Chicago, Illinois, spending his youth in Minneapolis, Minnesota, and Oakland, California. He graduated from Concordia Seminary in St. Louis in 1969 with the Master of Divinity degree. His first call was to Grace Church in Needles, where he completed the construction of a new church, and he also served St. John's Church in nearby Bullhead City, Arizona. His wife, Mrs. Lenore, nee Krage, graduated from Concordia Teachers' College in River Forest, Illinois, and taught in Lutheran elementary schools in St. Louis for three years. At the time, they had two children, Erin Margaret and Jason Alexander.

After Rev. Rosenwald left, the Rev. William S. Graumann, retired pastor from Immanuel in Riverside, served as interim pastor at Trinity from November 1978 to September 1979. The Rev. Martin R. Greunke was installed as pastor of Trinity on September 9, 1979, having come from Mt. Calvary Lutheran Church, Greenville, Michigan, where he served from 1970 to 1979. After graduating from Midland Lutheran College in 1959, he taught at the junior and senior high school level until 1965 when he began his theological training, receiving his Master of Divinity degree from Concordia Seminary in Springfield, Illinois, in 1973. While at Trinity, the church continued to prosper with the 500 members supporting the building project of an addition to the parish hall in 1981, which housed 5 classrooms, 2 offices, and some storage space.

Following Pastor Greunke's call in 1987 to serve in Nebraska, Pastor Eugene L. Fenton Jr. was called and installed on July 19, 1987, as Trinity's pastor where he served until 2001, accepting a called to Trinity in La Junta, Colorado. He was born on October 31, 1931, in Chicago, Illinois, and attended the University of Illinois, graduating in 1971. After receiving his colloquy through Concordia Seminary at Springfield, Illinois, he was ordained and installed at Holy Cross, Shellbyville, Illinois, where he remained two years. He was called to Christ in Juniata, Nebraska, ministering two years before going to Lutheran High School in Orange, California, where he taught for five years. Pastor married Nancy Mohr, a Lutheran schoolteacher, in 1961, with their marriage blessed with six children.

During Rev. Fenton's pastorate, Trinity continued to evolve in meeting the changing needs of the community by adding a ministry to Spanish-speaking people in the neighborhood. Rev. Mark McKenzie was the pastor-at-large to the Spanish-speaking community along with a former "son of Trinity," the Rev. David Stirdivant. This Hispanic ministry had its roots in 1994 when some members of St. John's, Montebello, Rosa Urdiano and her family, moved to San Bernardino, requesting their pastor, the Rev. Douglas Jones of St. John's in Montebello, to come to the area and conduct a Spanish service for them. Since they lived close to Messiah in Highland, Pastor Jones received permission to conduct services there in the afternoon at about 4:00 p.m. Each Sunday, he and Yolanda Tolosa, who came along to assist, would drive from Montebello to Highland to conduct services in Spanish. Since it was a long drive for them, Pastor Stirdivant consented to help with the services. After discovering there were more Hispanics in Trinity's neighborhood, permission was granted from Pastor Fenton to hold services at Trinity beginning in 1995. In the fall of that year, Pastor McKenzie was called to do full-time work as missionary-at-large among the Hispanic population. Trinity opened its doors to the Hispanic group just as they had for the Eritrean community the previous eight years, providing office space for Pastor Mark McKenzie and allowing the mission to use the sanctuary for worship services.

On Sunday, September 10, 1995, during the 10:00 a.m. service, the McKenzie family was welcomed into Trinity's membership and his work as missionary-at-large was publicly acknowledged. Pastor McKenzie was installed on October 22 by the District as missionary-at-large and was assisted by Rev. David Stirdivant where he has been assisting in this ministry at Trinity since its inception. When Pastor Stirdivant retired after doing ministry to the Hispanics for almost 50 years, he felt more comfortable worshiping in Spanish than English. At the end of 1996, Pastor McKenzie accepted the call to serve a dual pastorate at St. John's Lutheran Church in Colton with a special emphasis in developing a Hispanic ministry, while continuing to serve Iglesia Luterana La Santisima Trinidad in San Bernardino, for at least one year. In the dual Hispanic Ministry, he continued working with Pastor Stirdivant and also with Mr. Marcello Gomez, a student in the Theological Education by Extension (TEE) Program. This arrangement of a dual parish lasted one year.

In Colton, outreach to the Hispanic community began with letters sent before the Vacation Bible School, and then another one was mailed in October. The Saturday before the weeklong VBS, a carnival was held at the church with music, a moon jumper, and food, helping to bring people to the church. Hispanic ministry was started through the VBS, contacting people who had associations with the church or were friends of members. According to Pastor McKenzie, some of the key persons were Lui Garcia, and Jorge and his wife, who were all member of St. John's attending the English service. The group also canvassed the neighborhood and distributed fliers. Through all this work, about 15 people began attending Spanish services. Toward the end of 1997, Pastor McKenzie realized that he really wasn't able to do justice to both the Hispanic and English ministries at St. John's and in San Bernardino. He thought at that time, it would be better for someone else to do the English ministry at St. John's and he would continue with the Spanish work. Since Rev. Don Wiley, who had just returned from the mission field in Panama and was living with his parents in Riverside, St. John's decided to call him to serve both the English and Spanish-speaking congregations at St. John's, because he was bilingual. For about two months in the following year, Pastor McKenzie and Pastor Stirdivant assisted with the Spanish work and introduced Pastor Wiley to people they knew. As the parish wanted to concentrate on strengthening the English-speaking congregation to be able to support a Hispanic ministry and continue with the Hispanic market, the Spanish mission was dis-

Rev. Eugene L. Fenton Jr. was installed on July 19, 1987, and served until 2001. (Pacific Southwest District Archives)

Rev. Mark McKenzie began full-time work as missionary at-large among the Hispanic population in San Bernardino in the fall of 1995. (Pacific Southwest District Archives)

In 1995, Iglesia La Santisima Trinidad is started in Trinity's church building.

continued at that time.

During the summer of 1996, the Spanish mission in San Bernardino participated in Trinity's Vacation Bible School, which had a small attendance. For about three years, they continued to work with Trinity's VBS and then finally decided to do their own when Trinity didn't have a Vacation Bible School. They changed it to one day a week, Wednesday evenings, for five weeks. The following year, they used the same procedures but changed it to Friday evenings. When it was started, the people really got involved, which was helpful in bringing in the neighborhood children. Letters were sent to Hispanic homeowners in the area, using the three zip codes nearest the church. Through this letter and the VBS program, many people were gained for the church. At Christmas time, the mission always celebrated the Posada with the Posadas providing an opening for members of the congregation to make follow-up calls on the participants and invite them to worship and fellowship events. The attendance at this event ranged from 40 to 70, with the celebration of Posadas a real blessing to the mission.

During the year 2000, Pastor McKenzie was conducting Bible classes on Thursdays, Fridays, and Sundays and teaching Catechism classes on Tuesdays and Saturdays. In the Bible studies, the principles of good were addressed and taught. On January 30, the mission received the first adults into church membership through the Rite of Confirmation. Also on that day, the first church council members were installed. One of the members had been inviting his extended family to attend church, as they had been living in the area. In this family, many of the young people had musical abilities that they used in the evening service. Special fliers were distributed to advertise the Ash Wednesday service and Holy Week services. Friendship Sunday was changed to Friendship Weekend on April 29 and 30, with a concert, dance, and special services. In June, the Friday Evening Home Bible Study Class was moved to the church, as that was the desire of those attending it. At that time, a class for children was also started with Pastor Stirdivant in charge. That summer, VBS was held on 5 consecutive Friday evenings, beginning on July 7, with a total registration of 52, including 43 children and 9 adults. Twenty-one teachers and helpers taught an average attendance of 33 children, bringing a total of 70 people involved in the program.

In the fall, an additional Catechism class was begun with Pastor Stirdivant teaching the children, preparing them to receive First Communion, and another class was begun for the younger children with one of the members teaching it, doubling the number of adults attending Bible classes and children attending Catechism classes. During December, Posadas were held on the 16th and continued until the 23rd, culminating on Christmas Eve, with a Christmas program which incorporated many elements of the Posadas. Each night a group met at the church, sang Christmas carols, read Scripture, had a devotion, and prayed. After people were chosen to play the roles of Mary and Joseph, the group went out into the neighborhood of the church to sing Christmas carols. During Christmas caroling, they were able to make new contacts with people in the neighborhoods and invited friends, family, and neighbors to participate in this activity. On 3 evenings, there were between 80 to 100 people attending the events. During the year, church attendance grew from 53 to 60 per Sunday.

At the beginning of the year 2001, the mission's main emphasis was on stewardship with the goal, "To provide opportunities for those that belong to our church to grow in their stewardship." Growth in stewardship became even more important that year as the Regional Mission Council challenged the mission to contribute to the District $5,000 toward the pastor's salary. Besides revising the budget and seeing what other funds were available to help meet this big challenge, the month of January was dedicated to a stewardship emphasis. In addition to the emphasis on the stewardship of treasures, the other objective was the use of members' personal talents for the church work. Church workdays were initiated each month for the care and maintenance of the church property in coordination with representatives of Trinity. At the end of February, a workday was organized to clean the sanctuary floor and at the end of March, the weeds in the church parking lot were removed.

On two Saturdays, February 24 and March 3, members of the mission distributed fliers at supermarkets frequented by the Hispanic community inviting the community to the Ash Wednesday and Friendship Sunday services. Since a special service was planned with unique activities for Friendship Sunday, the morning and evening services at 9:00 a.m. and 6:00 p.m. were combined into one service at 12:00 noon. After the worship service, the congregation gathered in the parish hall for a meal with entertainment provided by some of the young women that included youth and older children who had learned and performed some Mexican folklorico dances. Following the meal, Dr. Victor Rodriguez, a Lutheran sociologist and professor in the Department of Chicano and Latino Studies at California State University, Long Beach, give a presentation on the Hispanic family. The Ash Wednesday service had 78 people in attendance and the Friendship Sunday had 79 people present.

On May 12 and 13, a total of 14 children received their First Communion with 125 people in attendance in the May 13 service. On Pentecost, June 3, 93 people witnessed 5 young people confirmed that day. Following both of the services, all of those in attendance were invited to celebrate with the families in a meal and festivities in the parish hall. The Vacation Bible School was held Friday, July 6, from 6:30–8:30 p.m. and continued for 5 consecutive Fridays with 58 children and youth and 9 adults registered assisted by 25 people who were teachers and helpers. Twenty-four of the people attending were new to the church. During the summer, the worship service attendance fell from 61 to 56; but by September, it had increased to 80 exceeding the year's goal of 75. Also during September, the Lord had blessed the Friday evening Bible class with an attendance of 33 children and youth and 133 adults. On November 11, the mission canvassed the neighborhood along with members from Trinity and students from Concordia University in Irvine. The year concluded with the annual Las Posadas held nightly from December 16 through Christmas Eve with 40 to a 100 people in attendance. Each evening a family was designated to receive Mary and Joseph and those that accompany them into their home or the parish hall with that family providing a meal or refreshments inviting their friends and family to participate. By means of the Las Posadas, they were able to make contact with new families through Christmas caroling and through invitations of the host family and other families. When the Las Posadas were done at the church, the group would sing at homes surrounding the parish. That year's attendance increased significantly from the previous years. Through the Las Posadas, at least one new family started attending church. At the end of the year, Pastor David Stirdivant and Teodoro Lopez, the music director, began to teach some of the younger youth in the 4th to 10th grades to play keyboard instruments for the worship services, meeting with them each Tuesday evening.

When a sister of one the members was killed at the end of January of 2002, Pastor Stirdivant and Pastor McKenzie visited and counseled the family members in the hospital and led the family and friends in prayer, sharing the hope of eternal life with them at both the viewing and the funeral service. On March 2, one of the young ladies of the congregation celebrated her 15th birthday (Quinceñera) with a special worship service. Previously, she and her family had attended church infrequently. In preparation for this special celebration, she and her family started attending the Friday evening First Communion, Confirmation, adult Bible study classes with Pastor having several special classes with her and her parents in preparation for the event. Because of this opportunity, the family started to attend the church on a regular basis. Two new Bible studies were begun with the one on Tuesday nights for the parents of children attending the music class and another on Wednesday nights in the homes of the families of the congregation.

Due to a decrease that year in the District's mission support grant for the Hispanic mission at Trinity and since the mission was not able to make up the difference to continue to pay the pastor's salary and benefits on the same level that he had been receiving the past two years, he was forced to secure part-time employment and become a worker-priest. When some members who lived in Fontana and who infrequently attended Trinity's mission requested that Spanish services be held in Fontana, Pastor McKenzie met with First Lutheran's Board of Elders who granted permission for services to be conducted at First with the initial one being held on June 9, 2002. From this time forward, Pastor McKenzie has conducted services both at Trinity and First each Sunday. With pastor preaching at two different churches, the attendance at Trinity's mission fell from an average of 67 on Sunday to 48. Pastor said, "God has been faithful in providing for my needs and those of my family. The concern is what the challenge did to our ministry and attendance. In trying to present the challenge, and in trying to figure out how to meet the challenge, and in deciding what we were going to be able to do, some people were 'turned off' because it seemed that all we were talking about was 'money.' Then there was the issue that 'the pastor was making so much more money than we are, why does he need so much?' I have been told that this is a factor in our drop in attendance. I know that there have been other factors in people's

Pastor McKenzie begins Hispanic minstry at First, Fontana, in 2002.

lives that may have also contributed to the drop."

Even with the disappointment of lower attendance during 2002, the new year of 2003 brought many blessings from the Lord, as attendance at services increased, averaging 68 with a high of 98 in the first quarter of the year. On February 14 and 15, Trinity had activities that reached out to the community creating a presence where the members could invite their friends, relatives, and neighbors to the church. On Friday, February 14, flowers were sold in front of the church for Val-

entine's Day and on Saturday, February 15, a Valentine's Day fair was conducted where there was food, games for children, a youth Mariachi Band, and dancing. During May and June, two rummage sales were held at Trinity to bring in people from the neighborhood. Since the most pressing area of need at the mission was financial, Pastor McKenzie was not only doing ministry in two places but was also having to develop a business to supplement his income to adequately support his family as he continued being a worker-priest.

First Lutheran Church
Iglesia Luterana La Santisima Trinidad
Fontana, California

The city of Fontana is located in the Inland Empire of Southern California where the three major freeways, the 10, the 15, and the 210, intersect. The city also has the Metrolink rail service running through the center of town, connecting it to the greater Los Angeles area and is only 10 minutes away from Ontario International Airport. The 2000 Census showed the population to be 139,100 with 57.7 percent of the residents culturally defined as Hispanic, with 23.9 percent Caucasians, 11.2 percent African-Americans, and the Asian population was at 4.5 percent. Fontana's population is now more diverse than the Inland Empire generally. The city was incorporated in 1952 and now encompasses an area of 36 square miles, with a sphere of influ-

ence of 56 square miles.

The earliest recorded landowner in the Fontana area was Don Antonio Maria Lugo, who received a land grant in 1813 with a second grant secured as Rancho de San Bernardino for his sons. The Lugo sons sold a portion of their land, which included part of what is now Fontana, to a group of Mormon settlers in 1851. The Mormon settlers eventually returned to Salt Lake City, and the Semi Tropical Land & Water Company gained control of the Rancho, subdividing into tracts in 1888 and calling it Rosena, but no development took place at that time because there wasn't a reliable source of water. Active development of the area, however, did not begin until the early 1900s when the Fontana Development Company acquired the acreage in 1903 and began a community, changing the name to Fontana in 1913. Fontana's early roots can be traced to an old farmhouse located on Pepper Avenue where the home was once used as part of Camp 1, a settlement that developer and farmer A. B. Miller started in the early 1900s to establish his Fontana Farms operation. Workers who lived in the camp with their families planted vineyards and orange groves for Miller who also secured 75 percent of the flow of water from Lytle Creek in 1906, making the land productive.

The town-site of Fontana was founded in 1913, when A. B. Miller, playing an active part in the development of agriculture in Southern California, developed it into a diversified agricultural area with citrus, grain, grapes, poultry, and with swine, the leading commodity. From 1922 to 1950,

The corner of Sierra Avenue and Foothill Boulevard, Route 66, as it looked in 1926 lined with orange and palm trees on the north and eucalyptus windbreaks on the south.

Fontana accepted 500 to 600 tons of garbage a day from Los Angeles to feed the hogs, the manure used to fertilize the citrus groves. In 1926 when Route 66 was completed, it cut through the town on Foothill Boulevard linking the city to westerly migration of segments of the American population that sought relief from the Midwest Dust Bowl during the Great Depression. Locations such as the Wigwam Motel and Bono's Deli, landmarks on Foothill Boulevard, provide nostalgic reminders of an era still treasured by many visitors to Fontana and some of its "old time" residents. In this mass migration west were many Lutherans who settled in the Inland Empire.

In 1942, the community faced a gigantic transition when Fontana was selected by Henry J. Kaiser as the site for his steel mill, which manufactured steel plates for 1,490 Liberty ships, changing the rural town to a blue collar city. He chose the site at the beginning of World War II as it was far away from the coast, had water, and would not be susceptible to a Japanese air attack as it was so far inland. When the city was incorporated on June 25, 1952, it had a population of 13,695, becoming Southern California's leading producer of steel and related products with the steel industry dominating the city's economy since the mill was built, employing 7,000 people at its height of operation. However, in the late 1970s, Kaiser Steel began to reduce production and manpower with the steel mill closing in 1984.

In the 1920s with an increased growth in population in Fontana, Lutherans were traveling to San Bernardino to attend church at Trinity, as there was no other Lutheran church in the area. Seeing the influx of Lutherans continuing to increase in Fontana, Rev. William J. Lankow of Trinity, deemed it his duty to canvass the Fontana field, conducting the first Lutheran service on November 29, 1925, in one of the Fontana Junior High School classrooms with 17 persons present. Thereafter, regular services were held twice a month, transferring the services to a grammar school auditorium after a few weeks. In January 1929, the Mission Board heeded the petition and requests of Pastor Lankow for assistance, asking Mr. Herbert Glock, a student at Concordia Seminary in St. Louis, Missouri, who later became a professor at California Concordia College at Oakland, to do supply work at Fontana where he served faithfully from January 6 until June 1929. On August 11, 1929, Mr. Harold Tietjen, another student at Concordia Seminary, St. Louis, who later became the director of missions for the Southern California District, assumed the work of student Glock.

On Sunday, January 26, 1930, Pastor Lankow conducted the services in Fontana where 28 adults and 8 children were present, preaching on Ephesians 2:19–22, using the text as the basis of his sermon, explaining the foundation, cornerstone, and building of the Holy Christian Church. After the service, he explained to the 15 adults, the constitution, which had been circulated among the people for a number of months. After the explanation of the constitution with its revisions, five men and five women voted to organize, naming the parish, First Evangelical Lutheran Church of Fontana, California. The congregation was now officially organized with 30 communicant members, being served by Student H. B. Tietjen from August 1929 to July 1930. On August 2, 1930, Rev. O. Henkel was installed as the first resident pastor of First of Fontana. Two years later, the first church building at the corner of Juniper and Valencia streets, was dedicated on April 3, 1932. On May 27, 1940, Rev. O. H. Henkel retired as pastor of the congregation with Rev. Edgar Brohm of Scotia, Nebraska, called and installed on June 14, 1940. By 1941, the membership numbered 92 baptized members and 70 communicant members. In April of 1942, the congregation purchased the parsonage from Rev. and Mrs. O. H. Henkel. With World War II raging in Europe and the Pacific, Rev. E. Brohm resigned his pastorate at First on August 17, 1942, to enter the Army chaplaincy.

The first church building, Juniper and Valencia streets, was dedicated on April 3, 1932. (Pacific Southwest District Archives)

Rev. R. F. Knaus, pastor of First from November 8, 1942, to 1962. (Pacific Southwest District Archives)

When Rev. Rheinold F. Knaus was installed on November 8, 1942, the membership was 94 baptized members with 64 communicant members and 24 in the Sunday school. In January of 1944, the congregation accepted a lot adjoining the church property at Juniper and Valencia streets as a gift from Mr. R. H. Guse. At the beginning of 1945, the congregation voted to become self-supporting. The following year, they purchased two additional lots for future expansion at Juniper and Valencia streets. By 1947, a proposed plan for future expansion of the parish was developed with the decision reached to establish a parochial school in 1948. At the same time, the congregation was presented a new Hammond organ by the Mary and Martha Club. Since the congregation had grown to 303 baptized members, 149 communicant members and a Sunday school of 90, it necessitated enlarging and remodeling the small church in 1949 doubling its size. The work was started on August 17, with the members volunteering over 5,000 hours in labor. Mr. O. J. Bruer, the architect, designed the building so that the front was extended toward the street enlarging the nave, doubling the seating capacity with a cornerstone laying service on October 19, 1949, at 3:00 p.m.

As the parish continued to grow, an evening service was conducted but was terminated in 1952 when the 8:00 a.m. service was inaugurated. Since the property at Juniper and Valencia streets was inadequate to meet the needs of the growing congregation, a five-acre site on the corner of Citrus and Randall Avenue was purchased on July 12, 1952, to relocate the church which had grown to 490 baptized members, 318 communicant members, and 182 in the Sunday school. The present spacious sanctuary, designed by Architect Jay D.

Wheaton, with all its appointments was dedicated on January 25, 1959. On October 25, 1959, the public dedication of the completed first unit of the church buildings, sanctuary, educational wing, and parish hall, the original church that was moved from the old location, was dedicated with an open house held for the community on November 1, 1959. At the time, the congregation had grown to 750 baptized members and 436 communicant members with a Sunday school enrollment of 288.

In the front of the church for all to see as they passed by was a 38-foot tower in a reflection pool rising majestically as a reminder of the towering strength to be found in the Gospel of the Lord, Jesus Christ. As the worshiper entered the large narthex on the west end of the nave, the eye was focused toward the chancel with the huge brass cross on a red brick wall over the altar. The nave, having long stained-glass windows on each side, seated 420 people on the main floor with an additional 55 seats in the choir loft. On the north side of chancel was the pastor's private study. On the south side of chancel was the sacristy with a sink and cabinets where Communion ware and altar cloths were stored. The mother's room on the south side of nave in a semi-sound-proof room was provided for mothers with small children. Some of the features of the new church included upholstered pews, an outstanding public address system, varied lighting effects, intercommunications, a remote control room for tape recordings, a player for recordings over the chimes tower, and facilities for radio or television broadcasts. The educational wing was composed of the church office and a supply room and three school-size classrooms, which could be divided into four Sunday school rooms. The parish hall served many purposes: Christian

The new sanctuary, educational wing and parish hall located at Citrus and Randall avenues. (Pacific Southwest District Archives)

fellowship dinners, Sunday school classrooms, and for meetings of various organizations. At the parish hall entrance was the church library and in the east end of the hall was a stage for presentation of plays with a large kitchen directly east of the stage. The area between the church and parish hall had a courtyard designed for recreation use with the possibility of using it for outdoor services. On the south side of the church was a paved parking lot.

After completing 20 years of ministry at First during its rapid period of growth and relocation, Pastor Knaus accepted a call to St. Paul's in Orange during 1962. Rev. Herbert Schulenburg became the interim pastor until Rev. William Siefkes was installed on November 24, 1963. During the installation service, Rev. Lawrence Rudolph of Redeemer, Ontario, delivered the sermon and Rev. Herbert Schulenburg served as liturgist.

Pastor Siefkes was born November 27, 1922, at Primghar, Iowa, receiving his elementary and high school education at Mitchell, South Dakota, and pre-ministerial training at Concordia College, St. Paul, Minnesota. Following his graduation from Concordia Seminary, St. Louis, Missouri, with the Bachelor of Arts and Bachelor of Divinity degrees, he served parishes at LaMoure, North Dakota, and Grand Forks, North Dakota. For the previous nine years, he had been pastor of the 1,700-member Messiah in Minneapolis, Minnesota, where he also served as evangelism chairman of the North

Minneapolis area for The Lutheran Church — Missouri Synod. At the time of his installation, he and Mrs. Siefkes were the parents of three children, Jane, Cynthia, and William Robert.

During Pastor Siefkes' ministry, the Lord blessed the congregation with renewed vigor and new incentives. The parochial school was started in 1966 with Mrs. Roberta Kregel as teacher of the kindergarten. In 1968, ground was broken for the construction of the much needed east wing of classrooms and the multi-purpose gymnasium building. By 1983, the school had grown to 120 students providing a Christian education to children in kindergarten through eighth grade. To complement the parochial school and accommodate the needs of the community, a preschool/nursery was begun in 1970 under the direction of Mrs. Gladys Patterson. In order to alleviate overcrowding of the school facilities, a beautiful, new preschool building, accommodating up to 100 children, was dedicated on February 13, 1983.

After Pastor Siefkes went to St. Paul's in Ames, Iowa, Rev. Robert F. Hoeft went to First in August of 1970 from Redeemer Lutheran Church, St. Clair Shores, Michigan, where he had served since September of 1968. During his years there, he worked with the Michigan District Youth Committee and in 1970 was appointed to the District's public relations staff. He served Christ the King Lutheran Church, Nashua, New Hampshire, 1964 to 1968. He was born on July 28, 1929, in Detroit, Michi-

Rev. William Siefkes was installed as pastor of First on November 24, 1963 and remained until 1970. (Pacific Southwest District Archives)

The interior of the new church on Dedication Day, October 25, 1959. (Pacific Southwest District Archives)

Rev. Robert F. Hoeft, pastor of First from August of 1970 until July of 1971. (Pacific Southwest District Archives)

Rev. Clarence A. Kindschy was installed on November 26, 1972, and remained until September of 1983. (Pacific Southwest District Archives)

gan, where he attended Detroit Business Institute, graduating in June 1956 with a Bachelor of Science degree. He received a Bachelor of Divinity degree from Concordia Seminary, Springfield, Illinois, in 1964. His vicarage was at Grace Lutheran Church, Fallen, Montana. Before studying for the ministry, he was a professional baseball player and also served in the Navy for four years. He and his wife, Patricia, had five children at the time of his installation, Rebecca, Roberta, Tamara, Amy, and Robert. At his installation service, Rev. Eugene R. Paulus of Redlands delivered the message entitled "Successful Ministers."

Following Pastor Hoeft's departure in July of 1971 to Trinity, Hammond, Indiana, after a short tenure at First, retired pastor, Rev. Luther Loesch, served the congregation well as interim pastor until the installation of Rev. Clarence A. Kindschy on November 26, 1972. Pastor Kindschy was born in Dearborn, Michigan, on May 30, 1926, and was ordained into the holy ministry in 1946 as a pastor of the General Council of the Assemblies of God where he served parishes in that denomination in Colorado, Kansas, Ohio, and Rhode Island. He received his initial ministerial training at Central Bible Institute, Springfield, Missouri, and Rockmont College, Denver, Colorado. Upon his graduation from Concordia Theological Seminary, Springfield, Illinois, in 1967, he was ordained into the ministry of The Lutheran Church–-Missouri Synod serving as pastor of Peace Lutheran Church, San Bernardino. He was active in civic affairs as a member of the Board of Directors of the San Bernardino Boys' Club, Del Rosa Community Center, and Uptown Exchange Club of San Bernardino where he served as an officer. He served the church-at-large as a member of the Board of Directors of Arrowhead Lutheran Camp, a member of the Committee for Outdoor Ministries of the Southern California District of The Lutheran Church — Missouri Synod, and the evangelism representative for his Circuit. Pastor and Mrs. Kindschy, the former Helene Butz, had three children, Mrs. Darrell (Willene) Esa, who was a teacher at Wheatridge Lutheran School, Denver, Colorado; a married son Lowell, who was in his third year of pre-ministerial training at Concordia Senior College, Fort Wayne, Indiana; and Jon, a senior at San Gorgonio High School in San Bernardino.

After serving the congregation for 11 years, Rev. Kindschy accepted a call to Peace Lutheran in Flagstaff, Arizona, in September 1983. Pastor Harold Boeche, who had been serving as assistant

to the pastor, then assumed the responsibilities of interim pastor until Rev. Donald Dannenberg was installed as pastor on June 30, 1985. He was born on July 2, 1937, in Hinsdale, Illinois, and married Janis Heinz on August 13, 1961, with their union blessed with three children: Kari, Kirk, and Kent. Following his graduation from Concordia Seminary, in Springfield, Illinois, in 1962, he was installed and ordained on July 8, at Immanuel, in Daykin, Nebraska. In 1965, he started Holy Cross, a mission, in Kearney, Nebraska, followed by a call to Trinity, West Chicago, Illinois, in 1967. After he and his wife became managers of the Walther League Hospice in Los Angeles in 1973 for one year, he served at Redeemer in Perris, California, until 1985.

When Pastor Dannenberg arrived at First in 1985, the congregation had 400 members, growing to 650 in the early 1990s. In 1988, the congregation purchased two additional acres of property east of the church for future development, giving the church six acres, and the sanctuary was renovated along with improvements made to the gym. With the recession in the mid-1990s came a great transformation not only to First but also the whole area as many large employers, Norton and March Field Air Force bases, either closed or reduced staff along with the old General Dynamics Plant closing and moving to Arizona, causing widespread unemployment and people moving from the community. With all these changes, there was a gradual decline in membership as the area around the church saw a shift in demographics also, with more Hispanics moving into the neighborhood.

In order for the congregation to minister to the membership more effectively and to be a resource to the community, members were trained as Stephen's Ministers, providing greater care for the membership and community at large. After Pastor received his Ph.D. in pastoral counseling in 1997, the parish established the Family Life Counseling ministry, opening another door for outreach to the community. Through the years, First Lutheran was also active in supporting a food pantry and clothes closet for the city. Concerns for the needs of it members and for ministering to the community were always a high priority of the congregation.

In order to minister to the people in the neighborhood, the parish requested help from the District in securing a Spanish-speaking pastor. Since none was available, the congregation decided to rent the building to a Guatemalan group who were not Lutheran and to a Korean Presbyterian church. After a short time, the Hispanic group left the premises. During this time, a member who had a large piece of property in the northern part of Fontana offered to give it to the Board of Directors of the church if his relatives would agree to it. Since they wouldn't agree to give it to the parish, the idea of relocating died. In the late 1990s, the school also faced many challenges with the student body reaching 125. One of the challenges was that few members had children to send to the school so it became a private school for other denominations or the unchurched who had no interest in joining the church. Due to the proximity of Fontana High School, parents were hesitant to send their children to the school as problems at the high school spilled over to the day school property with lockdowns at the high school causing First to also lockdown, and police would sometimes chase students through First's property. Since parents didn't feel it was any longer a safe environment for their children, enrollment began declining.

In 2000, the church had an offer to sell the property to a corporation who wanted to use the facilities as a vocational school for adult education. The congregation decided to sell the property as the area around the church had changed, moving to the north end of town where there were new housing developments, relocating the church and school in portable buildings. When the offer was presented, it was far less than the asking price. The congregation counter offered and never heard anymore from the corporation. During the time of negotiations, the rumor spread that the school was going to close, which affected the student population of 86 pupils. Even with letters sent to parents explaining that the school wouldn't close, only 40 pupils were enrolled in the next school year, forcing the school to close for lack of enrollment.

Finally in 2001, the congregation made its first attempt to do work among the Hispanic population in the neighborhood when Victor Aldaña came to begin Spanish services, which he continued until April of that year. Due to financial problems, he moved to the San Fernando Valley to live with his daughter. At this time, Pastor McKenzie of Trinity in San Bernardino proposed to Pastor Dannenberg and the president of the congregation, Tom Kutansky, to expand Trinity's Hispanic work to Fontana. He began by visiting families who had attended worship services in San Bernardino but lived in Fontana and others including the father and sisters of Pastor Alfonso Conrado of Panorama City. He then organized a social event and meal on

Saturday, June 1, since these families didn't know each other but would become the nucleus of the new mission. At the social, the people expressed an interest in beginning worship services at First in Fontana. The following Sunday, June 9, 2002, a worship service was conducted at 12 o'clock. The plan for these initial worship services was to solidify a core group, to organize, and to train people to function in different capacities such as the Altar Guild, ushers, and acolytes. The first worship services were very informal with more time dedicated to making plans and training people. As the weeks went by, the worship became more formal with people making commitments, having everything in order for worship on Sundays. In August, the decision was made to reach out to the community through a yard and rummage sale. On 2 Saturdays, September 21 and the 28, a group of people from First and Trinity distributed 800 fliers in the neighborhood surrounding the church. At the worship service on Sunday the 29th, there were 70 people in attendance. In October, classes were begun preparing children to receive their First Communion, Confirmation, and adult Confirmation. By October, the mission had approximately 23 different families who had attended worship and who were enrolled in classes.

During 2003, attendance at the Hispanic mission continued to climb, averaging 96 by April with 123 at the Easter service and the Sunday school growing to 23. There were four Baptisms and one Quinceñera where, during the services, there were opportunities to share the Gospel with new people. In May and June, two rummage sales were held which helped to introduce the mission to the community. Pastor McKenzie stated, "The Lord has placed a huge challenge before us, especially in Fontana, in reaching out to the Hispanic community. There is more than enough work for me to dedicate myself full-time to ministry in Fontana. I especially would like to have time to call on visitors. However, I am not only having to do ministry in two places, I am having to develop a business to supplement my income to adequately support my family."

The church buildings were also rented to the Hispanic Seventh-day Adventist congregation who worshiped on Saturday and to a Korean Presbyterian Church who used the facilities on Sunday. The Hispanic Lutheran group used the church free of charge at noon each Sunday. First runs a preschool with 40 children, a day-care center, and a summer camp program for the children

Rev. Donald Dannenberg was installed as pastor on June 30, 1985, serving until his retirement on July 7, 2002.

Rev. Mark McKenzie, who began work among the Hispanics at First on June 1, 2001. (Pacific Southwest District Archives)

In 2001, the congregation makes its first attempt to do work among the Hispanic population in the neighborhood.

in the area who are almost all Hispanics.

When Pastor Dannenberg retired from full-time ministry on July 7, 2002, taking an interim ministry at Mt. Olive, La Mirada, Rev. Maynard Saeger served as vacancy pastor along with Rev. Harold Boeche who would also assist. To aid First Lutheran to meet its many challenges, Mission &

Ministry Facilitator Gary Norton led the congregation leadership through the first four workshops of the Twenty-first Century Workshop Series in the summer of 2003. He stated, "The vision is cast and the congregation, having a clear understanding of its ministry to its community, feels ready to begin the call process for a full-time pastor."

First Lutheran Church
Iglesia Primera Luterana
La Santisima Trinidad
Pasadena, California

The land where Pasadena is located today, with a population of 133,936 of which 33.40 percent are Hispanic, and 39.11 percent are Anglo, is now famous for the Tournament of Roses, the Rose Bowl, the Jet Propulsion Laboratory, and the California Institute of Technology, but was once occupied by the Hahamogna Tribe of Indians who subsisted on local game and vegetation, living in villages scattered along the Arroyo Seco and the canyons from the mountains down to South Pasadena. With the arrival of the Spaniards who established San Gabriel Mission on September 8, 1771, the Indians were subjugated, converted, and forced to labor for the mission.

When the San Gabriel Mission, the fourth in California, grew to be prosperous, with abundant orchards, vineyards, and herds, the vast lands, which it administered for the Spanish Crown, were divided into ranchos. After the Mexican Revolution, the new government secularized the

mission lands in 1833 awarding them to individuals with the northeast corner of San Gabriel Mission, consisting of the 14,000 acres known as Rancho el Rincon de San Pascual, previously given as a gift to Doña Eulalia Pérez de Guillen in 1826 by the padres, as she was noted for her advanced age as well as her devoted service to the mission. On February 18, 1835, it was formally granted by the Mexican government to her husband, Don Juan Mariné who with his sons subsequently lost the land, which changed ownership a few more times before being granted on November 28, 1843, by Governor Manuel Micheltorena to his good friend, Colonel Manuel Garfias, son of a distinguished Mexican family.

In 1852, two years after California was admitted as a state to the Union, Garfias built an adobe hacienda on the east bank of the Arroyo, where he and his family proceeded to live in grand style, until he could not meet the interest payment due on a loan. Title to the land was then transferred

Downtown Pasadena at the corner of Colorado Boulevard and Fair Oaks Avenue in 1890. (SECURITY PACIFIC COLLECTION/Los Angeles Public Library)

The Pasadena Grand Opera House where Lutherans held services in the fall of 1892. (SECURITY PACIFIC COLLECTION/Los Angeles Public Library)

in 1859 to his lenders, Dr. John S. Griffin and Benjamin "Don Benito" Wilson who sold portions of the Rancho San Pasqual, leaving them with 5, 323 acres in 1873.

In 1886, Pasadena incorporated, mainly as a means to rid the city of its saloons. In the ensuing decade, not only were amenities such as sewers, paved streets, and electric street lighting installed but also on January 1, 1890, the Valley Hunt Club initiated a mid-winter festival with a procession of flower-bedecked horses and carriages known as the Rose Parade. It became a yearly tradition in 1898 when the Tournament of Roses Association formally sponsored it. An added tourist attraction, opened in 1893, was the Echo Mountain incline railway that included a mountain chalet resort and the Alpine Tavern at Crystal Springs.

The city also had a cultural and educational side that included an educational system, which was expanded in both the public and the private sector. Throop Polytechnic Institute (first named Throop University) was founded in 1891, later to become the California Institute of Technology. Pasadena had a Shakespeare Club, a Grand Opera House, although never very successful, and numerous civic and cultural organizations. By 1900, the city's population had grown to 9,117 and by 1910 was 30,291. The population also included many Germans who came from different backgrounds of Lutheranism, the Reformed Church, and the Evangelical Reformed.

When a small group of Lutherans in Pasadena, the remnants of a so-called Lutheran congregation, requested the services of Pastor Runkel from Trinity in Los Angeles, he preached in the hall of the Grand Hotel on the corner of Colorado and Fair Oaks Avenue twice a month on Sunday afternoons. After serving the mission for a number of years, the mission was placed in charge of the Rev. William F. Seeger of Monrovia who had left Synod at the time of the predestinarian controversy within the Synodical Conference. After a few months, Rev. Seeger aided the group to organize as a congregation on May 29, 1892. The eight men who were present adopted a good Lutheran constitution. On that day, the congregation extended a call to Rev. Seeger, which he accepted. He had immigrated to America from Europe where he had received his theological training. He submitted himself to a colloquy before the Missouri Synod Buffalo Conference where he served in New York City in 1873, in Lockhaven, Pennsylvania, in 1875, and in Long Green, Maryland, in 1878. Before

moving to Pasadena, he resided in Monrovia. In the fall of 1892, the mission congregation moved to the Pasadena Grand Opera House on the corner of Raymond Avenue and Bellevue Drive, using the hall on the second floor of this imposing building giving it a church-like appearance with an altar and pulpit, which were built for $35. After holding services in the Pasadena Grand Opera House for about one and one-half years, the small congregation purchased its first property on the southeast corner of Vernon Avenue and Walnut Street for $3,800. A small chapel was built at a cost of $856 and was dedicated on March 11, 1894. In the September 6, 1896, Voters' Meeting, the relationship between the congregation and Pastor W. F. Seeger was dissolved.

Thus, when the pastorate had become vacant, the congregation appointed Rev. Henry Teichrieb, who was connected with the Reformed Church, as pastor on December 1, 1896. Within 11 months, Rev. Teichrieb was dismissed in October 1897, and the congregation again came under the supervision and leadership of Pastor George Runkel. On December 27, 1897, a resolution was passed to seek affiliation with the Evangelical Lutheran Synod of Missouri, Ohio and Other States and to apply for membership in the California and Nevada District of that body. Thus the faithful labors of Pastor Runkel were finally crowned with success. The congregation now received subsidy from and came under the supervision of the Mission Board of the District.

First Lutheran's first chapel at the corner of Vernon Avenue and Walnut Street dedicated on March 11, 1894, built at a cost of $856. (Pacific Southwest District Archives)

Rev. August Hansen, pastor of First from 1905 to 1930. (Pacific Southwest District Archives)

In 1907, First Lutheran establishes English services.

Rev. Frederick Reiser, a former Methodist who for a time attended the Lutheran conferences and passed a colloquy, next filled the pastorate of the congregation from February 20, 1898, to February 28, 1901. On April 22, 1898, the congregation was incorporated as St. Paul's Evangelical Lutheran Church of Pasadena, California, and also joined the Missouri Synod that year. During the first part of Pastor Reiser's ministry, some noteworthy progress was made in establishing the congregation, which was due to the influence of Pastor Runkel. In the year 1900, an assembly hall was annexed and an addition was made to the chapel at a cost of $728.52.

However, stormy days were ahead for this little band of Lutherans. Fortunately, among the great influx of people from the Middle West in 1900, were some staunch orthodox Lutherans who also settled in Pasadena, giving strength to the congregation. The question of opening a Christian day school was discussed in a number of meetings, but no satisfactory agreement could be reached. Pastor Reiser and a group of members tried to take the property, but the faithful Lutherans had to go to court to have the matter settled with the court judging in favor of the orthodox Lutherans. In the end, Pastor Reiser's ministry was terminated. Again Pastor Runkel, now President of the California and Nevada District, came to the rescue of the congregation and helped to preserve its Lutheran character and even its property. However, Pastor Runkel could not prevent the withdrawal of a large number of members and the formation of a new non-Lutheran organization under the leadership of the former pastor. The voting strength of the congregation was reduced to 10.

During the long vacancy lasting from February 1904 to July 1905, Rev. J. W. Theiss of Los Angeles and Rev. E. P. Block served the congregation. The fourth pastor to be called was Missouri Synod trained Rev. August Hansen, the son of Rev. and Mrs. Peter Hansen of Worden, Illinois, who was born February 21, 1880. After attending the Christian day school at his father's congregation at Worden and at his uncle's congregation at Pittsburgh, Pennsylvania, he entered Concordia Seminary, Springfield, Illinois, in 1891 where he finished the pre-seminary in 1896 entering the seminary in the same year at the age of 16. After serving a two-year vicarage at Sturgis, Michigan, he graduated from the seminary in 1902. His first call was to Newman and Tracy, California, where he was ordained on September 14, 1902, by President G.

Runkel at St. Paulus Lutheran Church, San Francisco, and was installed at Newman on September 28, 1902. In 1905, Pastor Hansen received the call to Pasadena where Rev. E. P. Block installed him on July 3, 1905. After serving the congregation for a quarter of a century, he accepted the call of the California and Nevada District as director of missions in 1930. While pastor of First Lutheran Church, he also served the District as member of the Mission Board (1921–1927), as District visitor for two terms, as vice president of the District (1924–1930), as students' patron, as member of the Electoral College of California Concordia College and as a member of the Young People's Board. He was united in holy matrimony in 1904 with Bertha Klehn of Newman, California, and they were blessed with four children: Edwin A. Hansen, Arthur H. Hansen, Helen Marie Hansen, and Theodore Albert Hansen.

As the Lord blessed the work of the new pastor, a spirit of cooperation was demonstrated by all of the members. In October of 1905, the congregation, although numbering only 13 voting members, became a self-supporting church. The congregation conducted its first mission festival on June 2, 1907, and also established English services that year. In January 1910, the voters passed a resolution to open a parochial school with Pastor Hansen undertaking the work of teaching in the school that September in addition to his congregational duties and his care of the new missions at Covina, Upland, and San Bernardino along with exploring several mission fields in Arizona. After five years during the beginning of World War I, the school was forced to close when a number of members moved from the area, and the influx of new people was at a low ebb.

Due to the missionary spirit of Pastor Hansen and the encouragement of the members of his congregation, First St. Paul's Lutheran Church of Pasadena became the mother church of a number of congregations. In 1920, a mission station was opened in Van Nuys leading to the organization of First Lutheran Church of Van Nuys. A large number of members living in Alhambra were dismissed in 1921 to form the nucleus of First Emmaus Lutheran Church of Alhambra. In the winter of 1922–1923, work was begun in Monrovia resulting in the founding of First Lutheran Church of Monrovia with a number of communicant members also released to this young congregation.

Under the leadership of Pastor Hansen, on December 7, 1913, the second property, 135' × 187', on

East Orange Grove Avenue west of Los Robles Avenue, was purchased for $3,300. The cornerstone for the second grand edifice was laid on June 21, 1914, and the dedicatory services were held on November 22, 1914. The new building, 72' × 38' with a 65-foot spire, including furnishings and a new pipe organ cost $13,121. On the 30th anniversary of the congregation in 1922, the entire debt was paid off. In 1924, the California Nevada District met at First St. Paul's new church edifice for a large convention.

When in 1930, the California and Nevada District sought a capable and experienced man to supervise its far-flung mission fields, Pastor Hansen's record as an outstanding missionary was their choice extending him a call as director of missions. In the best interests of the church-at-large, the congregation on May 5, 1930, voted to grant him a peaceful release after 25 years of faithful service. The pastoral conference together with the local congregation celebrated his 25th anniversary on June 20, 1930, and wished him God's richest blessing in his new field of labor. He served

First's second grand building with a 65-foot spire was dedicated on November 22, 1914. The building cost $13,121 and included furnishings and a new pipe organ. (Pacific Southwest District Archives)

the California and Nevada District in that capacity until 1949, opening many new mission fields.

In the same meeting in which Rev. Hansen was given a peaceful release, the Rev. George E. Theiss, pastor of Emanuel Lutheran Church in Los Angeles from 1923–1930, was asked to serve as vacancy pastor. In a special meeting on August 25, 1930, a call was extended to Rev. George E. Theiss. Rev. G. H. Smukal, president of the Southern California District, held the installation services for Rev. Theiss on October 19, 1930.

The Rev. George E. Theiss was born on November 29, 1894, in Oakland, California, the son of Mr. and Mrs. J. G. Theiss. George's father was the principal of Zion Lutheran School in Oakland from 1883–1931. After completing the eighth grade of Zion Lutheran School, Rev. Theiss attended California Concordia College from 1909–1913; Concordia College, Milwaukee, Wisconsin, from 1913–1915; and Concordia Seminary, St. Louis, Missouri, from 1915–1918. His first call was to Eugene, Oregon, where he was installed in September of 1918. While in Eugene, Oregon, Rev. Theiss attended the University of Oregon as a graduate student. During his ministry at Eugene, not only was Grace Lutheran Church organized but also a church and parsonage were purchased. In 1923, he received the call to Emanuel Lutheran Church of Los Angeles where the church and parish hall were built in 1925 during his ministry. Rev. Theiss served for a term of three years as executive secretary of the Southern California District Mission Board, from 1936–1939, and held the office of transportation secretary for the District since 1925. In the year 1921, Rev. Theiss married Emma Bertha Ristow of Salem, Oregon, with their union blessed with three children, George Herman Theiss, Margaret Marilyn Theiss, and Phyllis Arlene Theiss.

Not many years passed before the congregation was again confronted with the task of providing more facilities for a growing congregation and an expanding Sunday school. For years, at almost regular intervals, the voters' assembly considered the same subject, *more* facilities; however, the problem was not an easy one to solve. A Building Fund was created and began to grow with $5,827.35 in 1931, $9,601.47 in 1933, and $11,708.40 in 1935. In the April meeting of 1935, the congregation appointed a Building Fund Promotion Committee and a Planning Committee for a new church, with the Building Fund Promotion Committee immediately going to work, reporting in July that in addition to a bequest of $2,000 from the Deden Estate,

Rev. George E. Theiss served First from October 19, 1930, until September 13, 1959. (Pacific Southwest District Archives)

The congregation is again confronted with the task of providing more facilities for a growing congregation.

Rev. Walter F. Fisher was installed on September 20, 1959, as the pastor of First. (Pacific Southwest District Archives)

$6,304 had been pledged by the members. In 1936, the congregation purchased the present property, 100' × 317' at North Los Robles Avenue and Buckeye Street for $7,000, engaging well-known architects Frederick Kennedy Jr. and David Ogilvie for the new, large Mission Revival cathedral-like church. The cornerstone laying ceremonies were held on February 21, 1937, with the new edifice dedicated to God on June 13 of that year.

After the debt of $10,000 on the new church had been reduced to less than $5,000 within three years, the congregation, in April 1940, felt encouraged to proceed with building a parish hall. With the limit set at $20,000, a Promotion Committee was appointed and immediately went to work. In the July meeting in 1940, the committee was able to report that $10,001.50 was available. Scott Quintin was engaged as architect and on December 9, 1940, bids were received with the contract awarded to B. J. Bennell Jr. On May 18, 1941, the new parish hall was dedicated in a joyous service.

In February of 1944, the 1913-vintage Heineman Brothers home at 838 N. Los Robles was purchased as parsonage for the pastor and his family, which today serves as Church Administrative Center. The day school was opened in 1944 with Herbert Gatzke serving as the first principal until 1952. In September of 1948, First Lutheran School building, which now is called "Koch Hall," was dedicated. The official church name was abbreviated to "First Lutheran Church of Pasadena" in April 1951, dropping the name "St. Paul's." The installation of Rev. Richard Z. Meyer as assistant pastor was conducted on September 13, 1953. During his

four and a half years in Pasadena, he performed valuable service to the congregation. In October of 1956, he was married to Carrie Matthias at First Lutheran with their marriage blessed with two children: Kevin Richard and Susan Carol Moyer. During the Lenten season of 1958, he accepted a call to Prince of Peace Lutheran Church in San Diego. One year later on September 13, 1959, Pastor George H. Theiss, preached his farewell sermon, after serving First Lutheran for 30 years during which membership increased from 185 to 750.

On September 20, 1959, Rev. Walter F. Fisher was installed as pastor of First. Pastor Fisher was born at Platte Center, Nebraska on July 23, 1923, the son of the Rev. and Mrs. Henry A. Fisher. He received his early education in the Christian day school of Trinity Lutheran Church, Los Angeles, California, and was confirmed by his father at St. Matthew's Church in East Los Angeles. His preparatory study for the holy ministry was at California Concordia College at Oakland, California. After graduating in 1943, he entered Concordia Seminary, St. Louis, Missouri, for his theological training. He was vicar at Ridgecrest and Trona, California, graduating in 1947 from Concordia Seminary with Bachelor of Arts and Bachelor of Divinity degrees and was awarded a Resident Fellowship at Concordia Seminary, receiving the Master of Sacred Theology degree in June of 1949. He was united in holy matrimony to Miss Dorothy Hesemann of Chicago Heights, Illinois, on June 15, 1947. Their marriage produced two children, Ruth Ann and Thomas Mark. On September 21, 1947, he was ordained and installed as the assistant pastor of Concordia Lutheran Church, Kirkwood, Missouri. Two years later on October 2, 1950, he was installed as the head pastor of the congregation. In 1959, he accepted the call of First Lutheran Church.

First had the privilege of celebrating the 25th anniversary of the dedication of the church building on Sunday, June 3, 1962, with Pastor Theiss, who was pastor of the congregation at the time of the erection of the building, serving as the anniversary speaker at the two services held at 8:30 a.m. and 11 a.m. The congregation previously completed the re-landscaping of the church properties and the erection of a new church sign. The neighborhood had undergone considerable change, becoming a "downtown church" with efforts being made to gear the congregation's program to meet this changing situation as blacks moved into the area. In the fall on October 20, a

First Lutheran's new large, Mission Revival cathedral-like church was designed by the well-known architects, Frederick Kennedy Jr. and David Ogilvie, and dedicated on June 13, 1937. (Pacific Southwest District Archives)

consecration service was conducted on the newly acquired site, 175' × 300', with half prepared as a parking lot for 61 parking cars and the other half used as the new playground. In addition, the congregation purchased a home and five units in a court that projected onto the property, thus assuring opportunity for future expansion. The actual cost of these property acquisitions and improvements was $102,000. The program was the result of studies made by a long-range planning committee during the preceding years.

When Pastor Fisher took the call to Immanuel, a large parish in Elmhurst, Illinois, to serve as head pastor, Rev. Walter C. Gerken was installed as the new pastor of First on March 12, 1967. During the service, Rev. Armin W. Hesse, Faith, Pasadena, delivered the sermon, and the circuit counselor, Rev. Reinhardt E. Schulz, First, Temple City, performed the Rite of Installation. Other pastors participating were Rev. Louis F. Brighton, interim pastor of First, Pasadena, and Rev. Richard W. Gerken, Peace, Bremerton, Washington. Anthems were sung by the adult choir under the direction of Walter J. Koch, minister of music and organist, and the day school choir, directed by Hubert O. Firnhaber, principal.

Rev. Walter C. Gerken was born in Leduc, Alberta, Canada, son of Rev. and Mrs. August Gerken, where he attended parochial schools, graduating from Concordia Seminary, St. Louis, in 1937. His first parish was in Thawville, Illinois. While serving as an Army chaplain for five years, he attained the rank of major. In 1960, he became assistant executive director of the Lutheran Deaconess Association and since 1961 served as its executive director. Pastor Gerken married Elizabeth Hagemann of St. Louis. Their five children were Pauline, wife of Rev. Carl M. Kummer; Faith; Richard, a pastor of Peace, Bremerton, Washington; Herbert, a missionary-at-large, in Rockford, Illinois; David, a vicar at Saint Stephen, Hickory, North Carolina; and John, employed at General Electric in Fort Wayne. They had six grandchildren, and he also had three brothers in the ministry: Theodore, La Grange, Illinois; Erwin, Puyallup, Washington; and Oscar, Cape Girardeau, Missouri.

With the growth of the day school, a new educational building, called the "North School Building" today, was dedicated on October 18, 1970, where Dr. Erwin Kurth was the speaker and Dr. Herman Meyerhoff, counselor of Christian education for the Southern California District, gave additional remarks. The congregation's senior

choir, children's choir, and the Lutheran Laymen's League chorus provided music for the service. By 1977 with decreased enrollment, the congregation decided to close the school in June after providing the children of the congregation a Christian education since 1944.

When Pastor Gerken left to take the call to Our Savior First Lutheran in Granada Hills, Rev. Carl R. Lampitt from Grace English Lutheran Church in Pine Bluff, Wyoming, was installed on March 28, 1976, who was followed by Rev. Robert O. Faga of St. Paul, Ashland, Kentucky, in December of 1981. Pastor Faga was born in Audubon County, Iowa, on September 19, 1929. Before entering Concordia Seminary at Springfield, Illinois, he served in the United States Air Force from 1948–1951, marrying Sonnie Jean Remmeres on November 27, 1954, with their union blessed with five children. Following his ordination at St. John's in Adair, Iowa, in 1961, he served a mission in Montgomery, Alabama, along with Selma Academy and College. In 1962, he had dual parishes at St. Paul's, Hackensack, and Emmanuel, Backus, Minnesota, followed by St. Paul's, Latimer, Iowa, and Our Savior, Leon, Iowa.

During his tenure as pastor, the neighborhood surrounding the church experienced a shift in demographics with a Hispanic population moving in. Seeing a need to minister to this new group, First decided to do work among the Hispanics. To help support this new ministry, the congregation received $5,000 from New Hope Lutheran Church in Minnesota. Many calls were issued with the Rev. Victor M. Aldaña accepting it to be missionary-at-large for the Hispanic community in Pasadena, being installed on September 24, 1989.

Pastor Aldaña was born on February 14, 1954, in Guatemala receiving his Bachelor of Science from Colegio de Ilustración of Guatemala in 1972. He also received his Bachelor in Theology with emphasis in church growth and evangelism from the Presbyterian Theological Seminary of Guatemala, beginning his ministry in Guatemala in 1972 several weeks after he entered the seminary. He planted two churches in Guatemala, remaining there as pastor for nine years. In 1978, he married Emma Haydee; they were blessed with three children: Victor Jr., Cindy, and Heidi Karina. He became acquainted with the Lutheran church in 1981, when he met Rev. Juan Martin, receiving instruction in doctrine under him, becoming a member of Holy Trinity Lutheran Church in Chicago, Illinois. He entered the Lutheran Institute for Hispanic Ministry in 1985, finishing his formal

Rev. Walter C. Gerken was installed as the new pastor of First on March 12, 1967. (Pacific Southwest District Archives)

Rev. Robert O. Faga became pastor of First in December 1981, serving until his retirement on September 30, 1991. (Pacific Southwest District Archives)

Rav. Aldaña begins work among the Hispancs in the neighborhood in 1989.

Rev. Victor M. Aldaña was installed on September 24, 1989, as missionary-at-large for the Hispanic community in Pasadena. (Pacific Southwest District Archives)

La Santisima Trinidad Mission has its beginning in August 1989.

A Bible study in the Aldaña home was the basis for missionary work in this new ministry. (Pacific Southwest District Archives)

studies in 1987. For his vicarage year, he was assigned to Emmanuel Lutheran Church in Aurora, Illinois, under the supervision of the pastor, Rev. Burneal Fick. During his vicarage year, he started a Hispanic mission, Cristo Principe de Paz, under the auspices of Emmanuel and St. Paul's Lutheran churches in Aurora. He was issued a call by Emmanuel and St. Paul's Lutheran churches and was ordained and installed as pastor of Cristo Principe de Paz, on March 6, 1988.

La Santisima Trinidad Mission had its beginning in August 1989, when Pastor Aldaña initiated his work the month before he was installed on September 24, by walking through the area, introducing himself and explaining the Lutheran mission to Hispanics. Noting those expressing an interest, he returned to visit, leading prospects in Bible study and explaining what the Lutheran church teaches. A telephone ministry for Pasadena and neighboring communities was established in October "to provide a friendly voice in response to spiritual needs." On December 18, 1990, members of First Lutheran brought groceries as a price of admission to a fellowship dinner. The groceries and money were distributed through the auspices of a newly formed Hispanic Lutheran congregation. Pastor Aldaña, his wife, Emma, and their children Victor Jr., Cindy, and Heidi, all participated in small-group Bible studies involving 20 residents of the community by February of 1990. His strategy or ministry philosophy was to make disciples for Christ through home Bible studies and others types of evangelism. He regularly visited all hospitals in the community and volunteered his services to the Pasadena Police Department to assist in communicating with Hispanics. He also made himself available to community agencies to assist people with problems with immigration, employment, and drug addiction.

The first Spanish worship service was conducted on February 11, 1990, under the direction of Pastor Aldaña in the facilities of First Lutheran. Worship services averaged 32 to 40 people with 49 communicant members and 59 baptized members. By 1992, due to some problems at the Hispanic mission, Pastor Aldaña's ministry was terminated. After Pastor Faga retired on September 30, 1991, as the pastor of First during a long pastoral vacancy, September 1991 to June 1994, First was lovingly led by interim pastors, Rev. August Hauptman and Rev. Dr. Lee Settgast with Rev. Erwin Norden conducting a shut-in visitation program. Also, during the vacancy period, the congregation celebrated its 100th anniversary on November 8, 1992, with former pastors, Rev. R. Z. Meyer and Rev. Walter Fisher, participating in the service, and at Easter of 1994, a two-day "Fun Day" was conducted for the community. On June 26, 1994, the congregation's prayers were answered when Rev. Christopher Schaar was installed as pastor of the church.

Pastor Schaar was born in Chicago, Illinois, on June 26, 1968, receiving his bachelor's degree from Christ College, Irvine, in 1990. After graduating from Concordia Seminary, St. Louis, Missouri, in 1994, he was ordained at the worship center of Christ College, Irvine, and installed as pastor of First and Iglesia Primera of Pasadena. The following year, 1995, seeing a need to reach the community, a member, Matthew Helmkamp, started a weekly community basketball program, which today is called the "Good Friday Youth Outreach" with attendance at times exceeding 60 youth. On August 25, 1996, Director of Christian Education Thomas Edelen was installed as director of youth and community outreach ministries with the specific purpose of starting an outreach to Hispanics who were 70 percent of the neighborhood where he directed a Spanish Ministry until 1998. Before coming to First, he served for two years in Venezuela. The vibrant youth program attracted youth and volunteers alike, having an average attendance of 44, and joined with outside organizations to provide community service in many areas.

At a meeting at Historic Trinity Lutheran Church in Detroit, Michigan, in October of 1996, First Lutheran Church became a founder of the Association of Downtown Lutheran Churches. In June of the following year, First celebrated its 105th anniversary, which included Rev. Dr. Oswald Hoffmann, the former "Lutheran Hour" speaker, as the preacher followed by a bratwurst barbecue on the school field. The Family Resource Center,

Rev. Christopher Schaar (right) was installed on June 26, 1994, pictured with Dr. Loren Kramer, District President, in 1997. (Pacific Southwest District Archives)

a cooperative community program between First Lutheran Church and The Sycamores, was opened in July of 1998, being housed in "Koch Hall." On September 27, 1998, a formal rededication of "Koch Hall" as the Family Resource Center took placed on the building's 50th anniversary.

With the installation of Maria Garcia-Bratton as director of community outreach ministries on January 9, 2000, the Hispanic outreach program began again. At the beginning of Maria's work, Spanish services were conducted, but few people attended. She then began posting notices on telephone poles around the church advertising the Spanish Bible class. Through the "Good Friday" youth outreach, two children attended Sunday school. On May 31, 2002, ESL classes were started on the church campus with a total of nine people meeting three days a week for two hours. Through these classes, new friendships were formed. Also, a Thursday morning Spanish Bible class was formed. By May, two ESL classes had been formed, bringing more people into the Resource Center. As a means of outreach, the mission was expanding its ESL class offerings as well as beginning a citizenship preparation class. Maria continued trying to connect with the parents of children who participated in the congregation's "Good Friday" youth outreach. The congregation's goal was to continue to be not only a social resource in the community but a spiritual resource as well. Food baskets were provided during special holidays at Thanksgiving and Christmas.

Christmas Festival at First Lutheran with children breaking the piñata.

The biggest opportunity for outreach during the first quarter of 2001 was when two Spanish devotional services were held on Ash Wednesday with 13 people at the second service. During Holy Week, Maria made home visits to some of the families that attended Festival de Navidad in December of 2000 with the children given punch out scenes of the Resurrection. The parents were given "Portales de Ordción" ("Portals of Prayer") as well as invited to Maundy Thursday, Good Friday, and Easter services. While work was going on in the Hispanic community, another struggle was taking place in the congregation as there was a rumor spreading that the Pasadena Unified School District needed a new public school in the area of First Lutheran and wanted to take the church's buildings by eminent domain for the new school. After a great deal of letter writing and meetings with city officials, the Pasadena City Council, on April 23, 2001, designated First Lutheran's church building, parish hall, and "Koch Hall" as Cultural Heritage Landmarks thus saving them from the "wrecker's ball." In April of 2001, an extensive remodeling of the gymnasium in the parish hall was completed with the project funded by special gifts collected in honor of First Lutheran's 109th anniversary. On December 16, the annual Festival de Navidad was hosted with a total of 173 people in attendance; 129 were Spanish-speaking people.

Pasadena City Council designated First Lutheran's church building, parish hall, and "Koch Hall" as Cultural Heritage Landmarks.

Rev. Marcelo Gómez, the new Hispanic pastor of First, was installed in May 2004.

They enjoyed an afternoon of fun and games, listening to Mariachis, free food, a raffle of two grand prizes, and a Christmas message shared with them in English and Spanish. On Christmas Eve, mothers from the ESL classes came to the Jazz Candlelight Service bringing not only their children but also nieces and nephews.

At the beginning of 2002, Maria made changes in the outreach program by revamping the ESL classes, which grew to 25 students, and she added a preparatory citizenship class with an average attendance of four. On June 2, First Lutheran celebrated its 110th anniversary, with Rev. Dr. Jacob A. O. Preus III, president of Concordia University Irvine, as preacher. Other special events celebrated at this time included the 65th anniversary of the beautiful sanctuary, and the rededication of the parish hall, 61 years after the original dedication. The anniversary gifts that were collected established a scholarship endowment for church-work students at Concordia University, Irvine.

During the summer, Aaron Rosales Smith, a 2002 graduate of Concordia University Irvine, was a summer intern at the church, a full-time staff member, to begin developing a "Word-and-Sacrament Ministry" in Spanish, working closely with Maria Bratton under the pastoral auspices of Pastor Schaar, where he did follow-up on referrals, leading Bible studies, and worship services in Spanish. Aaron lived in the gymnasium at the church, shopped in the local stores, washed his clothes at the neighborhood *lavanderia*, and walked the neighborhood, talking with people daily. Each day he opened the sanctuary where people came to pray. On Sunday, August 18, a special collection of $1,034 was gathered to support Aaron as he began his studies at Concordia Seminary, St. Louis. Through Aid Association for Lutherans, Branch #1323 "Helping Hands" matching dollars, he received $2,063. After completing his work in August, Aaron began his studies for the ministry by attending Concordia Seminary, St. Louis.

In 2003, Historic First Lutheran joined the Los Angeles Nehemiah Project, making it one of 12 Los Angeles urban churches "Partnering Together in the Gospel." Also during the year, Maria Bratton left her position as the church's community outreach director. During the summer, Aaron Rosales Smith returned to First to continue his work in the community. First Lutheran continues to provide services to the community through the Food Pantry, ESL classes, tutoring, citizenship classes, computer lab, youth programs, summer camp, and Christmas festivals. In April of 2004, the congregation's prayers were answered when Rev. Marcelo Gómez of Iglesia Luterana San Pablo of Harvard, Illinois, accepted the call to serve as missionary/church planter for First Lutheran and the Nehemiah Project, leaving Illinois during April to begin his ministry in Pasadena the first of May, opening a new chapter in the Hispanic work at First.

Holy Cross Lutheran Church
Holy Cross Hispanic Church
La Puente, California

The city of La Puente, Spanish for "the bridge," is located on Puente Creek, at the foot of the Puente Hills near Los Angeles, with a population today of 41,063, of which 83 percent are Hispanic and 6 percent are Anglos. The area's major manufacturers produce air-conditioning equipment, chemicals, and processed food. The city, once part of large La Puente Rancho, was established by a group of 25 people; 3 were scientists, half, including "Don Benito" Wilson, were settlers; and the others were adventurers. John Temple and William Workman, two Taos miners, led the group. The group drove sheep across the blistering desert, came through the Cajón Pass, and camped at Mission San Gabriel on November 25, 1841. Their arrival aroused the suspicions of the Mexicans as they thought they were political "meddlers." Within four years, Workman and Rowland allayed the fears of the Mexican government and were granted a tract of 48,000 acres, known as the La Puente Rancho.

From this rancho developed the small town of Puente, a commercial center for crop farming, poultry, and cattle raising. After World War II, the area changed from agriculture to tracts of middle class homes, with the small town of Puente incorporated as the city of La Puente in 1956 after thousands of families, almost all with children purchased the thousands of new homes erected in the new community. As the period of the late 1950s and early 1960s was a time of unprecedented housing construction throughout the United States, Southern California was no exception, and particularly the San Gabriel Valley, the biggest booming area in the country. Construction of the San Bernardino Freeway with easy access to Los Angeles, attracted to La Puente not only residents of Los Angeles but also many newcomers from "back East" coming to California at the rate of 2,000 per day. Most three-bedroom homes in the area sold for $10,000 to $12,000 with as little as $500 for a down payment with veterans of the armed services buying a home for a mere $99 closing cost. By 1956, La Puente had earned the nickname "kidsville, U.S.A," as a typical cul-de-sac of 8 to 10 homes had 40 or more children romping around—more children per square mile than anywhere else in the United States. Since the community building of this period presented a challenge to the people of The Lutheran Church—Missouri Synod, a challenge to which the Synod members did not fail to respond, several 100 new congregations were established during this time. In 1955, the Southern California District Mission Board purchased sites for churches in La Puente and Hacienda Heights. The three-acre site that became the property of Holy Cross Lutheran Church was purchased for $30,000. On the site stood two old, small, frame residences and a barn. Amar Road, known as Elliot Street then, was a two-lane country road with a row of walnut trees standing where crepe myrtles screen the church from Amar Road today.

Rev. Herbert Schulenburg, missionary-at-large in La Puente in 1955. (Pacific Southwest District Archives)

The Mission Board called Rev. Herbert Schulenburg, a 1933 graduate of Concordia Seminary at St. Louis who served Mt. Calvary in Holdrege and Zion in Imperial, Nebraska, and St. John's in Sherwood, Ohio, to serve as missionary-at-large, with the directive to organize a congregation. After Pastor Schulenburg arrived in La Puente on July 26, 1955, taking up residence on Amar Road, he canvassed the neighborhood, making calls on Lutherans, mostly members of Immanuel Lutheran in West Covina, which had organized in 1954. With the help of Mr. Paul Mueller, Mr. Sharp, and Mr. Dale Reeves, the pastor and his family prepared the two dilapidated residences for use as church and Sunday school.

In October, pastors from the valley came to help demolish the old barn on the property. While hauling off debris from the barn, their good will was somewhat tried by a local policeman who gave them a ticket for letting the remnants of the barn protrude from the truck beyond legal limits. With the help of his clergy brothers, Pastor Schulenburg conducted the first service in the little renovated house on October 16, 1955, where there were 22 people in attendance with 18 in Sunday school. At a second service in the afternoon, Pastor Schulenburg was commissioned with his son, Mark Schulenburg, playing the organ for the services. By the end of 1955, the congregation consisted of 10 families, 18 communicants and 16 baptized members with a Sunday school of 58.

The Workman home in the 1880s with Mr. William Workman standing on the front porch. (SECURITY PACIFIC COLLECTION/Los Angeles Public Library)

At the beginning of 1956, the average Sunday attendance was 46. By June, it had climbed to 68, making a second service necessary. Also in June, 90 children attended Vacation Bible School. By the end of year, the average Sunday attendance was 96 with 143 enrolled in Sunday school having an average attendance of 86 children. On November 25, the congregation was officially organized as Holy Cross Lutheran Church of La Puente with 38 charter members, having also purchased a parsonage at 14626 Ansford in Hacienda Heights for $16,000. With the increase in attendance at services in the old buildings, a great strain was put on the physical facilities with the floor in the little house of worship beginning to sag from the sheer weight of people attending, necessitating reinforcing the floors. During the winter rains, the roof leaked with steady drips falling from the ceiling during Sunday services. Because the house was so small, some people sat under umbrellas while others stood on the front porch, as there was no seating inside. By 1957, the capacity of both of the older buildings was overtaxed as the church and a Sunday school had grown. The men removed several interior walls to make an L-shaped room for worship. In May, the congregation received generous gifts of an altar, pulpit, lectern, and baptismal font from St. Matthew's Lutheran Church in East Los Angeles, a congregation that had been disbanded.

The summer of 1957 marked the end of the services of Pastor Herbert Schulenburg to Holy Cross as he had been called by the Mission Board as missionary-at-large, a non-permanent arrangement, and he subsequently accepted a call to Yucaipa, California. Rev. Paul Hinrichs, the first called pastor, took over the parish in September 1957. Pastor Hinrichs went to La Puente from Aiken, South Carolina, where he had served a mission congregation for five years. He was the youngest of Rev. and Mrs. Carl Hinrichs' eight children, who was born in Marengo, Iowa. While attending Concordia College in St. Paul, Minnesota, he mixed studying for the ministry and playing pro ball. In 1948, he was picked up by the New York Yankees and later played for the Boston Red Sox, graduating from Concordia Seminary, St. Louis, in 1950. He married the former Frances Rauscher of St. Louis on December 16, 1948, with the marriage blessed with three children, Mark, Rebecca, and Heidi, at the time. He was installed as the first resident pastor of Holy Cross Lutheran Mission of La Puente on Sunday, September 1, at 4:00 p.m. with services conducted outdoors on the church property behind the old house that was used for worship services. The speaker for the service was Rev. James Berner of Pomona, the liturgist was Rev. William Tensmeyer of West Covina, and the officiant was Rev. Lawrence P. Rudolph of Ontario.

At the time of the installation, the congregation numbered 126 communicants with 160 children filling the two little houses, which were "bursting at the seams." Sunday school classes were taught "back to back" indoors with many classes spilling outside in the warm weather. In cold weather to avoid the "organized pandemonium," one teacher taught her class in her station wagon. With the need for larger facilities paramount in the congregation's mind in 1958, Architect O. J Bruer drew plans from which a model was made showing the future church plant: the church/parish hall

The old house on three acres of land that was used as the first chapel of Holy Cross. (Pacific Southwest District Archives)

The first altar used for services in the old house on Amar Road. (Pacific Southwest District Archives)

Rev. Paul Hinrichs, the first called pastor of Holy Cross, assumed the pastorate in September of 1957. (Pacific Southwest District Archives)

with 250 seating, the adjoining 8-classroom Sunday school unit, kitchen, sacristy, and office. At the time, the church numbered 132 communicant members with a Sunday school enrollment of 250. On February 16, 1958, groundbreaking ceremonies were conducted for the new chapel. The chapel and Sunday school wing were constructed at an approximate cost of $55,000, largely with volunteer labor, under the supervision of Dale Reeves, an elder of the congregation who was hired as full-time supervisor of construction. The men of the congregation, who gave over 3,000 hours of voluntary labor, would come to the church property at 4:00 a.m., put in a few hours of work, then went to their daily place of employment, returning after supper to work until 10:00 p.m. Weekends saw many volunteers at work with even the ladies painting and scraping putty and paint from window panes. By November 27, Thanksgiving Day, construction

was far enough along to enable the congregation to worship in the unfinished building.

On March 1, 1959, Holy Cross formally dedicated its new house of worship with a dedicatory service at 10:45 a.m., conducted by Pastor Hinrichs. The public dedication service was held at 3:30 p.m., with Circuit Visitor L. P. Rudolph of Ontario delivering the sermon. After the festival service, members of the Lutheran Women's Missionary League served refreshments in the Sunday school rooms. Two services, 8:00 a.m. and 10:45 a.m., had to be conducted each Sunday to accommodate the growing congregation. The Sunday school department averaged almost 200 children filling not only the new Sunday school rooms but also the 2 small houses on the property. Because La Puente was a rapidly expanding community with a congregation consisting mostly of young couples with children, the Sunday school enrollment continued to grow each Sunday.

By January of 1961, the parish had grown to 325 communicants, 595 baptized members, and 23 voters with church attendance averaging 283 per Sunday and Sunday school averaging 350 taught by 30 teachers. Plans were made to build a new Sunday school wing. Since the nave could accommodate only 250 people, the congregation decided to lengthen the nave, adding 18 feet to its north end, and also to add a "youth wing" parallel to the Sunday school wing, again recruiting volunteers who gave many hours and weeks completing the second project at a cost of $15,000. The dedication was on November 23, 1961. Pastor Hinrichs designed the unique columnar backdrop to the chancel with the Holy Spirit emblem above the al-

Holy Cross's new house of worship with Luther's seal above the entrance was dedicated on March 1, 1959. (Pacific Southwest District Archives)

The interior of Holy Cross with the altar, pulpit, lectern, and baptismal font, gifts from St. Matthew's Church in East Los Angeles. (Pacific Southwest District Archives)

Rev. Waldemar Petzoldt became the second pastor of Holy Cross on July 7, 1963, remaining until 1965. (Pacific Southwest District Archives)

Rev. Hilmar T. Rosenberg was installed on November 14, 1965, as the third pastor of Holy Cross serving until his retirement in 1971. (Pacific Southwest District Archives)

tar. Allen Biang constructed the Luther seal above the church's main entrance. The building additions had barely kept pace with the congregation's growth, which had 420 communicants with 490 children enrolled in the Sunday school and 65 enrolled in the Bible classes. The church building plus the two small houses were filled to maximum capacity each Sunday.

When Pastor Hinrichs accepted a call to Trinity Lutheran Church, Manchester, Missouri, in November of 1962, two retired pastors, Henry Kringel and Theodore Gohlke, a former missionary to Brazil, served the congregation. On July 7, 1963, Rev. Waldemar Petzoldt, a graduate of Concordia Seminary, St. Louis, who did graduate work at Pacific Lutheran Seminary, Berkeley, and had served parishes in St. Francis, Kansas, and Salinas, California, became the second pastor of Holy Cross. He was born in Perry County, Missouri, on November 9, 1927. Following his graduation from the seminary, he married Sandra Richter of Quincy, Illinois, with their marriage blessed with two children, Rhonda and John, at the time he was installed. He faithfully visited the members and led the congregation in establishing a Helping Hand Fund, which provided interest-free loans to members in need. In the two years of Pastor Petzoldt's tenure, Holy Cross reached into its Sunday school membership 3 times, baptizing 26 members each time. Petzoldt accepted a call to Lompoc, California, in April 1965. Once again the congregation was without a pastor with services conducted during this period by pastors Lawrence Wachholz, Oswald Waech, and George Theiss.

The third shepherd at La Puente was Rev. Hilmar T. Rosenberg from Williamsburg, Iowa, where he had served St. Paul's Church the previous seven and one-half years. Earlier, he had held pastorates in the mid-west and served as corresponding radio secretary for the International Lutheran Hour and director of music for Radio Station KFUO. Pastor and Mrs. Rosenberg had three children: Lois, who was a parochial school teacher at First Lutheran, Long Beach; Robert, who was in his final year at Concordia Seminary, St. Louis; and Richard Mark, who was a junior at Concordia Teachers College, River Forest.

When Pastor Rosenberg was installed on November 14, 1965, the congregation was comprised of 465 communicants with the Sunday school enrollment decreasing to 371, after reaching its peak in 1962. With the establishment of sister congregations in Hacienda Heights and Walnut, some

members had either transferred or were "on the move," being transferred elsewhere by employers or simply prospering and buying larger homes in other communities.

In 1967, the congregation numbered 484 communicants with 724 baptized souls. That year the congregation razed the smaller of the two frame residences on the property. In 1969, the congregation refinanced its indebtedness and added a $10,000 construction and remodeling project to its goals. A parking lot was constructed west of the church, carpeting was installed in the chancel, a new memeograph machine was purchased, and plans were laid to add a storage shed to the church. Following the retirement of Pastor Rosenberg at the end of 1971, Pastor Melvin Gohdes served as vacancy pastor during the first half of 1972. On July 9, 1972, Rev. Paul Rosnau became the fourth and final resident pastor.

Rev. Paul O. Rosnau was born in Chicago, Illinois, on March 11, 1931, the eldest of two sons of Mr. and Mrs. Otto Rosnau where he attended Lutheran elementary schools and Luther Institute in Chicago. He attended Concordia High School in Milwaukee, Wisconsin, and studied two years at Concordia Jr. College at the same campus, entering Concordia Seminary, St. Louis, in the fall of 1951. He spent his vicarage at Zion, Belleville, Illinois. His first call was as missionary-at-large in San Antonio, Texas, where he was ordained at St. Paul's, San Antonio, on July 29, 1956. By August, Immanuel congregation was organized and on June 1, 1958, the church building was dedicated. On June 9, 1956, he was united in marriage to Theola (Sue) Kulpa of St. Louis, with their marriage blessed with four children: Lynn, Alan, Dean, and Jill. Their love of sacred music brought them together as they met while singing in the St. Louis Bach Society Choir. In 1961, Pastor Rosnau accepted a call to Trinity, Hinsdale, Illinois, serving until 1964, when he accepted a position at Concordia Publishing House, St. Louis, Missouri, as proofreader and manuscript editor contributing several devotional studies to the *My Devotions* publication. Pastor Rosnau and his family moved to California in 1969 where took a position as proofreader at National Timemaster Corporation in Commerce, becoming members of Holy Cross, La Puente. Longing to return to the parish ministry, he accepted the call to Holy Cross as their pastor.

In January 1973, the congregation demolished the original house of worship with a few pushes of a bulldozer and later that year, constructed the storage shed that was planned earlier. During the summers of 1972 through 1979, a week of camping for the young people at Yosemite National Park was shared with the young people from Holy Trinity in Hacienda Heights.

By the 1980s, Holy Cross's Sunday School was but a shadow of its former size, due to such factors as few members having children at home any longer and many families of the community having no tradition of Sunday school although La Puente was still a "kidsville." On May 10, 1987, Holy Cross sustained smoke and soot damage during an arson fire set in the church, when the arsonist broke a window, poured gasoline, and ignited it. In 1990, the congregation opened its doors to the Lutheran Braille Workers as it prepared to become an assembly and distribution center for Circuit 11, specializing in large print literature.

By 1996 with Holy Cross sitting in the midst of a growing Hispanic community, the congregation was seriously considering how they could reach out to this community. Rev. Ken Behnken, the District's administrative assistant to the president–missions, met with them in January to help them begin this process and was assisted by Rev. Frank Brundige of Bell Gardens, who had been working with the congregation. On November 3, 1996, Young Dae Kim, who was in the Korean colloquy program, held the first Korean service at Holy Cross for the Korean ministry of the Eastern United Korean Church. With the retirement of Pastor Rosnau at the end of 1996, the English congregation disbanded, turning over its facilities to the District in January of 1997, allowing the two new ministries, the Spanish and the Korean, to begin work in the buildings.

In 1997 after Pastor Jesús Martinez left La Santa Cruz in Los Angeles, he was contracted to do Hispanic ministry at Holy Cross in La Puente, which was situated in a middle class Hispanic neighborhood. Due to a conflict with the Koreans, some of the members who came with him from La Santa Cruz stopped attending church. In 1998, Pastor Martinez applied for a $10,000 Lutheran Brotherhood Grant with the goal of establishing a Lutheran Hispanic congregation by 2005 that would "have and share their life in Christ with all people" which they received in 1999. At the time, there was an average of 15 people attending worship services. During 1998, the congregation along with a youth team from Concordia University helped canvass the neighborhood, visiting and leaving fliers at 600 homes. They participated in

the Lutheran Laymen's League program, "Living for Tomorrow," and the Spanish equivalent, "Viviendo Sabiamente," with the results of 18 leads in Spanish-speaking homes and about 30 leads in English-speaking homes, mailing the appropriate materials to the 48 homes. In four homes, materials were hand delivered with the others followed up with a personal visit. Several of the visits resulted in Bible studies with the parents. After canvassing the neighborhood and studying the demographic information, the mission decided to reach primarily the English-speaking Hispanics who were in the majority in the community with the long-range goal to have a congregation of all nations.

There were six committed and dedicated Christians who were the core group for the English-speaking ministry with a worship service held every Sunday in English. When Baptisms were scheduled on Sundays, there were usually 45 people in attendance. Also, in the mission were several Spanish-speaking families who were leaders, having several Spanish worship services for them, which were well attended. In September of 1998, one Spanish worship service per month was scheduled until they were able to gather more Spanish-speaking families. The mission had a Christmas dinner, a picnic, and a barbecue.

Pastor Martinez conducted five small-group Bible studies in the community. He identified the natural leaders who had influence in their network of family and friends and trained those persons, with the leaders in turn ministering to the people in their network. Each family was encouraged to utilize their primary responsibility of teaching their children, using Martin Luther's *Small Catechism* and *A Child's Garden of Bible Stories* by Arthur W. Gross to prepare them for First Communion. Each father and mother were shown the materials and taught how to use them in their homes. When Pastor Martinez visited homes, he modeled how to utilize the materials and monitored the progress of the children. At the time, there were six children who would make their First Communion in May of 1999. He had 12 adults and 8 youth preparing for Confirmation. By 1999, he was ministering to 20 families with an average attendance of 20 at worship services. At the end of the year, eight children attended the Saturday Bible study classes, representing five families. By the year 2000, the mission consisted of people who resided in the community: a Japanese-American woman, a black man and his wife, several Anglo women, and the rest were Mexican-Americans. Pastor Martinez

Rev. Paul O. Rosnau was installed on July 9, 1972, becoming the fourth and final resident pastor of Holy Cross. (Pacific Southwest District Archives)

Pastor Jesús Martinez came to Holy Cross in 1997 to do work among the Hispanics in the area. (Pacific Southwest District Archives)

and his flock continued to minister to the people of La Puente, working to build a congregation for "all nations."

Following Pastor Martinez's retirement in the summer of 2003, the small group he had assembled disbanded. Pastor Brundige of Bell Gardens took the challenge of starting a Hispanic church by beginning Bible study classes in Holy Cross's old building. This Bible study class was a result of his three years (1987–1990) ministry at La Santa Cruz in East Los Angeles where he met the Margarito Castellano family. Mr. Castellano had worked in the meat market across the street from La Santa Cruz. Originally the family had lived in East Los Angeles but moved to Baldwin Park where they now reside. Over the years, Pastor Brundige conducted a Bible study in their home with family, neighbors, and friends attending. The family continued going to church in East Los Angeles, eventually attending services between Holy Cross in La Puente and San Pedro y San Pablo in Bell Gardens.

In 2002, Pastor Brundige conducted another Bible study in the home of Margarito and Rosario Castellano in Baldwin Park. In the winter of that year, the Bible study group decided on a mission plan which involved visiting different churches to see how they ministered to the Hispanic population around Holy Cross in La Puente, as well as visiting schools, shopping centers, the city hall, and a swap meet, thus carrying out the mission plan reaffirming the necessity of beginning work in Spanish and English at Holy Cross.

The Bible study group began meeting at Holy Cross after Easter of 2003 where they continued to walk the area around the church to meet the neighbors, beginning a Bible study class at the church on Tuesday evenings at 7:30 p.m. By the end of 2003, the Bible class had an attendance of between 12 to 19 people. With an offering ranging from $20 to $50 per week, they gave a tithe to the District for missions, paid the District $50 per month for use of Holy Cross's facilities, and compensated Pastor Brundige with $40 for gas mileage.

The group not only planned open house events such as yard sales and Posadas to get acquainted with the neighbors in the area of the church but they also assumed the responsibility of cleaning the sections of the church building they were utilizing. An English Bible study was begun in 2003 with Pastor Jesús Martinez, the retired pastor of Holy Cross, teaching the class, using the series "That I May Know Him." Margarito and Rosario Castellano assumed the role of teaching the Spanish Bible class allowing Pastor Brundige to teach the children and youth the Bible and the Catechism, with the younger children remaining with their parents. Pastor Brundige began the evening with devotions in the Spanish Bible class using hymns, the Kyrie, Lord's Prayer, Apostles' Creed, prayers, and a small section of the Catechism. After teaching the children and youth, he ended the evening with the English Bible class's devotions using responsive prayers from *Lutheran Worship*, Lord's Prayer, Apostles' Creed, prayers, and singing of hymns with the children and youth participating in both the Bible class's devotions. At the close of both the Spanish and English Bible classes, there was a group prayer with all people participating by adding their own petitions.

The lay people were active and supportive in planning a neighborhood walk the spring of 2004, as well as a yard sale and a car wash for outreach. They also assisted with repairs, upkeep, and maintenance of the buildings. The group continued tithing to the District missions, giving the District $50 for the use of the facilities, and giving $100 to San Pedro y San Pablo for the pastoral assistance given by Pastor Brundige. The mission was supported by 15 to 20 people coming from 6 families who supported it with offerings of $30 to $50 per week. One of the goals for 2004 was to have First Communion and Confirmation of the youth and receive adults into the mission by Profession of Faith. The prayer of the mission is to engage the neighborhood in Bible study and eventually worship services on Sundays.

In 2003, Pastor Brundige of Bell Gardens takes the challenge of starting a Hispanic church by beginning Bible study classes in Holy Cross's old building.

Trinity Lutheran Church
Iglesia Luterana Trinidad
Central Trinity Lutheran Church
Fuente De Agua Viva
Los Angeles, California

With Trinity's property at Eighteenth and Cherry in downtown Los Angeles sold in 1959 to the State of California and with all the buildings demolished to make way for the Harbor and Santa Monica freeway interchange, the congregation moved farther west to 987 Gramercy Place at Olympic Boulevard and South Wilton Place to begin a new ministry and continued to operate the day school. The beautiful new church designed by Walter Hagendohm, a member of Synod's Committee on Church Architecture, was dedicated on May 8, 1960. In the fall on a Sunday afternoon, October 23, Dr. Irene Robertson, head of the organ department of the University of Southern California, presented a recital dedicating the rebuilt organ. The Holzinger Organ Company of Los Angeles rebuilt the Austin pipe organ from "old Trinity" at Eighteenth and Cherry. The 3-manual, 26 rank organ was especially designed for the service of the church of the Reformation. That Christmas on December 18 at 4:00 p.m., a candlelight service was presented by the choir under the direction of Mr. Theophil M. Goehring.

In June of 1961, Pastor Seebeck resigned as pastor of Trinity. On January 14, 1962, Rev. Harold Maleske, professor of sociology at Concordia Senior College of Fort Wayne, Indiana, was installed as Trinity's fifth pastor. He was born in Chicago, Illinois, on March 17, 1916. Following his graduation from Concordia College, Milwaukee, Wisconsin, in 1936, he attended Concordia Seminary in St. Louis, graduating in 1940. He served Trinity, Norman, Oklahoma, for one year following his graduation. In 1941, he was ordained and installed at Trinity, Paw Paw, Michigan, and married Dorothy C. Kuhlman on November 12, 1941, with their marriage blessed with four children, Allen, Kenneth, Madeline, and Michael. During the war, he was on leave from Trinity to serve as a chaplain in the U.S. Army and Air Force. In 1948, he went to Trinity, Center Line, Michigan, where he served until 1955. He moved to Northbrook, Illinois, serving Grace until 1958, when he went to Concordia Senior College at Fort Wayne where he taught for three years. He received a Master of Arts degree in sociology from Wayne State University and a Ph.D. in social psychology from the University of Southern California and was an author of the book, *Natural Therapy,* which was a culmination of 30 years of research and counseling. In 1971, Pas-

Trinity's fourth house of worship was designed by Walter Hagendohm. (*Pacific Southwest District Archives*)

The striking interior of the new church located at 987 Gramercy Place with the marble-angel baptismal font from the old church on the left. (*Pacific Southwest District Archives*)

Rev. and Mrs. Harold Maleske, at the twenty-fifth anniversaries of his ordination and their wedding. He was Trinity's fifth pastor, serving from 1962 until 1971. (Pacific Southwest District Archives)

tor Maleske left Trinity to accept a teaching position at Texas State University and in 1975 accepted a teaching position at Concordia Teachers College, River Forest, Illinois.

Rev. Adam D. Lautenschlager was installed as the full-time pastor in 1972 after serving Trinity as assistant pastor during 1957 to 1965 and 1967 to 1972, while teaching at Lutheran High School in Los Angeles. He was born on January 27, 1916, in Endicott, Washington, attending one-room schools around Endicott and Monse, Washington. He completed his high school education at Concordia, Portland, Oregon, followed by his graduation from California Concordia in Oakland in 1936. After graduating from Concordia Seminary at St. Louis in 1940, he served congregations at Idaho Falls, Idaho; Camos, Washington; Rupert, Idaho; and Twin Falls, Idaho. While doing his vicarage in a rural congregation, Trinity near Buhl, Idaho, he met Arlene Lutz and later married her on August 3, 1941, with their marriage blessed with two children, William and Sharon. In 1953, he was called to teach at Los Angeles Lutheran High School where he served until 1965, accepting a call to three parishes in Oregon: All Nations at Newport, St. Mark's at Toledo, and St. Peter's at Lincoln City. In 1967, he was called back to Lutheran High School in Los Angeles. After serving Trinity until 1980, he went to Redeemer Lutheran Church in Wickenburg, Arizona, remaining until 1986.

In 1964, Trinity was forced to close the school, as the Sunday school rooms where it met didn't meet the city's Building and Safety Commission's code. However, the school was reopened in 1968 with a kindergarten in remodeled rooms that met the city's building codes. By 1975, a new unit was

built allowing the school to expand to 6th grade with an enrollment of 96. At the 90th anniversary of the congregation on June 25, 1972, the parish had grown to 550 souls with 392 communicant members averaging 139 in church each Sunday, with 47 students in the day school, and 80 in the Sunday school.

On June 22, 1980, the next pastor to serve Trinity was Rev. Dr. Alfred Freitag, who was born on April 14, 1916, in Chester, Nebraska, where he attended the Lutheran school and graduated from the local high school. After graduating from Concordia Teachers College in Seward, Nebraska, he was an elementary principal and teacher in Lutheran schools in Nebraska and Michigan from 1938 to 1945, an instructor in Detroit Lutheran High School from 1945 to 1947, and its principal from 1947 to 1953, when he came to Los Angeles to establish Walter A. Maier Memorial Lutheran High School where he became principal and superintendent. After receiving his Master of Arts from the University of Michigan, he completed his doctoral from the University of Southern California with the thesis subject, "The Centennial of Concordia Teachers College, River Forest, Illinois," later being published as a book. He was married on July 28, 1940, to the former Doris Bachmann, whose parents were missionary teachers in India, and who also graduated from Concordia Teachers College in Seward. They had three children: John, who became a pastor, and Carol and Mary, who became Lutheran teachers. After finishing his career in Lutheran education, he went through the colloquy program at Concordia Seminary in St. Louis, receiving a call to be pastor of Zion Church in Glendale.

As the area surrounding the church began to change during Rev. Dr. Alfred Freitag's ministry at Trinity, he was instrumental in establishing Hispanic and Korean ministries. In 1984, the first full-time Hispanic pastor at Trinidad was Felipe Luna, who was born on December 7, 1943, in Merida, Yucatán, Mexico, the oldest of 12 brothers and sisters. At the age of nine, his father died leaving him to help support the family by shining shoes and later learning the shoe repair trade. He attended the Bible Institute in Mexico City graduating in 1971. When he attended a Wisconsin Synod Lutheran church in Mexico City, he met his future wife, Vida Coria, whose father was not only the pastor of the church but also confirmed young Felipe, encouraging him to become a Lutheran minister. He was ordained in the Wisconsin Synod in

The first full-time Hispanic pastor at Trinidad is Felipe Luna.

Rev. Adam D. Lautenschlager was installed in 1971 as the full-time pastor after serving Trinity as assistant pastor at various times. (Pacific Southwest District Archives)

Trinity's Centennial in 1982 with participating pastors: Rev. Young Hwan Hong, pastor of Trinity's Korean mission; Rev. Dr. Oswald Hoffman, Lutheran Hour speaker; Rev. Dr. Alfred Freitag, pastor of Trinity; Rev. Felipe Luna, the first full-time Hispanic pastor at Trinidad (Trinity).

1972 in Mexico City, doing a two-year vicarage in Juarez, Mexico, and El Paso, Texas. Following his ordination in 1972, he was called as the pastor of Cristo Resuciado Lutheran Church in Mexico City where he stayed until 1975. He married Vida Coria on December 12, 1973, with their marriage blessed with two children, Emera, who was born on July 18, 1975 in Mexico, and David who was born on January 25, 1979 in Los Angeles.

When Pastor Luna and his family left Mexico in 1979 and came to Los Angeles, they were introduced to Trinity Lutheran Church in Los Angeles where he became a part-time lay pastor from 1981 to 1984. After going from door to door canvassing the area around Trinity, he began Spanish services where only he and his family were present at the first two services with the services gradually increasing to 25 and 30 a Sunday. At first, services were held at 5:30 p.m., but were later changed to 11:30 a.m. with the English congregation worshiping at 10:00 a.m. and the Korean congregation worshiping at 1:00 p.m. In 1984, Pastor Luna was colloquized in The Lutheran Church—Missouri Synod becoming pastor of Iglesia Trinidad. His wife reported that he had a passion for ministry, especially for new arrivals to this country, who were un-Christian. He and his wife, Vida, lived in the parsonage along with their two children, as Dr. Freitag had his own home in Glendale. That year Trinity became known as "The Church of All Nations" with one service in English, one in Spanish, and one in Korean every Sunday. Black, white, Hispanic, and Asian people of several dif-

ferent heritages worshiped and worked together as a happy and creative family of faith. There was a multicultural Sunday school, where all the congregation's children — of all races, languages, and cultures — met together to learn about and celebrate the risen Savior of all mankind. Only one thing stood in the way of an evangelism explosion through this unique program—the lack of a large van with which to transport children to Sunday school. Pastor Luna drove all over the area picking up children every Sunday morning. Rev. Young Hwan Hong served in the Korean-language ministry, leading a Korean-language service at 1:00 p.m. every Sunday, as Koreatown was practically next door to Trinity.

By 1987, the Hispanic mission had 35 baptized members, through the good work of Pastor Luna reaching the Hispanic population with his wife serving as secretary to the English and Spanish congregations. The small mission also grew through the day school as the children's parents who spoke Spanish became interested in the Lutheran church. The Hispanic mission always had bilingual services in Advent and Lent with the English congregation, sharing meals before the services with joint picnics held and all three groups participated in the anniversaries of Trinity.

In 1990, Trinidad was the setting for "Encuentro de la Mujer Hispana," a workshop designed for Hispanic women sponsored by the Pacific Southwest District Lutheran Women's Missionary League (LWML), the first to be conducted entirely in Spanish. Pastor Luna welcomed approximately 95 women attending the event, representing 13 different countries: Mexico, Nicaragua, Argentina, Guatemala, U.S.A., Brazil, Cuba, Puerto Rico, Venezuela, El Salvador, Chile, Ecuador and The Dominican Republic. By 1991, the church had grown with an average of 45 on Sunday mornings and a mailing list of over 150 families. Since Pastor wasn't proficient in English, they didn't have ESL classes, but he did teach a Wednesday evening Bible class and Confirmation and First Communion classes on Saturdays. Two weeks before the Confirmation class was to be confirmed, he died of a heart attack at the age of 47 on July 16, 1991. Following his death, Pastor Artigas came to Trinity to confirm the class, which also included David Luna, Pastor's son. After her husband's unexpected death, Mrs. Luna received support from the Synod. In 1992, Mrs. Luna moved to Arizona with her children where she worked for the

In 1984, Trinity becomes known as "The Church of All Nations."

Arizona Board of Medical Examiners until 1997 when she took a job as secretary for the Chair at Arizona State University's Secondary Education Department. She worked at the Schaller Community Center part-time and also volunteered her time to assist Pastor Artigas in his ministry in the Hispanic churches in the Phoenix area, teaching Sunday school and Saturday school.

Following Pastor Luna's death, Rev. Cris Artigas served as interim pastor for the congregation and stayed until June 30, 1992. To celebrate nine years of Hispanic ministry at Trinity, a trilingual service was conducted with Pastor Robert F. Gussick preaching simultaneously in Spanish and English, while the Korean pastor gave a synopsis of the sermon in Korean. In September of 1992, Alfonso Conrado was installed as lay pastor and was contracted to do work at the Hispanic mission at Trinity, which had a communicant membership of 50. In 1994, Trinity Lutheran merged the Anglo, black, Hispanic, and Korean congregations into a unified church selecting the name, Trinity Central. With Pastor Conrado's departure to El Redentor in Panorama City, Pastor Raul Saldaña became the vacancy pastor at Trinity from October 1998 to April 1999. After Pastor Conrado left, leaving only two families, Pastor Saldaña was able to increase the Hispanic congregation to 20 people per Sunday. Deacon Edgar Arroyo, who worked closely with the English and Korean language congregations through new member classes, Confirmation, and catechism classes, followed him.

Also, started at Trinity was the Brazilian church, which served as a starting place for immigrants speaking Portuguese who needed a place to worship, spiritual support, and a familiar cultural setting. The congregation worked in cooperation with not only Brazilian churches but with several other churches around the world. Their ministry included hunger and disaster response programs, substance abuse and marital counseling, jail, nursing home, and hospital visitation. Pastor Kirn served with Deacon Renato Helbrio Sbrana, who was studying for the ministry.

Deacon Edgar Arroyo joined the Nehemiah Project Staff, a joint ministry coalition of the greater urban Los Angeles area churches affiliated with the Pacific Southwest District of The Lutheran Church–-Missouri Synod, on August 1, 2002, as Hispanic missionary/church planter. The Los Angeles Nehemiah Project was organized in 1993 with the seven participating churches looking for new directions that could be used to address the problems of the urban community, equipping congregations for healthy, productive ministries through shared resources. By 2003, 11 congregations were participating in this program, with the primary goal to see changed lives through the Gospel of Jesus Christ, dealing with the life situations of addiction problems, runaway youth, gangs, prostitution, children from none traditional families and from single-parent homes with the belief that the only way broken lives can regain hope and congregations can be renewed is through changing communities by coming together to witness Jesus Christ in the daily life of the church in their communities.

Deacon Arroyo, a certified deacon of the Pacific Southwest District, had considerable experience in Hispanic ministry. He had been serving the Hispanic mission which met on the campus of Trinity Central, Los Angeles, for the previous two years and also had been working with the Hispanic mission at Trinity, Santa Ana, his home congregation. With the Nehemiah Project, he would be ministering full-time in two areas for Hispanic ministry, developing a new mission in the area surrounding Grace Lutheran Church on Vernon Avenue in Los Angeles. The Hispanic mission at Trinity Central came under the supervision of the Nehemiah Project with Deacon Arroyo continuing to serve that mission and further develop its outreach. Some of Nehemiah Project activities included the Children's Christmas Outreach, backpack and school supplies distribution with the Los Angeles public schools, the Youth Outreach Athletic League, a planned Children's Crafts Day as well as Vacation Bible Schools. Emphasis was placed on organizing small home Bible study groups, training leaders

In 1994, Trinity Lutheran merges the Anglo, black, Hispanic, and Korean congregations into a unified church selecting the name, Trinity Central.

Deacon Edgar Arroyo of Nehemiah Project with children in the Hispanic program at Trinity. (Pacific Southwest District Archives)

for the groups, and continuing services at Trinity Central. The commissioning of Deacon Edgar Arroyo took place on Sunday, September 29, 2002, at 3:00 p.m. in Grace Lutheran Church in Los Angeles, with Rev. John Durkovic of Trinity, Santa Ana, pastor of Deacon Arroyo's home church and former missionary, speaking at the service.

At Christmas of 2002, Deacon Arroyo held a Spanish-language Christmas service at Trinity Central with 49 people attending, and he began Hispanic services at Grace on January 5, 2003. In the new year of 2003, he continued to see significant growth at Fuente de Agua Viva, Fountain of Life (Trinity Central's new name for the Hispanic mission) with worship attendance increasing and with the start of two new Bible study groups. The Iowa District West provided a beautiful reconditioned 1973 Volkswagon for him when his car was wrecked in a hit-and-run collision. In the spring of 2003, the average church attendance was 40, with services held every Sunday and every Thursday evening. Deacon Arroyo continued having Bible classes on Wednesdays and training classes where a couple of members of the congregation were being trained as lay workers. He continued the distribution of fliers and making contact with people through phone calls and visits. On Palm Sunday and Easter, Trinity Central's English-speaking congregation joined the Spanish-speaking congregation in a joint service where the liturgy and sermon were bilingual. They joined the Spanish-speaking congregation at Grace in Los Angeles for Easter breakfast. During the year, the average attendance at worship services was 40, and Bible studies and evangelism training classes were held during the week. Through jointly sponsored worship services at Advent, Lent, and Reformation, nearly 500 people were reached with the Gospel. The mission participated in the Nehemiah Athletic League's basketball team involving 75 youth in 6 teams.

Since members were more actively inviting people to church, the attendance and giving continued to grow with the Hispanic mission opening its own checking account, the first in its 23-year history. Some of the members still wondered about the "convenience" of being dependent or becoming independent. They felt they didn't make enough money to tithe and support the church, but other members understood that even with the difficulties of being self-supporting, sooner or later they would have to face this big challenge. Even after 122 years, old Trinity continues to be a vibrant force in proclaiming the love of Christ in the downtown area of Los Angeles to all people, Korean, Hispanic, and Anglo

Fuente de Agua Viva, Fountain of Life, becomes Trinity Central's new name for the Hispanic church.

Redeemer Lutheran Church
El Redentor
Panorama City, California

Panorama City has the distinction of being known as the San Fernando Valley's first truly planned community. Since it had a strategic location at the geographical center of the valley, Fritz B. Burns and Associates purchased an area of 1,000 acres from the Panorama Dairy and Sheep Ranch in 1947. The associates' initial 33,000 homes were eventually supplemented by an additional 1,000, built by independent developers on curved streets isolated from the valley's commercial and industrial areas. On Valentine's Day in 1948, Burns received permission to begin commercial development in the town, transforming Panorama City's local business scene. One of the first offices opened in 1948 was that of Bank of America. Since 1948, Panorama City has seen many changes with major department stores comprising the nucleus of the renovated Panorama Mall, which opened in 1955 along with some 60 shops, boutiques, and services. The town of Panorama City, covering 5.5 square miles, is currently the home of more than 65,000 people.

As the city was transformed from a rural area to large housing tracts, many Lutherans moved into the area seeking a church. In July of 1955, Rev. Eugene Krieger, missionary-at-large, came to Pacoima-Panorama City to develop and start a Lutheran mission. During the middle of September of 1955, a staff of three teachers conducted Sunday school classes for a few weeks with the children, their parents, and friends, developing the new mission field. The first worship service was conducted on October 9, 1955, in the American Legion Hall in Pacoima. A two and one-half acre plot of ground

Redeemer congregation worshiping in the American Legion Hall in Pacoima. (Pacific Southwest District Archives)

Rev. Robert Cardaro, the congregation's second pastor, was installed on October 26, 1958. (Pacific Southwest District

N. Steiner serving as chairman of the Building Committee. On February 1, 1959, groundbreaking ceremonies were held. Due to adverse weather conditions and the slow process of the city checking the plans, the building was not started until early March 1959. The building, designed by architect Herbert J. Kaiser, covered approximately 6,000 square feet with a chapel seating 250, having an overflow room that would seat an additional 80 persons. The Sunday school wing had a large meeting room that could be divided into four large rooms with the installation of folding doors, a nice size kitchen, and a cry room for mothers with small children.

The exterior of the building featured combed brick and stucco with a slag roof and was completely air-conditioned. In order to construct the building, men of the congregation volunteered their time to help, with the women serving them meals. A member of the congregation built the altar, lectern, pulpit, and hymnboards, designed by the architect; the altar linens were hand-sewn by ladies of the congregation. The chapel was located at the far end of the pie-shaped lot facing Terra Bella Street, allowing for a large church to be built when the need arrived.

on which stood a five-room house, serving as a parsonage, was purchased for $32,000 through the Mission Board. After the congregation organized in October of 1957, Pastor Krieger accepted a call as assistant pastor in Traverse City, Michigan, the following month with Chaplain Edmund C. Manns becoming the vacancy pastor for one year. In October 1958, Rev. Robert Cardaro accepted the call to be the congregation's second pastor, being installed on October 26 at 7:30 p.m. in First Lutheran Church in San Fernando. Pastor Cardaro, a graduate of Concordia Seminary in Springfield, Illinois, was vicar in Providence, Rhode Island, and served a congregation in Hillsboro, Texas, for one year. At the time, Redeemer numbered 75 communicants with a Sunday school enrollment of 60.

Shortly after Pastor Cardaro's arrival, plans were developed to build a chapel with Robert

On June 12, 1960, 250 members and guests attended the official dedication of the new Lutheran Church of the Redeemer. Rev. Edmund C. Manns, the vacancy pastor, was the dedication speaker with Rev. Oswald Skov of First Lutheran Church in San Fernando as the liturgist, and Rev. Robert G. Cardaro conducted the Rite of Dedication. Featured in the dedication service was the Lutheran Laymen's League Chorus of Southern California, under the direction of Mr. Ray Linson, render-

Redeemer's new church buildings were dedicated on June 12, 1960. (Pacific Southwest District Archives)

ing the anthems "Come, Let Us Adore Him" by Johann Sebastian Bach, the "Lord's Prayer," and closed the service with the "Benediction."

In April of 1962, Pastor Cardaro accepted a call as chaplain in the armed services being stationed in Colorado. On October 29, 1962, Rev. Arthur Walther was installed as the pastor of the Lutheran Church of the Redeemer in Panorama City. By 1964, Redeemer had grown to 210 baptized members with 125 communant members having a Sunday school enrollment of 80 pupils. Following Pastor Walther's departure, after a period of particular difficulty which gave rise to talk of dissolution, the congregation was served for one and one-half years under a dual parish arrangement under Rev. James Hoppes who served Redeemer and Peace, Lake View Terrace. During this time, changing social and economic factors were altering the face of the community with construction of new dwellings limited almost exclusively to apartment buildings and multiple-dwelling complexes producing many challenges for Redeemer. To meet the challenge in the community, the plan was to use the Sunday school as an arm of evangelism to reach out to some of the children in the area who were unchurched.

After a two-year vacancy, the Rev. John M. Simon was ordained and installed on August 13, 1967, as pastor of Redeemer. He was the son of Pastor and Mrs. John E. Simon, and was born in Billings, Montana, on June 29, 1940. After attending grade school in Toledo, Oregon, he attended high school in Hood River, Oregon, and in Portland, Oregon. Following his graduation from Concordia Junior College in Portland, he attended Portland State College, and Concordia Senior College in Fort Wayne, Indiana, graduating in 1963. In December of 1963, he enrolled as a student at Concordia Theological Seminary, Springfield, Illinois, serving his internship at Immanuel Lutheran Church Milwaukee, Wisconsin, and receiving his Bachelor of Divinity degree in July 1967. In 1968, the parish had 260 baptized members, 134 communicant members with a Sunday school enrollment of 120. In order to survive, the congregation continued to receive District subsidy.

On October 21, 1973, Harlan Heyer was installed as a worker-priest director of Christian education serving both Redeemer and Peace in Lake View Terrace. He was born in Minneapolis, Minnesota, in 1946, and raised in Osseo, Minnesota, where he received his elementary and high school education. He held many offices in the Walther

League and enjoyed working with young people. He entered Dunwoody Industrial Institute receiving an education in basic electricity and obtaining his journeyman's license in 1972, as an electrician; he then entered Concordia College, St. Paul, Minnesota, to seek a church-related vocation, graduating from the director of Christian education program.

In 1975, the Rev. Michael Drews, began his ministry at Redeemer where there were only 90 communicants, all of whom were Anglos. In 1978 and 1979, Redeemer had VBS in conjunction with Calvary, an ALC congregation in Pacoima with 70 children enrolled each year, having 90 percent Hispanic children the first year and 30 percent the second. In the summer of 1979, Redeemer hosted a summer school each day for 70 enrollees with the average attendance of 45, all Hispanic youth. Enrique Vela and Pastor supervised 10 SPEDY workers (high school youth paid by the city) who did the tutoring; lunches were served under a federal program through the Latin American Civic Association. Badly needed in that program was a good curriculum and assistance. They also conducted a Saturday school, Escuelita, for about 15 Hispanic children with the mothers cooking lunches. Pastor, his wife, Jan, and Enrique tutored the children and trained some of the mothers in the tutoring program. Two members of Redeemer were involved with the cooking. Redeemer also had a Head Start program renting 3 classrooms for 45 children with about 80 percent Hispanic, with some black, Anglo, and oriental children.

By 1980, there were about 70,000 Hispanic people in the area of Redeemer. The Hispanic ministry developed mainly as a result of Pastor Drews' involvement with the Center of Community Promotion, a program developed by Rev. Juan Montoya, a Hispanic American Lutheran Church pastor, in connection with Calvary, ALC, in Pacoima (one mile from Redeemer) and the ALC Synod; it was a Social Service ministry assisting people with housing, 30 percent of the cases; employment, 60 percent; clothing, 2 percent; emergency food, 8 percent; furniture; translation; etc. The center also had programs in conjunction with Redeemer's summer school, camping, Saturday school, and celebrations. Lutheran Social Services in conjunction with United Way provided two CETA workers to handle the casework. Pastor served on the Board of Directors as Chairman of the Board.

The optimism of the '50s and '60s led to Redeemer's growth, which seemed to slow in the

Rev. John M. Simon was ordained and installed as pastor of Redeemer on August 13, 1967. (Pacific Southwest District Archives)

Rev. Michael Drews began his ministry at Redeemer in 1975, serving until July 15, 1984, when the congregation disbanded. (Pacific Southwest District Archives)

Rev. Esaúl Salomón was installed as mission-ary-at-large in the fall of 1982, serving the San Fernando Valley and El Redentor. (Pacific South-west District Archives)

Because the English-speaking congregation at Redeemer has dwindled, the congregation decides to disband in 1984.

'70s and even died for lack of people who would serve in the LWML, quilting, Sunday school, and the choir. But in the 1980s, Redeemer, struggling with its sense of mission, continued to relate to the surrounding community by offering vital wor-ship programs in Spanish and English, religious instruction in two languages, Hispanic camping, summer school, and social service needs. Spanish-speaking Rev. Harold Deye, formerly a missionary to Venezuela and Calexico, California, enhanced this outreach to the community; he was serving Bethany Church in Hollywood, at the time. He be-gan a series of six Sunday evening Lutheran Span-ish worship services beginning October 12, 1980, at 7:00 p.m. Pastor Drews said of this endeavor, "We see this as one of the best opportunities to at-tempt a Word and Sacrament ministry to Hispanic people." He added with enthusiasm, "We walk through the door God has opened at this time. To God be the glory!"

By 1981, there were 35 people attending the Spanish services. In the summer of 1981 after Mark McKenzie graduated from Christ College, Irvine, he worked with Pastor Drews at Redeemer where he assisted with the social ministry pro-gram distributing produce and other supplies on Saturdays and also worked at the social ministry office in Pacoima one day a week. Beginning on January 1, 1982, Rev. Napoleon Artigas, a pastor from El Salvador, did volunteer work at Redeemer visiting the families who had participated in Re-deemer's Hispanic program, where he located 20 or more families, with over 90 children. About 40 of these children were said to have been interested in Baptism, Confirmation or Communion prepa-ration. With that interest, Saturday classes were begun with 11 in attendance.

A major need of the congregation was a van to transport families to church services and activities. A "Van Fund" was established after an individual from another congregation donated $1,000 for the Hispanic ministry at Redeemer. Since people had to come to Redeemer from one-, 4-, and 6-mile dis-tances, worship attendance was about 30, but had a promising potential if there was transportation. Such a van could be used for the 80 youth campers the parish sent for one week at El Camino Pines, a Lutheran Camp, via *LA Times* scholarships each summer, and the 50 children in summer school could have field trips. At the time, four or more families were being given rides to church on Sun-day mornings. Since the youth couldn't go to the Sunday evening Hispanic worship because of a

lack of transportation, the parish applied to the District's Youth Ministry Grant Hospice Fund for $1,000.

Due to Pastor Drew's lack of ability to converse in Spanish, there was no opportunity to do follow-up ministry such as Confirmation and Bible stud-ies. Because the English-speaking congregation at Redeemer continued to dwindle, the congregation decided to disband, concluding its final English worship service on Sunday, July 15, 1984. As the Hispanic ministry should be the focus at Redeem-er, they recommended to the District to sell the property and relocate in an area where Hispanics were more dominate.

In the fall of 1982, Rev. Esaúl Salomón was called as missionary-at-large and placed in Circuit Two of the San Fernando Valley. Pastor Salomón was born on November 17, 1948, in Vera Cruz, Mexico, where he was raised in the Presbyterian church. After his mother died when he was seven years old, the family moved and started attending the Evangelical church, as it was the closest Protestant church to them. Following his graduation from the Mexican Bible Institute in Mexico City at the age of 18, he planted his first church in Mexico City. In 1975, he decided to come to the United States to get his master's degree and return to Mexico to be a worker-priest. While at the University of Chicago working on his master's, he worked with the American Bible Society. In making a presen-tation at a Lutheran church, a pastor said there was a need for Spanish-speaking pastors in the denomination. After reading the *Book of Concord*, he discovered that he had been a Lutheran all his life and didn't know it. In 1979, he attended Con-cordia Seminary at Fort Wayne, Indiana, receiving a Master of Theology in 1982, after doing his vicar-age at Bethel in Chicago in 1980 through 1981. Also in 1979, he married his wife, Melissa, where their marriage was blessed with two daughters.

Following Pastor Salomón's graduation from Fort Wayne in 1982, the Pacific Southwest District called him as a missionary-at-large for the San Fernando Valley, but his desire was to go back to Mexico. His first six months in the valley were very difficult because of having no facilities in which to do ministry. When Redeemer in Panorama City disbanded, he wanted to develop a ministry there, but the District wanted to sell the property to help defray the cost of his ministry. He reached out in a circuit-sponsored program with Bible studies in Pacoima and Sunday afternoon services in a Reseda park with Trinity Lutheran of Reseda also making its facilities available. He had two families taking Confirmation instruction there. He saw the greatest potential for ministry in the San Fernando and Pacoima areas because of the high concentration of Hispanics. He was able to go door-to-door or speak to people in the parks often leaving tracts as follow up to the spoken word. He once stated, "The people have a great love for music and singing," which led him to spend time each week teaching hymns, many of which he had translated and adapted, so that the people might enjoy using them in their worship. He used the traditional liturgy because of its beauty, and because it encompasses so well the elements of worship.

After the District relented and gave Pastor Salomón Redeemer's buildings for Hispanic ministry, which were in very poor condition, he spent months making repairs to the buildings and property so it would be presentable for a new congregation. After some time, Circuit Two recruited people to help restore the buildings of Redeemer each Saturday, making them quite beautiful and attractive to the middle-class Hispanic population he was trying to reach. The first service was conducted on Thanksgiving Day of 1983 with four people in attendance, all with Anglo names. He conducted Bible study classes gaining more new members.

According to Pastor Salomón, within 10 years he had 300 to 400 members who were middle class Hispanics with good educations; some were teachers and one was a public school principal. The church parsonage was rented and a preschool/day-care was started in 1987 with $5,000 seed money from the District, bringing people to the Lord. While in Panorama City, he worked on his doctoral thesis. In 1989, Rev. Paulus Voelzke was assisting Pastor Salomón in Panorama City with the English program, with the District hiring him from October 1, 1989, to December 31, 1990, to continue with the work. Through the Lord's blessings, El Redentor became a strong, stable Hispanic congregation in the Panorama City area, continuing to grow and eventually becoming self-supporting. On one Sunday in November of 1992, a dozen new believers were received into membership at El Redentor. At that time, the congregation represented Hispanics from 12 Latin American countries.

Since 1986, hundreds of people heard the Gospel through the evangelistic work of El Redentor with members dispersed throughout the United States, often returning to their countries of origin. The major ministerial focus was preaching, then equipping, and then sending lay missionaries to different parts of the world to continue the work begun at this evangelistic center, all done in accordance with the Great Commission. Through the combined efforts of Grace, Lancaster; El Redentor, Panorama City; and a core of El Redentor's membership, a mission at California City was established in 1992 with Pastor Salomón leading worship services on a bi-monthly basis. The city was expected to grow rapidly with additional personnel from the Edwards Air Force facility. The core of this new community had come from El Redentor families, living in the valley, who had transferred to Grace, Lancaster.

After Pastor Salomón was asked by the District to go to the San Diego area to begin a new Hispanic ministry in 1992, Rev. Jorge Garcia Jr. was installed at El Redentor. El Redentor's communicant membership was 107 with a baptized membership of 183. On February 12, 1994, a month after the Northridge earthquake, which caused some damage to the church, the LWML ladies of Zone 2 gathered at El Redentor for a time of prayer and praise. Although the occasion was not earth shattering, it was nonetheless of historical significance as the ladies of El Redentor were the first Hispanic LWML local in the Pacific Southwest District to receive a charter. To make the occasion more momentous, the charter, LWML pledge, and LWML mission statement were translated into Spanish and presented to the ladies. The vision for reaching out to Hispanic ladies through the LWML program began several years before under the leadership of Melissa Salomón, wife of Pastor Esaul Salomón. After the Salomóns moved to San Diego to begin a new Hispanic outreach, Brenda Garcia, wife of Pastor Jorge Garcia, provided additional organizational leadership.

In 1994, El Redentor received a $500 grant from Aid Association for Lutherans to defray the cost of radio station broadcast fees for a Spanish "Lutheran Hour" radio program broadcast in the Los Angeles area. During Lent and Easter season of 1997, many men were leading their families to church to hear God's holy Word proclaimed. The following was the church schedule:

10:00 a.m. Misa En Español
11:30 a.m. Hora de companerismo Cristiano
11:30 am. Estudio Biblico
1:30 p.m. Estudios Teológicos
7:00 p.m. Jueves Estudios Biblicos
10:30 a.m. Sábado Catecismo

El Redentor's first service is conducted on Thanksgiving Day of 1983.

The ladies of El Redentor are the first Hispanic LWML local in the Pacific Southwest District to receive a charter.

Pastor Alfonso Conrado was installed on February 5, 2000, as pastor of El Redentor. (Pacific Southwest District Archives)

The Thanksgiving Festival was held where the whole congregation enjoyed turkey and all kinds of food from different countries with 125 people at the worship service. Of the students who took the theology classes at El Retendor that year, Mr. Guillermo Jere was working with the Hispanic mission in Faith Lutheran in Tujunga, Mr. Romeo Martinez worked in the Hispanic Mission at Trinity, Reseda, and Mr. Efrain Erazo was beginning the canvassing in Hollywood and Burbank with Pastor Garcia working with the Canoga Park Hispanic Mission. During the state of disaster in Honduras and Nicaragua, the congregation sent 20 boxes of food and clothing, which was a great deal for this small congregation. In working among African-Americans, the congregation rented facilities to a multicultural learning center with an African-American as director. At Christmas, there were 110 present with 60 children receiving gifts, lighting their faces with bright smiles. The congregation continued to have bilingual worship services.

In 1999, Pastor Garcia received and accepted a call from El Buen Pastor Lutheran Church at Toppenish, Washington. He had helped the congregation to regroup and to open their eyes to the responsibility of each of the members during his ministry. During the interim, Pastor Conrado worked with the Church Council, bringing the congregation's members together while maintaining unity and harmony for all members. On February 5, 2000, Pastor Alfonso Conrado was installed as pastor of El Redentor. During the year, the average church attendance was 30. On September 30, a food fair was held as an outreach event. By October 20, the congregation distributed "share food" for the first time to help the community and share the Gospel. At the Christmas play, 66 persons attended including members, their friends, and relatives with all the children of the congregation participating in the events.

El Redentor celebrated its 15th anniversary on Saturday, October 6, 2001, with a festive day of worship at 4:00 p.m., followed by an authentic Hispanic reception and sit-down dinner. The men of the congregation hosted a Mother's Day breakfast on May 12, 2002, honoring the mothers and wives; at 9:30 a.m., the families began lining up with the children accompanied by a parent or guardian. Since it was so successful, the ladies of congregation decided to hold another breakfast on Father's Day to honor fathers, husbands, brothers, and uncles. These events were a good outreach to witness the love of Christ among families, neighbors, and friends. During this time, the average Sunday worship attendance was 37. Pastor Conrado has led the congregation in establishing an active Church Council to carry out the work of the parish.

St. John's Lutheran Church
Centro Cristiano Redwood
Oxnard, California

The city of Oxnard is located on the Pacific Coast of Southern California approximately 62 miles northwest of downtown Los Angeles and 35 miles south of Santa Barbara. As of the year 2000, Oxnard had a population of 172,887 with 20.6 percent Anglos and 66.2 percent Hispanic, making it the largest city in Ventura County. The name Oxnard comes from the family that developed one of the first industries in the area, a sugar beet factory. Its founder, Henry T. Oxnard, intended to name the city after a Greek word for "sugar," but finally, being frustrated with trying to communicate his desires to a state bureaucrat, he gave up and named the city after his family. The city, surrounded by some of the richest agricultural land in the world, has a variety of business parks and shopping areas and is the home of the county-operated Channel Islands Harbor, gateway to the Channel Islands National Park.

The first residents of the Oxnard area were Chumash Indians who lived in round, thatched houses and were known for their well-constructed plank canoes and fine basketwork. Later, in 1542, a Portuguese explorer, Juan Rodríguez Cabrillo, sailed into Point Mugu Lagoon, which he dubbed "the land of everlasting summers" and claimed it for King Charles I of Spain. After a number of Spanish explorations, Jose de Galvez, utilizing powers bestowed upon him by King Charles III, appointed Father Junípero Serra to head missions in Alta California. Mission San Buenaventura, established in 1782, was the halfway point between the San Diego and Monterey missions. Pueblo life and sprawling ranchos began to spring up around the mission, with "Californio" families exerting their influence until the State of California was added to the Union in 1850.

During the mid-nineteenth century, immigrants began to pour in from the east coast and Europe. The major industry, agriculture, produced great crops of barley and lima beans. In 1897, ranchers Albert Maulhardt and Johannes Borchard believed sugar beets would be a profitable crop for the area, and invited Henry Oxnard to construct a local factory to process the harvests. Oxnard and his three brothers operated the American Beet Sugar factory in Chino, California, and encouraged by a pledge of 18,000 acres of sugar beets from local farmers, built a factory in the heart of the rich fields. The Southern Pacific Railroad constructed a spur right to the factory site so the processed beets could be shipped out. A town quickly developed near the factory. Almost overnight businesses and residences appeared around the town square, called the "Plaza," and schools and churches emerged almost as rapidly with the city of Oxnard incorporated in 1903.

The factory attracted many Chinese, Japanese and Mexican workers to Oxnard with the sugar beet industry bringing diversification to agriculture. Major crops then included beans, beets, and barley, and businesses in town consisted of general merchandise, restaurants, laundries, saloons, and banks. Oxnard built its first public library, a classically styled, Andrew Carnegie gift, on the northwest corner of the Plaza in 1907. The building stands today as a county historical landmark and is the only remaining structure from the early days of the Plaza. Two years previous to Pastor Hemann's (he later dropped the last "n" on his surname) arrival in Oxnard in 1900, he described life in Oxnard, "there had been no town, but merely a vast bean field instead, until the Oxnard brothers of the American Beet Sugar Company decided to locate there. Then the town of Oxnard mushroomed forth. Inside of 2 years the town had 1,000 inhabitants, 3 churches (Baptist, Methodist, and Presbyterian), about 20 saloons, and became known up and down the coast as the sportiest wide-open town on the coast, but gradually sobered down and developed into a nice little city."

The attraction of the agricultural community also brought many German Lutheran farmers. The history of Lutheranism in Ventura County dates back to about 1897 when the first services were conducted for a number of these Lutheran families who had settled in the area. Services were held at various intervals in the little Baptist church at Hueneme, in the Springville Baptist Church near Camarillo, and later in the Oxnard Baptist Church. Among the pastors who came to

C Street in Downtown Oxnard with the large Carnegie Library on the right, circa 1908. (SECURITY PA-CIFIC)

Rev. Martin H. Hemann, first pastor from 1900 to 1903. (Pacific Southwest District Archives)

Ventura County by train during the late 1890s to conduct Lutheran services were Pastors G. Runkel of Los Angeles, J. Kogler of Orange, F. Reiser of Pasadena, and J. W. Theiss of Los Angeles.

In 1899, another group of Lutherans moved to the Oxnard area from Palmdale, a German town then called Palmenthal. This group of energetic Germans established Zionsgemeindein Church in 1887 in Palmenthal. They had been lured to the area by glowing literature sent to them at the farm homes in Nebraska and South Dakota. Dr. Voght, previously a practicing physician and pharmacist in St. Louis, was among the farmers who had planted orchards and vineyards before the days of irrigation. Since the reverses of this congregation came with the drought of 1896, 1897, and 1898 when the meager supply of water from the reservoir in the mountains was inadequate to meet their needs, they gathered their remaining household goods, boarded up their homes, left their withering farms and orchards, and migrated with their families to Oxnard. With the arrival of this new group of good, industrious farmers and loyal Missouri Synod Lutherans to Oxnard's El Rio vicinity, where things were booming and farmers were prospering due to the abundance of water from artesian wells for both domestic and irrigating uses enlarging the flock in Oxnard, arrangements were made with the California and Nevada District Mission Board to call a resident pastor, the Rev. Martin H. Hemann, who had recently gradu-

ated from the seminary.

Pastor Hemann in his May 22, 1951, letter to Rev. August Hansen described his ministry at St. John's. He came to the West Coast in response to a handwritten call by Rev. J. M. Buehler, Missouri Synod's pioneer pastor west of the Rockies. It was difficult to find lodgings in the new, young, overcrowded, two-year-old town of Oxnard, with half of the 1,000 inhabitants living in tents or rough board shacks. A German, Mr. Mendelsohn, son of a minister in Germany and employed as chief chemist at the sugar beet factory, took pity on Pastor Hemann, who had arrived in August, and offered to share his modest, rented shack with him. The following Sunday, September 9, 1900, Pastor Hemann conducted his first service in the Baptist church, where he met the people who were to be the charter members of the congregation. After the service, a meeting was held in which it was decided to organize and be incorporated as St. John's Evangelical Lutheran Church of Oxnard, with 14 men signing the constitution, making it Ventura County's pioneer Lutheran congregation. They also signed a paper pledging various amounts that they each volunteered to give toward the pastor's monthly salary. The following Sunday, Rev. Runkel came from Trinity, Los Angeles, to ordain and install Pastor Heman as the regular pastor of St. John's.

A real estate company, Colonia Improvement Company of Oxnard, donated two 50-foot lots at the corner of Seventh and C streets for the church and parsonage. Construction of the church began immediately so that within three months after Pastor Hemann's arrival in Oxnard, preaching every Sunday afternoon in the Baptist church, St. John's dedicated on Sunday, October 28, its new house of worship built at a cost of $1,200 by Mr. Albert Johnson of Oxnard, a member who served the parish for 45 years. According to Pastor Hemann, dedication Sunday was a "gala affair" with "the interior of the church superbly decorated with an abundance of garlands, plants, and flowers supplied by U. S. Senator Bard from his beautiful estate near Hueneme." The event was highly publicized by both Oxnard newspapers with the *Sun* devoting its entire front page to this big day. The church was packed to capacity in both the German morning service and the afternoon English service. At the time, St. John's had an active Ladies Aid society, which furnished a noonday meal in an unoccupied restaurant that was placed at their disposal for the occasion. The ladies fed about 400

St. John's first church and parsonage at Seventh and C used from 1900 to 1945. (Pacific Southwest District Archives)

Rev. P. Schmidt, pastor from 1904 to 1909. (Pacific Southwest District Archives)

Rev. C. K. Kaiser, 1909–1912. (Pacific Southwest District Archives)

Rev. L. J. Meyer, 1912–1913. (Pacific Southwest District Archives)

P. Zimmermann, 1913–1915. (Pacific Southwest District Archives)

William G. Ruehle, 1915–1918. (Pacific Southwest District Archives)

people at 2 long tables. Upon completion of the church building and recognizing the importance of religious education, Pastor Hemann established a Christian day school on January 3, 1901, which he continued to teach until he left for Wisconsin in October of 1903. The school continued until 1913. The following year on July 6, 1902, the Sunday school was officially opened.

According to the call that Pastor Hemann had received, he was to be missionary-at-large serving Santa Barbara, Ventura, and Los Angeles counties exclusive of the cities of Los Angeles and Pasadena, which were in care of pastors Runkel and Reiser. He did quite a bit of traveling, surveying Santa Barbara, finding a number of Germans who were not affiliated with the Catholic church, but who were not too interested in starting a preaching station. However, he did find a number of Norwegians in Santa Barbara and in the hills in Conejo, who were receptive. Pastor Hemann began preaching to each group once a month. They had Norwegian Lutheran hymnals from their

home country that they used for singing, while the rest of the service was in English. He served the three families who were left in Palmdale once every three months. At the time when he departed for Wisconsin in November 1903, St. John's had a church, parsonage ($800), and a barn for a horse and buggy, all surrounded by a neat picket fence, with the complete property worth well over $3,000. With the congregation's offerings paying all the bills, there was no need for subsidy from the District's Mission Board.

With the arrival of Pastor P. Schmidt of Walla Walla, Washington in October of 1904, a Young People's Society was organized on November 26, 1904. Within a few short years of the building of the church, all the congregation's organizations were well established, with the congregation growing to 35 communicant members in 1907. In November of 1909, Pastor C. K. Kaiser was installed at St. John's, remaining until February 1912, resigning due to ill health. Pastor L. J. Meyer immediately followed him in February of 1912 and remained

Interior of St. John's first church decorated for Easter. (Pacific Southwest District Archives)

Rev. Bruno Saager, 1919–1922. (Pacific Southwest District Archives)

Rev. G. Ferber, 1924–1927. (Pacific Southwest District Archives)

Rev. M. J. Von Der Au, 1927–1938. (Pacific Southwest District Archives)

Rev. William Faasch, 1939–1941. (Pacific Southwest District Archives)

Rev. Elmer E. Atrops, 1941-1966. (Pacific Southwest District Archives)

A few days before the Building Committee is to travel to Redwood City to see a church building, Pastor Faasch has an appendicitis attack and dies.

until September of 1913. Pastor P. Zimmermann of San Diego came in September of 1913, staying until May 1915, followed by Pastor W. G. Ruehle who arrived in May of 1915 from a congregation in Florida and left during December of 1918. During his pastorate, St. John's joined the Missouri Synod having been served by Synod's pastors for 18 years. Pastor Bruno Saager came in January of 1919, leaving in January of 1922 to go to Riverside. During his pastorate, the congregation celebrated its 25th anniversary in 1925, having grown to 92 baptized members, 74 communicants, with 16 voting members.

From January of 1922 to February of 1924, Pastor P. Lebahn of Santa Barbara served as vacancy pastor. In February of 1924, Pastor G. Ferber of Bruedersheim, Alberta, Canada, came to Oxnard to shepherd the flock. When Pastor Ferber accepted a call as missionary to the deaf in Southern California in April of 1927, the congregation extended a call to the Rev. M. J. Von Der Au of Chula Vista, California. He was installed on August 28, 1927 serving St. John's for a period of 11 years, until on October 23, 1938, when the Lord called this faithful servant to his eternal home. During his pastorate, the congregation had 104 souls with 72 communicant members, and 11 voting members with a Sunday school of 22. When the vacancy occurred, the Rev. E. J. Fleischer of Ventura served the Oxnard congregation as vacancy pastor, suggesting that a new location and a new church plant would better serve the cause of Lutheranism in Oxnard. While such an undertaking seemed impractical at the time, some consideration was given the matter.

After the installation of the new pastor, the Rev. William Faasch, on July 16, 1939, the activities of the congregation were reorganized and a build-

ing fund was established. In a voters' meeting on October 7, 1940, Mr. A. Schroeder announced that he would furnish a new church site at Fifth and H streets, if the congregation was sufficiently interested in undertaking a building program. The congregation gratefully accepted the offer and on November 6, 1940, officially resolved to proceed with plans for a building program with Mr. A. Schroeder elected to serve as chairman of the Building Committee. The Building Committee met the following week to organize its work and discuss preliminary plans. To obtain ideas on the type of church architecture desired, arrangements were made to visit the new Lutheran church in Redwood City, California. A few days before the scheduled trip, Pastor Faasch was suddenly stricken with appendicitis and, following an emergency operation, passed away on March 8, 1941. He had served the congregation only 19 months when the Lord of the Church, in His infinite wisdom, also summoned this servant to his eternal rest.

A call was extended to the Rev. Elmer E. Atrops, who was temporarily serving First Lutheran Church in Ventura from October 1940 until May 1941 while the Ventura pastor was on a year's leave of absence. Previously, he had assisted his father, the Rev. Herman Atrops, at the Garvey Mission from June to September 1940. He was born in a parsonage in Argo Township, South Dakota, on November 7, 1912. He attended California Concordia College in Oakland, California, from 1927 through 1933. Following his graduation, he attended Concordia Seminary in St. Louis, Missouri, graduating in 1940. He received a call to be a missionary in China, but could not obtain passage on a ship due to the uncertain conditions in the Orient at that time. He married Ruby Velma Stize on August 11, 1940, with their marriage blessed with nine children, Martin and David, who both became pastors; Judith; Janet; Joanne; Arthur; Jeanine; Jenilyn; and Julene.

Pastor Atrops accepted the call to Oxnard, and was installed on June 1, 1941. During the following months, plans for the proposed new church plant were prepared and discussed with Mr. Walter E. Erkes of Los Angeles who was engaged as the architect, with the congregation officially approving the completed plans on July 21, 1942. However, due to the war and restriction on building materials, the congregation decided to postpone the actual construction, putting forth every effort to gather the necessary building funds among the 93 communicant members.

With the development of the naval base at Port Hueneme, resulting in a large influx of war workers needing housing facilities not only for the workers but also for naval personnel, the government took possession of the land surrounding the congregation's new building site, including the right of way of the street. The advisability of obtaining another church site became apparent, and on May 28, 1944, the congregation resolved to dispose of the property at Fifth and H streets and select a new site. The original owner agreed to refund the purchase price of $2,800, allowing an additional sum of $750 to compensate for the advance preparations already made by the parish for the new church plant.

After an unsuccessful attempt to obtain a new site in the northern section of Oxnard, the congregation resolved to purchase property on H Street, comprising the eight lots or half a block between Second and Third streets, on July 10, 1944, with negotiations of the purchase price of $6,000 completed in 1945. That year the congregation's 137 communicant members celebrated their 45th anniversary with Rev. Armand Mueller as guest speaker. During November of the same year, the old church property at Seventh and C streets was sold to the Foursquare Gospel Church for $7,200. Because of continued restrictions on building materials, the congregation was unable to proceed with the building of its new church plant as anticipated, and because of an agreement to vacate the old parsonage by January 1946 and the church by July of that year, arrangements had to be made for temporary quarters. Three members purchased a large home at 407 Magnolia Avenue, making it available to the congregation for use as a temporary parsonage. After considering various plans as to a temporary place of worship, the congregation decided to erect a permanent Christian day school building at the new location, temporarily using it as a chapel and parish hall.

Following groundbreaking ceremonies for the new building on August 4, 1946, the new structure was dedicated to the glory of God, with Rev. A. G. Webbeking as the speaker at the dedication on December 22. During the previous five months, church services were held in the Diffenderffer and Son Mortuary Chapel, with all other meetings held in the parsonage. The cost of the building, furnishings, and the entire street paving improvements amounted to approximately $25,000. Up to this time $38,653.37 had been gathered for the Building Fund and $1,691.99 for an Organ Fund.

Early in 1948, the congregation resolved to proceed with the construction of the new church and parsonage as soon as financial arrangements could be made. Ground was broken for the new buildings on Sunday, May 9, 1948, with the cornerstone-laying service held on the afternoon of July 25, 1948. On Sunday, January 30, 1949, St. John's dedicated its new church and parsonage. During the previous eight years, receipts for the Building Fund alone totaled $65,557. The cost of the church was $60,000 with the parsonage costing $22,000. The congregation's property at that time, including improvements, buildings, and equipment represented an investment of approximately $120,000.

The beautiful, new English Gothic church of St. John's was built by Mr. Adolph Schroeder, local builder, a member of the congregation since 1908, and chairman of the Building Committee since the congregation began its expansion program during the previous eight years. The high, slender spire, capped with a stainless steel finial and small gold-leaf ball, the steep roof lines with a slight sweep along the bottom, the series of windows with shaped heads and splayed jambs, and the simple Gothic arched entrance with plank, redwood doors and transom, all combined to present a picture of churchly beauty. The plans were originally prepared in 1942 for a Gothic sanctuary including an adjoining parish hall. Due to a change in the building site and the growth of the congregation since that time, the decision was made to eliminate the parish hall. Other revisions of the original plans included lengthening the nave of the church to provide additional seating space with the narthex enlarged to permit the addition of a gallery for the choir and organ console, which caused

> St. John's builds a large English Gothic church in 1949.

other changes to be made at the east end of the building thus eliminating the parish hall.

When entering the church through the arched entrance, the narthex opened into the center and side aisles of the nave. A mothers' room was located on the left side. Included in the narthex was a registration desk with tract racks, a bulletin board, two small chair closets, an ushers' desk, shelving for a small church library, and a small room in which the organ blower was installed. The real beauty of the interior of the nave was in its worshipful atmosphere and the simplicity of architectural design with the steep-pitched, redwood roof of the nave and chancel rising to a height of 30 feet, with purlins running horizontally the full length. The heavy scissor trusses gave a feeling of refinement, attaining a Gothic effect by means of graceful corbels at their base. From the corbels in the nave hung lantern-style light fixtures, enhanced by ornamental iron brackets. The two long side aisles had redwood ceilings intersected by the piers with a series of arches. The aisles were separated from the nave proper by splayed arches, which extended the full length of the nave and into the chancel. Through each archway appeared a set of cathedral glass windows with shaped heads and beveled jambs. The 11, beautiful art glass windows were part of a proposed plan which included an entire series of 24 more windows depicting familiar scenes pertaining to the life and work of Jesus Christ all made by Judson Studios of Los Angeles.

Separating the spacious chancel from the nave was a simple wood screen where the pulpit and

lectern also stood. The focal point of the entire interior was the stunning chancel with its high Gothic arch, black walnut altar and reredos, enhanced by a rich bronze cross and candelabra, redwood ceiling, Communion rail, and art glass windows. The three art glass windows portraying "The Ascension of Christ" formed a continuation of the altar reredos. The simple Gothic treatment of the Communion rail and wood screens was carried out similarly in the west end of the church where the gallery projected over the narthex. The gallery, with its arched ceiling and flush ceiling lights, provided ample room for the choir, the two-manual pipe organ console built by the Reuter Organ Company of Lawrence, Kansas, at a cost of $5,600, a sizable organ chamber housing the 800 pipes of the organ, and an additional closet. The gallery was reached by means of a stairway in the narthex.

The floors of the gallery, mothers' room, narthex, pastor's study, and waiting room were covered with cork laid in an attractive tile pattern. The print room, working sacristy, and most of the nave proper had maple hardwood floors. The side

St. John's stately English Gothic church building and parsonage were dedicated on January 30, 1949. (Pacific Southwest District Archives)

The focal point of the interior was the stunning chancel with its high Gothic arch and black walnut altar and reredos. (Pacific Southwest District Archives)

aisles, center isle, and the space between the front pews and the chancel, as well as the entire chancel, were carpeted. At the east end of the church were the pastor's study, a waiting room, print room, restrooms, and a working sacristy completely equipped with shelving, cupboards, sink, and other conveniences for use in connection with the care of the Communion and altar ware, paraments, linens, and vestments.

At the time of dedication, St. John's had 284 baptized souls with 186 communicant members having doubled its communicant membership since 1940. The Sunday school enrollment was 65 with an additional 45 children enrolled in the Cradle Roll Department. Oxnard had a population of 21,500 and agriculture remained the major industry. The military bases established at Port Hueneme and Point Mugu during World War II, and the rise of electronic, aerospace, and other manufacturing industries, contributed to the growth of the city and surrounding areas, helping to increase church membership.

In 1950, Mr. Oscar F. Suelter, who served the school for 24 years, was installed as principal of the re-established Christian day school, opened that September, seeing the school grow from one room with 14 pupils to 209 students with 7 teachers in 1974 when he retired. When the congregation celebrated its 50th anniversary, the Rev. William G. Ruehle, a former pastor, was the speaker. At the time, baptized membership was 365 and the communicant membership was 228. When the day school had outgrown the three-classroom facility in 1954, a temporary classroom was purchased for $1,000 from the Hueneme School District with a fourth teacher added to the staff. Due to the growth of the parish, two services were conducted for the first time in 1956. With the continued increase in membership, the congregation purchased the present site, 435' width with a 500' depth that fronted C Street for $142,500 in 1964. With the H Street property sold for $145,000, a solution had to be found to house the congregation and the school temporarily. That solution in 1965 was to build the 8-room day school, 65' × 190' containing 10,640 square feet. The building was constructed of steel reinforced concrete block, with hot-mop roof and concrete floors covered with vinyl tile. Five classrooms were completed; four were used for the 141 pupils. There were also eight Sunday school rooms, teachers' lounge, library, supply room, and restrooms. The three unused classrooms, forming an L-shaped area, were used

for church services while the new church building was under construction. The last service was held in the H Street church at the beginning of 1966, just 17 years after its dedication. Before Pastor Atrops could see the new building completed, the Lord called him to his heavenly home on November 20, 1966, at the age of 54.

The Rev. Calvin R. Fiege, a member of the Michigan District office staff beginning in 1962, accepted St. John's call to become St. John's new pastor in 1967. He was born on March 25, 1925, in Benton Harbor, Michigan, and attended Concordia High School and College in Fort Wayne, Indiana, followed by his graduation from Concordia Seminary in St. Louis in 1948. Following his ordination in Emmaus, South Bend, Indiana, he was installed as assistant pastor at Immanuel, St. Charles, Missouri, in 1948 where he served until 1952 and then took a call to St. John's in St. John's, Michigan. On November 5, 1950, he married Doris Lucille Finck, and their union was blessed with three children. After serving St. John's in Oxnard, he joined the staff of the Southern California District as administrative assistant to the president stewardship in 1984, later becoming vice president of the Lutheran Church Extension Fund of the Pacific Southwest District.

On September 15, 1968, the new sanctuary was dedicated with the pastor of St. John's, the Rev. Fiege, serving as liturgist and the Rev. Victor L. Behnken, president of the Southern California District, as the speaker. As worshipers entered the C Street property, they beheld a free-standing bell tower with pre-cast concrete legs and a "TITANALOY" spire and cross containing a 25 note carillon located near the northwest corner of the sanctuary, rising 70 feet above the sanctuary floor level. The oak paneled front door was decorated with an eight and one-half foot bronze Chi Rho, the first letters of Christ in the Greek alphabet or the Latin Christus Rex, Christ the King. The conventional contemporary church building designed by the architects, Strange, Inslee, and Senefeld, sitting three feet above the sidewalk, was constructed of steel reinforced "Dutch White" face brick walls and stucco clerestory structure with a concrete roof. The building had a width of 65' and a length of 120', containing 9,272 square feet of floor space seating 498 in the nave plus 40 in the balcony, which also accommodated the 28-rank Moeller pipe organ.

When entering the nave with its exposed wood purlin and wood deck ceiling reaching a height of

Rev. Calvin R. Fiege became St. John's new pastor in 1967. (Pacific Southwest District Archives)

On September 15, 1968, the new sanctuary of St. John's is dedicated.

Rev. Mark E. Beyer pictured in 1991. (Pacific Southwest District Archives)

In 1978, St. John's dedicates its long-awaited fellowship hall.

31 feet, the eye is drawn to the large chancel area with the free-standing oak altar, surrounded by an oak Communion rail, accented by a red grille cloth extending from floor to ceiling on the back wall having a 14-foot Latin cross of anodized aluminum with oak inlay against the back wall of "Dutch White" brick with the three pavement candle holders and vases of bronze. The alcove to the left housed a seven-rank Robert Hall pipe organ. The chancel and narthex had black slate floors, with the nave and side chapel aisles carpeted, and with vinyl tile laid under the pews. All the woodwork, paneling and doors, pews and Communion rail, were oak, stained in a rich medium brown color. The nave lighting, with pendant fixtures extending 10 feet from the ceiling having the sound system installed in them, and the chapel and the chancel lighting were all dimmer-controlled for lighting modulation. Thirty-three stained glass windows adorned the worship area, narthex, and bride's room, portraying in figures and symbols, the meaning of the Christian faith and doctrine, setting hearts and minds toward thoughtful worship of the risen Lord and Savior of the church. Seven new stained glass windows in the clerestory depicted the great "I AM" statement of Christ contained in the Gospel of John, after which the church was named. A fully carpeted bride's room with restrooms and supply rooms were also all located off of the narthex. The pastor's office, reception and secretary's office, and the working sacristy were located adjacent to the chancel. Exposed

face brick was used extensively in these areas with all rooms having acoustical ceilings. At the time of the church dedication, the church had grown to 1,055 baptized members with a communicant membership of 638, and with the city of Oxnard having a population of 68,400.

In 1978, St. John's dedicated its long-awaited fellowship center with 600 members and friends worshiping and enjoying fellowship around the theme, "To Serve with Love." The service began in the church sanctuary as three of the congregation's choirs and the handbell choir participated with the service led by Rev. Fiege and Rev. Mark Beyer. The congregation concluded the service in the fellowship center with the dedication of the building and open house tours conducted by George Dockweiler, chairman of the Building Committee, and members of the committee. The ladies of the congregation served a luncheon.

The new fellowship center, designed by Architect Redge Crowell and built by a congregational member, Charles Schroeder, son of A. Schroeder who built the H Street facilities, included a large hall that could seat 800 or dine 400 people with several smaller rooms surrounding the main section of the building. At one end was the stage area and on the other were the administration offices. A large kitchen facility and two multi-purpose rooms were along one side. A warm atmosphere was created in the main room, which had a multi-purpose carpet designed to be used for everything from basketball to volleyball and from box

St. John's new sanctuary was dedicated on September 15, 1968. (Pacific Southwest District Archives)

The remodeled chancel with the 12-foot wide video screen. (Pacific Southwest District Archives)

lunches to Vespers.

In 1998, St. John's embarked on a huge building program which was culminated in a festival service on May 3 with combined adult and children choirs of 220 voices singing at the dedication of the renovated church which was completed in a 14-month building project resulting in the addition of 2 new school classrooms and a highly innovative worship space. The renovated campus also included a large outdoor fellowship patio, with a free-standing coffee and food gazebo adjacent to the parking area's sanctuary entrances. Rev. Kenneth Hahn, associate pastor, serving as liturgist and Rev. Mark E. Beyer, senior pastor, serving as dedication preacher, led the worship service. Also included in the service was the music of the new three-manual organ, brass, handbells, worship band, and piano.

Cutting edge technology was a large part of the vision for the remodeled church with the completed sanctuary utilizing a 12-foot wide video screen, a sound system designed with a 32–channel mixer with MIDI playback capabilities, CD, and tape player. The acoustics of the church were improved to enhance congregational singing, sound system, all types of music performance, and the new three-manual and pedal organ. The chancel was designed to be a flexible space with all furnishings moveable to provide varied arrangements for concerts, drama, large music ensembles, and all worship settings.

At the time, Pastor Mark Beyer commented, "Technology has not been our focus. It is also a tool to reach the worshiper, and the community with the Gospel. The technology is a 'now' resource for a 'now' church. The Gospel of Christ has been the focus in everything we have done." A few months earlier, the R. G. Neumann Education Building was dedicated, housing a new kindergarten classroom, and a new library, also used as a meeting room for St. John's Church and kindergarten through eighth grade Christian day school.

By 1980, there was a large shift in the population of Oxnard with more and more Hispanics moving into the area. With the increased Hispanic populace, St. John's saw a need to minister to this group of people. Pastor Fiege stated that the congregation began its Spanish outreach program through nine Vacation Bible Schools held in parks, yards, and people's homes where Hispanic children were invited to attend. After they procured trucks to take furniture to the sites, they had three teams that did the teaching, crafts, and music. When the Vacation Bible Schools were completed, they discovered that south Oxnard was where they received the best response. Following the request to the District Mission Board in the beginning of 1982 to supply the congregation with a Spanish-speaking pastor, Candidate Dennis Bradshaw was placed in Oxnard in 1983 to do Hispanic ministry where he was ordained at St. John's. He was born in Monrovia, California, on October 21, 1955, and graduated from Christ College, Irvine, in 1980. Following his graduation from Concordia Seminary in St. Louis, Missouri, in 1983, he was called as missionary-at-large to Oxnard. That summer he continued conducting a VBS having between 60 to 70 Hispanic children. Following the VBS, he made home visitations, beginning Spanish Bible study in homes of several families, and was preparing to begin a Spanish language Lutheran radio program in the area. A Spanish Saturday school and worship services were conducted at St. John's where Pastor Bradshaw met regularly with 15 to 20 children and adults in the church. He conducted services in the carports of apartment complexes and in the city parks in south Oxnard. In 1985, he and Tara Elise Lashley, who were both bilingual, were united in marriage with their union blessed with two children. She held a master's degree in public health from UCLA, taught parenting classes at the local hospital, and had participated in cross-cultural missions in Latin America.

Rev. Dennis Bradshaw was placed in Oxnard in 1983 to begin a Hispanic ministry. (Pacific Southwest District Archives)

With the increased Hispanic populace in 1980, St. John's sees a need to minister to this group of people.

Bev Byer teaching children in the apartment house carport, the first attempt to gather people for ministry in 1983.

In 1985, Centro Educacional Cristiano de la Iglesia Luterana is established in Oxnard.

Since St. John's best response for VBS was from south Oxnard, Pastor Bradshaw rented a storefront facility in South Oxnard in 1985, close to the families of the children with whom he worked, establishing Centro Educacional Cristiano de la Iglesia Luterana. St. John's shared the Christmas message with its neighbors in the Oxnard community at the Candy Cane Festival on December 6, 1986, with puppeteers from the congregation presenting a puppet show in Spanish and English based on "No Room at the Inn." Tracts in Spanish and English were distributed integrating the story with the presentation of the Gospel message of salvation along with Bibles and punch-out nativity sets given to the children. Included in the pamphlets was information on St. John's and its mission work with Pastor Bradshaw.

In 1988, Pastor Bradshaw administered First Communion to 10 new children on Palm Sunday in the young fellowship of Centro Educacional Cristiano de la Iglesia Luterana. The Hispanic congregation continued to experience some growth and stability during the previous year with the ministry effectively reaching Hispanics in the community. By 1990, the parish was averaging 40 people per Sunday. In 1991, the ministry had to be moved out of its facilities, because the new landlords had established a very high rent structure. They found a new building much closer to their ministry area and entered into a lease agreement, making it financially easier to handle. Pastor Bradshaw had expressed that the move, which they first thought would be a hindrance to the ministry, had proven to be a blessing.

In the May 1992 issue of *This Month*, Pastor Bradshaw reported, "We have had some wonder-

ful gatherings over the past few months, opening our facilities and providing diverse programs to the community of Southwinds. We have especially directed our outreaches to the many boys and girls who live in the apartment complexes within our immediate neighborhood. We offer devotions to lead young people to God's Law and God's Good News for them. We offer craft projects to encourage creativity and cooperation. We make many new friends! For many of these young people our Boys'/Girls' Group Program is the highlight of their week, and, oftentimes, the only interaction they have with a caring, loving, Christian, adult." Some of the activities were group devotions, a fishing workshop on the Hueneme Pier, a craft day, a Health Faire, and a neighborhood clean up. The food and snacks left over from Desert Storm packages were given to assist the ministry in Oxnard. The mission welcomed more than 20 visitors in the final months of 1992, generating a strong prospective member list. The mission, supported by member congregations within Circuit One and the Pacific Southwest District, had 66 baptized members, and 13 communicant members.

In 1993, a ministry team from St. John's went to Costa Rica through Latin American Mission to help struggling congregations and do some street witnessing. The following year, a 12-person mission team from Central America came to the Southwinds community to help the Oxnard congregation do door-to-door visitation. The location of the mission was visible and available to the neighborhood as apartments, often housing more than one family in each unit with Hispanic immigrants, surrounded it. Since many were on low incomes with tight food budgets, bread,

Pastor Bradshaw giving a boy his First Communion certificate on Palm Sunday, 1988.

The Hispanic mission that met in the Southwinds area of Oxnard, circa 1993.

courtesy of a local bakery, was distributed every Thursday. Through being open to the families' basic needs, this presented a good opportunity to talk to them about the real "Bread of Life." Other means that brought positive results were the storefront preaching station, worship in the park, active door-to-door evangelism, and strong circuit support which accepted the responsibility for this ministry through financial support having a council that met once a month to share in the success stories and bring back needs of the mission. Pastor Bradshaw once said, "Where 'Greenland's Icy Mountains' were once the mission field, the mission field has come to us. As immigrants continue to arrive in California, our circuit is sharing God's Word in its own backyard."

This small mission, a young congregation, consisting mostly of new Christians who were first generation Hispanic immigrants from either Mexico or Central America, joined Synod in 1997. By 1998, this small mission, now known as Centro Cristiano Redwood, had grown to between 80 and 100 Hispanics worshiping each Sunday. The mission also was involved in the SEAN lay leadership-training program with several members being trained. Through this program, work was begun to plant a mission in Carpinteria, alongside of Faith Lutheran's congregation. As Pastor Bradshaw moved into that mission, Pastor Marco Lozano began a part-time ministry in the Oxnard area. He was born on December 12, 1965, in Zacapú, Michoacán, Mexico, where he graduated from the high school. When his mother sent him to America to earn money to marry a girl in Mexico, he came to Oxnard where he worked in the fields, in a restaurant, and went to a mechanics school where he graduated. He met his wife, Francisca Leon, was married in 1986, and was blessed with two children, a boy and a girl. They were raised Catholics, but when his wife and daughter met Pastor Bradshaw through the VBS, they joined the Centro Cristiano Redwood becoming Lutherans. When Pastor Bradshaw asked to meet Marco, he came to church and was later confirmed in 1989. He decided he wanted to become a pastor as he had compassion for the needy. At the time, there was no way for him to study, as there was no program in Spanish. One day after he heard about the Theological Education by Extension (TEE) program, he enrolled.

By 2000, two groups from the mission were doing evangelism work in the community. During the month of June, the worship focus was on stewardship with the youth doing two successful car washes. The youth group went to an event in Santa Paula, called "Action House," where they made many different items designed specially for the youth of the different ministries. That summer a special evening event for the community was held after the VBS at the park with over 40 enthusiastic children participating. At the beginning of 2001, church attendance rose to 70 per Sunday with 2 new families attending. In the spring, the mission distributed food to the needy families and had a yard sale in order for the community to get know them. On September 29, the Circuit 1 Hispanic Mission Society and St. John's Mission Board sponsored a mission celebration with a bilingual service, followed by lunch, with displays of mission and ministry. The focus of the celebration was on how God was working to reach people of all cultures to deliver the Good News of Jesus Christ.

On a Wednesday during prayer time in the summer of 2001, a man visited Pastor Lozano with whom he hadn't been in contact for about three years. He told him, "Pastor, I have been looking for you; I was just not listening when you ministered to me. Today, I have seen an evangelism campaign and I want to serve the Lord in the church in which I first heard the Good News." Pastor said, "For me, it was such a joy to see how a soul that was lost came looking for Jesus. 'Til this day, he is faithful." At the beginning of 2002, church attendance had increased to 80 people per Sunday and Bible class attendance was at 50 with the Lord blessing the mission with new families. At the same time, the parish had shared about 30 baskets to needy families in the community. Three men, Marco Lo-

By 1998, this small mission, now known as Centro Cristiano Redwood, has grown to between 80 and 100 Hispanics worshiping each Sunday.

The Marco Luzano family with Pastor Bradshaw in 2000.

Centro Cristiano Redwood at the ELCA church where congregation worships.

zano, Javier Velasco, and Marcelino Velasco, were commissioned into the deaconate on June 9, having completed the SEAN Pastoral Theology Training Program. They served the Centro Cristiano Hispanic Ministries of Circuit 1 at Santa Ynez to Agoura Hills, while Deacon Lozano was leading the "mother congregation," Centro Cristiano Redwood in Oxnard. Pastor Dennis Bradshaw focused his energy on mission development in Carpinteria and in Santa Paula.

According to Deacon Lozano, the community of Oxnard has changed in the twenty-first century for Mexicans as they no longer toil in the fields, but now live in a more stable condition, as they work in steady jobs, since the agricultural fields have been displaced with homes. Centro Cristiano Redwood has between 60 and 70 members in a multi-cultural ministry where they work with the community and in the parks taking the Word to where people

are gathered. Redwood is a training place for new pastors and deacons, with the congregation having three deacons. The activities include parking lot sales, park visits, and visiting people, which is the most successful. Worship services are conducted in an ELCA church on Sundays at 6:00 p.m. with a Sunday school at 5:00 p.m., Wednesday evening services at 7:00 p.m., and a Friday Bible class at 7:00 p.m. There is also a youth program called Club de Niños. Deacon Lozano stated that the mission is a loving, caring, and warm church embracing the needy. St. John's of Oxnard continues to support the ministry with the District at one time supporting 20 percent of its funding. Office space is rented at 905 Redwood Street in Oxnard for the administration of the ministry and for meetings of the parish. The Lord has blessed this mission with dedicated people.

Faith Lutheran Church
Centro Cristiano
Carpinteria, California

he Carpinteria Valley has a total of 11.6 square miles, with the city of Carpinteria, incorporated in 1965, now having about 15,194 residents, covering 2.5 land miles. The Carpinteria Valley is located in the southwest corner of Santa Barbara County, midway between Santa Barbara and Ventura. Off

Highway 101, El Camino Real, Carpinteria is just a few hours drive from major metropolitan areas, Santa Barbara 12 miles north, Ventura 15 miles south, and Los Angeles 80 miles south.

Over many centuries, the Carpinteria Valley has felt the impact of three distinct cultures giving it a unique and colorful history. The valley's first inhabitants were the remarkable Chumash Indians whose exquisite woven baskets, projectile points, shell money, and rock paintings remain as evidence of their highly complex culture. Through the boat building work of the Chumash, the soldiers of the Portola expedition of 1769 were prompted to name the valley Carpinteria, meaning the carpenter's shop. During the Mission and Rancho periods, between 1786-1848, the Chumash were driven into forced labor, and the valley was set-aside as pueblo lands. Small parcels of land were commonly given to retiring presidio soldiers who built adobe homes for summer use. Not until 1850 when California became a state, did the valley open to American settlement. The earliest settlers were mainly disillusioned gold seekers from the north, becoming farmers and shopkeepers.

One hundred years later in the late 1950s, through the urging of several families in the area and the circuit counselor, Rev. V. W. Neemeyer of Santa Barbara, the Mission Board elected to serve the area with a vicar. Since a vicar was not available, Rev. Loren Kramer, missionary-at-large serving the Goleta field as pastor, was requested to initiate the work. Pastor Kramer was born on October 19, 1934, in Clay Center, Kansas, where his father, Rev. Dr. Fred Kramer was pastor, and later professor at Concordia Seminary in Springfield, Illinois. Loren received his pre-theological training at St. John's in Winfield, Kansas, graduating from Concordia Seminary, St. Louis, in 1959 and doing his vicarage year in Beloit, Wisconsin. At Winfield, he met Arlene Klaustermeyer, a native of Orange, California; they were married in her home church, St. John's, by Rev. W. Gesch, on July 6, 1959. In their first five years of marriage, they were blessed with three children: Mark, Katie, and Karen. Rev. Kramer served 26 years as pastor of Good Shepherd in Goleta, where the congregation became the largest parish in the circuit. He would later become District president, serving from 1985 to 2000.

Pastor Kramer took with him a box of hymnals and a check for $25 to open the first bank account when the first Lutheran worship service was held

Rev. Loren Kramer, missionary at large serving the Goleta field, began services in Carpinteria in 1959. (Pacific Southwest District Archives)

at 8:30 a.m. on October 4, 1959, in the Carpinteria Women's Club with 48 persons in attendance and with Sunday school classes attended by 15 pupils. At the time, the population of Carpinteria was approximately 3,000 with about 5,000 in the surrounding area to be served by the mission. General Electric and several other large companies were planning to erect offices and factories in the area, assuring a corresponding expansion in population.

By January 1960, the mission had 27 communicant members and 53 baptized members with an average church attendance of 40 and 21 in Sunday school. The District subsidy paid to the pastor for mileage was $50 per month, and the mission was able to meet all other regular operating expenses. Planning for further development of the work, the Mission Board was giving consideration to the purchase of real estate, as the facilities of the Women's Club were convenient and adequate at the time; however, the parking lot had to be shared with the Community Church, which was the predominant church in Carpinteria. Pastor Kramer stated in a 1960 report, "Until we get out of the 'shadow of their steeple' success in attracting newcomers will suffer. The members of the mission are faithful in attendance and are zealous in publicizing the fact that there is now a Lutheran church in the community. Prospects for future growth are encouraging."

In 1960, the growth of the mission under Pastor Kramer was steady, numbering 78 baptized members and 38 communicants with a Sunday school of 32. With the more rapid development of Goleta, coupled with increasing responsibilities of student work in the expanding campus of Santa Barbara State College, the Mission Board decided to divide this work and place a candidate in Carpinteria for more intensive activity in the growing area or request the services of a vicar, to work under the supervision of Pastor Victor Neemeyer of Santa Barbara. Since neither one of these suggestions came to fruition, Pastor Kramer continued to serve both parishes. By 1962, the congregation was not yet formally organized but did have an average attendance of 40 to 50 with 36 communicant

The first Lutheran worship service is held on October 4, 1959, in the Carpinteria Women's Club.

Rev. Philip Ilten was commissioned on September 17, 1962, as missionary-at-large serving as pastor of Faith Church, Carpinteria. (Pacific Southwest District Archives)

members, 76 baptized members, and a Sunday school of 33 children. The District loaned the congregation the necessary funds to purchase a site for future building, a four and three-quarter acre lot with a nine-room home purchased for $56,000. Growth in the Carpinteria area was slowed by several factors. No new homes had been built in the area for quite some time because of a poor sanitary disposal system. A bond issue solved that problem with several industries purchasing land in Carpinteria and starting plant construction. As part of the growing Santa Barbara metropolitan area, Carpinteria was a promising area of the future. The people of Faith Lutheran Church felt they had gotten in on the ground floor of Carpinteria's coming growth. They had a deep faith that with the God's hand of blessing, the congregation would grow and flourish.

Finally, on September 17, 1962, the congregation's desire to have its own pastor came through the commissioning of Rev. Philip Ilten as missionary-at-large in the Southern California District, serving as pastor of Faith Church, Carpinteria. Rev. William Ilten of Montebello, California, preached the sermon entitled "Serve the Lord with Gladness." Rev. Loren Kramer served as liturgist, and Rev. Elmer Atrops was the officiant. The commissioning service was followed by a reception for 150 guests in the parish hall of Emmanuel Church, Santa Barbara.

Pastor Ilten was the son of the late Robert C. Ilten and his wife, Hulda, of Cedar Rapids, Iowa,

and the youngest in a family of five children. In preparation for seminary training, he attended Concordia College, Milwaukee, Wisconsin. He completed his vicarage year under Rev. William L. Bartling, pastor of Apostles Lutheran Church, Franklin Park, Illinois, completing his formal studies at Concordia Seminary, St. Louis in 1962, earning a Bachelor of Divinity degree. On July 5, 1959, he married Sheila Meyer, a parochial school teacher from Springfield, Illinois, with their marriage blessed with a daughter, Jennifer, a year old at the time of pastor's installation at Faith.

On June 14, 1964, the much-awaited day finally arrived with the dedication of Faith's new $75,000 chapel designed by architect Dennis Wehmueller of Los Angeles, and the installation of Rev. Philip Ilten as its first full-time pastor. The two events took place the same day during the summer, with Rev. Frederic Brick, chairman of the Institutional Ministry Department of the Mission Board, delivering the dedicatory sermon, and Rev. William Ilten, pastor of St. John's Church in Montebello, speaking at the installation service. Officiant at the installation was Rev. Carl Mehlberg, circuit counselor. Also dedicated in the afternoon service was a Holzinger pipe organ, a gift to the congregation by Mr. Emil Schnackenberg of Orange. The building construction was supervised by Alvin Gnuse, a member of Faith Church with much of the labor supplied by the members, saving the congregation $25,000.

By 1966 with the aid of adequate new facilities, the parish had grown to 188 baptized members and 110 communicant members with a Sunday school enrollment of 105. The community also saw significant growth with new tracts of homes constructed along with two new shopping centers making Carpinteria a residential area for the Santa Barbara and Ventura commuters. Even though growth of the congregation had been gradual, the extended outlook was quite gratifying with the Lutheran church well established in the area as the population began to soar.

After Pastor Ilten accepted a call to Wausau, Wisconsin, in 1967, Rev Ronald Timmons became the second full-time pastor of Faith, installed on August 27, 1967. He was born in Riverside, California, on May 5, 1939. After graduation from Riverside Polytechnic High School, he attended one year at Riverside City College, followed by a job at the University of California at Riverside's Department of Air Pollution. In September of 1959, he entered the ministerial program at Concordia Theo-

Faith's new $75,000 chapel/parish hall was dedicated on June 14, 1964. (Pacific Southwest District Archives)

logical Seminary, Springfield, Illinois, serving his vicarage year at Evergreen Lutheran Church in Detroit, Michigan. Following his graduation from Concordia, he accepted a call to Ascension Lutheran Church in Cleburne, Texas in July of 1965. During his pastorate in Cleburne, he also served both Weatherford and Hillsboro, Texas, as vacancy pastor. He was active in the Christian Camping program in the Texas District serving on the Board for Camping in the Greater Dallas area, as well as dean of the camp at Sky Ranch. In Cleburne, he served not only as chaplain of Johnson County Memorial Hospital but also was active in civic affairs. He married the former Janet Mae Trinkle of Long Beach, California, on August 3, 1963. She had attended Concordia High School and Junior College at Oakland, California, and Concordia, River Forest, graduating in 1962 teaching in both parochial and public schools. At the time of his installation, they had been blessed with the birth of a daughter, Teri Loraine.

In October of 1969, Faith celebrated its 10th anniversary with a special service and fellowship dinner with Dr. William Carty, president of the congregation, serving as master of ceremonies, Pastor Kramer giving the keynote address, and the weekday school choir providing musical selections. The congregation had grown from the 48 persons who attended the first service to 125 members.

Ten years later on October 7, 1979, Faith celebrated its 20th anniversary with the theme, "God With Us — 20 years." Present at the celebration as guest pastors in the festival worship service were all of Faith's former pastors, Rev. Loren Kramer, Rev. Philip Ilten, Rev. Ronald Timmons, plus its pastor, Rev. David Thierfelder. A luncheon prepared by the ladies of the congregation provided a time of reminiscing for members and guests. Four years later, the congregation observed Rev. David F. Thierfelder's 25th anniversary in the ministry with a festival worship service at which the Rev. Calvin Fiege, administrative assistant to the Southern California District president, was the guest speaker, followed by a congregational dinner, where Roland Sylwester and his puppets were featured.

Two of Faith's members received awards for their work in the community. Alain Welty, a senior at Carpinteria High School and Carpinteria Boys Club Youth of the Year, was named 1985 Southern Santa Barbara Youth of the Year, where he participated in the national competition sponsored by the Boys' Clubs of America and the Reader's Digest Foundation. Also that year Soroptimist International of Carpinteria named Jean Harris, founder and director of Carpinteria Project Re-Entry, a rehabilitation program for stroke patients, "Woman of Distinction."

Marking the end of the yearlong 25th Anniversary Celebration of Faith in 1986 was the 40-voice choir and the handbell choir of Christ College, Irvine, presenting a Festival of Hymns. An organ recital and rededication ceremony featured guest organist Dennis Gano, pastor of Bethany, Hollywood, who demonstrated the capabilities of the newly rebuilt organ as part of the anniversary celebration. Four years later, Faith reached into the community with a week of Vacation Bible School taught by senior high students from St. Paul's Lutheran Church in Orange, with housing provided by members of Faith for the student teachers. In 1988, Pastor Thierfelder took a call to Bethany in Vacaville in northern California being replaced by Rev. Brian Hooper, assistant pastor at Gethsemane in Tempe, Arizona, who was a 1984 graduate of Concordia Seminary in St. Louis. By 1993, Faith had grown to 160 baptized members and 157 communicants members.

On May 5, 1996, Faith's newest pastor, Rev. David L. Bloedel, was installed in a colorful ceremony attended by a full house of worshipers and many fellow pastors. Participating in the service were the Rev. Phil Ilten, installer and counselor for Circuit One, of Christ the King Newbury Park; Rev. Dennis Bradshaw, Centro Cristiano Oxnard; Rev. La Mar Miller, Our Redeemer Ojai; Rev. Kenneth Hahn, St. John's, Oxnard; Rev. James Schmidt, past minister, Emmanuel, Santa Barbara; Rev. James Johnson, Good Shepherd, Goleta; Rev. Dr.

Rev. Ronald Timmons was installed on August 27, 1967, as Faith's second full-time pastor. (Pacific Southwest District Archives)

In 1988, Rev. Brian Hooper became pastor of Faith. (Pacific Southwest District Archives)

Faith's 20th anniversary celebration with former pastors: Rev. Timmons, Rev. Kramer, Rev. Ilten, Rev. Thierfelder, pastor at the time. (Pacific Southwest District Archives)

Rev. David L. Bloedel was installed as pastor of Faith on May 5, 1996. (Pacific Southwest District Archives)

In 1999, Rev. Dennis Bradshaw is asked to begin work among the Hispanics, beginning a small mission, Centro Cristiano, working side-by-side with Faith.

Loren Kramer, president of the Pacific Southwest District; Rev. Stanley Quebe, Zion, Anaheim; Rev. Richard Swanson, First Lutheran, Ventura, and the Rev. Cliff Kenyan, interim pastor at Faith.

Pastor Bloedel was born and raised in Janesville, Wisconsin, where he attended St. Paul Lutheran School before enrolling at Concordia Lutheran High School and Junior College, Milwaukee. In 1963, he graduated with a Bachelor of Arts degree from Concordia Senior College, Fort Wayne, and spent the summer touring Europe. After he received his Master of Divinity degree at Concordia Seminary, St. Louis, he and two classmates were ordained at their home church, St. Paul in Janesville, on June 18, 1967. He and Barbara Abrams, also of Janesville, were married in 1966 with their marriage blessed with two sons, Philip and Christopher. For eight and a half years, he served as pastor of Trinity Lutheran Church and School in Alamosa, Colorado. Prior to that, he served as a campus pastor at Central Missouri State University in Warrensburg, as pastor of Christ Lutheran Church, Elk City, and Our Savior, Weatherford, and as vicar/intern at Zion Lutheran Church in San Luis Obispo, California.

Faith broke ground on September 24, 1996, for an additional building to accommodate the pastor and secretary's offices, a nursery, recreation room, and storage area. It was almost to the day, 35 years before, when ground was broken for the first church building by then-pastor, Loren Kramer. Laborers for Christ, a Lutheran volunteer group, assisted in the construction of the additions. With the addition of space, the ministry could be broadened to reach into the community that was changing to a growing Hispanic population who worked in the agricultural industry. In order to work in this large mission field, the Rev. Dennis Bradshaw was asked to begin work among the Hispanics in 1999 beginning a small mission, Centro Cristiano, working side-by-side with Faith.

Throughout 1999, the ministry progressed with an ongoing study of the Hispanic community and neighborhood concentrations of Hispanics with canvassing done door-to-door in three particular areas of population. One cell group was formed in a home for several months but was terminated due to a rejection of the ministry on behalf of the prospective leader. Pastor Bradshaw stated, "This was a disappointment, yet there is peace in our decision to let this situation take its course as we are beginning to develop in another home a prospective base for cell group development. The ministry

is also working in the neighborhoods to develop other cell group bases." The outreach and visitation work sought to establish an evangelical Lutheran presence within the Hispanic community through the following: yard sales that ministered to the needs of the Hispanic community and provided an opportunity for personal contacts, the publication and regular distribution of the evangelistic newsletter called *El Noticiero del Carpintero*, "The Carpenter's Newsletter," the placing of a sign in Spanish in front of the mission location that would communicate the ministry and the Word of God to the Spanish-speaking community on an ongoing basis, and regular outreaches into the parks and public places where the Hispanic community gathered.

The lay leaders from Centro Cristiano Redwood (CCR) in Oxnard were also working with Pastor Bradshaw and his wife Tara in planting in neighboring Centro Cristiano Carpinteria (CCC). In addition to the evangelism tools in place at CCR, the mission in Carpinteria was also using specialized cell groups such as knitting and family and marriage counseling groups. In order to reach out and minister to the needs of the Hispanic community, which often was in search of affordable housing and employment in agriculture, CCC carried out a social ministry program, delivering bread, food, clothing, bedding, layettes, and other needed items to families. Pastor Bradshaw also led a conversational Spanish course with the supportive membership of Faith, Carpinteria. The class had to be closed after over 30 people had registered. CCC offered English as a Second Language (ESL) courses to the Hispanic community of Carpinteria.

For 20 years, Pastor Bradshaw had been educating Hispanic leaders for ministry and, as missionary-at-large, he led the mission planting of Centro Cristiano Carpinteria in Carpinteria. At the end of 1999, regular informal worship services were begun on Sunday at 5:00 p.m., with an average of 10 people, and one Sunday service a month was dedicated to evangelism. Through yard sales and park events, more names were gained for the contact list. One of the joys of the work was when a neighbor, who began attending Sunday worship regularly, opened her home to mid-week Bible study. In January 2000, she offered a knitting class to the ladies of the community.

At the end of the first quarter of 2000, worship attendance had increased to 16 with 5 people attending Bible class and 7 children attending Sunday school. The "Jesus movie" campaign that was started in that quarter had a limited response; yard sales continued to be a good outreach along with door-to-door visits. In June, a summer Bible school outreach ministry was begun with members inviting their Spanish-speaking neighbors. The program reached into the community sharing Bible stories, songs, crafts, games, and prizes with neighborhood children. A Spanish course continued to be offered to the English-speaking members of Faith and the community on Thursdays with the response from the leaders of Faith being very positive. Due to the mobility in the Hispanic community, regular worship services were suspended until another group of people was developed. Within the community was a reluctance to accept a Protestant ministry. Pastor Bradshaw stated in his year-end report, "Creativity and patience must be employed as we proceed with the support of Faith, Carpinteria; Centro Cristiano Redwood; the Hispanic Mission Society of Circuit One; and the Region One Mission Council of the Pacific Southwest District. We ask for your prayers that God would lead us to receptive key leaders within the Hispanic community and that God would lead these into the mission work and form a worshiping community."

The goal for the year 2001 was that the Hispanic mission of Centro Cristiano Carpinteria existed "to seek out and evangelistically call the lost, lead and bring in the responsive, build up the people of God, and send them out in mission to the Hispanic community of Carpinteria, Circuit One, and the world. The mission also existed to strengthen and support the pastoral training and lay training of Hispanic Lutherans within Circuit One." During the first half of the year, no services were conducted, as there was not yet a nucleus of people to begin services. Through the ESL class, contacts were gained for evangelism and Bible study. Weekly door-to-door evangelism visits were conducted to gain people for the church and children's events: Kids Ministry, Retreat, and Movie Night. Pastor Bradshaw taught family and marriage counseling workshops based on biblical principles. During the third quarter, worship services were resumed with an average attendance of 10. Sunday morning services emphasized the training of the worshiper in the basics in the profession of faith. Even though numerical growth was slow, the people in attendance were enthusiastic and wanting to grow in the faith. The Sunday school had an average attendance of eight with the adult Bible study having five. By July, Lay Pastor Marco Lozano was doing

full-time work at Centro Cristiano Redwood, freeing Pastor Bradshaw to do the tremendous expansion of outreach to Carpinteria and Santa Paula.

In February of 2002, Holy Communion was initiated with two children receiving First Communion and three adults being received into membership. ESL classes were held on Thursday at 6:30–8:00 p.m. with an average attendance of 10; the Children's Club met on Thursday at 6:30–8:00 p.m. averaging 12 students; "Dia de Amistad"–-Valentine's Day–-was a ministry of friendship to ESL students. Canvassing approximately 50 homes in the neighborhood was done on Sundays after services prior to the Easter celebrations. Pastor Bradshaw reported, "We are excited about gaining new students continually in the ESL outreach. Some come in as others go out. This maintains a number with which to work. We invite these folks to worship. Most don't come, so we plan other social activities with 'Word' ministry–-a short Bible lesson and an evangelistic call to them. We see some folks come to these and some seem to be contemplating Sunday attendance. In all, we are building personal relationships slowly." On Sunday, February 16, at 3:00 p.m. Faith, Carpinteria, rededicated its newly renovated sanctuary with a light meal served following the service, continuing in their partnership in ministry with Centro Cristiano Carpinteria

On June 9, three men, Marco Lozano, Javier Velasco and Marcelino Velasco, completed the SEAN pastoral theology training program and were commissioned into the deaconate serving the Centro Cristiano Hispanic Ministries of Circuit One, which reached from Santa Ynez to Agoura Hills. Deacon Lozano was shepherd to the "mother congregation," Centro Cristiano Redwood, in Oxnard, while Pastor Bradshaw focused his energy on mission development in Carpinteria and in Santa Paula. With the tremendous expansion of outreach to Carpinteria, and the newly established mission in Santa Paula, Pastor Bradshaw and Deacon Lozano joined forces to advance the Kingdom of God in Ventura County with greater focus and zeal.

In the first six months of 2003, church attendance increased to 18 with 10 children in Sunday school and 7 in Saturday classes. The ESL classes continued to be a good means to invite people to worship services and Bible classes; new classes were begun every 10 weeks. Through the sharing of the Gospel in ESL class, a young man invited a couple of his friends to attend. Special outreaches

> The goal for the year 2001 is that the Hispanic mission of Centro Cristiano Carpinteria would exist "to seek out and evangelistically call the lost...."

The Deaconate Commissioning of three men on June 9, 2002: Rev. Jim Johnson, Rev. Dave Bloedel, Rev. Dennis Bradshaw, Deacon Marco Lozano, Deacon Marcelino Velasco, Rev. Tim Seals, and Deacon Javier Velasco. (Pacific Southwest District Archives)

were planned at Mother's Day, Easter, and Father's Day, with evangelism and publicity visits on Saturdays during the spring. It was a struggle to develop new friendships in the community as the missionary-at-large, Dennis Bradshaw, spent half his time in Carpinteria and the other half in the new mission at Santa Paula. Since the communi-ties being served were economically depressed, there was a need for mission dollars in order to minister to community over the long term. In this process, the Lord was raising leaders and present-ing wonderful opportunities to establish District congregations to do mission work in Hispanic communities.

Trinity Lutheran Church
Centro Cristiano Hispano
Santa Paula, California

he city of Santa Paula is located 65 miles northwest of Los Angeles and 14 miles east of Ventura along the coastline of the Pacific Ocean. Santa Paula is the geographical center of Ventura County, situated in the rich agricultural Santa Clara River Valley surrounded by rolling hills and rugged mountain peaks in addition to orange, lemon, and avocado groves, making it known as the "Citrus Capital of the World." Santa Paula, covering an area of 4.6 miles, has a population of 28,598, which is 23.4 percent white, 71.2 percent Hispanic and 2.4 percent all other races according to the 2000 Census.

The original community that later became known as Santa Paula was established by the Chu-mash Indians as the villages of Mupu and Seswa. The land was later given away as part of a Span-ish land grant to Rancho Santa Paula and Saticoy in 1840 with the area subdivided into small farms in the 1860s. Oil was discovered in Santa Paula in 1880, leading to the formation of the Union Oil Company in 1890. The city of Santa Paula, in-corporated on April 22, 1902, was considered the pre-Hollywood film capital, the *Queen of the Silver Screen* in the early 1900s. Even today, Santa Paula is noted for its movie personalities, both silent and sound, who resided in and adjacent to the city with TV and movie crews not an unusual sight in the community. The city is a major distribution point for citrus fruits in the United States and is also noted for avocado producing and process-ing. The community has a quaint, small-town im-age, ideal climate, and reasonably priced housing, which is why Santa Paulans refer to their city as "Hometown USA."

In the early 1950s, many Lutherans felt the lure of Santa Paula, moving there to establish their homes in this rural valley. After a preliminary

The city of Santa Paula has a quaint, small-town image, which is why Santa Paulans refer to their city as "Hometown USA."

meeting with a few Lutheran families in the Santa Paula-Fillmore area who had been attending and were members at First Lutheran Church, Ventura, and St. John's Lutheran Church, Oxnard, the voters' assembly at Oxnard resolved to sponsor a new Lutheran mission at Santa Paula. The first service was held on May 23, 1954, at 9:00 a.m., in the Bixby Mortuary Chapel, at 128 South Eighth Street in Santa Paula, with 41 persons in attendance. Pastor Atrops of Oxnard conducted services, with the members living in Santa Paula and Fillmore taking charge of the Sunday school and Bible class, which was attended by 15 children in Sunday school and 4 adults in Bible class taught by 7 teachers. The renovated Bixby Chapel provided excellent facilities for services, having additional smaller rooms for the Sunday school. Pastor Atrops continued to serve until Pastor Kurt Klein took over the work, being installed on June 10, 1956. He had served in the Navy during World War II, attended Oklahoma A. & M. College, and was a graduate of Wartburg Seminary in Dubuque, Iowa. Before coming to Trinity, he served the Lutheran Church of the Master in La Habra. He and his wife had

Rev. Kurt Klein was installed on June 10, 1956, as Trinity's first pastor. (Pacific Southwest District Archives)

a three-year-old son, Warren, at the time. While residing in Santa Paula, he also served Redeemer congregation of Ojai as a combined parish.

On November 10, 1957, at 3:00 p.m., Rev. Lorenz H. Speckman, who resided in Ojai, was installed as pastor of Trinity Lutheran Church, Santa Paula, and of the Lutheran Church of Our Redeemer in Ojai with the service conducted in the Woman's Club in Ojai. The 2 parishes were approximately 25 miles apart. Pastor Speckman was born on March 22, 1914, near Kankakee, Illinois, to Henry and Anna Speckman, the youngest in a family of four boys and one girl. He attended the local elementary schools until seventh grade when he attended Zion Lutheran School at Chenanse, Illinois. After graduating from Concordia College in Fort Wayne in 1934, he attended Concordia Seminary at St. Louis, graduating in 1938. During his vicarage year, he served St. Paul's Lutheran Church in Kankakee, Illinois. His first call was to Emanuel Lutheran Church in Hamlet, Indiana, where he was ordained and installed on July 17, 1938. This was followed in 1945 by serving Bethlehem Church in Saginaw, Michigan, where he was associate pastor to Rev. An-

> The first service of Trinity is held on May 23, 1954, in the Bixby Mortuary Chapel in Santa Paula.

Main Street in Santa Paula in the 1920s.

Rev. Lorenz H. Speckman was installed as pastor of Trinity Lutheran Church, Santa Paula, and the Lutheran Church of Our Redeemer in Ojai on November 10, 1957. (Pacific Southwest District Archives)

To build Trinity's chapel/ parish hall, members and friends donate 4,000 hours of volunteer labor.

drew Zeile, president of the Michigan District. He married Lydia R. Burger on September 16, 1939, in St. John's at La Porte, Indiana, with their marriage blessed with two children, Paul and Barbara.

Formal organization of Trinity at Santa Paula was effected on March 13, 1955, with 42 communicant members, 71 baptized members, 10 voting members, and a Sunday school of 36 with an average church attendance of 50. The Southern California District purchased 4.3 acres of land at a cost of $22,500 as a site for a future church home of Trinity in January of 1956. In July of 1959, work was begun on a chapel/parish hall with Sunday school facilities. Members of the parish observed Labor Day of 1959 in a very special way deciding to "labor for the Lord" by working on their new chapel/parish hall designed by Mr. Otto J. Bruer. The chapel/parish hall was a stucco-frame structure with a white gravel roof having 5,000 square feet of floor space accommodating 250 people in the chapel with an overflow area for an additional 50. On the front of the church facing Harvard Boulevard, a 24-foot high laminated cross reached skyward. The building was erected under the supervision of Mr. Arnor Boehme, working foreman, with members and friends donating some 4,000 hours of volunteer work. The structure represented an investment of $50,000 exclusive of furnishings, paved parking area, and sidewalks.

Exactly nine months after breaking ground for its new building, Trinity dedicated the new facilities on Sunday, April 3, 1960. The first resident pastor to serve the congregation, Rev. Kurt Klein of First Lutheran in Manhattan Beach, returned to

deliver the dedicatory sermon with Rev. Lorenz H. Speckman conducting the dedicatory rites and serving as liturgist. The church choir under the direction of Homer Bardahl, sang "The Church's One Foundation" and the Sunday school children sang "We are In God's House Today" accompanied by the organist, Ronald Handrock. At the 3:30 p.m. festival service, Rev. Elmer Atrops, pastor of St. John's Church, Oxnard, preached the sermon with liturgists Rev. Victor Neemeyer, circuit counselor and pastor of Emanuel congregation, Santa Barbara, and Rev. Victor Craft, pastor of First Lutheran, Ventura. About 550 members and guests attended the dedication services.

By January 1, 1960, the congregation had numbered 63 communicant members, 11 voting members, and 124 baptized members. On Sunday, July 18, 1962, Candidate Arthur H. Puls, a spring graduate of Concordia Seminary, Springfield, Illinois, was installed as the pastor of Trinity. Rev. Lorenz H. Speckman, who had been serving Trinity, preached the sermon, taking as his topic, "Lessons from Peter's Installation"--John 21:15–17. Rev. Victor Craft of Ventura served as liturgist with the circuit counselor, Rev. Elmer Atrops of Oxnard, conducting the Rite of Installation. With the installation of Candidate Puls as pastor of Trinity Congregation, Santa Paula, Rev. Lorenz H. Speckman devoted his full-time to the Ojai congregation.

Pastor Puls was born in Cleveland, Ohio, where he completed his elementary education at Christ Lutheran School of Cleveland, graduating from West Technical High School in 1950. During his high school years, he was training for future em-

The new chapel/parish hall designed by Mr. Otto J. Bruer and dedicated on April 3, 1960. (Pacific Southwest District Archives)

ployment as a cabinetmaker, working in this field for a year after graduation. During his enlistment in the United States Air Force, he made his decision to serve his Lord in a full-time capacity. Also during this time, he was married to Miss Gloria Biberdorf in Rapid City, South Dakota, on August 28, 1955. In 1956, Mr. and Mrs. Puls moved to Springfield, Illinois, where he began his ministerial studies. He spent his vicarage year at Christ, La Mesa, California. During his seminary days, they also raised a family of three boys, Kent, David and Danny. While in Santa Paula, their fourth son, Timmy, was born.

By 1966, Trinity had grown to 192 baptized members having 115 communicant members with a Sunday school of 118. In March of 1965, Trinity observed its 10th anniversary. The growth had quickened with the completion of the new Santa Paula Freeway into the city. By 1968, the congregation had grown to 237 baptized members having 148 communicant members with a Sunday school of 84. Trinity was one of the older missions of the District, which had moved ahead slowly but steadily, finally becoming a self-supporting congregation on June 30, 1968. That year the American Lutheran Church terminated its mission in Santa Paula in the interest of good stewardship, as the growth in the area didn't materialize.

The year 1969 proved to be a disastrous year for Trinity, as flooding conditions on January 20, prohibited holding worship services at the church. However, some of the families held home services with fellow church members and neighbors. The church was spared water and mud damage, although tons of debris in the church parking area and on the lawn required a road grader, skip loader, and repeated pick ups by city trucks. The men of the congregation worked many hours shoveling and hosing in an effort to get things ready for the services the following Sunday. Church members, the Robert Hanneman Family, suffered the misfortune of mud and water in their home, garage, and yard; however, they also experienced the joy of Christian love in action as 20 members immediately joined to help in the clean-up operation. Pastor Puls wrote, "Many in our area have suffered tremendous loss, and all in a moment. Certainly the words of the psalmist have become a reality for us: 'He uttered His voice, the earth melted. . . . Be still and know that I am God.' " On September 21, 1969, Trinity held a farewell fellowship for Pastor Puls, who had served them seven years, and had accepted a call to Christ Church in La Mesa,

California, where he remained until his retirement in 1996.

After a short vacancy, Rev. Lenard Galster was installed as the new pastor of Trinity on November 30, 1969, with Rev. Harold B. Tietjen, District executive secretary of missions, delivering the sermon, Rev. Arlo Krueger the liturgist, and the circuit counselor, Rev. Loren T. Kramer of Goleta, performing the Rite of Installation. The choirs of Trinity and Redeemer, Ojai, united in singing for the service followed by a reception with a light lunch served by the ladies. A food shower was also held for the new pastor and his wife.

Pastor Lenard Galster was born in Hazen, North Dakota, April 9, 1930, the son of Mr. and Mrs. Bernhard Galster. After his elementary schooling in Hazen, North Dakota, he attended Concordia High School in St. Paul, Minnesota, and Los Angeles City College during the summer of 1951. He began military training in 1952, taking him to California, Kansas, and Massachusetts. From 1953 to 1955, he was stationed in Ethiopia, returning in 1955 to Fort Sheridan, Illinois. After military service, he attended Concordia Theological Seminary, Springfield, Illinois, from 1955 to 1960; the Mission School of Concordia Seminary, St. Louis, Missouri, in 1960; and the University of Hong Kong from 1960 to 1962 on a part-time basis. He married the former Ruth Ann Niemoeller on July 24, 1960. After his graduation from the seminary, he served as pastor of Holy Trinity Lutheran Church in Hong Kong during 1961 and 1962; All Nations Lutheran Church and Hong Kong International School from 1962 to 1966; and the Lutheran church in Thailand from 1966 to 1969. At the time, Pastor and Mrs. Galster had one son, David Michael.

By 1993, Trinity had only 127 baptized members with 67 communicant members. After Pastor Galster retired in January 1998, and moved with his wife, Ruth, to Roseberg, Oregon, Rev. Richard Swanson became interim pastor. Pastor Swanson was born in Minneapolis, Minnesota, in 1945, but was raised in St. Louis and Aurora, Colorado, graduating from high school in Aurora in 1963. He attended Concordia College in St. Paul, Minnesota, and Concordia Senior College in Fort Wayne. Following his graduation from Concordia Seminary in 1971, he became pastor of Redeemer in Nacogdoches, Texas, followed by an associate pastorate in Albuquerque, New Mexico. Other parishes he served were Peace in Arroyo Grande and First in Ventura, both in California. He also

Rev. Arthur H. Puls was installed on July 18, 1962. (Pacific Southwest District Archives)

Rev. Lenard Galster was installed as the new pastor of Trinity on November 30, 1969, and remained until his retirement in January 1998. (Pacific Southwest District Archives)

Rev. Richard Swanson, interim pastor of Trinity in 1998–2000 and 2001–2002. (Pacific Southwest District Archives)

In 2001, Trinity decides to transition to a Hispanic ministry, since the parish is located in a flourishing agricultural valley with a predominantly Hispanic populaton.

served as interim pastor at Trinity, El Reno, Oklahoma; Trinity, Ardmore, Oklahoma; Trinity, Santa Paula and Our Redeemer, Ojai, California; First, Camarillo; and again in 2001, Trinity, Santa Paula and Our Redeemer, Ojai, California.

In 1998 during Pastor Swanson's ministry at Trinity, Santa Paula, the president of Immanuel Lutheran Church, an ELCA parish in Ventura, requested the use of Trinity's church facilities as the building that Immanuel had rented had been sold. After a number of meetings, it was decided to allow Immanuel to use Trinity's building for worship services, with Trinity worshiping at 8:30 a.m. and Emmanuel at 11:00 a.m. each Sunday. Pastor Ron Dybvig, his wife, and the members of Emmanuel became "co-workers with Trinity in the Lord's vineyard."

On August 12, 2000, Rev. Eric Malmstrom, a Fort Wayne seminary graduate, was installed as pastor of the duel parishes, Trinity, Santa Paula, and Our Redeemer, Ojai. He was born on January 1, 1967, in Mountain View, California and was raised in San Jose. After graduating from Concordia University, Irvine, he entered the U.S. Navy and was honorably discharged in 1993. Before his graduation in 2000 from Concordia Seminary, Fort Wayne, in 1993, he served his vicarage as the chaplain at Lutheran Homes, Incorporated, in Fort Wayne. After he was ordained at Bethany Lutheran Church in Fort Wayne on July 9, 2000, he was assigned to serve as pastor of Trinity in Santa Paula and the Church of Our Redeemer in Ojai, remaining until August of 2001 when he took a call to First Lutheran Church in San Fernando. He married Leslie on June 9, 1989, in Irvine with their marriage blessed with twin boys, Thomas and Timothy, on July 9, 1999.

In September of 2001, Rev. Rick Swanson retuned to serve as interim pastor of Trinity with his wife, Linda, serving as organist. They have two sons, David and Andrew. That year as the congregation contemplated its ministry and future, the decision was made to transition to a Hispanic ministry, since the parish was located in a flourishing agricultural valley east of Ventura with its population predominantly Hispanic whose dominate language was Spanish. The leaders of Trinity worked with the Hispanic Mission Society of Circuit One, Region One's Mission Council, and other Pacific Southwest District leaders to effect the transition in the smoothest way possible.

In September of 2001, Rev. Carlos Hernandez of Synod's Board for Human Care worked with Pastor Dennis Bradshaw, the Hispanic missionary-at-large, to study the community of Santa Paula for future ministry. Having conducted a demographic analysis and resident interviews, these leaders initiated a Hispanic mission and ministry plan for Santa Paula and the new Hispanic ministry, Centro Cristiano Hispano. On April 14, 2002, the congregation of Trinity conducted its last formal English Sunday worship service at 3:00 p.m. with

Rev. Eric Malmstrom with his wife, Leslie, and twin sons, Timothy and Thomas. (Pacific Southwest District Archives)

Deacon Marco Lozano, Pastor Bradshaw, and Pastor Randy Wilkens from East St. Louis, Illinois.

Children at the first Easter service at Centro Cristiano Santa Paula in 2003.

A yard sale at Centro Cristiano Santa Paula.

Pastor Swanson serving as liturgist and Pastor Arthur Puls preaching the sermon; District President Larry Stoterau addressed the congregation and officiated in the transition from Trinity to Centro Cristiano Hispano entrusting the facilities to the Pacific Southwest District in order to be used for a new Hispanic ministry. At this service, the congregation was presented a booklet, *History of Trinity Lutheran Church of Santa Paula 1954 to 2002*, compiled by Ruby Adair, a charter member, and Lorraine Engelsgaard. Centro Cristiano Hispano began its ministries in the facilities, refurbishing and beginning outreach to the Hispanic community of Santa Paula. The current facilities also were providing the headquarters for the Theological Education by Extension Program, for lay training, and for resources for the ministries of Centro Cristiano Redwood, Oxnard, and Centro Cristiano Carpinteria.

Also in 2002, Centro Cristiano Santa Paula received a grant from the Lutheran Brotherhood Foundation to start the ministry to Hispanics in Santa Paula. Outreach to adults, youth, and children included English and health classes, summer Vacation Bible Schools, family game and movie nights, after-school programs, home Bible studies, and Sunday family fellowship. That summer Centro Cristiano Hispano entered into Phase 1 of its property improvement program. There were many areas of need, re-landscaping through cutting down trees and trimming bushes and a major one, a new roof. Pastor Randy Wilken led a Youth Mission Team of 40 youth and adult leaders from East St. Louis, Illinois, who visited Centro Cristiano Hispano, July 21–28, to work on facility improvements which included installing a new roof and changing the church overflow room to an office for Pastor Bradshaw; they made the Santa Paula church facility their home during their stay

and had fellowship with the other Hispanic ministries in the circuit.

On March 16, 2002, at 4:00 p.m., the Hispanic Mission Society (HMS) of Circuit One hosted an appreciation fellowship dinner for circuit churches, pastors, HMS reps and circuit and District leaders at Centro Cristiano Santa Paula. The financial and personal assistance of these member churches continued to assist in the growth of Hispanic mission sites at Centro Cristiano Redwood, Carpinteria, and Santa Paula under the leadership of Hispanic Missionary for Circuit One, Dennis Bradshaw, Centro Cristiano Hispano.

By 2003, worship services were conducted at Centro Cristiano Santa Paula at 1:00 p.m. each Sunday with an average attendance of 25 with 10 in the Sunday school. It was through the ESL classes that doors were opened immediately for ministry with worship services begun the third week after the ESL class began. The ESL class was conducted Saturdays at 4:00 p.m. along with a children's club at the same time. Deacon Javier Velasco used outreach opportunities through sports activities. The greatest priority was to garner funds to launch a day-care and/or preschool outreach. During the second quarter, the Sunday worship service grew to an average of 45 with a continued attendance in the ESL program. The mission had negotiations with the Ventura County School District to share facilities with the Gateway School for high-risk youth, which would help the mission economically and open doors for ministry to many young Hispanic people in need of Jesus' presence in their lives. Centro Cristiano's first Easter that year had 120 people present to worship the risen Lord. Following the service, a jumper was rented to entertain the children.

The ESL program was discontinued during the summer so that the mission could minister to

On April 14, 2002, Trinity conducts its last formal English worship service. By 2003, Spanish worship services are conducted each Sunday.

families at regular family nights. The ESL was a wonderful instrument, which the Holy Spirit used to bring people under the influence of the mission in a very rapid manner. It continued to bring in new people, even as some moved from the area or had schedule changes and could no longer attend classes. The ministry demonstrated to the people that the mission was there for them in a very practical way and had a desire to help not only them but also the whole family. The Friday Bible study had grown from about 8 regular attendees to over 15 where Deacon Velasco, the teacher, was involved with the people in the group, as he was very committed and gave more of his personal time than was required. He saw and recognized the window of opportunity that the Lord placed before him and was utilizing it in his ministry. Through the work, new families, single people, young men, and youth were being touched by the mission with some coming from other congregations in town where they had been hurt. The mission was trying to build rapport with the pastor of the congregation from which these people came.

The mission had yard sales with the purpose to aid people in need and to introduce them to the church and the Gospel. Through ESL classes and yard sales, the Hispanic community has become aware of Centro Cristiano Santa Paula. People came into the church to pray on bended knees making their petitions known to God before the altar during the week. The Easter of 2004 had 110 men, women, and children in worship service to praise the Lord. In a short period of time, the Lord of the harvest had blessed this small mission outreach to the Hispanic population of Santa Paula!

Blest be the tie that binds
Our hearts in Christian love;
The fellowship of kindred minds
Is like to that above.

Let the Vineyards Be Fruitful, Lord!

St. John's Lutheran Church
Orange, California
Inglesia Cristo Rey
Orange, California

The original inhabitants of the area now called Orange were the Native Americans, named Gabrielios by the Spaniards. The first landholder in the area was Juan Pablo Grijalva, a retired Spanish soldier who had marched through California from Mexico with one of the early expeditions. In 1801, he was granted permission by the Spanish colonial government to ranch "the place of the Arroyo de Santiago," an area that ran from the Santa Ana River and the foothills above Villa Park to the sea at Newport Beach. Grijalva lived in San Diego but built an adobe ranch house on what is now Hoyt Hill. After Grijalva's death, the rancho, known as the Rancho Santiago de Santa Ana, was taken over by his son-in-law, José Antonio Yorba, and grandson, Juan Pablo Peralta. Both Yorba and Peralta had nine children with their children and grandchildren who settled on various portions of the enormous rancho. Soon new acreage was added to the property until the family holdings extended from Riverside to the ocean. In 1848, California was ceded to the United States by the Treaty of Guadalupe Hidalgo with the boundaries of the Rancho Santiago de Santa Ana confirmed in 1857, allowing the Yorba and Peralta families to continue living on the rancho.

In the early 1860s, one member of the extended family — Leonardo Cota — borrowed money, placing his share of the rancho as collateral, from Abel Stearns,

> **"O God of Hosts: look down from heaven, and behold, and visit this vine and the vineyard Your right hand has planted."**
>
> — PSALM 80:14-15

the largest landowner in Southern California. When Cota defaulted on the loan in 1866, Stearns filed a lawsuit in the Los Angeles Superior Court to demand a partition of the land, trying to claim Cota's section. The case took two years to sort the complicated relationships among the families and to determine how much land each one owned with the rancho divided into 1,000 units parceled out to the heirs and to the claimants in the lawsuit.

The two sharp Los Angeles lawyers involved in the lawsuit were Alfred Beck Chapman and Andrew Glassell, who took some of their fees in land; they had already started buying other sections of the rancho as early as 1864. By 1870, they owned about 5,400 acres in what is now downtown Orange, which seemed like a good location for a town. Since the nearby Santa Ana River provided water, the soil was rich, and a stage road ran nearby. After Chapman hired a surveyor to divide the land into tracts of 40, 80, and 120 acres, he called the area Richland and began selling lots. Although Chapman later liked to call himself the "father of Orange," the real development of the city was actually guided by Captain William T. Glassell, Andrew Glassell's brother, who laid out the downtown area, bounded by Maple, Grand, Almond, and Lemon streets, with Chapman and Glassell streets meeting in a central "Public Plaza." Captain Glassell's home and office, on the west side of the Plaza Square, was the first building in Richland.

The captain also supervised the construction of the A. B. Chapman Canal from the river to provide irrigation for farm sites. Part of that canal's path may today be traced along Canal Street, behind the Mall of Orange. Since he was such an excellent salesman, there were a dozen houses in and around Richland by the end of 1871. The first school was started in a private home on March 26, 1872. By August, a one-room schoolhouse was opened at the corner of Sycamore and Lemon. The year 1873 saw the opening of the first local store, Fisher Brothers, on the north side of the Plaza, the first civic organization, the Orange Grange, and the first church, the Methodist Episcopal.

When Richland's application for a post office was refused in 1873 because there was already a Richland in Sacramento County, the townspeople selected the name Orange instead. The town of Orange began as a farming community, even though it took several years of trial and error for the settlers to discover the most successful agricultural crop. The first crops planted were grains such as barley, oats, wheat, corn, and rye. Many of the farmers then planted grapevines, primarily for use as raisins, with grapes becoming the major crop until the 1886 blight killed thousands of vines in Orange and surrounding communities. Settlers also tried growing tropical fruits such as bananas, pineapples, and guavas, but without

much success. Finally, the farmers found the ideal produce, orange trees that were planted in groves in 1873.

After the Southern Pacific Railroad built a depot in Orange in 1880, seven years later, the Santa Fe Railroad extended a line into the town. The two competing railroads dropped their passenger fares to attract customers, sparking the "boom of the '80s" in Southern California. Thousands of visitors came from the East, with many of them purchasing land in Orange County. The 1880s were also "boom times" for the city of Orange as well. To help attract tourists, promotional fliers were sent across the country, and three hotels were built in the downtown area. New subdivisions and town sites were offered for sale. Among those lured to Orange in the late 1870s were mostly single, German Lutheran men from Germany. In a short time, several related families from Wisconsin, Minnesota, and Germany joined them, thirsting for good farming land and German Lutheran services in their new homeland. Soon these Lutherans looked for a minister of the Gospel who would serve them according to the tenets of the true Lutheran faith. They found to their dismay that there were, in all California, very few ministers of The Lutheran Church — Missouri Synod. The first Lutheran minister with whom they came in contact was Rev. Martin Wyneken, who had been

Orange Plaza on Glassell and Chapman in the early 1900s. (Santa Ana Public Library History Room)

forced to relinquish his parish in Cincinnati, Ohio, because of failing health, coming to Los Angeles in the hope of restoring it. Rev. Wyneken visited the Lutherans of Orange several times in 1881, but because of his physical disability, he was unable to serve them as pastor. In November of 1881 another 35-year-old Lutheran minister came to Los Angeles from Belle Plaine, Minnesota, also in the quest of restoring his health. He, too, had had to relinquish his parish due to severe throat problems and could not think of again stepping into active service at that time. Yet, in spite of all this, he was the young man whom God had chosen as His vessel to build the kingdom of the Lord in the community of Orange, through St. John's Lutheran Church, building upon the foundation of Jesus Christ as the chief cornerstone. This man was Rev. Jacob Kogler, founder and pastor of St. John's Lutheran Church at Orange, California, for 35 years.

Pastor Jacob Kogler, born in the province of Wurtenberg, Germany, on January 6, 1847,

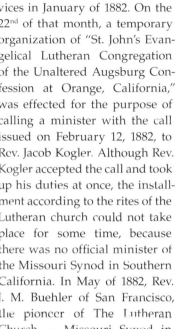

Rev. Jacob Kogler, founder and pastor of St. John's for thirty-five years circa 1881. (Pacific Southwest District Archives)

was raised by his grandparents, attending schools in Wurtenberg until the age of 14. He continued his studies in Stuttgart and Ludwigsburg with the original intention of doing missionary work. Later, however, he was urged to enter a seminary which prepared students for Lutheran churches in America. Since the demands for teachers and pastors in America was so great, after one year of seminary study this studious young man embarked on the long, six-week passage to the United States. After completing his training in 1874, he was then assigned to St. John's Church in east Minneapolis, Minnesota, where he met and married Dora Schultz in 1875, who remained by his side the rest of his life.

When Pastor Wyneken met the Koglers and their three children upon their arrival in Los Angeles, he drew Rev. Kogler's attention to the needs of the people in the small town of Orange who were desperately anxious to start a congregation of their own. Since Pastor Kogler had been in Los Angeles only a short time when Rev. Wyneken called his attention to the situation in Orange, he felt a deep compassion for these brethren who

were without a spiritual shepherd, which induced him to visit them at once. He took up active service among them immediately, preaching the first German sermon in Orange on December 10, 1881, and baptizing the first child, that of Peter Schmetgen and his wife. The second service was the Christmas festival of 1881 followed by several more services in January of 1882. On the 22nd of that month, a temporary organization of "St. John's Evangelical Lutheran Congregation of the Unaltered Augsburg Confession at Orange, California," was effected for the purpose of calling a minister with the call issued on February 12, 1882, to Rev. Jacob Kogler. Although Rev. Kogler accepted the call and took up his duties at once, the installment according to the rites of the Lutheran church could not take place for some time, because there was no official minister of the Missouri Synod in Southern California. In May of 1882, Rev. J. M. Buehler of San Francisco, the pioneer of The Lutheran Church — Missouri Synod in California, visited in Los Angeles and went to Orange to conduct the installation of the pastor of St. John's and also help organize St. John's twin sister, Trinity in Los Angeles. In the meantime, a permanent organization of the congregation took place on February 19, 1882, when a constitution was adopted, subscribed by 13 charter members, and the first officers were elected. The charter members were Juergen Schmetgen, William Hillebrecht, J. Kordes, Peter Schmetgen, Peter Ficken, H. Pohndorf Jr., F. Steskal, J. Gathmann, R. Rohrs, Klaus Seba, Johann Broederhoeft, Karl Struck, and W. Pribernow. The first officers elected as elders and trustees were F. Roehrs, chairman; Karl Struck, secretary; J. Gathmann, treasurer.

Through the grace of the Lord, Pastor Kogler's health was strengthened and restored, so that he could attend to all the pastoral duties of his small flock from its very inception. He served them when the workload increased with the growth of the congregation. He even went far beyond the confines of his field of labor in Orange to do pioneer mission work among the few Lutherans in other localities, from Los Angeles to San Diego and from the ocean to the foothills. Untiring

Pastor Kogler preaches his first German sermon in Orange on December 10, 1881.

activity marked his whole career as pastor of St. John's for 35 years until the infirmities of old age compelled him to relinquish the shepherd's staff to younger hands.

For one year after the organization of the congregation, members met in the homes of different families for services. In the summer and fall of 1882, a number of new arrivals to the area wanted to become members, but there was no private home large enough to house them for the services. To remedy this situation, steps were taken for erecting the first house of worship. On November 15, 1882, the congregation resolved "to buy two lots for church and school purposes" for $250. They also acquired a corner lot, located at the northeast corner of Almond Avenue and Olive Street, which had been generously donated by the firm of Chapman and Glassell, the original planners and developers of the city of Orange. At the same time, part of a public school building, a frame, 24' × 24' structure, was acquired from the city of Orange for a nominal sum and moved to the lots just purchased. After the members remodeled it for church and school use, the building was dedicated on February 11, 1883, as the first church of St. John's, serving also as the school. Pastor Kogler served for six years as the teacher of the school which began with nine pupils that year, along with teaching the first class of six catechumens who were also confirmed that year. The plain wooden benches without backs did double duty as church pews on Sunday and as school desks the rest of the week. A small reed organ provided music, and a wooden piano crate was used as an altar as this was not a congregation of means at the time.

With the news that a Lutheran church and school had been established at Orange, California,

Both St. John's and the city of Orange grow in the 1880s.

reaching many states beyond the Rockies, an even larger number of people were drawn to Orange. The result was that after the adoption of the revised constitution, scarcely three years had passed before it again became necessary to consider the question: How can we provide more room for the growing congregation? In a special meeting of the voters on January 31, 1886, it was resolved to build a 24' × 24' addition to the present church. As more room was urgently needed, not only for the church services but also for the school which had 30 pupils, the plan to expand the church building was carried out without delay, resulting in an enlarged church, which was dedicated to the service of the Lord in April of that year. Since St. John's now had a house of worship that could adequately seat the congregation, the members felt secure that they could settle down for many years to quiet spiritual building of souls. In January of 1887, a reed organ was purchased to lead the congregational singing of the "singing church." In February, a resolution was adopted and accepted that the congregation join the "Evangelical Lutheran Synod of Missouri, Ohio and other States." Because the school had grown to 65 pupils, the congregation called its first teacher, Mr. Fred Folkmann, late in 1889.

At the same time that St. John's was experiencing tremendous growth, the city of Orange was also feeling the same growth. Two local newspapers were founded in 1885 and 1888: the *Orange Tribune*, later renamed the *Orange Post*, and the *Orange News*, later renamed the *Orange Daily News*. The first public library opened in 1885. Asphalt sidewalks and gas streetlights were added to the downtown area along with operation of two streetcar lines. In 1886, the town's first bank, the Bank of Orange, was organized and a circular park with a fountain was set up in the middle of the Plaza. The most significant event of the "boom years" was the incorporation of the city in 1888, having a 3.10 square mile border bounded by Batavia Street, La Veta Avenue, Santiago Creek, and Collins Avenue. Today the city covers almost 25 square miles with a population of more than 120,000. The following year, the southern half of Los Angeles County voted to form Orange County, with both Anaheim and Orange hoping to become the new county seat, but that honor went to Santa Ana.

At a special voters' meeting in the month of April 1887, a grave question was brought up for consideration. A number of members of St. John's, residing in or near Santa Ana, petitioned for a peaceful release in order to organize a separate

St. John's first church and school building located on Almond and Olive was dedicated on February 11, 1883. (Pacific Southwest District Archives)

congregation in that community. St. John's, although it had never received support from outside its own ranks, had just become able to support itself. At this time, a weakening of the congregation through withdrawal of a number of its members threatened the welfare of its entire future. Because of the seriousness of the matter, the Rev. George Runkel of Los Angeles was brought in for counsel. The main reason against granting the petition for dismissal was on the advice of Synod, which had just published in the church periodical that smaller congregations should seek to combine, as there were not enough Lutheran ministers to serve them all. Since Rev. Runkel concurred with Synod's position, the congregation unanimously decided that it could not grant the petition at that time. A few months later, the pastor of St. John's was given permission to preach in Santa Ana if requests were made of him.

At the time of the dedication of the enlarged church in 1886, the members of St. John's assumed that they would have ample room for many years to come. That assumption proved to be false; already in 1892, the attendance at the services taxed the capacity of the building, often with standing room only at services. On April 3, 1893, the congregation resolved to build a new church, 72' × 36' with a tower and an altar niche, on the corner lot originally donated by Chapman and Glassell. After architect Bradshaw submitted the plans, the contract was given to Meacham and Pratt with the costs not to exceed $4,000. When it was discovered that $500 more would be required to complete the building as planned, Dr. Carl Mueller generously extended a five-year interest-free loan, which the congregation accepted. The building was a simple frame Gothic style with a small vestibule under the tower and a gallery in the west end. On May 28, 1893, the cornerstone was laid with the singing of "A Mighty Fortress," by St. John's choir under the direction of teacher F. A. Folkmann, the first time a chorale was sung in English at St. John's. At the dedication of St. John's new house of worship, which took place November 19, 1893, Pastor J. M. Buehler, president of the California and Oregon District, traveled all the way from San Francisco to preach the morning sermon in familiar German. District vice president, Pastor George Runkel of Los Angeles, took his entire Trinity congregation on the 30-mile train trip, and preached an afternoon sermon entirely in English. Pastor Buehler reported some time later, "The American population came out in great numbers," crowding the

little church to the doors. St. John's was reaching out to the English-speaking population.

Since the small reed organ was inadequate for the larger church building, a hand pumped pipe organ, the first in Orange, was purchased in the early part of 1894 from the Jackson Company for $1,500 and placed in the gallery. When in 1900, a former member of the congregation, Christ Zum Malln, who had moved back to Chicago, offered to donate $100 for a bell (making it the incentive for further similar contributions) within a few months, a larger bell was purchased from the Stuckstede Company of St. Louis, Missouri. This same bell, which was placed in the belfry tower of the new church, continues to call the faithful of St. John's to divine services to this day.

In 1891, land for the Evangelical Lutheran Cemetery, bordered on the south by what is now Santa Clara Avenue, was purchased from Henry Hockemeyer with plots selling for $10 at that time. Later, in 1911, more land had to be purchased from Rudolph Frick, which later became known as St. John's Cemetery, maintained today under perpet-

St. John's second church with its tall steeple was dedicated on November 19, 1893. (Pacific Southwest District Archives)

On May 28, 1893, the cornerstone is laid with the singing of "A Mighty Fortress," the first time a chorale is sung in English.

ual care provisions established in 1931. St. John's Cemetery is now surrounded by Fairhaven Memorial Park, bearing witness of the careful planning of the early congregational fathers.

Relieved of some of his teaching responsibilities by Mr. Folkmann, Pastor Kogler immediately turned to canvassing the area. By 1895, he had gathered a regular group of worshipers in Anaheim where he preached on Sunday afternoons, sometimes taking along his twin sons, William and Henry, who sang duets as a special treat for that small congregation establishing Zion Lutheran Church of Anaheim. Pastor Kogler, with his unending zeal, continued to reach out into the spreading county to establish and nourish still more German Lutheran congregations. After his usual Sunday morning sermon, the faithful pastor could be seen traveling by horse and buggy down the dusty roads to Oliveheim, later known as Olive, establishing St. Paul's in 1907, and then across to Santa Ana to preach an afternoon or evening sermon where he was instrumental in organizing Trinity in 1909. When teacher Folkmann resigned, Mr. William Batterman of Chicago was installed in 1903 and continued to serve as teacher and principal for 33 years.

In order to meet the needs of 124 pupils in the school, the sounds of carpenters' hammers were again heard across town as the congregation built a second and larger school in 1904. Dedicated on

In its first 25-year history, St. John's contributes $27,000 to the church-at-large.

February 12, 1905, the new 2-story modern school contained 4 spacious classrooms and a full cement basement where the children spent their recess periods on rainy days. They were summoned to class by the bell donated by Henry Dierker. Miss Emma Wyneken, sister of Pastor Martin Wyneken, became the first women teacher in 1906. In her prim white shirtwaist and long dark skirt, she was the model of a well-disciplined schoolmistress of the day. She was in delicate health, however, and was obliged to leave her position in 1907 with the vacancy filled by Mrs. Eda Gorath, who remained, with only a short interruption, until 1944.

The 25th anniversary of the congregation, February 17, 1907, was a joyous day for St. John's, marking both the founding of the parish and Pastor Kogler's 25-year pastorate among them. On that day, the lovingly decorated church was filled with natural garlands of fresh flowers, as the 540 members and an overflow crowd of visitors gave thanks to God for the bountiful blessings they had received. Not only had St. John's been given the means to be self-supporting during its 25 year history, it had also contributed $27,000 to the church-at-large for missionary work throughout its existence.

At the time of the dedication of the new church in 1893, St. John's numbered 59 voting members with the new building providing ample room for both members and guests. The artificial boom of the 1880s, which had also increased the size of Orange, had collapsed with the usual slowing and setback in all business activities following in its wake. All this had its effects on St. John's congregation. Since its existence and for 10 years, the parish had been blessed with a phenomenal growth. For a few years, the increase in membership had not kept the same pace as in the past, but that was only

St. John's second and larger school building built in 1904 and dedicated on February 12, 1905, served the congregation until 1929. (Pacific Southwest District Archives)

The interior of the second church decorated for the congregation's 25th anniversary celebration on February 17, 1907. (Pacific Southwest District Archives)

temporary. The first reaction from the collapse of the 1880s was a healthy and steady development of the citrus industry with the surrounding cities sharing in the new prosperity, thus stimulating the influx of new settlers in large numbers, and again St. John's with its church and Christian day school became the central point of attraction in the Southland for many Lutherans. This, combined with natural growth from within the congregation, soon filled every available seat in its house of worship. In 1907, the congregation celebrated its silver anniversary with 116 voting members, thus doubling its membership since 1893. At every service, the worshipers taxed the seating capacity of the church, and for the third time the question again confronted St. John's: What shall we do to provide more room?

By 1912, the situation had become desperate, as there was a serious danger of loss of members in the church. Even though a few years earlier, a large number of members who lived in and around Olive and Santa Ana were released from St. John's to organize separate congregations, it gave only temporary relief from overcrowded

conditions in the Orange church. On December 1, 1912, the resolution was unanimously passed to build a new church large enough to accommodate the present membership and future growth. Through much delay, the decision on the site and costs of the proposed new edifice finally occurred on June 30, 1915, when a decisive step was taken as the congregation passed a resolution to buy 6 lots on Almond Avenue, between Center and Shaffer streets for $3,500 and to build the church at the corner of Almond Avenue and Center Street. A building committee, given ample powers, was appointed and consisted of the following members: H. Grote, H. Fitschen, George Dierker, L. D. Gunther, A. Dittmer, William Batterman, and Rev. J. Kogler. The committee engaged Frederick H. Ely of Santa Ana as architect, with the plans calling for a brick veneered building, 119' × 72' × 56', outside dimensions, and 2 towers, 119' and 80' high respectively, all built in Gothic style of the Second Period. With the plans accepted by the congregation, the general contract given to Duker, Miller, and Loescher on their bid of $25,674. The church as it stood complete, including all furnishings, organ, and all private donations represented a total cost of $51,250.

The cornerstone of the new impressive church edifice was laid on September 21, 1913, with Rev. W. J. Lankow of Santa Ana giving the German ad-

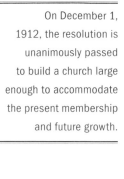

On December 1, 1912, the resolution is unanimously passed to build a church large enough to accommodate the present membership and future growth.

St. John's massive, beautiful, new house of worship that would seat almost 1,000, was dedicated July 19, 1914. (Pacific Southwest District Archives)

The interior of the magnificent, new church showing the large, ornate altar with the statue of Christ and the Johnston Pipe Organ. (Pacific Southwest District Archives)

On July 19, 1914, St. John's dedicates its large house of worship.

dress and Rev. George Mieger of Olive preaching the English sermon. By July of 1914, the building had been completed and on the 19th of that month, St. John's dedicated its large, beautiful house of worship to the service of the Lord. On that festival day, the first service was held in the old church with Rev. J. W. Theiss of Los Angeles preaching the farewell sermon. Rev. George Mieger conducted the dedicatory service in the new building with the afternoon service conducted by Rev. A. Hansen of Pasadena, and in the evening service, Rev. Edward J. Rudnick of San Bernardino preached in English. Practically all the congregations in the southern half of the state had sent participants. Since the main purpose of the church was for public worship, no provision was made for anything else in this large sanctuary that had a seating capacity of 1,000. In the base of the large tower was the ladies' restroom, and back of the pulpit was the vestry with outside entrance. The basement room provided accommodations for only the furnaces, the fuel room, and the electric motor, blower, and dynamo for the pipe organ. For religious training

of children, activities of different societies, and socials and entertainment, ample accommodations were provided outside of the church edifice in the school building.

The interior finish, the tinting, and decorations all harmonized well with the oak pews and one of the most impressive features of the building, the rich stained glass windows crafted by the Ford Brothers Glass Company of Minneapolis at a cost of more than $3,000 donated by individual members. In the gallery were large windows depicting "The Good Shepherd" and "Jesus and the Woman at the Well." The two windows in the nave were "Easter Morn" and "Gethsemane." The ornately carved white Gothic altar, with the central figure of Christ with outstretched hands gave reassurance to the worshiper of His love. Behind the altar in the chancel area, the walls were painted to resemble large flowing draperies. The electric lighting system consisted of 260 separate lights distributed in the Gothic arches and other parts of the building, so wired that they could be controlled by a number of light controls. A 2-manual, 27-rank,

The gigantic Good Shepherd window in the north gallery above the choir loft. (Pacific Southwest District Archives)

The immense, south gallery window depicting Jesus and the woman at the well. (Pacific Southwest District Archives)

pipe organ, built by the Johnston Company of Los Angeles had 1,475 pipes to produce its wide range of harmonic tones and was installed at a cost of almost $7,500. The organ was taken to Our Savior's Lutheran Church in Palm Springs, California, when the Zimmer Organ was built in 1981.

The dedication of the sanctuary took place at a time when threatening war clouds hung over the world-at-large. Dr. Richard T. DuBrau, in his *Romance of Lutheranism in California*, summed up the atmosphere of that day in one profound sentence: "A few weeks before the brittle peace of the world was shattered for a long time to come, the new church stood finished, firm as a rock, ready to weather many a storm." The glass for the leaded stained glass windows in the impressive new sanctuary arrived from Germany on one of the last shipments allowed out of the country before World War I closed all commercial sea lanes.

A few years later the United States entered into a war against Germany, which was painful for some of the people of St. John's who maintained strong loyalties, not only to their own German background but also with many relatives and dear ones still living in Germany. In an atmosphere of obvious coolness from the community as services were still conducted in German, the members of the congregation conducted themselves in the only manner in which they could. As good Christian citizens, several young men of the congregation served in the armed forces. Without much fanfare in the city, it was later reported that the people of St. John's had been among the largest purchasers of liberty war bonds in the area.

Failing health and increasing deafness made Pastor Kogler's duties more and more of a hardship, and calls for an assistant pastor went unfilled. He and his faithful wife, Dora, who had borne him 11 children, had devoted their lives to the Lord's work in St. John's. By 1917, Pastor Kogler made the heart-wrenching decision to retire from the pulpit. With deep reluctance, the congregation honored the request of their beloved leader who remained an active figure in the church and community, assisting whenever possible until he was called to his heavenly home on January 14,

Pastor Kogler about the time of his retirement in 1917, having served St. John's 35 years. (Pacific Southwest District Archives)

1926. Pastor Kogler was laid to rest on January 18 in the Lutheran cemetery; hundreds attended the funeral. The Reverend August C. Bode, who was by then pastor of St. John's, conducted the funeral sermon in German. He said, "This frail, modest, and unassuming man might well have said with St. Paul, 'We need no letter of commendation from you. Ye are our epistle, known and read of all men.' " The frail body, worn out in the service of the Lord, was at rest, the soul with its Master. Pastor Kogler had indeed been a tireless servant of the Lord, living to see his small flock expand into what was then the largest Lutheran congregation on the Pacific Coast, with over 700 communicant members. Several of his direct descendants are numbered among the members of St. John's today.

Upon Pastor Kogler's retirement, Rev. N. F. Jensen, who had served the deaf mission on the Pacific Coast and frequently conducted English services at St. John's, was called on July 15, 1917, as successor to Pastor Kogler and installed in September of the same year. He served St. John's for the next five turbulent and unhappy years. Through deep anguish and suffering came the splintering and splitting of the congregation in 1922, when some 200 members withdrew their membership from St. John's to establish Immanuel Church on Chapman Avenue a few blocks east of St. John's. Those were sorrowful and bitter years, during which Pastor Jensen was forced to resign, but the work of the Kingdom continued without looking backward. Fortunately, the spirit of Christian love and forgiveness eventually prevailed with wounds healed and apologies exchanged. St. John's has for many years enjoyed a healthy and happy fellowship with the sister congregation of Immanuel.

Since Pastor Kogler owned his own home, during his pastorate of 35 years, the congregation hadn't found it necessary to provide a parsonage. When a successor was called, he needed a home. For a few years, a house was rented which proved unsatisfactory. In 1921, it was decided to build a modern two-story stucco parsonage on Center Street just north of the church with a one-story addition at the rear of the house. The contract for the

The glass for the leaded stained glass windows arrives from Germany on one of the last shipments allowed out of the country before World War I closes all commercial sea lanes.

building was awarded to the Orange Contracting and Milling Company at a total cost of $12,588. The new parsonage was in harmony with the group of fine buildings owned by the congregation.

On February 12, 1923, St. John's extended a call to the Rev. August C. Bode of Good Thunder, Minnesota, and he accepted, bringing with him the emotional and spiritual maturity, which restored harmony and unity to the congregation. The Rev. William Schmoock, who had served the congregation as interim pastor, inducted Pastor Bode into his new office in April of that year. He would remain 25 years, well loved for his calm and clear-sighted leadership abilities. The transition from the German language to English in St. John's took place gradually. In 1914, it was resolved that services in English be conducted once a month. Two years later, two services a month were held in English. In 1918, all evening services were to be conducted in English. Since 1923, there were double services every Sunday and every holiday in German and English, with all business meetings conducted in English beginning in 1930. There were now two services every Sunday, one in English and the other in German. Through Pastor Bode's pastorate, the congregation experienced many blessings, resulting in an increased workload which caused the congregation to call an assistant to its pastor, Candidate Armand Mueller, of St. Louis, Missouri, who was ordained and installed on July 5, 1931.

> St. John's makes a slow transition from German to English.

Rev. August C. Bode, the third pastor of St. John's who served 25 years. (Pacific Southwest District Archives)

Charles K. Walker, a year or two before his death, had the intention of donating a very large sum of money for a Christian educational institution to be built in the southland, or for a similar purpose for St. John's congregation, but his death intervened. In 1926, the widow of the deceased, Mrs. Helena Walker King, made St. John's a magnificent, generous offer by donating up to $75,000 for the erection of a social hall on the lots east of the church, appropriate in every way for the large congregation with the contingency that the building be a memorial to her late husband naming it after him. The tablet at the east entrance of the building reads: "This Social Hall of the Evangelical Lutheran St. John's congregation was erected to the Glory of God, in loving memory of Charles K. Walker, died June 12, 1925, by Mrs. Helena Walker."

E. A. Schaefer, a member of the Building Committee, drafted the plans and was superintendent of the construction of the hall, a superb building in ornamental brick. By April 1927 with the work completed, the dedication took place on the 27th of that month. In the Sunday morning service that day, the 45th anniversary of St. John's congregation was commemorated with the dedicatory services held in the spacious 600-seat auditorium of the hall in the afternoon. The Rev. Walter Troeger of Pilgrim in Santa Monica gave the English address and the Rev. A. E. Michel of Trinity of Los Angeles spoke in German. Walker Memorial Hall was one of the finest of its kind in Southern California, embodying every convenience for the social life of various societies and the congregation. From its splendidly equipped gymnasium, immaculate kitchen, and spacious dining room to the elaborately furnished lobby and gorgeous auditorium, it was a marvel

Walker Memorial Hall with its spacious 600-seat auditorium, large gymnasium, immaculate kitchen, and spacious dining room that would accommodate 612 diners. (Pacific Southwest District Archives)

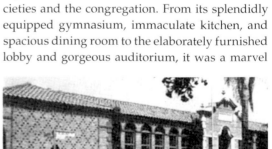

St. John's one-story school with ornamental brick and tile roof was dedicated on November 4, 1929. (Pacific Southwest District Archives)

of beauty, appointment, and compactness seldom found in structures of its type. The superb kitchen and dining room equipment for the hall, with its complete service for 612 persons, was personally selected and donated by Mrs. Carl Schumacher, a member of St. John's and sister of the donor of the building.

In 1928 when the school reached the 200 mark, it became imperative to employ permanently a fifth teacher. This necessity also involved another demand of St. John's that it could not avoid — the need for more room. A basement room in the building erected in 1904 was temporarily utilized and a female teacher was employed. Early in 1929, the congregation passed a resolution to build a new modern school and to acquire the necessary grounds, purchasing the northeast corner of Almond Avenue and Shaffer Street. After settling the question of a two-story versus a one-story building, the Building Committee took the work in hand without delay, employing J. H. Fleming of Los Angeles as architect. On November 4, 1929, the new one-story school with ornamental brick and tile roof was dedicated for the children of St. John's. The new building cost $37,851, with the spacious grounds acquired at a cost of $21,625. The new modern school contained 6 classrooms, a large assembly room with composition floor, one classroom for instruction of catechumens, office, library, health room, storage rooms, the necessary lavatories with tile on the floors and walls, and 75 lockers around the assembly room. All the desks and all furnishings were the latest and best quality.

In 1932 when St. John's triumphantly celebrated its golden anniversary with its 820 communicant members, the *Orange Daily News* gave much space to reporting the festivities marking this very special year. A weeklong series of special services were planned in both English and German. Rev. A. E. Michel of Los Angeles gave the morning sermon on February 14, with Rev. Arthur M. Wyneken of Long Beach preaching at the evening service. Mr. Eugene Wunderlich, who had joined the teaching staff the previous year, directed the church choir. The ladies lavishly decorated the church with large bouquets of golden flowers. To quote from social notes of the *Orange Daily News*, "On the altar table proper were two large baskets of the choicest Amling roses, garnished with golden acacia." The book that had been published for the 50th anniversary on the history of the church was printed in German, with an English translation following in a separate section.

On Friday, March 14, 1933, a major earthquake rolled through Orange and Los Angeles counties with the greatest damage and loss of life sustained in Long Beach and the surrounding areas. In Orange, a lot of minor damage occurred with the home of a member of St. John's, Richard Kohl of Westminster, totally demolished, but the people of St. John's rallied to help their fellow member. Because of the after-shocks, St. John's school was closed for the entire following week. Ironically, the students of the eighth grade had chosen that day for a roller skating party at a skating rink in Long Beach. The group had left that building only minutes before the quake collapsed the roof of the building. With all the phone lines and communications cut off, the students' parents spent many anxious hours before learning that all were safe.

In 1936, Theodore Hopmann answered a call to teach at St. John's, but before he could assume the responsibilities of the classroom, Principal Batterman was taken seriously ill and was forced to retire, passing away soon thereafter. Mr. Hopmann agreed to take over the duties of principal, a tenure that was to last for 31 devoted years. At this time Rev. Bode was nearing 70 years of age and feeling the burdens of his office. Rev. Kenneth Ahl had been called as assistant pastor in 1934 and remained until 1940, when he accepted a commission in the United States Army Reserve. A second pastor, Rev. William G. Gesch, from Alton, Illinois, was called and installed on July 13, 1941. Pastor Gesch was born in Berlin, Germany, on February 14, 1893, and immigrated with his parents, Her-

St. John's new school building of six classrooms, an assembly room, and offices, cost $37,851.

Santa Ana Business District after the March 10, 1933, earthquake. (Santa Ana Public Library History Room)

Rev. William G. Gesch served St. John's from July 13, 1941, to 1955. (Pacific Southwest District Archives)

In World War II, the United States War Department requisitions Walker Hall for military headquarters and bivouacs.

man and Luise (nee Klitzke). After graduating from Concordia Seminary, St. Louis, Missouri, in 1918, he began his ministry in Appleton, Minnesota, where he remained until 1921. During his ministry at Appleton, he married Katherine W. Laux on January 6, 1921; their marriage was blessed with three children, Dorothy, George, and Katherine. He moved to Alton, Illinois, serving the congregation for 20 years, before going to St. John's in 1941. He wrote one devotional booklet for Concordia Publishing House and sermon outlines for *Concordia Pulpit*.

Pastor Bode continued to serve St. John's on a limited basis, leaving the bulk of responsibilities to Pastor Gesch. Pastor Gesch led St. John's firmly through the years of World War II, when the United States War Department requisitioned Walker Hall for military headquarters and bivouacs, strictly off limits to all citizenry, including the members of St. John's. Seventy young men from the congregation served their country in uniform, and five of them died. During World War II, thousands of servicemen were trained in Southern California with the 30th Field Artillery Battalion stationed in Orange, while the men went off company by company to train in the Borrego Desert. Many of the servicemen returned to California after the war, often bringing their families with them, resulting in the biggest growth boom in Orange County's history.

Again the language question arose and, after prolonged discussions, it was officially and tactfully decided to "drop the German" during the war emergency. Soon thereafter, all sermons were given in English with one German Communion service a month. Older members found this a hard adjustment to accept with a small group of them actually petitioning the Church Council for reinstatement of the German services, declaring that they could gain nothing of spiritual value from the English services. Again, after the matter was soberly discussed at length, the first decision was upheld. It was Pastor Bode who compassionately offered, according to the minutes of that time, "to spend more time visiting and counseling with the older members" so that their spiritual needs could be met. He continued in this manner even after officially retiring in 1948. He made Orange his home until his death in 1954. Pastor Gesch also maintained a warm and caring relationship with the older German members, continuing to provide the German Communion service for them.

The years following World War II saw the beginning of phenomenal westward migration of

the population with an increase of the populace in Southern California as well as Orange County. The familiar orange groves were giving way to real estate subdivisions with the once small country village of Orange growing into a small city of more than 10,000 people increasing to 26,444 in 1960. St. John's also grew and expanded with the community while the work of the Kingdom proceeded at an accelerating pace. By 1950, the communicant membership grew to 1,200, necessitating a call for a second pastor, Rev. John H. Geisler of Paris, Texas, who was installed as associate pastor on August 20, 1950; he became well known for his ready humor and wit and was deeply respected for his unwavering adherence to the pure Word of God. With deep reluctance, the congregation in 1955, granted a peaceful release to Pastor Gesch, who felt called to accept the challenge of serving as missionary-at-large in the east Pomona area that later would become Montclair. Pastor Geisler became senior pastor at St. John's. Pastor Gesch remained at Trinity, Montclair, until ill health forced him to retire to Huntington Beach in 1962 where he lived until the Lord called him home on November 30, 1967.

Pastor Geisler was born in Fort Worth, Texas, in 1923, receiving his education at Concordia College in Austin, Texas, and St. John's College in Winfield, Kansas. After graduating from Concordia Seminary, St. Louis, in 1946, he was ordained and installed at St. Paul's in Fort Worth, Texas, as missionary-at-large at Grace, Paris, Texas, remaining until 1950. In 1946, he married Betty Boetal with their marriage blessed with two children, Ruth and Carol. When he became the pastor of St. John's, the congregation was again left with only one pastor. Calls were sent for an associate pastor with one finally answered in 1957 by the Rev. Robert Bentz of Cottage Hills, Illinois.

The year, 1957, marked St. John's 75th anniversary with more than 1,500 communicant members participating in the yearlong observance of the diamond jubilee celebration. Dr. John Behnken, president of Missouri Synod, gave the opening sermon of February 17, which was televised on the program, "Great Churches of the Golden West." A historical pageant was staged in October, and Pastor Gesch returned to give the special service of Thanksgiving in November. Local papers gave much space to the anniversary celebrations and so did President Dwight Eisenhower who honored St. John's with a personal telegram of congratulations. St. John's had made another milestone in its history, illustrating the chosen scriptural anniversary theme of "Hitherto Hath the Lord Helped Us."

Pastor Bentz left St. John's in 1964 to answer a call to Long Beach with the Rev. Harry Scholz arriving to fill the vacancy in 1965. As St. John's approached its 85th anniversary, it had over 2,100 communicant members, 2 pastors, a full-time principal, 17 teachers, a youth director, and a director of music. Mr. Edmund Martens joined St. John's staff in 1951, and under his direction as director of music, the beautiful candlelight Christmas Advent service became a high point in the annual church observance. When he accepted a call from Concordia Teachers College in Seward, Nebraska, in 1966, Mr. David Held accepted St. John's call as director of music that same year. Under his direction several new choirs were added to an already active music program. With the generous gift of a complete set of Swiss handbells, Mr. Held added yet another dimension to the worship services on Sunday mornings. After receiving his doctorate in music before leaving St. John's in 1979, he also accepted a position at Concordia Teachers College in Seward, Nebraska.

As St. John's centennial approached in 1982, the congregation voted to acquire a new pipe organ for the church as the old Johnston pipe organ that was installed when the church was dedicated was in need of extensive repairs. The new 3-manual pipe organ with its 4 divisions, the Great, Swell, Positiv and Pedal, containing 47 ranks (sets) of pipes totaling 2,445 individual pipes, was designed by Dr. Paul G. Bunjes of Concordia Teachers College, River Forest, Illinois. The Centennial Organ was built by Wilhelm Zimmer & Sons of Charlotte, North Carolina, whose family heritage in organ building dated back to the 1600s in Germany. The dedicatory concert was held on September 27, 1981, with concert organist, Charles W. Ore, a professor at Concordia Teachers College, Seward, Nebraska.

In the years since World War II, the world had seen the Korean and Vietnam wars, and had witnessed man in space and walking on the moon. Crime and violence statistics had risen alarmingly. The task of meeting the spiritual needs of a congregation in such bewildering times was being met at St. John's in a variety of ways: Increased emphasis was placed on a deeper Bible study, with classes scheduled for almost any day or night of the week. Worship services were conducted on Sunday at 7:50 a.m., 9:30 a.m., 11:10 a.m. and 6:30 p.m. with over 4,579 baptized members, 2,987 communicant members, and an average attendance of

1,763 served today by Pastors Timothy Klinkenberg, Mason Okubo, Phillip Sipes, and Paul Wentz. The school, served by Gary Beyer, principal, had over 640 students in preschool through grade 8. The ever mindful love of the Father that had been lavished upon the people of St. John's had, as urged by Pastor Jacob Kogler over a century ago, remained "steadfast and true to the confessions of the pure and unadulterated Word of God."

In 1986 through 1987, Johnny Lopez was the vicar at St. John's, opening a new ministry for the church. He initiated the first Spanish Bible class (catechetical) that met at Immanuel Lutheran Church in Orange on April 26. On December 13, 1987, at 3:00 p.m., he was ordained and commissioned as missionary-at-large for Orange to initiate a Hispanic ministry in Orange with the new project conducted by Immanuel, St. Paul, St. John's, and Salem congregations. The 4 congregations of Circuit 12 hoped to finance the special project without District subsidy. At the time, the pastor at St. John's, Norbert Oesch, wrote, "It is simply a thrill to be able to launch this ministry and support it cooperatively with Orange Lutherans."

Pastor Lopez was born on December 3, 1943, to Baldomero and Maria Lopez in Los Angeles, California, one of nine children. His educational journey was varied and included studying at a monastery before graduation from Mater Dei High School in Santa Ana in 1961, attending several community colleges, but a 20-year professional career in music intervened where he worked with Tom Jones, Engelbert Humperdink, Tony Orlando, Ike and Tina Turner, the Righteous Brothers, Connie Stevens, and others. He married Sarah Gates who was instrumental in leading him to Jesus. They were blessed with five children: Maria, Johnny Jr., Tony, Gina, and Joseph. In 1976, God radically changed his life when he was introduced to the Bible and became a committed Christian, leading him to join Trinity Lutheran Church in Santa Ana where he served in many capacities. In 1982, he continued his studies by entering Christ College Irvine (CCI) now Concordia University, preparing for a lay ministry degree. His activities in Hispanic ministry led to the chairmanship of the Hispanic Support Group of Southern California. He enrolled in the colloquy program at Concordia Seminary, St. Louis, in 1984, graduating in 1986, completing his vicarage at St. John's Lutheran of Orange in November of 1987. He received and accepted a call to serve as missionary-at-large for the Southern California District of The Lutheran

Rev. John H. Geisler came to St. John's in 1950. (Pacific Southwest District Archives)

Johnny Lopez initiates the first Spanish Bible class in 1987.

Rev. Johnny Lopez came to Orange to begin a Spanish ministry in 1987. (Pacific Southwest District Archives)

In November of 1992, Cristo Rey starts branch in El Modena.

Church — Missouri Synod to serve the Hispanic population in Orange. His goal was to establish a mission, bringing Christ to the thousands of Hispanics in that area.

This opportunity to establish a Hispanic mission was the culmination of Pastor Lopez's dream of many years. This dream came true in the establishment of Iglesia Cristo Rey and the initial work in the Orange Hispanic community began in 1987 with home Bible studies, evangelism calls, and catechetical instruction. That same year the Orange Hispanic Task Force was formed from representatives of the four sponsoring LCMS congregations in the city, with a direction to support this ministry and its pastor. Immanuel was selected for the site with offices for Cristo Rey in its former parsonage while worshiping in St. John's old parsonage. On July 24, 1988, the mission realized more of God's blessings when it had a record-setting attendance of 49, celebrated its first Baptism, had its first Sunday school class, had 15 visitors — the most first-time visitors — as well as having 13 children, the most at any of the services. The mission also received its first grant, a $200 gift from AAL. Each Sunday, Pastor Lopez preached a sermon that was largely instructional. A Bible study preceded the service introducing people to the Gospel. One woman told him that the Bible was now like a magnet to her — she wants to read it all the time. He always felt that his musical ability was a gift from God, but now he knew that it was also a gift for God, as he used music as a tool to communicate the Gospel message. In giving up a successful career as a professional musician, he found the transition to Gospel ministry an easy one. The Hispanic ministry development received a $5,794 LWML Mite Box offering with the money used for outreach to the Hispanic population in Orange.

Iglesia Cristo Rey was begun in St. John's old parsonage next to the church. (Pacific Southwest District Archives)

In the summer of 1989, Pastor Lopez was the master of ceremonies at the 1989 Youth Gathering, a 5-day event from August 5 through August 9, with over 17,000 LCMS youth and adults participating in Denver, Colorado, celebrating the theme, "Blessed in the Journey." The following year on January 14, Iglesia Cristo Rey's baptismal service produced a record high attendance of 90 at the mission, which was now meeting at Immanuel Lutheran, as St. John's needed the parsonage for its ministry. In 1991, the financially challenged Hispanic mission with a host of pressing challenges and opportunities elected to send $1,000, a tithe on a larger donation designated by a friend of the mission for use outside the mission's regular ministry, to TOGETHER WE ARE ONE for mission opportunities in the PSW District and Christ College, Irvine. The little mission was now averaging 60 to 90 in worship service. Pastor Lopez spoke regularly to congregations and church groups about the mission's challenge. He stated, "When I preach, lead a Bible study or visit Vacation Bible Schools in area churches, I talk about cross-cultural ministry, . . . not just the Hispanic side of it."

Most of the adults in the mission held two or more jobs to make ends meet. Their industrious lifestyles made time and money very precious commodities. Following a series of fund-raisers, including tamale sales, car washes, AAL grants, and gifts, in September of 1991, the mission held a spiritual retreat with 53 people. This representation from Cristo Rey Luterano at a family retreat at Arrowhead Lutheran Camp was its first step in working toward forming a recognized LCMS member congregation, which was a sacrifice of both time and money for most of the church families. In November of 1992, Cristo Rey started a new branch of its ministry in the El Modena area, calling it Centro Cristo Rey. The idea was to train people in Bible study and eventually teach them so that some day they could repay by helping others in similar situations. On March 28, 1993, at 12:15 p.m., Rev. Mark McKenzie was installed at Cristo Rey to assist in the ministry doing preaching, the liturgy, and teaching a Sunday morning adult/ youth Bible class. He also assisted with computer work on projects such as the workshop on the new Spanish hymnal and the kick-off celebration for the Spanish radio program. The Hispanic Radio Ministry Celebration was inaugurated on May 8, at 6:00 p.m., at St. John's in Orange. Both pastors Lopez and McKenzie made calls on the people in the community around Centro Cristo Rey and continued to offer a Bible study there on Wednesdays having varied attendance.

Since Trinity in Santa Ana had granted use of some its buildings for the Hispanic ministry, Pastor McKenzie had visited people in Santa Ana enabling him to form a Confirmation class/Bible-study group in the home of one of the members of the class; the first class was held on a Saturday in June of 1993 having an attendance of 12 people with 11 not confirmed with another class also started in Orange. In July, a very successful Vacation Bible School was held at Centro Cristo Rey where a total of 76 children registered. Several of the youth and a few of the adults from the congregation helped with the classes. By September, Pastor McKenzie was leading three Bible studies per week, Tuesday and Saturday evenings in homes, and Sunday mornings at church. He preached twice a month in Spanish and served as liturgist twice a month, as well as preaching in the English service from time to time. The Lord had continued to abundantly bless the mission effort of Cristo Rey as growth climbed steadily to 35 communicant members and 95 baptized members, with 75 percent of the members from Mexico and 15 percent from Central America.

In October, the Circuit Reformation Festival was co-hosted by Cristo Rey and Immanuel where there was an ethnic food fair with tostadas, bratwursts, and Venezuelan food. During the dinner, a Mexican folklore-dancing group from Westminster High School performed directed by Jesús Rios, the congregational president. After the dinner, a trilingual worship service was conducted with Pastor David Stirdivant preaching and pastors Eric Kaelberer, Wynn Nguyen, and Mark McKenzie serving as liturgists. Pastors Norman Franzen, Johnny Lopez, Wynn Nguyen, and Maria Rios, a woman from Cristo Rey, served as lectors. Musical groups from St. Paul's, Garden Grove, and the Garden Grove Vietnamese Lutheran Church also participated.

Four of the adults who had been studying in the Tuesday and Saturday night Bible studies were confirmed on Sunday, February 27, 1994. Centro Cristo Rey office for the Spiritual outreach at the Villa Santiago Apartments in Orange was finally becoming a reality with the help of student work parties from Concordia University and Prince of Peace, San Diego. Pastor McKenzie was assigned to do social ministry in the apartment complex about three miles east of Cristo Rey, working in the Christian education office. Since the apartment complex was a bad environment run by slum landlords, the police department demanded that the owners donate four apartments for this social ministry. The ministry helped with food, health, tutoring, English, thrift shop, and a co-op with most of the funding to operate it supplied by St. John's in Orange. At the end of October, a beautiful Reformation service was held at Trinity, Santa Ana, involving the Hispanic congregations of Trinity, Cristo Rey, and Zion, Anaheim. The youth/adult choir at Zion, which was formed the previous month, participated. This combined service was a good way for the people at Cristo Rey and Zion to show their support for the new ministry at Trinity. A Catechism class for children to prepare for their First Communion was started at Cristo Rey with three children coming from Anaheim to attend the classes. Pastors Lopez and McKenzie traded teaching the classes on Saturdays.

On December 10, 1994, a Christmas party/Bible study was held at Pastor McKenzie's home for Saturday night Bible study at Cristo Rey with nine adults and seven children attending. On Christmas Eve, the service was well attended with over 60 people. In the fall, Pastor McKenzie was assigned to be missionary-at-large in San Bernardino, leaving the Orange field to Pastor Lopez to work solo. The 1995 Reformation Sunday service was the "first ever Spanish-English service" held at Immanuel. The congregation invited Iglesia Cristo Rey to worship with them on the fifth Sunday of every month. For the first experience of uniting the English- and Spanish-speaking groups, a brass choir, school choir, Spanish choir, and chancel choir performed with the worship folder presenting the order of service side-by-side in English and Spanish.

One of the members of Iglesia Cristo Rey, Jesús Rios, received national attention in August of 1997 when he and his group, Itzamná Folkloric Dancers, performed at the "150th Anniversary Celebration Extravaganza" in St. Louis in conjunction with the National Great Commission Convocation before a crowd of 15,000 at Kiel Auditorium. The name "Itzamná" was chosen because it means "keeping our traditions alive," one of the objectives of the group. In June, the dancers presented their colorful program at the Pacific Southwest District Equipping Conference at the Westin Hotel near LAX. With Pastor Lopez, fellow members of Iglesia Cristo Rey, and other talented musicians, the troupe also danced at the 1996 "One in the Spirit" event sponsored by the District in South Gate. Mr.

The 1995 Reformation Sunday service is the "first ever Spanish-English service" held at Immanuel.

Jesús Rios, Director of It-zamná Folkloric Dancers and leader of Spanish Bible class at Iglesia Cristo Rey. (Pacific Southwest District Archives)

Itzamná Folkloric Dancers: Front: Lizbeth Perez, Yuri Vidalis, Heidi Fuentes, Janessa Garduno, Jennifer Garduno, MiLinda Valverde, Teresa Dever; Middle: Cesar Franco, Israel Solis, Stephanie Garduno, Franklin Mendez, Cesar Puga; Back: Jesús Rios, Director. (Pacific Southwest District Archives)

Rios, employed by the A & J Cheese Company and the Westminster Boys and Girls Club, served as the dance academy instructor. He was also an instructor of Quinceñera presentations, a member of the choir at the Iglesia Cristo Rey, and was doing theological studies at the Institute Hispano de Teologia. He was trained at and performed for the Institute Folklorio Sinaloense in Mazatlan, Sinaloa, Mexico.

In 1998, the church had a complete youth handbell choir and had expanded the adult choir. A Spanish Bible class was started and led by Jesús Rios. A prayer group met with each individual praying for two visitors who had been invited by congregational members to return to worship service. After six months of prayer, each person was invited to a special church service and a luncheon. In December over 100 people attended the "Noche Buena" Christmas Eve worship service, which concluded with Las Posadas, a pageant that re-enacted Joseph and Mary's search for lodging. The year ended with an average of 39 people at the 2 worship services and 7 people at Bible classes. In an effort to increase attendance, two new Bible studies were offered in English as well as in Spanish. Through efforts to merge the ministry with

Trinity's Hispanic ministry in Santa Ana, Cristo Rey wanted to assist them in winning more souls through community outreach.

In an outreach effort in 1998, a Folklorico dance class was started on the 29th of January. In April, the offices of Cristo Rey in the old parsonage were dedicated at a special service. Since the offices were in very poor condition, a select group of members worked very hard over a six-month period to renovate and improve them. Also in the first months of the year, the average church attendance swelled to 47 people in 2 services. The year ended with an average of 66 in worship services. At the end of 2000, a children's choir was begun on October 28 with congregational visits made by Vicar Ramón Contreras. On November 18, evangelism outreach was conducted in downtown Santa Ana and on December 2, 10 Cristo Rey families participated at the Mission Festival Community Outreach to Hispanics at Abiding Savior, Lake Forest, by selling tamales. Plans were being made to have a demographic study done through Human Care Ministries of the LCMS and investigating the feasibility of relocation. The relocation is discussed later in the chapter.

Trinity Lutheran Church
Misión Trinidad
Iglesia Cristo Re
Santa Ana, California

Today, the city of Santa Ana is over 27 square miles having a population of 343,700, with 76 percent Hispanic, 12.4 white, 8.7 Asian, and 1.3 black, located 33 miles south of Los Angeles and 12 miles inland from the Pacific Ocean. The first to explore the area was Don Gaspár de Portolá, a leader of a Spanish expedition party, who discovered a picturesque valley and river in Southern California, which he christened Santa Ana, in honor of Saint Anne, on July 26, 1769. The Santa Ana River with its smaller tributary, Santiago Creek, is usually dry but can be unpredictable in wet years. José Antonio Yorba, one of the expedition's soldiers, and his nephew Juan Peralta, were given a Spanish land grant for the area in 1810, developing Rancho Santiago de Santa Ana for cattle grazing and productive farmland.

Jacob Ross purchased 650 acres from the Yorba family's vast Rancho Santiago de Santa Ana. When William H. Spurgeon, a Kentuckian, rode through on horseback on October 10, 1869, the land was covered with tall yellow mustard that was so high he had to climb a sycamore tree in order to view the land. Enchanted with what he observed, he paid Jacob Ross Sr. $595 for 74.2 acres. Here he built his town with 24 blocks of about 10 lots each naming it Santa Ana. The boundaries were First Street at the south; West Street (now Broadway) at the west; Seventh Street, north; and Spurgeon Street, east. He spent the rest of his life in active service for what became his city, dying in 1915 at the age of 88.

Spurgeon opened a small general store that was also patronized by families to the south and west of town. In 1869, his artesian well and small water tower supplied the residents' water. In 1870, he became the postmaster, keeping the mail in a wooden shoebox. He became the first mayor when the city incorporated on June 1, 1886, with the town having a population 2,000. In order to meet the Wells Fargo stage with its mail and passengers, he built and paid for a road through the mustard fields to make easier access to Anaheim with Wells Fargo opening an office in Santa Ana in 1874. When Orange County was separated from Los Angeles County in 1889, Santa Ana was designated the county seat, making it the financial and governmental center of Orange County and a major city in the state today. By 1887–1888 when the Santa Fe trains reached Santa Ana, it was stated, "10 horse cars went to Tustin and 2 trains to Fairview, while 41 trains or trolleys touched Santa Ana each day." In 1906, the Red Car from Los Angeles ran along Fourth Street on the new Pacific Electric line, but by the 1950s, the route was abandoned and the tracks were removed. In 1953, the Santa Ana Freeway was opened between Broadway and First Street.

Santa Ana's first schoolroom was located in a private home at Fifth and Main in 1870, presided over by Mrs. Annie Cozad as the teacher. The first school building, called Central School, was a two-story building on the site of the present day YMCA. The school began with only elementary grades, but in 1892 it had graduated its first class of three high school boys who were taught on the upper floor; by 1898, 27 graduated from high school classes. Later a high school was built at 520 West Walnut Street with that school sharing the building with junior college classes in 1915. With increased enrollment, the college classes took over an entire building on the campus and then moved to 1010 North.

With all the growth in Santa Ana in the late 1800s, many German Lutherans also arrived with

> A high school is built at 520 West Walnut Street with the school sharing the building with junior college in 1915.

The business district on East Fourth Street in Santa Ana, circa 1900. (Santa Ana Public Library History Room)

the new Lutheran population wanting a church of their own as they were traveling to Orange to attend services at St. John's. As was mentioned earlier, they petitioned St. John's in April of 1887 to establish their own parish in Santa Ana with that request being denied. After 22 years of waiting for a congregation to be established, the Lutherans in Santa Ana were finally able to organize a parish of their own when an organizational meeting occurred on October 12, 1909, adopting a constitution naming the new congregation "Die Erste Deutsche Evangelisch-Lutherische Dreieinigkeits Gemeinde," the first legal name of Trinity Lutheran Church, and electing a board of directors. Trinity was now on its way to becoming a full-fledged congregation except it had no pastor, no building, nor any real estate. For the first year and a half of its existence, Pastor Kogler served as vacancy pastor, conducting services in the homes of various members.

On July 24, 1911, a new day dawned for Trinity as that was the day their new pastor, Rev. Herbert O. H. Michel, was ordained and installed. Since the congregation didn't have a building, the service was held in the Unitarian Church on the southeast corner of Eighth and Bush streets with the service conducted by the father of the new pastor, the Rev. Arthur Michel, pastor of Trinity Lutheran Church in Los Angeles being assisted by pastors Kogler of Orange, Schmelzer of Anaheim, and Mieger of Olive. Rev. Herbert Michel was a 1911 graduate of Concordia Seminary in St. Louis. On October 3, 1911, he mar-

After 22 years of waiting for a congregation to be established, the Lutherans are finally able to establish one of their own on October 12, 1909.

Rev. Herbert O. H. Michel with his wife, Bertha, was ordained and installed as Trinity's first resident pastor on July 24, 1911. (Pacific Southwest District Archives)

Trinity's first church building was dedicated on November 19, 1911, and located on a triangular plot of land bordered by Brown, Sixth, and F streets. (Pacific Southwest District Archives)

ried Miss Bertha Ellerman of Los Angeles. After the wedding, his salary was raised from $50 to $60 a month. One would think that wasn't a great deal of money, but one must realize that five pork chops cost 15¢ and a 6-room house rented for $15 a month.

Following the installation service on July 24, 1911, after most people had filed out of the church, the congregation had a voters' meeting with its three voting members, as a large number of families had become discouraged over the years and either returned to St. John's or joined the Ohio Synod church which was organized a few weeks before Pastor Michel arrived. Even with this disappointment, the congregation put their trust in the Lord and purchased a triangular plot of land bordered by Brown, Sixth, and F, later named Lacy, streets. They awarded a contract to the general contractor E. W. Smith to build a church for them, and made arrangements with the Unitarian Church to hold services there on Sunday afternoons until their building was completed. Pastor also organized and conducted the first Sunday school on August 6, 1911, three weeks after his arrival. On November 19, 1911, the joyous day had arrived as the little flock dedicated its first house of worship with pastors A. E. Michel, Schmelzer, and Mieger officiating at the ceremonies. This happiness was very short lived, as Pastor Michel, early in 1913, developed serious eye problems resulting in his resignation from the ministry. After his eyes were healed, he took a call to St. John's in Covina where he also served as missionary to the Upland mission and in 1920, he was missionary to St. Paul's in Pomona establishing the mission. In 1933, he developed serious eye problems, which resulted in complications forcing him to resign from the ministry.

When Rev. William J. Lankow, formerly of Salt Lake City, was called, he was serving as missionary-at-large in the San Diego area. He was installed as Trinity's second pastor on June 29, 1913, by pastors J. Kogler, Mieger, and H. G. Schmelzer. When the new parsonage was built behind the church on Brown Street, Pastor Lankow and his family occupied it in October of 1913. In 1914, he was forced to resign his pastorate due to throat problems. In September of 1914, Pastor Rudnick left San Bernardino to accept the call to Trinity, Santa Ana. With his throat problems healed, Pastor Lankow was installed on September 20, 1914, at Trinity in San Bernardino where Pastor Rudnick had served six and a half years, building a mission with no church to a congregation with a beautiful, new church building.

Rev. William J. Lankow was installed as Trinity's second pastor on June 29, 1913. (Pacific Southwest District Archives)

During Pastor Rudnick's tenure at Trinity, Santa Ana, a Walther League was organized on February 13, 1915, with his sister-in-law, Miss Barbara Sandler, elected president. The group pledged a substantial amount of money for the building of a parish hall, which was located between the parsonage and the church on Brown Street. The money they earned purchased the building materials, which was assisted by selling bonds ranging from $5 to $100. After the funds were raised, the young people built the parish hall by themselves assisted by some adults when necessary. With the building completed in September of 1915, the congregation had a hall for social functions for 30 years. Pas-

Rev. Edward Rudnick and his family in 1916. Front: Alma, John (Pastor's father), Robert on John's knee, Martin, Caroline (Pastor's mother), Helen, Beata; Back: Natalie, Arthur, and Pastor. (Pacific Southwest District Archives)

tor also organized the first church choir in 1916, having a membership of 18 by the end of its first season.

Before the great flu epidemic hit Santa Ana in the fall of 1918, Pastor's three little sons had severe dysentery in mid-May. Robert, age three, and Arthur, age two, died and were buried in St. John's Cemetery. In the fall, everyone in the house except Mrs. Rudnick contracted the flu. Following Pastor's bout with the flu, his tuberculosis reoccurred, forcing him to resign his pastorate at Santa Ana as the doctor had recommended he move to the desert with his family of nine. He and his wife and five children plus his parents took up residence in Banning in 1919. While living in Banning, his health was restored and he started a small mission in the city's theatre. The Banning experience was a real struggle for the Rudnick family as they received only $35 a month from the District for support. The rest of their funds came from raising goats and selling goat's milk and from his father doing odd jobs. In 1922 with renewed health, he took a call to Immanuel in Fresno where he ministered, building a large congregation just as he had done in Santa Ana. He retired in 1947 and was called to his heavenly home a short time later.

Following Pastor Rudnick's departure, Rev. William Schmoock was installed on November 2, 1919. He was born in Janesville, Minnesota, in 1880, receiving his preparatory training at Concordia College, Milwaukee, Wisconsin, graduating from Concordia Seminary, St. Louis, in 1905. His first call was to North Dakota where he served as the secretary of the North Dakota-Montana District. Due to ill health, he was forced to leave, taking a call to Bellingham, Washington, for three years, leaving there for a pastorate in St.

Lake City, Utah. At the advice of his doctors, he went to Southern California where he alternated serving Escondido and San Pedro churches on a part-time basis. He married Katherine Krumsieg, daughter of Rev. Theodore Krumsieg in 1908 with their union blessed with three children, Irmgard, who died in early childhood, Gerhard, and Enno, who both became pastors.

On May 7, 1922, all the Missouri Synod Lutheran churches in Southern California held a joint service in the Hollywood Bowl in honor of the 75ᵗʰ anniversary of The Lutheran Church — Missouri Synod with Pastor Schmoock as one of the principal speakers. By 1927, Trinity had grown to over 200 members with 50 members in the voters' assembly. During the following years from 1930–1939 with economic pressures of the Great Depression and internal conflict, the membership dropped to half of its size with only 17 voting members. After 23 years of faithful service at Trinity, Pastor Schmoock took a call to Grace in Banning where his son Gerhart, who was pastor in Santa Barbara, installed him on January 7, 1943. During the vacancy at Trinity from January 7 to December 18, 1943, Rev. Schmelzer in his retirement served as vacancy pastor.

Trinity's new pastor was the Rev. William L. Duerr who was born in Beaufort, Missouri, on March 29,1911, spending most of his boyhood at St. Paul's Lutheran Church in Union, Missouri, where he was confirmed. After completing his preparatory training at St. John's Winfield, Kansas, he attended Concordia Seminary in St. Louis graduating on June 5, 1936, and the following day marrying Miss Ruth Nolte in St. Louis. After accepting the call to St. Paul's in Beaufort, Missouri, he and Rev. Maack conceived the idea of a trailer mission making numerous trips throughout the Middle West doing evangelistic work resulting in forming many new congregations. This program was later developed into the Synod's successful

Rev. William Schmoock was installed as Trinity's fourth pastor on November 2, 1919. (Pacific Southwest District Archives)

Rev. William L. Duerr was installed as Trinity's fifth pastor on December 12, 1943, and served until his retirement in 1976. (Pacific Southwest District Archives)

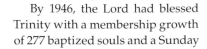

Trinity officially drops Dreieinigkeits as their name on May 6, 1944

P.T.R. (Preaching, Teaching, Reaching) movement. At the time Pastor Duerr received Trinity's call, he was engaged in a very strenuous missionary campaign in the Chicago area while still serving his parish in Beaufort, Missouri.

Rev. and Mrs. Duerr arrived in Santa Ana on December 8, 1943 with their two children, Ruth and Bill. Pastor Duerr was installed the following Sunday, December 12, by circuit counselor, W. G. Gesch, who was assisted by pastors H. G. Schmelzer, A. G. Webbeking, L. E. Eifert, and H. Wiechmann. At the time of Pastor Duerr's installation, Trinity had only 35 families with 88 baptized souls and 72 communicant members with 15 in the Sunday school. Things would change as the country was in the second year of World War II with thousands of defense workers migrating to Southern California. Among the many new people to move to the area were Mr. and Mrs. Walter Ott who became members at Trinity in September 1942; he had served in the Lutheran schools in Lincoln, Seward, and Scribner, Nebraska, and was in charge of the Adult Extension Department at the University of Nebraska. When the congregation decided to open a Christian day school, it immediately called Mr. Ott in July of 1944, who then proceeded to open the school in the parish hall with 40 students on September 9, 1944. With the changing population and the congregation using English exclusively, the parish decided on May 6, 1944, to officially change its name from the German, Dreieinigkeits, given in 1909, to the English, Trinity.

By 1946, the Lord had blessed Trinity with a membership growth of 277 baptized souls and a Sunday school of 107; all the services filled the little white-framed church to full capacity with chairs placed outside the front door and under the windows. Since the Brown Street property was so small and inadequate, making future expansion impossible, three lots on South Broadway at the southwest corner of Cubbon were purchased in 1946 with a parish hall/chapel and two classrooms constructed on the two south lots. During construction from September 1946 to March 1947, all services, Sunday school, and the day-school classes were conducted in an old warehouse building at 2417 Main Street, which became affectionately known as the "tin house." On March 9, 1947, Pastor H. G. Schmelzer and Rev. G. L. Steinback, director of the "Southern California Lutheran Hour," dedicated the new parish hall/chapel to the glory of God, with a congregation that had grown to 327 baptized members and 235 communicants. With the congregation continuing to expand, it necessitated having two services each Sunday. With the day school increasing to 95 in 1949 making it necessary to expand to three classrooms, two lots west of the church plant on Birch Street were purchased, with Pastor and his family moving into a house on one of the lots and the old parsonage on Broadway becoming the third classroom. In 1950, the old building was sold and moved off the lot where a third classroom was built.

By 1951, the congregation had outgrown their parish hall/chapel, having reached 526 members. A building committee was selected to build a new church that would accommodate the membership. In October 1952, Mr. Walter R. Hagendohm, A.I.A. of Los Angeles, was engaged as the architect to design a sanctuary to accommodate 500 people. Groundbreaking ceremonies were conducted on October 17, 1954, by Pastor Duerr with Rev. Erick Oelschlaeger of First Lutheran Church in Long Beach as guest speaker. On the following day, construction of the new church began with the completion and dedication of the building on May 15, 1955. With the continued growth in the school, it became apparent that a new education building was needed. On September 20, 1959, the new build-

ing, which housed the 160 pupils, was dedicated. Three years before, in August of 1956, the Lord called His servant, Mr. Walter Ott, Trinity's first teacher and principal, home to be with Him. Mr. Ott was described as a man of calm and unruffled temperament, jovial, yet always full of sympathy and understanding. Another teacher who also hailed from Nebraska and would spend most of his career at Trinity School was Don Morner who came in 1959 to not only teach but also to serve as youth director.

In 1956 when the little Hispanic mission, Nuestro Salvador, in Santa Ana closed, the members were sent to Trinity where the congregation was unable to assimilate the Hispanic members as no one was conversant in Spanish with only a few of the members from Nuestro Salvador, who functioned in English, remaining. When Trinity celebrated its 50th anniversary in 1959, the parish had 1,142 baptized members, 762 communicants, 161 in the school, 250 in Sunday school, 102 in the Walther League, and a Confirmation class of 65. Also that year a new trend was appearing in Santa Ana as the downtown was in a state of deterioration. The Hispanic population was growing in 1965. By 1974, the area was experiencing white flight from neighborhoods with retail commerce leaving the

> The Hispanic population of Santa Ana grows in 1965.

The interior of Trinity displaying the large mosaic mural in the chancel. (Pacific Southwest District Archives)

Trinity's beautiful, large new church building that would accommodate 500 people was dedicated on May 15, 1955. (Pacific Southwest District Archives)

Rev. Richard Dannen-bring, pastor of Trinity. (Pacific Southwest District Archives)

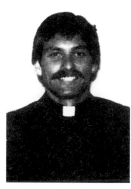

Rev. Robert E. Smith Jr. was installed as Assistant Pastor of Hispanic Ministry at Trinity on August 18, 1985, to begin a ministry to the Hispanic population. (Pacific Southwest District Archives)

Pastor Smith begins work in Hispanic neighborhood in 1985, after being installed at Trinity.

downtown area for the suburban malls. In order for Trinity to accommodate the changing neighborhood, a day-care program was begun in the patio building in 1975. The following year, Pastor Duerr retired after 33 faithful years as pastor of Trinity with Rev. Richard Dannenbring assuming the pastorate.

Pastor Dannenbring was born on April 5, 1947, in Chester, South Dakota. He attended Concordia Senior College, Fort Wayne, Indiana, and graduated from Concordia Seminary, St. Louis, in 1973. He was ordained at St. John's in Chester, South Dakota, and installed in a dual parish, St. John's in Laona and St. John's in Townsend, Wisconsin, where he remained until accepting the call in 1975 to serve Santa Ana. In 1988, he accepted the call to Christ, Brea, serving as pastor in a large parish and school. On January 30, 1993, he married his second wife, Kara J. Alspaugh. He also served on the Lutheran Credit Union Board of Directors.

By 1980, the densely populated neighborhoods in Santa Ana were experiencing rapid changes. In April or May of 1982, Elsie Porter, a member from St. John's in Orange, approached Johnny Lopez, who was then a youth director at Trinity to start a ministry to the Spanish-speaking neighborhood, after having offered money three times to Pastor Richard Dannenbring and being turned down three times. Elsie continued to feel the Lord's direction to start a Hispanic ministry with the money she had inherited from apartments when her husband had died. She and her husband used to take food and clothing to Tijuana in the 1960s, but she was now widowed. Johnny began a Wednesday night Bible study in the 921 S. Birch Street house that was converted into Trinity office space with Elsie supplying all the needed educational materials: Bibles, Sunday school materials, and Catechisms. Two families from the general area attended, one from Bristol Street and another from Orange Street. Planning was begun some time before with Frank Brundige, a student at Christ College, Irvine, who attended Trinity. The work stalled when the second family left because they wanted Johnny Lopez to baptize them, but he was not a pastor. Before Johnny went to Concordia Seminary in St. Louis in September 1984, he surveyed Orange County for potential Hispanic ministry for St. John's, a study that involved Rev. Bob Gussick.

Rev. Robert E. Smith Jr. was installed as assistant pastor of Hispanic ministry at Trinity on August 18, 1985, to serve beside the senior pastor,

Richard Dannenbring. He was born in Novato, California, on November 16, 1958, to Robert and Janice Smith, the eldest of six children. He lived in Novato until he was 10 years old when his family moved to Healdsburg, California, where he attended public school graduating from Healdsburg High School. While in high school, he took four years of Spanish, which he used and perfected in the vineyards in Healdsburg. There he was able to converse with Hispanic workers in the field where his boss involved him in translating. At the time while attending Santa Rosa Junior College, he wanted to be a vintner, but the Lord had different plans for him as he decided to go into the ministry. After graduating from Healdsburg High School in 1976, he continued his education at Christ College, Irvine, earning a Bachelor of Arts degree in theology in 1980. During his seminary training at Concordia, Fort Wayne, Indiana, which also included two years in Hispanic ministry in New York City, he was awarded the Master of Divinity degree in 1985.

During his vicarage, he spent two years at St. Matthew's in New York City, the oldest Lutheran Church in the United States, ministering to the people from the Dominican Republic where he had a difficult time breaking the Hispanic barrier. While instructing a well-known Dominican man from the neighborhood for church membership, he asked him to take him into the neighborhood to introduce him to people. This fellow knew many people in the neighborhood, which opened new doors for him to minister to the area. When he asked why the people were so indifferent to him, the man responded that he looked like a Marine, whom the Dominicans disliked and mistrusted due to their experience of the Marine involvement there during President Johnson's term of office.

After Pastor Smith was ordained in his home congregation, St. Luke in Santa Rosa, California, on August 4, 1985, he was installed at Trinity in Santa Ana two weeks later on August 18 to start a Hispanic mission in the old Church of Christ building on McFadden adjacent to Trinity, which Trinity had purchased and was in need of much work. Pastor and the people helped to paint and do repair work on the building to prepare for ministry in it. His office was in the old house next to the church. He began his ministry with Bible classes, ESL classes, and finally worship services where he had 10 people attending that swelled from 35 to 40 on Easter Sunday. He discovered that this was a very poor, transient Hispanic community with many families from Morelos in Michocán, Mexico. Because they were so poor, multiple families would rent and live in a single-family dwelling and even in the garage. The family of Brenda Luz, the first person he baptized, lived in the garage behind a house, having no furniture and sleeping on the cement floor. When he discovered this, he was able to secure furniture for the family and carpet for the floor. Shortly thereafter, when he went to pick up the family for church, he saw that they were again living on the cement floor as someone had stolen all their furniture including the carpet. A member of the church, Luis, who had come to America by swimming from Baja California to San Diego, would go with Pastor to help make evangelism calls.

The financial support for the Hispanic work at Trinity was funded by a combination of District and congregational funds, on a sliding scale with the goal of developing a self-supporting congregation over a period of five years, or the work would be taken over by Trinity alone. The work at Trinity proved to be a challenge greater than anticipated by the congregation at the outset. There was support given by Vera Saldaña, a member of Trinity who had become a Lutheran through the little Mexican mission in Santa Ana in the 1940s. Pastor Smith related that it was easy to get to know the people in Santa Ana. While at Trinity, he met his future wife, Bobbi Miller, marrying her on December 27, 1985, with their marriage blessed with three children, Samantha, Robert III, and Paul. Pastor Smith left Trinity in February of 1987, after taking the call to Zion in Rosemead where he was called to do bilingual work.

When Pastor Smith arrived at Zion, the church was rented on Sunday afternoons to a Chinese Pentecostal group. Since Zion wanted to do a Hispanic ministry using the church in the afternoon for its ministry, it was decided not to renew the Chinese church lease. Pastor worked the neighborhood inviting Hispanic children to Sunday school where his wife developed a children's choir that sang in two-part harmony. Their daughter was the only non-Hispanic in the group. Even when the children sang, the parents were reluctant to come to church to hear them. He started a service on Sunday at noon with most of the people coming from La Puente and Baldwin Park. The congregation did research with the help of personnel from the District office in the hope of beginning a preschool with the discovery that there were more Chinese than Hispanics in the area. The

suggestion was to begin a Chinese ministry, but the members felt they were not able to deal with such an effort. A Chinese Lutheran pastor came and wanted to do a side-by-side Chinese ministry with them, but the congregation voted against it. During the last three months of his ministry at Zion, he helped Pastor Brundige start a preaching station in Baldwin Park in the home of a former member of Santa Cruz Lutheran in East Los Angeles. In April of 1991, he was installed as pastor at Trinity in Indio, California.

The next pastor at Trinity was the Rev. Charles W. Pearson Jr. who was installed on August 14, 1988. He was born in Lubbock, Texas, on September 3, 1944. Charles's father was stationed there for part of World War II, and Charles spent his childhood in several cities before the family settled in Denver, Colorado. They were members of Bethlehem Lutheran Church in Lakewood, Colorado, and he attended the Christian day school there. After graduating from the Denver Lutheran High School in 1963, he attended Western State College in Gunnison, Colorado, where he received a Bachelor of Arts degree in music education in 1968. While attending college, he decided to study for the ministry, entering Concordia Seminary, Springfield, Illinois, in 1968, spending his vicarage year at Our Savior in Norwood, Chicago, Illinois. During his second year at the seminary, he married Marseda Kay Westermann of St. Louis on June 6, 1970, with their union blessed with three children, Charles, Rebecca, and Kristi.

From about 1988 to 1993, the Hispanic ministry seemed to flounder and cease, as there was no one on the staff to take charge of it. At the District Board of Directors meeting on September 30, 1993, it was reported "Initial meetings have been held with Trinity to discuss the possibility of beginning work with the Hispanics in Santa Ana." In 1994, the congregation developed a "business plan" to minister to the Hispanic community, which included receiving a two year $50,000 Lutheran Brotherhood grant plus congregation offerings to support Pastor John Durkovic who had been called as pastor of Hispanic ministry. The goal was that Pastor Pearson would increase membership in the English-speaking congregation that would support two pastors; if he didn't, the bilingual pastor would stay, and Pastor Pearson would leave. Rev. John G. Durkovic was installed at a 4:00 p.m. service on September 25, 1994, as the bilingual pastor in charge of Spanish-language ministries at Trinity.

Rev. Charles W. Pearson Jr. was installed as pastor of Trinity on August 14, 1988. (Pacific Southwest District Archives)

Pastor Durkovic was born on November 29, 1936, in Cheyenne, Wyoming. After graduating from Valparaiso University in 1959, he worked as a control systems engineer at Johns Hopkins University's Applied Physics Lab in Maryland. He married Janet Bahls on December 25, 1958, with their marriage blessed with five children: Catherine, Andrew, Joel, Timothy, and Heidi. After deciding on a career change to study for the ministry, he attended Concordia Seminary, Springfield, Illinois (1964–1969) with a two-year vicarage in Venezuela supported by faculty and students. He graduated with a Master of Divinity degree in 1969. Following his graduation, he served La Iglesia Luterana Cristo Rey (Christ the King) in Guatemala City, Guatemala, from 1969–1981. He then served in Guatemala, promoting Theological Education by Extension for leadership development in Central America-Panama (1981–1985). In 1985, his wife was called to her heavenly home. He continued serving Central America's mission field as missionary coordinator/counselor (LCMS-BFMS), in Guatemala, El Salvador, and Honduras. In May 1989, he returned to the United States, accepting a call to serve as part-time pastor of St. Paul's, Brooklyn, New York, and as Hispanic ministry coordinator in metropolitan New York City for the Atlantic District. He also served as tutor for the Hispanic Institute of Theology in New York City. He was a man of rich experi-

ence in cross-cultural ministry, with special gifts and aptitudes in the Spanish language. He had a profound understanding of the Hispanic culture, their people, and their language. On April 10, 1993, he married Nancy Nowak, a Lutheran parochial school teacher, who was teaching in Queens, next door to Brooklyn.

With the arrival of Pastor Durkovic at Trinity in Santa Ana, the congregation defined and accepted its mission statement: "to share the good news of salvation in Jesus Christ with all the people in our changing neighborhood," a neighborhood of about 80 percent Hispanics. The first person he met at Trinity the day he arrived was Edgar Arroyo who ran the day-care center but was not attending the Lutheran church, as he was a member of another denomination. Through the illness of Edgar's child, Pastor Durkovic ministered to him, bringing him and his family into the church. The first outreach in the Hispanic neighborhood started with a once-a-week food pantry. Next, Pastor began a conversational Spanish class for three English-speaking members of Trinity. In the spring, he trained to teach ESL classes and eventually invited members of the class to the Lenten soup suppers followed by a Spanish lay service in a member's home, transporting people from the church to the members' homes. During the third week, a member of the class offered his home with 15 to 20 Hispanic people attending the Lent-

Bi-lingual Reformation Service held at Trinity on October 31, 1998, with the participating pastors: Mason Okubo, Joe Simpson, Johnny Lopez, John Durkovic, Dave Stirdivant, and Deacon Edgar Arroya.

en soup suppers and informal service. Through this beginning, a Spanish service was begun. In 1996, Pastor began to train lay members, using the SEAN materials approved by the District's Lay Leadership Training Program. SEAN used the Gospel of Matthew to successfully train lay leaders in Third World countries throughout the world. He prepared five students to be lay leaders at Trinity, one being Edgar Arroyo, a Guatemalan who was a self-taught English speaker.

In order to help fund the work of Edgar Arroyo as the Hispanic ministry pastoral assistant while he worked as director of the day-care center, a change would occur for Pastor Durkovic. He taught kindergarten at the beginning of September 1996. The half-day income he received was channeled into support for Edgar. Since the English congregation hadn't grown in membership or financially, and as the grant was depleted, Pastor Pearson was asked to leave Trinity, eventually taking a call to Gethsemane in La Crescenta. Pastor Durkovic was asked to serve the English-speaking congregation along with the Spanish work. He began the ministry to both the English- and Spanish-language groups in January 1997. Since there was a lack of moral and financial support by the Church Council, Edgar was counseled in June of 1997 to secure full-time employment elsewhere in order to support himself and his family. What had grown in two years was effectively abandoned for lack of full-time workers, lack of funds, and lack of support. The development of a new Hispanic ministry was indeed a full-time job. Since Edgar's position as a Hispanic ministry leader was never formally accepted at Trinity, he procured a position as "trainer" with the Curtis Association contracted by Orange County Social Services to train people on welfare how to find gainful employment. A couple years later, Curtis lost the contract with Orange County, and Edgar secured the same position with Catholic Charities. He eventually became one of the supervisors at the Catholic Charities branch office in Santa Ana. During all this time, he continued serving Trinity as a lay assistant, conducting the Spanish services.

Pastor and Edgar succeeded in getting some church and family members to provide the music in Sunday services. They made visits, doing some evangelism in the community, and conducting weekly worship services in Spanish but with no significant growth. For the most part, they ministered to the bilingual, Hispanic members of Trinity and their family members, doing both English

and Spanish ministries for three years.

In 1999, Dr. Ken Behnken, the District's mission executive, extended an invitation to interested District pastors to participate in a project to help their congregations "ReFocus" their ministries into accomplishing what God had planned for them. Pastor Durkovic accepted the challenge, thinking this would be an excellent way to apply those learned principles toward reaching Trinity's mission statement goals. The first part of the "ReFocus" process was to learn how to apply the principles to one's own life, as pastor. Then part way through that process, a small team of congregational leaders would be involved, with the pastor leading them through the process. This team became the "ReFocus" team, which led Trinity as a congregation through the "ReFocus" process.

In May 2000, Edgar Arroyo became eligible to be a District certified deacon, and do what a pastor does, preach, teach, and administer the Sacraments, under ordained pastoral supervision. He had completed the lay training program of the District, interviewed with District President Loren Kramer, and was certified under contract with Trinity, Santa Ana, for the remainder of the year. As a deacon, contracts had to be renewed every year in December. Almost immediately, Deacon Arroyo was asked to assist at Trinity, Los Angeles. Trinity, Santa Ana, agreed to temporarily loan Edgar's services to Los Angeles, so his time was now split between the two Trinity congregations. After every early morning service in Los Angeles, he rushed back to Santa Ana for the 11:45 a.m. service. At Trinity, Los Angeles, he blossomed. His deacon contract for 2001 was renewed, and the loaned services were extended. He joined Los Angeles Nehemiah Project in August–September 2002 as a full-time worker with the goal to plant Spanish language ministries in Los Angeles, being stationed at Grace, Los Angeles, where he began Spanish services.

In February of 2001, Cristo Rey, Orange, a Hispanic mission led by Rev. Johnny Lopez, accepted Trinity's invitation to move its ministry onto the church property in Santa Ana. Hispanic worship at Santa Ana was combined into one service at 11:00 a.m. with Pastor Johnny Lopez serving as coordinator, since Cristo Rey's Hispanic ministry was more fully developed than Trinity's. With the move to Santa Ana, there was less resistance from the new sister church and greater opportunities available to do mission work in the community with Pastor Lopez's assistant, Vicar Jesús Rios. An

Cristo Rey of Orange moves to Trinity, Santa Ana in 2001.

Rev. Johnny Lopez, pastor of Trinity-Cristo Rey Lutheran Church of Santa Ana. (Pacific Southwest District Archives)

Trinity's day school closes in 2002.

eight-week art project for children was initiated in February, running through the first part of May, with the hope of making it an on-going program. The "Evangelism Walk" in the neighboring community took place on March 8 with moderate success. The average church attendance increased to 47 and shot up to 90 in the second quarter. Other outreach opportunities were mosaic art classes, VBS, neighborhood campaigns (canvassing), and Spanish contemporary worship. After visiting a non-member while in the hospital, Pastor Lopez was asked to perform the lady's funeral. Through that opportunity, two family members began attending church regularly.

During the summer of 2001, Cristo Rey and Trinity each received a Hispanic vicar from the Concordia University (Ethnic Pastor Certification Program). The Lord also blessed the Spanish work when an entire family developed a praise band for the Spanish worship. Deacon Arroyo, at that time, had to spend most of his Sunday mornings in Los Angeles, so the Santa Ana worship had to be moved to a contemporary style Sunday evening service, using some parts of the praise band. While the family members played for worship services in Spanish, Pastor Durkovic was instructing them weekly in their home for church membership. In December 2001, the eight members of this family were baptized and confirmed. The church was thankful for an abundance of workers, 2 Spanish services, a praise band, and 8 new members doubling the size of the mission in less than 10 months, after 3 years of no growth. Even with the growth, there was a loss within Trinity's school staff because the congregation was unable to subsidize the school as it had done in the past, causing a downsizing of the school to only three staff members, which included the principal. Seeing the problem, Pastor Durkovic donated his services as a temporary school administrator from September 1, 2001, through February 2, 2002. With all the problems, the school year began with only 30 students in kindergarten through 6th grade as the 7th and 8th grades had been eliminated. On March first, Tim Surridge assumed the school administrative position on a part-time basis. By 2001, Santa Ana had the highest concentration of Spanish-speaking residents in the United States with 74 percent of all Santa Ana residents speaking Spanish according to the 2000 Census as quoted in the November 20, 2001, *Los Angeles Times* article.

On March 1, 2002, Pastor Durkovic officially retired from the active ministry and began working under contract as part-time pastor at Trinity. He also began traveling as regional coordinator for Hispanic Institute of Theology in a team ministry with the Pacific Southwest District. The objective was to inform District pastors of the institute's program for leadership training for Hispanics, and to encourage Hispanic pastors to better prepare their members for service using the educational materials produced by the institute. With Pastor Durkovic's retirement, both pastors Durkovic and Lopez were offered part-time stipend contracts with Trinity, and with Cristo Rey approving this new working relationship. Monies that had been used to pay for Pastor Durkovic's salary and benefit package funded these workers. On Thursdays, May 9 and May 30, at 6:30 p.m., Pastor Lopez conducted English-language contemporary praise and worship services featuring the Promised Land Worship Band. Since there had to be more decreases in the school program, it was decided to close the school in June 2002, retaining only a preschool class. In November, Pastor Durkovic resigned his role at Trinity, Santa Ana, to take a part-time position as pastor of Palabra de Dios (Word Of God) Lutheran Church, a Hispanic Mission in Maywood. Pastor Lopez was eventually called as full-time pastor of both Trinity and Cristo Rey in Santa Ana. In 2003, the congregation decided to close the preschool.

In 2003 when a community health clinic needed classroom facilities, the church provided space and also received three health clinic sessions per week in the facilities. A continued effort was being made to reach out to the neighboring community with invitations to Sunday school and Vacation Bible School. The average church attendance continued to remain steady with an average attendance of 46 per Sunday. The prayer of the mission was that the Lord would open the hearts of the members to accept the people of the community with genuine love of Christ.

Sunday, January 25, 2004, was a milestone for Trinity when a combined church service was conducted at 10:30 a.m. to celebrate the merger of Trinity and Iglesia Cristo Rey with Dr. Jack Preus, the president of Concordia University at Irvine, as guest speaker. During the festival service, the Board of Directors for new Trinity-Cristo Rey Lutheran Church of Santa Ana was installed. Following the joyful service, a potluck lunch was served in the parish hall for all the guests and members of the congregation.

Zion Lutheran Church
Iglesia Luterana El Buen Pastor
Iglesia Luterana Sion
Anaheim, California

Anaheim was established in 1857 by German colonists from San Francisco whose intent was to develop a settlement with vineyards as the source of income. George Hansen surveyed the original 200 acres, which now comprise the city's downtown area, bounded by North, South, East and West streets. The city's name is a derivation of "Ana" from the nearby Santa Ana River and "heim," the German word for home. Known as "The Mother Colony," Anaheim is the oldest city in Orange County, except for San Juan Capistrano, which was founded by the Spanish and is Orange County's second largest city. Today, Anaheim has a population of 348,014 with 48.8 percent of Hispanic origin.

Farming was the major occupation and lifestyle when the city was founded, with the major crop being the production of grapes grown for wine until a plague in the 1870s destroyed the vineyards. In their place, groves of orange trees, referred to as "Anaheim gold," were planted, with the first commercial oranges in Orange County cultivated in Anaheim. The growers attributed their success to the local hills protecting the fruit from cold wind coming down the mountains.

The first settlers were not only farmers but were also writers, artists, and musicians whose first public buildings were not administrative facilities, but rather a school and an opera house. When the city was incorporated with a population of 881 in 1876, it was a small rural community, growing slowly, but steadily for the next several decades. In 1887, the construction of the Santa Fe Depot linked Anaheim's citrus growers with the East, providing vital markets for their "golden crop." According to the Orange County Directory of 1899–1900, Anaheim "…is surrounded by very rich and fertile country. Abundant water is supplied for irrigation. There are many fine business blocks, an opera house, hotel, and prosperous merchants, also a large brewery. Immense quantities of the finest sugar beets are raised, while walnuts, oranges, lemons, and other citrus and deciduous fruits grow to perfection here. Anaheim is on both the Southern Pacific and Santa Fe railroads, has one band and two weekly newspapers, and the population consists mostly of Germans."

Anaheim's small town atmosphere continued through the first half of the twentieth century with Center Street, now Lincoln, the hub of community

> By 1900 Anaheim has many fine business blocks, an opera house, hotel, and prosperous merchants, also a large brewery.

Center Street (Lincoln Avenue) in Anaheim, circa 1890, looking west from the corner of Los Angeles Street (Anaheim Boulevard). (Anaheim Public Library)

activity with the populous gathering to celebrate local events, festivities, and to mark such national and international events as the end of both World Wars. On Sunday evening, January 7, 1945, the nation's favorite radio entertainer, Mr. Sunday Night himself, Jack Benny, would place Anaheim on the map and in the nation's vocabulary when the show's radio announcer stated that Jack's entourage was heading to New York, saying: "Train leaving on Track Five for Anaheim, Azusa, and Cucamonga!" The Anaheim residents were in shock, as they were known locally as the capital of the Valencia orange empire and the pre-war training grounds of Connie Mack's Philadelphia Athletics. Beside that, the three stops weren't even on the Santa Fe Railroad line!

In the late 1940s and 1950s, California experienced its third population explosion, the economic and industrial boom following World War II. The first boom happened with the discovery of gold in the late 1840s, and the second was the great real estate boom caused by the railroad rate wars. In 1950, Anaheim, the sleepy little town of 14,556, would soon be propelled into the modern era. From downtown Los Angeles, sprawling tracts of homes mushroomed as far as the eye could see, replacing agricultural fields and small towns. Highways and roads were paved overnight with Angelenos moving to the new emerging towns and cities that had been farms the year before. The nation's new affluence brought leisure time for families. A man by the name of Walt Disney would change life in Anaheim forever when he purchased acres of orange groves for his new theme park, Disneyland, opened on July 17, 1955.

The story of Anaheim must also include an important event that occurred on Christmas Day of 1895. On that day, Zion Lutheran Church of Anaheim was born when Pastor Jacob Kogler conducted the first service for the Lutheran Christians of the Mother Colony. Also, that day he met with a

Rev. Jacob Kogler of St. John's, Orange, conducted services from 1895 to 1903 in Anaheim. (Pacific Southwest District Archives)

Rev. A. W. Lussky was installed as first resident pastor of Zion on October 15, 1903, remaining until 1908. (Pacific Southwest District Archives)

committee which chose Zion or "der ev. luth. Zions Gemeinde zu Anaheim," as referred to in the minutes, as the new name of the embryonic congregation and elected five officers to act as trustees with very clear instructions, "...a committee to build a church." Zion was the sixth church to be established by the Missouri Synod in Southern California. This German Lutheran Church was not the only German church in Anaheim as there was the German Methodist Church, the German Baptist Church, and the Catholic Church, St. Boniface, named for the Irish monk who evangelized Germany. Anaheim was truly a German town having a population 1,456 in 1900. In 1899, the telephone directory showed 35 phone numbers in Anaheim, 2 of them residential, 2 for saloons, and the balance for business and professional subscribers.

Three meetings of the committee were held in January of 1900, regarding the merits of several parcels of land with none approved. A budget of $154.29 was mentioned for the first time in one of the meetings. In the meeting on February 16, 1902, two lots owned by Anaheim's pioneers, Richard and Mary Melrose, were available for the price of $150 with the committee accepting the offer. On March 14, 1902, title to two lots on the corner of Emily and Chartres streets passed to "Evangelische Luthersche Zions Gemeinde." Also at this meeting, Pastor Kogler was instructed to contact Synod for a list of candidates from which a pastor could be called. With no list forthcoming, they continued to meet in 1903 trying to raise funds for a church as they only had $5 left in the treasury after paying for the lots. By April, the plans for the new church, created by Mr. Williams, estimated to cost $1,500, were accepted with him being paid $20 for his services. Also, Pastor Kogler was instructed to contact Synod for a pastor for Zion at an annual salary of $250. Pastor Kogler also presented "a surprise gift of a lovely Communion goblet" or *Abendmahl Gefase*, from St.

John's. On April 12, 1903, a big step was taken by Zion, as the Articles of Incorporation of Evangelische Lutherische Zions Gemeinde were signed by Henry Burdorf, William M. Hildebrandt, J. H. Brunworth, Jonathan Bayha, and Fred Dettmer, filed with the Secretary of State of California on April 16, 1903, and from that date, Zion has been a non-profit corporation with April 16, 1903, treated as the official founding date. In May, the contract by Williams and Dunn, building contractors, was signed for $1,400, building materials ordered, and construction begun. During the eight years before the erection of the building, the congregation had worshiped in the Anaheim Episcopal Church and other locations.

Rev. A. W. Lussky, a recent St. Louis Seminary graduate, was called on July 3, 1903, accepted it on July 19, and arrived in Anaheim in September of 1903. On October 15, the congregation experienced a double joy, as their new church was dedicated with Pastor Kogler officiating and Pastor Reisner from Pasadena delivering the sermon. In the afternoon, Pastor Lussky was installed, preaching his first sermon in the evening service in English even though most services at Zion were conducted in German over the years. At his installation service,

the collection for the evening was $106. In 1904, an organ was purchased for $30 and a youth choir was started. A small parsonage was built for Pastor Lussky at a cost of $437, with donations of $225 given by the congregation.

Between 1905 and 1908, the congregation faced financial problems having difficulty meeting the pastor's salary and paying bills. In 1907, Pastor Lussky was authorized to preach every other Sunday afternoon in Santa Ana. At the January 8, 1908, Voters' Meeting, the congregation, after hearing of the desperate needs of the church in India, voted to collect money for the mission over the next three years, even though they only had 50 cents in the treasury at the time. At a special meeting called on December 20, 1908, Pastor Lussky announced that he had received a call from Jehovah Lutheran Church in Chicago, informing the Board that he had decided to accept it, requesting a release from Zion. When he was asked to remain, as the Board was rather reluctant to release him, he gave the following reasons for his release: "1. The congregation cannot pay my salary; and 2. The house is too small and there are no plans to enlarge it." He informed the congregation that his last and farewell sermon would be given the following Sunday. With the release granted, a collection of $50.75 was taken applying it to the unpaid portion of his salary. Arrangements were made with Pastor Berman of Olive to assist Zion during the vacancy with the congregation paying him $5 each Sunday, and the time of the Sunday service was changed from 10:00 a.m. to 2:20 p.m. to accommodate Pastor Berman's schedule.

> Pastor Lussky receives call from Jehovah Lutheran Church in Chicago and leaves Anaheim in 1908.

Zion's first church building, located on the corner of Emily and Chartres, was dedicated on October 15, 1903. (Pacific Southwest District Archives)

The interior of Zion's first church building with the large, high pulpit. (Pacific Southwest District Archives)

On February 21, 1909, Rev. H. G. Schmelzer of Portland, Oregon, was installed as second pastor of Zion with the Rev. Jacob Kogler officiating, and the Rev. A. Berner of Olive assisting. In September 1909, Christian education came into its own, as Christian day school classes were begun in the old Chennitzer residence with 18 pupils instructed by Pastor Schmelzer. On April 3, 1910, the congregation purchased an old house next to the church for $800 from Mr. Backs, remodeling it so that it could be used for school purposes. In the summer of 1910, Pastor Schmelzer and Mr. Dettmer traveled to Los Angeles to purchase an 800-pound bell for $85, which was installed in the church tower. The Ladies Aid Society came into being in May of 1911. At a cost of approximately $2,000, the school was built in 1913, which was later used as a parish hall with a kitchen and stage added. In September of that year, the congregation called its first teacher, Mr. Carl Goetz, with other teachers in those early years being Mr. C. F. W. von Neibelschuetz and Mr. G. H. Grefe. In the August 1918 Voters' Meeting, a letter was read from the United States Department of Defense, requesting that German no longer be taught or spoken in the school or Sunday school due to the troubled times that the country had faced during World War I. Since this was the wish of the federal government, all instruction in the educational units of Zion was then conducted in English except for church

Rev. H. G. Schmelzer was installed as pastor of Zion on February 21, 1909, and remained until his retirement in 1941. (Pacific Southwest District Archives)

In the 1918, a letter is read in the Voter's Assembly from the United States Department of Defense, requesting that German no longer be taught or spoken in the school or Sunday school.

services, which continued in German. With the continuing financial problem facing the congregation in 1919, the school was closed that fall.

By 1920, Anaheim had grown to 5,526 with Zion also experiencing so much growth that their small church building couldn't seat all the members. Architectural plans were submitted by a Mr. Gaw of Los Angeles with the bid of $44,016 by H. Pibel of Anaheim accepted in October of 1921 for the construction of the new sanctuary. The cornerstone was laid for the new brick church building that would seat over 500, which they believed would meet their future needs for years to come. A jubilant, thankful Zion sang dedication praises to the glory of the Triune God on August 13, 1922, in 2 services in German and one in English for which 100 English hymnals were purchased accompanied by the new 2-manual Estey Pipe Organ which supplied the music for the choir, soloist, and congregational singing with a total cost for the edifice and furnishings amounting to approximately $42,500. In January of 1924, Zion voted to conduct an English service in the morning at 9:45 a.m. with Sunday school at 8:45 a.m. and a German service at 10:45 a.m. By 1928, the English service was conducted in the morning with the German service held in the afternoon. On the occasion of the 25th anniversary in 1928 marked by two special services, Zion had 75 voting members, 195 communicants, and 460 souls with 102 children enrolled in

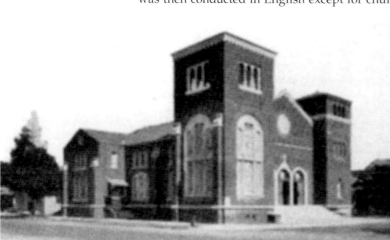

Zion's large, new 500-seat sanctuary was dedicated on August 13, 1922, with two services in German and one in English. (Pacific Southwest District Archives)

The interior of the new church with the choir and the organ in a balcony above the altar. (Pacific Southwest District Archives)

the Sunday school, 11 in the German department, and 91 in the English department. In 1923, the Walther League Society, the young people's group, was organized.

On July 2, 1930, the newly established Southern California District with 47 congregations, 45 pastors and 4,900 communicants, held its first convention at Zion. In Zion's 33rd year on April 13, 1936, the congregation called a young Pastor Lorenz E. Eifert to assist Pastor Schmelzer. Three years later the church again entered the field of Christian education, buying an acre of ground on North East and Cypress streets for a school site placing a former public school building with a double classroom on the property with Pastor Eifert teaching 14 pupils the first year in the one-room school. In 1941, Pastor Eifert was called as pastor when Rev. Schmelzer retired after 32 years of continuous service to Zion; he remained active in civic and church work until the Lord called him to his eternal home in June 1951.

When America was drawn into World War II on December 7, 1941, with the bombing of Pearl Harbor, the old question of the use of the German language in worship services came back to haunt Zion as they had two services on Sunday mornings, German at 9:00 a.m. and English at 11:00 a.m. Shortly after the attack on Pearl Harbor, the Southern California District recommended that all Missouri Synod congregations cease holding German language services. All churches immediately dropped German services except for Zion in Anaheim, which continued conducting services into January of 1942. When the Associated Press picked up the story of Zion's decision to continue German services, Zion received a firestorm of letters from area Lutheran churches, Trinity, Whittier; Trinity, Los Angeles; Christ, San Pedro; Zion, Maywood; and First, Culver City, all stating that it was unpatriotic to continue German services and would give the impression that the Lutheran church was a foreign church. With all this criticism, Zion voted at the end of January to discontinue the German service because of "...the present war emergency," leaving the church with

Rev. Lorenz E. Eifert served as pastor from 1936 to 1950. (Pacific Southwest District Archives)

Rev. Edwin H. Pflug was installed as Zion's pastor on August 13, 1950. (Pacific Southwest District Archives)

only one service on Sunday, English.

In 1940, Walter Knigge was called as teacher later serving as principal of the school. In 1942, Mrs. Velma Knigge assisted him, and in the following year Vicar Norman Widiger assisted in teaching in the school for a year. Harold Franzen was called as second teacher in 1944. When he resigned in 1946, Paul Lohr took his place. Also that year a school bus was purchased. Until then, the school had been using a car, a station wagon, and a bus loaned by members of the congregation. In 1947, additional land was purchased adjacent to the school with a new school building, consisting of 3 classrooms for 95 students in the 8 grades, a confirmation-library room, office, waiting room, four restrooms, and several utility rooms, built in 1948 for approximately $50,000 including furnishings. Members and friends of the congregation donated many hours of volunteer labor. Miss Frances Luke, who later became the wife of a Lutheran pastor in Washington, was employed in 1948, and the next year Miss Maxine Geisert was employed to take her place as third teacher. Miss Geisert became the wife of Richard Heitshusen Jr. who was called as the fourth teacher in 1950.

The year 1950 was a year of many changes for Zion as the urban sprawl was just beginning to spread into Orange County. When Pastor Eifert accepted a call to Laguna Beach, Pastor R. Elmer Gunther then served the congregation temporarily. During the vacancy, the sanctuary was remodeled, redecorated, and strengthened, as it had been found unsafe in case of an earthquake, all at a cost of over $22,000. After Rev. Edwin H. Pflug of Chicago accepted Zion's call, he was installed as pastor on August 13, 1950 in an afternoon service; in the morning service, the refurbished church was rededicated. When school opened that September, there was an enrollment of 109 students. In 1951, the congregation began conducting German services again each Sunday with German at 8:45 a.m. and English at 11:00 a.m.

By the time Zion celebrated its Golden Jubilee on April 12, 1953, it demonstrated its missionary zeal by organizing a parish planning council,

After many letters requesting Zion to discontinue German services, they vote at the end of January 1942 to terminate the German service.

Rev. Elmer W. Matthias was installed as Zion's pastor in December 1956. (Pacific Southwest District Archives)

made of representatives of all the societies within the congregation, who scheduled four open-air services yearly during the latter part of May and the first part of June in the Greek Amphitheater in the beautiful Anaheim City Park with a total attendance of 2,500 worshipers, conducted annual three week Vacation Bible School at the end of the regular school year, and did extensive house-to-house canvassing of Anaheim and surrounding territory to gain new members for church, school, and Sunday school. By the time of the jubilee celebration, a branch Sunday school was opened at the parochial school at 205 North East Street in Anaheim. For the summer months beginning in June, early services were conducted on a trial basis. In order to provide more room for the Sunday school and Bible classes at Emily and Chartres streets, the Christian Science Church was purchased giving Zion control of the south frontage of Chartres. At the time of the 50th anniversary, the congregation numbered 715 communicants with 1,021 souls.

With the program of the church and the Christian day school expanding so rapidly, new facilities were sorely needed. The decision was made to erect a parish hall at the church site with additional property purchased to make this possible, and at the same time two additional classrooms were erected at the school site. The parish hall, a 2-story structure with 24 Sunday school classrooms which could be opened to provide 4 large con-

ference rooms, meeting rooms, an office area, a lounge, a chapel seating up to 100, and an upstairs kitchenette and a fully equipped kitchen downstairs together with a combination auditorium-gymnasium seating 500 having a regulation basketball court with a full stage, and dressing rooms and showers under it. The building, designed by Architect O. J. Bruer and built by Leonard Bouas, cost an estimated $140,000. This fine facility and the two classrooms at the school site were dedicated in March 1956. There were 587 children enrolled in the entire Sunday school, which operated two branches in the eastern and western sections of Anaheim

When illness did not permit Pastor Pflug to shoulder full responsibilities of the church program at Zion, he requested to become assistant pastor and Rev. Elmer W. Matthias of Galena Park, Texas, was called and installed as pastor in December 1956. He was born at Riceville, Iowa, the son of Rev. and Mrs. A. W. Matthias, attending St. Peter's Lutheran School at Sac City, Iowa. Following his years at Concordia College, Milwaukee, Wisconsin, in the high school and college departments, he attended Concordia Theological Seminary at St. Louis, Missouri, graduating in 1945. After a year of graduate work at Concordia Seminary, he entered the ministry, accepting a call to Galena Park, Texas, in September 1946 where he organized Peace Lutheran Church in November of that year, serving 10 years. On November 12, 1947, he was united in holy matrimony with Miss Ruth Weinhold, the daughter of Rev. and Mrs. P. G. Weinhold, Whittemore, Iowa. Their union was blessed with two children, Bruce and Steve, at the time of his installation at Zion.

The '50s and the '60s were years of rapid growth, not only for the city of Anaheim and surrounding communities with the population reaching 55,000 in 1956 but also for Zion as the communicant membership reached 1,000. After a series of stokes and failing health, the Rev. Edwin Pflug relinquished all pastoral responsibilities in 1957, and the Lord called him home on January 24, 1960. The Rev. Herbert Kluck of Del Rio, Texas, joined the staff as assistant pastor in 1958. He had a fruitful ministry for almost eight years. These years were growing years for Zion because many Lutherans from the mid-west were moving into Orange County, at that time the fastest growing county in the nation. In the early '60s, church attendance at Zion averaged over 900 per Sunday and frequently hit the 1,000 mark. Also that year Mr. Milfred C. Schlieske of

Zion's chancel after the remodeling and redecorating of the church in 1950. (Pacific Southwest District Archives)

Colorado Springs, Colorado, was called as teacher and director of music, installed in August of 1958. In the growing and expanding school and congregation, he began a program of music education and training, initiating the Christmas candlelight concerts that became a tradition at Zion. He revitalized the school chorus, and after a few years organized a junior choir reaching a membership of over 60 high school students. Since he was an accomplished church organist, he was instrumental in encouraging Zion to purchase a new $20,000 Wicks organ, which was dedicated on May 19, 1963. After 43 years of faithful service to the Lord and His Church, Mr. Schlieske's retirement was recognized with a special service on November 3, 1974.

In June of 1961 with a great deal of foresight and vision, Zion purchased, for $19,000 per acre, an 8½-acre orange grove, the last sizeable piece of property in the area, on East Street, across the street from the school. With no immediate need for the development of the property, the growth of the community, the congregation, and the future expansion of the church indicated the immediate purchase of the property for future use. Ten years later the new church plant was dedicated on the site. After Pastor Kluck accepted a call to Arapahoe, Nebraska, in 1965, the Rev. Kenneth Behnken of Lubbock, Texas, accepted the call as associate pastor of Zion in 1966, beginning an eventful and meaningful 5-year pastorate where he began a youth program centered around Sunday evening meetings at which Christians from the evangelical community were invited to give their personal testimonies. He was born in Fort Worth, Texas, the son of Rev. and Mrs. Victor Behnken. He attended St. John's Academy and Junior College in Winfield, Kansas, followed by two years at Concordia Senior College in Fort Wayne, Indiana. After graduating from Concordia Seminary in St. Louis, he received a call to Our Savior in Lubbock, Texas, where he was also student pastor at Texas Tech University for two years. When he arrived at Zion, he was a bachelor; in 1969, he married Mildred Schulz, a member of Zion's school staff. In the early months of 1972, he accepted the call to St. Matthew Lutheran Church, Minneapolis, Minnesota. He returned to Southern California District as head of the Department of Mission Services where he served 21 years. He left there to take the call as director of the Center for U.S. Missions, a joint ministry of LCMS Board for Mission Services, North America Mission Executives (NAME), and Concordia University at Irvine, California.

Since this was also a period of planning for the new church, parish hall, and administrative unit, Mr. Robert Inslee of the architectural firm of Orr, Strange, Inslee, and Senefeld from Los Angeles was selected as architect. The Building Committee under the chairmanship of Mr. James Burnette worked carefully and faithfully "with the Lord of the Church blessing their efforts with one of the finest Lutheran church plants in function and beauty west of the Mississippi." This massive structure was dedicated on August 29, 1971, with 1,289 at the 10:00 a.m. service and 1,395 at the 4:00 p.m. service to hear Dr. Oswald Hoffmann, speaker of "The Lutheran Hour." The architectural approach was a blending of traditional and contemporary forms with the red tile roof and contemporary arch-forms in the windows suggesting the Spanish mission flavor of the area. The open bell tower with 25 bells topped by a cross and crown, the symbol of Zion, is almost Byzantine. The dominant feature of the chancel area of the church is the 24-foot high free-standing crusader's cross behind the altar. Behind the cross is the chancel screen concealing the pipes of the organ in its chamber. The free-standing altar has 12 metal figures representing the 12 apostles of the Lord. The lectern, baptismal font, and pulpit are made of the same material as the altar, a special blending of fiberglass and plastic in a deep blue.

The stained glass windows executed by Henry Lee Willet of Willet Stained Glass Studios of Philadelphia, Pennsylvania, are done in faceted glass of brilliant colors an inch in thickness with an epoxy mixture poured around the glass to hold it in place. The windows are in three sets: (1) the nave, aisle, and narthex windows, (2) the transept windows, (3) the chancel windows, depicting Old and New Testament symbols of the church. In the north transept window is the Zion window depicting the church above and the church on earth; a unique feature shows the Sleeping Beauty Castle of Disneyland as the symbol to identify Anaheim as the place where the Christians who built the sanctuary live and work in the Kingdom. In the south transept window is a display of the Means of Grace with the Word of God and the Sacraments of Holy Baptism and Holy Communion symbolized in a unique manner.

On February 1, 1976, the Emma Wagner Early Childhood Education Center was dedicated. Zion's preschool and day-care, temporarily housed in the parish hall, was moved into the new fa-

Rev. Kenneth Behnken was installed as associate pastor of Zion in 1966 where he remained five years. (Pacific Southwest District Archives)

Zion dedicates its massive new church on the 8½-acre property on East Street on August 29, 1971.

cilities with the program becoming one of Zion's most successful enterprises. Since most of the children came from the community, with only a small percentage from the membership, the pre-school and day-care responded to the needs of working mothers in the community, doubling the size of the kindergarten program, becoming a firm base for the expansion of the Christian day school program. In the fall of 1977, Zion resolved to build a new Christian day school on the church site, selecting Mr. Ulysses Bauer as the architect who designed a 10-classroom building clustered around a library-learning center together with appropriate offices comprising 15,000 square feet. It was also resolved to have the congregation act as its own contractor and again erect this structure with volunteer labor with the building and the structure valued at $400,000. In 1991, a new fellowship hall/gymnasium was dedicated followed by a 9-room school addition that was completed and dedicated in 2003.

When Zion celebrated its 75th anniversary in 1978, the parish had 1,551 communicants with 2,059 baptized souls. One of the goals for the anniversary was the expansion of the organ from 14- to 50-ranks as part of Zion's 75th anniversary thank offering, which was spearheaded by Mr. William J. Heide, minister of music who came to Zion in September of 1974. He had expanded the music program by adding two bell choirs, as well as beginning the Zion Concert Series, bringing a variety of music experiences to the church throughout the year. Throughout Zion's history, the parish has always been bilingual with the pastors serving the German speaking population of

> When Zion celebrates its 75th anniversary in 1978, the parish has 1,551 communicants with 2,059 baptized souls.

Orange County. During the post-war years, there was a sizeable immigration of German-speaking people from Germany and central Europe with a large number of them settling in Orange County, which was growing and expanding rapidly; Zion was the only Lutheran church that had a ministry to the German-speaking people, meeting a clear need for that segment of the population.

Zion celebrated its 75th anniversary from April 1978 through March 1979 having guest speakers Dr. J. A. Preus, president of The Lutheran Church — Missouri Synod, and Dr. Guido Merkins, vice president of the LCMS. In May of 1978, Rev. Thomas Klinkenberg accepted the call to serve as Zion's associate pastor. He was born and raised in Wisconsin, later attending Valparaiso University in Indiana. Upon completion of two years of military service, he entered Concordia Seminary, Springfield, Illinois, graduating in 1964. He was commissioned as missionary-at-large where he formed parishes in Chandler and east Mesa, Arizona, being called as the first pastor of Eternal Life in Mesa. In 1970, he accepted a call to Iowa, returning to Arizona as pastor of Peace Church in Flagstaff in 1972. He married Kay Schrieberg with their marriage blessed with three children at the time. After graduating from Concordia Teachers College, River Forest, Illinois, she taught school in New York and Illinois and held a master's degree in guidance and counseling. She also was author of numerous devotional materials and a second-grade Sunday school course entitled "I'm a Disciple Too."

Also in 1978, Rev. Dr. Elmer Mathias, Zion's senior pastor, accepted the call to be associate profes-

Zion's beautiful, new, massive sanctuary was dedicated on August 29, 1971.

The chancel area of the new church with the twenty-four-foot free-standing crusader's cross behind the altar. (Pacific Southwest District Archives)

sor of practical theology at Concordia Seminary in St. Louis, giving his farewell sermon on July 23. In 1979, Pastor Klinkenberg became the senior pastor at Zion. In January of 1981, the Laubach Literacy classes were started to assist the Hispanic and Vietnamese populations' acquisition of English. Zion celebrated its 80th anniversary in October of 1983 with a Lutheran heritage renewal evening series of events that included a "Lutherfest" featuring a German potluck dinner followed by a history of Martin Luther. On October 30, a special commemoration of Martin Luther's birth was held in the sanctuary with special organ music provided by Michael Burkhardt who later became the music director accepting the full-time minister of music position in 1987 serving until 1991. During his tenure at Zion, he became well known as a leading concert organist and composer in the United States. Early in 1985, Pastor Klinkenberg was stricken with cancer, being called to his eternal rest on June 18, 1985, having served Zion for only 6 years. In 1989, Rev. Thomas Meyer accepted the call and was installed as Zion's senior pastor on November 1. He remained until February 11, 2001, when he left for a pastorate at St. Mark's in Kentwood, Michigan. By the end of November, the loan of over a half-million dollars for the sanctuary, parish hall and church offices taken out in 1971, was paid-off making Zion's property debt free.

In 1990, Zion hosted a Korean congregation, which had been worshiping at St. Luke's in Westminster. In June of that year, Zion's school celebrated its 50th anniversary with a special service at 10:45 attended by 701 worshipers followed by 365 attending a luncheon where the former principal, Mr. Walter Knigge, was honored for 50 years in the teaching ministry. The following year, 1991, the elementary school grew from 235 to 285 students with a total enrollment in the preschool and day school reaching over 400. On September 8, the new gym/fellowship hall was dedicated. The year ended with Zion having grown to 1,602 souls and 1,217 communicant members. Through the years, Zion had become an area church, as opposed to a neighborhood church since 48 percent of the membership lived within 3 to 8 miles of the church, and an additional 8 percent lived 9 or more miles from the church in 1978. Today that number has changed, as very few members live near the church.

Seeing a shift in demographics surrounding the church facilities over the last 2 decades with the Hispanic population growing from 17 percent to 31 percent, Zion tried to reach this new population, who had migrated to Anaheim. In a report to the District Board of Directors in January of 1992, it was stated that Zion had a lay-led Hispanic ministry reaching out to 70 or more Hispanics through home Bible study groups and other ministries. A Christ College student, Ernilda Milla whose home was in Peru, was working with the group using Hispanic pastors to help with worship services on special days having up to 90 people present at these services. Ernilda graduated from Christ College in May, but her desire was to find a job in Orange County and continue to help, part-time, with the ministry she had started. Because of the great need for Hispanic ministry throughout the western section of Orange County, Zion took the challenge to their circuit to see if any other congregations would be interested in helping them reach the Hispanic population. One congregation, Christ, Brea, expressed an interest and willingness to commit funds to this ministry with the understanding that they could also begin work in La Habra, a community near to the community served by Christ Lutheran Church. Zion was working with Christ, Brea to develop a proposal to call a pastor or a Hispanic lay minister to serve this group and start a new group in the Brea area.

The strategy for implementing work with the Hispanic communities around Zion and in La Habra was to call a full-time Hispanic worker who understood the meta-church model and was willing to work with it in these two communities. The mission developer was to begin by organizing small groups in both key areas with the goal of having 15 small groups by the end of the second year, training leaders in each of the groups. These leaders would also be responsible to train leaders who could then begin, develop, and lead new groups. When the groups were ready to begin worship services, Zion, Anaheim, would share its facilities for worship. The mission developer would also search for a congregation with which facilities could be shared or look for rented facilities where the group could meet for worship in the La Habra area. He would initiate his work at Zion working with the groups of people gathered by Ernilda. The goal was to develop a total of 50 small groups within 5 years in Anaheim and La Habra. The ultimate goal was to merge the Anaheim Hispanic congregation with Zion, with the La Habra groups either merging with an existing LCMS congregation or developing an individual

Rev. Thomas Klinkenberg became pastor in 1978, serving until his death in 1985.

Rev. Thomas Meyer was installed as Zion's senior pastor on November 1, 1989, remaining until February 11, 2001. (Pacific Southwest District Archives)

Zion and Christ Lutheran Church in Brea develop a proposal to call a Hispanic pastor to work in the area.

congregation. By the year 2000, there would be 50 new Hispanic worshiping groups in Anaheim and La Habra. A big goal!

In 1993, Zion and Christ formed a joint mission society to help organize and fund a Hispanic ministry in both of the areas. They interviewed candidates for the pastoral position. In the fall of 1994, at the suggestion of the Joint Hispanic Ministry Committee of Zion and Christ, the Hispanic group at Zion chose a name to identify itself, "Iglesia Luterana El Buen Pastor," or Good Shepherd Lutheran Church. On Sunday, October 16, El Buen Pastor had a picnic and service in a park with about 35 people attending. Pastor Mark McKenzie was serving the group part-time with Saturday night Bible studies twice a month with families from Buen Pastor. He and Pastor Johnny Lopez at Cristo Rey conducted First Communion/Catechism classes of three children from Anaheim and three children from Cristo Rey in December. At Buen Pastor, Pastor McKenzie conducted successful Las Posadas on 5 different nights, December 16, 17, 18, 20, and 22, attended by the members with each night having some new people from the community join the group with an attendance ranging from 25 to 35 people. The major Christmas celebration was on Friday, December 23, with a 6:30 p.m. service attended by 35. After the service, there was a short drama in which Pastor and his wife participated followed by a meal. On Christmas Day, a regular service was conducted at 10:00 a.m. with 25 people in attendance. After the service, everyone participated in breaking two piñatas. A new family, which was contacted through the Posada on December 22, attended both Christmas services. Ernilda, through the Social Ministry Committee at Zion, was able to provide toys and a box of food for each family. During May and June of 1994, Pastor McKenzie began conducting a Spanish service at Zion.

During May of 1995, Pastor McKenzie started canvassing an apartment complex near Christ in Brea where, at 12 apartments, people were willing to answer his questionnaire. Out of those 12 apartments, 4 families had Bible studies in their homes. At Christ, Brea, on Tuesday mornings from 9:00 to 10:00 a.m., the food pantry was opened where

Iglesia Luterana El Buen Pastor is formed in 1994.

Iglesia Luterana Sión is formed in 1997.

Rev. Cesar Sifuentes was installed on January 21, 2001, as assistant pastor and as director of the Joint Hispanic Association, a joint mission effort of Zion and Christ, Brea. (Pacific Southwest District Archives)

Pastor assisted. Before he started making contacts in the neighborhood, practically no one was coming for help at the food pantry. Since canvassing the apartment complex, many of the same people who had been attending the Bible studies received help at the food bank. On June 18, he preached his last Sunday sermon at Buen Pastor (Zion) as he had been reassigned to San Bernardino, thus completing his ministry in the Anaheim-Brea area. That Easter there were four services in English, one in Spanish, and one in Korean with Zion becoming a truly bilingual church.

In the summer of 1997, John Pavasars, a 25-year-old who was born of Lutheran Missionary parents and raised in Colombia, South America, had come to California and married Michelle Sloan, the director of youth and education at Christ, Brea. He was asked to work in the Hispanic ministries at Christ by Rev. Richard Dannenbring and at Zion by Rev. Tom Meyer where he was extremely well received with the work finally growing after a four-year delay. He served as a lay minister for a number of years at Zion and Christ where the ministry was called Iglesia Luterana Sión. In 1998, he was commissioned as a deacon in The Lutheran Church — Missouri Synod. On Saturday, March 16, 1997, in Zion's sanctuary, Feidi Benites, celebrated her Quinceñera, a service recognizing God's protection for a girl in the past and asked His continued protection in the future, a first in Zion's history but not the last. In July of 2000, Deacon Pavasars resigned as leader of the Joint Hispanic Ministry to prepare for another calling in the ministry.

In 2000, the Rev. Cesar Sifuentes, who with his wife, Elly, were an evangelistic team in the Michigan District working out of Redeemer Lutheran Church of Saginaw, Michigan, was called to be full-time pastor to do Hispanic work at Zion and Christ. The need for someone to develop this ministry from the small band of people who were gathered was great with a potential of making it an active, growing, worshiping community. He would be accountable to the Joint Hispanic Ministry Association Board, working with the pastors at Christ and Zion to plan and develop this ministry where there were 20 worshipers with a Sunday school of 15 with 2 teachers. He was installed on January 21, 2001, as assistant pastor and as Director of the Joint Hispanic Ministry Association, a joint mission effort of Zion and Christ, Brea. He began the Spanish worship service and Bible study at Zion on February 11 at 12:30 p.m. and Bible study at Christ in Brea. On November 5, Zion started a new type of class for the community, an ESL class, English as a Second Language, spearheaded by the Ethnic Ministries Committee, and led by Manuel Andrade with 50 people in attendance. Since the class was so large, it had to be moved from the portable building to the large Zion Room.

On February 17, 2002, Rev. Mark Rossington was installed as senior pastor, having served as associate pastor of Zion since 1997. (Pacific Southwest District Archives)

On February 17, 2002, Rev. Mark Rossington, associate pastor of Zion, was installed as senior pastor with Rev. Ralph Juengel officiating and Rev. Richard Dannenbring delivering the sermon. Pastor Rossington was born in Newport, Arkansas, on May 20, 1962. After he received a degree from Christ College, Irvine, in 1985, he attended Concordia Seminary at Fort Wayne, graduating in 1993. That summer he was ordained at Shepherd of Peace in Irvine and installed as pastor of Our Savior in Granbury, Texas. On May 18, 1996, he married Alison D. Fellows with their marriage blessed with one child. In April of 1997, he came to Zion in Anaheim as the new associate pastor.

By 2002, Zion's Spanish worship services had an average of 34 people with 22 children in Sunday school. Pastor Sifuentes and his wife went out once a week knocking on doors inviting people to church and leaving cards and other information about services and church activities. Bible classes in the homes were held, along with a Hispanic Ladies Society, which also met in homes once a month. Following the service, a reception was held once or more a month. He also talked with the people who came to the food distribution centers at Zion and at Christ.

To aid Pastor Sifuentes in reaching out to the Hispanic community, his wife, Elly Sifuentes was working on completing deaconess training at Concordia Seminary, St. Louis, Missouri. Pastor and Elly Sifuentes continued to counsel people on family matters such as domestic violence, alcoholism, and drugs, and with spiritual problems. Also, one or two congregation members regularly rode along with Pastor Sifuentes as he made calls in the neighborhood. By 2003, 14 children participated as acolytes after receiving their First Communion; the children also participated in special music during the worship service. One of difficulties in ministering to the Hispanics was in trying to correct the Lenten misunderstandings of the people who came from a Catholic background. Many still thought that by denying themselves something, they could make up for their sins. Pastor continued to explain that they were saved by what Christ did for them not by what they had to do. These old habits and beliefs "die hard." By mid-2003, 2 children were baptized, 4 children and 2 adults were confirmed with Sunday worship averaging 33 per Sunday.

To celebrate Zion's centennial year in 2003, special events were planned each month commemorating the decades of Zion's history beginning with 1895 through 1999 with former pastors, who were either pastors of Zion or were members who had entered the ministry, preaching in the services. Each month, the congregation received an installment describing the decade so that by the end of the year, they had a complete history of not only what occurred at Zion in its 100 years but also what transpired in the United Sates and Anaheim during the same time period. Art Gray, who wrote most of the chapters of the book, headed

Pastor and Elly Sifuentes with a group of children who had celebrated their First Communion. (Pacific Southwest District Archives)

the Book Committee. This festive celebration was a unique affair as people dressed in costumes of the era and had cars and other items on display from each of the decades.

Also, another Orange County congregation, Christ Lutheran Church in Costa Mesa, which was established in 1953, saw a need in its community to work among the growing Spanish-speaking population by beginning outreach to the community in June of 2002, with Bible studies in the homes of believers. This came about through an effort of the congregation to explore the possibility of establishing a Hispanic ministry as the neighborhood surrounding the church had changed to a Hispanic community. Jorge Almaraz, an elder of the church, was one of the people participating in these early outreach meetings. He became a member at Christ through his children, who were attending the Christian day school. Since he was a Catholic, he decided he had better learn what his children were being taught in the day school, so he started attending adult information class led by Pastor Tornow. Through his children attending the school, he became a member of Christ.

During the organizational meetings for a Spanish outreach, it was decided to reach the neighborhood through Spanish Bible study classes to be conducted in the homes of church members who lived in the area. It was also decided to hold classes on Wednesday evenings in a member's home, as it was easy for people to attend. Some of the members who lived in the neighborhood asked Jorge if he would lead the Bible study group. The decision was made to use the Christ Care Program that Pastor Strubbe had used with the English-speaking congregation. Since this Bible study centered on the book of John in English only, Jorge decided to translate the lessons into Spanish. When the Bible class first met in June of 2002, 10 people attended where the ages ranged from 13 through 85 with the group continuing to meet at this writing.

The objective of the class was to get people reading the Bible. Jorge Almaraz stated, "Be gentle and do not destroy their Spanish heritage." Through this Bible class a number of people started attending Christ Lutheran Church. The hope was to build this group into a Spanish-speaking worshiping community, which would take time.

Trinity Lutheran Church
Messiah Lutheran Church
Iglesia Santa Maria
San Diego, California

 an Diego is the 7th largest city in the country and the second largest in California having 1,223,400 residents of which 25.40 percent is Hispanic. Even with this large population, San Diego has maintained a comfortable, small town atmosphere. Before the first white men arrived in San Diego, the Diegueño Indians dwelt in the area. Juan Rodríguez Cabrillo, a Portuguese explorer in the service of Spain, was probably the first European to see the area, sailing into San Diego Bay in 1542. The first white settlers didn't arrive until 1769, when Spanish soldiers built a presidio in what is now the Old Town area of San Diego. California's first mission, San Diego de Alacalá, was established in the presidio that year by Father Junípero Serra, who had journeyed from Spain to settle the area in order to Christianize the local Indians, founding the first of California's 21 missions in San Diego. During

the early 1800s, trading cattle hides became an important activity in San Diego's beautiful port, helping to make the settlement the center of the Pacific Coast hide trade.

After Mexico achieved independence from Spain in 1821, San Diego became part of Mexico as well as the rest of present-day California. An *alcalde* or mayor was the head of the local government governing a very sparse population at the time. The mission and surrounding ranches dominated the San Diego landscape with San Diego organized as a town in 1834. The next big event in San Diego's history was the Mexican-American War with the 1846 Battle of San Pasqual, the major battle in California, fought in the Lake Hodges-San Pasqual area. Following the United States' victory in the War, the Treaty of Guadalupe Hidalgo was signed in 1848, ceding the areas of California, Arizona, New Mexico, and Texas to the United States.

With the discovery of gold in northern California in 1848, the population of California increased rapidly, making it possible to qualify the territory for statehood. California was admitted to the Union in 1850 with San Diego incorporated as a city on March 27, 1850. In the same year, the first mayor, Joshua Bean, brother of the famous Judge Roy Bean, known as "The Law West of the Pecos," was elected. Within 10 years, 1860, San Diego had a population of 731.

In 1867, Alonzo E. Horton, a businessman, bought the land in what is now downtown San Diego, laying out an area called New Town near the city's wharf, which soon became the new center of San Diego. The California Southern Railroad, the first railroad in the city, reached San Diego in 1885; its arrival created a land boom with business expanding rapidly. By 1887, San Diego's population had jumped to 40,000, but when the boom ended suddenly by 1890, the population of San Diego had decreased to about 16,000.

In 1890, the Rev. Jacob Kogler, pastor of St. John's in Orange and one of the pioneer missionaries of Southern California, received a request by the Mission Board to make a trip to San Diego to "seek and visit" German speaking Lutherans bringing them God's Word in regular worship services. In a short time, he had gathered quite a number of souls who eagerly awaited his every visit. He placed the following notice in the *San Diego Union* church page on September 14, 1890:

> German Lutheran service will be held at the Holt House, 15th and H Street. Sunday school 9:00. Church 10:00 a.m. H. J. Hack (pastor) 1138 13th St. Preaching by R. Gertel of St. Louis

The Holt House at 15th and H Street, where the first German Lutheran services were conducted. (Pacific Southwest District

Rev. Hack also served St. John's Lutheran Church in Otay Mesa, a small city south of San Diego on the Mexican border; the mission paid his rail fare from San Diego to Otay Mesa. The records are sketchy as to services conducted and who served these San Diego Lutherans from 1890 to 1896, but in 1895 in the *German Synodical Report of California District,* two items appeared as to the mission work in San Diego. First, "mission work should begin in San Diego, and the brethren were instructed to serve there until further steps become necessary." Second, G. F. W. Kiesel was "newly accepted" into the Missouri Synod, having formerly been with the General Synod. The following year on March 29, 1896, Missionary Kiesel who was also a pastor of a church in Monrovia, gathered 14 men and 14 women in the Seventh-day Adventist Church on 18th and G streets for a worship service. By November, the Board of Commissions transferred Pastor Kiesel to the San Diego church where services were held on a regular basis. On January 3, 1897, a church organizational meeting was held adopting the name, "Trinity First German Evangelical Lutheran Congregation of the Unaltered Augsburg Confession of San Diego." When Pastor Runkel of Los Angeles visited San Diego, he was so pleased by the work of the missionary that he was convinced that San Diego was a "hopeful field." When he preached at the service in March, there were 70 people present.

On June 19, 1901, Trinity was accepted into membership of The Lutheran Church — Missouri Synod, having 20 voters, 108 souls, and a Sunday school of 46 pupils. The pastor also conducted services once a month in German and English for 7 families at the preaching station in Otay Mesa, 20 miles from San Diego. On July 17, Der Deutche Evangelische Lutherische Trinitatis Frauen Verenin, the Ladies Aid, was officially formed with the goal of "strengthening of Christian fellowship and to be active in any way possible." On September 6, 1902, the congregation purchased its first church building at the corner of Wollman Avenue (now Oceanview Boulevard) for $900 from a disbanded Presbyterian congregation; seven members and friends held title until it could be transferred to the parish. The dedication of the church was held on September 15, with Rev. Jacob Kogler preaching the dedicatory sermon. In 1903, the preaching station in Olivenhain, a community between Rancho Santa Fe and Encinitas, was added to Pastor Kiesel's preaching schedule along with Trinity and Otay Mesa. In September of 1904, when the congre-

Seventh-day Adventist Church on 18th and G streets where Trinity worshiped from 1896 to 1902. (Pacific Southwest District Archives)

Rev. Fred Leimbrock, Trinity's second called pastor, who served from 1906 through 1914. (Pacific Southwest District Archives)

Rev. Paul Scherf became Trinity's third pastor in 1914, serving the parish until 1921. (Pacific Southwest District Archives)

Rev. K. Knippenberg became Trinity's fourth pastor on May 1, 1921, and served until he resigned in July of 1933. (Pacific Southwest District Archives)

gation was incorporated, the property was transferred to Trinity. Pastor G. W. Kiesel resigned on March 26, 1906, and Pastor Fred Leimbrock, a new seminary graduate, accepted the call and arrived in September as Trinity's second called pastor.

Since the congregation continued to grow and wanted to have a day school, the building was renovated and enlarged at a cost of $1,911 with the church now 31' × 43' and with the schoolroom of 31' × 22'. The lot adjoining the church was purchased for $800 for a parsonage that was built at a cost of $1,851. Between 1908 and 1911, the congregation grew to 160 souls with Pastor Leimbrock not only teaching the German-English school but also serving Otay Mesa and the preaching station in Escondido. To help Pastor Leimbrock, a St. Louis Seminary student, Lawrence Acker, was hired in 1912 to assist with teaching in the day school, and preaching at Trinity and the preaching stations at Otay Mesa and Escondido. The pastors would travel either by train or by horse and buggy to reach the preaching stations. Vicar Acker used "his ingenuity and commuted over the rough roads with a motorcycle," before he returned to the seminary in 1914. Due to the language problem at Trinity where there were German services only, some of the members left in 1912 to form an English-speaking sister congregation, Grace, with Pastor Clarence Damschroeder.

In 1914, the pastor was relieved of his school teaching duties when William Wall, a Seward, Nebraska, graduate, arrived to serve as Trinity's first day-school teacher under the new school motto, "Whoever has the youth, has the future." In November, Pastor Leimbrock accepted a call to Denver, Colorado, with Rev. J. Meyer of Orange serving as vacancy pastor. In April of 1915, Rev. Paul Scherf of Covina, California, became Trinity's third pastor. San Diego also became a naval cen-

ter during World War I (1914–1918) with the North Island Naval Air Station in San Diego Bay established in 1917. In 1915, San Diego played host to the Panama-California Exposition, an international fair with the exposition bringing worldwide attention to the city making Balboa Park a popular tourist attraction. During 1916–1920, the congregation, which had peaked at 500, had dropped to 120 with a Sunday school enrollment of 37 children. In 1917 when Mr. Wall was released from his contract in the spring semester, accepting a call to Berkeley, the day school closed. By 1920, the city had grown to almost 75,000 persons, and in December of that year, Pastor Scherf accepted a call to Alsace, France.

On May 1, 1921, Rev. K. Knippenberg, formerly of Germany, was called from London, England, to be Trinity's fourth pastor with the cost of moving him from London to San Diego being a grand total of $200. The congregation decided to conduct two services, one in English and the other in German in 1922. The Ladies Aid had collected $1,000 for the purchase of "a new church" by 1925, as the old building was too small. Trinity's 30th anniversary was celebrated on October 23, 1927, with a German service in the morning and an English service in the afternoon where Rev. Otto W. Wismar, pastor of Grace (the first English-speaking congregation in Los Angeles), was the preacher. By 1932, Trinity had 110 members with 16 voting members and the pastor still serving the two mission stations at Otay Mesa and Olivenhain. After Pastor Knippenberg resigned in July of 1933, District President Rev. G. Smukal, installed Rev. William A. Theiss of Santa Barbara as Trinity's fifth pastor on December 3 with Rev. Damschroeder, who served as the vacancy pastor at Trinity while still serving his own church, officiating at the service. Pastor Theiss faithfully served the congregation until his

Trinity's first church building on Ocean View and Dewey Street that was used from 1902 through 1941. (Pacific Southwest District Archives)

The interior of the new church at Christmas time. (Pacific Southwest District Archives)

untimely death on January 26, 1940. Rev. Paul Hilgendorf Sr. of Hood River, Oregon, was called and installed by Rev. G. Smukal, the Southern California District president, on June 23, 1940.

The dream of having a larger church building finally became a reality in 1941 when Trinity purchased Our Savior's Lutheran Church on Twentieth and F streets from the Norwegian congregation. They also purchased for $100, the beautiful 1725 white altar with a painting of Christ praying in Gethsemane in the middle of the reredos, brought from Norway. At the time, the name of the congregation was changed from "Trinity First German Evangelical Lutheran Congregation of the Unaltered Augsburg Confession of San Diego, California" to "Trinity Evangelical Lutheran Congregation of the UAC of San Diego, California." On the occasion of the dedication of the new church property at Twentieth and F streets on October 5, District President Rev. G. Smukal and Rev. A. Amstein were speakers at the 10:30 a.m. service and Rev. Louis Jagels of Grace, Escondido, was the speaker at the 3:00 p.m. service. After the Japanese attacked Pearl Harbor on December 7, 1941, bringing the United States into World War II, Trinity's last German service was conducted on December 21, 1941.

During World War II (1939–1945), San Diego's airplane plants attracted thousands of workers from throughout the United States. In addition, the armed services built new military bases in the city. By 1943 with San Diego's population continuing to grow, Trinity's communicant membership grew to 200. Also, all the debts on the church building and the parsonage were liquidated. After the war, thousands of members of the armed forces who received military training at the bases in San Diego settled in the San Diego area. By 1946, Trinity's membership had climbed to 300 with the

congregation purchasing two lots at the corner of Twenty-first and F streets for a Christian day school, but sold them in November of 1949. Seeing a need to be of service to the men in the armed forces, the congregation opened a service center in 1949. That same year they purchased a pipe organ from Spencer Organ of Pasadena and dedicated it on September 19.

By 1950, the population of San Diego had soared to 334,387, with more Lutherans to moving to the area, desiring Lutheran churches to be established in their neighborhoods. There was Bethany, which was started in 1937, St. Paul's in 1943, and Messiah in 1950. Also in 1950, Trinity's baptized membership had grown to 565 with 345 communicant members. Paul Hilgendorf Jr. graduated from the seminary at that time and was ordained in Los Angeles. Ten years later, he became the seventh pastor of Trinity. In 1958, the congregation was forced to sell its property on Twentieth and F streets due to the construction of the new 94 Freeway. They purchased a 5½-acre piece of property for $25,000 to build their new A-frame church, incorporating the old white Norwegian altar in the chancel.

In 1945, seeing a need to work among the black population of the city, a canvass was conducted in the Logan Heights area of San Diego. After several years of consultation with the District Mission Board, the Synodical Conference Mission Board, and in cooperation with the pastors of San Diego County, efforts were made to establish a mission among the black people of San Diego with the vicinity blessed with success when the Synodical Conference Mission Board, in the spring of 1948, agreed to open and support the field, under the supervision of the Southern California District Mission Board. After that time, the District Mission Board decided to completely assume the field

Rev. William A. Theiss was installed as Trinity's fifth pastor on December 3, 1933, serving until his untimely death in 1940. (Pacific Southwest District Archives)

Rev. Paul Hilgendorf Sr. became Trinity's sixth pastor on June 23, 1940. (Pacific Southwest District Archives)

Rev. Paul Hilgendorf Jr. became Trinity's pastor in 1960. (Pacific Southwest District Archives)

Trinity's church and parsonage on 20th and F streets purchased in 1941 from Our Savior's Lutheran Church. (Pacific Southwest District Archives)

The interior of Trinity's new church showing the beautiful 1725 white altar that came from Norway. (Pacific Southwest District Archives)

as a mission of the District, beginning on July 1, 1949. The Rev. Kurt Brink entered the field in the last week of August 1948. He had graduated from Concordia Lutheran Theological Seminary in Springfield, Illinois, in 1941, spent his vicar year at Christ Lutheran Church, Peoria, Illinois, and served there most of the year following his graduation as a candidate for the ministry. He served several years under the Mission Board of the Southern California District, first at Christ Lutheran Church, Redlands, from 1942 to 1948. He and Mrs. Brink had four children, Lois, David, Ruth Ann, and Paul, who became a pastor.

Pastor Kurt Brink began missionary work in the Southeast San Diego area in 1948, where he founded Messiah Lutheran Church. With no Lutheran nucleus — only the names of two possible prospects — a Sunday school was opened on Reformation Day, 1948, in the Community Center at 2936 Imperial Avenue in the heart of the Logan Heights' black neighborhood with an attendance of six. In 1949, the enrollment was above 80 with an average attendance of 65. Members of the local churches, most of them from Grace, served as helpers in the Sunday school. The first Sunday service was held Easter morning with 75 in attendance, mostly children. Pastor Brink reported, "We believe that this field offers fine possibilities for the future because there is so little Bible preaching being done in the existing colored churches, and the church practice in many cases is deplorable."

In the fall of 1948, the District Mission Board purchased a lot, 100' × 140', on Thirty-first Street

and Clay Avenue at a cost of $3,400, with the board making application for a $15,000 loan from the general Church Extension Board for the erection of a chapel. On January 4, 1949, the missionary and his family moved into a rented house in the heart of the Negro population. He conducted church services in his home, 235 South Thirty-second Street at 6:30 p.m. every Sunday in order to pave the way for regular church attendance when services were inaugurated at the Community Center. A Lutheran woman, a native of Mobile, Alabama, came from Coronado twice each Sunday in order to attend Sunday school and church, being very grateful for the opening of a mission in San Diego. Pastor wrote in a District report, "This has done much to put our work in a favorable light among our neighbors, and we are very happy in our home and in our work." At the time, the unorganized mission numbered three communicants and six baptized members. Sunday offerings averaged about $12, sufficient to cover the rent of the hall, Sunday school expenses, and many miscellaneous items. Pastor Brink addressed the Orange County Zone Rally of the Lutheran Women's Missionary

Pastor Brink establishes Messiah Lutheran Church in 1948 for the black population of Southeast San Diego.

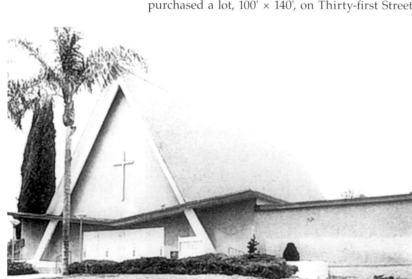

Trinity's new A-frame church built in 1959, located at 7210 Lisbon Street, San Diego. (Pacific Southwest District Archives)

The chancel of the new church with the white ornate Norwegian altar and pipe organ. (Pacific Southwest District Archives)

League at Zion Lutheran Church in Anaheim, as the mission was one of the projects supported by the organization.

On November 6, 1949, ground was broken for the new 2,500-square-foot chapel in Logan Heights designed by Architect O. J. Bruer. When the plans were put out to bid, the bids ranged from $21,000 to $23,000 with the District having only $15,000 to build the chapel. At this point, the stymied members of the Mission Board and the Church Extension Department gave an ear to the insistent pleas of the missionary to build the chapel with the assistance of volunteer workers from all congregations in San Diego County. After sending out letters for assistance, approximately 100 laymen returned their cards donating 3,500 man-hours of labor, with Lutheran businessmen supplying materials at wholesale and also giving valuable supervision. The Lutheran ladies' groups from various parishes served hot meals every Saturday at noon, and hot coffee on the regular Monday and Thursday evening work nights. Through this, there had been a cash saving of between $8,000 and $10,000, a closer bond of fellowship among dozens of San Diego County Lutherans, increased missionary zeal by all who participated, a thrilling adventure

in Christian race relations, and a new and deeper faith in the hearts of pastors and people that "with God truly nothing is impossible."

With the devoted zeal of all the volunteers, the building was completed in four months, and was dedicated to the glory of God in two special services on March 12, 1950, with over 500 members, interested friends from the community, members of sister congregations in San Diego County, and visiting Lutherans from as far away as the Los Angeles and San Bernardino areas in attendance. Rev. Paul Lehman, pastor of St. Paul's, Los Angeles, was the guest speaker in the 4:00 afternoon service with total offerings for the new building amounting to nearly $400 on dedication day. The new building, which consisted of an auditorium seating 150, a mothers' room, a pastor's study, 2 Sunday school rooms, a kitchen, and restrooms, was completely furnished with beautiful chancel furniture, finished in ash, a 50th anniversary memorial gift of the Southern California District Walther League.

In 1950, a 3-bedroom parsonage was completed with the aid of a loan from the District Church Extension Fund and over 1,500 hours of donated labor by San Diego County Lutherans. By 1951, the

> Messiah Lutheran dedicates the new church on May 12, 1950 with 500 people present.

Christmas program with Pastor Kurt Brink at the extreme left and his wife third from the left. (Pacific Southwest District Archives)

mission had a baptized membership of 75, a communicant membership of 25 and an average attendance of 40 with Sunday school, which had one Lutheran child when established in October 1948, now having an average attendance of 60 children per Sunday. Pastor Brink was installed as pastor of the Logan Heights congregation on January 28, 1951, with 135 worshipers in attendance at a service conducted by Rev. Clarence Damschroeder, District vice president, with the sermon delivered by Rev. Paul Lehman of St. Paul's, Los Angeles, the Rite of Installation performed by Rev. L. H. Jagels, circuit visitor, and assisted by pastors Victor Herrmann and Arthur Brommer. The goal of the parish for the year was to double the communicant membership through a community-wide distribution of Gospel tracts by the members of the congregation. Through the generosity of Bethany, San Diego, the congregation became the recipient of a Mason-Hamlin motor-driven reed organ which was dedicated to the glory of God in a solemn service in church Sunday afternoon, December 7, at 3:30, with an organ recital.

With the Lord's blessing in the growth of the Sunday school, additional Sunday school rooms were required. Members of the congregation, aided by a few members of sister parishes, built the addition in just six weeks, under the supervision of Mr. Fred McCann, a member of Grace, San Diego, and a foreman for a large local construction firm who donated his services, a fact which helped to keep the cost of the addition to only $2,500, less than half of the contracted price. The new two-room Sunday school annex of the Logan Heights church was dedicated in two festival services on Sunday, November 7, 1954, with Rev. Victor Behn-

> In the summer of 1955, Pastor Brink resigns due to his wife's illness.

ken, vice president of the District, preaching in the afternoon service, and the music supplied by the 65-voice San Diego County Lutheran Oratorio Society. Rev. A. G. Webbeking, who represented the Mission Board and Church Extension Department, spoke words of encouragement. An appreciation dinner was given on November 21, 1954, to take note of the more than 500 hours of donated labor and the women of the congregation who faithfully supplied snacks on the work nights and dinners on Saturdays.

In the summer of 1955, Pastor Brink resigned due to his wife's illness. On September 11, he preached his farewell sermon, having served the congregation for seven years. He accepted the call to Concordia Lutheran Church in Barstow, where he served from 1955 to 1956, and then took a call to be pastor of Immanual Lutheran Church in Albuquerque, New Mexico. Pastor John K. Sorenson, who succeeded him, was born in San Francisco, graduating from Concordia College, Oakland, California, and from Concordia Seminary, St. Louis in 1956. On August 15, 1956, he was installed as the congregation's second pastor. He was chairman of the Southern California District Committee on Human Relations and a member of the Board of Directors of the San Diego County Association for Retarded Children. At the January 6, 1957, congregational meeting, the voters decided to change the name of the church from Logan Heights congregation to Messiah Lutheran Church in order to have a spiritualized designation for the congregation rather than a localized name. The parish had grown to 125 communicants with an average church attendance of 83 per Sunday and a Sunday school of 89. Pastor John Sorenson received a call in late 1959 to form a mission in the Lake Murray area of San Diego, which he accepted, and where he became pastor of Christ the King Lutheran Church. By 1960, Messiah's membership and the Sunday school had grown to 140 with 90 in attendance on Sunday mornings. Three additional lots, two with rentals, were purchased with the intent of expanding.

On August 21, 1960, Rev. Edgar Robinson was installed as the new pastor of Messiah. He was born in Mansura, Louisiana, on November 27, 1913. In 1928, he began his study for the Lutheran ministry as a student of Luther Preparatory Academy of New Orleans, followed by seven years including two years vicarage spent at Immanuel Lutheran College and Seminary in Greensboro, North Carolina. In 1946, he was honorably discharged

Messiah Lutheran Church at 31st Street and Clay Avenue was built by the volunteer labor of Lutherans in the San Diego area and was dedicated on March 12, 1950. (Pacific Southwest District Archives)

from the chaplaincy as a first lieutenant in the Army. Since 1946, he had served Good Shepherd Lutheran Church of Gary, Indiana, as pastor. In 1952, he was awarded a master's degree in education by Indiana University. His wife, Iago Robinson, previously served as a public health nurse for nine years holding an R. N. degree; their daughter, Jeanne, was in the seventh grade. By 1964, Messiah had grown to 338 baptized members, 174 communicants, and 120 Sunday school children. The giving of the congregation had been reduced by unemployment in the county, which made the church the first to feel the cut. Due to unemployment in the area, the anticipated large influx of new people into the community from which new membership was drawn didn't materialize.

Since the immediate area surrounding the parish was becoming more and more a commercial area, it was difficult to draw new members. Another situation in the community was an abundance of churches, 15 to 20 within a half-mile-radius, necessitating a greater emphasis on members making door-to-door calls in the immediate area of the church. By 1968, improved working conditions for the members had helped the congregation assume a greater share of budget responsibility with a minimum of subsidy assistance. There were 336 baptized souls, 184 communicant members with a Sunday school enrollment of 77. Pastor Robinson served for 10 years with dedication until an unusual illness forced him to resign. He resided at Friendship Manor in San Diego, a victim of a rare brain disease. After an extended effort to obtain a pastor, Rev. Wayne Bayer, a candidate from the seminary, accepted a call to serve Messiah and was installed July 13, 1969. Pastor Bayer brought youth and zeal, fresh innovative ideas, and served with vigor until he accepted a call to serve a parish in Kent, Washington. Following his acceptance of that call, an interim pastor, Rev. G. L. Hoemann, was assigned, who later accepted the call to become Messiah's full-time pastor.

Pastor Hoemann's ministry at Messiah witnessed an outstanding milestone in the history of the parish. After more than 20 years of struggling, scrimping, saving, and sacrificing, the property of Messiah finally became debt-free in 1972. In 1973, Messiah celebrated its 25th anniversary with the founding pastor, Rev. Kurt Brink, returning to preach at this joyous celebration. After Pastor Hoemann's acceptance of a call to Blythe, several visiting pastors served intermittently until Pastor Erwin L. Lueker Jr., accepted the assignment

to conduct a 6-month self-study, which began October 1974. On May 16, 1976, Pastor Lueker was commissioned by the Southern California District of the LCMS, to serve as Messiah's missionary-at-large. By the time Messiah celebrated its 30th anniversary in 1978, the area surrounding the church was changing with more Hispanics moving into the vicinity. In 1983, Luisa Hernandez, teacher at Christ, La Mesa, began weekday Spanish language religion classes with 30 to 40 children in attendance. By 1984, the parish had declined to 97 communicant members with 129 baptized members. In 1986, Rev. George Gunter was ordained and installed as the pastor of Messiah. Participating in the service were the Rev. Richard Dickinson, synodical executive secretary of Black Ministry Commission, who was the preacher, the Rev. Steven Cluver, Circuit 21 counselor was the officiant, and the Rev. Gerhard (Gary) W. F. Harms, Messiah's vacancy pastor, liturgist.

In May of 1985, Rev. Mark McKenzie was called as missionary-at-large to do work in the Hispanic neighborhood surrounding Messiah. He was born on August 5, 1958, in Santa Monica, California, but was raised in Huntington Beach, California, where he attended junior high and high school taking Spanish classes with an interest in becoming a missionary. After graduating from Christ College, Irvine, in 1981, he attended Concordia Seminary in Fort Wayne, Indiana, graduating in 1985. He spent his year of vicarage at St. John's in Montebello and was ordained at his home congregation, Redeemer, Huntington Beach, in 1985, and was installed at Messiah, San Diego, as missionary-at-large also in 1985. On December 21, 1987, he married Elvira (Leticia) Rodriguez, whom he met through one of the members of the church as she spent weekends with them; their marriage was blessed with four children, Francisco, Jessica, Isaac, and Rebecca.

Since Iglesia Santa Maria was a side-by-side ministry with Messiah, the Church Council at its August 3, 1987, meeting, approved Pastor McKenzie's use of the parsonage for his Hispanic ministry as the parsonage had been rented. Since the black congregation was also using Messiah church plant, Pastor McKenzie starting Spanish worship service at noon and finally had a 6:30 p.m. service, as that time was better for the people. During the first year of his ministry, the name Iglesia Santa Maria was chosen. Since most of the Hispanics in the area were poor, working as housekeepers in hotels to earn a living, there was a great deal of

Rev. Mark McKenzie established a Hispanic church, Iglesia Santa Maria, a side-by-side ministry with Messiah. (Pacific Southwest District Archives)

Iglesia Santa Maria is established as a side-by-side ministry with Messiah in 1987.

transiency during his seven-year ministry there. At Easter, there would be a large celebration as a means of gathering people from the neighborhood. Every year around August 15, the mission celebrated St. Mary's Day where they would have a fair or carnival selling food and have some games. During the summer, funds were made available through the District for children to spend a couple days at Camp Caroline. At Christmas time, they celebrated Posadas going through the neighborhood singing carols.

In October of 1992, an additional 8:00 a.m. worship service was conducted with 10 people to accommodate those people who preferred not to be out after dark. In the 6:30 p.m. evening service, attendance was 26. Santa Maria had 3 communicant members with 76 baptized members with an average Sunday attendance of 27 and had a VBS enrollment of 25. A special challenge to this ministry was its location in a very poor neighborhood with a mobile population. One-on-one ministry was most effectively done by Pastor McKenzie. Since Santa Maria hadn't grown enough to support itself after seven years, and since the District financial situation was forcing it to re-evaluate all of its ministries, the difficult decision had to be made of whether to continue to fund ministries at the same amount as in the past. The pastors and congregations of the San Diego area, who were

supporting the ministry at Iglesia Santa Maria for six years with funds over and above their regular mission offerings, decided to redirect these funds to establish a new Hispanic ministry in Chula Vista under the direction of Rev. Esaúl Salomón. The redirection of these funds would cause a shortfall of the money the District had available to conduct the ministry at Iglesia Santa Maria. Pastor Mark McKenzie was relocated to serve in team ministry in the Orange County area with Pastor Lopez at Cristo Rey.

Pastor Salomón tried to follow-up with the people at the Santa Maria mission, but Chula Vista was about 10 miles away. With transportation always a big problem for the people of the mission, they tended not to go to church in Chula Vista. Ted Martin, who was a member at Pilgrim in Chula Vista and had been a missionary in Guatemala and Mexico, was also helping Pastor Salomón in Chula Vista at the time. With the demise of Santa Maria, a new Hispanic mission was established in Chula Vista. Since Messiah faced the same problem of a poor, changing neighborhood, the congregation voted to merge with Trinity in San Diego, signing merger papers on July 7, 1996, conducting their last service at Messiah on September 1, 1996, with their first combined service at Trinity on September 8, 1996.

Iglesia Santa Maria and Messiah both close in 1996.

Pilgrim Lutheran Church
Concordia Lutheran Church
Iglesia Luterana Concordia
Chula Vista, California

 The earliest inhabitants, who lived in the area known as Chula Vista, were the Yuman-speaking people who began moving into the area around 3000 B.C. Many of the Native American Indians who live in San Diego today are descendants of the Kumeyaay tribe who roamed the area for hundreds of years. In 1542, a fleet of 3 small ships sailed into San Diego Harbor commanded by Juan Rodríguez Cabrillo, who led the explorations for Spain, laying claim to the land. Chula Vista became part of a Spanish land grant known as Rancho del Rey or "The King's Ranch" in 1795. When Mexico formed its own government in 1831, Rancho del Rey be-

came known as Rancho del la Natión or National Ranch encompassing the area now known as National City, Chula Vista, Bonita, Sunnyside, and the Sweetwater Valley with the Mexicans using it as grazing land for their cattle and horses. In 1845, the land was granted to John Forster, the son-in-law of Pio Pico, the last Mexican governor of California. When the United States claimed California following the Mexican-American War in 1847, the land grants were allowed to continue as private property under American law even when California became a state in 1850.

John Forster continued to operate the ranch for 10 years until he sold it to a French developer with the land again sold to the Kimball brothers in 1868 for $30,000. The Kimball brothers, Frank, Warren and Levi, intended to develop the land into productive American-style cities and farms. Through Frank Kimball, the Santa Fe Railroad was brought to San Diego, with its first terminus in National City.

Several directors of the Santa Fe Railroad and Colonel W. G. Dickerson, a professional town planner, formed the San Diego Land and Town Company with the company developing the lands of the National Ranch for new settlers. Through their promotional material issued to attract settlers that read: "Upon the best part of this tract, 5,000 acres are being subdivided into 5-acre lots with avenues and streets 80 feet in width running each way, the steam motor road passing though the center. This tract, known as Chula Vista, lies but a mile from the thriving place of National City." The boom of the 1880s was begun with this announcement. These 5-acre lots sold for $300 per acre in 1887 with the purchaser required to build a home within 6 months on the land. By 1889, 10 houses were under construction and land sales were excellent, thus, creating the city of Chula Vista. A resident, James D. Schulyer, suggested the Spanish name Chula Vista, roughly translated as "beautiful view," which the San Diego Land and Town Company adopted.

Rev. Loren A. Rumsch, who served Pilgrim for over 40 years. (Pacific Southwest District Archives)

In 1888 with the Sweetwater Dam completed bringing water to Chula Vista residents and their farming lands, Frank Kimball, the new state commissioner of agriculture, discovered citrus trees to be the most successful crop for the area, eventually establishing Chula Vista as the largest lemon-growing center in the world for a period of time, with the local farmers continuing to grow lemons as their primary crop using over eight packing houses in the city. The National City and Otay Railroad was built to connect San Diego, National City, Chula Vista, and Otay; it flourished for many years. On October 17, 1911, the populace voted in favor of incorporating Chula Vista.

World War II ushered in changes that would affect the city of Chula Vista forever with the relocation of Rohr Aircraft Corporation to Chula Vista in early 1941, just months before the attack on Pearl Harbor. Rohr employed 9,000 workers in the area at the height of its wartime production.

With the high demand for housing, the land never returned to groves again. After the war, many factory workers and thousands of servicemen remained in the area, resulting in a gigantic growth in population. During those years, numerous schools, homes, banks, restaurants, gas stations, and shopping centers opened to accommodate the expanding number of residents. With the loss of the citrus groves and produce fields for homes, Chula Vista became one of the largest communities in San Diego. The population of Chula Vista tripled from 5,000 residents in 1940 to more than 16,000 in 1950. Its present population is 174,319, where 49.6 percent are Hispanic and 31.7 percent are Anglo.

In 1941 just before the outbreak of the Second World War, many Lutherans had arrived and settled in the Chula Vista area. The beginning of the first Lutheran Church — Missouri Synod came about in a unique manner, as it was through the Young People's Society of Grace Church in San Diego. At one of their meetings that year, there was a lively discussion on mission work in Southern California. Through much discussion on the topic, it was agreed that there should be more Lutheran churches and pastors in San Diego County to minister to the spiritual needs of the ever-growing Lutheran population in that vicinity. They were ready to leave it at that when a young man suddenly arose and challenged the group, "Well, let's do something about it!" With those words, the young people accepted the challenge, pledged their financial support, and voted to begin a Lutheran mission in Chula Vista to serve the people of the South Bay area. In August of 1941, Loren A. Rumsch, a recent graduate of Concordia Theological Seminary of St. Louis, Missouri, who had completed his studies at the University of Minnesota, was requested to conduct a religious canvass of the South Bay area with Grace establishing a mission board consisting of Mr. Oswald Boltz, Mr. Elmer Kogler, Pastor Damschroeder, and Pastor Rumsch, paying Pastor Rumsch $40 a month with Mr. and Mrs. J. C. Rumsey offering free board and room.

Rev. Rumsch was born in Butterfield, Minnesota, on October 2, 1914, the second child of William and Meta Rumsch. After attending Concordia College in St. Paul, Minnesota, and the University of Minnesota, he attended Concordia Semi-

Pilgrim Congregation
in Chula Vista begins
with the help of Grace,
San Diego in 1941.

nary in St. Louis where he graduated in June of 1941. In 1945, he married Mary Moore and during their marriage adopted two children, William and Mary Colleen. In 1979, the Lord called his beloved wife, Mary, home to be with Him. After serving Pilgrim over 40 years, he retired on December 31, 1981, marrying Janet Jolliff two days after his retirement.

Following the canvass, the first Lutheran service was conducted on Sunday, September 28, 1941, in the Chula Vista Women's Clubhouse at 357 G Street attended by approximately 50 people of whom the majority were visitors from the mother church, Grace Lutheran of San Diego. Eight children were in attendance at the Sunday school. From its inception, Pilgrim Church made slow but steady progress with days of encouragement and days of discouragement for the congregation and the pastor. Due to the transient population during the war years, the transfer of members to other parts of the country to a great degree nullified the gains made in church membership. Enthusiasm would run high when 15 children were present at Sunday school and 40 people were in attendance at the divine service. Since the pastor, who didn't own a car, had to make daily trips by bus to Chula Vista from his home in San Diego, the Grace Lutheran Mission Society purchased a 1932 Dodge in January of 1942 for the pastor's transportation.

On January 12, 1942, a meeting was held to discuss plans for the formation of a congregation with the election of temporary officers tak-

ing place, Mr. Carl Boltz Jr., chairman; Mr. E. A. Bonnoront, treasurer; and Mr. M. L. Roberts, secretary. In the February 4, 1942, meeting, the Grace Lutheran Mission Society decided to request the English District Mission Board for financial assistance, with the board granting a subsidy of $90 per month. During the ensuing months, this amount was steadily decreased with Pilgrim congregation receiving a subsidy of $765 in 1942 and $420 in 1943. In January of 1944, the congregation became self-supporting, having received only $1,185 from the English District Mission Board to start the church.

On March 2, 1942, the officers of the Chula Vista mission met with the members of the Grace Lutheran Mission Society, and each group decided to send a divine call to Vicar Loren A. Rumsch; one was for assistant pastor of Grace Lutheran Church, the other for pastor of the Chula Vista Lutheran mission. After prayerful and thoughtful deliberation, the pastor accepted the call to the Chula Vista mission and was ordained and installed by Pastor Damschroeder on May 17, 1942.

The first official meeting of the Chula Vista mission was held on May 27, 1942, where a constitution was formulated and adopted with the name Pilgrim Evangelical Lutheran Church chosen as the official name of the parish. The charter members of the congregation were Mrs. Bertha Armer, Mr. and Mrs. Carl Boltz Jr., Mr. and Mrs. E. A. Bonnoront, Mrs. Emma Dalton, Mrs. W. A. Praser, Mrs. Paula Hansen, Mrs. E. J. Hill, Mrs.

The large building of Pilgrim Lutheran Church, located at 497 "E" Street, would seat 500 people and was dedicated in 1956. (Pacific Southwest District Archives)

The beautiful interior of the church at the time of dedication. (Pacific Southwest District Archives)

E. Jewell, Mr. and Mrs. Robert Long, Mrs. Marie Popelar, Mr. and Mrs. M. L. Roberts. Several lots were purchased by the congregation on the corner of Fifth Avenue and E Street in September of 1944, with the hope that a church and parish hall would be erected in the near future. However, that didn't materialize due to wartime government restrictions; building plans were delayed until the fall of 1946. Finally, on September 28, 1947, exactly 6 years to the day that the first service of the Chula Vista mission was held, Pilgrim congregation held groundbreaking ceremonies for the new parish hall. The new parish hall, 58' × 72', was of reinforced concrete construction containing the pastor's study, a social room, a fully furnished kitchen, and Sunday school rooms. The architect was Mr. Earl Giherson with Mr. L. C. Anderson serving as the contractor. The completed building with furnishings cost approximately $47,000.

The Lord blessed the efforts of the members of Pilgrim and their pastor. Within the short history of 6-½ years, 130 children were baptized, 15 children confirmed, 57 adults baptized or confirmed with the pastor performing 57 marriages and officiating at 12 funerals. There were 462 baptized souls with 203 communicant members and a Sunday school enrollment of 185. In 1956, a magnificent, new church, seating 500, was built of reinforced concrete at an approximate cost of $140,000.

Following the war years, the Chula Vista area continued to grow with the spread of new tract homes increasing the population. The Mission Board of Southern California District purchased 10 acres of property for $20,660 at 267 E. Oxnard Street for a future church site in southeast Chula Vista. In 1962, construction was begun on the $69,384 chapel, designed to hold 175 worshipers comfortably with a choir loft for 20 people and an education wing, which now housed Concordia congregation. Architect, Mr. Dennis V. Wehmueller of Los Angeles, designed the building with Mr. Ted Schiermeyer of Hemet serving as the contractor. The building was planned in the shape of a cross with the south extension incorporating the church entrance, nave and chancel; the west arm was the choir loft and sacristy; the north extension was a large educational unit; and the east arm was for the office and kitchen with the additional land provided for future expansion. An asphalt parking lot provided room for about 50 cars with the landscaping done by the members. The Southern California District owned six acres of land that adjoined Concordia's property that was later sold.

Pastor Norman A. Schneider, a recent graduate from Concordia Seminary, St. Louis, was called by the Mission Board to serve as missionary-at-large in the area, arriving in August of 1962, to begin mission work in the southeast section of Chula Vista. He was also called by the Mission Board to serve the already existing Atonement mission at Spring Valley where he devoted most of his time in the beginning. He was the son of Mr. and Mrs. Otto L. Schneider of St. Louis, Missouri, and began his schooling at Bethlehem Lutheran School in St. Louis, graduating from the first Lutheran High School in 1950. After attending Concordia Teachers College, River Forest, for one year and graduating from St. John's College, Winfield, Kansas, in 1953, he was a student at Concordia Seminary in St. Louis from 1953 to 1956. From June of 1956 to February of 1960, he served in the U.S. Air Force where he taught bomb-navigation electronics at Lowry Air Force Base in Denver, Colorado, via the first Air Force closed-circuit educational television system. He returned to Concordia Seminary in March 1960, was a vicar at Calvary Lutheran Church, Baltimore, Maryland, and graduated from the St. Louis Seminary July 25, 1962.

Pastor Schneider was ordained in his home congregation on July 29, 1962, by his pastor, Rev. Lorenz E. Eifert. The Rev. John C. Jacobsen commissioned him as missionary-at-large on October 7, 1962, at Atonement Lutheran Church, Spring Valley. He was married to Miss Rose E. Wilder, daughter of Rev. and Mrs. Alfred C. Wilder of Denver, Colorado, on January 22, 1961. He and Mrs. Schneider lived in Spring Valley in the parsonage at 3406 Scenic Terrace.

Some canvassing of the area had been done in September, October, and November of 1962 by the Elmer Buchhorn family, the Del Bunker family, the Frank Roseman family, together with Mrs. Margaret Schneider, and Mrs. Betty Mehlenbacher and her children, all from Pilgrim Lutheran Church in Chula Vista, forming a hard-working nucleus which helped organize a Sunday school, built Sunday school equipment, and sent out publicity for the start of first services. With their prayers and hard work, Concordia mission got off to a flying start at the dedication of the sanctuary and educational building on December 9, 1962, at 3:00 p.m., having 167 people in attendance. The guest speaker was Rev. Harold B. Tietjen, acting executive secretary of the Southern California District Mission Board with Rev. John C. Jacobsen, pastoral counselor for Circuit Sixteen of the

Rev. Norman A. Schneider, was called as missionary-at-large in August of 1962, to begin mission work in the southeast part of Chula Vista. (Pacific Southwest District Archives)

Work for Concordia Lutheran Church starts in 1962.

District, and Rev. Norman A. Schneider, pastor of Concordia, serving as liturgists. The choir of Our Redeemer Lutheran Church, San Diego, provided special music.

The first service and Sunday school was held on December 16, 1962, with 102 attending worship followed by 75 on December 23, 69 on December 30, and 88 on January 6. The Christmas Eve service was attended by 160 people with 47 on Christmas Day, and 20 on New Year's Day. By the first Sunday in January of 1963, the Sunday school, which had met only on the previous 4 Sundays, had a total enrollment of about 80 or more children and young adults, and a staff of 8 teachers. Also in January, the ladies of the congregation organized to give their services to help furnish the kitchen, care for the altar, and to give service to the Lord in every area possible. On the first of April, the first junior Confirmation was conducted for two young people. May 5 was Confirmation day for 11 members of the first adult class. On June 9, 53 communicants, 2 families of the nucleus group and the 11 adult confirmands, signed the new constitution as charter members. During the summer months, a very able graduate of the Lay Institute and his wife, Mr. & Mrs. William Coplin, assisted Pastor Schneider and the congregation in the Lord's work at Concordia. By October, Pastor William Gieck and family arrived to undertake the work as missionary-at-large and was commissioned in a special service on October 27, delivering his first message on November 3, 1963.

By 1964, Concordia had grown to 151 baptized members with 78 communicant members and a Sunday school enrollment of 177 with an average attendance of 150. The educational wing was divided, so that 4 rooms housing 8 classes, was configured for 12 classes with a number of the classes

In 1966, Concordia's membership consists of 60% of families from the Navy.

conducted in the chapel. A combined junior and senior Confirmation class, numbering 11 children in the 7th to 9th grades, was being conducted with an adult Confirmation class, numbering 4. Concordia had drawn and continued to draw adults and children from the immediate area surrounding it. Training of evangelism callers was done in February using "Families For Christ" mission. It was the opinion of the pastor that the field was limited only by what Concordia was willing to provide for those in her area; by what her membership was willing to do for them; by how zealously her members worked; and by how earnestly they prayed for the Lord's strength, guidance, and success. In April, Concordia was organized and accepted into the Missouri Synod.

In April of 1965, the congregation called its first permanent pastor, Rev. William R. Gieck, who was serving as missionary-at-large with the call accepted and the installation service held on May 16. Due to the rapidly growing Sunday school department on October 10, 1965, ground was broken for an additional 3,600 square foot educational facility at the cost of $36,000 with the completion and dedication of this new wing taking place the first of 1966. It was the hope and prayer of the congregation that this much needed space would help to meet the challenge that faced them in this young, fast-growing community that overflowed with children. A new development of 1,000 homes canvassed by the membership when new units opened was a rich source of new membership for both children and adults. One of the blessings, as well as a handicap, was the sudden influx, and also the sudden transfer of the more than 60 percent of the Navy families who made up the membership. That year baptized membership had reached 216 with communicant membership at 115 and a Sunday school enrollment of 284.

After Rev. Gerhard (Gary) W. F. Harms finished the colloquy program in 1965, he served Trinity in Tolley, North Dakota, and Bethel, Bismarck, North Dakota, and came to Concordia in the 1970s. Following his stay in Chula Vista, he served Messiah and Trinity in San Diego.

Concordia's next pastor was Rev. Edmond Aho, the son of Gustaf A. and Helia (Tuikka) Aho, who was born in Ely, Minnesota, on August 27, 1930, and was a 1955 graduate of Concordia Seminary, Springfield, Illinois. He was married to the former Alma Johnson of Deer Creek, Minnesota, with their marriage blessed with two sons, Joel and Stephen. He served parishes at New York Mills

Concordia's sanctuary and educational building was dedicated on December 9, 1962. (Pacific Southwest District Archives)

and New Hope, Minnesota; Banning and Simi Valley, California; Sheboygan, Wisconsin, Yuma, Arizona, and retired from Concordia, Chula Vista, in 1992. He was called to his heavenly home on February 4, 1998.

At the time of Pastor Aho's retirement, Concordia had 175 communicant members with an average Sunday attendance of 112. Rev. Douglas W. Lutz Jr., a 1989 graduate of Concordia Seminary, St. Louis, followed him. After his graduation from the seminary, he was the assistant pastor of Good Shepherd in Pasadena, Texas, where he served until going to Concordia.

Rev. Richard Schmidt came to Concordia in 1996 from Mt. Calvary in Cahokia, Illinois, where he served from 1993 to 1996. He was born on July 19, 1961, in Milwaukee, Wisconsin, and was a graduate of Concordia Teachers College in Seward, Nebraska, in 1983. Following his graduation, he taught at Zion in Terra Bella, California, for three years. He moved to Zion Lutheran School in Dallas, Texas, where he served as a teacher and Director of Christian Education for three years. He decided to enter the ministry, attending Concordia Seminary in St. Louis and graduating in 1993. He was ordained and installed at Mt. Calvary in Cahokia, Illinois, in 1983. He married Michelle Kaasch on July 11, 1987, with their marriage blessed with two children, Michael and Kristin.

With demographic changes in the neighborhood surrounding the church in the late 1980s and early 1990s, Concordia Lutheran Church requested the District to help start a new Hispanic outreach program from its parish in 1991. This start had to be delayed because of the financial situation of the District at the time. In June 1992, the District called Pastor Esaúl Salomón as missionary-at-large to the San Diego South Bay area and the Mexican border. He was installed as pastor to the Hispanic community in Chula Vista with the installation conducted on October 4, 1992, at Concordia, Chula Vista, at 2:00 p.m. With his installation began the implementation of a new side-by-side ministry at Concordia, which had just observed its 30th anniversary and the retirement of Pastor Edmond F. Aho, after 37 years in the ministry of The Lutheran Church — Missouri Synod. Pastor Aho and his wife, Alma, remained in the Chula Vista vicinity.

Rev. Salomón, who came to Chula Vista from Panorama City where he served as senior pastor at El Redentor Spanish Lutheran Church for 10 years, received his doctorate at Concordia Theo-

Rev. Gerhard (Gary) W. F. Harms, who served Concordia in the 1970s. (Pacific Southwest District Archives)

Rev. Edmond Aho served Concordia until his retirement in 1992. (Pacific Southwest District Archives)

Rev. Douglas W. Lutz Jr. (Pacific Southwest District Archives)

logical Seminary in Fort Wayne, Indiana; he and wife, Melissa, an attorney, and their two daughters resided in the Rancho Del Rey area of the city. Financial support for his Hispanic ministry came from several sources, including the congregations of the San Diego circuits, the District, and grants from Aid Association for Lutherans and Lutheran Brotherhood. Before a Hispanic worship service was conducted, Pastor Salomón spent three to six months canvassing, gathering names, distributing fliers, talking to people and giving them his business card, and finally calling all the people he had met to invite them to the initial service. He conducted Bible classes on Monday, Tuesday, Wednesday, and Friday evenings and on Saturdays and Sundays, with the mission established in a middle-class Hispanic area.

After one year of outreach, Iglesia Luterana Concordia, started by Pastor Salomón, had an average church attendance of 40. Beginning with zero in January of 1993, he confirmed the first communicant members in June with the second adult Confirmation class in November swelling the ranks of communicate members to 21. At the November Confirmation service, Dr. Loren Kramer, president of the Pacific Southwest District, delivered the sermon through an interpreter with the 15-member Hispanic youth choir and the Anglo choir from Concordia Lutheran singing. Following the service was a time of celebration with food and entertainment provided by mariachis. At the congregation's first Christmas, the ladies made tamales as a means of raising funds to attend the LWML District Convention in June. Through the Bible study groups that met in homes during the week, Pastor instructed between 80 and 100 Hispanics in a non-threatening home environment. With a vision to reach many more Spanish-speak-

In 1993, Concordia begins side-by-side Hispanic Mission, Iglesia Luterana Concordia.

Rev. Esaúl Salomón was installed as pastor to the Hispanic community in Chula Vista on October 4, 1992, at Concordia, Chula Vista. (Pacific Southwest District Archives)

Dr. Salomón and his wife, Melissa, jointly write a booklet "Harvest Waiting: Reaching Out To The Mexicans."

ers in the San Diego and in Tijuana areas, Pastor Salomón worked with the Lutheran Laymen League's "Cristo Para Todas Las Nactones" to produce radio broadcasts in Spanish, with spot messages in December; this outreach continued to expand to a 15-minute, locally produced program that began in February 1994 on KRPZ, 1210 AM. He instructed four Spanish Confirmation classes in 1994 that helped to double church attendance that year.

When interviewed, Pastor Salomón recalled that within 2 years, he had 120 members who supported the church with their offerings of $3,000 a month. He worked to develop the concept of having an extension of Christ College in Irvine in Baja California to train pastors for the Hispanic mission field in a Bible institute where they would continue their education at the seminary. He established the Instituto Biblico Concordia de las dos Californias (Concordia Bible Society for the 2 Californias) which had 35 students with bachelor's degrees, sending 40 of these students to Concordia University, Irvine.

Beginning on November 23, 1994, 700, 32nd spot announcements were aired on 5 of the largest secular Spanish radio stations in the San Diego/Tijuana area advertising a 4-day family conference on December 15–17, offering some 6,000 copies of a wonderfully written, Christ-centered, 24-page booklet on being a family, being a couple, and raising a family in troubling times. Ten telephone lines were installed to take the requests of listeners who desired a free copy of the booklet as well as to take registrations for the family conference which was entitled "Trayendo Paz a la Familia" (Bringing Peace to the Family) consisting of three days of workshops and culminating in a concert, conference (evangelistic sermon message), and a dinner. The presenters were a couple from the "Lutheran Hour" office in Caracas, Venezuela, Drs. Jaime and Rut Paredes, each of whom had a doctorate in education, and post-graduate work in marriage and family counseling. He had a master's in theology and she had a master's in Christian education. Half-page ads were purchased in three Spanish-language newspapers to advertise the workshops. This was an experiment for LLL, as no other such campaign had been conducted in the Spanish-speaking community in this country. On the final day of the conference, which was a Sunday, five new families attended the morning worship service. New families enrolled in Confirmation classes, requesting home Bible studies.

Unique to this ministry was the importance of family; Pastor Salomon stated, "The Hispanic defines himself by his family, so it follows that the entire family must be evangelized and thought of as a unit. Home Bible studies and visits are a major key to our work."

On the first Sunday in January of 1995, five children were baptized. The 5 included 2 sets of twins, and the mission recorded the highest number of people in worship, 85, with 35 in the adult Bible class following the service. That January, the mission requested the District to allow the mission to formally organize as a congregation since it now had 40 communicant members and 120 persons who worshiped and worked at the mission. In addition, the offerings from the mission were averaging more than $1,000 each month. As the mission grew, plans were discussed to open a mission outreach to the northern San Diego County, as they had seven families that resided in the area of Vista, Oceanside, and San Marcos who needed a ministry there. It was exciting times knowing that God would accomplish great things among the Spanish-speaking community of that geographic region that numbered nearly 3,000,000. By mid-1995, Pastor Salomón had three missions going, Escondido, Imperial Beach, and Tijuana. Also, at that time Dr. Salomón and his wife, Melissa, a practicing attorney, who had lived and worked among the Mexican people for many years, jointly wrote and published a booklet that summer, "Harvest Waiting: Reaching Out To The Mexicans," combining their experiences with practical tips for churches contemplating Hispanic outreach in their own communities. Noting the 1990 U.S. census report of a 54 percent Hispanic growth, totaling some 13.5 million Mexicans entering the states in the previous 10 years, the 44-page booklet outlined plans for meeting specific spiritual needs of the Hispanic community. Their main focus was to alert readers to common mistakes and cultural pitfalls to avoid.

On May 8, 1995, while attending a pastors' conference, Pastor Salomón was playing a game of tennis; as he jumped over the net of the tennis court, he caught his foot on the net, fell on the cement court, and injured his head, sustaining a severe concussion. Within a few weeks, his head started to swell causing a deep depression and personality change affecting his marriage and church work. Even through the pain and distress it caused, he continued his work, establishing the thriving Instituto Biblico Concordia de las dos

Californias in January 1997, with the objective of preparing young men in solid Lutheran doctrine and evangelism theory and practice. The staff included Rev. Dr. Esaúl Salomón, Mike Rodemeyer, M. A., lay leader of Iglesia Luterana Concordia and instructor for the institute; Mario Gurisatti, M.A., lay leader of Iglesia Luterana Concordia and instructor for the institute; and Melissa Salomón, J.D., administrator, Iglesia Luterana Concordia and instructor for the institute. Through the use of the "Lutheran Hour" facilities in Tijuana, beginning in December 1997, worship and a developing ministry for the central region of Tijuana was begun.

Some time in the summer of 2001, Pastor Alan Wyneken and Vicar Raymond Fellers met with Pastor Salomón to discuss doing a Hispanic ministry at Pilgrim in Chula Vista as the area surrounding the church was 50 percent Hispanic. When interviewed, Vicar Fellers recalled that Pastor Salomón might have moved the Hispanic mission from Concordia to Pilgrim in July of 2001. Due to a loss of funding at Concordia, he worked with the Lutheran Border Concerns Mission in Tijuana Pastor Salomón started work at Pilgrim but also continued to work for Lutheran Border Concerns Ministry (LBCM).

As a result of his health problems from the accident, Pastor Salomón's ministry took a different direction. He left Chula Vista in March of 2002 to take a call as associate pastor to develop a Hispanic ministry at Holy Trinity, an English District church in Tucson, Arizona. The first year at Holy Trinity, he had 45 members in the Spanish service, which grew to between 80 and 100, while the Anglo church had 25 to 30 people in the English service during the summer, swelling to 120 in the fall when the "snow birds" returned to the area. In May 2003, the head pastor resigned leaving Rev. Salomón as pastor for both the English-speaking

and Hispanic congregations. The area around the church consisted of poor Hispanics who lived in apartments.

In 2002, Juan Garcia, a TEE student and part-time drywall hanger, was asked to become the guest lay pastor at the Hispanic mission at Pilgrim in Chula Vista where he helped with Spanish services and Bible studies. He was born on May 6, 1960, in Hostotipaquillo, Jalisco, Mexico, and attended Emiliano Zapata School in Mexico for nine years. He married Maria del Pliar Garcia in 1978 and was blessed with five children. In 1993–1994, he attended church at San Pedro y San Pablo in Bell Gardens. From there, he became a member at El Redentor in Panorama City followed by membership at Grace, Escondido, in 1998, moving to St. James in Imperial Beach in 2001. He continues pursuing his studies, which he hopes will lead to full-time ministry in the church in 2009. While continuing to work in the construction field, he ministers to the mission at Pilgrim where 20 faithful souls attend Spanish services each Sunday with an average of 8 attending Bible classes and 8 children in Saturday school. He follows up with telephone calls to new members of the Hispanic ministry to see how they are doing or if they need assistance, making sure they feel welcome and return to the mission. He remembers their birthdays by sending cards. The main struggle at the time was that he felt he needed to be working full-time at the mission in order for it to grow.

In December of 2003, Juan Garcia left for Texas to do his vicarage. The Hispanics at Pilgrim who didn't speak English were encouraged to go to St. James in Imperial Beach where a Spanish service was conducted, with those who spoke English staying at Pilgrim. At the time of this writing, there is no Spanish worship service being conducted at Pilgrim.

> In 2001, the Hispanic mission is moved to Pilgrim, Chula Vista.

St. James Lutheran Church
St. James Hispanic Lutheran Mission
Imperial Beach, California

 mperial Beach, incorporated on July 18, 1956, claims the unique distinction of being the "most southwesterly city" in the continental United States, located only 5 miles from the Mexican border and 11 miles from downtown San Diego in the southwest corner of San Diego County. Imperial Beach comprises an area of 4.4 square miles with a population of 28,002 of which 52.26 percent are white and 40.08 percent are Hispanic. R. R. Morrison, a developer who subdivided the area, founded Imperial Beach in June 1887. George Chaffey later bought a large section of the land to build a resort for residents of the Imperial Valley. Through this venture, it is believed that is where the name of Imperial Beach is derived. During the 1880s, the area was part of a larger land boom with many homes, businesses, and hotels erected. The first pier was built in 1909, with the hope that the wave action would help to generate electricity; this was never accomplished. The pier was finally washed out to sea in 1948 after gradually falling into disrepair.

Imperial Beach, described by some as quaint, has a rare innocence and a relaxed atmosphere. The climate is like spring or early fall year round with temperatures ranging from 50 to 80 degrees. At a leisurely pace, a person can walk the 3.5 miles of the city beachfront in about an hour, viewing surfers, boogie borders, surf fisherman, and several species of shore birds. Looking south of the city across the international border with Mexico is the Plaza de Monumental, Tijuana's famous "Bull-ring by the Sea." Near the southeast corner of Sea-coast Drive and Imperial Beach Boulevard is the edge of the Tijuana Estuary, or the sloughs, as it is commonly referred to. Walking east is a dirt path angling off to the right.

A few years before the Lutheran church began work in Imperial Beach, the population of Imperial Beach and Palm City comprised approximately 2,500 people in the early 1950s. During that time, large automotive and aircraft industries and other subsidiary factories developed along San Diego Bay, southeast of San Diego and west of Chula Vista. These industries and factories employed thousands of people, many of who resided in Chula Vista; as a result, the city of Chula Vista increased in population. Many of these workers had

permanent residences in Imperial Beach and Palm City. When the U.S. Navy developed additional large installations in the general San Diego area, many of the civilian workers as well as enlisted Navy men had their residences in the Imperial Beach and Palm City area. These developments resulted in a comparative population and residential growth in the area, increasing the population to 9,000 in the early 1950s. Immediately south of Imperial Beach, the Standard Oil Company held hundreds of acres of land where large oil deposits were located.

Into this area came The Rev. Frederick L. Oberschulte of Lake Route, Pequot Lakes, Minnesota, a retired pastor who was formerly active in the English District, to visit his married son and married daughter living in Chula Vista and Imperial Beach, respectively. Pastor Oberschulte and his wife spent several months with their family and realized an opportunity to share the Gospel to some of the large population in the area. There was only a Methodist church and one or two Pentecostal groups in the area. Pastor Oberschulte secured permission from the Methodist church to conduct Lutheran services in its church building on Tuesday evenings during the Lenten season of 1954, having an attendance ranging from 11 to 37.

During his short stay, Pastor Oberschulte caused the organization of a Lutheran group in the area to be effected. When he returned to his residence in Pequot Lakes at the end of April, he requested his District president to pursue placing a vicar in charge of the work in San Diego County beginning in May. Without knowledge of Pastor Oberschulte's work and the development of this mission, the Mission Board of the Southern California District entered a request through its District president for a vicar to serve this area and

First Lutheran services held in Imperial Beach during Lent of 1954 by retired pastor from Minnesota, Rev. Oberschulte.

St. James Lutheran Church and School as it looked in 1959. (Pacific Southwest District Archives)

another promising field in the San Diego region, Lemon Grove, beginning some time in the middle of July, contingent upon having of a vicar. In the meantime, tentative arrangements had been made with pastors of the San Diego area to conduct services at the beginning of May following the departure of Pastor Oberschulte.

The Rev. Walter Lossner, Pastor of Our Redeemer Lutheran Church, San Diego, was placed in charge of the new mission conducting services at 7:00 a.m. with Sunday school at 8:00 a.m. in Imperial Beach churches and the VFW Hall, preceding the services at his own church. In September 1954, Mr. John Rath, a student at Concordia Theological Seminary, St. Louis, Missouri, was assigned to Imperial Beach and served the church in a full-time capacity until July 1955, when St. James installed its first resident pastor, the Rev. Paul A. Hilgendorf Jr., where he served until 1958. When Synod had the need for men to represent her in the Navy chaplaincy, Pastor Hilgendorf accepted the call, as he had never had active military duty and felt very strongly that the Lord wanted him in this field for a two-year active duty. During the same month, the congregation called Pastor William McMurdie of Faith Lutheran Church, Sonoma, Washington. He accepted the call, arriving on July 1, 1958, with his wife, Jean, and children, Mary and Johnny. On July 6, he was installed as pastor of the congregation. In 1961, he left Missouri Synod to join the Evangelical Synod.

A 5-acre plot of land at the corner of Ninth and Coronado was purchased in December 1954 with official groundbreaking ceremonies for the first unit of the church plant, the chapel/parish hall, conducted on January 22, 1956. A member of St. Paul's, Pacific Beach, Mr. A. L. Porry, supervised

construction, and with members of the church donated volunteer labor on Saturdays. The building of approximately 4,700 square feet, provided seating for 250, and included a church office, kitchen facilities, and Sunday school rooms. A parsonage was built in 1957. Chapel construction was made possible by a loan from the District Church Extension Fund. By January 1, 1958, the congregation had become self-supporting, and on Sunday, April 27, 1958, groundbreaking for the new school was conducted.

When work was begun in 1954, no one would have dreamed that by September 15, 1958, a beautiful three-room Christian day school for pre-first through seventh grades would have been completed by volunteer labor with 100 children attending the school under the supervision of 4 full-time teachers: Dr. Herman Meyerhoff, principal and teacher, and his wife, Mrs. Anna Meyerhoff; Miss Joanne Ehlen; and Miss Mary Kimball. One of the rooms in the parish hall was used for the kindergarten. Also, at that time, 56 adults were taking adult information courses, with 40 teenagers attending Confirmation classes. With such a fast-growing community, the future held great opportunities for the church. With 164 communicant members and a Sunday school of 330, the average church attendance was 220; the VBS held that summer averaged 210, even though it was held in August.

ST. James School was started on September 15, 1958, with four teachers.

Dr. Herman Meyerhoff, principal and teacher, Rev. McMurdie, and teachers, Miss Joanne Ehlen and Miss Mary Kimball. (Pacific Southwest District Archives)

The chancel of St. James' chapel/parish hall in 1959. (Pacific Southwest District Archives)

The Kennedy Plan, an evangelism program, is used in 1969, increasing membership.

In 1959, groundbreaking services were held as construction was begun on the first Lutheran junior high school south of Los Angeles. It contained six attractive classrooms, the principal's office, a reception room, a large supply room, restrooms, and showers. Begun in 1958, the building had been constructed with volunteer labor of friends and members of the congregation. Furnishings and equipment had been carefully selected in order to combine quality and good taste with economy. Desks, chalkboards, tile, etc., were carefully chosen to make the rooms inviting. A covered breezeway around the quadrangle allowed easy access to centrally located lavatories. The kindergarten room and the teachers' lounge were located in the parish hall. St. James was situated in one of the fastest growing areas in Southern California. From the original 12 members, the congregation had grown to 246 communicant members with 16 young people confirmed on Pentecost Sunday, May 17. Also in 1959, the members of St. James honored Dr. Herman Meyerhoff in a special service for his 35 years of service as an outstanding educator in the church with the Rev. G. C. Schramm, first vice president of the District, delivering the address. The children and parents of the congregation presented a gift to Dr. Meyerhoff.

At a 3:30 p.m. service on Sunday, January 21, 1962, Rev. Gerhardt Rusch of Duluth, Minnesota was installed as the new pastor of St. James with Rev. John Jacobsen of Grace in San Diego preaching the sermon. He was followed by Rev. Jack W. Keenan, a 31-year-old, who was born in Illinois

Mr. Larry Matthew, principal of St. James School, viewing the full-academic National Science Foundation scholarship he received. Looking on with their approval are Rev. Gerhardt Rusch, right, and Dr. Herman Meyerhoff, District counselor of education. (Pacific Southwest District Archives)

and was a graduate of the University of Iowa with a degree in business administration and a degree in psychology before graduating from Concordia Seminary at Springfield, Illinois. He had served congregations in Illinois and Texas. In 1971, he was elected to the Journal of Outstanding Young Men in America for his volunteer work among servicemen returning from the Vietnam conflict. He married Marlys Widmark of Little Falls, Minnesota, on June 9, 1974.

During Pastor Keenan's second year at St. James, he instituted the mission project using the "Kennedy Plan," a method of evangelistic training for lay members devised by a Florida Presbyterian minister, Rev. James Kennedy. This plan called for the pastor to personally train a few members in making evangelism calls to unchurched people with each trainee then training a few other members. Through this approach, 35 members were received shortly after Easter and a total of 109 new members were taken in on another Sunday in the fall as the climax of a membership drive, which was launched in January of 1969. Of the 109 members received, the largest majority were new converts with 65 adult communicants, ranging in age from a 15-year-old convert to a 73-year-old man who had transferred his membership from another Lutheran church with the total church membership at 703, which included 380 adults.

As a result of a specially designed evangelism program, the congregation had increased by more than 100 members in 1970. Pastor Keenan, stated: "The Kennedy Program grew out of a need to evangelize the community which is very transient but which offers a great opportunity to spread the Gospel of Jesus Christ worldwide." In 1971, the sanctuary was remodeled with Rev. Gerhardt Rusch, former pastor of the congregation, the guest speaker for the special service. The remodeling included the chancel being completely refurbished, adding a 10-foot Celtic cross on the wall behind the altar, the pipes of the organ were refinished and set behind the green oak-leaf design of the symbol of new life in Christ, and padded pews and kneelers were also added.

In 1974, Pastor Keenan took a call to Our Savior's First in Granada Hills; in the spring, Rev. John Jacobsen, circuit counselor, installed Rev John C. Rumsey as pastor of St. James with pastors Loren Rumsch (a cousin), the speaker; Clarence Damschroeder (childhood pastor), the lector; Lawrence Rudolph, interim pastor, and other clergymen from the circuit participating in the service. After

Pastor Rumsey graduated from Concordia Seminary, Springfield, Illinois, he served parishes in Florida and Oklahoma and Redeemer Church in South Gate. In 1956, he married Dorothy Meyers of Oklahoma City with their marriage blessed with five children: John, Rebecca Judith, Grace Ann, David, and a foster daughter, Lora O'Reilly. When St. James celebrated its 25th anniversary on July 1, 1979, the Rev. John H. Rath of Faith Church in Topeka, Kansas, the vicar who conducted services for the congregation during its organizing efforts in 1954, preached at special services. Following the afternoon services, a program and buffet dinner was served in the parish hall.

During Pastor Rumsey's pastorate, a preschool was opened in October 1979 with Dorothy Rumsey serving as director. A new organ was dedicated on January 10, 1982, and on October 17, the congregation held a special service to celebrate Pastor Rumsey's 25th anniversary in the ministry with a 5:00 p.m. Hawaiian program held in the parish hall where the congregation presented Pastor and Dorothy a trip to Hawaii. On October 5, 1983, groundbreaking ceremonies were held for the low-income senior housing behind St. James' parking lot. On December 1, the new kitchen and conference room adjacent to the fellowship hall were completed. The occupancy lottery was conducted on July 17, 1984, for the 100 units in the new St. James Plaza, with the tenants occupying their units in August and with the dedication on September 9, 1984. On May 22, 1988, the first of a series of stained-glass windows, "The Good Shepherd," depicting the life of Christ and Old Testament scenes, was dedicated along with a hand-crocheted Lord's Supper wall hanging. In November of 1990, the church pews were refinished and re-

The refurbished chancel with a 10-foot Celtic cross above the altar. (Pacific Southwest District Archives)

upholstered in blue, the exterior and interior of the church was refurbished, with new church light fixtures added in June of 1991.

On June 6, 1993, Pastor Rumsey's retirement service was conducted as he had completed 36 years in the ministry of which over 19 years were at St. James. During the service, Rev. Edmond Aho was liturgist; Rev. James Tyler was the preacher with Dr. Loren Kramer, District president, giving words of greeting. Also participating in the service were Pastor Rumsey's sons, John and David, and son-in-law, Kelly Session, reading the Epistle and Gospel lessons. Following the service was a retirement dinner in the fellowship hall. From June 13 through August 15, 1993, Rev. Edmond Aho served as interim pastor.

In an afternoon service on August 15, 1993, Rev. Bruce Jeske was installed as the new pastor of St. James. He was born on April 11, 1942, in Salt Lake City, Utah, and attended California Concordia College in Oakland, graduating in 1962. In 1964, he graduated from Concordia Senior College in Fort Wayne, Indiana. Following his graduation in 1968, from Concordia Seminary, St. Louis, he served Trinity, Akron, Colorado; St. Mark in Provo, Utah; and Christ, Costa Mesa; where he was associate pastor beginning in 1982. He married Ilze Veiss on December 27, 1966, with their marriage blessed with 3 children. On April 25, 1984, she died and on October 12, 1985, he married his second wife, Carol Pappas, who had a child by a previous marriage. Their four children are Marta, Beata, Wendy Hunter, and Timon. Pastor also did community service through the Lions Club, Optimist Club, and served as a high school exit interviewer.

During his ministry at St. James, the congregation celebrated its 40th anniversary on May 15, 1994, where Rev. Paul Hilgendorf, the first pastor, preached the sermon with Rev. Jeske, Rev. Rumsey, and the church choirs participating. Also in 1994, the congregation established a Christian martial arts ministry, an after-school afternoon program for 6- to 18-year-olds who practice martial arts self-defense techniques in karate attire, gearing the students towards the development of mental strength. It was a Christ-centered, evangelical outreach of St. James, with the goal of reaching the community-at-large with the Gospel. The ministry began with 6 students and in 1998 had an enrollment of 64. Each class, for members and non-members, began with prayer and ended with a 30-minute Bible study and prayer.

Rev. John C. Rumsey at the time of his installation as pastor of St. James in 1974. (Pacific Southwest District Archives)

Rev. Bruce Jeske was installed as the new pastor of St. James on August 15, 1993. (Pacific Southwest District Archives)

Hispanic ministry
begins in 1996 with
Spanish Bible class.

Since Imperial Beach is the city closest to the Mexican border in the southern San Diego area, St. James under the guidance of Pastor Jeske and Pastor Salomón of Iglesia Concordia in Chula Vista, recognized a need to minister to the large Hispanic population in sharing the Gospel. With the combined effort of the two congregations, Efrain Erazo, a lay minister, was hired to develop a mission to minister to the needs of the growing Hispanic culture. He started with a list of names of Hispanics who had contact with St. James through their ministry and through the school, making visits to these people. Through the contacts, Spanish Bible classes were organized in homes and at the church, with the first meeting on January 15, 1996. Canvassing of the community with fliers distributed, helped to advertise the mission's presence, which was willing to serve them in Spanish. From this small beginning, the classes grew to 25 adults with 9 children ranging from ages 8 through 14. During the second Bible study, a lady from Imperial Beach who had registered her daughter for karate class and stayed for the Bible class, told how her mother was a Jehovah Witness, how she couldn't accept the doctrine, and when she married, she stopped going to church gatherings. Through this Bible class, she continued to study the Word, which she said was a new beginning for her life.

On August 1, 1998, Deacon Gabriel Ochoa, the former pastor of El Redentor in Tijuana from July 1995 through July 1998, came to St. James to continue the Hispanic work mainly drawing together people of Hispanic background to learn, grow in the Word, and to worship. Through contacts made at St. James School, the Christian martial arts ministry, St. James Place, and the VBS, he began canvassing the neighborhood around Peace Lutheran Church. Since this ministry was a joint effort of St. James and Peace Lutheran Church of San Diego, he was welcomed into this ministry in a service at Peace on August 9, 1998. A Vacation Bible School was conducted on August 3 through the 8. After the VBS, he did follow up calls on all who attended and did canvassing in both neighborhoods of the churches. He called on prospective visitors at both the congregations, reporting to the pastors, attending the Hispanic ministry meetings, administering the Sacraments at both parishes, and working with the Christian martial arts ministry at St. James.

As Deacon Ochoa's ministry continued to grow, he worked exclusively at St. James. By 2003, he held Sunday evening services attended by 26 and a Sunday school. The Hispanic congregation participated in a friendship dinner at the church where the members had an opportunity to get to know each other better, inviting some of their friends. They had bilingual Lenten worship services on Wednesday evenings with scripture readings and hymns in both Spanish and English. Through a fundraiser, they purchased two cases of Bibles, which were presented to visitors, members who might need one, and to families or friends who might be interested in studying the Word of God.

Deacon Ochoa participated in the pre-school and kindergarten program by singing to the students in Spanish, teaching the children to have an ear for the Spanish language. The Hispanic members were excited and happy that their mission was part of St. James. They were faithful in their worship and Bible study, distributing fliers to their neighbors, inviting them to worship at the mission. Through the work of the mission, the members' lives were more stable, they had more personal relationships, and they participated in prayer. In order for the mission to grow, the hope was to start an advertising campaign in several of the area's Spanish newspapers. Another goal was to have spot announcements on Spanish radio stations. In the spring of 2003, the ladies of the mission had a tamale sale, selling 1,000 tamales; the net raised was $600.

Deacon Ochoa stated the following:

When we were brought here to initiate a mission, we thought with God's help, and dedication and persistence on our part, the mission would be established. Thanks to God we see the presence of the mission in the Hispanic community at St. James. People are coming to church, homes are being blessed, and children are learning about God and His Word. Youth are learning about a meaningful life. God keeps showing us the way to run His mission and opening doors and hearts in the community.

We have made a list of the people and family members, friends of our congregation. First, we pray for them and then we invite them to church. Lately, we have learned about the importance and the power of prayer and that God gives us the opportunity to ask him our petitions with supplication. That is why we take every project, every plan first to the Lord in prayer.

Grace Lutheran Church
Iglesia Luterana Gracia
Escondido, California

he Shoshonean groups of the Great Basin Indians who migrated to southwest California and originated the San Luis Rey culture over 1,000 years ago once inhabited the land where Escondido stands today. The Luiseño Indians had long established villages and campsites along the Escondido Creek and in the north and north central portions of present-day Escondido. The Native American Kumeyaay were Yumans who migrated from the Colorado River area and occupied San Pasqual Valley with sites along water sources in the southern and western portions of Escondido, especially along the San Dieguito River. In 1776, Juan Bautista de Anza, a Spanish explorer, was the first white man to discover and identify the location of Escondido. Later, a land grant of 12,653 acres was bestowed to Juan Bautista Alvarado in 1843, by the Mexican Governor, Manuel Micheltorena, with the area becoming part of the Rancho Rincon del Diablo, meaning the devil's corner, nestled in a beautiful valley, completely surrounded by rock-ridged mountains, studded with many enormous boulders, whose bald knobs formed various landmarks for its present inhabitants, a valley where Indians once left many vestiges of their habitation appropriately named by Spanish, *escondido*, the word for hidden.

The course of history for Escondido took a dramatic turn when soldiers of the United States Army attacked Mexican forces of Alta California in the neighboring San Pasqual Valley on December 6, 1846, with a number of American soldiers being either wounded or killed. Within a few years of the Battle of San Pasqual, California was annexed into the Union in 1850. Early in the American period, the rancho was sold to Oliver S. Witherby, a San Diego judge, who continued the cattle business and began mining gold on the property in 1860. The following year a small gold rush ensued with the name "Escondido" appearing on legal records in the "Escondido Mining Company" filing claim. Attempts at gold mining in that portion of the city continued into the 1920s. In 1868, Witherby sold the ranch to the Wolfskill Brothers with John Wolfskill, part owner and ranch manager, occupying the southeast part of the ranch where he employed the San Pasqual Indians. Cattle herds

were reduced as the Wolfskills built a sheep ranch. In due time, the Wolfskills not only started planting grapes and orange groves but also pursued other forms of agriculture.

On March 1, 1886, another change would occur in Escondido when Richard Thomas and his four brothers, along with several other investors, created a land boom with the development of the area by organizing a land survey of the old rancho. Land promoters sold Escondido's climate as ideal for growing crops and varied agriculture. Since they wanted Escondido to be more than an ordinary frontier town, they donated free land for churches, a 100-room hotel was constructed, and a branch of the University of Southern California was established. Within a short time, banks were opened, a weekly newspaper was published, and Escondido was linked by railroad to the rest of the country. Since supplies such as brick and lumber were needed to build the town, labor was needed and supplied by Chinese workers who were brought to Escondido to make bricks and to build schools, churches, and other buildings. When construction was completed, the Chinese workers found employment in restaurants, laundries, and small farming. The little boomtown of the Escondido Land and Town Company was incorporated as the city of Escondido on October 8, 1888.

Into this rural "hidden valley" came many German Lutheran pioneers who decided to settle in this agricultural community, a far outpost of San Diego, with no paved streets. They had come from San Diego, Olive, Orange, and Santa Ana in

The city of Escondido is incorporated on October 8, 1888.

Grand Avenue (circa 1900) where the city of Escondido began. (Escondido Public library)

Grace Evangelical
Lutheran Church is
organized on May 25,
1919, by Rev. William
Schmoock of Santa Ana.

the earliest years and later from other communities. This group of Germans, who communicated
in German among themselves, saw the need for
spiritual aid almost immediately. Being few in
number and relatively poor financially, they requested the California and Nevada
District for pastors to serve them
intermittently if not regularly with
help forthcoming very quickly. Arrangements were made with the
Seventh-day Adventist Church to
use those facilities to hold services
for the German Lutherans. They
called on the Rev. F. Leimbrock,
then pastor of Trinity Lutheran
Church of San Diego, to serve the
few scattered families with the
Gospel of Christ in 1908. The Rev.
Louis Meyer, who served Olivenhain for a year during 1911, kept in
touch with these members in the
valley. Then Vicar Lawrence Acker,
who was assisting Pastor Leimbrock, followed him. In order to get
to Escondido, his rough trips were made from San
Diego on a motorcycle over un-surfaced roads. In
the intervening years up to 1918, there were inter-
mittent services conducted by the Rev. J. Kogler

*Rev. William F. F. Hoff-
mann was Grace's first
resident pastor from
August 1, 1920, to June
1930. (Pacific Southwest
District Archives)*

of Orange, Rev. J. W. Theiss of Los Angeles, Rev.
W. A. Theiss of Olive, Rev. E. Rudnick of Banning,
and Rev. N. F. Jensen and Rev. E. Pargee of Orange. Then, beginning in 1919, came Rev. William
Schmoock of Santa Ana, who agreed to preach
regularly taking the train or driving
his car each Sunday, until the church
was organized at a meeting on May 25,
1919, where he submitted a constitution and the name, "Grace Evangelical
Lutheran Church of Escondido, California," was adopted. The first officers
elected to serve the new congregation,
as deacons were F. W. E. Huefner, Julius Knappe, and Frank Singer; president, William Luchau; secretary, Rev.
William Schmoock; treasurer, William Luchau.

Pastor Schmoock continued to
minister to this small group until the
summer of the following year, when a
call was extended to the Rev. William
F. F. Hoffmann of Amherst, Nebraska,
who arrived on July 17, 1920, and was
installed as the congregation's first resident pastor
on August 1, 1920, by Rev. Schmoock. Pastor Hoffmann who was born in 1881 in Adrian, Wisconsin,
was ordained in 1907, going to Escondido after
serving parishes in South Dakota and Nebraska.
He died at his home in Escondido on January 18,
1979, and was survived by four daughters, Martha
Thompson, Esther Eden and Eleanor Pratte, all of
Escondido, and Selma Heman of Windsor; three
sons, Walter of Burbank, Karl of San Diego, and
William of Escondido; 15 grandchildren, 19 great-
grandchildren, and one great-great grandchild.

Since the congregation had no church building of its own, it was eager to acquire property for
future development. An opportunity arose when

*Grace's first church on Grand and Ivy was dedicated
on September 4, 1921. (Pacific Southwest District Archives)*

*The large, hand-made altar and pulpit designed and
built by Louis Junge for Grace's first church. (Pacific
Southwest District Archives)*

the First Methodist Church offered its property on East Grand and Ivy Street for sale. Action was taken immediately at the July 12, 1920, meeting, only a few days prior to the arrival of the newly called pastor, with the parish voting to purchase the Methodist Church, which was being offered for $2,500, seeking a loan of $2,000 from the District Church Extension Fund, and asking Rev. Schmoock to solicit the balance of the money needed to secure the purchase from the congregations at Orange, Olive, Santa Ana, Los Angeles, and San Diego. At the following meeting, the purchase price of the Methodist Church was loaned to the congregation by Mr. Henry Moennich, of Olive, California, effecting the immediate acquisition of the property.

Rev. Louis H. Jagels was installed on January 11, 1931, as the second pastor of Grace, remaining until his retirement in 1954. (Pacific Southwest District Archives)

Before the church could be dedicated, much had to be done to make it ready for occupancy. The bats in the roof and belfry had to be brought under control. This "battle of the bats" was to continue for 32 years until the building was again vacated. The interior was painted and cleaned, new windows were installed, and a platform was built for an altar which was constructed by August Junge, a skilled carpenter, who designed it from pictures and also from personally viewing the altar at St. John's Lutheran Church in Orange, California. Upon completion of the altar, Mr. Robert Bergander did the painting and decorations on it. With the altar completed, Mr. Junge built a pulpit, lectern, baptismal font, and hymn board to match the altar, which was used by Grace for nearly half a century. These items were given to Camp Caroline, Valley Center, when the camp's chapel was built in 1967 through the effort of Grace's members.

The joyous day of the dedication took place on September 4, 1921, with Pastor William Schmoock preaching the dedicatory sermon. In the afternoon service, the Rev. W. F. F. Hoffmann delivered the dedicatory address. Mr. Henry Moennich, who had so kindly loaned the necessary funds for the purchase of the church a year earlier, made an outright gift to the congregation by the cancellation of the entire note at the time of the dedication of the church. While regular services were being conducted in both English and German, the dedication service was in English. During Pastor Hoffmann's pastorate at Grace, he performed 36 Baptisms, 33 Confirmations, 12 marriages, 7 burials, and communed 641. He also served the St. John Lutheran Mission at Olivenhain where, from April 1921 until December 1932, he baptized 25, confirmed 4, communed 283, and buried 4. After 10 years of service, Pastor Hoffmann terminated his services in June 1930, with his resignation accepted by the congregation. He continued to reside in Escondido following his retirement. During the ensuing vacancy, the congregation was served by the Rev. K. Knippenberg, of Trinity Lutheran, San Diego, until the beginning of January 1931. The Rev. Louis H. Jagels of Deshler, Nebraska, accepted the call extended to him by Grace, arriving with his wife, Eugenia, and daughter, Helen, on January 7, 1931, being installed the following Sunday, January 11, by the Rev. K. Knippenberg, assisted by Pastor A. C. Bode of Orange, and Rev. Charles Wehking, pastor emeritus of San Diego. He was an intellectual, who could discuss issues on a wide range of topics, a skillful carpenter, and, as the church records revealed, he had meticulously neat handwriting. He was also very active in building the congregation, in serving the Southern California District, and in taking an active interest in civic affairs

By 1931, the city of Escondido had undertaken steps to improve the downtown area by paving the streets and installing sidewalks and streetlights, with many of the trees that surrounded the church on both Ivy Street and Grand Avenue removed. The congregation followed suit by improving its property with new stairs and railings, installing new light fixtures and a layer of sheet metal on all the walls and ceilings. In March 1933, an organ was purchased and reconditioned with a motorized blower. The same year another change was effected — resolved that English would be used exclusively in all the services. When Grace was started in 1919, there were just a handful of people, but by 1929, the congregation had grown to 66 communicants. With the crash of the stock market that year, the congregation dwindled to 50 communicants by 1930. From that point on with the one exception of the years 1944 through 1945, the communicant membership increased steadily. With this growth, the congregation purchased

Grace's membership increases steadily.

the adjoining property at 419 E. Grand Avenue in August 1944 with its spacious house, naming it Lutheran Hall. The house was remodeled with volunteer labor of members who enlarged the first floor to encompass a spacious 28' × 42' assembly room for social functions and meeting place for all of the organizations plus a modern kitchen was added. The second floor had three rooms for Sunday school classes.

On November 21, 1934, Grace notified the Southern California District, that at the beginning of 1935, the congregation would become self-supporting, thus ending 14 years as a subsidized mission congregation. The first mission festival was held at Felicita Park in 1936, where the members gathered in a service on a Sunday afternoon in September to hear guest speakers exhort them to do their utmost in furthering the cause of mission work throughout the world. In December of 1938, Grace broke the long-standing German-Lutheran custom of requiring the men and women to sit in different sections of the church by allowing men and women to sit together and to Commune together. The children still had to be seated in the front rows of the church with one of the deacons appointed to sit with them to avoid disturbances during the service. At the time, the congregation sat in folding chairs until used pews were purchased from Trinity of San Diego in 1941. At the beginning of the Second World War, the congregation placed a U.S. flag and a Christian flag in front of the church to show loyalty to God and country. The common cup had been used when the church was started in 1919, and the Ladies Aid purchased a set of individual glasses for Communion in 1953.

During Grace's first 25 years, she became the mother of 2 other congregations in northern San Diego County. On April 11, 1943, Pastor Jagels began preaching services in the Chapel of The Pines at Oceanside, serving the faithful members in the area who were affiliated with Grace, and also ministering to the servicemen at Camp Pendleton. Pastor Jagels continued until March 1945, when Candidate Waldemar Meyer began his work in that field, thus releasing Grace's members. Further releases from Grace came with the establishment of a new mission in Encinitas during 1944, when St. Mark's was established where members of the former St. John in nearby Olivenhain supplied a nucleus. Even with the release of members to form daughter churches, Grace had a communicant membership of 160 by 1945.

In December of 1938, Grace breaks the long-standing German-Lutheran custom of requiring the men and women to sit in different sections of the church by allowing men and women to sit together.

As was previously mentioned, Pastor Jagels had a talent and love for woodworking, making small and decorative objects in wood. In 1946, with congregational approval, he crafted the crucifix, a set of candelabras, the cross on the baptismal font, and the kneeling bench for marriages. His wife, Eugenia Jagels, embroidered all the paraments for the altar, lectern, and pulpit, along with Pastor's stoles. In the fall of 1949, Pastor Jagels celebrated his 35th anniversary in the ministry as well as his 35th wedding anniversary. To honor this dedicated couple, the congregation collected funds to purchase a new 1949 Chevrolet, presenting it to him after an anniversary service, which was conducted by Rev. Clarence Damschroeder of San Diego.

Christian education always held a paramount position in the minds of the members of Grace, particularly in regard to training youth and children. A Vacation Bible School was conducted as early as 1947 with 55 children. By 1964, they had a VBS enrollment of 199 children. With the congregation experiencing growth in membership and in the Sunday school, in the April 1950 Voters' Assembly, the voters decided that something would have to be done to enlarge the facilities for education and worship. An ensuing study showed that the present location on Grand and Ivy had too many building restrictions and little room to expand unless additional lots could be purchased. It was decided to establish a building fund and to investigate all of the neighboring properties. None were available for purchase. With this information, the congregation was trapped within the confines of its present quarters or it would have to relocate. Through a questionnaire that was sent to the members to determine if relocation was a possibility, the response clearly showed that a majority of the members were willing to relocate if no other satisfactory arrangements could be made with the present property. With that in mind, a Building and Grounds Committee was established.

By the end of 1951, the adjoining property south of the church was on the market with canvass of the congregation to provide funds to purchase the property, but the owner refused to sell. As this one hope for a solution to expand suddenly faded, the relocation plan came to the forefront again. At the February 3, 1952, meeting, 75 percent of the congregation favored relocation, asking the committee to return the following week to give a report on the seven different parcels of land it had investigated. In the Voters' Meeting of February 10, an official vote was taken on whether or not to relocate. The relocation was favored 34 to 10. The seven parcels of land were quickly narrowed to two, four acres at Thirteenth and Redwood and a parcel on Grand and Ash, with the congregation voting to purchase the 4-acre vineyard at Thirteenth and Redwood for $11,000 and to proceed immediately with relocation plans.

The first priority of the property was to install streets, sewers, and other utilities and grade the land. After plans were drawn and all the land improvements made, a groundbreaking ceremony was held on November 9, 1952, for the construction of a parish hall with an adequate kitchen and a Sunday school wing. The "modified Spanish" designed building of wood frame construction with steel truss ceilings, concrete floors, and stucco sides was valued at about $80,000. After a year of sweating with members giving 8,500 hours of volunteer labor, the congregation had finished the parish hall containing 8,500 square feet and the Sunday school wing 2,700 square feet. The pews, organ, altar, and other furnishings, along with the church bell, which had been a prominent feature of the Escondido landscape since before the founding of the city in 1889, were all relocated to the new site and placed in the new building. With the building ready for dedication on Sunday, December 6, 1953, the morning service was conducted with Rev. W. G. Gesch of Orange as the guest preacher, and the afternoon service had Rev. Kurt Brink of Logan Heights in San Diego as guest preacher, having all three choirs participating in the services. The next major project was the construction of the parsonage with work begun in August of 1954 and completed the following December 19. This $16,000 home of 3-bedrooms, study, and 2 baths was completed for about $7,000.

In 1955, the property on Grand and Ivy was finally sold for $42,000, helping to reduce the indebtedness of the congregation. However, the congregation was offered the 3-acres of land adjoining the property on Fifteenth Avenue, which they quickly purchased for $10,000, installing curbs and gutters on Thirteenth Street from Quince to Redwood. Since the Sunday school facilities were filled immediately, it was still a major problem providing adequate space for all the children. With this in mind and also wanting to begin a day school, it was resolved in 1956 to build a three-room school building designed by Mr. George Linhardt, a retired architect and member of Grace, which was completed and dedicated in March of 1957.

In 1952, after 19 faithful years of service to Grace, Pastor Jagels' health began to fail. His doctor advised him to spend some time in the desert, away from the humid night air so that his lungs could heal. After two weeks in Borrego Springs brought him relief, he was instructed not to go out in the evening fog. He followed these instructions, which aided his health. With the increasing problems of relocation and the inability to attend evening meetings, the congregation became aware that an assistant pastor was needed, with Rev. John Schlichting becoming an assistant to Pastor Jagels on June 15, 1953. Pastor Schlichting, who entered the ministry in 1908, had resigned from his congregation in Pasadena in 1951 and retired to a turkey ranch, which he gradually converted to a home on Sixteenth Avenue. He assisted the congregation in whatever areas pastoral services were needed, having much success in effecting

Grace relocates, purchasing a 4-acre vineyard at Thirteenth and Redwood for $11,000.

The parish hall of "modified Spanish" design at 13th and Redwood was dedicated on December 6, 1953. (Pacific Southwest District Archives)

The interior of the new church on dedication day, showing the beautiful altar, pulpit, and hymnboard from the old church. (Pacific Southwest District Archives)

Rev. Emil Geistfeld was installed on November 28, 1954, as Grace's third pastor; he remained until 1957. (Pacific Southwest District Archives)

Rev. Arnold G. Kuntz (circa 1972) was installed on June 2, 1957, as pastor of Grace. He later became the District president. (Pacific Southwest District Archives)

transfers, evangelizing in the community, spearheading mission ventures such as the Vacation Bible School, and teaching adult instruction classes.

Since Pastor Jagels had an opportunity to go on a six-week trip to the Holy Land, the congregation granted him a leave of absence, with him embarking on the trip on July 29, 1953. In March of 1954, he made a trip to Warrensburg, Missouri, even though not well himself, to visit his son-in-law, Aris Green, who was extremely ill. While there, Pastor suffered a stroke, which hospitalized him. In June, he submitted his resignation as pastor of Grace effective in September, as he would be 65 and eligible for retirement. Pastor Jagels returned in September, still recuperating from his stroke, sold his home, and moved back to Missouri where he lived until the Lord called him to his heavenly home.

With the congregation still having the services of Pastor Schlichting, they called Rev. Emil Geistfeld of Lewiston, Minnesota, who was installed on November 28, 1954, with the Rev. Kurt Brink of Logan Heights delivering the sermon; the Rite of Installation read by Rev. Roy Gesch, Oceanside, visitor of the San Diego Circuit; and Rev. Schlichting serving as liturgist. Rev. Geistfeld was a graduate of Concordia College, St. Paul, Minnesota, and Concordia Seminary, Springfield, Illinois. He had a rich musical background, having directed the radio choral group of Concordia Seminary, Springfield, Illinois, and having sung with the Minneapolis Opera Company, the Minneapolis Symphony Orchestra, and also with the Twin Cities Walther League Chorus. Mrs. Geistfeld was a registered nurse, a graduate of Bethesda Lutheran Hospital, St. Paul, Minnesota. At the time, the Geistfelds had five children, Vinton, Thomas, Ruth, Theodore, and Luther. When they moved to Escondido, after spending a few weeks living in the Al Kuehl residence, they moved into the newly completed parsonage. Pastor Geistfeld and Pastor Schlichting worked together until Pastor Schlichting resigned in August of 1955. Shortly after his resignation, he saw the need for a church in the community of Ramona and used his talents to start this congregation.

Early in 1957, Pastor Geistfeld's doctors told him that living in Escondido's climate was impairing his health. Feeling that his health could be completely restored, he accepted a call, which returned him to Minnesota. On Sunday, June 2, 1957, Rev. Arnold G. Kuntz was installed with Rev. Herman Mitschke of Our Redeemer Church,

San Diego, the speaker; Rev. Frederic E. Brick of St. Mark's, Encinitas, was liturgist; and Rev. R. G. Gesch, circuit visitor of Immanuel, Oceanside, performed the Rite of Installation. Pastor Kuntz was born in Clintonville, Wisconsin on March 2, 1926, to Arnold and Beata (nee Habenicht) Kuntz, a parochial school teacher and principal. Pastor Kuntz attended Concordia College in Milwaukee and Concordia Seminary in St. Louis. Following his graduation, he was called as associate pastor at Emmaus First Lutheran Church in Alhambra, California. He married Marlene Meyer on August 9, 1953, and their marriage was blessed with two daughters, Terry and Susan.

As Pastor Kuntz assumed his pastoral duties, plans were being made for the opening of a parochial school in the beautiful, functional classrooms and playground facilities that already had been completed on the spacious property at Thirteenth and Redwood streets. Mr. Carl Witt and Mr. Allen Freudenburg were installed as teachers of the new school on August 11, 1957, in a special afternoon worship service. Mr. Witt assumed the responsibilities of principal and teacher of the upper grades; Mr. Freudenburg taught the middle grades and served as choir director; and Mrs. Freudenburg taught primary grades. Mr. Witt formerly taught at Redeemer School in Ontario, and Mr. and Mrs. Freudenburg taught previously in Chester, Illinois. The three modern classrooms had a total enrollment on the opening day of 68. In 1960, Grace School received national attention when Joyce Netzke, Mark Ruhm, Ann Beth Hoffmann, and Paul Bergquam, pupils at the school, were guests on the Art Linkletter television program and received a large globe and a television set for the school. After 2 years, a 4th classroom was opened, allowing 2 grade levels per classroom with the enrollment rising in excess of 90. In order to accommodate the fourth classroom, the society room, attached to the parish hall, was used to serve this purpose on a temporary basis.

In the spring of 1961, Carl Witt accepted a call to Peace congregation in Pico Rivera, California, with Mr. Allen Freudenburg then called as principal. Mr. Freudenburg resigned his office in the 1965–1966 school year in order to pursue his interest in linguistics. After appropriate training at the Summer Institute of Linguistics at the University of Washington, followed by six months of instruction and training in jungle survival in southern Mexico by the Wycliffe Bible Translators, he and his wife and three children made their services available to the Lutheran Bible Translators in New Guinea in 1967. The congregation gave full support to this dedicated family and began supplying more than one-half of their support in 1967.

In the congregation's years of remarkable growth under Pastor Kuntz, he helped the parish to understand the principle of Christian discipleship where each individual was a missionary for Christ seven days a week. As the calendar year of 1960 closed, so also closed the pastorate of Pastor Kuntz at Grace as he had accepted a call to Bethany Church in Long Beach where, under his guidance, that parish also grew. In 1969, he was elected president of the Southern California District, and he served until his retirement in 1985. During that time, he also was the author of a Lenten sermon series, devotions in "Portals of Prayer," and Sunday school materials for Concordia Publishing House.

During the vacancy period, the congregation was served by a number of pastors. In January of 1960, Grace called Rev. F. W. Boettcher of Berkeley, California, but he respectfully declined. After a number of unsuccessful calls, Pastor Boettcher was again called; after accepting it, he was installed on September 24, 1961. Following his graduation from Concordia Seminary, St. Louis, in 1940, he was ordained at Big Falls, Wisconsin, serving congregations in Green Bay, Wisconsin, and Salinas and Berkeley, California. During his tenure, the church continued to grow, reaching 1,000 communicants in 1969. The emphasis was still being placed on personal evangelism as so many individuals came to Escondido with little or no knowledge of salvation through the grace of Jesus Christ.

As the community of Escondido grew, Grace continued to grow under the blessing of God. Once again, the members of Grace had outgrown their facilities. In 1963, a Building Committee was appointed along with a funding committee. After Walter Hagendohm, A.I.A., a Los Angeles architect, was engaged, the promise of a loan of $275,000 was secured from the Church Extension Fund of the Synod. A campaign to gather $35,000 a year was launched under the leadership of Dr. Erwin Kurth of Los Angeles, beginning at Easter 1961 and completed at Easter 1967, that was eminently successful.

The master plan included a 500-seat sanctuary, 3 additional schoolrooms, school office and library facilities, 7 additional Sunday school rooms, and a new church office space. When the

Mr. and Mrs. Allen Freudenburg with their three children were commissioned as Lutheran Bible Translators to New Guinea in 1967. (Pacific Southwest District Archives)

time came to open bids, it became apparent that the entire project could not be completed due to the cost of the project and the amount of money available through the loan from Synod and the accumulated Building Fund. It was decided to build in several phases with Phase I, the sanctuary, to be undertaken immediately and other phases to follow when that was completed. A local contractor, Leonard O. Minor, was the successful bidder on Phase I; volunteer labor was used whenever possible. Following the groundbreaking ceremony on July 31, 1966, 92 pieces of pre-cast concrete, some of which weighed as much as 48 tons, were poured and cured on the site, then lifted by a giant crane, assembled, and welded into place.

The chancel area featured a central altar of Spanish marble, where 40 communicants at a time could be served. A walnut cross with encircling brass rings, suggesting a modern technologically oriented world, was suspended over the altar. Along the east side of the nave designed and constructed by Erwin and Leonard Schroeder, was a garden containing green plants and four fountains symbolizing the four Gospels. Erwin Schroeder, a member of the congregation, designed and constructed the baptismal font. Mounted above the font was a sculpture, done in marble and hammered brass, depicting the descent of the Holy Spirit. John Barlow, a church member and head of the art department of Palomar College, San Marcos, made this sculpture. The Holy Spirit window of leaded glass above the choir loft showed the Spirit of God in the form of a dove with His blessings radiating down upon His church. Above the

Rev. F. W. Boettcher was installed as Grace's pastor on September 24, 1961. (Pacific Southwest District Archives)

top of each sidewall were stained glass windows along with a series of seven windows on each side depicting stories of the Bible from creation to the ultimate glorification portrayed in the Book of Revelation. These windows, as well as others which adorned the stairways to the choir loft, mothers' room, and nursery, were faceted glass set in reinforced concrete fabricated by Roger Darricarrere of Los Angeles. The Conn-Tellers organ consisted of a full Conn electronic concert organ and a four-rank Tellers pipe organ, which could be played independently of each other or together, using the same console. Generous members gave many of the furnishings in the new sanctuary as memorials.

The day, September 10, 1967, finally arrived to dedicate this fine house of worship to the glory of God with more than 1,200 people in attendance. Pastor Boettcher spoke on the theme "A Monument to the Grace of God" with the guest speaker for the afternoon service, the former pastor of the church, Rev. Arnold G. Kuntz, first vice president of the District and pastor of Bethany Church, Long Beach, and the liturgist was Rev. Paul Bergmann, pastor emeritus, of Escondido. On the last Sunday in Advent 1968, the mosaic of "Christ of the Open Hands" by the Carmel artist, Geza St. Galy, the gift of Mrs. Donald Reedy in memory of her husband, was dedicated.

With exhaustion setting in from the work to complete Phase I of the master plan, Grace proceeded to build Phase II in the fall of 1968, constructing a Sunday school unit consisting of five rooms, one of which was large enough to accommodate a day-school class that was formed in September 1969. The additional classroom was a God-send when circumstances forced the opening of another classroom for the day school. Some time later, the third phase of the project — three additional classrooms, a school office, and library — was completed.

By the end of its 50th year, God's grace was evident, as the congregation numbered among its children, churches at Oceanside, Ramona, and Poway, and claimed a grandparent's interest in churches at Vista and Fallbrook. Later, two new mission stations in Escondido, Gloria Dei and Community, would be opened and would grow into large parishes. The $2,500 that once purchased its first house of worship was a weekly "budgeted need," helping to pay salaries of 8 full-time employees, maintain a school for 130 children, and a Sunday school for 400. Their mission contribution, once measured in terms of $22 or $55 per month, was now $1,500 per month, plus $300 for the support of the Freudenburgs. In the congregation's 50th year, the parish decided to add a full-time assistant pastor to the staff to work especially with the youth and give help in all the other ministerial responsibilities, calling the Rev. Darrill D. Sandberg of Palmdale, California, who accepted and was installed two weeks before Easter of 1969. Grace had much for which to be thankful as it concluded its 50th anniversary year.

After Pastor Boettcher accepted the call to Gloria Dei in Escondido, the Rev. Charles W. Keturakat was called as Grace's new pastor in 1978. He was born in the parsonage of Rev. and Mrs. William Keturakat and was raised in Wisconsin, coming from a line of pastors. His grandfather, Rev. David Keturakat, served parishes in Russia and later in Lithuania. After graduating from the

The exterior of Grace as it looked in 2004 with the remodeled exterior.

The chancel in 2004 with the mosaic of "Christ of the Open Hands" and pipe organ.

Lutheran Seminary at Thiensville, Wisconsin, on June 10, 1947, he married his wife, Ruth, on August 24, 1947, with their union blessed with three children, Carla, Charlie, and Kathy. His ministry began in St. Paul's in Oklahoma, which led him to Christ Lutheran in Perry, Oklahoma, in 1952, later moving to St. Paul's in San Antonio, Texas, in 1958. He came to California in 1964, serving St. Luke's in Santa Rosa followed by his call to Grace in 1978 where he retired in 1988. In his retirement, he received a Doctor of Theology degree and served as interim pastor of the new mission, Community Lutheran Church, established by Grace until the first pastor, Rev. William Vogelsang Jr. was called in 1988. He was also involved in Pathway Ministries, an organization devoted to helping congregations in establishing fund-raising programs for the building and construction of Lutheran churches and schools.

In 1986, the Rev. James P. Young was installed as the associate pastor of Grace. He was well known to the congregation as he served his vicarage there in 1979–1980. He was born in Los Angeles on April 15,1946, attended Los Angeles Lutheran High School, where he was captain of the football, basketball, and baseball teams and received numerous athletic honors. Following high school, he attended Concordia Teachers College, Seward, Nebraska, where he played football and baseball, graduating in 1968 with a Bachelor of Science degree in education. Afterward, he served as a graduate assistant in physical education at Seward while earning his master's degree in physical education from the University of Nebraska. In 1969, he was called to teach and coach football and baseball at Los Angeles Lutheran High. During his teaching career, the Lord began to redirect his life toward the ministry. Following his graduation from Concordia Seminary in Fort Wayne, Indiana, he was called in 1980 to St. Matthew Lutheran Church in Harbor City, California, where he served until the spring of 1986. He married Betty Maier in 1966 with their marriage blessed with two children, Cari and Tim. Mrs. Young received her Bachelor of Science degree in education from Concordia Teachers College, Seward.

In 1989, Rev. Young was installed as the new pastor of Grace. Through his leadership and vision, a five-year expansion plan was formulated and adopted by the congregation. Phase I was a total renovation of the sanctuary, two multi-purpose rooms, restrooms, two modular classrooms, and a total "face-lift" of all the existing buildings

and property. The outdoor area, The Grove, was enhanced with a gas grill, sound system, and landscaping, and a dedication celebration was held on November 3, 1991.

Since the area surrounding the church was changing, Grace tried to educate the congregation to advance the need for a Spanish ministry. On October 20, 1991, Rev. Ken Behnken, administrative assistant to the president, missions, gave the sermon at 8:00 a.m. and 11:00 a.m. as well as taught the 9:30 Bible class to bring the congregation a step closer to Hispanic ministry. Also in October, a Spanish class was given for the congregation, not only to teach Spanish but also to incorporate the social and physical aspects of the Hispanic culture. Later in the year, a Saturday morning workshop was conducted with several speakers discussing Hispanic ministry. Special meetings were planned with the purpose of discussing the importance of a Hispanic missionary program. In the May 1992 Voters' Meeting, a plan was presented for the approval of the congregation.

By 1996, Grace had experienced a demographic change where there were approximately 14,000 Hispanics living within a 3-mile radius of the church. Area studies revealed that a great number of the people had no formal religion or just did not attend church regularly, with less than .05 percent attending church. Since the spiritual needs of these people were urgent, Grace decided to open Misión Hispana Gracia on March 24, 1996, marking the beginning of an extensive effort to reach out to the rapidly growing Hispanic population in Escondido with Samuel Gómez called to develop a Hispanic ministry in the Escondido area where he was a lay pastor conducting Spanish services. He was born on September 29, 1969, in Mexico City and received his bachelor's degree in communications in 1994 from Universidad Autonoma Metropolitana, Mexico (Metropolitan University of Mexico). In 2000, he completed the Hispanic Institute of Theology program from Concordia Seminary Saint Louis, Missouri, and he received his master's degree in theology and culture from Concordia University Irvine in 2002. He took classes at Oblate Seminary, San Antonio, and Universidad Interamericana de Puerto Rico for a further degree. He was a member of the Hispanic Task Force of the North American Mission Board of the LCMS from 1997–2003. In 1998, he was assigned as vicar at Grace Lutheran Church until he accepted the call to be associate pastor. His wife, Damaris, attended National University

Rev. Charles W. Keturakat became Grace's new pastor in 1978 and retired in 1989 after 41 years in the ministry. (Pacific Southwest District Archives)

Rev. James P. Young was installed in 1986 as the associate pastor of Grace, becoming senior pastor in 1989. (Pacific Southwest District Archives)

Grace opens Misión Hispaña Gracia on March 24, 1996,

Pastor Samuel Gómez came to Grace to begin a Hispanic ministry in 1996.

By September 2002, Misión Hispaña Gracia's average attendance at worship services is 83.

in Mexico City.

Pastor Gómez conducted the Spanish services in 1996, when attendance ranged from 25 to 30. On Sunday, June 15, 25 people were in attendance; about half of them were children who were taken to another room for Bible study by his wife, Damaris Gómez. They conducted a home Bible study on Tuesdays and Thursdays; on Saturday mornings, Damaris conducted a children's program of art and Bible study; Sunday at 11:00 a.m. was the Spanish worship that also coincided with the English service which was very intimidating to the Spanish-speaking visitor who had to work his way through crowds of English-speaking people. Because of this, the schedule was reviewed.

On 3 Sundays in February of 1997, 72 people were in attendance, giving opportunities to share the message of Jesus Christ. At the time, there were 4 groups in the Sunday school with 12 adults enrolled in 3 Bible studies during the week. The mission had an average church attendance of 50 with 30 children in the Saturday school and Sunday school. In March, the mission received a $10,000 grant from the Lutheran Brotherhood Foundation with the grant used to help support the Hispanic ministry along with the Pacific Southwest District's support of $9,600 for the year, and for the first time, the Hispanic ministry was a line item of $12,000 in Grace's budget. On May 4, 1997, the Hispanic mission celebrated its first anniversary, celebrating the reception of 4 new members and one Baptism with the attendance close to 50 people. Also, the worship service time was changed to 12:30 p.m. with membership class at 10:00 a.m. and Sunday school at 11:00 a.m. The mission now had 43 people, representing 15 families, 16 adults and 25 children. Bible study was conducted on Wednesday and Friday evenings at 7:00 p.m. with the children's choir practice and Confirmation class at 10:00 a.m. on Saturdays. One dedicated family, who lived in San Diego and attended Grace for almost a year, went every Sunday to Bible study and to the worship service.

When the mission celebrated its third anniversary in 1999, the Sunday school consisted of four groups — adults, teens, and two children's groups, age three to five years and age six to nine — meeting in Grace's Fireside Room for an opening at 9:30 a.m. and from there, each group went to its designated areas. The youth group of between 12 and 13 teenagers met every Saturday, having a short Bible talk and socialized. They were also in charge of the worship service on the last Sunday of every month.

During the 4th anniversary of the Hispanic ministry, membership had grown to 25 with 12 Baptisms, 17 Confirmations, and an average of 40 at worship services. The Love Escondido Evangelistic Campaign took place during the summer. This was an outreach to the Hispanic community of Escondido. Its goal was to share the Gospel of Jesus Christ with 50 Hispanic families in the area through the distribution of the Jesus film during summer. During the year, the high school ministry combined the Hispanic and the English high school ministries in an outreach to Enseñada, Mexico, with the two youth groups traveling to Enseñada three times that year.

On September 22–24, 2000, both youth groups combined efforts to take the Word of God to a non-denominational congregation in Enseñada. Pilar Garcia, one of the high school translators, had an opportunity to experience the power of God's Word. Following the service, the youth group showed the Spanish version of the "Jesus" video on a borrowed white sheet nailed to a 2' x 12' rafter in the church; the Word of God was never more profound than that night. An audience of 30–35 people sat together as the story of the Savior unfolded where the Holy Spirit reached out and touched two unbelievers. On Sunday, October 24, there was a joyous celebration as there was one Baptism, 26 First Communions, and 6 Confirmations. By the end of the year, church attendance had risen to 52 and the ministry was being extended to Zion in Fallbrook.

The year 2002 proved to be a year of bountiful blessing for Misión Hispaña Gracia as the Ash Wednesday service had 120 people in attendance. As the ministry grew, it was necessary to have a youth leader to work with the 16–20 teenagers and college students. A secretary was also needed to send reports and cards and to do the bulletins and other publications. By September, the average attendance at worship services was 83. At the time, Pastor Samuel Gómez, was completing his ordination certification through Concordia Seminary, St. Louis. During the year, 11 people were baptized and 24 were confirmed with 17 children participating in First Communion. The Sunday school was taught by Alma Salaiza and Jazmin Salaiza with Pastor teaching the adults where there were 38 people attending Sunday school. Larry Dee was the organist on Sundays with Karen Gibelman assisting in the services.

Pastor Gómez with the First Communion and Confirmation classes on Reformation Sunday 2003.

Once a month, Pastor Gabriel Ochoa from Saint James Lutheran Church in Imperial Beach and Pastor Gómez would exchange pulpits, giving the members an opportunity to hear a different person preach. Pastor Ochoa's son, Gabriel Ochoa Jr., also helped once a month, accompanying the congregational singing on the piano and was the song leader. Pastor Jesús Lopez, who was continuing the Hispanic ministry at Zion in Fallbrook, directed the liturgy and sermons on special occasions.

Pastors are called upon to do many things in their ministry, but few are called to rescue a person from a burning building. On November 17, 2002, as Pastor Patrick Miller, the 30-year-old associate pastor of Grace, and Pastor Jim Young completed the third service that morning, they noticed a dark cloud of smoke billowing from the Greencrest Mobile Home Park near the church. After quickly driving to the park, they discovered a man with a garden hose trying to extinguish the fire. As the pastors began warning people in other mobile homes, a woman was yelling in Spanish and pointing to the burning mobile home that a woman was trapped in a wheelchair inside. Pastor Miller raced into action, running through the intense smoke in the mobile home. He rescued the 88-year-old invalid by scooping her up, as her caregiver could not pick her up, and carrying her out. Pastor Young and the women followed and saved the lady's wheelchair.

Pastor Miller said, "We were in the right place at the right time. It was like one of those heroic scenes from a movie. I'm wearing my clerical collar

and running out of the house through the flames and smoke with a lady in my arms. You don't have time to really think." When looking back, Pastor Miller suggested that going into the house may not have been the smartest thing he ever did, but he was glad he was in the position to do it. For his act of heroism, the American Red Cross honored him at a breakfast on May 1, 2003, along with four other San Diego North County heroes.

On August 3, 2003, a 11 piece Mariachi band played in all the English services and the Spanish service that day. On September 14, the 12:15 p.m. Spanish service was changed to 11:45 a.m., and that fall an ESL class was begun with over 20 people enrolled, meeting on Tuesday, and Thursday evenings from 7:00 p.m. to 9:00 p.m. On Sunday, October 12, at 3 p.m., Pastor Gómez was ordained and installed as associate pastor and liaison to Hispanic ministry at Grace. This was not the first ordination at Grace. In the 1990s, Grace also ordained the following from among their midst: Rev. Allen Freudenburg in 1991, Rev. Howard Barth in 1995, Rev. Dennis Schmelzer in 1995, Rev. Herb Keistman in June 1996, Rev. Wiley Smith in June 1996, and Rev. David Floyd in May 1998. This mission-minded congregation also sent and supported the following missionaries in the mission field: the Allen Freudenburg family, the Frank Fitzgerald family, the Clint Souligny family, the Dean Nicks family, and the Glenn Fluegge family. The congregation's mission zeal continues as it reaches into the Hispanic neighborhood surrounding Grace.

On August 3, 2003, a 14-piece Mariachi band plays in all the English services and the Spanish services.

Zion Lutheran Church
Zion Hispanic Church
Fallbrook, California

The community of Fallbrook, a quiet, hidden little gem nestled among the hills of Southern California, is in the northernmost corner of San Diego County about 15 miles due east of the Pacific Ocean, bordered on the west by Camp Pendleton Marine Corp Base, and a short drive east to Interstate 15, providing easy access to Los Angeles, San Diego and Orange and Riverside counties. As an unincorporated part of San Diego County, the community, having a population of 29,100 with 57.3 percent Anglo and 37.3 Hispanic, is administered by the County Board of Supervisors.

Fallbrook began in the area that is known today as Live Oak County Park, three miles east of the present-day town, with the first permanent recorded settlement in 1869, when Antonio and Charles Vital Reche and C. F. Fox settled in the area naming the new community Fall Brook after their former Pennsylvania homestead. They wandered across a rolling mesa between the San Luis and the Santa Margarita River canyons finding the country good for agriculture. Cold air drains off of the mesa into the low riverbeds, leaving the fertile table free of frost. The present town site was plotted in 1885, with one of the community's churches constructed in 1890 still in use today. Main Street has preserved a turn-of-the-century charm with many of the commercial buildings dating back to the late 1800s. The original Fallbrook School,

closed in 1939, still serves the community as the Reche Clubhouse.

Oak trees were the original primary trees in Fallbrook with olives becoming a major crop by the 1920s and continuing through World War II, eventually phased out in favor of the present avocado and floral industry. A favorable year-round climate is one of the most valuable assets of Fallbrook having pleasant summers and mild winters at elevations between 500 and 1,500 feet, with an average around 685 feet. The area enjoys an annual rainfall of roughly 16 inches, which comes mostly between November and April, making it ideal for avocados, fruits, strawberries, tomatoes, many sub-tropical fruits, vegetables, and flowers. Since Fallbrook's primary business is agriculture, she is known as the Avocado Capital of the World, having been a primary avocado growing area since the fruit was first planted locally in 1912, with annual revenues from avocados reaching approximately $26 million, earned mostly on small groves of 2- to 10-acres.

Into this rolling rural countryside came a number of loyal Lutheran families, who, through the request of Mrs. E. Cooper in 1948 that Lutheran services be conducted in Fallbrook, received worship services. In early 1948, Rev. William Duerr of Santa Ana (a member of the Mission Board) went to an evening meeting at the Herbert Mann home in Fallbrook to discuss the feasibility of beginning services in Fallbrook with interested Lutherans. The first service was conducted for 32 people in the Fallbrook Methodist Church on April 25, 1948, at 7:30 p.m. by Rev. A. C. Young of the Corona and Elsinore Mission. The first infant, little Jeannie Louise Bohn, daughter of Mr. and Mrs. Sidney Bohn, was baptized that evening. Pastor Young also preached the first sermon on "The Good Shepherd." After 8 months of activity, the group numbered 27 souls, 14 communicants and 12 families, with a Sunday school of 6 and an average church attendance of 16. Upon the request made by Pastor Young, the work was taken over by the Southern California District Mission Board, with Rev. Luther Schwartzkopf, pastor of Immanuel, Oceanside, placed in charge of assisting this very faithful nucleus of families with services conducted for 16 to 25 people on the second and fourth

Main Street in Fallbrook as it looked around the turn of the twentieth century.

Sundays of the month at 7:30 p.m. in the Methodist Church. He conducted his first service on June 6, 1948, one week after being installed as pastor of Immanuel, also providing adult instruction and Catechism classes for children. On November 7, 1948, services were moved to the recreation room in the Community Building of the Federal Housing Project beginning at 9:15 a. m. followed by a move to Berry-Bell Mortuary Chapel, and then the change was made to evening services in the old Episcopal Church. By the end of 1949, church attendance had dwindled to 10 and the Sunday school dropped as a number of members moved to Twenty-nine Palms.

In 1950 when Pastor Schwartzkopf took a call to Trinity, San Bernardino, the services were suspended. According to reports at the time, the mission had a potential of 27 souls, 14 communicants, 12 families, and 10 children enrolled in Sunday school with the project self-supporting. From December 3, 1950, through May of 1952, Mrs. Theodora L. (Felix) Garnsey corresponded with Rev. Roy Gesch of Immanuel in Oceanside, listing the members who were previously active in Fallbrook. In May of 1952, she wrote that they had received 32.5 inches of rain in their valley.

On September 12, 1954, the Rev. Martin W. Lankow arrived as the first resident pastor in Fallbrook, beginning his work on Sunday, September 19, 1954, preaching his first Sunday morning sermon, "Co-workers with Christ" in the Seventh-day Adventist Church at 10:45 a.m. where three Sunday school sessions were held at 9:30 a.m. This lovely little church with three separate Sunday school rooms was rented for $10 per month, with the rent doubling to $20 in the winter season, which began the first of November. Pastor Lankow had received 20 of *The Lutheran Hymnal* from Pastor Gesch of which 15 belonged to the mission and 5 were a gift from Pastor Gesch. He had come from Bethany Lutheran in San Diego where he organized the church and the school in 1937, serving as its first resident pastor. His arrival in Fallbrook was heralded with thanksgiving by the group, which had conducted the Lutheran Sunday school in the Seventh-day Adventist Church for some time.

Pastor Lankow was born in the parsonage of Rev. and Mrs. (Martha Reitze) William J. Lankow

Rev. Martin W. Lankow arrived in Fallbrook on September 12, 1954, to serve as Zion's first resident pastor. (Pacific Southwest District Archives)

in Tacoma, Washington, on October 31, 1903. He graduated from California Concordia College, Oakland, in 1924 and Concordia Theological Seminary of St. Louis, Missouri, in 1927. His first congregation was Grace Lutheran Church, Lancaster, California, where he also established preaching stations in Bishop, Brown, and the Randsburg District, and served as Lutheran chaplain at the Institute for Women at Tehachapi. He did extensive traveling throughout the Pacific Coast states on behalf of the International Lutheran Hour, which was heard in 56 languages and over 1,150 radio stations. He married Thelma Edith Johnson in May of 1931 and was blessed with two daughters, Donna and Martha, who were enrolled in Fallbrook High School as senior and junior students.

At the close of December 31, 1955, the Fallbrook mission numbered 65 baptized members, 31 communicants with 35 in Sunday school and a staff of 6. During Pastor Lankow's pastorate from September 1954 until January 31, 1956, 7 children were baptized and 8 adults received Baptism or Confirmation. At the end of January of 1956, Pastor Lankow announced his acceptance of a call to serve Zion Lutheran Church of Cornelius, Oregon. The Mission Board arranged for Rev. Carlton Kjergaard, who had been stationed in Perris, to serve the two fields as one parish. Pastor Kjergaard preached his first sermon on February 5, 1956, while Pastor Lankow preached his farewell sermon on January 29, 1956, with 58 in attendance. At the 22d of January Family Night potluck dinner at the Reche Club, Pastor Lankow introduced Pastor Kjergaard to the members of the Fallbrook Lutheran Mission. Rev. Carlton Kjergaard, vacancy pastor for over six months, served only on Sunday and Thursday each week with the church showing little growth. Four acres of land were purchased February 1956 at a cost of $14,000. Formal organization of the congregation took place in December of 1958 with 52 charter members. The church numbered 50 communicants, 11 voters, and 83 baptized members.

In June of 1959, Rev. Roy Gesch of Oceanside began to serve Zion as vacancy pastor conducting Sunday evening services. After several unsuccessful attempts to call a pastor, Candidate Thomas Dudley was placed by the Mission Board to serve

Formal organization of Zion takes place in December of 1958 with 50 communicants, 11 voters, and 83 baptized members.

Rev. Thomas Dudley was commissioned in a special service at Zion on June 26, 1960 as missionary-at-large to serve the Fallbrook–Vista field. (Pacific Southwest District Archives)

as resident pastor in June of 1960. In a special service at Zion on Sunday, June 26, at 6:00 p.m., he was ordained into the Lutheran ministry and commissioned as missionary-at-large of the Southern California District to serve the Fallbrook-Vista field; the preacher for the ordination was Arnold G. Kuntz of Escondido with Circuit Counselor Roy G. Gesch of Oceanside performing the Rite of Ordination and commissioning. Rev. Richard Z. Meyer of San Diego was liturgist with Rev. Luther P. Steiner of Perris assisting.

Pastor Dudley, a 1960 graduate of Concordia Seminary, Springfield, Illinois, came from Detroit, Michigan, after preparatory training at Concordia College of Fort Wayne, Indiana. After several years in the military service and private business, he finished his ministerial studies at the Springfield seminary. While he was at Fort Wayne, he met Charlene Desmonds, his future wife. At the time of his ordination, their marriage was blessed with three children, Dawn, Thomas, and Nathan. With his commissioning, morning services were now possible at Fallbrook with the establishment of a mission in Vista. Worship services were held each Sunday at Vista at 8:00 a. m. in the Women's Club Building, and at Fallbrook at 11:00 a.m. at the Seventh-day Adventist church building. Zion grew to 88 baptized members, 55 communicant members, 17 voting members, and had a Sunday school enrollment of 92 in 1961 with the congrega-

tion owning a church site plus a parsonage.

Groundbreaking services for Zion's first building were held in July of 1961. The church and adjoining parish hall were completed and dedicated in 1962, with Rev. Schwartzkopf giving the dedicatory sermon. During succeeding years, several additional parcels of land were added, with the property expanding close to five acres. Also in 1962, Rev. Dudley was called by the congregation as the permanent pastor. By 1967, Zion had 234 baptized members, and 147 communicant members with a Sunday school of 129 children. Many military families had left as the war in Vietnam had intensified, but many retired people were moving into the community to fill the void.

After a division in the congregation, Rev. Dudley left in 1971 with Pastor Beryl Droegemueller of Faith, Vista, leading the parish from November 1971 until April 1972 in Sunday worship in addition to 2 services at his own church. During this period, the membership showed a decrease to 106 communicates with 136 baptized souls having an average attendance of 84 at worship. Rev. Jerome Rossow accepted a call to Fallbrook and was installed on April 23, 1972, serving the congregation until August 1, 1976, when he received a call to Kenesaw, Nebraska. When Pastor Rossow left, the parish had grown to 167 communicates with 214 baptized members and a weekly attendance of 116. The vacancy from August 1, 1976, through May 1978 was filled with a retired Navy Chaplain Herbert C. Albrecht, Ph. D. The Rev. Richard Onnan then served the congregation until the installation of Rev. Mark C. Behring of San Jose on September 24, 1978, who served the congregation until June 1, 1989.

Zion marked its 25th anniversary with a celebration on October 7, 1979 at a 3:00 p.m. service. Guest speaker for the occasion was Rev. Roy G. Gesch, executive director of the Lutheran Bible Translators, who had served as a visiting pastor early in Zion's history. Also participating in the service were lector, Rev. Luther Schwartzkopf, another early visiting pastor, who was director of Arrowhead Lutheran Camp, and the present pastor, Rev. Mark G. Behring, was the liturgist. The anniversary service included the dedication of the recently completed renovation of the church's interior, as well as a large office addition. The focal point of the renovation program was the beautiful, large stained glass window over the altar which incorporated a gold-colored cross in the center, donated by Mrs. Rosetta in honor of her husband.

The interior of the church in 1962 when it was dedicated. (Pacific Southwest District Archives)

In 1979, Mrs. Ken Moeser, publicity chairman for Zion, stated, "Fallbrook was just a little friendly village when Zion was first organized and until 1977 remained just that. Zion's membership, accordingly, showed only a slow growth in the early years. Even today Fallbrook is an unincorporated area, reluctant to change, and rather unwilling to accept the increase in its population. But people are moving in, and Zion church recognizes the challenge presented by these larger numbers. Already the congregation is working on a master plan and thinking in terms of a larger church and the possibility of a Christian day school. For this opportunity and privilege we praise the Lord." The dream of having a Christian day school in 1979 became a reality in 1984 when Zion's new educational building was dedicated with Ms. Kris Dickerson beginning her duties as the first principal of the school, having an enrollment of 21 students that fall. In 1985, the school grew to 135 students. In the following year, a preschool was added with the school having an enrollment of 137 and a new principal, Mr. Chris Baxter. In 1987, Mr. Tim Timm became the new principal of the school, which had 141 students increasing to 240 students in 1989. The preschool through grade 8 enrollment peaked in 1999 at 380 students.

During the 1980s the congregation experience a marked growth not only in membership but also in spiritual growth. The congregation grew from 159 communicates, 205 baptized members with an average attendance of 97 to a peak at 424 communicant members, 617 baptized souls and an average attendance of 252 per Sunday. In order to accommodate this growth with ministries to the youth, evangelism, and education, the parish decided to enter the vicarage program in 1980 with Gary Frost arriving that summer for a one-year internship. Carl Carlson, Joe Judge, Chuck Deckert, and Gary Rohwer succeeded him. Even though the vicarage program was a success, it was decided that a full-time church worker would give more continuity to the program with Mr. Steve Hayes, a certificated lay minister, hired in 1986 to work full-time with youth, evangelism, and education, resigning in late 1988. While trying to replace him, Rev. Behring accepted a call to Lake Worth, Florida, with Dr. Elmer Mathias serving as interim pastor and was assisted by Rev. Herman Mueller, a retired pastor and a member at Zion. Rev. Charles Deckert of El Cajon accepted the call to serve as pastor of Zion and was installed on December 17, 1989.

Zion continued to grow, becoming one of the fastest growing church/school combinations in the Pacific Southwest District with addition of many families from the community through the day-school ministry. To accommodate the growing school enrollment, the preschool was relocated in 1990 to its own location in rented quarters at 203 Laurine Lane. Upon completion of Zion's new Fellowship Center in March of 2004, the preschool was moved back to the main campus. In order to meet the needs of the growing congregation, the pastoral staff was increased, with Mr. Gregg McCaslin serving as director of Christian education from July 1990 to September 1994 when he accepted a call to Plano, Texas. Mr. Steve Hayes returned as lay minister in May 1991 to April 1996, where he served in the areas of administration, worship, and evangelism.

On August 25, 1996, Zion celebrated two milestones: the installation of Steve Mattoon as minister of youth and education and the 50th anniversary of Zion's assisting minister, Pastor Herman Mueller, as an ordained minister in The Lutheran Church — Missouri Synod. On behalf of the congregation, Zion's president, Peter Bardeen, and Pastor Chuck Deckert, presented Rev. Mueller with a plaque honoring him for his service to the church-at-large. He began his career in 1946 as a mission developer of young churches at Bethel Lutheran Church in Sweet Home, Oregon, where he was instrumental in building a small parish hall and helped build the parsonage—literally, as local sawmill workers and loggers set up a min-

Rev. Mark C. Behring was installed as pastor of Zion on September 24, 1978, serving the congregation until June 1, 1989. (Pacific Southwest District Archives)

The renovated church during Christmas of 2001 with the large stained glass window over the altar. (Pacific Southwest District Archives)

iature "cutoff" to transform logs into lumber for both buildings. During his service to the church, he and his wife, Dicie, had served many western parishes in Washington, Oregon, Idaho, Arizona, and California.

Prior to his arrival in Fallbrook, Mr. Mattoon, a 1988 graduate of Christ College Irvine who returned to pursue the director of Christian education degree from Concordia University, served for two years as a called director of Christian education at Shepherd of Peace Lutheran Church, Irvine, the same congregation where he served his internship year. From 1984 to 1992, Mr. Mattoon, who was raised in Mission Viejo, toured Uganda, Austria, and Italy with Vanguard Ministries, a Christian semi-professional soccer team with an international ministry. He and his wife, Janette, also a graduate of Christ College Irvine who worked as a Christian educator, had a 2-year-old son, Joshua at the time. In October of 2000, he accepted a call to serve as Interim Youth Director at Christ, Costa Mesa.

The congregation sadly accepted the resignation, for personal reasons, of Pastor Deckert in October of 1997. Zion's vacancy was served by Rev. Allen Rudow for 11 months who had retired 8 months before from Church of Joy in Chula

Zion's spiritual leaders in 1991 were Rev. Deckert (left), Mr. Steve Mattoon (center), and Rev. Mueller. (Pacific Southwest District Archives)

Vista. Chaplain Warren Neagele, who introduced Telecare Ministry to Zion, followed him for four months. On March 21, 1999, Rev. Mark Demel of Bethlehem Church, Carson City, Nevada, was installed as pastor of Zion. The preacher was Vicar Erik Herrmann of Bethlehem, Carson City, with Chaplain Mark Steiner serving as liturgist. Rev. William Vogelsang, pastor of Community Lutheran Church, Escondido and circuit counselor, was officiant, and Steve Mattoon of Zion; Rev. Fred Page III, of Immanuel, West Covina; and Rev. Paul Miller of Desert Hot Springs, as lectors.

Pastor Demel was born on June 14, 1955, in Pomona, California, one of five children of Bill and Elaine Demel. He attended various public elementary schools, graduating from Covina High School in 1973. He received an Associate of Arts degree from Mt. San Antonio College, Walnut, California, and a Bachelor of Arts degree from California State Polytechnic University, Pomona, California. He was united in marriage to Cathy Jo Clarke on December 11, 1976, at Immanuel First Lutheran, in West Covina. Two years before in November of 1974, he met Cathy through the circuit youth group called "Ongoing Ambassadors for Christ." The Lord blessed their marriage with four daughters, Jennifer, Rebecca, Erica, and Melody.

In May of 1978, Pastor entered Concordia Theological Seminary, Fort Wayne, Indiana, graduating on May 28, 1982, with a Master of Divinity degree. During his vicarage year, he served at Peace Lutheran Church, Arvada, Colorado. Upon graduating from seminary, Mark accepted the call to serve as pastor of St. Peter's Lutheran Church, Davenport, Nebraska, and was installed on July 18, 1982. He served there until accepting the call to serve as pastor of Bethlehem Lutheran Church, Carson City, Nevada, where he was installed on October 25, 1987.

With Mr. Mattoon's departure in October of 2000, Mrs. Elisa Dufresne was hired as an interim youth director. In May 2001, the voters decided to hire her as full-time youth director. Elisa's husband, Scott, was Zion School's assistant principal. Also in 2001, with the approval of the Church Council and elders, the church applied for a vicar through the LCMS Seminary Program, receiving Vicar Aaron Pingel and his wife, Kara, on August 15, 2001, to serve his one-year vicarage at Zion. In July of 2002, Mr. Timm relinquished the office of school principal, becoming the director of facilities and development with Mr. Scott Dufresne becoming Zion's principal. The long anticipated

Rev. Mark Demel is installed as pastor of Zion on March 21, 1999.

Vicar Gómez (right) and Pastor Demel (center) with fourteen children who received their First Communion at Zion on Reformation Sunday of 2002.

construction of a 20,000 square foot multi-purpose building, housing a parish hall/gymnasium, upper-grade classrooms, a large kitchen, locker room, and other rooms was begun. One unique feature of the building was 200 solar panels on the roof that were to provide the electrical needs of the structure. On August 10, 2003, Zion installed Vicar David Bergelin, a St. Louis seminarian, for his one-year vicarage. Amid much joy, the large fellowship center and educational wing was dedicated on Sunday, February 29, 2004, at 3:00 p.m. with the school youth choir, handbell choir, and adult choir participation in this joyous occasion with the hall filled to capacity to hear Pastor Demel give the dedication message with Vicar David Bergelin serving as liturgist. Following the service, the ladies served hors d'oeuvres and cake to all who attended. The Lord had blessed the congregation in 2003 with 644 baptized members, 561 communicant members, having an average church attendance of 331.

Seeing a need to do mission work among the Hispanic population in Fallbrook, Dr. Phil Roberts and some other men at Zion asked Vicar Samuel Gómez of Grace, Escondido, to work with them, thus beginning Spanish outreach at Zion in the fall of 2001 in the area. Vicar Gómez went to Zion on Sunday mornings to teach a Sunday school class in Spanish with the ministry involving 10 to 15 children. The congregation supported the ministry both financially and physically by helping in the work.

During this time, Pastor Jesús Lopez from Tijuana also came to help Vicar Gómez for about nine months. Rev. Esaúl Salomón brought him into the Lutheran church, as he had served in the ministry of Church of God in Tijuana. He came to the United States when his one-and-one-half-year-old daughter had health problems and needed heart surgery. Through the help of pastors Ochoa and Gómez, she found needed help.

For a while, the parish transported Hispanic children to Grace in the church van each Sunday to be instructed by Vicar Gómez. Through instruction in Lutheran doctrine, 14 children took their First Communion at Zion on Reformation Sunday of 2002. Vicar Gómez continued having a Spanish Sunday school class where some of the parents of the children also attended. He conducted a few Spanish worship services. After the vicar was ordained and installed as an assistant pastor at Grace, his schedule didn't permit him to continue his work at Zion on a regular basis. With Pastor Gómez able to teach the children at Zion only on one Sunday every couple of months, Dr. Roberts, Ray Runkel, and Tim Kressin transported the children to Sunday school at Zion each Sunday. The ministry hasn't grown much beyond the children who were gained in 2002. The children are now integrated into the regular English Sunday school classes. Dr. Roberts and other people from Zion continue to work in this ministry to share Christ with their Hispanic neighbors.

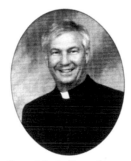

Rev. Mark Demel was installed as pastor of Zion on March 21, 1999. (Pacific Southwest District Archives)

Zion asks Vicar Samuel Gómez to work with them, thus beginning a Spanish outreach in the fall of 2001.

**Let the vineyards be fruitful, Lord,
And fill to the brim our cup of blessing.
Gather a harvest from the seeds that were sown
That we may be fed with the bread of life.**

Land of the Sun

Trinity Lutheran Church
Indio, California

"...And the desert shall rejoice, and blossom as the rose."

— ISAIAH 35:1

 Indio, located within the Colorado Desert, surrounded by the San Jacinto Mountains to the east, the Santa Rosa Mountains to the south, and at the eastern end of the Coachella Valley, began as an Indian village where Native Americans found palm oases along the San Andreas Fault zone in the Indio Hills with the Whitewater River flowing through the Valley to ancient lakes that attracted native settlers. In the late 1700s, Spanish and Mexican exploratory and military expeditions traveled through the Coachella Valley on their way from Sonora in Mexico to Los Angeles. American miners and settlers also passed through the area using the San Gorgonio Pass for access to their California destinations. The arrival of the Spanish in 1819 in Cahuilla territory brought several mission outposts. In general, the Spanish, Mexican, and early American presence did not greatly affect the Native American Cahuilla society, which was estimated to have a population of 6,000–10,000, but the Cahuilla did develop economic and political strategies to deal with Hispanic immigrants by taking the form of confederations of clans.

The earliest U.S. Government surveys of the area, which located township and section boundaries, date to 1855–1856. Cahuilla outnumbered Euro-Americans, but the smallpox epidemic of 1863 and continued immigration would change that. Epidemics and possession of Indian land by new settlers led to the creation of Indian reservations by 1877 which included Agua Caliente, the Augustine Reservation, the Torres-Martinez, and the Cabazon Band of Mission Indians. Lieutenant Robert Williamson of the U.S.

Topographic Engineers explored the region for the Southern Pacific Railroad in 1853, surveying it as the halfway point between Yuma and Los Angeles in 1872. The area was chosen as a suitable location for a railroad depot since Indian reservations were near, supplying construction labor with crew houses, a siding, and building a roundhouse. In 1876, trains began running from Los Angeles to Indio, with the route to Yuma completed in 1877. Originally called Indian Wells, the name was changed in 1877 to Indio, the Spanish word for Indian, to avoid confusion with other locations.

In 1888, a formal survey was made for the Indio town site with a map filed with the San Diego County Recorder. In 1893 as part of the newly designated Riverside County, Indio became one of the 12 townships having had 50 inhabitants by 1896. In 1890, the United States Department of Agriculture (USDA) sent date palms from Algeria to the region with the USDA establishing a date experiment station near Mecca in 1904. By 1909, the Indio school census indicated the school district had 43 families with 82 children. In 1914, the Southern Sierras Power Company completed an electric power line to the Coachella Valley to provide power needed to pump water because artesian wells ceased functioning as the water well levels had dropped. The Coachella Valley Water District (CVWD) was formed in 1917 to find water sources for the valley, which eventually led to construction of the All-American Canal, completed in 1948, bringing Colorado River water to the valley. Construction of the All American Canal allowed expansion and growth of the agricultural industry, which then brought retail, service, and processing and packing facilities to Indio. Additionally, an underground distribution system was built to irrigate the agricultural lands. In 1915, CVWD also began the construction of a four-mile levee around Indio to divert the Whitewater River to protect the city from flooding.

With a population of 1,875, Indio was incorporated as a city in 1930, becoming the Coachella Valley's first city. After Highway 99 was completed in 1923 and Highway 60-70, which eventually became Interstate 10, was completed in 1936, the highways brought travelers and continued growth of service industries. Indio's population grew from 5,300 in 1950 to 13,450 in 1964. Today, Indio has a population of 49,800 with 75.4 percent Hispanic. Indio is the geographic mid-point of both Riverside County and the Coachella Valley that is 50 miles long running from Palm Springs to the Salton Sea, and Indio is also known as both a desert resort and a major agricultural area. The city is about 75 miles north of the California-Baja California Mexican border, 125 miles east of the center of the metropolitan center of Los Angeles, and 15 miles east of Palm Springs. It is the halfway point for Southern Californians who make the weekend and holiday trips to the Colorado River and the Glamis Off Road recreational facilities.

In addition to beginning as a railroad town, tourism played a major roll in Indio's formation and growth. In 1901, the *Riverside Press* newspaper reported, "amusement included tennis, croquet, baseball, mountain climbing, and tramps along the desert." In 1903, a tennis health camp opened near the Indio railroad depot to take advantage of the much publicized health benefits from the valley's climate. Since Indio was also known as a crossroads with Interstate 10, old Highways 60-70, and Highway 99 now U.S. 86, the city became known as the service center to travelers. Between 1905–1907, maintenance work on a manmade canal system near the Mexican border led to an accidental flooding of the Colorado River resulting in the creation of the Salton Sea. Vast salt deposits over 1,000 acres, considered one of the largest in the country, filled with water, which accounts for the Salton Sea's salinity.

The area was devoted to date culture, grape, citrus, and truck farming, drawing a number of Lutherans who worked in the vicinity. They requested that worship services be conducted, since there were many former Lutherans in the Valley who had joined the Episcopal and the Methodist churches. Mission work began in 1939 with the first service conducted by Rev. R. Knaus of Banning, on January 7, 1940, in the Women's Clubhouse in Indio. The Mission Board had authorized the work in the Indio and Coachella Valley field, conducting two services per month on each second and fourth Sunday at 7:30 p.m., which was discontinued after Easter. The work was resumed in 1941 with encouraging results, an average attendance of 19 and 8 communicants. Services were held in Women's Clubhouse in the nearby city of Coachella every other Sunday with the group desiring morning services and a Sunday school. Contributions had met all expenses each month. When Pastor Knaus accepted a call to Fontana in 1942, the work was discontinued. Following a more thorough survey and a partial canvass of the area in 1945 by pastors of Imperial Valley churches, under the guidance of circuit visitor, Rev. Elmer Boxdorfer of Yuma, Arizona, the Women's Clubhouse of Coachella was secured for worship purposes. Services were resumed, conducted on Sunday evenings, with the pastors of Imperial Valley alternating in rendering their services for this purpose. By 1945, the Rev. William Schmoock of Grace Church, Banning, was serving the Indio and Coachella fields.

By October of 1947, Rev. E. C. J. Boxdorfer of Yuma, Arizona, began preaching at services again with the new preaching mission being sponsored by the pastors of the Desert Circuit. During the

Aerial view of the El Mirador Hotel in Palm Springs during World War II, when the government took it over in 1943, renaming it the Torney General Hospital. The District purchased one building, moving it to Indio in three sections for use as a chapel and parsonage for Trinity.

previous year, regular evening services were held in the Women's Clubhouse at Coachella. This was not too successful, because the place of worship was considerably outside of the main population area. Also in October of 1947, the Mission Board purchased a piece of real estate on the corner of Park and Requa in downtown Indio, and extended a call to Candidate R. Moehle to be placed in charge of the field. He served only a short time with the Rev. George Fisher, who had replaced Pastor Schmoock of Banning, assuming the responsibility of serving the area in September of 1948. Worship services were moved to the Women's Clubhouse in Indio, the center of activity and development in the valley, proving to be a definite boon to the mission.

Early in 1948, the Mission Board purchased a well-constructed Army hospital building, 30' × 150', at the former Torney Army Hospital unit located on the property of the old El Mirador Hotel in Palm Springs with the building divided into three sections and moved to Indio. One unit was remodeled to serve as a chapel with a second unit converted into a spacious two-bedroom and den parsonage. The third unit was placed on a foundation, finished externally, and sold. The total cost of the project was $33,888 of which the District Lutheran Women's Missionary League assumed $6,000 toward the cost of remodeling the chapel. The director of missions, Pastor Webbeking, spent many weeks in Indio working with a hammer and saw, as well as encouraging, recruiting labor, and designing the chapel. At a special service conducted on May 9, 1948, in the Indio Women's Clubhouse, Rev. W. Duerr of Santa Ana preached the sermon, and Rev. Robert Moehle served as liturgist. Following the service, the cornerstone lay-

ing for the new chapel was held with Rev. T. H. Joeckel of Redeemer, South Gate, and Rev. Moehle officiating. Among those present, besides the guest pastors, were Mrs. T. H. Joeckel, president of the District LWML, Rev. and Mrs. Gesch of Brawley, and Rev. E. W. Heckenberg of Holtville. After the services, the ladies of the congregation served refreshments. The beautiful, spacious chapel was dedicated to the service of God on Sunday afternoon, October 17, 1948, with Rev. E. H. Kreidt, District vice president, delivering the sermon.

Pastor Fisher of Banning, who had also started preaching services in Palm Springs, was asked to serve as vacancy pastor when Rev. Moehle resigned. Rev. Fisher was very successful in re-establishing the group and developing the mission with a formal organization of the 10-member Voters' Assembly completed on May 12, 1949. A class of 10 children was confirmed on May 22, with nearly 100 people at the service. Services were conducted regularly on Sunday evenings with attendance ranging from 40 to 60 and the Sunday school averaging 25. At the time, Pastor Fisher wrote: "Prospects in Indio look bright." A number of calls by the Mission Board to supply the field with a resident pastor had been fruitless. A call was now issued to the Rev. Arthur F. Otto of Lone Rock, Iowa.

Rev. Otto was installed in a special service on Sunday afternoon, August 7, 1949, at 4:30 p.m. in Trinity's new chapel. At the installation and commissioning service, Rev E. H. Kreidt, pastor of First Lutheran Church of Monrovia and second vice president of the District, preached the sermon; and Rev. E. C. J. Boxdorfer, pastor of Calvary Lutheran Church of Yuma, Arizona, and circuit visitor, was in charge of the installation and commissioning

Early in 1948, the Mission Board purchases an Army hospital building at the former Torney Army Hospital unit located on the property of the old El Mirador Hotel, using part of it as Trinity's first chapel.

The former Army buildings remodeled for use as Trinity's chapel and parsonage. (Pacific Southwest District Archives)

The congregation assembled for the installation of Rev. Arthur F. Otto (center in a black robe) on August 7, 1949. (Pacific Southwest District Archives)

portion of the service. Due to the intense heat of the summer, many people left the area for recreation in a cooler climate; hence, the entire membership was not present at the time of the installation. Pastor Otto served this congregation for only about six months when he accepted a call to Iowa. After another vacancy of about 15 months, Pastor Paul A. Hilgendorf Jr. was installed on May 6, 1951. Pastor George Fisher served the congregation during the first vacancy and during the first part of the second. Pastor William C. Schmoock served as resident vacancy pastor during the latter part of the second vacancy. At the time, there were about 37 communicant members with 67 souls.

In 1954, Trinity embarked upon an ambitious missionary program of preaching the Gospel in the community. Beginning on March 1, they presented a 15-minute program of morning devotions called, "The Coachella Valley Lutheran Hour," every Monday through Friday from 7:30 to 7:45 a. m. over Indio's radio station, KREO with Pastor Hilgendorf serving as the daily speaker. This program was the only Protestant religious radio program that the station carried during the week, consequently receiving a very favorable response from the community. To make this radio program possible, individual members and friends of Trinity pledged to pay, over and above their regular church contributions, for one radio program a month for one year. For most of them, this meant a yearly contribution of $72 to the Radio Fund alone. The station manager estimated that the program enjoyed perhaps their largest daily audience, with a high estimation of 18,000 daily listeners.

The congregation numbered 75 communicant members and was still being subsidized monthly by the District. In January of 1954, due to the Sunday school space becoming entirely inadequate, the congregation proceeded to convert the parsonage into a Sunday school annex and, in turn, rented a parsonage for the pastor and his family. At the time, Trinity was the only Missouri Synod Lutheran Church in the Coachella Valley. On Sunday, October 16, 1955, at 4:00 p.m., Rev. Paul R. Schmidt, formerly of Wood River, Nebraska, was installed as the resident pastor of Trinity Lutheran with Rev. G. H. Hillmer of Hemet, delivering the sermon; Rev. William Tensmeyer, circuit visitor and pastor of Grace Church in Banning, served as officiant; and Rev. LeRoy Hass was the liturgist. Pastor Schmidt also served Eagle Mountain, a small mining community 60 miles from Indio. He was born in Kansas and moved to Maywood

in 1936 with his parents where they were charter members of Zion Lutheran Church. He attended California Concordia High School and College in Oakland, California, graduating from Concordia Seminary, Springfield, Illinois, in 1950.

Through an enthusiastic "self-help" project, the congregation completed extensive renovations of both their buildings. On Washington's Birthday, February 22, 1958, the float, designed and built by Trinity's Walther League, was viewed by 30,000 people attending the annual Riverside County Fair and Date Festival parade that year. The float, identifying the church and drawing attention to Synod's television program, "This Is the Life," was the only float entered by a church or religious organization. The central focus of the float, designed by Alien Unrine, was a nine-foot silver cross before which was depicted the Law of God on the symbolic tablets of stone with four robed Junior Choir members riding on the float. Members of the Walther League had made all decorations for the float.

On January 4, 1959, Rev. Hugo M. Warnke was installed as pastor of Trinity with Pastor G. Hillmer serving as liturgist, Pastor L. Schwartzkopf delivering the sermon, and Pastor A. H. Herkamp installing him. Pastor Warnke, a 1937 graduate of Concordia Seminary, Springfield, Illinois, came to Trinity from Klamath Falls, Oregon, where he had served since 1955. He had previously served parishes in Boylestown, Wisconsin; Green Lake, Wisconsin; Browne Valley, Minnesota; and Covina, California. At the time, he and Mrs. Warnke had four children: William, Paul, Loretta, and a married daughter who lived in Oregon. He remained until April of 1963 when he accepted a call to Paso Robles, California.

Rev. Paul R. Schmidt was installed as Trinity's pastor on October 16, 1955. (Pacific Southwest District Archives)

In 1954, Trinity presents a 15-minute program called, "The Coachella Valley Lutheran Hour," that has an estimated 18,000 daily listeners.

Rev. Hugo M. Warnke (1959–1963) with a Confirmation class in 1960. (Pacific Southwest District Archives)

In 1951, there were 40 communicants at Trinity with slow growth and a transient membership. There were internal and external troubles with the summer church attendance alarmingly small due to the desert heat. The facilities were inadequate and unattractive in a community that was growing beyond all expectation. In 1959, 5 acres were purchased in the growing residential area northwest of the city for $25,000 for the relocation of the church with a parsonage built on the new property at a cost of about $16,000. The old church property including the buildings was sold to the Methodist Church for $27,500. The communicant membership was 84 with an average church attendance of 88, and a Sunday school of 76. Pastor Warnke stated at the time: "We learn to thank God even for the few whom He calls from the heat of the desert to the cool fountains of refreshing waters of Life."

In mid-1962, Trinity dedicated its unique house of worship, an unusual Inca design by the architect, Herbert Kaiser, of Los Angeles. The church was built on an A-frame Old Testament tabernacle style with Inca stonework covering the exterior. As one approaches the church, attention is focused upon the theme for the structure — the stone wall near the entrance which serves as an introduction to the entire church, carrying the eye onward through the glass doors into the narthex up the aisle to the chancel steps, the altar, and then the 13-foot hammered bronze resurrection cross made by Clarence Moe who also crafted the decorative wrought iron Trinity symbol that adorns the altar and the Communion rails with the Alpha and Omega symbols. The exterior and interior walls were of native stone laid according to an ancient

> Due to the mobility of the population, the membership of Trinity fluctuates from year to year along with the changing pastors.

In 1962, Trinity dedicated its unique house of worship with its unusual Inca design. (Pacific Southwest District Archives)

Inca design, which may be the only church of this style in the United States. In addition to the sanctuary, the facilities contained a parish hall, kitchen, and seven Sunday school classrooms of buff cement block. Much of the construction work was done by members of the congregation with approximately 6,000 hours of donated labor by skilled and unskilled help by men, women, and children, friends of members, and sometimes comparative strangers. The parish was thankful to the Southern California District, which made this distinctive and attractive chapel a reality in the Indio desert area.

On November 3, 1963, the Rev. Gastav A. Chatt was installed as Trinity's new pastor with Pastor Walter Reuning of Palm Springs conducting the service, Pastor Martin Wahl of St. John's in Hemet reading the Rite of Installation, and Pastor Paul Hilgendorf of San Diego delivering the sermon. Pastor Chatt was born October 22, 1903, graduating from the seminary in 1930. He and Mrs. Chatt had one child, a daughter, who was married to Phillip Maggart. Pastor Chatt served in Argonia, Kansas, from 1930–1941, and then served in Lahoma, Oklahoma, from 1951–1953. Upon his arrival in Canoga Park, he found a small mission congregation in a semi-rural community. Under his leadership, the congregation grew to over 800, reflecting the development of the community; a new parochial school building was dedicated in 1957, housing 165 pupils from kindergarten to 8th grade, and a new red brick sanctuary of contemporary design was dedicated in December 1960. He also served as District counselor for the Southern California District. Upon his arrival in 1963, Trinity had 135 communicant members and 285 members with a Sunday school enrollment of 135.

When the congregation celebrated its 20th anniversary in 1969, it had a membership of 275 souls with 164 communicants. Due to the mobility of the population, the membership of Trinity fluctuated from year to year along with the changing pastors. After Pastor Chatt left in 1970, Pastor Bruce G. Dahms, a 1966 graduate of St. Louis seminary, succeeded him. Under his guidance, the officers of Trinity undertook several projects designed to foster a congregational support system. At the time, he stated, "The efforts are based on a belief that the congregation will fulfill its ministry to the world and community best as it realizes its family characteristics through mutual love and concern. These grow in direct proportion to the amount of open communication between members, especially in the sharing of faith in Christ." The elders began cottage meetings with small groups of members in their districts to promote fellowship and obtain feedback for the congregation's programs and efforts. The Sunday school staff along with Pastor Dahms began a series of home Bible studies to encourage mutual help and growth in spiritual matters. Also, he began a monthly newsletter entitled "T. L. C.," which stood for "Trinity Lutheran Commentary."

Pastor Winfred B. Schaller served as vacancy pastor for Trinity from 1979 through 1983. Rev. Gregory S. Stringer of Mt. Clemens, Michigan, was installed as pastor of Trinity in an afternoon worship service on January 16, 1983. The preacher for the installation service was Professor Robert Dargatz of Christ College, Irvine, with Pastor D. Scott Hewes of Palm Springs as liturgist, Pastor Victor E. Lehenbauer of Banning as lector, and Pastor Dean H. Boernke of Hemet, Circuit 18 counselor, as officiant, along with other members of the circuit clergy. Representing the Southern California District was Pastor Lothar V. Tornow of Costa Mesa, second vice president. Pastor Stringer was a June 1982 graduate of Concordia Seminary, St. Louis, where he received his Master of Divinity degree. He had previously attended Wayne State University, Detroit, and Concordia College, Ann Arbor, Michigan, where he received his B. A. degree in 1978. He served his vicarage year at St. Paul Lutheran Church in Westlake, Ohio and was ordained into the holy ministry on November 28, 1982, at Christ Lutheran Church, New Baltimore, Michigan.

During Pastor Schaller's tenure, Trinity's Child Development Center was established with the Center opening in 1981, having an enrollment of 36 children. As the enrollment continued to increase, the facilities became inadequate. A new 7,000-square-foot building was constructed by Laborers for Christ and members of the church giving volunteer labor; the new building was completed in the fall of 1989. The commercial refrigerator/freezer in the preschool kitchen was a gift of the Southern California District Lutheran Women's Missionary League who had 40 years before, given its first Mite Box project of $6,000 for Trinity's first church building. The following year, 1990, Pastor Stringer left Trinity with Rev. Walter Bussert serving as interim pastor until Rev. Robert E. Smith came in 1991.

Rev. Smith was installed as pastor of Trinity on the second Sunday of Easter, April 7, 1991,

with Rev. Irwin D. Goehring, Circuit 18 counselor and pastor of Prince of Peace Lutheran Church in Hemet, the officiant; and Rev. Paul Miller, pastor of Prince of Peace, Anaheim, and father-in-law of Pastor Smith, the preacher. Other participants in the service were Rev. Walter E. Bussert, Indio's interim pastor; Rev. Paul Harting, emeritus, Yucca Valley; Rev. George A. Lepper of Grace, Banning; and Rev. Michael Coppersmith of Our Savior's, Palm Springs. After the service, the women of the congregation hosted a dinner-reception honoring Pastor and Mrs. Smith. The day of the installation there was a large congregation present, but with each succeeding Sunday, it grew smaller and smaller as the snowbirds, who worshiped there, left to go back north for the summer.

Pastor Smith had served Zion Lutheran Church in Rosemead in an Anglo-Hispanic ministry from 1987 to 1991, and Trinity Lutheran Church, Santa Ana, from 1985 to 1987 where he served entirely in the Hispanic ministry. His vicarage was spent at St. Matthew Lutheran Church, New York, also in Hispanic ministry. He and his wife, the former Roberta Kay Miller, had three children at the time. When he arrived, the District had a Mobility Ministry in Indio that was phased out, with the remaining $2,500 applied to the Hispanic ministry at Trinity. Before he accepted the call, the congregation had expressed a strong desire to have a Hispanic ministry. When Pastor Smith got there, it became apparent to him that only a few people shared that strong desire. At the time, the congregation had a preschool of over 200 children with most of them Hispanic, but it was hard to get parents involved in the church. Eloise Freeman was the director of the Child Development Center. By 1993 the majority of the children attending Trinity's preschool and day-care were Hispanic, and Trinity was working to develop a Hispanic ministry. Since Pastor Smith was bilingual, the circuit expressed an interest in helping with this new venture. In 1993, Trinity had 240 members and 180 communicant members.

In 1993, Pastor Coppersmith from Our Savior's in Palm Springs contacted Pastor Smith about doing some Hispanic work in the valley as his congregation had sent money to do mission work throughout the world and wanted to shift donations to the valley for a Hispanic ministry. After two years of meetings with circuit churches and pastors, the Coachella Valley Hispanic Ministry was incorporated as a nonprofit organization and ready to do work in the valley. It had been desig-

Rev. Gregory S. Stringer served as pastor of Trinity from 1983–1990. (Pacific Southwest District Archives)

Rev. Robert E. Smith was installed as pastor of Trinity in 1991 and initiated work among the Hispanic population of Indio. (Pacific Southwest District Archives)

The Coachella Valley Hispanic Ministry is incorporated as a nonprofit organization and ready to do work in the valley.

Rev. Francisco Ruiz began work on January 5, 1998, in the Hispanic community and continued until 2002. (Pacific Southwest District Archives)

nated as a mission project of the Pacific Southwest District, and had been receiving funding support from LCMS congregations and AAL. With a solid financial base in place, the association had spent the last half of 1997 in a thorough search process for a worker for this ministry. Ken Behnken, administrative assistant to the president missions, had been especially helpful in the process, making contact throughout Synod to find a worker. The goal was to get someone from Mexico, as the Hispanic population in the valley was self-contained, having not been integrated into the American community, with most of the people coming from Mexicali. They had pastors Salomón, Bradshaw, and Brundige go talk to the association on the style of ministry, with each suggesting his chosen style, but were all in agreement that a worker should be found.

Pastor Smith's vision was to start a storefront church in Coachella as that city had a large Hispanic population. The need in the city of Coachella was great, as the population was 20,775 with 95 percent Hispanic; of them, 81 percent were Spanish-speaking. Every year a large number of migrant farm-worker families passed through Coachella with 90 percent of the population of Coachella claiming to be from Roman Catholic background, but the large share of this population did not get involved in regular Christian worship activities. This, in turn, opened a door for reaching these people with the saving Gospel of Jesus. The non-profit Coachella Valley Hispanic Ministry Task Force provided ongoing leadership for this ministry with member congregations making a commitment to contribute at least two percent of their annual un-designated offerings to the work of the Coachella Valley Hispanic Ministry. A five member Board of Directors, elected from among the members of Task Force, provided ongoing direction and leadership to the ministry. The purpose of the Coachella Valley Hispanic Ministry was to establish Hispanic missions in or near the Coachella Valley, to reach the Hispanic Community with the saving Gospel of Jesus Christ, and in His love minister to their spiritual needs.

Pastor Salomón suggested Rev. Francisco Ruiz, whom he had known through the Church of God

in Mexico even having Ruiz's wife as a parishioner. With Pastor Salomón's assistance, a worker, Francisco Ruiz a 52-year-old native of Mexico, was located and began work on January 5, 1998, with Pastor Smith giving him a tour of the area. He had served as a pastor in the Church of God in Mexico from 1965–1981. Since 1982, he had been planting Hispanic churches in Southern California. His study of Scripture and Lutheran confessional documents led him to a place where he desired to minister within The Lutheran Church — Missouri Synod; Pastor Esaúl Salomón had taken him and his family through the process of Confirmation and was in an ongoing weekly in-depth program to mentor with Francisco, who served as a licensed deacon under the supervision of the Board of Directors Coachella Valley Hispanic Ministry. He arrived in Indio with his wife, Eunice, and sons, Israel, Hiram, Isaac, and Benjamin, to start Hispanic ministry, with the Coachella Valley Hispanic Ministry financing the project and Trinity allowing the mission to use the building rent free. In order for Pastor Ruiz to be ordained in the Lutheran church, he had to take classes through the St. Louis Seminary.

The Hispanic ministry used Trinity's facilities at 1:00 p.m. for Sunday services and Bible classes, which also were conducted in people's homes. The Spanish service averaged between 10 and 15 people each Sunday with the church filled for the occasion of the 25th wedding anniversary of Pastor and Mrs. Ruiz. When Pastor Ruiz was away taking classes in St. Louis, Pastor Smith would preach for him. He had established youth groups — one meeting each Friday to practice music, and another that was involved in sports. For a short time, Riverside County had vocational classes teaching Hispanics reading and writing skills. Pastor Ruiz started having Bible classes at the Salton Sea as a family lived there. Due to actions taken by CVHM, Pastor Ruiz's ministry at Trinity was terminated in 2002, after four years of working in the Hispanic community. At the present time, Spanish services are not being conducted at Trinity, but the CVHM continues to work toward the establishment of a storefront mission somewhere in the valley.

Grace Lutheran Church
Iglesia Evangelica Alfa Y Omega
El Centro, California

The city of El Centro, county seat of Imperial County in southeastern California 120 miles east of San Diego, is a desert community located 52 feet below sea level with the unique distinction of being the largest settlement in the United States below sea level. In 1905, El Centro was laid out by W. F. Holt and developed as a commercial and transportation center for the Imperial Valley. It is also the home of the National Parachute Test Range, and in the 1980s, geothermal energy was being developed based on local well drilling. The city now has a population of 37,835, 74.58 percent Hispanic and 18 percent Anglo.

The first to have the dream of changing the desert to a blooming oasis of a rich agricultural empire was Dr. O. M. Wozencraft, who originally came to California for the Gold Rush. In his vision, he saw the Colorado River diverted to bring water to the Imperial Valley, even persuading the California State Legislature to support this quest by granting him the right to the land if he could get water to it. Unfortunately, the Civil War intervened with all support going to the war effort. Following the war, others came to the valley to try their hands at getting Colorado River water to the area. Some came to make surveys revealing a total of two million acres could be irrigated in the Salton Basin and Baja California from a single canal project with the Salton Sink to serve as drainage for the area. Finally, George Chaffey, who established the city of Ontario, along with his brother William, began dredging a canal bed in August of 1900 with water supplied to Calexico by 1901 causing 1,500 acres to be cultivated and bringing potable water to the populace instead of being hauled by railroad cars, thus starting a population boom.

In 1901, few white men inhabited the Imperial Valley other than the surveyors working on the canal. By 1905, the residents had increased to 12,000 with irrigated land going from 1,500 acres to 67,000 acres. Since the heavy silt deposit in the canal created growing problems for the irrigation project, it was decided to dredge a bypass from the canal with no control or floodgate. A series of floods in 1904–1905 caused rapid erosion with the widening of the bypass opening, resulting in the Colorado River flowing full-force through this channel into the Imperial Valley settling in the Salton Sink. The Southern Pacific dedicated tons of large boulders, rock, and gravel, transporting it in railroad cars to close the breach in the canal. Finally, the river was diverted back to its original channel, but this disaster had made a 50-mile by 15-mile body of water covering 285,000 acres making it the largest saltwater sea, the Salton Sea, in North America.

With the increase in population, there came a demand for transportation to import goods into the Imperial Valley and ship out agricultural produce. In 1903, the Southern Pacific built a branch line into the valley with El Centro linked to San Diego by 1919. The abundant crops of alfalfa, cantaloupes, lettuce, melons, grapefruit, dates, and flax were shipped west to coastal markets. With this large increase in population came many Lutherans who gathered for worship services in the home of T. D. Ehmke in the early 1900s with the first official worship service conducted in 1910 by the Rev. Jacobs of the Ohio Synod. Between 1910 and 1922 occasional worship services continued with the help of visiting Lutheran pastors: Rev. Clineline of Los Angeles, Rev. Shults of Pomona, Rev. Hohberger of Los Angeles, Rev. Peters of Los Angeles, Rev. Herman Meyer, Rev. Mangold of Pomona, Rev. Satzsaenger, and Rev. Carl Saenger, with the majority of this early work conducted by pastors of the Ohio Synod.

Beginning in 1923, The Lutheran Church — Missouri Synod began work in the Imperial Valley with pastors, Rev. H. G. Schmelzer of Anaheim, Rev. J. W. Theiss of Los Angeles, Rev. A. Harrsere, Rev. G. H. Smukal of Los Angeles, Rev. C. Damschroeder of San Diego, Rev. R. Jeske of Whittier, Rev. Arthur C. Keck of Alhambra, involved in this initial work. In about July of 1926, Rev. Theodore C. Schoessow, missionary-at-large, did work at El Centro for more than two years, holding services there once a month until November 17, 1927, when the Rev. A. W. Kaiser was installed as the first full-time Lutheran pastor in the Imperial Valley with 25 people attending the installation service. During this time, worship services were held in both El Centro in English and in Holtville in German where 50 to 70 adults, who were members of a Swiss colony, came regularly to services. From the very beginning, they had welcomed these services, organizing St. Paul's Lutheran Church of Holtville on December 1, 1929. The El Centro Lutherans worshiped at various locations including the Odd Fellows Hall at Fifth & Main, the old Lincoln School at Fourth & Olive, the Japanese Hall at Fifth & Commercial, the Methodist church at Sixth & Commercial, and the Seventh-day Adventist church at Tenth & Holt. At the time, the Imperial Valley was an area 30 by 60 miles with some 65,000 inhabitants — an immense field for one missionary to cover!

When Rev. A. W. Kaiser was called to Holtville, it was combined with the mission in El Centro until the beginning of 1936. Though the city of El Centro and the surrounding territory had experienced marked developments, the mission little more than continued to exist. Encouraged by the new interests experienced by the mission at Yuma, Arizona, having secured a candidate worker about a year before, the small El Centro group approached the Mission Board in January of 1935, with a request to procure a candidate worker with the mission promising free lodging or its equivalent for the worker, and $15 per month toward his salary. The request was granted, with the provision of a District subsidy of $10 per month; in April of 1935, Candidate Joseph Galambos was sent into the field. On April 18, 1935, the El Centro group officially organized as First Evangelical Lutheran Church of El Centro with 8 voting members, 26 souls, and 17 communicant members, meeting in the Seventh-day Adventist Church. By 1936, the congregation had grown to 72 souls, 40 communicants with 12 voting members having an average of 42 in worship services with 34 pupils enrolled in the Sunday school averaging 15 per Sunday. On June 25, 1937, First Evangelical Lutheran Church of El Centro was officially received into The Lutheran Church — Missouri Synod.

During 1937, Rev. Paul Neipp was installed as the first resident pastor of First Lutheran Church with the president, Pastor G. H. Smukal, delivering the sermon from II Corinthians 5:10–15, and serving Holy Communion; assisting in the service were Pastors J. Galambos, O. Tietjen, and Circuit Visitor W. A. Theiss. The service was filled to capacity with some of the worshipers coming from as far as Redondo Beach, San Diego, and Yuma, Arizona.

Since the congregation had no church building of its own, and held services in the Seventh-day Adventist Church, the work was greatly hindered, as they could use the church only on Sundays

and couldn't advertise, as they would like. While the congregation experienced a slow but steady growth, it was not in proportion with the growth of the city. Within the next 5 years, the population of the entire valley was expected to double from 70,000 to 140,000 when the All-American Canal was completed, reclaiming 500,000 acres of desert land. Several problems confronted the church work as men who wished to attend services on Sundays often were not allowed to because of their work schedules; there was much transiency with people constantly coming and going; the lodge problem was great as many considered the lodge their church; and finally, there were no Lutherans from which to draw. All the work was purely missionary work, gaining converts largely from adults. In 1938, eight adults and five children were confirmed. At the time, there was a building boom in El Centro with the previous year recording over $250,000 to build new homes.

While El Centro had an unexcelled winter climate drawing many tourists and health seekers, it had extremely hot summers with everyone who could do so leaving, which meant that church work had to begin anew every fall with people getting back into the church-going habit. Pastor Neipp reported, "Our congregation is quite scattered and the members are of the poorer class, but they have a zeal for the Lord's work and have started a Church Building Fund. We have a well-indoctrinated Sunday school staff and a Women's League was recently organized." Fourteen miles north of Grace, Pastor Neipp organized a daughter congregation, Trinity Lutheran in Brawley in 1938.

In 1939, the congregation changed its name to "Grace Evangelical Lutheran Church" and purchased 3 spacious lots, 140' × 176', for a new sanctuary on South Eighth Street with construction beginning in April of 1940. The church dedication was held on Reformation Sunday, October 27, 1940, in three special services with the Rev. George Theiss of Pasadena preaching both the morning dedicatory sermon and the evening sermon. In the afternoon, the Rev. A. G. Webbeking of Orange occupied the pulpit with Pastor O. Tietjen of Yuma, Arizona, and Rev. Paul Neipp also participating in the impressive ceremonies. The well-attended services were composed of the local membership as well as a number of visiting Lutherans and townspeople. Between the afternoon and the evening services, the women of the church served an excellent turkey supper, using their "modernly"

Pastor Neipp reports, "Our congregation is quite scattered and the members are of the poorer class, but they have a zeal for the Lord's work...."

equipped new kitchen for the first time. After the meal, fellowship songs were sung, and prominent persons present gave a number of short talks. At the time of dedication, the parish numbered 47 communicant members and 90 souls.

The new building had an exterior of white stucco, with a cedar-shingle roof topped with a blue neon cross, which could be seen at night from a considerable distance. Contractor for the building was Mr. Hugh Johnston of El Centro, who, through sacrifices on his part, kept the building costs down to about $5,000 with a generous loan from the Southern California District Extension Department. The nave, with ceiling of Weatherwood, was 21' × 48', seating 140 people with a chancel measuring 21' × 12' deep. The nave could be divided with folding doors into two rooms, which was to be used for day-school classrooms in the future. A beautiful hand-carved wooden crucifix was suspended over the altar, prominently standing out against a dossal curtain of rich red and gold damask. At each end of the Philippine mahogany altar was a wooden candlestick with the pulpit and baptismal font also made of Philippine mahogany. Extending west of the nave was a wing, 9' wide and 58' long, which contained a sacristy, a meeting-room, the vestibule, restrooms, and a kitchen. Members and friends of the congregation donated all the furnishings of the church, amounting to over $700.

In 1943, the valley could boast of having the world's largest irrigation project, where 40,000 dollars' worth of crops were grown annually in

Rev. Albert Nickodemus was ordained and installed as the pastor of Grace and of Trinity in Brawley on September 19, 1943. (Pacific Southwest District Archives)

an all-year-growing climate, where more cattle and sheep were fed than in any other place on the Pacific Coast. With growth and rental property at a high premium, the congregation was compelled to purchase a dwelling at 1025 El Centro Avenue through donations and loans of the membership, together with a loan from the District Extension Department, as the home occupied by the pastor was sold with no other rental available. When the parish was able to do so, it intended to reapply its investment in a new parsonage that was to be erected on the church property. The membership included 115 souls with 75 communicants. When Pastor Neipp left in 1943, Rev. Albert Nickodemus, a 1943 graduate of Concordia Seminary in Springfield, Illinois, was ordained and installed as the pastor of Grace and of Trinity in Brawley. His vicarage year was spent as dean of boys and athletic director at the Lutheran Child Welfare Association in Addison, Illinois. On June 25, he married Miss Anna Dickman of Silverton, Oregon.

On Sunday, October 28, 1945, Grace celebrated the fifth anniversary of the dedication of its church building with a special anniversary supper and a program held the following Wednesday evening where Pastor Nickodemus served as master of ceremonies, introducing the guest speakers of the evening: Rev. E. Heckenberg of Holtville, who had served the congregation as vacancy pastor in 1943; Rev. J. Galambos, who served as pastor from 1935 to 1937; and Rev. Paul Neipp, who served from 1937 to 1943. During the previous five years, Grace erected its church,

Grace's first church building, which was dedicated on Reformation Sunday, October 27, 1940. (Pacific Southwest District Archives)

Rev. Paul Neipp at the altar of Grace's new sanctuary. (Pacific Southwest District Archives)

purchased a parsonage, and on its anniversary day also celebrated the fact that it was now debt free. After Pastor Nickodemus left in 1947, Rev. Gordon Mackensen came in 1948. On May 22, 1950, the congregation's dream of having the parsonage on the church property materialized as they dedicated the new home, a white stucco house with 3 bedrooms, built at a cost of $11,500. Less than a month before, on April 28, Pastor and Mrs. Mackensen had a baby girl, Susan Jane, bringing much joy to their new home.

Also in 1950, Grace opened a Sunday school branch at the El Centro Naval Base with the four Lutherans living at the Base forming the teaching staff. Teachers' meetings were held under the direction of Rev. Gordon Mackensen. During the first two weeks, the enrollment reached over 50. The congregation first assumed the financial support of the project; however, the Navy took over this phase of the program. The school on the base was used for Sunday school sessions with a Navy bus transporting the children to and from the adjoining housing area.

With the growth of the congregation, it was decided that a new church sanctuary was much needed with ground broken on Sunday, January 3, 1954; participating in the ceremony were Rev. Gordon Mackensen, pastor of the parish; Mr. E. Shaw, president of the Chamber of Commerce; Mr. B. Painter, mayor; and Mr. Ted Ehmke, chairman

> Much of the superstructure of the new church building is erected through the cooperative efforts of the sailors at the Naval Air Base in Seeley located near El Centro.

of the congregation. Members of the congregation built the block wall church, costing approximately $45,000, with funds raised by gifts and loans from members of the parish. The building, erected under the direction of the congregation with no contractor, had Mr. Tom Hall, trustee of the congregation, as the general building foreman for the project with members and friends of the congregation donating $10,000 worth of time. Much of the superstructure was erected through the cooperative efforts of the sailors at the Naval Air Base in Seeley located near El Centro. With the aid of volunteer services of the sailors and members, the 108' × 48' sanctuary, seating 300 worshipers, was quickly completed and dedicated on December 5, 1954. The dedicatory services in the morning were lead by Pastor Mackensen. At the special "Festival Service" held in the afternoon, Rev. Paul Neipp, former pastor of the congregation, preached the sermon. The old church building was used as the parish hall and is still being used today.

In 1957, Grace released 32 communicants to carry on the work in the new mission in Calexico where Vicar James Profitt was establishing a new parish. When the congregation celebrated the 25th anniversary of its organization in 1960, it had grown from 16 communicants and 26 souls to 182 communicant members, 375 souls, and had a new pastor, Rev. Paul W. Harting, who came in 1958 and remained until 1977. He was born in Kimms-

Groundbreaking on Sunday, January 3, 1954; participating in the ceremony were Rev. Gordon Mackensen; Mr. E. Shaw, president of the Chamber of Commerce; Mr. B. Painter, mayor; and Mr. Ted Ehmke, chairman of the congregation. (Pacific Southwest District Archives)

Grace's beautiful, new, 300-seat church was dedicated on December 5, 1954. (Pacific Southwest District Archives)

Rev. Paul W. Harting served Grace from 1958 to 1977. (Pacific Southwest District Archives)

Rev. Donald T. Heiderich was pastor of Grace from 1977 to 1982. (Pacific Southwest District Archives)

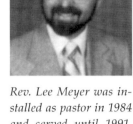

Rev. Lee Meyer was installed as pastor in 1984 and served until 1991. (Pacific Southwest District Archives)

Rev. Lewis Busch was ordained and installed at Grace in 1992, serving until 2002. (Pacific Southwest District Archives)

wick, Missouri, on September 30, 1923, to Rev. and Mrs. H. C. Harting. Before graduating from Concordia Seminary, St. Louis, in 1948, he attended St. Paul's College at Concordia, Missouri. He was ordained and installed in 1948 to serve in missions at Prosser and North Richland, Washington. In 1953, he accepted the call to Peace in Philomath, Oregon, where he remained until going to El Centro in 1958. On August 22, 1948, he married Betty Klyver with their marriage blessed with three children. In 1977, he accepted a call to Yucca Valley where he retired in 1988. He was called to his heavenly home on June 28, 1999.

Rev. Donald T. Heiderich, who was born in Milwaukee, Wisconsin, to Gilbert and Alice Heiderich and graduated from the St. Louis Seminary in 1961, succeeded Pastor Harting. Before going to El Centro, he served parishes in Conroe, Texas; Hooker, Oklahoma; Racine, Wisconsin; and Walnut, California. He married Ellen Eiden with their marriage blessed with four children, Monica, Mary, Martin, and Matthew. He left El Centro in 1982, to teach at Faith Lutheran High School in La Verne, California, going back to the parish ministry at Ephrata, Washington; and Burbank and Perris, California, retiring in 1997 and called to his heavenly home on July 27, 2000.

After a vacancy, Rev. Lee Meyer, a 1973 St. Louis Seminary graduate who had served in Papua, New Guinea, was installed in 1984. The same year a long time dream came true when Grace started a Christian day school which was served by a number of principals, Micky Johnson from 1984 to 1992, Betsy Smith from 1992 to 1994, and Barbara Beard from 1996 to 2000, and presently by Dr. Joe Dikerson. The kindergarten through 8th grade school had 101 pupils, 40 to 50 percent Hispanic. At one time, 15 students came across the border from

Mexicali to attend the school. One of the problems at the school was getting Synod-trained teachers, as none of the graduates from Synod's schools wanted to live in the desert.

After Pastor Meyer left Grace in 1991 to serve Allelujah in Tempe, Arizona, Rev. Sheldon Klietz, a 1960 St. Louis Seminary graduate who came from Faith, Oaklawn, Illinois, became the new pastor in 1991, leaving in 1992 to take a call to serve as assistant pastor at St. John in Chicago, Illinois. Rev. Lewis Busch, was ordained and installed at Grace in 1992 as its pastor after he graduated from Concordia Seminary in St. Louis in 1992. He was born on March 21, 1962, in San Diego, California, where he attended Christ Lutheran School. After graduating from Grossmont High School, he received a bachelor's degree from California State University in Chico in 1985 followed by his studies at Christ College, Irvine graduating from Concordia Seminary in St. Louis with a Master of Divinity. While at Christ College, he met Edith Morrison of Bishop, California, marrying her in December of 1987 with their marriage blessed with three children, Joshua, Lauren, and Katherine.

When Pastor Busch arrived, he observed that the congregation was a seasonal one with 105 people in church during the winter and only 70 people in church during the summer as the heat was so intense, and that the area was mainly a Hispanic community. The church now had 260 members and 180 communicants with an average attendance of 125 at worship. In order to meet the needs of the community and the school, Spanish-speaking teachers were hired. Through these efforts, some of the Spanish-speaking parents, who were also fluent in English, became members of Grace. From 1994–1996, Pastor Busch also served

In order to meet the needs of the community and school, Spanish-speaking teachers are hired.

as school administrator, since the school couldn't obtain a principal and had grown from 60 to 90 pupils at the time. He also went into each classroom three days a week teaching religion classes and conducting a chapel service once a week for the school. He served the community in the Kiwanis Club, as the Imperial County Sheriff chaplain, and a Naval Reserve chaplain.

When the ELCA church in El Centro tried to have bilingual services after the English-speaking pastor left, the ELCA stopped supporting the Spanish congregation, Santa Isabel; hence, Santa Isabel lost its building, forcing the Spanish congregation to leave. In 1995, they requested that Grace allow them to use their building for worship services. With permission granted, they began worshiping at Grace on Sunday afternoons, eventually leaving the ELCA to become an independent congregation. Deacon Jesús Jimenez, a lay pastor and worker-priest, who was in the TEE program working with Pastor Smith in Indio and the Coachella Valley Hispanic Ministry, started a Hispanic ministry in El Centro in a storefront building. When Pastor Busch heard of Deacon Jimenez's situation

in 1997, he encouraged Grace to be supportive as the Hispanic ministry was something they needed to do. The congregation also opened their doors to this ministry, allowing Iglesia Evangelica Alfa y Omega to use its buildings rent free for worship on Sunday evenings at 6:00 p.m. and also on Friday nights at 7:00 p.m. Since Pastor Busch didn't speak Spanish, he worked with Deacon Jimenez in doing some evangelism. Deacon Jimenez also assisted Pastor in the English services. As Deacon Jimenez worked cleaning carpets during the day to support his wife and children while attending classes to become a Lutheran pastor, Grace allowed his children to attend the day school tuition-free. In 2003, Pastor Jimenez began a Spanish worship service on Tuesday evenings at 6:30 p.m. at Trinity in Brawley. He also helped Santo Tomas, a congregation in Mesa Rica in Baja California, by conducting services on Saturday afternoons. He, along with congregational members, put a new roof on the chapel and installed a drop ceiling and insulation, which helped cool the building during the summer. In 2002, Pastor Busch left Grace to accept a call to Good Shepherd in Downey.

Faith Lutheran Church
Calexico, California

 ince Calexico represents the mixing of two cultures and areas, and with its proximity to the Mexican border, the name Calexico was coined as a combination of California and Mexico. A fence separates Calexico from Mexicali, its Mexican sister city, with immigration agents patrolling the area on bicycles. The climate in Calexico is very arid and hot as this desert area has little rainfall with extremely hot temperatures at least half the year, normally sunny year-round. Today Calexico has a population of 27,109 with 95.3 percent having a Hispanic background. In 1900, Calexico began as a tent city of the Imperial Land Company, growing into a larger, thriving city on the U.S./Mexico border. Before the repeal of prohibition in 1933, Calexico was primarily a weekend town visited by workers in the Imperial Valley for the pursuit of fun and games, dance halls, and saloons in adjacent Mexicali outside the United States and unaffected by the Volstead Act which prohibited alcoholic beverages of any sort in the U.S. Gaining a reputation

as a typical U.S.–Mexico border town with all its immoral aspects, the modern city of Calexico is a far cry from what is was in its early history, as now there are hundreds of acres devoted to industrial-park use with commercial and retail incentives being offered to encourage industrial development.

Following the incorporation of Calexico in 1908, the Women's Improvement Club, and the Farmers and Merchants Club, encouraged the city to apply for a Carnegie Grant in 1914 for a "more metropolitan" library "more in keeping with the progressive spirit of the town." Calexico was growing rapidly with the introduction of irrigation from water in the new canal. Well-known architects, Allison and Allison, had drawn plans for a beautiful building at a cost of $25,000. The $10,000 offered by Carnegie in 1915 fell far short of the $25,000 on which the plans were based. After much discussion with Carnegie, they accepted the $10,000 in 1917, but the full concept of the building was never realized. The library used this small building until 1986, when a new library was built. The old building is still standing, waiting for rehabilitation.

During the years of the Second World War with gas-rationing being particularly acute, a group of Lutherans released from Grace in El Centro met at the home of Mr. and Mrs. U. L. Press, 847 Heffernan Avenue in Calexico and asked Rev. E. W. Heckenberg, pastor of St. Paul's in Holtville, to attend to their spiritual needs. He began conducting services in Calexico at the Seventh-day Adventist Mission School until transfers depleted the small congregation. When the war ended, with gas rationing no longer needed, the remaining members of the Calexico congregation returned to either the El Centro or the Holtville congregation.

In 1952, Lutheran missionary work began again in Calexico as a branch Sunday school was begun under the supervision of Rev. Gordon Mackensen of Grace, El Centro, and Mr. Fred Johnson of Calexico with Sunday morning church services added in November of 1955. On July 15, 1956, the members of Grace in El Centro, who lived in Calexico, were released by Pastor Mackensen and placed in the care of Vicar James M. Profitt to establish their own church in Calexico. Faith Lutheran Church of Calexico became a formal organization, signing the constitution of The Lutheran Church — Missouri Synod at the Southern California District Convention in San Diego in April 1957. After Vicar James M. Proffitt accepted the call to be the pas-

Rev. James M. Proffitt began work in Calexico in 1956, establishing Faith Lutheran Church. (Pacific Southwest District Archives)

tor of Faith in May of 1957, he was ordained and installed in an installation service conducted at Grace in El Centro on Sunday, June 23, 1957; he remained at Faith until 1962. He was born in 1920 in Westville, Oklahoma, graduating from Concordia Seminary in Springfield, Illinois in 1957. He married Virginia Raney in 1942 and was blessed with one child.

In June of 1959, plans for church and parish hall were set with initial sketches adopted. On January 17, 1960, ground was broken with construction beginning on February 22, 1960. As Faith was its own contractor, they engaged Mr. Tom Hall, a consecrated Christian from Grace, El Centro, to supervise the building of their "House of God" with the building completed in August of 1960. On October 9, 1960, the beautiful little church was dedicated "to the glory of God and the welfare of mankind."

In 1965, Rev. Arlo Krueger was installed by Rev. Paul Harting of El Centro, as the new pastor of Faith with Rev. Harold B. Tietjen, executive secretary of the Mission Board, delivering the sermon. Prior to Rev. Krueger's going to Calexico, he was pastor of Our Savior Church in Sparks, Nevada. He and Mrs. Krueger had four children, Mrs. Gary Cooper, Judith, Dennis, and Donald.

In 1974 with the Hispanic population continuing to grow in Calexico, Grace in El Centro and Faith in Calexico cooperated in calling Vicar Robert J. Paulson of Concordia Seminary in Springfield, Illinois, to further Hispanic work in communities of the Imperial Valley primarily El Centro and Calexico. The vicar was fluent in Spanish and

Rev. Gordon Mackensen with the teachers and children at the branch Sunday school in Calexico at the Seventh-day Adventist Mission School in 1954. (Pacific Southwest District Archives)

Faith's beautiful little brick church was dedicated on October 9, 1960. (Pacific Southwest District Archives)

sought exposure to this type of ministry during his year of vicarage. They placed a heavy emphasis on reaching Mexican-Americans, having plans for a large bilingual school in Calexico that never materialized. The following proposal was made to the District Mission Board: "The Mission Board make an official request to the Synodical Board of Parish Education to provide the services of a qualified survey conductor to look into the possibilities of a bilingual and bicultural school effort in Calexico." Faith continued to request a pastor from the Mission Board, but the board stated that Faith should continue to receive pastoral services from area pastors.

Finally, Faith's prayers were answered when the Rev. Harold A. Deye was installed as pastor on August 8, 1976, in a service conducted by Pastor Harting of El Centro with Rev. Walter Niermann of Ascension Lutheran Church in Garden Grove, the father-in-law of Pastor Deye, preaching the sermon. Pastor Deye was the son of the Rev. and Mrs. Armin U. Deye of St. Martin's Lutheran Church, Winona, Minnesota. He attended prep school at Concordia, St. Paul, Minnesota, graduating from Concordia Sr. College, Fort Wayne, Indiana, with a B.A., receiving his Master of Divinity degree from Concordia Seminary, St. Louis, in 1968. He received additional special training at the Missionaries' School, St. Louis, with Spanish-language training, CIDOC, in Cuernavaca, Morelos, Mexico. He served as a missionary in Southern

> A matrix, Latin for womb, was a cultural exposure designed so that participants would "conceive" new concepts and understandings about a different culture or life style.

Monagas, Venezuela, before serving as the pastor of Epiphany Lutheran in Chandler, Arizona, in 1971. His wife, Kathleen Deye, the daughter of Rev. and Mrs. Walter Niermann of Garden Grove, was a music major having played with the Philharmonic Orchestra in St. Louis and Phoenix. At the time, she and Pastor were the parents of two children, Holly and Paul.

Pastor Deye's assignment in Calexico was to provide Spanish ministry exploration and outreach to the Hispanic people of this border area. Within three miles of the Calexico church was Iglesia San Juan, a congregation in Mexico, served by Rev. Juan Rosas. The congregations of Circuit 22 in the Southern California District supported Pastor Deye's ministry in Calexico. In early September, Miss Patricia Muehrer, intern of The Lutheran Deaconess Association, arrived to assist in that outreach several days a week. Since both were fluent in Spanish, they were working with the people in various ways, such as starting cooking and sewing classes in order for the people to develop relationships with them, thereby being able to share Jesus Christ with the people. They hoped to begin Spanish services in a short time. A matrix was conducted in Calexico–Mexicali, May 25–26, at Faith Lutheran Church in Calexico under the leadership of Pastor Harold Deye, assisted by Deaconess Patti Muehrer. A matrix, Latin for womb, was a cultural exposure designed so that participants would "conceive" new concepts and understandings about a different culture or life style. The program consisted of in-depth presentations on the Hispanic culture by Rev. Sam Hernandez, pastor of an ALC church in Fresno; Rev. Mike Cooper, LCA pastor of Angelica Lutheran Church in Los Angeles; and Pastor Robert Gussick of LBCM of San Diego. In addition, the motion picture, "The Unwanted," was shown, highlighting the situation of the undocumented worker. Several other visual presentations plus cultural games enlivened the program. Part of the exposure was that all meals, except breakfast, were eaten at Mexican restaurants in Mexicali where Spanish was spoken. The group also visited the Mexicali Lutheran Church and School where Pastor Juan Rosas served.

In 1979, a mission festival was held at Faith where nearly 250 people attended from the Lutheran congregations in Calexico, El Centro, Holtville, Brawley, Blythe, Yuma, and Mexicali. A bilingual festival worship was held to encourage support of the outreach mission work being done through

Rev. Arlo Krueger (center) was installed as pastor of Faith in 1965 by Rev. Paul Harting (left) of El Centro, and Rev. Harold B. Tietjen, executive secretary of the Mission Board. (Pacific Southwest District Archives)

Faith in Calexico and to draw the members of the various congregations closer. The service began with a banner in the procession, which led the mass adult and children's choirs into church with pastors from all the circuit's congregations participating. The Spanish sermon was given by Rev. Juan Rosas, Iglesia San Juan, Mexicali, with Rev. LaVern Brack of Trinity, Brawley, addressing the worshipers in English. Russ Renninger of Yuma directed the choirs with Mrs. Susan Waterman of El Centro as the organist, and Deaconess Dawn Riske of Calexico playing the guitar and singing. The festival day ended with a potluck supper held outside. Since the mission festival was so well received, a Circuit-wide Reformation Festival was planned for October. The Calexico mission was supported by the Circuit Cluster, which included the 6 other congregations in Circuit 22 with part of their mission offerings sent to Hispanic outreach programs in Calexico.

In 1979, Rev. LaVern Brack of Brawley discovered the availability of time for a regular one-half hour Lutheran-Spanish radio program each Sunday on Station KICO Calexico, which was a very helpful mission arm for the church since the station beamed a majority of its programs into Mexico with Circuit 22 pledging its support for the program providing several hundred dollars for the broadcast. The Radio and TV Committee encouraged Rev. Brack to go forward with this program assuring him of the support of the Committee and the California Lutheran Program with both financing and the format of the broadcast. By 1985, the Spanish Lutheran broadcasts were heard on radio stations KICO and KGBA FM 100.

When Pastor Deye accepted the call to Bethany, Hollywood, Rev. Harting from Grace, El Centro, served as vacancy pastor until Rev. William L. Brunold arrived to serve Faith where he also conducted Spanish services. Pastor Brunold was born on December 29, 1951, in San Diego where he attended San Diego State University graduating in 1973 and Concordia Seminary at Fort Wayne, Indiana, graduating in 1978. He was ordained the same year at Christ, La Mesa, California, and installed as pastor of El Calvario, Brownsville, Texas, serving until 1980 when he went to Calexico. He married Patti L. Inglis on September 28, 1974, with their marriage blessed with two children. He also served as a U.S. Army Reserve chaplain. In 1984, he left Calexico to accept the call at Emmaus, Alhambra, staying until 1998, when he went to First in Burbank.

Rev. Harold A. Deye was installed as pastor of Faith on August 8, 1976, where he began a ministry to the Hispanic population in Calexico. (Pacific Southwest District Archives)

Rev. William L. Brunold came to serve Faith from 1980 to 1984, where he also conducted Spanish services. (Pacific Southwest District Archives)

In August of 1984, Rev. Jose Lopez of Mexican descent and a Mexican citizen, was placed at Faith to maintain the small English-speaking congregation while he worked primarily with the Hispanic population. When he arrived on the scene, he reached out to the people in the area with a concerned ministry, forming youth groups, initiating ministries to serve the elderly, and provided an excellent Word and Sacrament ministry with the congregation doubling in number. The ministry was funded largely by gifts from the circuit congregations. Since Pastor Lopez didn't have the proper papers allowing him to remain in the United States, he was deported, the church was closed, and a replacement was needed immediately. After Pastor Lopez left, Rev. James Harris went to Faith as the pastor.

By 1989, Faith faced some Anglo/Hispanic problems with Anglos slowing the Hispanic work and the circuits not giving support that was promised. By May, Rev. Juan Rosas, pastor in Mexicali, was contracted to work with a Hispanic ministry in Calexico for six months. At the end of six months, the Department of Mission Services was to make a final decision in regard to the Calexico mission station. By September, it was reported that it was very difficult to keep the Hispanic ministry going at Faith. The facilities were being rented to a Chinese congregation and the members of the Anglo congregation were worshiping in El Centro. By 1991, the property was sold, the Hispanic work discontinued, and the life of Faith Lutheran Church in Calexico ended.

By 1985, the Spanish Lutheran broadcasts are heard on radio stations KICO and KGBA FM 100.

Centro Cristiano Fuente de Vida
San Jacinto, California

San Jacinto, a city of 23,779 with 40.3 percent Hispanic and 56.6 percent Anglo, is 1,546 feet above sea level located near Hemet, about 85 miles east of Los Angeles and 90 miles north of San Diego. It is the oldest incorporated city in Riverside County with the name, San Jacinto, coming from Juan Bautista de Anza who came to the valley in 1774 to begin his rancho, naming it for St. Hyacinth, "San Jacinto" in Spanish. The San Jacinto Rancho was a gigantic Spanish grant, which extended from the mountains to Corona. The grant from the Mexican government was originally given to the Don Jose Antonio Estudillo family in 1842 where, for many years, they remained basically alone in the valley. When other people finally starting migrating to the area, he sold portions of his holdings, eventually deciding to establish a town with the first school built in 1868. In 1884, the first newspaper in the county, the *San Jacinto Register*, was published and by 1888, San Jacinto was incorporated as a city. San Jacinto High School was established in 1885 with the first

Rev. Juan D. Herrera, founding pastor of Centro Cristiano Fuente de Vida, with his wife, Eva, in 2002. (Pacific Southwest District Archives)

campus located at what is now Monte Vista Middle School. The middle school name was changed with the building of the new middle school, North Mountain.

For more than 70 years, the valley had been the home of the Ramona Pageant, an outdoor love story from California's early days based on the novel, *Ramona*, written by Helen Hunt Jackson in 1884. The Ramona Pageant, a California tradition since 1923, returns every year in the spring to the Ramona Bowl in the hills above Hemet with a cast of more than 400 actors, singers, dancers, and horsemen, telling the story of the timeless love of Ramona and her Indian hero, Alessandro.

The Hispanic Lutheran Mission in San Jacinto, Centro Cristiano Fuente de Vida, is the most unique Spanish mission in the District as it wasn't originally started by the Pacific Southwest District,

but was started by Rev. Juan D. Herrera, who was a pastor in the Church of God. He was born into the Christian home of Eusebio Herrera León and Natividad Domínguez García on July 26, 1950, in the city of Tijuana, Mexico, where he had eight siblings, five sisters and three brothers. He stated he has always felt a calling to become a minister. "When I was five years old, my father made me a small pulpit. People would come to my home and listen when I preached." He studied from 1967 to 1969 in Bethsaida Theology Institute in the city of Durango, Durango, Mexico. Following his graduation, he received his first minister's credential as an Exhorter Minister in June of 1969. From 1969 to 1970, he was the youth director at several churches in Tijuana, Tecate, and Mexicali, which was followed by his first position as pastor in Tecate, Mexico, lasting to 1973. In July of 1973, he married Miss Eva Alcalá Esparza with their marriage blessed with two daughters, Keren, born on August 9, 1974, and Denise, born on November 28, 1975.

During July of 1973 and through March of 1979, Pastor Herrera directed the Los Angeles based radio program, "Maranatha," while he also worked as youth vice president for the Church of God district in South Los Angeles and had the position of secretary/treasurer of the district. In April 1979, he took his second position as the pastor of the Church of God in Whittier, California, which he held until March of 1991. During that time, he received his second minister's credential as a licensed minister on March 21, 1980. He served as district supervisor, member of the Credential Committee, member of the Conduct and Discipline Committee, and member of the Board of Counselors of the Territory. On May 27, 1981, he received his third and last credential certifying him as an ordained minister in the Church of God. In 1987, he wrote *Proezas*, a book of plays and poems for the holidays. He received his third position as pastor in Moreno

Valley in March of 1991, staying until May of 1994. From May 1994 to July 1995, he gave lectures and workshops wherever he was invited.

In July of 1995, he received his fourth position as pastor of a small Church of God congregation of six people in San Jacinto, renting the Methodist Church for services. During this time, he wrote three pamphlets in Spanish for personal evangelism entitled "Aunque Usted No Lo Crea" ("Though You May Not Believe"), "Amigo Cual Camino Llevas" ("Friend What Road Are You Taking?"), and "Aprovecha La Oportunidad," ("Take Advantage of the Opportunity"). He also established and directed the radio program "Luz Para Los Perdidos" ("A Light For the Lost").

In 1997, the mission that he established decided to purchase an old body shop at 540 S. San Jacinto Ave. and the mechanic shop behind it, as they were paying the Methodist Church $450 per month to use the building on Sundays with the rent being raised to $500 a month. Since they were paying so much for rent, the 100 members of the congregation decided they wanted to purchase the San Jacinto Avenue property. When they went to the Church of God for financial aid, the superintendent told the group they were not to purchase any property, as they were too small and it might fall back on the main body to pay the mortgage. Since the mortgage payment on the property was only to be $600 a month, the congregation decided to go ahead with the purchase of the building as they felt they could handle the payments. Previously, the Church of God had given them $5,000 to help support the congregation. With that money and some of their own, they proceeded to purchase the property because they had sufficient funds for the down payment. When they did that, the

The auto repair shop that was purchased in 1997 for use as Centro Cristiano Fuente de Vida's church. (Pacific Southwest District Archives)

Church of God cut them off, no longer having fellowship with them even after Pastor Herrera continued to call the superintendent in order to work things out.

The asking price for the property with the 2 buildings was $112,000 with the congregation securing it for $84,500. While the property was in escrow, the city required the congregation to have more land for parking. When they inquired about the three lots south of the church, the 2 neighbors told them they wanted $375,000 for the lots, making it impossible to purchase that property at the time. The day escrow closed, after receiving the keys to the building, the pastor noticed that the house west of the property was for sale for $75,000 for the house and the adjoining lot. The congregation offered $40,000 for the 2 pieces of land with the owner taking $50,000, making a total mortgage payment of $1,228 a month for all the property. In 2003, the neighbor who wanted $255,000 for the property south of the church sold the 2 corner lots to the church for $54,900.

After the Church of God severed all relationships with the congregation in 1997, the officers of the church decided in 1999 that they wanted to be in fellowship with a church body. That summer Deacon Francisco Ruiz from Trinity Lutheran Church in Indio, who came into the Lutheran Church through Pastor Salomón, called Pastor Herrera asking the congregation to join The Lutheran Church — Missouri Synod. After Pastor Smith from Trinity in Indio talked to the congregation, Pastor Herrera decided to also discuss the matter with Pastor Salomón and the Coachella Valley Mission Society. They officially began as a Lutheran congregation on November 11, 1999. After many deliberations, the congregation voted to join The Lutheran Church — Missouri Synod in January of 2000.

In the mean time, Rev. Dr. Loren Kramer, president of the Pacific Southwest District, told Pastor Herrera to send all of his papers to the District office to be reviewed in order for him to qualify for the colloquy program. When Rev. Dr. Stoterau became the president of the District, he thought that Pastor Herrera should attend the Spanish Institute of Theology in St. Louis, Missouri, and San Antonio, Texas, as he wasn't proficient enough in English to pass the colloquy test. Pastor Herrera's great joy was being part of The Lutheran Church — Missouri Synod, where his congregation could count on the support and encouragement not only of District officials but also the local

Pastor Herrera's great joy was being part of The Lutheran Church — Missouri Synod, where his congregation could count on the support and encouragement.

Lutheran churches in the area.

During the first six months of 2000, Pastor Herrera was training his congregation in Lutheran doctrine and worship. In the summer, the pastor and congregation were invited to attend the Hispanic Support Group meeting at Trinity in San Bernardino on a Saturday, where there was a high liturgical service. When he returned home that evening, many members called him saying they were very upset, as they had left the Catholic Church because of all the high liturgical practices. The next day at Sunday Bible class, the Bible topic couldn't be studied as many people expressed their concerns about the service they had attended the previous day with many leaving the class that day never to return to the church. Within a short time, there was a mass exodus of 90 people leaving the congregation. Only 10 members remained. With so few members and a high mortgage payment on the property, Pastor Herrera decided to get a secular job, as the congregation couldn't pay his salary. His two daughters told him that they thought it was more important for him to stay in the full-time ministry to lead souls to Christ with both daughters securing employment so that the family would have a means of support. In his sermons Pastor Herrera often stressed the importance of family saying, "If we have a good, strong family, we will have a strong church and a strong community." His daughters certainly demonstrated the words that he preached.

The year 2000 began with the women and men's groups having prayer and Bible study services in homes of families every Tuesday. They had potluck lunches with the goal of developing good relationships among themselves, inviting their neighbors to share in the meal, and in the Word of God. Some of the needs at the time were Spanish Bibles, *Cantad al Senor* hymnals, and Sunday schools materials in Spanish. Another priority was to help poor families in the San Jacinto Valley, which included San Jacinto and Hemet. In August, the Coachella Valley Hispanic Ministry loaned $24,714.30 as an unsecured loan to pay the second mortgage on the church property of Centro Cristiano Fuente de Vida. It was a temporary loan until a full loan could be secured from LCEF. Also during the summer, Pastor Herrera attended the seminar at San Antonio, Texas, and the Hispanic Conference at Concordia University at Mequon, Wisconsin. The church had its first Vacation Bible School and Pastor was invited to preach at a LWML rally at Prince of Peace in Hemet even though he said his English was limited. Rev. Carlos Hernandez, director of human care, came from St. Louis, Missouri, to work in San Jacinto Valley.

On Sunday, December 12, 2000, at 4:00 p.m., Rev. Robert Smith, circuit counselor and pastor of Trinity Lutheran Church in Indio, joined Dr. Ken Behnken of the District office to welcome the Centro Cristiano Fuente de Vida congregation into the Lutheran church. At the time, this church was one of only two Lutheran churches in Riverside County to conduct services in Spanish. Pastor Herrera stated, "Our group is very strong in the faith. They are courageous and hard working, also." An example of that hard work could be found at the church, as members converted the former garage on San Jacinto Avenue into a sanctuary with a large chapel using pews they had received from Lamb of God in Ontario when it disbanded and other pews they had purchased. Both Prince of Peace in Hemet and Shepherd of the Hills in Rancho Cucamonga had each given them an organ and many other congregations had given support and Christian love. A second large building on the property was used for Sunday school rooms and a storage room for materials sold at periodic rummage sales. The year ended with an average of 22 people attending worship services with 8 in the Sunday school and 17 in the Bible class.

The year 2001 began with the need to do repair work on the church facilities and property. The incorporation papers of the congregation had been completed and were accepted by the state. Also, Pastor Herrera's wife became disabled and was confined to her bed, having total knee replacement surgery in the fall. During the second quarter of the year, through the loan from LCEF, the church property and parsonage were secured. One of the big projects was to remodel the church when funds were available. That summer Pastor

> Pastor Herrera states, "Our group is very strong in the faith. They are courageous and hard working."

The congregation at worship in the converted auto repair shop. (Pacific Southwest District Archives)

Herrera completed the first level of work at the Hispanic Institute of Theology, visited Concordia Seminary in St. Louis, and assisted at the installation of Dr. Gerald Kieschnick, the new President of the Synod; in November, he began the second level of classes at the seminary in St. Louis.

The one big goal for 2002 was to reach the San Jacinto Valley's 26,000 Hispanic population. On March 15, Region 3, represented by all the pastors in the region, met at Centro Cristiano Fuente de Vida. During the first part of the year, the congregation was invited by the Chamber of Commerce to participate in a fair in the Hemet Valley Mall; Fuente de Vida was the only church to participate, and they were able to share the Gospel with those in attendance. Through their efforts, an aggressive evangelism campaign was developed in the valley, bringing some new people into the church. With the help of Deacon Edgar Arroyo of Trinity in Santa Ana, there was a special outreach activity using his musical ministry. A new style of evangelism was developed using plastic bags containing Christian literature, which were delivered to homes in the area.

During the summer, Pastor Herrera attended the Frontera Ministries Conference, a ministry of LCMS that coordinated the efforts of all the districts along the Mexican border with the synodical work in Mexico. The goal was to reach one million Mexican citizens and train 500 new workers. Once again a Vacation Bible School was conducted in August. Also in August, Pastor Herrera worked with Pastor Samuel Gómez of Misión Hispaña Gracia in Escondido. Pastor Herrera baptized 3 children in the city of Perris with close to 150 participating in the baptismal reception. He was helping coordinate the development of Bible studies in the Perris area. The year ended with the congregation making plans to build a beautiful new chapel

and parish hall when funds could be raised for the project.

The new year of 2003 began with the first quarter worship attendance averaging 35 persons per Sunday with the Sunday school growing to 15. The congregation maintained an aggressive outreach program throughout the year. In July, the congregation voted to begin the construction on a new sanctuary and the other facilities by August of 2006. During the summer, Pastor attended the Hispanic Institute of Theology on the campus of Concordia Seminary in St. Louis. Vacation Bible School was conducted on August 18–23 with the theme, "Portraits of the Family" where children from the church and neighborhood as well as adults read and learned about Cain and Abel, Joseph, Moses, and the Prodigal Son. In the fall, the outreach to the Hispanic community began with the ESL classes, which were conducted on Monday evenings from 6:00 p.m. to 7:00 p.m. with 41 students registered and taught by 2 teachers, Mr. Dorman Dimmitt and Mr. Chuck Bentz, along with Mr. Leo Garcia teaching a computer class. On September 6, 2003, the church had a rummage sale even though it began to rain on the day before with Pastor, his wife, and her sister putting away items so they wouldn't be damaged. Even with the problem of rain the previous day, the rummage sale was a big success with a huge amount of donated items coming from Prince of Peace Lutheran Church in Hemet. The mission conducts four rummage sales a year along with the ladies of the mission making Mexican tamales with the proceeds used to balance the budget.

Through the years as Pastor Herrera continued to do evangelism work in the community, he discovered that some of his former members had placed fliers on the doors of the people in the town, stating that he had changed from Church of God

Model of proposed new church buildings for Centro Cristiano Fuente de Vida. (Pacific Southwest District Archives)

Rummage sale on church property. (Pacific Southwest District Archives)

to Lutheran; what would he be next? Through these fliers, it made evangelism very difficult, as San Jacinto was a middle class city with the Hispanic population owning their own homes. One of the first summers that the pastor was away for classes, one of the young men of the original congregation convinced a number of the members to leave the church and return to the Church of God.

Even with all the difficulties, the church today has grown to over 35 members who support the parish with their love offerings of $2,500 a month along with the Coachella Valley Mission Society giving $900 a month, the District providing about $833 a month, and Prince of Peace in Hemet helping with $200 a month. The church has been blessed with faithful members and friends.

Arizona
Land of the Sun

rizona is known as the Copper State due to its rich and numerous copper mines, having the motto, *Ditat Deus* — "God enriches," which is certainly true in all aspect of Arizona's rich history and the history of The Lutheran Church — Missouri Synod in the state. When tourists crisscrossed the state in 1950 or when the "snowbirds" who came from the cold, frigid north to spend the winter in a mild, warm climate, they would look for a Missouri Synod church in the *Lutheran Annual* for the nearest place of worship, only to discover that there were about 38 stations listed with 33 belonging to the Wisconsin Synod, one to the Southern California District, and four to the English District, a nongeographical District of Synod. One might wonder why the Wisconsin Synod dominated the Arizona landscape as Wisconsin was so far away, and the Southern California District of The Lutheran Church — Missouri Synod was so close at hand. This disparity was the result of a "gentlemen's agreement" between the two synods, scrupulously observed by Southern California District. At the time, Arizona had 65,000 Indians with 6 major Indian reservations in the state having 23 Wisconsin Synod Indian missions.

The Wisconsin Synod's work began in 1893 when two Indian missionaries, John Plocher and Paul Mayerhoff, arrived at their field of labor at Fort San Carlos welcomed by the Apache Indians even though they didn't speak Apache or English well. They established two missions, one at Fort San Carlos and the other at Camp Apache. The U. S. Government gave the mission a plot of land for the erection of a chapel with the Mission Board of the Wisconsin Synod appropriating $1,000 toward the building. The Rev. Gustav Harders eventually became "the grand old man" of the Apache mis-

sion and eventually "wrestled" the gentleman's agreement not to enter Arizona from the California Mission Board of the Missouri Synod. Before an annoying throat problem forced him to seek relief in the arid Arizona climate in 1904, he had been the very well-liked pastor of Jerusalem Lutheran Church in Milwaukee. He was also a talented and gifted writer, who wrote three Indian mission novels, *La Paloma*, *Will Against Will*, and *Jualahn*, published in Hamburg, Germany. These novels had a strong emotional appeal to Germans, becoming German literary classics as they were widely read by the religiously indifferent in Germany before the 1918 collapse of the country. Up to the time of his death in 1917, he was the general superintendent of Wisconsin's Indian missions that had headquarters at Globe, Arizona.

Until 1909, the Wisconsin Synod's sole interest in Arizona was comprised of the Indian mission work to the exclusion of all others. A chance meeting would change the history that finally forced the Wisconsin Synod to concern itself with the needs of Lutherans who were settling in Arizona. During October 18 through 29 of 1909, at the request of the California and Nevada Mission Board and the local Los Angeles Conference of the Missouri Synod, Pastor August Hansen of Pasadena was asked to explore Arizona. His trip came about through a letter from a Missouri Synod layman, Charles Kage, who had married and settled in Tempe. He inquired of his former pastor, Rev. Charles Panhorst of Petoskey, Michigan, about the possibilities of having the services of the Missouri Synod for his family. Pastor Panhorst sent a letter to Rev. G. A. Bernthal, president of the California and Nevada District of the Missouri Synod, who in turn referred it to the local Los Angeles Conference for action with their exploits resulting in the Arizona survey by Rev. A. Hansen. Before he embarked on his trip to investigate Arizona for the Missouri Synod, a notice was published in *The Lutheran Witness* and *Der Lutheraner* about the canvass that was to be conducted. With this notice, names and addresses of 11 families were sent to him referring him to people in Phoenix, Tucson, Tempe, Warren, and Bisbee. After arriving in Phoenix on the Southern Pacific Railroad, he held services on October 24 at the downtown Methodist Church with 19 adults and 4 children in attendance, who also requested regular services. In Tucson, services were held at the W. Dittus home with four persons being communed. He stayed at the home of Mr. and Mrs. F. Hann, whom he had met on the day he had installed Rev. Fred C. Leimbrock in San Diego in 1906. He knew Mrs. Hann, as she had been a member of his congregation in Pasadena. At Bisbee Warren, a service was held where three communed. On October 27, 28, and 29, he canvassed Bisbee finding 10 Lutherans living there.

When he left for home, Pastor Hansen promised the Arizona Lutherans that he would recommend to the California and Nevada District Mission Board that a missionary for Arizona should be called for the area. While having lunch en route home in the Southern Pacific diner, Superintendent Gustav Harders boarded the train at Benson, Arizona, looking for the Lutheran pastor from California. Pastor Hansen discussed Missouri Synod's plans for inaugurating services for the Lutherans in Arizona with Harders suggesting that in the interest of his Indian mission, the Wisconsin Synod should be allowed to take over the Phoenix work planned by the California and Nevada District Mission Board of the Missouri Synod. This would assure a more effective continuance of Wisconsin's Indian mission, as Indian wards could be directed to such congregations established in the cities. He went on to suggest that a worker from the Wisconsin Synod might serve where the Missouri Synod had done exploratory work. With this suggestion, Pastor Hansen added this proposal to his Arizona survey report. After considerable correspondence, it was finally agreed that the California and Nevada District would temporarily desist from carrying out their plans, permitting the Wisconsin Synod to serve the Lutherans there with a more or less clear understanding that the Wisconsin Synod would not duplicate efforts and extend its operations to the area of the California and Nevada District.

With this agreement, cordial relations were maintained and good counsel prevailed, leaving no doubt that the Wisconsin Synod was willing to occupy the field with Pastor Harders going to Tucson for services once a month. Because of Arizona's distances, the rest of the state had to depend on "outside" help, in this case whatever assistance the Missouri Synod was able to furnish. From a great deal of correspondence that reached Southern California, it seemed that the Lutherans of Phoenix, Bisbee–Warren, Douglas, Tucson, and other places did not object to being served by Missouri Synod pastors who happened to be in Arizona. At Bisbee, there were some 500 Finns in the Finnish settlement, who worked in the mines. Since the Wisconsin Synod was unable to supply the field, the Board for Foreign-Tongue Missions of the Missouri Synod sent Pastor C. S. Klemmer in 1911 to serve the Finns.

After World War I when the Douglas field became vacant, the Wisconsin Synod gladly used the services of a Missouri Synod Army chaplain, Chaplain A. J. Schliesser of the 32nd U.S. Infantry stationed at nearby Camp Davis. When the chaplain transferred, a Missouri Synod pastor, Rev. John C. Schmidt, from Milwaukee, who was in Arizona for his health, served the Douglas area. Afterwards, he went to Southern California serving congregations in San Pedro and Redondo Beach.

In 1914, Zion Lutheran Church of Phoenix joined the Wisconsin Synod five years after the agreement between the synods had been put into operation. But when the congregation became vacant in 1925, Pastor Richard G. Deffner, a Missouri Synod clergyman, was unanimously called and installed on February 1, 1926, rendering 13 years service to the congregation before accepting a call to St. John's in Covina, California, in 1939. Zion's next pastor again was a Missouri Synod man, Rev. Robert W. Schaller, who subsequently married Lorna Smukal, the daughter of the Southern California District's President Smukal, thus making it impossible for California ever to lose sight of the work in Arizona. At the 50th anniversary of the California and Nevada District in 1937, congratulatory letters came from Arizona with the same sentiments as in 1909, California is nearer than Wisconsin and the Arizona pastors and members wanted to affiliate with the Missouri Synod.

In the October 15, 1940, issue of the Southern California *District News*, it reported a "Macedonian call" from Arizona with numerous groups of Lutherans of Missouri Synod origin insisting on being served by the Southern California District. Since requests had come to the California District from Kingman, Seligman, Williams, Flagstaff, Tucson, Phoenix, and other places, the District was satisfied that the Wisconsin Synod was unable to give adequate service, and it was resolved to occupy the field immediately. However, the administration of the Southern California District remembered the gentleman's agreement and abided by it.

Yuma, Arizona, was situated on the California line with the Colorado River separating it from the Golden State, and was the center of a prosperous, irrigated valley surrounded by jagged mountains. In 1930, Pastor Arthur W. Kaiser of Holtville in the Imperial Valley began the initial work in Yuma. The first years were difficult, but the Southern California Mission Board did not lose sight of this strategic location, establishing Calvary Lutheran Church, a member of the Southern California District of The Lutheran Church—Missouri Synod. During 1934 and 1935, Student E. A. Wessel served Yuma. On May 19, 1935, Candidate William H. Klaustermeyer was installed and ordained at Yuma, remaining only a year in this hot desert area. Missionary Ottomar H. Tietjen carried on the work and organized the congregation in 1939 with Calvary Church extending a call to him to be its permanent pastor, being installed on November 16, 1939, by President Smukal. During his pastorate at Yuma, Pastor Tietjen joined the California National Guard as chaplain and entered Federal service in 1943. He served with distinction in Luzon and at Manila. He gained a wide military experience from serving with the airborne soldiers of the 82nd Airborne Division to service with the chair-borne soldiers of the Pentagon.

> Missionary Ottomar H. Tietjen carries on the work and organizes Calvary Lutheran Church in Yuma, Arizonza, in 1939.

Rev. Elmer C. J. Boxdorfer, pastor of Calvary, Yuma, 1944 to 1950, conducted survey of Phoenix along with Rev. Webbeking and Rev. R. Finke. (Pacific Southwest District Archives)

From 1944 to 1950, Rev. Elmer C. J. Boxdorfer was pastor in Yuma where he not only had opportunities to serve many hundreds of troops stationed in the desert and at the Yuma Army Air Corps Base but he also served Germans in the prisoner-of-war camps in Yuma County. As circuit visitor during his ministry in Yuma, he was engaged in helping to establish churches in Blythe, Brawley, Needles, and Indio along with preaching at each station. Before he was called to Zion in Maywood, California, where he spent the last 28 years of his ministry, he was requested by a group of Missouri Synod Lutherans to establish a preaching station in Phoenix.

As early as 1948, the Southern California District's interest in Arizona was rekindled as the Board of Directors in its session on December 14, 1948, passed a resolution asking the Mission Board to consider entering Phoenix, Arizona, with a new mission. The decision was made to run an ad in the Phoenix papers, the *Arizona Republic* and the *Gazette,* for a week requesting all unaffiliated Lutherans of the Missouri Synod to send their names and addresses to a designated box number of the newspaper. Pastors Webbeking, Boxdorfer, and Finke spent several days in Phoenix following up on eight replies received from unaffiliated communicant members of the Missouri Synod. The reactions they received were very encouraging with the committee convinced that the people in Phoenix wanted a Missouri Synod Church even though there were three Wisconsin Synod churches, one United Lutheran Church and two American Lutheran churches in Phoenix.

By April of 1949, after further investigation into the Phoenix, Arizona, mission possibilities, and after consultation with members of the South Wisconsin District Mission Board of the Wisconsin Synod, the Mission Board had "come to the conclusion that the interests of the kingdom of God are best served if the Southern California District, The Lutheran Church — Missouri Synod, does not at this time enter the Arizona field." The Mission Board resolved "that at this time the Southern California District will not enter this field and be it further resolved that this resolution be referred to the Board of Directors of the Southern California District." With this resolution, the Missouri Synod Lutherans were once again left with no church of their own. One year later Phoenix had grown to 106,000 people with many more Lutherans arriving in the Valley of the Sun.

Mt. Calvary Lutheran Church
Sola Fide (FE) Lutheran Church
Phoenix, Arizona

undreds of years before any of the cities in the eastern section of the United States were so much as a clearing in the wilderness, a well-established, civilized community occupied the land that is now known as Phoenix with the Pueblo Grande ruins testifying to the city's ancient roots, between 700 A.D. and 1400 A.D. The wide Salt River ran through the valley, but there was little rain or melting snow to moisten the brown, parched earth from river to mountain range on either side; the former industrious, enterprising, and imaginative residents had built an irrigation system consisting of about 135 miles of canals, in order to channel water to this dry, arid land making it fertile farm terrain. The ultimate fate of this ancient society is a mystery with the accepted belief that it was destroyed by a prolonged drought. When the roving Indians observed the Pueblo Grande ruins and the vast canal system the people left behind, they gave them the name "Hohokam," the people who have gone. The 90Maricopa and Pima Indians lived there when John Y. T. Smith, a white trader, arrived in the mid-1860s.

The modern history of Phoenix began in the second half of the nineteenth century, when Jack Swilling of Wickenburg stopped to rest his horse at the foot of the north slopes of the White Tank Mountains in 1867; looking down and across the expansive Salt River Valley, his eyes beheld the rich gleam of the brown, dry soil turned up by the horse's hooves and saw fertile farmland, free of rocks, and a place beyond the reach of heavy frost or snow. The only thing that was needed was water! After returning to Wickenburg, he organized the Swilling Irrigation Canal Company, moved into the valley, and began digging a canal to divert some of the Salt River water onto the land in the valley. By March 1868, water was flowing through the canal with a few members of the company raising meager crops that summer, and a small colony was formed approximately four miles east of the present city with Swilling's Mill adopted as the new name of the area. It was later changed to Helling Mill, Mill City, and years later, East Phoenix. Darrell Duppa suggested the name Phoenix, as the new town would spring from the ruins of a former civilization with Phoenix officially recog-

nized on May 4, 1868, when the Yavapai County Board of Supervisors, the county in which it was located at the time, formed an election precinct.

A post office was established in Phoenix on June 15, 1868, with Jack Swilling as postmaster. The Richard Flour Mills, built in 1869, was the first steam mill in the Valley. With the rapid influx of pioneers continuing, a town site was selected on October 20, 1870, with the official designation of the North Half of Section 8, Township 1 North, Range 3 East, which today encompasses the downtown business section, bounded on the north by Van Buren Street, on the south by Jackson Street, on the east by Seventh Street, and on the west by Seventh Avenue. To administer this new town site, the Salt River Valley Town Association was formed. Captain William A. Hancock, a surveyor, did the first survey of the town site laying out the lots and the town, which was one mile long, a half-mile wide containing 96 blocks with the 100 feet wide Washington Street designated the main street in town. The east and west streets were named after U.S. presidents with Washington Street in the middle and Adams, the first street to the north, Jefferson, first street south of Washington with the pattern following — one to the north and one to the south — until recent years. The north-south streets originally carried Indian names, but these were changed in favor of the more easily remembered numbers, with streets being to the east of Central Avenue and avenues to the west.

In the December 7, 1870, issue of the *Prescott Miner*, the following advertisement was listed: "GREAT SALE OF LOTS AT PHOENIX, ARIZONA, on the 23rd and 24th of December." The first effort to market Phoenix resulted in the sale of 61 lots with an average sale price of $48 each. The first lot, purchased by Judge William Berry of Prescott, located at the southwest corner of First and Washington streets, sold for the rather steep price of $116. The first store building to be erected in the new town was Hancock's Store, an adobe general store on the northwest corner of First and Washington streets, which opened in July 1871, and also served as the town hall, county offices, and general meeting place of early Phoenix. Although churches had been formed by 1870, the first church building erected in Phoenix was the Central Methodist Church built in 1871 at the corner of Second Avenue and Washington Street. In 1872, the first Catholic priest came to Phoenix conducting Mass in the Otero home until 1881, when an adobe church building at Third and Monroe streets was built for the Sacred Heart of St. Louis. The first school opened for the youth of Phoenix on September 5, 1872, with about 20 children studying under the guidance of Jean Rudolph Derroche in the courtroom of the county building. By October 1873, a small adobe school building was completed on Center Street (now Central Avenue), a short distance north of where the San Carlos Hotel now stands. The first female schoolteacher in Phoenix was Miss Nellie Shaver, a newcomer from Wisconsin. In 1895, the Phoenix Union High School was established with 90 students enrolled.

On February 12, 1871, Yavapai County was divided, with Maricopa County, the sixth county in the state, created by the Legislature. In 1874, downtown lots were selling for $7 to $11 each. Also that year, the first telegraph line entered Phoenix with Morris Goldwater, the first operator of this station, located in his father's store on the northwest corner of First and Jefferson streets. By 1875, there were 16 saloons, 4 dance halls, 2 monte banks and one faro table in Phoenix. A safe location was required for the money that was being made in the valley so the National Bank was established in 1878 with capital stock of $200,000. The first newspaper in Phoenix was the *Salt River Valley Herald*, which changed its name to the *Phoenix Herald* in 1880. In 1880, Phoenix had a population of 2,453, a school enrollment of 379 pupils, an ice factory, and a new brick sidewalk in front of the Tiger Saloon. In 1881, the 11th Territorial Legislature passed "The Phoenix Charter Bill," making Phoenix an incorporat-

ed city and providing for a government consisting of a mayor and four council members with the bill signed by Governor John C. Fremont on February 25, 1881. On May 3, 1881, the first election was held in the newly incorporated city, having a population of approximately 2,500 with John T. Alsap elected mayor, receiving 127 votes. Great strides were made toward making Phoenix a modern city, with one of the first electric plants in the west, a steam plant with boilers fired by mesquite wood, installed in Phoenix in 1886. That same year, the Phoenix Fire Engine Company Number 1 was organized comprised of a volunteer group that served the city for many years.

On November 5, 1887, the first horse-drawn streetcar line was built along some two miles of Washington Street with an additional line installed along Center Street on December 30, 1889. The streetcar system became rather extensive in later years, with tracks covering most of Phoenix and extending even to Glendale. The horse-drawn streetcar was replaced by electric cars in 1893 and then by the automobile with the streetcars discontinued on February 17, 1948. On July 4, 1887, the first Southern Pacific train arrived from Maricopa Wells; the advent of the railroad helped to revolutionize the economy of the area with merchandise flowing into the city by rail taking products quickly to eastern and western markets instead of by wagon. In 1889, the territorial government was moved from Prescott to Phoenix. On March 12, 1895, the Santa Fe, Prescott, and Phoenix Railroad ran its first train to Phoenix, connecting Phoenix to the northern part of Arizona and giving travelers another outlet to the east and west via the Santa Fe. The additional railroad speeded the capital city's rise to economic supremacy in the state.

The advent of the railroad helps to revolutionize the economy of the area with merchandise flowing into the city by rail, taking products quickly to eastern and western markets.

Washington Street in downtown Phoenix in the 1870s with adobe buildings on the right.

Horse drawn streetcars passing old courthouse in the 1890s.

On February 18, 1908, the Carnegie Free Library was opened with the library building donated to the city by Andrew Carnegie. By the turn of the century, the population of Phoenix had reached 5,554. The state capital finally got a permanent home when a 10-acre lot was donated at the west end of Washington Street with a building, constructed of native tufa in neoclassic style, erected at a cost of $130,000 and dedicated on February 25, 1901. An important event for the people of Phoenix and the valley occurred in 1902, when President Theodore Roosevelt signed the National Reclamation Act making it possible to build dams on western streams for reclamation purposes. The Theodore Roosevelt Dam, the first multiple-purpose dam to supply both water and electric power, was constructed under the National Reclamation Act and started in 1906. On May 18, 1911, the former President dedicated the dam, the largest masonry dam in the world, opening a new era in farming for the valley and securing the part of the economy that depended on water for its lifeblood. President William Howard Taft approved Arizona's statehood on February 14, 1912, making it the 48th state in the Union.

By 1930, Phoenix had grown to 48,118 with 120 miles of sidewalks and 161 miles of streets of which 77 were paved. The year 1940 marked another turning point in the life of Phoenix as the city had gone from a farming center to a distribution center with World War II rapidly turning Phoenix into an industrial city. Luke Field, Williams Field, and Falcon Field, coupled with the giant ground-training center at Hyder, west of Phoenix, brought thousands of men into Phoenix with their needs, both militarily and personally, met in part by the small industries in Phoenix. When the war ended, many of these men returned to Phoenix with their families. Suddenly large industries, learning of this vast labor pool, started to move branches to the city. In 1950, 105,000 people lived within the city limits of Phoenix, an area of 17.1 square miles, with thousands more living immediately adjacent to and depending upon Phoenix for their livelihoods. Today, the city covers almost 470 square miles with a population of 1.15 million of which 34.1 percent are Hispanic, ranking it 7th in the country with Phoenix the corporate and industrial center of the southwest.

By the late 1940s more Missouri Synod Lutherans were moving to Phoenix wanting a church of their own. One who disclaimed knowledge of the "gentlemen's agreement" was Ted Dallmann, a retired builder who helped organize Mount Calvary Church, the first Missouri Synod congregation in Phoenix, which came to be known as Synod's "Mother Church" in central Arizona. Before leaving Riverside, Illinois, in 1948, he and his wife, Helene, were advised that the Missouri Synod's English District had planned to start missions in Arizona and were given a list of Lutherans living in the area with the encouragement to get in touch with them.

At about the same time, a small group of Missouri Synod Lutherans living in Phoenix, who were mostly unaffiliated with any church, was anxious to have a Missouri Synod church established in the valley. Dr. Victor Behnken, president of the Southern California District, was contacted in regard to procedures in starting a church. He advised them to contact Rev. Boxdorfer in Yuma, the circuit visitor and pastor of Calvary Church, and the only Missouri Synod church in Arizona at the time. Pastor Boxdorfer suggested that they run an ad in the newspaper to ascertain how many people in Phoenix were interested in starting a church. If there were enough families interested in beginning a Missouri Synod mission, he would go to Phoenix to conduct services on Sunday evenings. After the ad ran for 2 weeks in the local newspaper, 15 interested families were found to form the nucleus of a church. The report was forwarded to Rev. Boxdorfer who, in the meantime, had accepted a call to Maywood, California. After Dr. Behnken was contacted again, he sent a telegram advising Mr. Vanatter, a leader of the group, that the reverends Streufert and Ted McRee of the English District were at a Tucson hotel as they were making arrangements to start a mission there. Unfortunately, Mr. Vanatter failed to make contact with them.

Some time later, the Rev. R. Jesse of the English District, began holding services in Tucson with the Vanatter family driving to Tucson to see him. He suggested they find two or more families not affiliated with any Synodical Conference congregation in Phoenix who would write to the Mission Board of the English District asking to start a mission in Phoenix; his advice was followed. Finally, with permission granted, the first service, attended by 78 people, was held in the music room at Grandview School, located at Eleventh Avenue and Camelback Road, on July 23, 1950. At this service, the congregation was organized as Mount Calvary Lutheran Church of Phoenix and elected Theodore Dallmann as temporary president with

Harold Griffith temporary treasurer. When this group outgrew the music room, they moved services to the auditorium of the school. The following year, the first Easter service was held in the garden courtyard of Grandview School with the altar decorated with palms and a white cross. The Rev. Emil H. Polster, missionary-at-large, who later accepted the call to serve as the congregation's first pastor, conducted both of the services.

Pastor Polster, the first pastor of the first Missouri Synod Lutheran church in the city of Phoenix not affiliated with the Wisconsin Synod, was a native of Kansas who had been serving a congregation in St. Paul, Minnesota, prior to being called by the Mission Board of the English District to begin a mission congregation in the Phoenix area. His family consisted of his wife, Margaret, and his daughter, Virginia, who at the time was a 22-year-old graduate of the University of Minnesota.

The Rev. Emil H. Polster, Mt. Calvary's first pastor, served from 1950 to 1954. (Pacific Southwest District Archives)

During the first four years of Mount Calvary's existence, Pastor Polster laid the groundwork for this growing congregation with Vicar Louis Nau assigned to assist him in this work until September 1953 when he returned to the seminary for his final year. He and pastor made hundreds of house calls, followed up on visitors, Lutheran Hour referrals, and other leads with the church growth steady and gratifying, growing day-by-day. Vicar Nau came back to Mount Calvary in 1954 for his ordination into the ministry, as this was his home parish. His first call was to the mountainous country of north-central Luzon in the Philippines as a missionary. During his missionary work there, he dedicated the Mount Calvary Chapel in Luzon in 1955, using the same logo of Mount Calvary in Phoenix, three crosses on a hill, placed over the door of the chapel.

With much foresight, the congregation purchased 10 acres of land in 1952 for $20,000 at the corner of Seventh Avenue and Colter Street, with a member advancing the first $1,000 as down payment on the property. The acreage selected was virtually on the edge of the Phoenix "suburban sprawl" in those early years. With ground broken in March of 1952, construction of the parish facility began with Chester Norris serving as chairman of the Building Committee. By the time the construction of the sanctuary was begun, the members volunteered using shovels and rakes, paint brushes and floor wax, sweat and sun, which were all part of this growing Lutheran community of believers who built this new house of worship. The cornerstone-laying service was held on May 11, 1952, with the dedication services held on September 28, 1952, while the total membership had increased to 376 souls with 259 communicants in just 2 years. Participating in the dedication ceremony was Rev. Harold H. Engelbrecht, who was to become Mount Calvary's second pastor, a few years later.

Mt. Calvary's first church building, dedicated on September 28, 1952, was of neo-Spanish design. (Pacific Southwest District Archives)

The modernistic design on the altar wall pointed to the hand-carved crucifix. (Pacific Southwest District Archives)

Mr. Ed Firant of the architectural firm of Lescher and Mahoney was engaged as the architect of the sanctuary. He designed a $105,000, neo-Spanish building which incorporated both traditional and modern techniques of architecture with a perlite brick, a material used for the walls noted for its insulating qualities, which was so necessary in Phoenix due to the great variances of temperature. Gold-colored draperies and Modernfold doors separated the parish hall and chapel, allowing conversion of the chapel into a larger area when needed. The Modernfold doors were also used to divide the parish hall into individual Sunday school rooms. The floor level of the parish hall was 16 inches higher than the chapel floor with the north wall made of arcadia doors that opened onto the patio. The Women's Guild furnished the completely modern and functional kitchen. In addition, the entire building was cooled by refrigeration. In the chancel, the altar, Communion rail, and pulpit were handmade by Mr. Bernard Schler, Mr. Walter Haake, and Mr. Theodore Dallman. The carpeting in the chancel and the aisles was a gift from the Women's Guild of the congregation. The altar and pulpit paraments and vestments were hand sewn by the Altar Guild. The members of the Men's Club dedicated much time and arduous work in preparing the building for occupancy.

The original church logo, a curved line with three crosses, the center cross representing the cross of Christ, flanked on either side by crosses representing the penitent and the impenitent thieves, was the symbol of Mount Calvary designed by Pastor Polster and displayed on the front of the church building. The reredos wall behind the altar in the sanctuary, painted in vivid shades of chartreuse, red, and yellow that literally danced, was painted by Virginia Polster, the pastor's daughter, who interpreted the "Passion of our Lord Jesus Christ" by use of ancient symbols in terms of modern expression, took eight months to complete. From this artwork, the church received the nickname of "The Red Rooster Church." The symbols used were the chalice and the cross, the shield and rope of Judas, the cock crowing at the third denial by Peter, the crown of thorns pressed upon the Lord's head, the nails driven into His hands and feet on the cross, the bowl of sour wine and hyssop reed used by the soldiers, and surmounting it all, the symbols of the bursting pomegranate, denoting the Lord's resurrection and the hope of everlasting life. All these symbols and the general design of the wall pointed to the cross of Christ, a hand-carved crucifix crafted by Richard Cook, artist and congregational member, taking more than a year to complete.

In mid-1953, a "Cross of Calvary" was installed at the corner of Seventh Avenue and Colter Street. On Arbor Day in 1953, each Sunday school class presented a tree of its choice that was planted in this park area forming a small park in which the cross with rocks placed around the foot, became the focal point of the landscaping. Ramadas were later built for cookouts. Over the years, the badly-deteriorated cross was replaced with a new one donated by the Heldt Lumber Company and installed by the Board of Trustees on April 10, 1979.

After four years of labor watching Mount Calvary grow, the Polsters left in October of 1954, as the pastor had accepted a call to become public relations director for the Lutheran Children's Friends Society of Minnesota. With his departure, lay people and visiting pastors Marcus Lang and William F. Dietz from Tucson conducted church services. After a 35-year career in the ministry, Pastor Harold Engelbrecht received and accepted the call to become Mount Calvary's second shepherd with his installation, taking place on February 20, 1955. He was born in Indiana on September 7, 1897. After attending St. Matthew's School in New York City and Concordia Collegiate Institute, Bronxville, New York, he graduated from Concordia Seminary, St. Louis, in 1920. He was married to Hulda Steege of New Britain, Connecticut, in 1922. They were blessed with five children: Mrs. Carl Kelley, Don, Ellen (deceased), Anthony, and Luther, a missionary to India. Pastor Engelbrecht served Missions in La Grande, Oregon; Immanuel, Puyallup, and Zion, Tacoma, Washington; Valparaiso University, Valparaiso, Indiana; Redeemer, Green Bay, Wisconsin; Trinity, Gary, Indiana; Sherman Oaks Lutheran, Sherman Oaks, California.

With Mt. Calvary and Phoenix continuing to grow, Pastor Engelbrecht assumed the leadership role of church building relinquished by Pastor Polster with incredible progress in the building program during his tenure. In 1955, there were one building, two small areas of lawn, nine palm trees, and a few shrubs with the entire north end of the property a desert covered with tumbleweeds and an unpaved south parking lot. In 1956, the new three-bedroom parsonage on the northeast corner of the property fronting Colter Avenue was dedicated. As the congregation continued to grow, the need for more education space was solved by the construction of an addition to the northwest

Rev. Harold H. Engelbrecht became Mt. Calvary's second pastor on February 20, 1955, remaining until 1966. (Pacific Southwest District Archives)

corner of the sanctuary. At the north side of the chapel, running parallel to Seventh Avenue, a new educational unit, known as Luther Hall, was dedicated September 28, 1957. In later years, this addition was used for the office area and church lounge. The new wing added an expanding Sunday school with the preschool and kindergarten classes held there. In the fall of 1958, this wing also served as the first day school, consisting of kindergarten and grades one and two with Arthur Weidner serving as the first principal until his departure to enter the ministry in 1964.

Continued growth of the parish sent Mt. Calvary back to the drawing board with another building program to remodel the original church structure. Shortly after the dedication of Luther Hall, the congregation decided to remodel the existing sanctuary with Richard Nelson, a member of the congregation, engaged as the architect for the project and with much of the actual labor being done by volunteer labor from the congregation. The entire chancel area was remodeled with a new flagstone altar placed at the east end of the nave having a print dossal curtain hung behind it with the carved crucifix hung in front of the dossal curtain. The gold-colored draperies separating the chapel and the overflow area, formerly the parish hall, were removed, and the overflow area was made into a chapel with a small altar. The old kitchen was converted into the pastor's study with a restroom added. Long windows of cathedral glass were installed on either side of the altar with three long, narrow stained-glass windows added in the south wall of the sanctuary. Dr. A. A. Kretzmann of Chicago, a noted Missouri Synod

Lutheran church leader, designed the windows and the Chicago firm of Hilgart and Giannini fabricated them. The installed windows were dedicated to God's glory on April 19, 1959. With the remodeling of the sanctuary and chancel completed, another service of dedication was held on November 8, 1959.

With the closing of Mount Calvary's first decade of existence, the facilities were in place to allow God's people to worship in comfortable surroundings. As the congregation was growing and vital, it was ready to share blessings with the expanding population of Phoenix. In this era of major change and growth, Mount Calvary joined the Southern California District, thus beginning an era of change and growth of its own. Mt. Calvary teamed with other Lutheran churches in the valley to sponsor a city-wide rally featuring Rev. Oswald Hoffmann's "Crusade," which began on June 24, 1960, in the Scottsdale Ballpark. In the summer, the congregation celebrated its 10th anniversary with Pastor Emil Polster, the first pastor of the parish, as guest preacher. Also, during the summer, Robert Orling, a member of Mount Calvary, served as the vicar. Two "daughter" churches, St. Paul's in west Phoenix and Holy Cross in east Phoenix, were opened, the first of 11 spun off of the "mother church" during this decade of rapid growth. In 1961, two more "daughter churches "were established, Beautiful Savior in Tempe and St. Luke's in Mesa. Once again during that summer, Robert Orling served as vicar at Mount Calvary. In 1962, two more churches, Lutheran Church of the Master and King of Kings, were started. The following year Peace Lutheran opened with Bethle-

> As the congregation was growing and vital, it was ready to share blessings with the expanding population of Phoenix.

Luther Hall, a new educational unit for Sunday school, the preschool, and kindergarten classes, was dedicated September 28, 1957. (Pacific Southwest District Archives)

The remodeled chancel with a Persian print dossal curtain hung the full length of chancel wall, was dedicated on November 8, 1959. (Pacific Southwest District Archives)

hem Lutheran beginning in 1964 calling to its new pulpit Rev. Robert Schaller, former pastor of Zion, a Wisconsin Synod church. Other "daughters" that would be born in the decade of 1960 were St. Mark's in Phoenix, Eternal Life in Mesa, Epiphany in Chandler, and Trinity in Casa Grande with Mount Calvary sending some of its own members as many as 50 at a time, to establish and worship in these new congregations.

On March 14, 1961, a groundbreaking ceremony was conducted for a $145,000, 5-year pay-as-you-go building project to construct a new school and auditorium designed by architect, Richard Nelson, as the expanding congregation needed additional space. Phase One was the building of classrooms on the east side of the property, directly opposite the east end of the sanctuary building with the classrooms constructed in a row running from north to south and completed in 1961. Phase Two began one or two years after the completion of Phase One when additional funds became available which included the construction of a kitchen and a library that were built to the west of the classroom building running parallel to it with a vacant area between the two reserved for an auditorium joining the classroom building on the east with the library/kitchen structure on the west. The 700-seat auditorium and classroom area was dedicated on October 2, 1966, by Pastor Harold Engelbrecht with the structure named Engelbrecht Hall in his honor. In succeeding years, the building became known as the Education Building. At a later date, the auditorium was converted into a gymnasium. Since it was not originally designed to be a gymnasium, the basketball court was not regulation size. All of the building had been accomplished in less than 10 years, with the projects dedicated debt free. The congregation had an architect, plumber, masons, electrician, painters, artist, carpenters, and other talented workers with 67 men and women working many days to complete the projects.

Pastor Engelbrecht was honored on June 5, 1960, with a surprise observance of his 40th year in the holy ministry. Pastor Harold Johnson of Mill Valley, California, a close personal friend of Pastor Engelbrecht, was the preacher at both services and also the principal speaker at a banquet at the Hiway-House in Phoenix that evening. At the banquet, Rev. E. E. Streufert of San Fernando, local pastors, and the officers of Mount Calvary Church gave congratulatory remarks. The program was interspersed with selections by the choir and vocal groups under the direction of Mr. Richard Cook. Another highlight of the evening was the presentation of personal gifts and a purse of money given to Pastor and Mrs. Engelbrecht by the organizations and members of the congregation.

On June 13, 1965, Mount Calvary honored Pastor and Mrs. Harold Engelbrecht again for 10 years of service at Mount Calvary and 45 years in the ministry of the Lutheran Church with a "bon voyage" dinner. The 1,300-member congregation honored its 64-year-old pastor with a world tour that included India, as the Engelbrechts' son, Luther, was a missionary there. Under his administration, the flock increased several hundred percent, built new facilities, and helped develop 11 other congregations.

In September 1966, Pastor announced that he would be leaving Mount Calvary to accept a call as assistant pastor of Zion Lutheran Church in Piedmont, California. October 2 marked the completion of Mt. Calvary's master building plan of 7 projects and the fruitful ministry of 11-½ years of Pastor Engelbrecht in the congregation. Pastor departed with the following statement, "I have great confidence and trust in the young people. The church will be in good hands when they assume the leadership." This statement was not unusual for Pastor Engelbrecht, as he had been active in Walther League work, having been vice president of the International Walther League and having served as International Walther League representative at LSV schools for 35 years. That October he continued his ministry by assisting at Zion Church in Piedmont. In California, the Engelbrechts had the opportunity to be with some of their family, as their son, Luther, and his family were on furlough from the India mission field with a year of study in Berkeley, and Anthony was a medical doctor at Stanford University Hospital in Palo Alto. On September 28, 1972, Pastor Engelbrecht died of a stroke at the age of 75, while visiting relatives in Hartford, Connecticut.

With Pastor Engelbrecht's official resignation on October 3, 1966, the congregation called a 37-year-old pastor to become the next shepherd of Mount Calvary. Rev. Eugene Beyer was installed on March 19, 1967. He was born in Hillsdale, Michigan, on May 4, 1929, the son of Rev. Arthur and Mrs. Beyer, receiving his grade school education in Fowler and Ypsilanti, Michigan. After attending high school and junior college at Concordia College, Fort Wayne, Indiana, he entered Concordia Seminary in 1949. During his vicarage in

In 1966, Pastor Engelbrecht's departing words are: "I have great confidence and trust in the young people. The church will be in good hands when they assume the leadership."

Rev. Eugene Beyer, third pastor of Mt. Calvary, was installed on March 19, 1967, leaving in 1978 to begin a mission in Scottsdale. (Pacific Southwest District Archives)

In April 1968, the Southern California District holds its first convention outside of California at the Del Webb Townhouse in Phoenix, attended by 1,000 delegates from 216 churches, with Mount Calvary hosting it.

Rockford, Illinois, he organized a mission congregation in nearby Loves Park. In June 1954, he was ordained into the holy ministry and installed as the associate pastor of Calvary Lutheran Church, Lincoln Park, Michigan, where his father had been serving since 1948. On June 18, 1955, he entered the holy estate of matrimony with Linda Schumaker, daughter of Mr. and Mrs. Leon Schumaker of St. Johns, Michigan, with their marriage blessed with four children, Ellyce, Paul, Eugene, and Erick. Upon the death of Pastor Beyer's father in January 1956, he was named pastor of Calvary, which was in the midst of a $500,000 building project of a new church, school, and gymnasium. During nearly 13 years at Calvary, he served the Michigan District as stewardship chairman for the Wyandotte Circuit, as District representative to the Detroit Metropolitan Lutheran Research Commission, and as a member of the Urban Study Committee of Detroit and suburbs.

In 1967, August Stellhorn was hired as teacher and principal of the Mount Calvary Day School and organist and director of the parish where he served until his death on September 5, 1976. Before going to Mt. Calvary with his wife, Rose Ann, a son, and four daughters, he served as teacher and organist at St. Paul's Church in Fort Wayne. In April 1968, the Southern California District held its first convention outside of California at the Del Webb Townhouse in Phoenix, attended by 1,000 delegates from 216 churches, with Mount Calvary hosting it. On September 21, 1968, David L. Freiberg was appointed as director of youth and education. His primary responsibility was working with the teenagers of the congregation, assisting with the Sunday school, weekday school, Vacation Bible School, and Bible class and also assisting Pastor Beyer in evangelism. He was a native of Wausau, Wisconsin, receiving his education at Concordia Teachers College, River Forest, Illinois. He had served parishes in Centralia, Illinois, as a day school teacher, and New Orleans, Louisiana, and Battle Creek, Michigan, as director of youth and education.

In 1968, Mount Calvary Day School was forced to close due to lack of enrollment with the transfer of Principal Stellhorn, Teacher Carol Reas, and 39 students to Christ Lutheran School. In 1972, David Freiberg accepted the position as coordinator of Christian education for six Lutheran churches in the Phoenix area, called the Martin Luther School Association; the congregations involved were an American Lutheran Church and five parishes of

The Lutheran Church — Missouri Synod: Christ the Redeemer, Church of the Master, King of Kings, Mount Calvary, and Peace. The school operated in the existing classrooms at Christ American Lutheran at Nineteenth Avenue and Glenrosa. In the early 1980s, the school was divided, with the upper grades, known as Martin Luther Junior High School, moving to Mount Calvary's campus with 55 students in the first junior high class.

As Lutheran families continued to flow into the Valley of the Sun, organizational meetings were conducted in early 1979 for the establishment of a Lutheran high school in Phoenix. These meetings led to Dr. Mark Silzer accepting a call as first principal of Valley Lutheran High School. The high school was governed by an association of Lutheran churches, both from the Missouri Synod and the Evangelical Lutheran Church in America (ELCA) with most of valley's students coming from these association member churches. The school itself began in September 1981 in a vacant school building at Twenty-third and Wilshire avenues with Mount Calvary as one of the supporting churches. With Mount Calvary's central location and open areas, VLHS was moved to its campus in 1985 with the school using modular units that were installed along the eastern boundary of the church property. The school of grades 9 through 12 had an enrollment of 100 to 120 during the latter part of the 1990s. Recent enrollments have seen an increase in non-Lutheran and non-church students who prefer the smaller school to the larger public high schools.

In the 1970s, a church library of 347 books was established in a small corner of Luther Hall, then later moved to a larger area on the west side of Fellowship/Engelbrecht Hall where the library grew to over 2,000 titles. In September 1970, Mount Calvary celebrated its twentieth anniversary and the 125th anniversary of The Lutheran Church — Missouri Synod under the theme, "A Rose to Remember — A Future to Mold." By 1973, work began on a project to redesign the sanctuary interior to accommodate more people. Francis Schultz, a member of Christ Lutheran Church, one of Mount Calvary's "daughter" churches, was engaged as the architect for another remodel project on the sanctuary. This time the changes involved a greater degree of construction than the previous remodeling.

The altar was moved to the south wall, and a wrap-around seating concept was installed accommodating 400 people. The contemporary version of the Greek cross over the altar was made of copper, enamel, and wood with a small ascending Christ on it with the wall candelabra, Communion candles, and the altar containing the same inlays. The chancel floor was a muted red Italian ceramic tile. The three stained-glass windows were removed from the south wall, made into one window, and relocated just to the south of the office entrance to the patio on the exterior of the south wall of the sanctuary. The floor of the elevated parish hall/overflow area on the north side of the building was removed making it level with the sanctuary floor and the center column was removed to permit a center aisle facing the altar. The arcadia doors on the north wall were replaced with a solid block wall with five, horizontal stained-glass windows inset across the top of the wall, each window depicting some of the last words of Christ on the cross. With the east end of the sanctuary extended farther east, large double door exits were installed which also contained a small narthex area, the chamber for the pipes of the pipe organ, and room for the heating/cooling system. New furnishings for the sanctuary and improved refrigeration systems for both the sanctuary and Luther Hall were installed with the total project costing $210,000.

Worship services were held in Engelbrecht Hall during the 1½-year renovation. Dedication services for the remodeled facilities took place on May 19, 1974, in a special afternoon service attended by over 400 people. Dr. Arnold G. Kuntz, District president, joined Pastor Beyer in the rededication service with celebration and thanksgiving to God for another completed milestone in the life of Mount Calvary. In January 1976, Mount Calvary had grown to 998 members, 790 communicant members and 189 Sunday school pupils. The church property was appraised on December 1, 1977, at $2.7 million, of which $1 million was in the land. A new 15-rank, 12-stop pipe organ for the remodeled church was dedicated on December 18,1977. The instrument, designed by David Harris of Whittier, California, especially for the liturgy of the Lutheran church, was the first organ in the southwest to have a combination card reader to control the combination action allowing the organist to preprogram any changes on a modified computer card offering a permanent record for future reference. The finest woods—poplar, Philippine mahogany and oak—were used in the organ's construction of 900 pipes that were made of tin, lead, and hardwood.

In June of 1978, Pastor Beyer left Mount Calvary to begin a mission congregation, Shepherd of the Desert, in Scottsdale. Following his retirement from that congregation in 1994, the District requested that he start another mission congregation in north Scottsdale that became Desert Foothills Lutheran Church. When Pastor Beyer left on June 25, 1978, his successor, Pastor Donald D. Smidt was installed as the congregation's fourth pastor on January 21, 1979. He was born and raised in the western part of the country, having attended St. John's College in Winfield, Kansas, where he met his future wife, Susan David, whom he married in August of 1964 with their marriage blessed with two children, Erich and Eileen. He received his Bachelor of Arts from Concordia Senior College, Fort Wayne, Indiana, and his Master of Divinity from Concordia Theological Seminary, Springfield, Illinois. He was ordained into the holy ministry in June 1968, at his home congregation in Holyoke, Colorado. Before coming to Phoenix, he was assistant pastor at Bethlehem, Lakewood, Colorado, and senior pastor at Christ Lutheran, Murray, Utah.

In the 1980s, Pastor Smidt began a program of intentional intergenerational ministry, which continued throughout his years at Mount Calvary with numerous new programs initiated and existing older ones expanded, including a Wednesday morning Bible class for senior adults, adult Bible classes, junior and senior high programs, athletic teams and programs, Marriage Encounter seminars, tape ministry, a care ministry for personal crises of members, parenting classes, Cub Scouting, blood pressure checks, singles and couples clubs, and a hiking club with the congregation responding enthusiastically to all of these programs.

Rev. Donald D. Smidt, fourth pastor of Mt. Calvary, served from 1979 to 1996. (Pacific Southwest District Archives)

A new 15-rank pipe organ is designed and built for the remodeled church by David Harris of Whittier, California.

Pastor Beyer standing in the remodeled nave of the church with its new central altar. (Pacific Southwest District Archives)

Rev. Dann Ettner, the present pastor of Mt. Calvary, was installed on January 4, 1998. (Pacific Southwest District Archives)

Ministry to Hispanics in the Phoenix area is Mount Calvary's primary missionary focus throughout the 1990s.

In the mid-1990s, he led a change in the governing body of the church from a church council format to that of board of directors.

During the 1980s, a master plan was adopted for the entire campus property, and the first phase of this plan called for the building of a day-care center. In 1989 Architect Richard Johnson, a member of the congregation, was engaged to draft plans for a day-care facility which would accommodate children who were a few weeks old to five years old. Caviness Construction Company, also members of the congregation, was hired to construct the building with the site chosen at the northwest corner of the property, on Seventh Avenue and Colter Street, formerly used as a park area by the congregation for outdoor gatherings in a garden-like setting.

The building, designed around a central courtyard, contained nine classrooms for children with a reception/office area at the front of the building opening to the east and a kitchen. The rooms consisted of three infant rooms with cribs and equipment, three toddler rooms containing small tables and chairs, toys, and other equipment, and three other rooms with tables and equipment for preschool-age children. Each of the toddler and preschool rooms had access to restrooms furnished with small toilets and sinks. The Christian Children's Center was a critically needed day care for 125 infants and preschoolers, also serving the families of children through parent-support programs. In September 1990, this new half-million dollar center was dedicated. In June of 1995, the $12,500, 90 square-foot Noah's Ark stained glass window, designed and fabricated by Maureen McGuire Design Associates, Inc., for the western wall of the lobby between the office and the courtyard, was dedicated.

After nearly 18 years, Pastor Smidt, Mount Calvary's senior pastor, was given a peaceful release in October 1996, due to health concerns sustained in a near fatal car accident in Germany in 1994. Upon leaving he stated, "I have genuinely mixed feelings. There is sadness in separating from Mount Calvary, but I also have gladness and high hopes both for the congregation and for what God may still do in my life. I'm thankful to Him and to the people here for what I've had the past 18 years. I've had a good time!" He headed Connecting Generations consulting ministry, a non-profit corporation that brought different generations together through education and participation in various activities. In addition, he was a part-time chaplain at Mayo Clinic Hospital, using his expertise with intergenerational ministry to assist patients in their recuperation and therapy. In 2000, he served as interim pastor at Holy Cross Lutheran in Scottsdale.

Between November 1996 and January 1998, an interim pastor, Rev. William Royer, a retired pastor from Illinois, served Mount Calvary assisted by a group of lay congregational leaders in various pastoral functions. The fifth and present pastor of Mount Calvary, Rev. Dann Ettner, was installed on January 4, 1998. He was born on February 27, 1957, in Long Beach, California, graduating from California Lutheran College in Thousand Oaks, California, in 1979. Following his graduation from Concordia Seminary, St. Louis, in 1983, he was ordained and installed as pastor of Zion Church, Rapid City, South Dakota, where he served until July 1986. His next parish was Holy Trinity in Atwater, California, serving to August 1994, taking a call to Faith, Pasadena, before going to Mt. Calvary. He was also a chaplain in the United States Army Reserve since 1991, attaining the rank of captain. On June 7, 1980, he was married to Barbara Bosse with their marriage blessed with two daughters, Rebecca and Mary. He was also an author of two books—*The Seven Days of Creation*, a children's book published by Concordia Publishing House, St. Louis; and *The Gospel According to Jesus' Enemies*, a Lenten series published by CSS Publishing. He is a contributing author for articles and worship services published through Concordia Publishing House.

Ministry to Hispanics in the Phoenix area was Mount Calvary's primary missionary focus throughout the 1990s. A District task force was established in 1990 with delegates from all the congregations. From its inception, the task force received considerable support and assistance from Mount Calvary. After being hired as missionary-at-large by the task force, Pastor Cristiano Artigas became a member of Mount Calvary. The associate pastor at the time, Pastor Will Krueger, served as president of the executive board of the task force, as did Pastor Smidt in 1998. At the end of 1999, Pastor Dann Ettner agreed to accept the position of vice president of the organization with other members of Mount Calvary serving on the board as Secretary and as delegate-at-large. Pastor Ettner's interest in multicultural ministry helped to foster the establishment of an Ethiopian/Eritrean Christian congregation that met in the gymnasium of Mount Calvary beginning in early 1999.

Pastor Artigas, before starting three Spanish-speaking churches in Phoenix — Santo Tomas, Gracia, and a small group, Sola Fide, that met at Mount Calvary on Saturday evenings — was the regular preacher at the English Saturday evening service at Mount Calvary from 1995 to 1998. He also headed the Schaller Community Center established by the Hispanic ministry with John Shaw, a lawyer and a member of Mount Calvary, volunteering his expertise as a legal aid to Spanish-speaking residents who went to the Schaller Center for assistance. Each year since the mid-1990s, Mount Calvary has had a special Christmas tree in the sanctuary decorated with "Little Angels" with each "angel" representing a child in one of Pastor Artigas' parishes. Church members take one or more of the "angels" with the name of the child, the age, clothing size, and desired toys listed, and purchase Christmas gifts for the child. After the gifts are wrapped, returned to the church, and placed under the "Angel Tree," Pastor Artigas and his helpers collect all the gifts about a week before Christmas, and distribute them at a Christmas party for the children.

When Pastor Artigas's wife, Sherrie, had a number of strokes in the late 1990s, the congregation arranged for meals to be taken to the Artigas home every other day. When she died on January 13, 2001, of complications from the strokes, the parish was there to support the pastor and his family. He stated this about the people of Mt. Calvary, "I really believe that the Lord wanted us here in Arizona among such a family, so that when we needed to be ministered to, all those beautiful members of Mount Calvary lovingly shared their gifts with us." He also said he always looked forward to doing the Saturday evening English service at Mt. Calvary and was now back doing the service in Spanish.

When Mt. Calvary opened its doors to the Hispanic people in 1999, ESL classes were offered to the community. Through these classes, Sola Fide (FE) Lutheran Church began serving the Hispanic community of Central and South Americans with a majority of Guatemalans who were more receptive to the Lutheran liturgy and had fewer misconceptions about the Virgin Mary. This area was a bountiful land in which to preach and witness to the various Hispanics nationalities. Worship services were conducted every Saturday night at 7:00 p.m. with an attendance of 37 people. The ministry reached into the community through ESL classes, Bible studies, Catechism, First Communion and Confirmation classes, Baptisms, Vacation Bible School, Back-to-School Program, Christmas Angel Program, Reyes Magos, rummage sales, Quinceñeras, and weddings with one of the men training to be a deacon. At the beginning of 2003, Pastor Artigas's name was also added to the church sign in front of the building.

On Saturday, October 11, 2003, the annual dinner for friends and supporters of the LCMS Hispanic Ministry in Arizona was held at Mount Calvary with a PowerPoint presentation about the goals and the achievements of this ministry presented by Ms. Emera Luna, an enthusiastic volunteer in the ministry. Among those present was the Rev. Jerry Kosberg the regional coordinator, and many church representatives from supporting congregations. Pastor Artigas gave a moving speech on how people's talents and gifts were best used when shared.

Phoenix's first Missouri Synod Church has been truly blessed since its inception in 1950, continuing to use its gifts to spread the Word not only to the English-speaking population but also to the Spanish-speaking people and other nationalities in the area. She was not the first to attempt to do work in Spanish in the Phoenix area. The work was really started in the 1970s.

Rev. Cristiano Artigas and his wife, Sherrie, in 1987. (Pacific Southwest District Archives)

Through ESL classes, Sola Fide (FE) Lutheran Church began serving the Hispanic community in 1999.

La Santa Cruz Mission
El Mirage, Arizona

El Mirage, a Mexican-American community adjacent to Sun City approximately 25 miles northwest of Phoenix, was a very poor area where many Mexicans had settled. The Lutheran mission work began in this predominately Mexican community when Ron and Marie Valenzuela, members of King of Kings in Phoenix, moved into the city in early 1971. On September 1, 1971, they along with members of King of Kings and Fountain of Life in Sun

The Peapenburg family in 1977, leaders in the El Mirage mission. Front: Todd and Mark; Back: Pete, Connie, and Char.

Mrs. Catalina Broyles, one of the leaders in the mission, with the children of the mission.

City, opened the mission with 25 to 30 children in Saturday School classes taught by members from Sun City, Phoenix, and Glendale. Every Saturday morning, a rummage sale was conducted to raise funds to pay the rent and utilities on the small, old Pentecostal church at 14302 Verbena Street in El Mirage. Also, from this facility was a food bank supported by Lutheran churches in the valley, providing food for farm workers or any family in need with food baskets distributed at Thanksgiving and Christmas time; shoes and medicine were also provided for the children. Sometimes gas money or transportation was provided to take people to the county hospital 30 miles away. Another project for the children in the area was the summer camp at Camp Aloma in Prescott where funds were provided by the AAL to send 60 children. A devastating blow befell this little group of concerned Lutherans who called themselves the El Mirage Mission Committee, when Mr. Ron Valenzuela, a dedicated Spanish-speaking Lutheran, accepted a job with the American Lutheran Church as the Mexican-American ministries coordinator in Corpus Christi, Texas.

Before the Valenzuelas' departure, a request was made to the Southern California District Mission Board to establish a preaching station in the area and continue the work started by the Valenzuelas and the El Mirage Mission Board that included Mr. and Mrs. Ron Valenzuela, Mr. and Mrs. E. H. (Pete) Peapenburg, Mrs. Catalina Broyles, all of King of Kings, and Mr. Norman Horen, Mr. Lou Bornamann, and Rev. William Pebler of Fountain of Life. On June 22, 1976, Rev. David Stirdivant, the father of Hispanic work in the District, was asked to investigate the area and advise the Mission Board of the possibilities of doing mission work in the vicinity. With a positive response forthcoming,

the District decided to continue to rent the small Pentecostal church. Rev. Stirdivant reported that Hilario Deniz, a member of La Santa Cruz in Los Angeles, was "qualified and would be interested in filling in for a period of time." The Board decided that Mr. Deniz, who had done an excellent job in assisting Pastor Stirdivant in Los Angeles and showed a love for people and the Lord, was to work in El Mirage for 6 months under the supervision of Rev. Stirdivant and the El Mirage Mission Committee at a salary of $475 per month with financial aid from the Phoenix area congregations.

Hilario Deniz was born on February 1, 1950, in the tropical seacoast town of Manzanillo, Colima, Mexico, the eldest son of a large family. Their home was adjacent to or in the shadow of one of the large Catholic churches in the city; one of his proud moments was serving as an altar boy in the church. In 1972, he left his home, moving to Tijuana, Baja California, Mexico, where Christ was revealed to him as his personal Savior. One day as he passed a Protestant church that was conducting a Vacation Bible School, he heard singing which moved him to go inside where he heard the Word proclaimed with the Holy Spirit leading him to Christ. When he moved to Los Angeles to work in a restaurant as a chef, he kept passing by La Santa Cruz Lutheran Church in the Boyle Heights section of Los Angeles. One day he went inside the church and met the pastor, Rev. Stirdivant, and they became friends. Through this meeting, he was confirmed and decided he wanted to become a pastor in the Lutheran church. Since he couldn't speak English and none of the Missouri Synod seminaries had classes in Spanish, his solution was to attend Instituto Biblico of La Puente where he studied three years while retaining his job and membership in La Santa Cruz. He was a gifted man who was a

Pastor Stirdivant and Mr. Hilario Deniz, who arrived in El Mirage on November 17, 1976, to begin work at the mission and establish Spanish worship services.

The front of the mission with the youth leaving for a trip to Concordia University, Irvine.

good preacher, teacher, and musician, playing the guitar and piano.

When Pastor Stirdivant accompanied Hilario Deniz to El Mirage on November 17, 1976, to begin work in this mission, they saw the very poor, poverty stricken community of El Mirage. After Mr. Deniz's arrival, he stayed at the Broyles' home some 10 miles from the mission for a couple of weeks, later moving into a house trailer. Since he had no transportation, a bicycle was loaned to him, and he pedaled from place to place, making calls. The first few weeks he was there he removed rummage sale materials from the building and cleaned, painted, and repaired it, as it had been used as a storehouse for food distribution. He created a chapel in the small storage room; he also resolved several problems with the mission committee, and gathered a small group of people in Bible study and worship in the church, naming it La Santa Cruz. Since he had a very charismatic personality and a love for music, he was able to draw many people to the mission. By December, he had established the following schedule: services were conducted on Sundays at 11:00 a.m. in the chapel that had a portable altar with appropriate appointments; Catechism classes were taught at 1:00 p.m. with music practice following; and sports activities were at 4:00 p.m. with an evangelistic service conducted at 5:30 p.m. On Tuesdays, he and Mrs. Broyles went to the Arrowhead Ranch to make calls and distribute food and clothing to the needy where there were 54 children. On Wednesday afternoons, there were volleyball games at 5:00 p.m. followed by an informal service at 6:00 p.m. with singing, prayers, and a Spanish movie; one of the movies was on the birth of Christ where 94 people were present of which 24 were adults, mostly mothers. After the service, there was more volley-

ball until 8:30 p.m. On other Wednesdays, a sports night was held with basketball, volleyball, and ping-pong along with guitar classes. On Thursday, another sports night was conducted followed by a Christian movie with over 90 people, which were mostly small children. In a short month, he had established a thriving mission.

Even with all this activity and growth, there were complaints from the El Mirage Mission Committee about not being able to use the chapel to store rummage sale goods and food bank items, along with the landlord who was a neighbor, complaining about the noise from the youth playing volleyball at night. Building a metal shed for storage and not having outdoor activities in the late evenings resolved the conflict. Pastor Stirdivant was asked to represent the Board for Missions in evaluating the mission work done among Mexicans in El Mirage. Since Hilario was placed under the supervision of Pastor Stirdivant, Pastor visited the mission on different occasions to assist and supervise him, reporting the progress to the Board for Missions.

In the beginning of 1977, Rev. Harold Deye and Rev. Stirdivant visited the El Mirage mission to consult with the group there, hoping to work out difficulties due to communication problems and to continue the ministry. In the April 19, 1977, Board for Missions meeting, it was recommended because of the unusual circumstances at El Mirage that the department request Dr. Kuntz to consider commissioning Hilario Deniz according to the guidelines of the program of the Lay Ministry School at Concordia, Milwaukee, to perform acts of ministry of Word and Sacrament at El Mirage only and that Pastor Deye would visit this mission regularly to supervise the work. It was decided to give Mr. Deniz the Concordia Plan (benefits), along

Rev. Dr. Waech, who served in the Pacific Southwest District from 1962 to 1979 as presidential administrative assistant. (Pacific Southwest District Archives)

with an additional $400 per month for expenses, building rental, and utilities. On June 14 at 7:00 p.m., Rev. Harold Deye of Calexico and Rev. David Stirdivant of Los Angeles confirmed 19 boys and girls in a "full house" attendance that included Dr. Oswald A. Waech, who spent two days at the El Mirage mission.

Dr. Waech served as presidential administrative assistant in the Pacific Southwest District from 1962–1979, promoting stewardship and evangelism in its 250 congregations with 85,000 members, laying the groundwork for opening of new missions, which included El Mirage. He was born on October 3, 1911, in the parsonage at Spring, Texas, where his father, Rev. C. A Waech, had been not only pastor but also the president of the Texas District. Soon after his birth, the family moved to Crete, Illinois, where his father served as pastor. He attended Concordia College, Milwaukee, Wisconsin, graduating from Concordia Seminary, St. Louis, in 1936. He did graduate work at Canisius College, Buffalo University, and Concordia Seminary, which conferred a Doctor of Divinity on him in 1979. After graduating from the seminary, he was ordained on September 27, 1936, and served as assistant to Rev. Francis Verwiebe, the District president, at Gethsemane Lutheran Church in Buffalo, New York, a bilingual congregation where he preached in German and English from 1936 to 1954. After the death of the president, he became the head pastor of the parish. While at Gethsemane, he met his future wife, Marion Korn, whom he married in 1939 with their marriage blessed with four children, Phyllis, Marcia, Judith, and David.

From 1954 to 1962, Rev. Waech was the first evangelism secretary of The Lutheran Church — Missouri Synod in St. Louis, directing Open House Mission (Preaching, Teaching, Reaching [PTR]) conducting over 200 and Spiritual Life Mission (SLM) that combined a congregational self-study with a five-day congregational workshop, designed to develop the congregation's potential strengths. He was the author of many tracts and pamphlets on evangelism and stewardship with his guidelines on "How to Witness" receiving wide distribution. He also wrote a Living Way Bible Study course and "The Pastoral Letters of Paul." For nine years, he was the Monday speaker on the Lutheran Program broadcast over KGER, Long Beach, California. After retiring from the District, he served as assisting pastor at Holy Cross, Cypress (1979–1981), Trinity, Whittier

(1981–1988), Shepherd of the Hills, Rancho Cucamonga (1988–1995), assisted Rev. Harold Boeche at Trinity, Montclair (1995–1997), and is presently pastor emeritus at Shepherd of the Hills, Rancho Cucamonga, California.

Since public transportation to the El Mirage mission was inadequate and unaffordable to the members, the mission requested that the District purchase a van to take Sunday school children, youth, and adults to the activities of the mission. By September 1977, the Board for Missions received permission from the Board of Directors to solicit the congregations of the District for a van to be used at the Hispanic mission. Since there was limited response from congregations, the board decided to loan Hilario Deniz a maximum of $4,000 from the District Auto Revolving Fund in order to procure a van for the mission with a group from First Lutheran of Culver City giving some money to the fund and the congregation in El Mirage committing $100 per month toward the loan. The van was purchased and owned by Hilario Deniz, but the District held the pink slip until the loan was paid in full.

Due to some interpersonal problems between Hilario Deniz and members of the congregation and for lack of support on the part of the local constituency, the mission activity at El Mirage was terminated by the District on February 12, 1978, with the Board for Missions instructing Dr. O. A. Waech to consult with Hilario about enrolling in the seminary in Mexico City, so that he could eventually work into a worker/evangelist status. Hilario Deniz was recalled for more training and returned to Bell Garden, California, where he assisted Pastor Stirdivant until more interpersonal relationship problems forced his termination. While at the mission for only 16 months, he had baptized 3 adults and 18 children, confirmed 60 adults and children and had a Sunday school of 57 children. This very talented person drew many people to the mission and to the Lord, but the flaw in his personality forced him to leave the ministry.

On Sunday, February 19, 1979, 53 people met in the little chapel for a final informal service even though all the utilities were disconnected with the building having to be vacated by the end of that month. The contents of the mission were a chalice given by members of the mission; two brass candlesticks donated by a church in Yuma; two plastic candles given by Catalina Broyles; two silver patens given by members of the congregation; one crucifix given by the Castillo family; one small brass crucifix donated by Marcelina Carrillo; $700 Kimball Organ given by the congregation; red, white, green, and purple paraments; one small chalice given by the Morales family; an incense bowl given by Petra Leyva; a candlelighter donated by members of the congregation; five chairs donated by the Castillo family; a Communion tray with glasses; two plastic plants given by the children of the church; a black and white satin rope given by Sun City; a Revere 8880 slide projector, table, and 4' × 4' screen given by Sun City; three boxes of slides; a baptismal font; a wood table given by the Castrillo family; and a pulpit given by Sun City.

At the March 21, 1978, Board for Missions meeting, Mr. Pete Peapenburg, a member of the El Mirage Mission Committee, encouraged the Mission Board to continue to have mission activities in the El Mirage vicinity. He stated that there were about 30 to 35 families consisting of about 175 souls, who needed ministering, expressing that "an ordained pastor would probably be a real blessing to the people in El Mirage and would help the mission to grow, not only in numbers, but also in faith toward their Lord." Unfortunately, no pastor or layperson was sent to minister to this group. It was the hope of the Mission Board and area congregations that the people would go to the Anglo churches in Phoenix even though they didn't speak English.

Mr. Carlos Hernandez, a member of Synod's Hispanic Task Force, was asked to accompany Mr. Ron Valenzuela on a visit to the El Mirage area, June 18–24, 1978, to contact the people of the former El Mirage mission. Due to a lack of interest on the part of the people and that a Spanish-speaking pastor was unavailable to minister to this group, the El Mirage mission was never reopened by the Missouri Synod, but work was continued by Mr. and Mrs. Ron Valenzuela. Mrs. Marie Valenzuela established a mission for the American Lutheran Church that became known as Pan de Vida and is now a congregation in the Evangelical Lutheran Church of America.

Bethlehem Lutheran Church
Schaller Center
Iglesia Gracia Luterana
Phoenix, Arizona

 On June 21 1964, Rev. Robert Schaller along with a group of Missouri Synod lay people founded Bethlehem Lutheran Church. Pastor Schaller and the group of Missouri Synod Lutherans had been members of Zion Lutheran Church, a Wisconsin Synod Church in Phoenix. When the Wisconsin Synod withdrew from fellowship with The Lutheran Church — Missouri Synod, Pastor Schaller expected Zion to leave WELS and be independent for a while which he had recommended in a carefully prepared study document that he had presented to the congregation. The presiding officer at the meeting called for a vote that gave ownership of the church facilities to those loyal to the WELS. With that vote passing, Pastor Schaller reported, "That left us Missourians [107 communicants] out in the street." As a result, Bethlehem Lutheran Church was organized and accepted into the Southern California District with Pastor Schaller serving as Bethlehem's pastor for the life of the congregation.

Rev. Schaller was born on June 14, 1910, in Concordia, Missouri, where his father, William, was professor of German at St. Paul's College. His grandfather Gottlieb Schaller was a professor on the faculty with the famous C. F. W. Walther with Robert's father born on the old campus of the Concordia Seminary in St. Louis. After graduating from St. Paul's College in Concordia, Missouri, he attended Concordia Seminary in St. Louis in fall of 1930, during the Great Depression where he heard Dr. Walter A. Meier's first "Lutheran Hour" sermon during a chapel service. While a student at Concordia Seminary, he went to Pasadena in the summer of 1931 with the seminary's Orpheus Quartet. Arriving late from an engagement in Tijuana, Mexico, the quartet decided, he could shave first and go in and entertain the congregation on the organ, as the congregation were already present. As an organist, he had memorized one Bach chorale, "Vater Unser im Himmelreich," of which he played several variations while the other members of the quartet prepared to come out and sing.

When the time for his vicarage arrived, Pastor Schaller figured he would not receive an assignment, as opportunities were very scarce during the days of the Great Depression. Finally, a letter arrived from the Rev. George Theiss of Pasadena inviting him to come as organist and choir director for one year. The Rev. Gotthold H. Smukal, president of the Southern California District and pastor of St. John's congregation in Los Angeles, persuaded the Pasadena congregation to release him to teach school at St. John's, which he did for two years. During his teaching days, he met Lorna Smukal, the president's daughter. After an appropriate time of engagement, they were married on October 12, 1941. When he returned to the seminary in 1935 finishing the following year, he served as organist, choir director and c.r.m. (pastor temporarily in an inactive status) under the Rev. J. L. Sommers at Hickory, North Carolina, for two years. Since there were no calls in the Missouri Synod, he accepted a call to serve a Wisconsin Synod Church, Zion Lutheran Church in Phoenix, where he was ordained on April 30, 1939, serving 25 years.

About 25 years later on June 21, 1964, Pastor Schaller established Bethlehem Lutheran of Phoenix with a group of 68 people first worshiping in the air-conditioned meeting room of the Phoenix

Rev. Robert Schaller with his wife, Lorna, celebrating fifty years in the pastoral ministry in 1990. (Pacific Southwest District Archives)

Public Library on Central Avenue and McDowell Road. Following the worship service, the unity of the group expressed itself in the signing of two letters, one requesting a peaceful release from membership in Zion Evangelical Lutheran Church, Phoenix, Arizona, and from the Wisconsin Evangelical Lutheran Synod, the other applying for membership in the Southern California District of The Lutheran Church — Missouri Synod. Fifty-five communicant members signed these documents with others who were not present indicating their intentions to do the same. Numbered among the small flock were 29 children. Also indicating the joy of this day was the adoption of the name "Bethlehem" for the new church established at that meeting. Bethlehem was derived from the Hebrew words "beth" and "lehem," meaning house of bread, as this new church would be a house in which Jesus, the Bread of Life, would be offered as spiritual food for all who came, and Bethlehem was that humble spot where the Son of God chose to become man with the angels of heaven proclaiming "on earth peace, good will toward men."

The following Sunday, June 28, 1964, the new parish met at Cedar Hall, 3232 North Twentieth Street, just south of Osborn Boulevard in a 10:00 a.m. service with Sunday school at 9:00 a.m., which would be their meeting place for over two years until they found a permanent home. The previous Tuesday, the ladies decided to form a women's group keeping the same officers as they had elected while in the Dorcas Guild of Zion congregation but changing the name of their new organization to the Mary-Martha Guild. The previous Sunday evening eight young people and six adults met in the home of Mr. and Mrs. Earl Gilbert to organize a youth group with their first outing, a swim party, on Sunday, June 28, from 6:30 p.m. to 10:00 p.m. at the Broadway Pool.

By Sunday, August 2, 1964, the parish had a new lectern, which also served as the pulpit, designed and built by Mr. Albert Wagner, using scraps of materials saved from construction materials of Mr. Wagner's former church in Chicago. The lectern also served as a cabinet for the new service books and hymnals. The first Communion service was conducted on August 16 with Holy Cross Church of Scottsdale supplying Communion ware for the service. On the previous Friday, August 14, at 7:30 p.m., the new congregation met with representatives of the Missouri Synod in The Church of the Holy Cross, Scottsdale, for the purpose of being accepted into the Missouri Synod, and to consider a permanent location for the new parish. The Rev. Victor L. Behnken, President of the Southern California District of The Lutheran Church — Missouri Synod, the Rev. Harold B. Tietjen, executive secretary of the Board for Missions, and the Rev. Karl H. Meyer, circuit counselor and pastor of The Church of the Holy Cross, represented the Missouri Synod at the meeting.

Since Bethlehem's members lived so close to other Missouri Synod parishes, the District asked that the members locate in those parishes and disband the newly established congregation, with the congregation not heeding their advice. In June of 1965 when Bethlehem asked the District for funds to purchase Creighton Methodist Church at Twenty-ninth and Mc Dowell, containing a sanctuary, educational building, and a parsonage for $120,000, the District denied the request as the parish only had 90 communicant members and 119 souls with an average Sunday attendance of 55 and a Sunday school enrollment of 15 with an average attendance of 10. Once again, the request was denied, as this property was in an older section of Phoenix too close to other Missouri Synod parishes.

In 1966, the congregation purchased a church building from the Wesleyan Methodist, which had originally been a Baptist church, located on the northwest corner of Twenty-fourth Place and East Portland Avenue. The building had been constructed sometime after World War II about when the Elsinore Subdivision was developed where it was located. The structure had approximately 3,872 square feet and was built of block construction that would accommodate typical church services and activities with the interior divided into a sanctuary, parish hall with a small kitchen, restrooms, offices, and eight small Sunday school rooms. Pastor Schaller subsequently purchased additional property, the northeast corner of 24th

Bethlehem Lutheran Church on northwest corner of 24th Place and East Portland Avenue in the Elsinore subdivision of Phoenix. (Pacific Southwest District Archives)

Street and East Portland Avenue that adjoined the church property on the west so that it could be available for possible future expansion. This adjacent property was improved with two duplexes, each having two one-bedroom apartments, and a large garage.

In an interview with Pastor Schaller, he stated that a problem developed in doing mission work at the Bethlehem site, as Missouri Synod Lutheran wouldn't settle below McDowell Street because of all the commercial businesses in the area and the demographics had changed to a Hispanic population. Bethlehem continued to decrease, getting smaller and smaller, not being able to grow due to being in the wrong location. At the end of the congregation's life, there were few people attending church services at Bethlehem. In 1987, Pastor Schaller's wife, Lorna who was also the organist and choir director, suffered a stroke that confined her to a wheelchair. After two or three more strokes, leaving her unable to speak, she was hospitalized with Pastor Schaller visiting her twice a day. They had no children. Pastor's eyesight grew weaker and weaker causing him to be unable to read the Scriptures. He also had to play the organ and preach at the services. Although by 1991, he was still officially the pastor of Bethlehem, the need to intensively care for his wife led him to relinquish many of his responsibilities. The Rev. Kenneth Hohenstein served as interim pastor while Bethlehem's pastor once again served as organist for the congregation, completing a career in ministry that began in a similar musical position. Pastor Schaller's ministry encompassed 51 years in the Phoenix area serving 2 congregations, Zion and Bethlehem.

Over the years, the area surrounding Bethlehem was in the midst of an almost total Hispanic community. The Phoenix congregations formed a Hispanic task force agreeing to provide funds to be used along with a grant from Lutheran Brotherhood for Hispanic ministry. The District Mission Board called Rev. Roberto Becerra of Shelby, Michigan, a bilingual pastor, to replace Pastor Schaller. Pastor Becerra was installed on January 13, 1991, to serve as the first Hispanic Pastor in the Phoenix area, serving the remaining flock at the Bethlehem congregation and also helping with the Hispanic ministry at Peace Lutheran. Pastor Becerra was born in San Jose, California, on July 17, 1939. Before graduating from Concordia Seminary at Fort Wayne 1987, he spent his vicarage year at Bethel Lutheran Church in Chicago, Illinois; he

Pastor Becerra is installed on January 13, 1991, to serve as the first Hispanic Pastor in the Phoenix area, serving the Bethlehem congregation.

also attended the University of New York and served in the Armed Services. His first call was to St. Stephen in Shelby, Michigan, in December 1987, a congregation of 261 members and 225 communicant members. He married Karen Klenk on January 25, 1964, with their marriage blessed with three children, Roberta, Sheila, and Julia. Due to his wife's health problems, Pastor Becerra resigned his position as missionary-at-large for Hispanic ministry in the Phoenix area on February 28, 1992, having served only 13 months.

When the District's Department of Mission Services called Rev. Roberto Becerra to serve in the Phoenix area, it was determined, in consultation with Bethlehem congregation, that he would be asked to serve south Phoenix from Peace congregation as well as reach out to Hispanics and other people surrounding the Bethlehem area. After Pastor Becerra and Pastor Robert Schoenheider studied the dual ministry between Peace and Bethlehem, they found that it was a very difficult task for one man to handle both ministries. It became apparent that the area for ministry around Bethlehem was very small, having natural boundaries: the north, East Papago Freeway (Highway 202); the west, the Papago Freeway; the east, a canal; and the south, the Sky Harbor Airport, making it difficult to reach out to other areas. These boundaries left a very small ministry area from which to draw people with the church building sitting in the middle of a neighborhood housing tract, making it very difficult to see from any of the main arteries and difficult to find.

Upon the request of the Valley of the Sun Hispanic Ministry Committee, pastors Cristiano Artigas of La Santa Cruz, Los Angeles, and Frank Brundige of San Pedro y San Pablo, Bell Gardens, conducted a survey of the Bethlehem and Peace neighborhoods touring the areas around these churches on January 21, 1992. From the study of the vicinity, it was quite evident that the population in the Bethlehem area was very mixed with poor renters consisting of one-third low income Anglo, one-third black, and one-third Hispanic, which seemed to be the entry point of the Mexican population before moving to other neighborhoods. They found one Roman Catholic Church with a Spanish mass and one Italian Protestant church. Bethlehem's major membership lived a distance from the church; five members resided in the area around the parish. In the summer of 1991, a very successful Vacation Bible School, averaging 36 neighborhood children who participated

each day, was conducted at Bethlehem. Due to the small membership of the congregation, the staff came from outside the congregation, making it very difficult to maintain. Pastor Becerra spent the majority of his Sunday mornings leading the worship services for 10–12 people at Bethlehem, where there had been no significant growth for many years, drawing him away from the Hispanic people who attended worship services at Peace. When he started Hispanic worship services at Peace, he found it difficult to prepare a sermon for the English service at Bethlehem and for the Spanish service at Peace each Sunday. Bethlehem's retired pastor and his flock were prepared to move on and leave their church as a gift for someone to do ministry in the neighborhood.

At Peace in south Phoenix, they found a Mexican working-middle class with a small population of Central and South Americans, a declining white "blue collar" population, and a black population. The Hispanic population was educated, bilingual, mobile, and consisted of homeowners; the area had "shacks" mixed with nicer houses; the region was developing from a semi-rural to suburban as evidenced by better homes and new shopping centers with a K-mart that was aimed at a middle class, having Spanish tapes and movies for adults and children. There was one Roman Catholic Church, which was not oriented to the Hispanic, 19 Baptist churches, 14 Pentecostal, 14 Independent churches, 9 Holiness, and some Spanish Protestant churches of various sizes. Across the street from Peace was an elementary school where the principal informed the reviewers that the population was mixed with the children speaking English on the playground, but translators had to be used in meetings with their parents.

The reviewers found that the ministry at Peace had Hispanic people who participated bilingually; the new Anglos in the congregation were open to change; and the long-time members were cooperative. The review committee found there was a need for a pastor who was people-oriented, hands-on, using the "go out and see and meet approach." Pastor Becerra had begun to use this type of approach, but at the time, it was crucial to the Hispanic ministry that this be the primary direction. They recommended that a bilingual pastor with inner city experience, be allowed to work exclusively at Bethlehem for at least a year in order to know the exact ministry situation and needs with a clear plan then developed; in the future, the pastor could work as a mission planter

---

The area for ministry around Bethlehem is very small, having natural boundaries: the north, East Papago Freeway (Highway 202); the west, the Papago Freeway; the east, a canal; and the south, the Sky Harbor Airport.

in other Hispanic regions of the city. In their visit, they discovered that Phoenix was quite different from Southern California as the Mexican migration, history, patterns, and origins were different with many of the Phoenix Hispanics being educated, bilingual, and mobile. "A people-oriented approach was needed, with missionary pastors chosen to match Hispanic needs using evangelism, oriented to nurturing discipleship which would produce indigenous Hispanic churches capable of functioning as mature Christians."

In the spring of 1992, the Valley of the Sun Hispanic Ministry, made up of representatives from 16 Phoenix congregations, called Rev. Cris Artigas to serve in the Hispanic ministry as missionary-at-large in the Phoenix area. He was installed on August 9, 1992, at Mt. Calvary Lutheran Church, where the Rev. Ken Behnken, district executive, delivered the message, and the Rev. Will Krueger conducted the installation. Rev. Artigas began his work centered at Bethlehem Lutheran Church in Phoenix, as the church buildings were made available for the new Hispanic outreach when the Bethlehem congregation closed its ministry, leaving the facilities to the Pacific Southwest District.

Rev. Cristiano Artigas had served in Hispanic ministry since his graduation from the seminary where he served Hispanic people at Redeemer, South Gate; La Santa Cruz, Los Angeles; Zion, Maywood; Iglesia San Pedro y San Pablo, Bell Gardens; Misión Hispana "Trinidad," Los Angeles; and also served as a teacher at Southeast Lutheran High School. For three years, he was stationed in Saudi Arabia as a military chaplain. He served as chaplain during the Gulf War where he conducted nine services on a Sunday, which prepared him for preaching many services in the Phoenix area on Sundays. He continued to serve in the National Guard for four more years. He and his wife, Sherrie, had three children, Cristiano, Amanda, and Benjamin, at the time. Sherrie was a trained schoolteacher who worked in the Phoenix area.

Pastor Artigas' main focus was around the Bethlehem church, but he also worked with the Hispanic people who had been gathered by Pastor Robert Schoenheider at Peace in south Phoenix. He was available to all the Lutheran churches in the Phoenix area to provide them with help and resources for reaching the Hispanic population. The ministry was financed by the congregations of the Phoenix area, over and above their regular mission offerings, and supplemented by the Pacific Southwest District. By February of 1993, two

to three families were worshiping at Bethlehem along with small Bible study groups being held. Spanish worship services were also conducted at Peace with 20 to 30 Hispanics in attendance each Sunday.

Since the facilities at Bethlehem were in need of repair and renovation for a community center to meet the spiritual and physical needs of a low-income, multi-ethnic community, the facility was refurbished through the joint efforts of Lutheran organizations: the Pacific Southwest District Department of Mission Services, Lutheran Social Ministry of the Southwest, Laborers for Christ, and the Valley of the Sun Hispanic Ministry, consisting of 16 congregations in the Phoenix area. A festival dedication service was held on Sunday, May 22, 1994, with many representatives of the city and neighborhood present. Pastor Schaller, who was the pastor at Bethlehem for over 25 years, joined the celebration, seeing his dream of continuing the ministry through the new center becoming realty. The church facilities were packed that day, which was a sight to behold! On June 1, 1994, the newly dedicated Schaller Neighborhood Center was ready to open its doors in Phoenix under the leadership of Arden Dorn, Lutheran Social Ministries of the Southwest, and Rev. Chris Artigas, PSW missionary-at-large, in the renovated Bethlehem Church to begin its unique ministry of meeting the spiritual and physical needs of the community.

The Schaller Neighborhood Center received the 1994 National Mission Projects award at the LCEF National Conference in Scottsdale, Arizona, with recognition given for the center's uniqueness in ministry, meeting needs of the community, and reflecting the goals of church extension to "supply space and place" for ministry. During the week, the center provided many programs and activities for all ages all day long: children's after-school tutoring and recreational programs, food and clothing distribution, A. A. programs, English as a Second Language, single mothers' program, community meetings, special community celebration events, tax services, and job referrals. Using the Schaller Center for her base beginning on July 16, 1995, Eunice Utteria, a trained missionary from Mexico and the mother of the Rev. Cris Artigas, did missionary work in the Phoenix area. That year Pastor Artigas's son, Cris, was the winner of an Arizona State University wrestling camp scholarship, where a wrestling move was named after him, "The Artigas Roll."

Rev. Cris Artigas was installed on August 9, 1992, as missionary-at-large in the Phoenix area to serve in the Hispanic ministry. (Pacific Southwest District Archives)

On June 1, 1994, the newly dedicated Schaller Neighborhood Center is ready to open its doors in Phoenix.

Pastor Schaller at the 2001 Hispanic Ministry Appreciation Dinner held at Mt. Calvary in Phoenix. (Pacific Southwest District Archives)

In March of 1997, Pastor Artigas conducted the first service for 27 people in the Schaller Center, naming the mission Iglesia Gracia. This worship service was an outgrowth of the Schaller Center community service program. Many of the families attending were the patrons who had gone to the Community Center seeking material help, food, clothing, job tutoring, ESL classes, and tax assistance. That first year, the worship service was held at 2:30 p.m. every Sunday; currently, services are at 11:00 a.m. In the following years, church attendance increased to 50 to 60 people a Sunday. The church also provided Bible studies, Confirmation and Catechism classes, First Communion classes, Vacation Bible School, Back-to-School Program, Christmas Angel Program, Reyes Magos, a food bank with weekly food baskets and holiday food baskets, along with ESL classes.

During the summer of 1998, the Schaller Community Center sponsored a two-week Vacation Bible School or, as it was called, the Back-to-School Program with the closing service held on Sunday, August 16, at Iglesia Luterana Gracia, where the children who attended received new backpacks and supplies for the new school year. Mrs. Vida Orea de Luna, the wife of the late Rev. Felipe Luna, became lay minister and director of the center during this time. The following year, the VBS had 90 children with an attendance of 65–85 children

during the two-week period of the school. The teachers were Pastor Artigas, Vida de Luna, and Emera Luna, each in charge of two groups, adapting each lesson to fit the age group. Before the closing service on August 15, a festive barbeque with hot dogs and hamburgers was served with 120 people attending the service conducted by Pastor Artigas where they sang "uplifting jubilee of songs to the Lord" and the children received backpacks with school supplies.

Also in 1999, Pacific Southwest District Lutheran Women's Missionary League (PSW LWML) gave a $9,850 grant for playground equipment that was installed at the Schaller Community Center. There were two sets of swings, slides, tetherball poles, climbing equipment, huge tractor tires, and large, painted sewer pipes for crawling and climbing activities. The youth from Apostles Lutheran Church and men from the neighborhood helped clean the vacant lot, and spread sand around and under the play equipment; a chain link fence enclosed the entire area. The Fountain Hills Lutheran Brotherhood Branch donated materials for an irrigation system and plants along the fence. The Schaller Center continues to meet the social needs of the Elsinore community, serving over 50 families each week with Iglesia Gracia meeting the spiritual needs of the area with church attendance averaging 80 people per Sunday.

Peace Lutheran Church
Iglesia Luterana Santo Tomas
Phoenix, Arizona

In October of 1961, a small group of Lutherans began meeting Thursday evenings in the Valley View School where plans were made to form a Lutheran church in south Phoenix, a community that was partially rural with groves and ranches and mixed classes of people. On November 4, 1962, three families gathered for the first worship service conducted in the Junior Chamber of Commerce building located at 5206 South Montezuma Avenue, as the building was made available free of charge. Rev. Kenneth Fuerbringer, missionary-at-large from Tempe, had served the group that would become known as Peace Lutheran Church. The Mission Board purchased five acres of land in the extreme southern section of Phoenix south of Baseline Road on Sev-

enth Avenue, across from Valley View School.

The Southern California District Board of Missions contracted Mr. Francis Schultz of Scottsdale to draft plans for the first unit, a chapel that provided seating for about 200 people with an overflow area space for an additional 100. Included in the wing of the first unit were a church office, pastor's study, kitchen, restrooms, mechanical room, and two classrooms. McKinney and Shank, contractors, were chosen to construct the building at an approximate cost of $75,000 for the building with parking lot and access drive. With the building completed, a dedication service was held on March 24, 1963, where Rev. Victor L. Behnken, pastor of St. Paul's Lutheran Church, Laguna Beach, California, and president of the Southern California District was the preacher with Rev. Kenneth Fuerbringer, missionary-at-large and pastor of Beautiful Savior Lutheran Church in Tempe, serving as the liturgist assisted by Beautiful Savior church choir and organist, Mrs. Fred Dase.

In the summer of 1963, Rev. Kenneth John Kilian, a 1963 graduate of Concordia Seminary in St. Louis, was called to Peace Lutheran Church as missionary-at-large. He was born in Warsaw, Wisconsin, on October 8, 1936, of Ewald and Hertha Kilian, one of nine children who, because of his poor health, moved with his family to Colorado Springs when he was seven. At 14, he entered St. John's Academy in Winfield, Kansas, to prepare for a career in teaching. After changing his career goal to a ministerial major, he studied at Fort Wayne, Indiana. In 1965, he married Nancy Precker, a teacher at St. Paul's in Olive with their marriage blessed with three children, Joel, Jason, and Nathan. He was installed as the pastor of Peace on January 15, 1967, with Dr. Erwin Kurth, vice president of the Southern California District, serving as the preacher assisted by Rev. Loel Haak of St. Mark's in the Paradise Valley section of Phoenix and Rev. Kenneth Fuerbringer. The results of a full-time spiritual ministry were apparent in the months that followed, as the congregation expanded to 90 members with 42 communicant members with a Sunday school of 35.

The previous year plans were made for construction of a $16,500 educational unit addition with the rooms used for Sunday school and Vacation Bible School purposes. Since Valley View School was across the street from Peace, the congregation started a mid-week school in 1966 with a class of eight fourth graders. The results of the class indicated that the other elementary age groups would be added that September. There was also a family worship hour on Wednesday

Rev. Kenneth John Kilian (center) witnessing Governor Sam Goddard signs a proclamation as the "Year of the Bible" in 1966. Looking on is Mrs. F. F. Shotwell, Regional Secretary for Women's Activities for the American Bible Society. (Pacific Southwest District Archives)

nights providing a fine opportunity for informal Bible study services. With a decrease in building activity in the Phoenix area in 1968, the parish also felt the impact of the decline of population. The result was the postponement of expansion plans as the growth of the Sunday school also ceased. That year, the congregation celebrated its fifth anniversary with guest speaker, Rev. Victor L. Behnken, president of the Southern California District, who also spoke at the original dedication service in 1963.

During Peace's celebration of its 10th anniversary in 1973, a special community Sunday observance heard community representatives, Judge Walter Bloom, justice of the peace for the south Phoenix area; City Councilman Calvin Goode; Mayor John Driggs; Pastor Kilian; and State Senator Alfredo Guteirrez, indicate what they thought the church's role in the community should be. In response to the community representatives, Pastor Kilian announced various commitments on behalf of the congregation. That summer a representative of the congregation participated in a five-week course in the Spanish intensification program in Illinois that included instruction in conversational Spanish, as

With a decrease in building activity in the Phoenix area in 1968, the parish also feels the impact of the decline of population.

Peace Lutheran's new church building was dedicated on March 24, 1963. (Pacific Southwest District Archives)

Rev. James Rath was installed as missionary-at-large at Peace in January of 1981, serving until his death on January 24, 1988. (Pacific Southwest District Archives)

As Pastor Rath sees a greater need to minister to the Hispanics surrounding Peace, he introduces Spanish in the Sunday worship services on October 19, 1986.

well as training in Hispanic cultural styles and experience in inner-city settings provided through a special grant from the Aid Association for Lutherans of Appleton, Wisconsin. The Hacienda de Los Angeles, a home for mentally and physically handicapped children, continued to receive gifts of money and time from members of the church. The director of Hacienda de Los Angeles, Ilene Butler, was a member of the congregation. In addition, the church would also continue to help the South Phoenix Community Medical Center where Junelle Mohr, another member of Peace, served as liaison with the center. The pupils from the weekday school had visited the center and presented its director with a poster entitled "Love is Kind," since the school had designated the center as its project for the year. Community contact with the City Council and the "South of the Salt" Planning Association continued. The congregation shared the Good News by distributing thousands of copies of "Good News for Arizona," a collection of Scripture readings with full-color photos of Arizona scenes. Also, copies of "A Touch of Fire" were distributed to guests at the community Sunday observance.

In 1974, Pastor Kilian was appointed to a six-year term on the Phoenix Planning Commission by the City Council. Also during that year, he received a public service award by the American Society for Public Administration for his outstanding contributions to good government. Bill Hermann, public information officer for the city of Phoenix stated, "For the last three years, Rev. Kilian has been in the forefront of every movement to knit together the people of South Phoenix." He was the founder of the "South of the Salt" Planning Association, a member of the South Phoenix Citizens Planning Committee, and a member of the Greater South Mountain Business Association. In 1976, he took the call to serve as assistant pastor at St. Paul's Lutheran Church in Orange, California, and as director of development and communication for Lutheran Bible Translators from 1976–1985. In 1986, he began work with the Pacific Southwest District as director of "His Love, Our Response," and later, editor of *This Month* newspaper. At the same time, he became a part-time assistant pastor at St. Paul's in Orange. In 1990, after suffering from various lung-related diseases since childhood, the Lord called him home at the age of 53.

After Rev. Kilian accepted another call to Orange, a five-year vacancy period at Peace caused membership to dwindle. In January of 1981, Rev.

James Rath, a 1958 graduate of Concordia Seminary, St. Louis, who had previously served Immanuel Lutheran Church in Steger, Illinois, was installed as missionary-at-large at Peace where the congregation, like the urban, racially mixed community it served, had a rebirth with the communicant membership growing to 115. On Sunday, March 1, 1981, there were 81 people in church with 31 in attendance on Ash Wednesday. The reason the church was so filled on Sunday was because of the Baptism of three children in a Mexican family and a baptismal party of 16 people. In June, pastor flew to Illinois to attend his son's graduation and then helped his wife prepare for the move, driving back to Arizona with their dog and cat at the end of June to continue his ministry at Peace with his family.

On November 3 and 4, 1983, Rev. Stirdivant and Rev. Phil Molnar from Bell Gardens, California, visited Peace to encourage Pastor Rath and the congregation in their Hispanic ministry in that vicinity and to advise the congregation in methods and materials for expanding the Hispanic outreach. At the time, the congregation had about 65 communicant members with Sunday attendance averaging 35 to 40, mostly middle aged, as the Sunday school had less than 10 children. They encouraged the parish to continue in the Church Growth Program, to be willing to be flexible and open to the new ways of "new people," and to be culturally sensitive to the people around their church. They were also encouraged to cultivate the friendship of the Jess Maduena family, a family the pastor had brought into the church, and to establish a VBS in the summer, Saturday doctrine classes, ESL classes, and Spanish services in the future.

As Pastor Rath saw a greater need to minister to the Hispanics surrounding Peace where he had married a number of Hispanic people, he introduced Spanish in the Sunday worship services on October 19, 1986, making Peace the first area LCMS church to have a Spanish service. Jesse Lopez, a young man who was married at Peace, assisted him in the service. He and his wife, Jessica, had their daughter, Usa, baptized in the church, with Pastor Rath conducting the baptismal service in Spanish. By 1987, the congregation had grown to 120 members with 70 communicant members. Pastor Rath served the congregation from January 1981 until his death on January 24, 1988. At the time of his death, the demographics of the area included a mixture of just about everything:

light and heavy industry, commercial, residential of all types, which included a high proportion of Hispanics, about 85 percent, and blacks. The area was a difficult one in which to minister, as the congregation struggled with problems of visibility and a changing population. With the help of the Department of Mission Services, an interim pastor, Rev. Robert Schoenheider, was secured in 1989 to serve the congregation. Representatives from nine Phoenix-area congregations officially organized the Valley of the Sun Hispanic Ministry in September of 1990. In cooperation with its member congregations and the Department of Mission Services, they worked to develop, support, and carry on various efforts of Christian ministry to and with Hispanic people with initial work beginning at Peace and old Bethlehem.

At a special meeting on Sunday, February 6, 1994, the members passed, by a large majority, a resolution to disband Peace Lutheran Church with April 15, 1994, set as the date for the termination of the congregation. All property and assets passed to The Lutheran Church   Missouri Synod's Pacific Southwest District when the congregation disbanded. After 31 years of proclaiming the Gospel as Peace Lutheran Church, the congregation held a final service with a special Service of Praise and Thanksgiving on April 10, 1994. A short time before the congregation disbanded, Pastor Artigas and two families started Santo Tomas Church with Spanish services conducted at 5:00 p.m. each Sunday at Peace. On Sunday, April 15, 1994, Santo Tomas began using the facilities for Hispanic ministries conducting services each Sunday at 10:00 a.m. When Peace closed, all the Anglo members were transferred to other Lutheran churches in the area. David Buchholz remained along with three Hispanic families who had been attending Peace since their teenage years. These three families were the mainstay of Santo Tomas, supporting the parish through their good stewardship. David was instrumental in aiding Pastor Artigas in locating Spanish-speaking people in the area and assisting in the establishment of Santo Tomas. Pastor spent 3 days a week beginning this new outreach among Hispanics, averaging 20 to 30 people a Sunday with a high of 66 people gathering for worship and study on a Sunday in May of 1994 — all from the immediate community.

During the summer of 1994, Santo Tomas had grown to 50 worshipers listening and growing in the Word, with four children attending Catechism class. By September 19, the buildings were ready for the dedication of Santo Tomas with the delegates of the Hispanic ministry meeting at the church preceding the dedication service. At the 4:00 p.m. dedication ceremony, the all female Mariachi band, "Las Femeniles," who helped dedicate the Schaller Center, participated, and the ladies of Santo Tomas provided a supper at 5:00 p.m. During the service, Rev. Kenneth Behnken, assistant to the District president missions and evangelism, preached in English with Rev. Cristiano Artigas translating the sermon into Spanish.

A group of approximately 70 leaders of the International Lutheran Women's Missionary League held its meeting in Phoenix in October of 1997. That week they had a worship service, designating the offering for the work at Iglesia Santo Tomas. By 1998 with the financial help from various groups and organizations, the parish operated a food pantry and a thrift shop with the assistance of people from the Hispanic ministry association churches in Arizona. The average attendance at worship services was 40. One Saturday each month, Santo Tomas sponsored a rummage sale at the church, which helped to pay the church's expenses. In the summer, a 10-day VBS, "De Regreso a la Escuela," was held with 87 children. That increased the names in the church's contact list and the number in worship, as attendance had increased to between 45 and 50 with Sunday school growing to 30. One of the highlights of the year was the Christmas Angel Program with people gathering

A short time before Peace disbands in 1994, Pastor Artigas and two families start Santo Tomas Church with Spanish services conducted at 5:00 p.m. each Sunday at Peace.

Pastor Artigas (right) with people in the 2002 Christmas Angel Program. (Pacific Southwest District Archives)

during Advent for Posadas and the Christmas Eve service attended by 219 people.

Pastor Artigas stated that the mission hadn't grown, as it was a sending place where people came for the Food Basket Program, were introduced to the church, and then started attending Gracia or other Spanish-speaking parishes in the Phoenix area. A thrift shop was located at the church where people came to purchase clothing and other items, and were introduced to the church with some coming to worship services and Bible study. Santo Tomas was a sending parish, bringing people to the faith and sending them to other Lutheran churches. In mid-2003, Pastor Artigas received a phone call from the pastor at Apache Junction stating he had received new members who were former members of Santo Tomas. At the time, Pastor Artigas was also training three candidates for certification as deacons to assist him in this ever-expanding ministry. Over the 7 years the Hispanic parish had been in existence, it had been able to reach over 400 families sharing the saving knowledge of Christ as their Savior.

King Of Kings Lutheran Church
Rey de Reyes
Phoenix, Arizona

By the grace of God, the Kingdom work for King of Kings was begun in northwest Phoenix, a community of 45,000, on July 27, 1962, at 7:30 p.m. at St. Paul Lutheran Church at 63rd Avenue and Indian School in Phoenix with the commissioning of Rev. Wesley Toncre as missionary-at-large for this area to start the eighth congregation of the Missouri Synod in the Phoenix area with six of them having been established since 1959. Pastor Toncre was born on December 26, 1939, to Walter and Emma Toncre in Cleveland, Ohio, where he spent his first 18 years, attending St. John's Lutheran School and Lutheran High School. Following his graduation, the family moved to Warren, Ohio, where he was in the first class at the newly opened Concordia Senior College at Fort Wayne, Indiana, meeting his wife, the former Esther Essinger a resident of Arlington, Ohio, who was in nurses training at Lutheran Hospital, later becoming a registered nurse. Before his 10-month vicarage in Miami, Florida, under Rev. C. F. Kellermann, he and Esther were married on June 4, 1960. During his days at the Seminary, he worked as a mechanic and service station attendant. Following his graduation in May of 1961, he was called by the Southern California District to begin missionary work in Phoenix, Arizona, and ordained at his parents' home church, Trinity in Warren, Ohio, in the middle of June.

Young people from neighboring congregations actively publicized the mission in the area with a nucleus formed that conducted the first service as King of Kings Lutheran Church, Phoenix, Arizona, on September 2, 1962, in the small Carousel Nursery School at Thirty-fourth Avenue and Rose Lane adjacent to the five-acre plot purchased by the Mis-

Pastor Wesley Toncre with first Confirmation class.

The altar in Carousel Nursery School where the first service of King of Kings was conducted.

sion Board as the home of King of Kings Church. Fifty people, most of them visitors and well-wishers from sister congregations in the Valley of the Sun and other places in the country, attended that first service. The Sunday school began on October 7 with an enrollment of 31 students and 6 teachers. Since God richly blessed the congregation in the small nursery school, they were forced by crowded conditions to adopt a two-service schedule in November 1962. On Christmas Eve, an assembly of 98 people crowded into a place usually inhabited by 21 very small children. One of the charter members, Frances Pleger, recalled, "No one minded having to set up the chairs and altar and Sunday school every Saturday" in the nursery school. Her daughter, Judy Rundquist, also recalled going to the nursery to set up chairs and put out hymnals for church services on Sunday. "Later, on Saturday, my dad, Gene Pleger, would set the mimeograph on our kitchen table and run the bulletins and... we kids would help fold them."

By January of 1963, King of Kings numbered 47 communicants and more than 90 members. In February, the blueprints for the new church were presented, and the congregation purchased a piano for $125 along with new hymnals. On March 10, 1963, groundbreaking services were conducted on a beautiful Phoenix day followed by a potluck dinner. In July, the District authorized the new parish to purchase a 5-rank Robert Morton Organ for $4,200. Construction of its worship education unit was in progress at that time with the congregation gathering on October 10, to consecrate its beautiful, new house of worship with 76 in the 7:45 a.m. service and 149 in the 10:15 service along with 120 in the Sunday school. At 3:00 p.m. on Sunday, November 3, 350 gathered in a dedication Vespers to hear Rev. Engelbrecht preach the dedication sermon with Pastor Toncre officiating. Miss Diane Hejhall served as organist, and the combined choirs of the Lutheran Church of the Master and King of Kings under the direction of Rev. John Kunz participated.

By 1964, the congregation had grown to 203 members with 113 communicant members having a Sunday school enrollment of 184. In the middle of the year, 50 percent of the congregation completed the accredited teacher training courses and became teachers in the triple-staffed educational department, teaching the Sunday school classes and weekday Bible classes. In September, a six-year graded religion course was initiated on Saturdays. In 1966, through their efforts, the congregation grew to 455 members, 193 communicant members with a Sunday school enrollment of 276. Thirty Sunday school classes allowed for building of close Christian relationships between pupil and teacher. Mrs. Leona Aubuchon, a charter member, remembered, "There were so many Sunday school classes that we used the church and dividers to separate the classes. We had folding chairs at that time and no pews, so everything had to be reset for second service." This rapidly growing parish was located almost in the center of the most densely populated area in Phoenix with 60,000 people in a "stone's throw" distance from the location of the congregation.

After Pastor Toncre took a call to St. Matthew's in Miami, Florida, King of Kings had a vacancy, which was filled when Pastor Richard Schinnerer took the call in 1967. He was born in Long Beach, California, on September 25, 1929, and was raised at First Lutheran Church, which his grandparents helped to establish in 1904. Following his gradu-

This rapidly growing parish is located almost in the center of the most densely populated area in Phoenix with 60,000 people in a "stone's throw" distance from the location of King of Kings.

The interior of the church at Christmas in 1982.

King of Kings Lutheran Church in 1980.

Rev. Richard Schinnerer came to King of Kings in 1967 and remained until 1973.

Rev. Steven Cluver became the third pastor of King of Kings in 1973. (Pacific Southwest District Archives)

Rev. Kenneth Piepenbrink was installed in October of 1980 as the fourth pastor of Kings of Kings, serving until his retirement in 2001.

ation from Oakland's California Concordia College in 1949, he attended Concordia Seminary in St. Louis graduating in 1954. The previous year he married his first wife, Kathryn Necker, a Christian day school teacher, with their marriage blessed with four children. He was ordained and installed at Holy Cross Lutheran Church in San Diego, California. In 1960, he accepted the call to St. John's in Covina, California, where he remained until 1967 when he went to King of Kings.

When interviewed, Pastor Schinnerer stated that his ministry at King of Kings was "extremely interesting and exciting." He recalled that Ron and Marie Valenzuela became members of King of King, and through their missionary zeal, the El Mirage Mission was established with the youth from King of Kings going to El Mirage to help with the Vacation Bible School. In 1968, the church reached a milestone by becoming self-supporting. During his ministry there, he purchased an eight-unit apartment complex that led him to resign from the ministry in 1973 to work as a salesman in the real estate field. He returned to the ministry at the urging of Rev. Beyer of Mt. Calvary in Phoenix, accepting a call to be pastor of Trinity, Prescott Valley, Arizona, in 1977. In 1982, he went to Calvary, Yuma, Arizona, where he stayed two years. During the succeeding years, he worked in the plumbing industry, taught at Lutheran High School in La Verne, California, married his second wife, Elaine Moderow Lloyd, on September 5, 1986, and served as vacancy minister at various Southern California Lutheran churches.

Following Pastor Schinnerer's departure, a vacancy occurred with Rev. Zitlau serving as vacancy pastor until Rev. Steven Cluver became the third pastor of King of Kings in 1973. He was born

in Watseka, Illinois, on October 9, 1943. Following his graduation from Concordia College, Milwaukee, Wisconsin in 1963, he attended Concordia Senior College, graduating in 1965. While attending Concordia Seminary in Springfield, Illinois, he married Karen Sue Weber on June 29, 1967, with their marriage blessed with three children. After his graduation from the seminary in 1969, he was ordained and installed at St. James Lutheran Church, Lafayette, Indiana. During his ministry at King of Kings, the charismatic movement was prevalent, causing many problems. Pastor Cluver left the parish in May of 1980, accepting a call to Trinity in San Diego, where he stayed until 1988, accepting a call to Christ in Boulder City, Nevada. After he left King of Kings, the church had a vacancy for a year with pastors Zitlau and Wessler serving as vacancy pastors. In October of 1980, Rev. Kenneth Piepenbrink was installed as the fourth pastor of Kings of Kings.

Pastor Piepenbrink was born on May 24, 1937, in Mt. Prospect, Illinois, where he attended St. Paul's Lutheran Church and School during his childhood. He went to Concordia College in Milwaukee, Wisconsin, for one year, transferring to Concordia Seminary, Springfield, Illinois, graduating in 1962. He was ordained in his home church, St. Paul's in Mt. Prospect and installed as pastor of First Lutheran Church in Phillipsburg, Kansas, in 1962. He married to Karen Wille on June 29, 1963 with their union blessed with two children, Mark, who became a pastor, and Dawn. His wife taught at Martin Luther Lutheran School in Phoenix. In 1965, he took a call to Tabor Lutheran Church in Chicago, Illinois, staying until 1972, when he went to Immanuel in Bridgman, Michigan. In 1974, he served two parishes, Trinity, Wautoma, and Grace, Deerfield, Wisconsin. In October of 1980, he was installed as pastor of Kings of Kings in Phoenix, Arizona, where he remained for over 21 years until his retirement on December 31, 2001.

During Pastor Piepenbrink's ministry, the congregation celebrated its 20th anniversary on November 6, 1983, with Rev. Toncre, the first pastor, preaching at the service with a dinner following in the educational wing. On May 1, 1988, a service of praise and thanksgiving was held to dedicate the remodeled interior of the church, the addition of the new choir room/altar room, the newly purchased organ and handbells with Pastor Schinnerer preaching and Pastor Piepenbrink serving as liturgist. The large lighted cross that had hung over the altar in the chancel was removed and

On May 1, 1988, a service of praise and thanksgiving is held to dedicate the remodeled interior of the church.

made into a table and cross for the narthex of the church. The church reached another milestone in its history on July 13, 1986, when the congregation gathered to celebrate being debt free by burning the church mortgage in a special service that day. At the time, Pastor's 14-year-old daughter, Dawn, with her partner, Rick Castaneda, after three years of competing in the national championships, were ranked sixth in the nation in the Junior Pairs division of the U.S. National Figure Skating Championship earning her ranking at the competition held in Salt Lake City, Utah, in February 1990. During her skating career, she went to Nationals about 11 times, ranked 10th in the nation and also skated internationally for the USA in France, Germany, South Korea, Poland, and Spain. Pastor and Karen Piepenbrink's son, Mark, received his Master of Divinity degree from Concordia Theological Seminary, Fort Wayne, Indiana, in May of 1990 and was ordained and installed as the new assistant pastor at Our Saviour Lutheran Church in Sedalia, Missouri, where he worked with the youth and evangelism programs.

By 1993, King of Kings had grown to 347 members with 275 communicants. On October 26, 1997, the congregation conducted a 35th anniversary service where Pastor Harms preached with Pastor Piepenbrink serving as liturgist, and the first organist Diane nee Hejhall Johnson returned to play the organ for this joyful occasion. This was not only the church's 35th anniversary but also Pastor Piepenbrink's 35th year in the ministry that was also noted along with the 150th anniversary of the Synod. Following the service, the AAL served a Bratwurst luncheon that was followed with Pastor Piepenbrink dedicating the new Memorial Garden at 1:00 p.m. Since there was dissension within the parish, some of the members transferred to other congregations. In the latter days of Piepenbrink's ministry at King of Kings, the neighborhood surrounding the church had changed to a large Hispanic population with Pastor Cris Artigas invited to start a side-by-side Hispanic ministry, beginning with ESL classes at King of Kings. Rey de Reyes started worship services on the fifteenth Sunday after Pentecost, September 24, 2000, with 38 people in attendance having a database of 150 families who visited in worship services during that year. The new mission provided the following services to the community: weekly worship services, weddings, Quinceñeras, Baptisms, Bible studies, Confirmation and Catechism classes (First Communion), Vacation Bible School, Back-

Pastor Cris Artigas with a child from the 2001 Vacation Bible School.

to-School Program, Christmas Angel Program, Reyes Magos, and ESL classes.

At the time of Pastor Piepenbrink's retirement in 2002, the congregation had 195 souls with 164 communicants, averaging 86 people in worship on Sundays. During 2000 and 2003, with the help of the vacancy pastor, Rev. James Swinford, the congregation began meeting to see how best to serve the area, canvassing the neighborhood, inviting people to the church, holding a special music service with Spanish songs which was attended by the members only, and a live nativity with a petting zoo. With the results of no new members, the congregation voted to sell the property. Before it became public, the New Life Korean Presbyterian Church, in April of 2003, purchased the property for $650,000, which included the sanctuary, parish hall, and Sunday school rooms, leaving the Hispanic congregation, Rey de Reyes, with nowhere to worship. The last service for King of Kings in its building was Easter Sunday, April 20, 2003. The English-speaking congregation moved to Good Shepherd Care Center Chapel, a Wisconsin Synod retirement home in Peoria at 103rd and Olive, where 70 people continued to worship at the new location about 12 miles from the old church. During April, Pastor Swinford accepted the call as pastor. The parish rented 3 storefront units at Seventy-fifth and Peoria to develop into a worship center and Sunday school, using the cross from over the altar of the old church, along with the beautiful banners, handbells, and grand piano.

The Hispanic congregation of 40 people didn't fare so well, as only 2 families stayed with the Lutheran church when it was relocated to Sola Fide Mission on Mt. Calvary's campus in Phoenix. With the sale of Kings of Kings' buildings, Pastor Artigas used this time to develop a new ministry

Rey de Reyes starts worship services on September 24, 2000, with 38 people in attendance.

at Holy Cross, Scottsdale, a church located on the south side of Scottsdale where there is a heavy concentration of Hispanics. The new ministry, La Santa Cruz, began on May 13, 2003, when 2 ESL classes were started with over 40 people in attendance. Through these classes, Pastor was able to gain two families, beginning worship services with an average attendance of seven. Mrs. Vida Luna taught Bible stories and the Catechism to children in a Saturday class. During August of 2003, a Vacation Bible School called "Back-to-School Program" was conducted for one week with eight children attending. On the last Sunday of the school, the children received a backpack with school supplies in a closing devotion held in the church sanctuary with two sets of parents and one father attending the closing activity. The ESL classes had an enrollment of 75 by January of 2004, serving Hispanics from Central and South America.

Hispanic Lutheran Women's Missionary League

On September 28, 2002, LCMS Hispanic Ministries gathered women from the 5 Hispanic worship sites for the first informational LWML meeting with 25 women attending this historic milestone in the life of LCMS Hispanic ministry in Arizona. Devotions were led by Rev. Cristiano Artigas with the session presided over by Mrs. Vida Luna. The women were excited and enjoyed learning about their sisters in the LWML. They reviewed the LWML brochure (Spanish version) and recited the LWML pledge, and adopted as their official hymn "Cantad Al Senor," a familiar tune from the Spanish hymnal. The women presented to the chairman of the circuit LWML, Ms. Chris Hutchins, five checks that were collected during the VBS offerings that year. Vida Orea de Luna translated the LWML brochure into Spanish with the design and layout done by Emera Luna; the translated brochure offered non-English speaking women an opportunity to understand how the LWML works. Through the establishment of the LWML (official Spanish abbreviation is SFHML), the SFHML held meetings every month with Ministry on Wheels as one of their projects where the women assembled toiletries along with hot beverages, water, and donuts, to be distributed each week to Hispanic men stationed in the parking lots of large home improvement stores who were seeking day jobs.

At the end of 2003, Pastor Artigas reported the following about the Arizona Hispanic ministry:

I wish there were words deep enough to make you feel the deep emotions of 12 years of LCMS Hispanic ministry in the Valley of the Sun. The Lord has poured His blessings abundantly towards this ministry. Programs such as Brown Bag, ESL, ESOL

The first meeting of the SFHML (a Hispanic version of LWML) occurred on September 28, 2002, in Arizona. (Pacific Southwest District Archives)

classes, Thanksgiving baskets, Christmas Angels, Easter baskets, are the continuing avenues used to reach the Hispanic community. The community is being reached for the sole purpose of bringing them to the Knowledge of Jesus' Redemption Plan for each one of us. Currently we are offering worship services at five different locations every Sunday, offering ESL classes in four different locations weekly, providing First Communion and Confirmation classes at various churches, providing seasonal programs such as the ones mentioned previously, teaching Sunday school and Vacation Bible School programs, and training and enabling Hispanic women to take over a vital role in church development through the SFHML (a Hispanic version of LWML).

Christ the Redeemer
Christo El Redentor
Phoenix, Arizona

rior to the establishment of a congregation in northwest Phoenix, the Southern California District purchased five acres of land at 8801 N. Forty-third Avenue; but it wasn't until a need was seen for another sister congregation in northwest Phoenix that plans were developed for the birth of Christ the Redeemer Lutheran Church. In May 1969, the District assigned Rev. John F. Pope, a 1969 graduate of Concordia Theological Seminary, St. Louis, to start a congregation named "Christ the Redeemer." He was born in Fort Smith, Arkansas, on April 7, 1943. He attended St. John's College, Winfield, Kansas, graduating in 1963, receiving his bachelor's degree from Concordia Senior College, Fort Wayne, Indiana, in 1965. He was ordained at Christ the Redeemer in Tulsa, Oklahoma, in 1969. He married Viola Wesche on May 29, 1966, with their marriage blessed with two daughters.

Rev. John F. Pope, first pastor of Christ the Redeemer, as pictured in 1993. (Pacific Southwest District Archives)

After Pastor Pope, his wife Vi, and their daughter Kirsten, moved to 6761 N. Forty-fourth Avenue, he was commissioned as missionary-at-large in Christ Lutheran Church, Phoenix, on September 14, 1969. The first service of the new congregation was held on Sunday, September 21, 1969, with 47 people in attendance giving an offering was of $107.95, at Alta Vista Elementary School, 8710 N. Thirty-first Avenue, where the congregation worshiped four years. On the following Saturday, September 27, the Redeemer Guild was formed in Pastor and Mrs. Pope's home. In December, the District purchased the parsonage at 4034 W. Hatcher Road

with the Popes moving into the house during the week of April 5, 1970. The following week on Sunday, April 12, the first Confirmation class of two, Brian Sherant and Doreen Meyer, was confirmed. By the parish's first anniversary, the membership had grown to 98 members with 70 communicant members.

On January 25, 1971, a new member was added to the congregational family with the birth of another healthy baby girl, Jennifer, to Pastor and Vi. In the spring on May 8, 1971, the first step was taken to prepare the property at 8801 N. Forty-third Avenue for the construction of a church building with a clean-up party clearing the property of debris, working diligently, and looking forward to the day when the church building would become a reality. In the fall, a sad day fell upon the congregation when they learned that Pastor Pope was leaving the congregation, as all loved him and his family. He had terminated his ministry on September 28, 1972, leaving on December 10, 1972. He served in the Arizona Highway Patrol from 1972 to 1992, retiring as a commander in October 1992. He directed the DARE Program in Arizona from 1985 to 1992 serving on the National DARE Board. He went back into the ministry to serve Beautiful Savior in Tempe, Arizona, where he remained until 1998 when he took a medical leave from the ministry.

Rev. Fred Rockett, a retired pastor, was asked to be the vacancy pastor. He and his wife had moved to Mesa, Arizona, from Pittsburgh, Pennsylvania,

Rev. Roger Hedstrom (circa 1970) served from 1973 to 1975. (Pacific Southwest District Archives)

When the chapel/parish hall is dedicated on January 27, 1974, the parish has grown from 12 families to 239 members, having an average of 200 in worship services.

after his retirement. He served faithfully until April 1, 1973, when the second pastor, Rev. Roger Francis Hedstrom, accepted the call extended to him by Christ the Redeemer. After he and his wife, Susan, and children, Andrei and Christina, worshiped with the congregation in the morning service on April 1, 1973, he was installed at King of Kings that afternoon. Rev. Martin Lundi of Tempe, representative of the District Mission Board, gave the sermon; Rev. Fred Rockett, vacancy pastor, served as liturgist, and the District counselor, Rev. Paul Strickert of Sun City, performed the Rite of Installation with the pupils of Martin Luther School of Phoenix singing under the direction of David Freiberg. A reception followed the installation to honor Pastor Hedstrom and his family.

Pastor Hedstrom was born on July 9, 1943, in Berkeley, California. Following his primary education in Chico, California, he attended California Concordia College, Oakland; Concordia Senior College, Fort Wayne; and Concordia Seminary, St. Louis where he received his Bachelor of Arts degree in classical languages, with a concentration in philosophy. He spent his year of vicarage at Zion, Detroit, Michigan. While attending college and seminary, he taught Sunday school for retarded children, served as organist for a Negro Lutheran congregation and was active on the social concerns committee of the seminary. After his graduation from the seminary in 1969, he served as assistant pastor of First Lutheran, Long Beach, California, where he was active in working with the Boards of Education, Adult Life, Evangelism, Stewardship and Youth, initiating the Kennedy Evangelism Program and the Bethel Bible Series. His wife, Susan, whom he married in 1966, was a graduate of Concordia Teachers College, River Forest, Illinois, who taught in parochial schools in St. Louis and Detroit.

Pastor Hedstrom preached his first service at Christ the Redeemer on April 8, 1973. Two months later, on June 10, the congregation voted to begin

Christ the Redeemer's first building dedicated on January 27, 1974. (Pacific Southwest District Archives)

construction of a new chapel/parish hall building. Sunday, June 17, 1973, was an important day in the history of the congregation as the groundbreaking ceremony was held at 9:45 a.m. that morning at the church site, 8801 N. Forty-third Avenue. The building was designed by architect Francis A. Schultz, A.I.A., and built by R. E. Spurr Construction Corporation. When the building was dedicated on January 27, 1974, the parish had grown from 12 families to a membership of 239 members, 173 communicants with 43 voting members, having 200 in worship services and a Sunday school of 77 in just 4 years.

In the summer of 1973, Christ the Redeemer conducted a joint Vacation Bible School with the Church of the Master in Phoenix with 181 children enrolled having a staff of 66. As their evangelism project, the children distributed a gift, "Touched by the Fire" Bible, to 1,000 homes in the neighborhood of Christ the Redeemer. Enclosed in the Bible was an invitation to the new Phoenix mission congregation of Christ the Redeemer. The pastors of both churches, Rev. Roger Hedstrom and Rev. John Kuntz, reported that both congregations enjoyed this cooperative venture. In 1974, a preschool was opened in the Sunday school rooms with the first instructor, Beverly Truett.

In 1975, Pastor Hedstrom left the parish, taking a call to St. Mark, Phoenix, where he remained until March of 1976. He married Theresa Yvonne Amon-Castleman on June 4, 1977, and was also installed as the new pastor at Epiphany, Chandler, Arizona, where he remained until December of 1982. He and his wife adopted a child. In January of 1983, he was installed as pastor of Hope in Daly City, California, remaining until 1998. In August of 1998, he became pastor of Mt. View Lutheran Church in Apache Junction, Arizona, where he served until 2002.

He was succeeded by Rev. John F. Meyer, who was installed as the third pastor on February 8, 1976, with over 200 people, including 13 clergymen, attending and participating in the installation service with the congregation's youth and children's chorus singing an appropriate anthem. Rev. William Graumann, first vice president of the District and pastor of Immanuel, Riverside, was the preacher.

Pastor Meyer was born in St. Louis, Missouri, on January 17, 1928, where he also received his elementary education. After attending the preparatory school at Concordia College, Fort Wayne, Indiana, he graduated from Concordia Seminary in St. Louis in 1952. His vicarage was at Miami, Florida; Riverton, Wyoming; and Freistatt, Missouri. His first pastorate was Pilgrim Church in Kilgore, Texas, followed by Mount Olive Church in Flint, Michigan; Christ Church in Cape Canaveral, Florida; Concordia Church in Oak Harbor, Washington; and Our Savior Church in Satellite Beach, Florida. During his ministry, he served on the District Boards of Youth, Evangelism and Public Relations, and also served as counselor for his synodical circuit. On September 1, 1951, he was joined in holy matrimony with Irma (nee Woods) of Edwardsville, Illinois, with the Lord blessing their marriage with three sons, John, Joel, and James. During his ministry at Christ the Redeemer, an educational building was built in 1979.

After Pastor Meyer left in 1980, Rev. Loel Haak was installed as the fourth pastor on August 9, 1981. He was born into the parsonage of Rev. and Mrs. William Haak in St. Paul, Minnesota, in 1938 and was raised in Lutheran parsonages in Minnesota, South Dakota, and Iowa. After his early educational training in Lutheran grade schools and high school, he attended Concordia College, St. Paul, Minnesota and Concordia Senior College, Fort Wayne, Indiana, where he graduated with a B.A. degree in 1960 completing his seminary training at Concordia, St. Louis, in 1964 where he also did post-graduate studies leading to a master's in sacred theology in 1973. In 1963, he married Annamarie Pfeffer, a native of Germany and a 1963 graduate from the University of Nebraska, who had a Bachelor of Science degree in textiles and merchandising. They had four children, Sarah, Miriam, Julia, and Lucas.

Following his graduation, Pastor Haak served as missionary-at-large in Paradise Valley north of Phoenix and as pastor of St. Mark until 1971. He took a call to Hope Lutheran Church in Seattle, Washington, where he served as associate pastor. During his ministry, he served as a circuit counselor and as pastoral advisor to zones of the Walther League, Lutheran Laymen's League, and Lutheran Women's Missionary League. He was chairman and secretary for the Puget Sound Pastoral Conference. For eight years he was a member of the Board of Directors of the Hearthstone, a Lutheran retirement community in Seattle. He served for three years as a member of the Northwest District Evangelism Committee and administrated three Evangelism Explosion Leadership clinics. He was a presenter at one of the workshops at Synod's Great Commission Convocation in St. Louis in

November of 1979 and at a Northwest District Evangelism Convocation in Twin Falls, Idaho, in February 1980. Pastor Haak was a charter member of the Lutheran High School in Seattle — a school which had completed its third academic year in 1980 — and served on the steering committee for its formation. He was active in Toastmasters International for three years.

When Christ the Redeemer Lutheran Church celebrated its 20th anniversary in 1981, the parish had grown to 900 members with 680 communicants. On November 3, 1991, Laborers for Christ was engaged, with the help of church members, in a six-month construction project at Christ the Redeemer to construct a new sanctuary and office and remodel the existing buildings. On October 31, 1993, the new 500-seat sanctuary, chapel, 5 new offices, and workroom/library were dedicated. The $1.2 million edifice took one year to occupy and two years to complete in terms of organ, artwork, and landscaping. The Rev. Calvin Fiege, assistant to the president of the PSW District, delivered the dedicatory address. The old sanctuary was renovated for a fellowship hall, and the original educational space became two new classrooms and a nursery. The parish numbered 924 souls and 714 communicants with pastors Loel G. Haak, Vernon T. Trahms (associate pastor), and Walter E. Lichtsman (emeritus) serving the congregation along with Vicki Nordbrock, director of the Christian Child Development Center. The preschool was closed in 1989 but was reopened in 1992. In 1995, a kindergarten was added, and in 1996 the school expanded to a first grade with another grade level added each year. The school presently has two classrooms per grade level.

At the beginning of 1996, Pastor Haak returned to the pulpit of Christ the Redeemer following a sabbatical study during the month of January where he wrote a 100-page paper entitled, "Evolution of a Neighborhood Church into a Metropolitan Church, the Story of Christ the Redeemer," completing the last requirement for a ministry program initiated six years before. The parish provided community services through the Jail Ministry, outreach (meals) to homeless, Braille ministry, quilts for various shelters, ESL classes, support groups for the divorced, parents, the grieving, and a Korean ministry in 1996–1997. The Korean ministry received a Lutheran Brotherhood Foundation $25,000 grant for the development of this new congregation helping it to become a self-supporting Korean Lutheran Church that was led by

Rev. John F. Meyer, who was installed as the third pastor on February 8, 1976. (Pacific Southwest District Archives)

Rev. Loel Haak was installed as the fourth pastor on August 9, 1981. (Pacific Southwest District Archives)

Rev. Donald E. Schoenback Jr. current pastor of Christ the Redeemer. (Pacific Southwest District Archives)

After placing a sign in front of the church in 2001, Pastor Schmidt conducts the first Spanish service with 19 people. Today between 130 and 175 attend.

Pastor Sael Chang.

When Pastor Haak retired, Rev. Donald E. Schoenback Jr., a graduate of Concordia Junior College, Ann Arbor, Michigan; Concordia Sr. College, Fort Wayne, Indiana; and Concordia Seminary, St. Louis, in 1982, was called as the new pastor. He began his ministerial career at Trinity, Shelton, and Zion, Gilman, Wisconsin. He served St. Peter and Trinity, Wausau, Wisconsin, and was mission developer in Mattawan, Michigan. Before going to Christ the Redeemer, he served St. Mark in Kentwood, Michigan. He and his wife, Cheryl (Reitz), a Lutheran schoolteacher, have two children, Kristin and Allison.

In 1997 after Rev. Gale Schmidt retired from El Buen Pastor at Jehovah Lutheran Church in Chicago and moved to the Phoenix area, he became a member of Christ the Redeemer. He was born on a farm near Daykin, Nebraska, on November 25, 1936. After he graduated from Concordia Seminary, St. Louis, in 1962, he was ordained in his home church, Immanuel, Daykin, Nebraska, and installed as pastor in First Immanuel in Chicago, Illinois, where he stayed for four and one-half years. He took a call to St. Matthew's, located in the Mexican community in Chicago, where he started a Hispanic ministry working with lay workers, remaining 12½ years. In 1979, he went to El Buen Pastor at Jehovah Lutheran Church of Chicago, which had 150 communicants and 240

members, retiring in 1997. He married Lois Mayer on July 10, 1960, with their marriage blessed with four children.

When Pastor Schmidt moved to Phoenix, he began a jail ministry, as there was a need for someone to minister to people in Spanish. He continues the ministry each Friday to 50 men and 50 women in chapel services separately as the chapel can hold only 50 people. Since so many inmates wanted to attend services, their names were placed on a waiting list. After he became a member at Christ the Redeemer in Phoenix, the parish decided to conduct ESL classes. In 2001, Pastor decided to start Spanish worship services at the church using the name Cristo El Redentor. After placing a sign in front of the church in September, he conducted the first service in the chapel at 12:00 p.m., where 19 people came, then 13, and then 20. Before long, the group outgrew the chapel and was worshiping in the sanctuary with between 130 and 175 people in attendance.

The work among the Hispanics at Christ the Redeemer included cultural activities and events such as house blessings, First Communions, Quinceñeras generally held on Saturdays, Posadas, and Ash Wednesday services. When Spanish worship services began, the people took ownership with one member, Marta, taking service folders with the scripture readings to people at work, inviting them to attend services. Pastor Schmidt trained lay workers to help lead the services. At one of the Baptisms held on a Sunday morning, the girl and her brother sang a duet. One Sunday at the time of the offering, an elderly lady got up and expressed the desire to sing a song of praise to God. Because a member who was a painter had to work on Sundays, he began his job at 4:00 a.m.

Christ the Redeemer's beautiful, new 500-seat sanctuary was dedicated on October 31, 1993. (Pacific Southwest District Archives)

The interior of the church with its unique cross, located on the wall behind the free-standing altar. (Pacific Southwest District Archives)

so that he could attend the 12:00 noon service that day. One Sunday there were eight Baptisms conducted during the service. Some months later, while pastor was conducting services in the jail, he met a fellow who had been arrested on drunk driving charges and who had been previously baptized at Cristo El Redentor. Many of the people attending Cristo El Redentor were laborers who lived in apartments with some of the people having a good education.

Pastor Schmidt started teaching Spanish through songs and Spanish phrases in the day school to the children in kindergarten through grade three. Some time later, a retired bilingual educator took over this work in the school. Pastor

is now involved in a social ministry program of feeding the needy. All his work at church and jail he does gratis. When the Hispanic ministry began in September 2001 with a handful of people, the ministry continued to be blessed. On June 30, 2002, 56 new Hispanic members were added to the congregation, with 100 families visiting the Hispanic mission the previous year. One of the new projects that was started that year was training back-up singers and musicians, especially guitar players, to assist in the worship services. In February of 2003, two ESL classes were conducted, with an average of 90 attending weekly worship. This new mission continues to grow under the Lord's guidance and blessing.

Rev. Gale Schmidt, a retired pastor who began work among Hispanics in the area. (Southwest District Archives)

Church Of The Master
El Divino Maestro
Phoenix, Arizona

Surveys of the Phoenix metropolitan area as early as 1959 indicated a steady development of home sites in a northerly direction which moved the Mission Board to effect the purchase of a 5 acre church site at North Twenty-third Avenue and Q Street in the Phoenix Deer Valley area in 1960. Deer Valley in north Phoenix was one of the choicest developing residential areas of greater Phoenix; even though it was still a sparsely settled area, this section of suburban Phoenix was experiencing the most rapid growth of any in greater Phoenix. In 1961, Rev. Harold Engelbrecht, pastor of Mt. Calvary, the mother church of The Lutheran Church — Missouri Synod in Phoenix, met with several gatherings of Lutherans interested in forming a Deer Valley Mission. In the summer of 1961, he was with a realtor, looking for a house in Deer Valley; they found a well-built one at 12211 North Twenty-fifth Avenue, Phoenix, fairly close to the church property, with three-bedrooms, living room, dining room, large lot, fenced, etc., with Pastor having the dream of starting a Sunday school there at the earliest possible moment. The parsonage was purchased on August 24, 1961, at a cost of $25,903.

Pastor Engelbrecht wrote the District the following in an August 1961 letter:

We just have to get ahead of the U.L.C. and have something to tell folks out there.

Time is of the essence and the tragic delay in obtaining a pastor is doing much harm. A Sunday school will help hold the field and prove that we are doing something.

As usual, we will start this new mission with two-dozen hymnals and an agenda. We will also loan them enough folding chairs to take care of the present. My Sunday school will provide the S. S. and Bible class materials. We will organize the folks out there to keep up the parsonage etc.

I am having the sign for the church property printed and hope to have it up the middle of next week. Don't you think we ought to have signs on our other properties to let people know that we intend to do something?

Pastor Engelbrecht was good on his word as his congregation began a Sunday school in the newly purchased parsonage that fall with the District calling Rev. John P. Kuntz of Wheatland, Wyoming, to serve as missionary-at-large. While the immediate area around the church property was not fully developed, the surrounding land area, a radius of one and one-half miles, was under the control of tract development, with an estimated population in the area to be served at 12,000 having a potential of rapid increase in housing. The Mission Board had contracted archi-

Rev. John Kuntz, who was commissioned on January 7, 1962, as missionary-at-large for the Deer Valley area of Phoenix. (Pacific Southwest District Archives)

As the growth of Phoenix moves steadily northward, the mission finds itself in the center of a constantly increasing population.

tect Dick Nelson to draft plans for a church building on the property with construction begun in the fall of 1961. On January 7, 1962, Rev. Kuntz was commissioned as missionary-at-large of the Deer Valley area of Phoenix at Mount Calvary Church, Phoenix. The officiant at the commissioning service was Dr. Henry Kumnick; Rev. Harold Tietjen, assistant executive secretary of the District, delivered the sermon; and Rev. Harold Engelbrecht, pastor at Mount Calvary, performed the commissioning. Assisting with the ceremony were neighboring pastors William Pebler, Arthur Inner, Karl Meyer, and Kenneth Fuerbringer. A reception for Rev. and Mrs. Kuntz followed the service.

Pastor Kuntz was born in Clintonville, Wisconsin, where his father was a teacher in the Christian day school. He prepped at Concordia College in Milwaukee, Wisconsin, graduating in 1952, followed by Concordia Seminary in St. Louis, Missouri, graduating in 1957. His year of vicarage was spent at St. Mark Church, Detroit, Michigan, under Rev. E. Kurth. After his seminary graduation, he was called to Trinity Lutheran Church in Wheatland, Wyoming, where he also served Zion Lutheran Church in Douglas, Wyoming. While serving the dual parishes, he met and married Marian Jans of Milwaukee, Wisconsin, in 1960. They had a son, Gary, on October 23, 1961, and some time later, another son, Mark. At the time, his father was a retired parochial school teacher at Emmaus Church, Alhambra, and his brother, Rev. Arnold Kuntz, was pastor of Bethany Church in Long Beach.

In January 31, 1962, letter, Pastor reported to the District that the people in Deer Valley "were an enthusiastic group, eagerly awaiting the establishment of the church and actively letting the neighborhood know that a Lutheran church was going to be there. There were between 25 and 30 families who were already a part of, or who had expressed an interest in, the mission. Several unchurched were interested in taking instruction with a class beginning the following Tuesday. On the 21st of January, a gathering at the parsonage filled the house to capacity in spite of heavy rain all day." The first meeting of the men, an orientation meeting, was held at the parsonage on January 29 where 17 men were invited. Seven were present at the meeting, while five called to indicate that work, night school, etc., would keep them away. The purpose of the meeting was to get acquainted and to seek talents and make decisions. The plans preceding the dedication were to complete a can-

vass of the area and publicize the church and Sunday school in local newspapers

Since the building wouldn't be ready until the end of February and since there was no suitable place in the area for conducting a temporary worship service, the first worship service would be held in the new building on Ash Wednesday, March 7, 1962, at 7:30 p.m. with 74 people in attendance. Because the building actually wasn't ready, as there were no heat or electric light fixtures, a few strategically positioned electric heaters and flood lamps served adequately for the service along with a borrowed Lowrey Holiday home organ. The Ash Wednesday service was the first in a series of six Wednesday evening Lenten services. On Sunday, March 11, a worship service was conducted at 10:00 a.m. and Sunday school was held at 8:45 a.m. with attendances during the following weeks, averaging approximately 110 and about 70 children in Sunday school. The first Communion service was celebrated on April 1, with 46 partaking of the Sacrament. By April 3, there had been five Baptisms and one adult Confirmation. With the building completed, the day finally arrived for the dedication of the chapel/parish hall unit on May 13, 1962, with Rev. Harold H. Engelbrecht as guest speaker. By the summer, the parish had grown to 90 communicant members.

As the growth of Phoenix moved steadily northward, the mission found itself in the center of a constantly increasing population. In 1963 for the second successive year in cooperation with other congregations of Synod, the Church of the Master advanced its growth though an aggressive evangelism effort with membership at 199, communicant membership at 93, and Sunday school enrollment reaching 147. By 1966, although growth

The Lutheran Church of the Master's chapel/parish hall unit was dedicated on May 13, 1962. (Pacific Southwest District Archives)

in the Deer Valley community had leveled temporarily, the Lutheran Church of the Master showed signs of favorable expansion even with a high rate of membership turnover, the parish experienced the blessing of growth and continued to serve a large Sunday school of 150. In the previous year, a growing segment of unchurched in the community had been seeking help from the church, a challenge, which had opened many new doors for the witness of Christ. Projected expansion of two large plants located in north Phoenix, General Electric and Sperry Company, was to bring the parish in contact with many more families. By 1970, the congregation had grown to 369 members and 216 communicant members.

In 1981, after serving 12 years at Church of the Master, Pastor Kuntz served as assistant pastor at several congregations, and, briefly, with the organizing staff of Christ College in Irvine while completing his master's program. He joined the staff of Lutheran Counseling Center, Community Counseling Service, Van Nuys, California, as associate director in 1978 until he accepted the call to Abiding Savior in El Toro, now Lake Forest, California, in 1982 where he retired in 1997. Rev. Robert W. Holstein became the second pastor at the Church of the Master. He had previously served in Alberta, Canada; Grand Forks, North Dakota; and Red Bud, Illinois. While in the Southern California District, he served on the District Education Commission and Social Ministries Committee. He was born on May 19, 1932, in Osmond, Nebraska, graduating from Concordia College, St. Paul, Minnesota, in 1953 and Concordia Seminary, St. Louis, in 1958. Following his graduation from the seminary, he was ordained at Grace in Hinton, Alberta, Canada, where he served along with congregations at Jasper and Edson. He married Lucille Beckman, a registered nurse, on June 8, 1958, with their marriage blessed with two children, Lisa and Bob. He served the LWML as both zone and District pastoral counselor.

Also in 1981, the congregation decided to open a preschool with six children, hiring the director, Pam Schimke, a Seward Concordia Teachers College graduate who was born in Nebraska. After staying three years, she was followed by Brenda Ludwig, who also was in charge of the church music program. In 2000, Pam returned to the preschool where there are now 17 children enrolled.

On October 16, 1983, in a special service followed by a potluck dinner, the congregation honored Pastor Holstein on his 25th anniversary

in the ministry and Pastor Robert Zitlau for his 30th year in the Lutheran ministry. That evening at 6:00 p.m., a program of music and entertainment was held at Valley Lutheran High School, 2536 N. Twenty-fourth Avenue. Pastor Zitlau had served at Grace Lutheran Church, San Diego, and Bethany Lutheran Church, Ocean Beach, California, before accepting a call to the institutional ministry in the Phoenix area in 1964. In 1985, Rev. Richard A. Heller, a graduate of Concordia Seminary, Fort Wayne, and his wife, Doris, came to the parish where he became the assistant pastor.

In 1992, Rev. Michael Harding came to the Church of the Master as the new assistant pastor to Pastor Holstein and Deaconess Ruth Fisher in ministering to the Church of the Master's 718 baptized members and 512 communicant members. When Pastor Holstein retired in 1994 to serve Fountain of Life in Sun City part-time, Rev. Harding became the new head pastor. He was born in Lockport, Illinois, on September 21, 1947, and graduated from Christ College, Irvine, in 1981 and Concordia Seminary, St. Louis, in 1985. He was ordained and installed at Faith, Andrews, Texas, in 1985. In 1987, he went to Messiah in Dallas, Texas, serving until 1991 when he went to the Church of the Master. He wed Brenda Cherry on July 12, 1967, with their marriage blessed with one child.

Since the Church of the Master wanted to take the Gospel to Hispanics, the parish began ESL classes with a retired English teacher who taught English grammar but nothing about Christ. By the year 2000, the congregation had invited Valley of the Sun Ministry to help with its community outreach through ESL classes, co-sponsoring an ESL class there twice a week with the hope to develop a more solid Lutheran presence among Hispanics in the area's changing neighborhood. In the summer of 2000, an arsonist destroyed a major portion of the preschool education building. All the churches in the Phoenix area, including other denominations, were very supportive and offered to help. The Lutheran Church of the Master was not the first church in the Phoenix area to be targeted by arsonists. Pastor Harding was vigilant in reminding the staff, members, media, and officials that God would work something good out of this tragic event. Today, the Church of the Master has 436 baptized members and 306 communicants with an average of 178 in worship on Sundays.

When Pastor Cris Artigas took over the ESL Program at the Church of the Master, he integrated the teaching of Christ into the curricu-

Rev. Robert W. Holstein became the second pastor of the Lutheran Church of the Master, retiring from the parish in 1994. (Pacific Southwest District Archives)

Rev. Michael Harding at the time of his installation as assistant pastor in 1992. (Pacific Southwest District Archives)

Rev. Cris Artigas with the children in the 2002 Vacation Bible School.

lum. Through the ESL classes and participation of various families previously involved in the "DE REGRESO A LA ESCUELA" programs, Iglesia El Divino Maestro was established on Easter Sunday 2001, as a side-by-side ministry of the Lutheran Church of the Master. The closing of the

Vacation Bible School that summer was the first worship service in this location. The 6 families gained through the ESL classes invited neighbors, friends, and relatives to join them in worship on a weekly basis with the average attendance ranging from 20 to 60. While Pastor Artigas conducted the ESL classes for adults on weeknights, Mrs. Vida Luna taught their little children Bible stories. She also worked part-time (20 hours per week) at the Schaller Center in Phoenix. This ministry not only reaches the community through ESL (English) classes and weekly worship services but also through Bible studies, Baptism, First Communion, Confirmation and Catechism classes, Vacation Bible School, Back-to-School Program, weddings, Quinceñeras, Christmas Angel Program, and Reyes Magos, providing the Hispanic community a variety of means in nurturing their faith in Christ Jesus as their Savior.

First Lutheran Church – Missouri Synod
Hispanic Convention
August 1-5, 2003

Since the Missouri Synod's Hispanic missions in the United States have grown to include a large number of pastors and congregations, the first LCMS Hispanic Lutheran Convention was held on August 1–5, 2003, at the Los Angeles Airport Marriott Hotel. The theme was "Under the Cross of Christ, Yesterday, Today, and Tomorrow," and 148 people registered for the event. The reason for the Pacific Southwest District to host this convention was that this District contains one of the largest numbers of Hispanic churches ministering to the Spanish-speaking community. The convention was conducted in Spanish, opening on Friday, August 1, at 2:00 p.m. with the president of the Hispanic Mission Society, Rev. Eloy González, presiding. Following devotions and singing, the president gave information on the convention and an orientation of the procedures that were to be used during the convention. At 3:30 p.m., the group adjourned to the pool area to attend a reception hosted by the Hispanic Institute of Theology where the 15-member Mariachi band from San Pablo Lutheran Church in El Paso, Texas, entertained the group. Throughout the convention, they provided beauti-

ful music for the conventioneers. In the late afternoon, more business was conducted.

The following day, Saturday, August 2, elections were held with the following elected: President, Rev. Dr. Alberto Gómez; Vice President, Rev. Alex Merlo; Secretary/Treasurer, Susan González; Board Members, Rev. Julio Flamenco and Rev. Enrique Orozco. Following the elections, Rev. Dr. Justo González, a noted church historian, spoke on the past — the early Spanish history in America. Rev. Dr. Jack Preus, president of Concordia University, Irvine, spoke on being one body in Christ with diversity in that body. In the evening, there was a Communion service with the Rev. Dr. David Stirdivant, the father of Hispanic ministries in the Pacific Southwest District, preaching on being an apostle.

Since Sunday, August 3, was a free day, the convention continued on Monday with the Rev. Douglas Groll, the head of Hispanic Institute of Theology, speaking on the "Church of Today" followed by Rev. Aurelio Magariño. Resolutions were passed for the 2004 LCMS convention to consider. One of the resolutions was that the Spanish-speaking churches form their own district like the English District of Synod. At the evening banquet, awards were given to Rev. Dr. David Stirdivant and Rev. Douglas Groll. Rev. Dr. Gerald Kieschnick, president of the Missouri Synod, concluded the evening with his presentation on the "Church of Tomorrow." The convention concluded the following day, Tuesday, August 5, with more resolutions being sent to Synod.

What is in store for the church as it continues to develop its ethnic ministries, especially to the ever-increasing Hispanic community? How does the church minister to the Hispanics? The Lord assures us with His words, "…My Word …shall not return to Me void, but it shall accomplish that which I please, and it shall prosper in the thing whereto I sent it." Isaiah 55:11, and "Go ye therefore, and teach all nations, baptizing them in the name of the Father, and of the Son, and of the Holy Ghost: Teaching them to observe all things that I have commanded you: lo, I am with you always, even unto the end of the world." Matthew 28:19–20.

Sent forth by God's blessings,
Our true faith confessing,
The people of God from His dwelling take leave….
His grace did invite us,
His love shall unite us
To work for God's kingdom and answer His call.

† Soli Deo Gloria! †

The Churches in the Pacific Southwest District

Year Established*

I was glad when they said unto me,
"Let us go into the house of the Lord."

— PSALMS 122:1

1882 Los Angeles, Trinity
1882 Orange, St. John
1887–1899 Palmenthal, Zion**
1887–1917 Otay Mesa, St. John**
1892 Pasadena, First
1895 San Diego, Trinity
1897 Oxnard, St. John
1903 Anaheim, Zion
1903–1936 Olivenhain, St. John**
1905 Long Beach, First
1905 Los Angeles, Christ
1906 Montebello, St. John
1906–1959 Los Angeles, Emanuel**
1906 Los Angeles, Grace
1906 San Bernardino, Trinity
1907 Orange, St. Paul,
1907–1927 Upland, Mission**
1908 Whittier, Trinity
1909 Riverside, Immanuel
1909 Santa Ana, Trinity
1911 Covina, St. John's
1912 San Diego, Grace
1913 Santa Monica, Pilgrim
1914–2002 Hollywood, Bethany**
1915 Santa Barbara, Emanuel
1919 Escondido, Grace
1920 Pomona, St. Paul's
1920 Van Nuys, First
1921 Burbank, First
1921 Lancaster, Grace
1922 Los Angeles, Fifth Avenue
      (Closed)**

1922 Orange, Immanuel
1923 Alhambra, Emmaus First
1923 Glendale, Zion
1924 Los Angeles, El Serino (Closed)**
1924 South Gate, Redeemer
1925 Fontana, First
1925–1962 West Hollywood, St. James**
1925 Los Angeles, Faith
1925 Los Angeles, St. Paul
1925 Pasadena, Mount Olive
1925 Rancho Palos Verdes, Christ (San
      Pedro)
1925 Redondo Beach, Immanuel
1926 Banning, Grace
1926 Monrovia, First
1927 Los Angeles, First (Culver City)
1928 Hemet, St. John
1928–1971 North Hollywood, St. Paul**
1929 Holtville, St. Paul
1929–1956 Los Angeles, St. Matthew**
1929–1940 Los Angeles, San Pablo**
1929 San Fernando, First
1930–1935 Los Angeles, St. Andrew**
1930–1933 Wilmington, Redeemer**
1931 Long Beach, St. John
1931–1976 Lynwood, Lynwood**
1931 San Diego, Faith
1931 Yuma, AZ, Calvary
1933–1934, Lake Hughes, CCC Camp
      Mission**
1933 Los Angeles, Pilgrim (Deaf)
1934 Ventura, First

1935 El Centro, Grace
1935 Inglewood, Good Shepherd
1936–1997 Maywood, Zion**
1937 El Monte, First
1937 Needles, Grace
1937 Riverside, Faith
1937 San Diego, Bethany
1938 Brawley, Trinity
1938 Rosemead, Zion
1938–1956 Santa Ana, Nuestro Salvador**
1940 Beverly Hills, Calvary
1940 Las Vegas, NV, First Good Shepherd
1941 Burbank, Christ
1942 Chula Vista, Pilgrim
1942 La Mesa, Christ
1942 Redlands, Christ
1943 Covina, Trinity
1943 Downey, Messiah
1943 Ontario, Redeemer
1943 San Diego, St. Paul
1944 Barstow, Concordia
1944 Colton, St. John
1944 Long Beach, Bethany
1944 South Gate, Peace
1944–1950 Trona, Trinity**
1945 Bishop, Grace
1945 Canoga Park, Canoga Park
1945 Corona, Grace
1945 Encinitas, St. Mark
1945 Laguna Beach, St. Paul
1945 Long Beach, Grace
1945–1946 Los Angeles, Concordia**

* *Information taken from* **The Lutheran Annual 2005**
** *Information gathered from District Archives*

1945 San Diego, Peace
1945 Temple City, First
1945 Venice, First
1946 Harbor City, St. Matthew
1946 Lake Elsinore, First
1946 Sherman Oaks, Sherman Oaks
1946 Tujunga, Faith
1947–1992 Azusa, Concordia**
1947 Bell Gardens, Bell Gardens
1947 Buena Park, Messiah
1947 Inglewood, Concordia
1947 Oceanside, Immanuel
1947 Ridgecrest, Our Savior
1948 Manhattan Beach, First
1948–1968 North Hollywood, Messiah**
1948 Pacific Palisades, Palisades
1948–1997 San Diego, Messiah**
1948 Victorville, Zion
1949 Indio, Trinity
1950 Blythe, Zion
1950, Chino, Immanuel
1950–1972 Compton, St. Peter**
1950 Norwalk, St. Paul's
1950 Phoenix, AZ, Mt. Calvary
1951 Boulder City, NV, Christ
1951–1954 Calimesa, Our Savior**
1951 Garden Grove, St. Paul
1951 Los Angeles, Hope Memorial
1951 Reseda, Trinity
1951 San Diego, Our Redeemer
1952–1998 Calexico, Faith**
1952 Henderson, NV, Our Savior
1952 Los Angeles, Our Savior
1952 Pasadena, Faith
1952 Pico Rivera, Peace
1953 Costa Mesa, Christ
1953 Palm Springs, Our Savior
1953 Phoenix, AZ, Christ
1953 West Covina, Immanuel First
1953 Whittier, Faith
1954 Arcadia, Our Savior
1954 Bisbee, AZ, Hope
1954 Camarillo, First
1954 Downey, Good Shepherd
1954 El Segundo, St. John
1954 Fallbrook, Zion
1954 Granada Hills, Our Savior First
1954 Imperial Beach, St. James
1954 Ojai, Our Redeemer
1954 Palmdale, First
1954 Rialto, Grace
1954 San Diego, Holy Cross
1954–2002 Santa Paula, Trinity**
1954 Torrance, Ascension

1955 Anaheim, Prince of Peace
1955–1960 Culver City, Mission**
1955 Glendora, Hope
1955 Kingman, AZ, Immanuel (Closed)**
1955 La Crescenta, Gethsemane
1955 Long Beach, St. Paul
1955 San Diego, Prince of Peace
1955 Twentynine Palms, Immanuel
1956 Coronado, Resurrection
1956 Eagle Mountain (Closed)**
1956 Fullerton, Our Savior
1956–1997 La Puente, Holy Cross**
1956 Tustin, Peace
1956 Yucaipa, Good Shepherd
1957 Anaheim, St. Mark
1957–1992 Azusa, Concordia**
1957 Buena Park, Bethel
1957 Fullerton, St. Stephen
1957 1998 Gardena, St. Thomas**
1957 La Mirada, Mount Olive
1957 Lake Arrowhead, Mt. Calvary
1957 Las Vegas, NV, Mountain View
1957 Los Angeles, La Santa Cruz
1957 Montclair, Trinity
1957–1984 Panorama City, Redeemer**
1957 Westminster, St. Luke
1957 Winnetka, Our Redeemer
1958–1989 Garden Grove, Ascension**
1958 Coolidge, AZ Christ
1958–1980 North Edwards, Christ**
1958 Perris, Redeemer
1958–1980 Pomona, Peace**
1958 Ramona, Ramona
1958 Riverside, Gethsemane
1958 Tucson, AZ, Fountain of Life
1958 Whittier, Hope
1959 Apple Valley, Ascension
1959 Carpinteria, Faith
1959 Cypress, Holy Cross
1959 Goleta, Good Shepherd
1959 Phoenix, AZ, St. Paul
1959 Simi Valley, Trinity
1959 Woodland Hills, Atonement
   (Merged)**
1960 Compton, St. Phillip
1960–1967 Downey, Immanuel**
1960 Highland, Messiah
1960 Poway, Mount Olive
1960 Scottsdale, AZ, Holy Cross
1960 Tehachapi, Good Shepherd
1960 Tempe, AZ, Beautiful Savior
1960 Vista, Faith
1961 Bellflower, Our Savior
1961 Desert Hot Springs, Christ

1961 Mesa, AZ, St. Luke
1961 Spring Valley, Atonement
1961 Yucca Valley, Good Shepherd
1962 Brea, Christ
1962 Hacienda Heights, Holy Trinity
1962 Lake View Terrace, Peace
1962 Las Vegas, NV, Redeemer
1962 Peoria, AZ, King of Kings
1962 Phoenix, AZ, Church of the Master
1962 Phoenix, AZ, Shepherd of the
   Desert (Closed)**
1962 Thousand Oaks, Redeemer
1962 Los Angeles, USC Chapel (Closed)**
1962 Wickenburg, AZ, Redeemer
1963 Hesperia, Faith
1963 Huntington Beach, Faith
1963 Huntington Beach, Redeemer
1963 La Jolla, University
1963 Los Angeles, University
1963 Rancho Palos Verdes, Mount Olive
1963 Salome, AZ, Community (Closed)**
1963 Ventura, Grace
1964 Casa Grande, AZ, Trinity
1964 Chandler, AZ, Epiphany
1964 Chula Vista, Concordia
1964 Mesa, AZ, Eternal Life
1964 Newberry Park, Christ the King
1964 Phoenix, AZ, Our Savior (Deaf)
1964 1974 San Bernardino, Peace**
1964 Santa Clarita, Bethlehem
1964 Walnut, Christ the King
1965 Alta Loma, King of Glory (Closed)**
1965 Agoura Hills, St. Paul
1965 Capistrano Beach, Faith
1965 Claremont, St. Luke
1965 Flagstaff, AZ, Peace
1965 Lake Forest, Abiding Savior
1965 Orange, Salem
1965–1970 Riverside, Mt. Calvary**
1965–1968 San Dimas, St. Matthew**
1965 Yuma, AZ, Christ
1966 Inglewood, Faith
1966–1972 Northridge, Resurrection**
1966–1968 Redlands, St. Mark**
1966 Sun City, AZ, Fountain of Life
1966 Wrightwood, Faith (Closed)**
1967 Phoenix, AZ, St. Mark
1967 Redlands, Christ the King
1968 Anaheim, Mt. Calvary (Deaf)
1968 Diamond Bar, Mt. Calvary
1969 Phoenix, AZ, Christ the Redeemer
1971 San Diego, Christ the Cornerstone
1972 Prescott Valley, AZ, Trinity
1973 Oceanside, Shepherd of the Valley

* *Information taken from* The Lutheran Annual 2005
** *Information gathered from District Archives*

1974 Bullhead City, AZ, St. John
1970 Cerritos, Concordia
1970 Cottonwood, AZ, Faith
1973 Tempe, AZ, Gethsemane
1974 Anaheim, Hephatha
1976 Camarillo, Peace
1976 El Mirage, AZ, La Santa Cruz (Closed)**
1976 Mammoth Lakes, Mammoth Lakes
1976 Tempe, AZ, Alleluia
1977 Big Bear Lake, Shepherd of the Pines
1977 Rancho Cucamonga, Shepherd of the Hills
1978 Escondido, Gloria Dei
1978 Moreno Valley, Shepherd of the Valley
1978 Prescott, AZ, Shepherd of the Hills
1978 Santa Ynez, Shepherd of the Valley
1978 Scottsdale, AZ, Shepherd of the Desert
1978 Valley Center, Light of the Valley
1979 Apache Junction, AZ, Mountain View
1979 Glendale, AZ, Atonement
1979 Hemet, Prince of Peace
1979 Peoria, AZ, Apostles
1980 Anza, Shepherd of the Valley
1980 Bell Gardens, San Pedro y San Pablo
1980 Irvine, Light of Christ
1980 Gilbert, AZ, Christ Greenfield
1980 Litchfield Park, AZ, Trinity
1980–1999 Ontario, Lamb of God**
1981–1989 Quartzsite, AZ, Covenant**
1983 Boron, Resurrection
1983 Chino Hills, Loving Savior
1983 Panorama City, El Redentor
1984 Los Angeles, Trinidad
1984 Pahrump, NV, Shepherd of the Valley

1984 Sierra Vista, AZ, Immanuel
1985–1993 Las Vegas, NV, Sunrise**
1985 Moorpark, Faith
1985 Oxnard, Centro Cristiano
1985–1993 San Diego, Iglesia Santa Maria**
1986 Kingman, AZ, Good Shepherd
1986 Menifee, Good Shepherd
1986 Sun City West, AZ, Crown of Life
1987 Orange, Cristo Rey
1988 Black Canyon City, AZ, Grace
1988 Mesa, AZ, Hosanna
1988 Los Angeles, Ark of Noah
1988 Quartz Hill, Resurrection
1989 Diamond Bar, Grace Chinese
1989 Escondido, Community
1989 Garden Grove, Vietnamese
1989 Long Beach, First Cambodian
1989 Sedona, AZ, Rock of Ages
1989 Temecula, New Community
1990 Carlsbad, Redeemer by the Sea
1990 Cordes Lake, AZ, Mountain of Faith
1990 Moreno Valley, Grace Korean
1990 San Diego, Living Waters
1991 Baldwin Park, Jesus de Nazaret (Closed)**
1991 Fullerton, True Light
1992 California City, Trinity
1992 Fountain Hills, AZ, Trinity
1992 Garden Grove, Good News Korean
1992 Las Vegas, NV, Lamb of God
1992 Laughlin, NV, Living Christ
1992 Los Angeles, Young Kwang
1992 Rancho Santa Margarita, Mount Hope
1992 San Diego, Shield of Faith
1992 Whittier, Faith Arabic
1993 Phoenix, AZ, Santo Tomas
1994 Chula Vista, Church of Joy

1994 Chula Vista, Santisima Trinidad
1994 Phoenix, AZ, Santo Tomas**
1994 San Diego, Grace Street Mission
1995 Los Angeles, Ark of Noah Korean
1995 San Bernardino, La Santisima Trinidad
1995 Scottsdale, AZ, Desert Foothills
1996 Chino Hills, Loving Savior, Chinese
1996 Escondido, Misión Hispána Gracia**
1996 Peoria, AZ, Mt. Zion
1996 Rimrock, AZ, Grace Community
1997 Castaic, West Valley Prince of Peace
1997 Los Angeles, Brazilian
1997 Maywood, Palabra de Dios
1997 Phoenix, AZ, Iglesia Gracia**
1998 Lake Havasu City, AZ, Lamb of God
1998 Las Vegas, NV, Faith Community
1999 Carpinteria, Centro Christiano**
1999 Mesquite, NV, Mesquite
1999 Phoenix, AZ, Soli Fide (FE)**
2000 El Centro, Alfa y Omega
2000 Fullerton, New Covenant
2000 Indio, Primera Iglesia
2000–2003 Phoenix, AZ, Rey de Reyes**
2000 San Jacinto, Centro Cristiano Fuente de Vida
2001 Anthem, AZ, Cross of Christ
2001 Fontana, La Santisima Trinidad**
2001 Phoenix, AZ, Cristo El Redentor
2001 Phoenix, AZ, El Divino Maestro
2002 Fullerton, Searchlight
2002 Queen City AZ, Saving Grace
2002 Santa Paula, Centro Cristiano**
2002 Surprise, AZ, Word of God
2002 Yuma, AZ, Shepherd of the Hills
2003 Litchfield Park, AZ, Summit
2003 Murrieta, Promise
2003 Scotsdale, AZ, La Santa Cruz**
2004 Peoria, AZ, Life in Christ

✠

𝕿𝖍𝖊 𝕮𝖍𝖚𝖗𝖈𝖍'𝖘 𝖔𝖓𝖊 𝖋𝖔𝖚𝖓𝖉𝖆𝖙𝖎𝖔𝖓
𝕴𝖘 𝕵𝖊𝖘𝖚𝖘 𝕮𝖍𝖗𝖎𝖘𝖙, 𝖍𝖊𝖗 𝕷𝖔𝖗𝖉;
𝕾𝖍𝖊 𝖎𝖘 𝕳𝖎𝖘 𝖓𝖊𝖜 𝖈𝖗𝖊𝖆𝖙𝖎𝖔𝖓
𝕭𝖞 𝖜𝖆𝖙𝖊𝖗 𝖆𝖓𝖉 𝖙𝖍𝖊 𝖂𝖔𝖗𝖉....

* *Information taken from* **The Lutheran Annual 2005**
** *Information gathered from District Archives*

Donors

"For God loveth a cheerful giver."

— Corinthians 9:7

Robert and Enid Anderson
Marcelyn Bohl
Robert and LaVerne Burwell
Centro Cristiano Fuente de Vida, San Jacinto,
   California
Concordia University, Irvine, California
Raymond and Pam Dabela
Anthony Dinardo
Michael and Mina Doyle
Douglas Dueker
Rev. John and Nancy Durkovic
Norman Everhart
First Lutheran Church, Los Angeles, California
Thomas and Verna Frinell
Mildred Grebing
Sharon Hartwig
Marilyn Hertz
Hispanic Mission Society of Circuit One
Hispanic Support Group, Los Angeles, California
Iglesia Luterana San Pedro y San Pablo, Bell
   Gardens, California
Immanuel Lutheran Church, Chino, California
Eloise Kennedy
Jim and Carole Klopschinski
Gene Knoppel

Rev. William Lindenmeyer
Lou Marting
Richard Meyer Metal Supply
Rev. Phillip Molnar
Rod and Colleen Nicks
Gladys Nye
Odle and Associates
Pacific Southwest District of The Lutheran Church —
   Missouri Synod
Pacific Southwest District Lutheran Women's
   Missionary League
Palabra de Dios Lutheran Church, Maywood,
   California
St. Luke Lutheran Church, Claremont, California
St. Paul's Lutheran Church, Pomona, California
Lawrence Schatz
Rich and Thelma Scheu
Cliffton Shout
Don and Olga Schulteis
Timothy Scoullar
Marjorie Sobosky
Rev. David Stirdivant
Donald Tietjen
Carlton and Margaret Williams

We give Thee but Thine own,
Whate'er the gift may be;
All that we have is Thine alone,
A trust, O Lord, from Thee.

Books and Manuscripts

Adair, Ruby and Engelsgaard, Lorraine. *History of Trinity Lutheran Church of Santa Paula 1954 to 2002.* Manuscript.

An Illustrated History of Los Angeles County California. Chicago: The Lewis Publishing Company, 1888.

City of San Bernardino. Contributed by Cultural and International Affairs — Mayor's Office, 2003.

Christ Lutheran Church, Los Angeles, California. 40th Anniversary Book, 1945.

Christ the Redeemer Church, Phoenix, Arizona. Dedication Booklet, January 27, 1974.

Cole, Martin. *Pico Rivera: Where the World Began.* Rio Hondo College Community Services, 1981.

Concordia Lutheran Church, Chula Vista, California. Dedication Book, December 9, 1962.

DeKay, Ken and Lydia. *Thirtieth Anniversary, History Messiah Lutheran Church.* Downey, California, 1973.

Doyle, Michael. *Sent Forth by God's Blessings, A History Zion Lutheran Church, Maywood, CA.* 1999.

Doyle, Michael. *Mother of the Valley, A History St. Paul's Lutheran Church, Pomona, CA.* Upland: Dragonflyer, 2001.

Du Brau, Richard T. *Romance of Lutheranism in California.* 1959.

Faith Lutheran Church, Whittier, California. Dedication Booklet, March 7, 1954.

Faith Lutheran Church, Whittier, California, Dedication Booklet, September 14, 1958.

First Lutheran Church, Fontana, California. Dedication Booklet, October 25, 1959.

First Lutheran Church, Pasadena, California. Golden Anniversary Book, 1942.

First Lutheran Church, Pasadena, California. 70th Anniversary Book, 1962

First Lutheran Church, Pasadena, California. 110th Anniversary Book

Fifty Years Under the Cross. Zion Lutheran Church, Anaheim, California. Golden Anniversary Booklet, 1953.

Grace Lutheran Church, El Centro, California. *Sixty-five Years of God's Grace.* 2000.

Grace Lutheran Church, Escondido, California. 25th Anniversary Book, October 13, 1946.

Grace Lutheran Church, Escondido. California. 50th Anniversary Book, October 1969.

Gray, Arthur. *A Centennial History of Zion Lutheran Church, Anaheim, California.* 2003.

Hansen, Rev. August. Presentation by Stereoptican and Moving Pictures. Summer, 1926.

Hill, Laurance L. *La Reina Los Angeles in Three Centuries.* Security Trust and Savings, 1929.

History of Los Angeles County. Chicago: Lewis Publishing Company, 1889.

Holy Cross Lutheran Church, La Puente, California. 25th Anniversary Booklet, November 22, 1981.

Huebner, Roberto. "Historical Account of US/Mexican Border Ministry." Manuscript.

King of Kings Lutheran Church, Phoenix, Arizona. Memory Book, 1998.

Los Angeles Birthday Pamphlet

Mayo, Morrow. *Los Angeles.* Alfred A Knoff, 1933.

Messiah Lutheran Church, Downey, California. Dedication Booklet, October 28, 1973.

Messiah Lutheran Church, Downey, California. Organ Dedication Booklet, September 10, 1978.

Messiah Lutheran Church, San Diego, California. 30th Anniversary Book, 1978

Mount Calvary Lutheran Church, Phoenix, Arizona. Dedication Booklet, September 28, 1952.

Mount Calvary Lutheran Church, Phoenix, Arizona. *Reflections….Fifty Years in God's Grace, 1950–2000.* Anniversary Book, 2000.

Newmark, Harris. *Sixty Years in Southern California.* Boston: Houghton Mifflin, 1930.

Overholt, Alma. *The Catalina Story.* Catalina Island: Catalina Island Museum Society, 1962.

Peace Lutheran Church, Phoenix, Arizona. Dedication Booklet March 24, 1963.

Peace Lutheran Church, Pico Rivera, California. Dedication and Installation Booklet, June 6, 1954.

Peace Lutheran Church, Pico Rivera, California. Dedication Booklet, March 12, 1961.

Pilgrim Lutheran Church, Chula Vista, California. Church Dedication Program, February 29, 1948.

Riedel, Dr. Erhardt H. *From the Land of Sinim — A Memoir.*

Robinson, W. W. *Los Angeles from the Days of the Pueblo.* The California Historical Society, 1981.

St. John's Lutheran Church, Montebello, California. 50th Anniversary Booklet, 1956.

St. John's Lutheran Church, Montebello, California. 75th Anniversary Book, 1958.

St. John's Lutheran Church, Orange, California. 50th Anniversary Book, 1932.

St. John's Lutheran Church, Orange, California. 100th Anniversary Book, 1982.

St. John's Lutheran Church, Oxnard, California. Church Dedication Book, January 30, 1949.

St. John's Lutheran Church, Oxnard, California. Church Dedication Book, September 15, 1968.

Schuiling, Walter C. *San Bernardino County: Land of Contrasts.* Windsor Publication, Inc., 1984.

Seidenbaun, Art & Malmin, John. *Los Angeles 200 — A Bicentennial Celebration*. Harry M. Abrams, Incorporated, 1980.

75 Years in Christ. Zion Lutheran Church, Anaheim, California, 1978

Stirdivant, Rev. Dr. David M. "Brief Sketch of Spanish Lutheran Work in the Southern California District." Manuscript, January 1979.

Time-Life Book. *This Fabulous Century — 1940–1950*, Volume V. Time Incorporated, 1969.

Theiss, John William *The History of the Lutheran Churches and Missions of Southern California 1881-1927*. Manuscript. Pacific Southwest District Archives.

Trinity Lutheran Church, Los Angeles, California. 50th Anniversary Book, 1932.

Trinity Lutheran Church, Los Angeles, California. 75th Anniversary Book, 1957.

Trinity Lutheran Church, San Bernardino, California. 25th Anniversary Service, 1931.

Trinity Lutheran Church, San Bernardino, California. Church Dedication Booklet, June 1961.

Trinity Lutheran Church, San Bernardino, California. 75th Anniversary Booklet, 1981.

Trinity Lutheran Church, San Bernardino, California. 90th Anniversary Booklet, 1996.

Trinity Lutheran Church, San Diego, California. 50th Anniversary Book, 1947.

Trinity Lutheran Church, San Diego, California. 75th Anniversary Book, 1972.

Trinity Lutheran Church, San Diego, California. 100th Anniversary Book, 1997.

Whittier A Pictorial History. Quaker City Federal Savings and Loan.

Ziegler, Albert. *Biographical Sketches of LC MS Mainland China Missionaries*. Manuscript, 1981.

Zion Lutheran Church Fallbrook, California. Church Dedication Book, April 29, 1962.

Zion Lutheran Church Fallbrook, California. 25th Anniversary Book, October 7, 1979.

Interviews

Ruby Adair, April 20, 2004.

Jorge Almaraz, October 28, 2003.

Rev. Cristiano Artigas, January 7, 2004.

Rev. Dennis Bradshaw, April 21, 2004.

Rev. Frank Brundige, August 13 and 14, 2002, November 15, 2002, March 24, 2004.

Rev. Lewis Busch, November 20, 2003.

Terry Carter, August 22, 2003.

Flora Chavez, May 6, 2002.

Rev. Dr. Donald Dannenberg, August 13, 2003.

Rev. John Durkovic, October 10, 2003.

Lorraine Engelsgaard, April 21, 2004.

Raymond Fellows, March 24, 2004.

Gilbert Flores, May 5, 2002.

Rev. Dr. Alfred Freitag, August 7, 2003, and April 21, 2004.

Arthur Gray, April 30, 2004.

Angelina Gómez, August 2, 2003.

Rev. Samuel Gómez, May 23, 2004.

Rev. Carlos Hernandez, August 5, 2003.

Pastor Juan Herrera, October 13, 2003.

Rev. Douglas Jones, April 18, 2003.

Deacon Marco Lozano, August 1, 2003.

Vida Luna, February 19, 2004.

Lay Minister Jesús Martinez, February 14, 2003.

Rev. Mark McKenzie, October 29, 2003.

Colleen Nicks, August 11, 2003.

Belen Perez, May 5, 2002.

Charlotte Peapenburg, May 1, 2004.

Rev. Kenneth Piepenbrink, February 24, 2004.

Sue Pleger, March 13, 2004.

Dr. Phil Roberts, March 24, 2004.

Rev. Dr. Alfredo Saez, July 31, 2002, and August 31, 2002.

Rev. Thomas St. Jean, April 23, 2003.

Deacon Raul Saldaña, May 13, 2003.

Vera Saldaña, May 6, 2002.

Rev. Dr. Esaúl Salomón, August 5, 2003.

Rev. Ricardo Sarria, April 23, 2003.

Rev. Richard Schirmer, February 24, 2004.

Rev. Robert Schaller, November 12, 2002, and January 19, 2004.

Rev. Richard Schmidt, May 18, 2004.

Pam Schmidke, January 7, 2004.

Rev. Gale Schmidt, August 2, 2004.

Rev. Luther Schwartzkopf, August 31, 2004

Mrs. Sherry Shaw, July 30, 2003.

Rev. Robert Smith Jr., December 11, 2003.

Rev. Dr. David Stirdivant, August 8, 2002, January 21, 2003, February 14, 2003, May 8, 2003, May 20, 2003, and January 26, 2004.

Rev. James Swinford, January 9, 2004.

Marie Valenzuela, April 30, 2004.

Rev. Dr. Oswald Waech, April 11, 2004.

Rev. Robert Wolter, October 4, 2002.

Interviews (Published)

Rev. Philip Molnar, interview by Jean Beres, February 15, 2002, Pacific Southwest District Archives.

Rev. Dr. David Stirdivant, interview by Jean Beres, 1997, Pacific Southwest District Archives; interview by Rev. Kenneth Behnken, 1991, Pacific Southwest District Archives.

Newspapers

The Arizona Republic Phoenix, June 20, 1964

Enterprise Fallbrook, January 20, 1956.

Evening Tribune San Diego, September 11, 1951; September 10, 1955.

Hemet News, December 8, 2000.

Industrial Post Bell/Maywood, September 6, 1953.

Los Angeles Times, March 22, 1913; February 27 1978; November 20, 2001.

Prescott Miner, December 7, 1870,

San Diego Union, September 14, 1890; December 5, 1953

Southeast News Downey, September 8, 1978.

Star Reporter, March 13, 1952.

Periodicals

California Historical Society, The. "Los Angeles 1781–1981." Vol. LX Spring 1981.

Concordia Historical Institute Quarterly, Du Brau, Richard T. "John William Theiss Pastor and President, Poet, and Painter." Vol. 54, No. 3, Fall, p. 130–135.

District Digest, December 1, 1938; February 1, 1940; July 1971; April 1, 1973; November 1974; January 1975; May 1975; January 1976; July 1976; April 19, 1977; October 1978; September–October 1980; December–January 1980–1981; August–September 1981; November 1981; December 1981–January 1982; February–March 1982; February–June, July 1982; November–December 1979.

District News, January 1, 1940; October 15, 1940; May 1942; November 1942.

In Focus, January/February 1998; September/October 1998; March/April 1999; January/February 2000; January/February 2002; May/June 2002; July/August 2002; November/December 2002.

Los Angeles City Directory, 1875; 1887; 1879–1880; 1881–1882.

Lutheran Woman's Quarterly, Vol. XIV, No. 4, October 1956.

PSW e-News, May 30, 2000; October 23, 2000; October 30, 2000; December 14, 2000; December 21, 2000; February 21, 2001; March 15, 2001; April 26, 2001; May 24, 2001; June 7, 2001; July 3, 2001; August 7, 2001; November 15, 2001; December 7, 2001; December 13, 2001; April 18, 2002; May 9, 2002; May 2, 2002; May 30, 2002; June 13, 2002; September 21, 2002; September 27, 2002; October 11, 2002; November 14, 2002; December 12, 2002; January 10, 2003; January 16, 2003; February 9, 2003; February 27, 2003; March 3, 2003; March 21, 2003; April 2, 2003; April 24, 2003; June 14, 2003; June 5, 2003; August 27, 2003; October 8, 2003; October 15, 2003; October 31, 2003.

Sharing the News in the PSW, January–March 2001; July–September 2001; January–March 2002.

Southern California Lutheran, April 1932; April 1935.

Southern California Lutheran, November 24, 1952.

The English District Supplement, March 8, 1960.

The Lutheran Witness, November 7, 1884; May 26, 1931.

The Lutheran Witness Supplement, January 19, 1943; July 6, 1943; October 12, 1943; January 4, 1944; February 15, 1944; May 11, 1944; March 27, 1945; April 24, 1945; June 22, 1945; July 31, 1945; October 9, 1945; December 18, 1945; November 5, 1946; April 8, 1947; December 2, 1947; March 23, 1948; May 18, 1948; June 1, 1948; June 15, 1948; July 18, 1948; August 8, 1948; November 16, 1948; November 30, 1948; December 12, 1948; March 22, 1949; August 23, 1949; October 4, 1949; December 29, 1949; January 10, 1950; April 18, 1950; June 13, 1950; June 20, 1950; July 12, 1950; August 22, 1950; October 3, 1950; October 17, 1950; January 1, 1951; March 6, 1951; May 27, 1952; August 31, 1952; September 19, 1952; November 11, 1952; November 24, 1952; February 3, 1953; April 28, 1953; May 12, 1953; November 10, 1953; December 22, 1953; January 19, 1954; February 2, 1954; March 2, 1954; May 11, 1954; April 14, 1954; July 20, 1954; August 17, 1954; October 12, 1954; November 10, 1954; November 23, 1954; January 1, 1955; January 18, 1955; March 29, 1955; April 26, 1955; June 21, 1955; August 30, 1955; September 19, 1955; November 22, 1955; February 28, 1956; April 10, 1956; July 3, 1956; July 17, 1956; September 11, 1956; February 26, 1957; July 2, 1957; October 8, 1957; October 22, 1957; December 3, 1957; December 21, 1957; December 31, 1957; January 1, 1958; February 11, 1958; April 22, 1958; June 6, 1958; July 29, 1958; September 9, 1958; September 14, 1958; October 21, 1958; December 2, 1958; December 16, 1958; February 10, 1959; February 24, 1959; March 10, 1959; April 21, 1959; June 16, 1959; September 14, 1959; September 19, 1959; September 27, 1959; December 29, 1959; May 3, 1960; July 12, 1960; July 26, 1960; October 4, 1960; October 18, 1960; November 1, 1960; January 24, 1961; March 7, 1961; April 4, 1961; May 30, 1961; September 1, 1961; September 15, 1961; January 9, 1962; April 3, 1962; May 15,

1962; July 24, 1962; August 7, 1962; September 4, 1962; September 18, 1962; November 12, 1962; December 25, 1962; January 8, 1963; February 1963; August 6, 1963; September 26, 1963; November 12, 1963; December 12, 1963; December 30, 1963; January 7, 1964; February 17, 1964; August 18, 1964; October 13, 1964; February 1965; April 13, 1965; July 1965; December 1965; January 1966; December 1966; January 1966; February 27, 1966; March 3, 1966; April 1966; January 1967; February 1967; March 1967; April 1967; July 1967; October 1967; November 1967; February 2, 1968; August 24, 1968; September 1968; November 1968; April 1969; October 1969; November 1969; January 1970; December 1970; February 1971; April 9, 1972; August 23, 1973; October 3, 1973; January 6, 1974; April 28, 1974; July 29, 1974; April 26, 1975; May 18, 1975; September 14, 1975; December 21, 1975; August 29, 1976; February 26, 1977; July 10, 1977; September 25, 1977; February 1978; April 1978; October 1978; March 1979; April 1979; July 1979; September 1979; November 1979; December 1979; April 1980; October 1980; November 1980; January 1981; September 1981; October 1981; November 1981; December 1982.

The Northern Light, September 2002

THIS MONTH, February 1983; March 1983; April 1983; June 1983; August 1983; October 1983; November 1983; January 1984; February 1984; March 1984; April 1984; August 1984; September 1984; November 1984; January1985; February 1985; September 1985; October 1985; November 1985; December 1985; March 1986; May 1986; June 1986; September 1986; October 1986; November 1986; December 1986; February 1987; April 1987; May 1987; June/July 1987; August 1987; September 1987; December 1987; January 1988; May 1988; June 1988; August 1988; October 1988; November 1988; April 1989; May 1989; June/July 1989; September 1989; October 1989; January 1990; February 1990; April 1990; March 1990; June/July 1990; September 1990; November 1990; January 1991; June/July 1991; September 1991; October 1991; May 1992; June/July 1992; October 1992; November 1992; December 1992; February 1993; April 1993; June/July1993; August 1993; September 1993; October 1993; November 1993; January 1994; March 1994; May 1994; April 1994; September 1994; November 1994; December 1994; January 1995; March 1995; April 1995; August 1995; November 1995; January 1996; February 1996; March 1996; May 1996; July 1996; August 1996; September 1996; November 1996; March 1997; April 1997; May/June 1997; September 1997; November 1997; December 1997.